THE
BUSINESS
OF AMERICA

THE

BUSINESS

OF AMERICA

edited by

IVAR BERG

Columbia University

HARCOURT, BRACE & WORLD, INC.

New York Chicago San Francisco Atlanta

Library of Congress Catalog Card Number: 68-15866
Printed in the United States of America

PREFACE

The size of modern business corporations and the resources their leaders control and administer assure them an enormously significant place on the American institutional landscape. The social impact of corporate action is thus a vital consideration in many business decisions, and teachers of business no less than their colleagues in political science, sociology, and economics must give it careful attention if they are to help their students achieve a realistic understanding of the American system of enterprise. This book is intended to help make such an examination of the interplay between business and the rest of society more useful and systematic.

Much has already been written about the impact of business on America. Unfortunately, however, many of the views expressed have been polemical, and references have been lacking to the evidence available in journals and monographs. Seven years of teaching the Conceptual Foundations of Business course in the Columbia University School of Business convinced me that a book of another kind was needed, and I found that many of my associates agreed and were willing to contribute to its realization.

After a period of discussion and analysis, several of the crucial political, economic, and sociological effects of business were identified, and a corresponding division of labor was established. Each contributor chosen had completed a major research project in the area he would investigate. Each undertook first to search his discipline, the public records, and the business archives for basic evidence and then to utilize and report this evidence in a way that would bring the discussion of business and society "back to the

v

facts" and would facilitate the work of teachers and students. I believe that these aspirations have in large part been achieved.

I am grateful to my colleagues James Kuhn, Leonard Sayles, and Eli Ginzberg for their professional and personal help and encouragement; to my contributors for their willingness to work within agreed-upon frameworks and for tolerating with good humor my editorial direction; and to my angelic secretary, Joyce Phelan, who never once complained about her formidable tasks in this enterprise.

Were editors able to single out and dedicate their contribution to a book like this one, I would dedicate mine to my teachers Irene Law and Arnold Sio.

IVAR BERG
Columbia University

CONTRIBUTORS

Ivar Berg, Associate Professor, Graduate School of Business, Columbia University. Author of *Values in a Business Society: Issues and Analyses* (with James W. Kuhn) and *Democratic Values and the Rights of Management* (with Eli Ginzberg).

Gordon C. Bjork, Associate Professor, Graduate School of Business, Columbia University. Rhodes Scholar. Author of several articles on U.S. economic history and a forthcoming book on the historical nature of capitalism.

Richard Eells, Executive Editor, Program for Studies of the Modern Corporation, and Adjunct Professor, Graduate School of Business, Columbia University. Author of *Corporation Giving in a Free Society: Conceptual Foundations of Business* (with Clarence C. Walton) and *The Corporation and the Arts.*

Alfred Eichner, Assistant Professor of Economics, Columbia University. Author of *The Emergence of Oligopoly* and other volumes.

Marcia K. Freedman, Senior Research Associate, Columbia University. Author of *Youth Employment Programs in Perspective* and *Getting Hired, Getting Trained: A Study of Industry Practices and Policies on Youth Employment.*

Karl B. Hill, Special Assistant for Research and Technology, U.S. Department of Housing and Urban Development. Editor of *The Management of Scientists* and formerly an officer of Associates for International Research, Inc.

James W. Kuhn, Professor of Industrial Relations, Graduate School of Business, Columbia University. Author of *Values in a Business Society: Issues and Analyses* (with Ivar Berg), *Bargaining in Grievance Settlement,* and *Scientific and Managerial Manpower in Nuclear Industry.*

Hyman Rodman, Senior Research Associate, Merrill-Palmer Institute. Editor, *Marriage, Family, and Society.* Author of numerous articles on the family and social structure. Editor of *Social Problems.*

David Rogers, Associate Professor of Sociology and Management, Graduate School of Business Administration, New York University, and Senior Research Sociologist, Center for Urban Education. Author of *Politics, Schools, and Segregation: The Case of New York City* and articles on political problems and business.

Constantina Safilios-Rothschild, Research Associate, The Merrill-Palmer Institute, and Adjunct Associate Professor, Wayne State University. Author of articles studying international contrasts in family patterns.

Arthur B. Shostak, Associate Professor, Drexel Institute of Technology. Editor of *Sociology in Action, New Perspectives on Poverty,* and *Blue-Collar World.*

Charles F. Stewart, Professor, Graduate School of Business, Columbia University. Author of *The Economy of Morocco.* Editor of *The Global Businessman.*

Clarence C. Walton, Dean, School of General Studies and Professor of Business, Columbia University. Author of *Corporate Social Responsibilities, The Business System: Readings in Ideas and Concepts* (with Richard Eells), and *Ethos and the Executive.*

Robert N. Wilson, Chairman, Department of Mental Health, and Professor of Sociology, University of North Carolina. Author of *Man Made Plain: The Poet in Contemporary Society* and *Community Structure and Health Action.* Editor of *The Arts in Society.*

Melvin Zimet, Administrative Assistant, New York University Graduate School of Business. Former business executive and board director in several industries.

CONTENTS

part **1**

chapter **1**

INTRODUCTION: THE IMPACT
OF BUSINESS ON AMERICA

IVAR BERG

"The business of America is business," Calvin Coolidge remarked confidently in 1925, and ever since this maxim has been cited by foreign critics to prove that the United States is a notably commercial and materialistic nation. In some cases the observation of these critics may have been prompted by envy, but that does not mean their opinion is entirely wrong; commercial and materialistic we undoubtedly are, in the sense that the output of our economy is enormous. In each year in the mid-1960's more than 8,000,000 automobiles rolled off assembly lines. From 1961 to 1968 the number of families that owned two cars doubled to include 25 per cent of American households. About 1.5 million households own at least three cars! Approximately a quarter of U.S. homes boast two or more television sets, while color TV may be found in one home in every seven that has television. Economic output on this scale would undoubtedly have been impossible without our rich endowment of human and natural resources, but it would also have been highly unlikely had the organization of these resources been attempted from the beginning by a business system radically different from the one we have known.

Great material abundance is the most obvious, thoroughly measured, and highly acclaimed effect of our business system, but the system has other effects, some of them equally praiseworthy and some not. With its associated pattern of income distribution, American business influences the operations of all levels of our government, the character of our political ideology and foreign policy, the rate of our economic growth and scientific advance, our patterns of family living and cooperation at work, and every phase of our artistic and intellectual endeavors. The essays in this book are

3

dedicated to describing and evaluating these important sociocultural effects of the American business system.

PROBLEMS OF DEFINITION

To assess the impact of business on other aspects of our society it is first necessary to define "business." Several definitions are possible, and the individual contributors to this volume have chosen among them according to their own needs. Some contributors clearly refer to the actions of business leaders individually or collectively, others focus primarily on the actions of corporations, and two treat business in a still more general sense by organizing part of their discussion of the family around the impact of socioeconomic employment and income distribution patterns that are influenced in substantial ways by business.

Even if it were a simple matter to define business, it would still be difficult to deal satisfactorily with the question of its general impact. It is by no means easy to differentiate the effects of business from those of other agencies whose policies and practices are similar in order to compare and to evaluate them. First, business, the government, and other components of our society influence each other; this suggests among other things that the effects of a corporate decision cannot simply be attributed to "business" alone. Second, important social phenomena are caused by an incredible diversity of factors and forces, and as a practical matter it is enormously difficult to evaluate the contribution of any one group or agency.

The question of what our business system contributed to American economic growth, for example, is a complicated one, the answer to which would require the use of a set of simultaneous equations taking account of the interplay of a host of forces and factors. These would include investments in what economists call "social overhead capital"—roads, waterways, public health facilities, and the like, whose financing was usually shared by business and government—as well as such "variables" as the western frontier, with its natural resources and its challenges to wit and intelligence, America's political stability and system of currency, and its legal structure of regulations, tariffs, and laws protecting property, patents, contracts, and personal liberties. An analysis of such a disparate array of quantitative and qualitative dimensions would necessarily be an imprecise overview, the more so since the contribution of business to economic growth is simply one aspect of the multitude that would have to be considered in assessing business' general impact on America.

In the face of these difficulties, it is judicious to postpone the attempt at an overall assessment and to deal first with three general questions that crosscut the detailed analyses offered by the contributors:

1. What has been the effect of business on American "capitalism"?
2. What has been the effect of business on American democracy?
3. What has been the effect of business on individuals in America?

It will readily be seen that these questions take one a few steps beyond the more specific ones to which the contributors address themselves, yet they stop short of a level of analysis requiring a grand synthesis; the inherent vagueness in such words as "capitalism" and "democracy," meanwhile, guarantees that an effort to reach a "middle range" estimate will indeed be a preliminary one. These questions do have the virtue, however, that they oblige one to deal not only with a number of realities in American life but with standards against which these realities might in one way or another be judged. These standards may be derived from a limited number of "theories in search of reality," or theories formulated to order our thinking about reality. By examining some aspects of the most conventional "theoretical" formulations in search of American realities, in the realms to which these three questions relate, it is possible to assess their adequacy.

BUSINESS AND CAPITALISM[1]

Businessmen have minimized their ability to affect the environment in which they are obliged to operate. Their tendency has been to regard themselves as "intervening" rather than "independent" variables in the complex equations by which the operations of the economy are measured. A great many businessmen see themselves as rational decision-makers guided by (1) the best information they can secure on prices, interest rates, tax policies, government expenditures, labor markets, the practices of competitors, the preferences, moods, and demands of consumers, investors, and union leaders, and so forth; (2) straightforward accounting criteria having to do with costs and returns; and (3) their individual ethical commitments.

This view of their function causes many sensitive businessmen to feel that one of the government's primary functions is to punish those responsible for perversions of information—deceit and fraud, for example. More and more regard education in "social responsibility" as an important part of training for a business career. Inefficiency, meanwhile, continues to be regarded as a serious crime against economic rationality, and summary punishment is assured by the harsh discipline of the marketplace.

The problem of business power in the economy is treated with despatch. According to the University of Chicago's Milton Friedman, whose views on economic matters often win the approval of the business community, the most important fact about monopoly in industry, as contrasted with monopoly in labor and governmentally produced monopoly, is "its relative unimportance from the point of view of the economy as a whole." While businessmen acknowledge the existence of large and powerful enterprises, a fact that has preoccupied critics of capitalism and of our business leaders for generations, they do not agree that these enter-

---

[1] Some of the themes of the next three sections of this introduction are illustrated at length in a volume that is in several respects a companion to this one: James Kuhn and Ivar Berg, *Values in a Business Society: Issues and Analyses* (New York: Harcourt, Brace & World, 1968); see especially Chs. 8–10. The editor has collaborated with Professor Kuhn for many years as co-teacher and co-author, and it would be difficult for him to single out here every strand of thinking that originally grew out of their association. This general acknowledgment must take the place of a more detailed expression of gratitude.

prises constitute a danger to our system of private enterprise. They tend to stress how many enterprises there are in America, rather than how few are in positions of unusual power. As Professor Friedman has observed,

> There are some four million separate operating enterprises in the United States; some four hundred thousand new ones are born each year; a somewhat smaller number die each year. Nearly one-fifth of the working population is self-employed. In almost any industry that one can mention, there are giants and pygmies side by side.[2]

Business as a Constrained Force

The businessman's view of himself as a reactor rather than as an active initiator in economic affairs is supported from "outside" by a number of ranking theoreticians and researchers. One is Arthur F. Burns, currently professor of economics at Columbia University and the president of the influential National Bureau of Economic Research and formerly chairman of President Eisenhower's Council of Economic Advisers. His views on the role of the businessman, at least as he has expounded them in his most popular book,[3] would seem to be shared by all but a minority of business leaders whose positions may be located at the liberal and conservative extremes of what John K. Galbraith has described as "the conventional wisdom." For Professor Burns, business—meaning business leadership—is an intervening variable between the causes of economic events and the events themselves. His review and appraisal of the growth, level of activity, and utilization of manpower of the American economy during the period since World War II gives enormous weight to public policies, union demands, and Presidential speeches as causes for the waxing and waning of business prosperity and attaches relatively little importance to the initiating actions of business.

The upsurge—or boom—in economic activity during the mid-1960's, Burns believes, can only partly be explained by reference to "the application of fiscal stimuli in a context of monetary ease"[4] underlined by adherents of the new economics.[5] "Rather," he writes, "the want of sufficient confidence . . . kept investment from expanding more vigorously during 1961,"[6] and prevented an earlier economic recovery from an "inventory recession" in 1960–61. He goes on to identify the mechanics of the businessman's and the economy's dependence upon the specific initiatives of others:

> The coming of a new [Kennedy] administration that was strongly supported by the trade union movement inevitably raised questions in the minds of busi-

---

[2] Milton Friedman, *Capitalism and Freedom* (Chicago: University of Chicago Press, 1962), pp. 119–32.
[3] *The Management of Prosperity, The 1965 Fairless Lectures* (New York: Columbia University and Carnegie Presses, 1966).
[4] *Ibid.*, p. 17.
[5] See, for example, James Tobin, "The New Era of Good Feelings," in *National Economic Policy* (New Haven, Conn.: Yale University Press, 1966), pp. 35–42.
[6] Burns, *op. cit.*, p. 18.

nessmen who were already concerned about the steady rise of labor costs and the erosion of profit margins during the late fifties.[7]

After outlining the fears of businessmen following President Kennedy's inauguration—fears of increasing federal budget deficits, union-wrought cost-squeezes, continued deterioration in payments balances, new taxes, and even price controls—he observes:

> The fears of the business community reached a climax in April 1962 when President Kennedy moved sternly to force the major steel companies to rescind [price increases] that they had just posted. This action by the President had no clear sanction in law and it caused consternation in business circles. . . . Since the beginning of 1962 economic recovery had shown some signs of hesitation. Now, with confidence shaken, its continuance became much more doubtful . . . the economy became sluggish in 1962.[8]

Thus when things begin to go badly in the economy it is because confidence among businessmen gives way to fear generated by the acts, or even the possibility of acts, by others. "Fortunately," however, writes Professor Burns rather colorfully of the period in question,

> An imminent recession was forestalled. President Kennedy had a quick and honest mind . . . he turned at once to the difficult task of rebuilding confidence. . . . By stressing the vital role of free markets and of profits in generating economic growth in a series of pronouncements, he helped to reassure the business community. . . . However . . . confidence . . . cannot be restored promptly or by verbal reassurances alone. Skepticism among businessmen lingered on until it became quite plain that the government was seeking to create a better environment for business enterprise.

Constructive actions were not long delayed. The actions Burns classifies as constructive reveal something of the substances of which the confidence of the business community is made:

1. The granting of liberalized, "more realistic" depreciation allowances.
2. An investment tax credit formulated in line with business wishes.
3. A sweeping tax reduction for corporations and individuals.
4. President Kennedy's "firmness in handling the Cuban missile crisis in the fall of 1962 [that] made Americans feel better about themselves and their country. . . ."
5. The rejection of larger federal spending, while favoring tax reduction, as a fiscal stimulant for the economy.
6. President Johnson's "judicious handling" of the office he inherited after the tragic assassination of Mr. Kennedy.
7. President Johnson's first budget, which "supplied new and more tangible evidence that our nation's fiscal policy was really changing."
8. President Johnson's proof of the "new mood of frugality . . . by announcing cuts in expenditures or by indicating that the new policy of tax reduction [would] be continued."

[7] *Idem.*
[8] *Ibid.*, pp. 19–20.

9. President Johnson's "business-like manner."

10. President Johnson's new appointments from which businessmen "drew encouragement."[9]

These and other passages in Burns's influential book well illustrate the significant elements of the most widely held theories of the role of the businessman in America's particular brand of capitalism. Presidents, labor leaders, and other personalities can cause fear or threaten confidence among businessmen; businessmen simply respond in proportion as they are fearful or confident. Their responses are rationally adapted to circumstances brought about by others.

On the one hand, confidence is high if circumstances are favorable, which is to say, (1) if government cuts back on its impact on the economy by reducing the tax bite it takes of the social pie and also its expenditures, (2) if unions and union members accept their current relative *share* of the national product as an equitable one and seek increases in the *absolute* amount of their rewards only in proportion to increases in their productivity-per-manhour, and (3) if the levers of political and regulatory power are not moved heavy-handedly. Waste attributable to mismanagement, meanwhile, can only occur in the short run in a given enterprise, for in the long run it will be penalized by the forces of competition and the related process of technological change.

Confidence is shattered, on the other hand, if government expenditures for welfare programs, measures to counter injustices against Negroes, or expanded public works drain off even a small part of the gross national product from the private sector. When funds and resources are controlled and allocated by government rather than by the market, it is impossible for businessmen and investors to count them among the prizes to be sought and among the incentives that are needed to grease the nation's economic machinery and to reduce the frictions generated by an immoderate squeezing of profit by cost. Business is helpless, or so the theory goes.

Business as a Constraining Force

The Marxist critique of the economic thinking underlying analyses of the kind symbolized by Burns's book is in some ways a progressively less interesting one.[10] As latter-day Soviet Marxists seek to find a rational way into a "consumer economy" in which relatively more economic planning is to be supplemented by something like a market and in which principles of cost accounting are considered highly relevant, their talk of the impersonality of economic forces under capitalism, of the "fetishism of commodities," and of the "exploitation" of surplus value and the rest takes on a particularly tedious and hollow ring. One can hardly avoid recognizing the tortured logic in distinguishing, in the abstract, between "socialist profit," of which much is written in the U.S.S.R., and plain old capitalist profit.

---

[9] *Ibid.*, pp. 20–23.
[10] The is not to suggest that the political and sociological content of the Marxist critique is uninteresting; the reference here is to its economic aspects.

Of somewhat greater interest is the degree to which neo-orthodox economic theory—blended with increasing proportions of Keynesian fiscal and monetary policy—is adequate to the job it is called upon to do, implicitly by businessmen and explicitly by economists like Burns. "More cannot be derived from a theory than is put in by assumption," says Gardiner Means,[11] who has labored many years to bring economic theory in line with reality. He has long maintained that the American economy is far different in reality from the way it is pictured in the theoretical apparatus employed in standard economics textbooks[12] and in conventional estimates of the businessman's role in the American economy. In an essay on capitalism and economic theory, Professor Means wrote:

> [No] comprehensive economic theory has been developed in terms of [a corporate economy, as contrasted with an atomistic or a factory economy] in spite of the fact that the collective enterprise of our great corporations sets the tone of today's economy. As a result we stand with a great deal of economic theory but with a major part built on an obsolete base [the atomistic economy] and another part disproved by events [the evolution of a subsistence economy into first a factory and then a corporate system. A] major reconstruction of economic theory is in order.[13]

Means concludes that in place of a theory that applies to atomistic conditions altered only to accommodate the facts regarding the pervasive separation of ownership from control and the size, wealth, and power of large business units,

> it is necessary to create a body of theory which applies to collective capitalism and modify it to the extent necessary to allow for the fact that not all enterprise is collective—i.e., corporate, large, and potent enterprise.[14]

In contrast to an analysis in the classical tradition, in which the firm is merely one entity, one *persona ficta*,[15] among many, in which the powers of corporate leaders are treated as "deviant cases," and in which the businessman is a rational but passive reactor, Means suggests a model in which the capacity of businessmen to shape reality be brought to stage center. Thus he would make major changes in "employment theory," the "theory of the firm," "allocation theory," "wage theory," and "growth theory"—which, in their present form, he argues, are special cases of neo-orthodox theory that has been rendered obsolete by the inability of traditional models of economic equilibrium to account for large corporations or

[11] "Collective Capitalism and Economic Theory," in Andrew Hacker, ed., *The Corporation Take-over* (New York: Doubleday, 1965), p. 63. This and the subsequent quotations from the paperback edition of Hacker's book are used with the permission of Harper & Row, Publishers, New York, publishers of the original edition, 1964.
[12] See, for example, Adolf A. Berle, Jr., and Gardiner Means, *The Modern Corporation and Private Property* (New York: Macmillan, 1932), and Gardiner Means, *The Corporate Revolution* (New York: Crowell-Collier, 1962).
[13] In Hacker, *op. cit.*, p. 67.
[14] *Idem.*
[15] For a striking analysis of this doctrine see Thurmond Arnold, *The Folklore of Capitalism* (New Haven, Conn.: Yale University Press, 1937). Yale published a paperbound edition in 1959.

for a good many modern unions. These large units are often powerful enough in the marketplace to administer the prices for materials, goods, services, and products. They are, in short, able to tinker with the market and, more particularly, with its governor, the pricing mechanism.

At the same time profits would appear to Means to have a different status in a corporate economy in which professional managers, rather than owners, direct the course of business policy. This status is not easily linked to the simplified role assigned to profits in classical theory in which owners risked their fortunes for returns on their capital as well as on their time, energies, and imaginations.

The differences between the two theoretical schools, here represented by Burns and Means, are a matter of approach. One group, for whom Burns may speak, believes that classical models—updated to take account of bigness in industry and the effects of big government, big labor, and other new developments—adequately equip one to discuss cause and effect in the American economy. Another group, in whose name Means speaks, feels that most intricate new theories of "oligopoly," "monopsony," industrial organization, and the rest consist simply of conceptual baggage that has been loaded on the classical train of thought and do not correct such basic classical assumptions as the commodity theory of labor, profit maximization, and price flexibility—all regarded as inapplicable in the modern American economy. For this group, our economy is one in which prices may be administered, in which managers rather than investors allocate much of the corporation's income, and in which numerous private and public goals compete with profits for the attention and energy of corporate decision-makers. Thus it is not considered amenable to conventional economic analysis. Professor Means writes:

> We need to start fresh and ask just what are the motivations of top corporate management—to increase their personal incomes, to serve the stockholders, to expand management's power to foster the status of the corporate collective, to serve the public interest? Clearly a new theory of the firm to apply to the corporate collective must start with an analysis of motivation in the big business bureaucracies. Such an analysis must be based on actual observation. This will not be easy, because motivation is itself elusive. Perhaps such investigations will require the joint action of economist, political scientist, psychologist and anthropologist. . . . The bureaucratization of industry requires still another extension of the theory of the firm—the study of the bureaucracy itself. How are the great corporations actually run? . . . In some degree this aspect of enterprise theory must deal with the same problems of administration as those dealt with by political theory in its analysis of government bureaucracy. [This] will be a new kind of allocation theory in which the unseen hand of Adam Smith is replaced by the visible hand of business bureaucracy.[16]

The editor is inclined to a sympathetic view of Professor Means's position and to be optimistic about the possibility of an evolution in economic thought that will carry us closer to the kind of theory to which Means is pointing. This is not to

[16] In Hacker, *op. cit.,* pp. 76–77.

say that Means himself has offered a wholly satisfactory picture of our economy, or that the views of Burns are radically incorrect; rather, it is the direction and emphasis of Means's thought that seem particularly attractive. The cooptation of liberal-intellectual ideas (discussed in Chapter 5), the increasing consciousness of the interdependence of business and government brought on by the space age, and the movement of sociologists into research on poverty, business management, and complex organizations point to a readiness and an empirically demonstrable need for revisions in "received doctrine."

Business as a Responsible Force

The degree of conflict between the two theoretical approaches to business should not be exaggerated, of course. Substantial changes have already taken place in the theoretical apparatus applied by proponents of more orthodox economic analysis. Much has been made by some business leaders themselves of their role as arbiters among employees, consumers, stockholders, and the public at large.

A growing literature points to the fact that many business leaders have a sense of "social responsibility" and that they increasingly consider the "public's interests" along with others' in their decision-making in respect to prices, employment policies, competitive practices, and even such "non-economic" matters as civil liberties, political action, and urban planning.[17]

According to one interpretation—perhaps the boldest and best-known of the efforts to deal with managerial *noblesse oblige* and the doctrine of the social responsibilities of businessmen—the Protestant ethic has operated as a "modifier of transcendent quality" in American capitalism. Borrowing from Max Weber's classic analysis of the role of ascetic Protestant ethics in western economic life, Adolf Berle sees a "transcendental margin" in the contemporary American value system, leading businessmen and the rest of us to pay tribute to the Golden Rule. Earlier, writes Professor Berle,

> prosperity resulting from economic activity was [seen as] proof . . . that the Lord had destined the fortunate one for greater fields of work and wider service.
>   That, however, did not mean that the fortunate one, having received his reward, could do as he pleased. To the contrary: The greater the reward, the greater the obligation [to serve] the community.[18]

[17] This issue is considered in Kuhn and Berg, *op. cit.*, Chs. 3–5. See Clarence C. Walton, *Corporate Social Responsibilities* (Belmont, Calif.: Wadsworth, 1967). See also Richard Eells and Clarence C. Walton, *Conceptual Foundations of Business* (Homewood, Ill.: Richard D. Irwin, 1961); Scott Walton, *American Business and Its Environment* (New York: Macmillan, 1966), Chs. 11, 22, and 32; Earl Cheit, ed., *The Business Establishment* (New York: John Wiley, 1964), Ch. 5; Edward Mason, ed., *The Corporation in Modern Society* (Cambridge, Mass.: Harvard University Press, 1960), Chs. 3, 5, and 10. This issue is also touched upon by several contributors to the present volume, but see especially those by Eells, Walton, and Rogers and Zimet.
[18] Adolf A. Berle, Jr., *The American Economic Republic* (New York: Harcourt, Brace & World, 1963), p. 191.

This obligation is still felt today, he suggests. Thus Berle, who had participated with Means in the earlier study[19] that constituted so significant an attack on the assumptions of traditional economic theory, in recent times seems relatively tranquil about the significance of his earlier findings. In 1933 he wrote:

> The divorce of ownership from control consequent on the translation of perhaps two-thirds of the industrial wealth of the country from individual ownership to ownership by the large, publicly financed corporations almost necessarily involves a new form of economic organization of society.[20]

And that therefore:

> The future may see the economic organism, now typified by the corporation, not only on an equal plane with the state, but possibly even superseding it as the dominant form of social organization.[21]

By 1963 Professor Berle had come about to the view that America is an "economic republic [that] will insist on dominating the economy"[22] and that

> A large and growing transcendental margin has been created. The cause for its creation was not search for gain or personal power. The motive, albeit mixed, transcended the calculable individual interest of the numberless men who contributed the capital. Either through their individual processes of conscience or through compulsion of a social conscience, they were led to recognize and give realization to a range of values arising more out of ethics than out of interest.[23]

Other social commentators are less sanguine about the correlates and consequences of a broadened and deepened sense of social responsibility. Believing in the older theory and the need to preserve institutional structures in the form in which traditional theory contemplated them, they deplore a variety of actions that might be assimilated only by a newer theory. Milton Friedman, for example, holds that the view that managers and labor leaders have a social responsibility that goes beyond serving the interest of their stockholders or their members

> shows a fundamental misconception of the character and nature of a free economy. In such an economy, there is one and only one social responsibility of business—to use its resources and engage in activities designed to increase its profits so long as it stays within the rules of the game, which is to say, engages

---

[19] Berle and Means, *op. cit.* This study first examined in empirical terms the extent of separation of corporate management from ownership of American capital. Many of the implications of this separation for legal and economic analysis were earlier adumbrated by Max Weber, *Theory of Social and Economic Organization* (New York: The Free Press, 1947), and by John P. Davis, *Corporations* (New York: G. P. Putnam's Sons, 1905). The manuscript for this volume was completed in 1897. It was reprinted under the same title by Capricorn Books, in paperback, New York, 1961.
[20] Berle and Means, *op. cit.*, pp. vii–viii.
[21] *Ibid.*, p. 357.
[22] Berle, *The American Economic Republic*, p. 127.
[23] *Ibid.*, p. 198.

in open and free competition, without deception or fraud. Similarly, the "social responsibility" of labor leaders is to serve the interests of the members of their unions. It is the responsibility of the rest of us to establish a framework of law such that an individual in pursuing his own interest is, to quote Adam Smith, "led by an invisible hand to promote an end which was no part of his intention. . . ."

Few trends could so thoroughly undermine the very foundations of our free society as the acceptance by corporate officials of a social responsibility other than to make as much money for their stockholders as possible. This is a fundamentally subversive doctrine.[24]

The Force of Reality

While theorists and their theories seek to locate and define reality, reality continues not only to change but to lend itself at once to diverse theoretical formulations. This is so because elements of reality support a variety of mutually inconsistent assumptions, depending on what is chosen for examination, and because these elements may be differentially construed depending upon the terms of the assumptions themselves. Sometimes the quest for reality is confounded by a kind of surrealism in the efforts of intelligent people to reach agreement on even fundamental terms used in theoretical discourse. The upshot, inevitably, is to make evaluation of the impact of business dependent to a significant degree upon terminology and to imbed evaluatory efforts in a morass of semantic considerations and extra-theoretical value judgments.

Thus U.S. Steel's board chairman, Roger Blough, told a 1957 Senate subcommittee investigating identical prices for some products that "the buyer has more choice when the other fellow's price matches our price."[25] This "theory," which contradicts the basic principle of a competitive economy and undermines the argument that businessmen cannot influence their environment, does recognize that corporations must protect their markets by offering a variety of services, benefits, and delivery commitments not easily reflected in the market prices of competitors. Further evidence that businessmen have something to do with their own fate and do not constantly behave according to any discernible theory is provided by the notorious electrical-equipment pricing conspiracy case of the early 1960's, touched off by a competition for the building of turbogenerators for the Tennessee Valley Authority. The rationality—or at least the arithmetic—of managers who explained their uniformly high bids on the basis of the cost of American labor was placed in considerable doubt when it was discovered that the winning bid of a British corporation would have been $4 million to $5 million lower even if one of the conspiring American corporations had obtained its

[24] Friedman, op. cit., p. 133.
[25] For a discussion of this and other gyrations in the logic of much of the rhetoric employed in economic debate see Ivar Berg, "The Confidence Game," in Columbia University Forum, Vol. 6 (Winter, 1963), pp. 34–40. See also Kuhn and Berg, op. cit., Section 4.

labor—including engineers, draftsmen, and other salaried personnel as well as hourly rated factory workers—entirely free![26]

An analogous problem with mathematics seemed in evidence when the Ford Motor Company proclaimed in its 1960 annual report that in negotiations with 120,000 production workers it was going to "hold the line on all costs, avoiding particularly any labor cost increases that would force us to raise prices" in order to help fight the inflation that was allegedly draining the confidence of businessmen and squeezing corporate profits. At the same time, however, it was reported that Ford was awarding $33.6 million in bonuses to 4,373 "executives." (Ford production workers earned a reported $29 million increase in wages in 1959.) Both items were carried in front-page news stories the same day by the Detroit *Free Press*.

Reports in the *Wall Street Journal* of similar stories in other industries are not easily interpreted in accordance with any economic theory, particularly with a theory that assigns the businessman very little weight as an initiator in the economic process. Businessmen would seem to have more responsibility than they readily admit for positive corporate actions, and the same may be said with respect to corporate failures and inaction. Thus, Ford was allegedly unable to locate even one person on whom basic responsibility could be fixed for the Edsel fiasco that cost the company upwards of half a million dollars.[27] And railroad executives almost persuaded the public in the 1950's and 1960's that unions, government regulations, and taxes were responsible for bleeding dry one of the largest arteries of industrial capitalism. The fireman who tends no fires on diesel locomotives has come to personify the slow death by leeching of a once great industry that survived at all only because its executives were alert to even marginal opportunities for profit.

These disclaimers are hard to accept. To those familiar with the railroad industry, the very fact of the diesel engine's use is surprising, because it looked for some time as if many railroad managers would manage to hold on to the old-fashioned, puffing "iron horse" forever in spite of its having been made technically and financially obsolete by the advent of the diesel. The president of the Pennsylvania Railroad, addressing a stockholders meeting in the late 1940's (many confident years after the diesel had proved itself), announced with an apparent mixture of nostalgia and resentment that since savings of 33⅓ per cent could be realized by the change from steam, the Pennsy was compelled to dieselize! Given the sad circumstances of so many of our railroads, one inevitably wonders how many other railroading decisions were reached with such studious, stout, and faithful confrontations with opportunity.

All these examples of the behavior of business leaders have involved mistakes

[26] For a fuller discussion of the history and details of this see Clarence C. Walton and Frederick Cleveland, *Corporations on Trial: The Electrical Case* (Belmont, Calif.: Wadsworth, 1964).

[27] This automobile failed in its first year (1957) on the market despite careful surveys alleging considerable demand for such a vehicle. A full-sized automobile, it appeared on the market at about the same time that small, imported-car sales reached their peak in the U.S.

and incompetence. American managers do, however, make astute decisions far more often than these cases may suggest. If they didn't, our economy would never have achieved the preeminence it enjoys today. But "right" decisions, and the profits following from them, seem to be their own reward; journalists and scholars have relatively little interest in recording for posterity the details of good managerial behavior compared to their interest in recording obtuseness and failure. As often happens, therefore, we are in large part reduced to learning from our mistakes, but it would be reassuring to have at least a little evidence that managers are no more bound to the "rationality" of our microeconomics textbooks in their successful operations than in their failures. Evidence of this sort would seem to have been provided by Margaret Chandler and Leonard Sayles, who report from an examination of decisions to contract-out (or subcontract) plant maintenance and construction work, that

> complex cost calculations were not employed universally [in determining whether it is cheaper to contract-out or to do the work inside] but rather were limited to about three-fifths of the group. Of the remaining 40 per cent, about 30 per cent made rough computations, and slightly over 10 per cent made absolutley no cost calculations. Surprisingly, the character of the computing system had no relationship to conclusions regarding relative cost. . . .
>
> Size of plant seemed to have some relationship to estimates of the relative cost of contracting-out versus in-plant operations. A significant majority of the larger plants considered contracting-out cheaper than inside work.[28]

It would be unreasonable to cite these particular findings as conclusive evidence of "irrational" decision-making; rather, they indicate that "cost . . . tended to be an 'iffy' matter, often yielding its key position to other considerations,"[29] and that high-level managers are often free to disregard cost calculations in their decision-making. The argument that information costs are high and that it might not pay to make cost calculations begs the question of how "rational" are economic decisions that can so often be made on the basis of non-economic considerations. Some rough answers to the question, however, may be found in a monograph based "on a series of interviews with top management of a representative group of large-scale enterprises . . . conducted . . . for the purpose of interpreting the general role of big business in the American economy. . . ." The authors report:

> It was evident that most of the executives with whom the interviews were conducted did not ordinarily concern themselves with pricing details; instances appeared in which they were not intimately aware of how their products were priced. Even those who were quite familiar with company policy in the pricing area were among those who could not illustrate the policy by a detailed follow-through of particular price decisions. The fact that in some of the companies there was a gulf between the top officials and the price makers is in itself significant.
>
> Even where the people doing the pricing tended to have certain staff informa-

[28] *Contracting-Out: A Study of Management Decision Making* (New York: Columbia University Graduate School of Business, 1959), p. 36.
[29] *Idem.*

tion placed before them while making up their minds, whether and just how that information was taken into consideration often remained obscure. . . . Repeatedly, reference was made to the "art" or "feel" of pricing rather than observance of a formula.[30]

Clearly, capitalism is an evolving system; its dimensions are sometimes rapidly and sometimes slowly modified by a variety of forces, not excluding those triggered and controlled by businessmen themselves. If prevailing theories do not do justice to reality it is at least partly because theorists resist the need to modify assumptions about reality that may be reconciled with "the facts" only by scholastic logic. The facts of our modern business world are that businessmen, their protests to the contrary, regularly influence the destinies of their enterprises. They also regularly liberate themselves from the very market forces they extol in their rhetoric, and they accept the subsidies, depreciation allowances,[31] and stockpiles that are part of the welfare system they decry. When they characterize government assistance to corporations as confidence-building and similar assistance to the dependent children of impoverished unwed mothers as confidence-shattering, they are partly correct, but only because they are in a position to fulfill many of their own dire predictions if the former assistance is cut back and the latter expanded. Reality can fulfill theory not because the theory is correct but because some of the conditions of its fulfillment are to a remarkable degree controllable by those who favor the assumptions that inform the theory.

Our discussion to this point causes us to reserve judgment on the issue of whether businessmen are simply (1) rational decision-makers (2) who respond to opportunities, (3) who are constrained to react to parameters controlled largely by others and (4) whose behavior therefore is at least described adequately in conventional economic analysis, except insofar as (5) they have added an element of social responsibility to their decision-making. Judgment must be reserved, on the one hand, because cases can be mobilized that do not fit such a model of reality and, on the other, because cases are "for instances" and "for instances" do not disprove a theoretical system that can cover all cases, however deviant, simply by distinguishing between the long and the short runs or by using rubbery categories that may be shaped to fit empirical exigencies.

BUSINESS AND DEMOCRACY

If it is not an easy matter to estimate the impact of business on American "capitalism," it is no less difficult to reach a straightforward answer to the question, "What is the impact of business on American democracy?" American democracy is distinguished partly because of our adherence to "constitutionalism," which provides that political power exercised in the public's name be fragmented

---

[30] Abraham D. H. Kaplan, Joel B. Dirlam, and Robert Lanzilotti, *Pricing in Big Business: A Case Approach* (Washington, D.C.: Brookings Institution, 1958), p. 5.

[31] Obviously depreciation allowances have not only the desirable effect of encouraging successful managers to make inventive investments but the effect, also, of helping to defray the costs to the firm of managerial misjudgment.

in order that its exercise be constrained and limited. Americans have long been committed to the belief that when power is shared by voluntary associations and by governmental units organized on different levels and split at most levels along the lines of "separate" powers, the result is a kind of "pluralism" that avoids, on one side, the centralized autocracy made infamous in totalitarian societies and, on the other, the anomic atomism contemplated by Hobbes of "the war of all against all."

In addition to its appeal as a defense against autocracy and anarchy, pluralism has also the positive attraction of appearing to be the political equivalent of the free-enterprise economic system. Like economic acts, political acts must not be of such scope and magnitude that they can do more than cause occasional tremors in the institutional landscape; if either type of power—economic or political— becomes too great, it may cause cracks in the foundations of our system. It is better that economic and political power be decentralized and dispersed among a multitude of decision-makers so that even their major undertakings will be of marginal rather than of central significance to the maintenance of the common-weal. This sociology of democracy, "adumbrated by James Madison and rein-forced by Alexis de Tocqueville," Hacker has written,

> is firmly fixed in our thinking. This model presupposes a wide dispersion of power among many interacting and overlapping groups in both society and the political system. Some measure of equilibrium among forces is assumed, and if there is conflict it results in compromises not overly oppressive to any of the participants.[32]

"Big Business" in a Pluralistic Society

The facts of American life have caused many observers to doubt whether plural-ism in the United States has actually resulted in the kind of democracy or capitalism our ideology commends. The atomistic market model is far less than fully applicable in the face of the emergence of large corporate structures like General Electric, American Telephone and Telegraph, and Standard Oil of New Jersey. And when these and other business behemoths enter the political arena, as Professor Hacker puts it,

> we have elephants dancing among the chickens, for corporate institutions are not voluntary associations with individuals as members but rather associations of assets, and no theory yet propounded has declared that machines are entitled to a voice in the democratic process.[33]

In a lively discussion of the emergence of powerful "corporate citizens" and their effect on the theoretical benefits of pluralism to America, Henry Kariel argues that we have witnessed a gradual decline in the public capacity to exercise power simply because the principles of federalism and separation of powers make for governmental disorganization and stalemate. At the same time, "private" power has grown enormously because of the integrating tendencies of technology and the fragmented nature of the public powers that might otherwise have acted as a

[32] Andrew Hacker, "Introduction: Corporate America," in Hacker, *op. cit.*, p. 7.
[33] *Ibid*, p. 7, cited in the contribution to this volume by Clarence C. Walton, p. 86.

countervailing force. The conclusions Professor Kariel draws from his review of the strategic role of a relatively small number of large organizations[34] are worth citing in full:

> Cooperating with the major organs of the national government and more or less peaceably disposed toward the leadership of the great labor unions, the corporate giants occupy a strategic economic position. Well-disciplined organizations with control of their material and financial resources, they have the means to promote not only their social but also their economic policies. Generously permitting smaller corporations and public governments at all levels to share a portion of their surplus, they constitute a formidable reservoir of public power. However sensitive to the aspirations of the groups that they govern, however inefficient their rule in practice, and however responsive to a government-endorsed national interest when it is virtually unanimous, they wield power in a stupendously large sector of our economic order. They determine the level and the distribution of national income. They direct the allocation of scarce resources, and they decide the extent and the rate of technological and economic development. They fix the level and the conditions of employment, the structure of wage rates, and the terms, tempo, and season of production not only for themselves but also for those who use their bargaining agreements as models. They decide which labor markets to exploit and which to reject. And they control the quality of goods and services as well as the standards and quantities of consumption.
>
> Insofar as corporate oligarchies effectively control industrial systems, and insofar as the systems manage to bring under their influence vast areas of the public, it is corporate oligarchies that control public life. As their environment remains at peace, they become secure; as the world outside becomes dependent, they become independent. Their law becomes *de facto* constitutional law; their economic behavior becomes statesmanship; their social conduct becomes public morality. The organizations they control emerge as self-maintaining political communities prospering in a social setting made ever more hospitable. Their professional duty becomes to govern well, to operate as self-appointed stewards, responsible but unaccountable, integrating a multitude of interests, not selfishly but for the sake of the enterprises they rule. Their systems are self-centered: once properly primed, they generate, replenish, and purify themselves. Above all, they provide their own validation, their own excuse for being. Ironically, they come to represent the sovereign, conscience-burdened individuals in whose behalf John Locke vindicated the Glorious Revolution.[35]

Kariel's thesis is not unlike that of the late Professor C. Wright Mills, who pointed out, besides, that no "conspiracy theory" is involved in recognizing that there is a "power elite" in America, since corporate and other leaders share a constellation of values, reach their positions from similar backgrounds, and have

[34] Regardless of whether there is a trend toward increasing concentration—a problem examined by Professor Eichner in this volume—the existing picture is "enough at odds with our economic mythology to justify attention. . . . One hundred and thirty-five corporations own 45 per cent of the assets of America's non-farm economy. Industries in which the four largest producing firms turn out half of the total value account for 57 per cent of the value of all manufactured products. In 22 industries the four largest do 80 per cent of their industry's business." Henry Kariel, *The Decline of American Pluralism* (Stanford, Calif.: Stanford University Press, 1961), p. 29.
[35] *Ibid.*, pp. 47–48.

a community of interests. Under these conditions, Mills argued, there is relatively little need for conspiracy tactics, though there is

> little doubt that the American power elite—which contains, we are told, some of "the greatest organizers in the world"—has also planned and has plotted.[36]

Professor Walton argues in his contribution to this volume that both Kariel and Mills have exaggerated the degree to which "private power" has gained in the face of a cumbersome and structurally differentiated public power, but there is no denying that we have moved far from the democracy Thomas Jefferson had in mind; our representative democracy has been obliged to make room for large oligarchies.

Compensatory Democracy

Granting that large private power blocs exist in America, some observers nevertheless maintain that these blocs are themselves democratic, that they are accountable to such sub-groups of American society as stockholders and constituent members. This argument also tends to stumble over a number of inconvenient facts. Certainly our large institutions do not behave like private democratic citizens in either the economic or the political spheres. To take one striking example, our large institutional investors, which have become increasingly important in the financial markets, each function "primarily as an investor, not as militant or crusading shareholders. [In] the Wall Street game of investing, you try to pass on to some unsuspecting buyer a security which you suspect will decline."[37] These insurance companies, banks, "funds," and investment houses do not, typically, extend their interests beyond voting for or against management and stockholder proposals on proxy statements; they rarely offer proposals in proxy statements or take the lead in proxy battles or other intracorporate activities. At least as regards institutional investors, John Maynard Keynes was right, to judge from Mr. Livingston's evidence, to liken investing to "a game of Snap, of Old Maid, of Musical Chairs."[38] The great English economist wrote of this pastime that it was one

> in which he is victor who says *Snap* neither too soon nor too late, who passes the Old Maid to his neighbor before the game is over, who secures a chair for himself when the music stops. These games can be played with zest and enjoyment, though all the players know that it is the Old Maid which is circulating, or that when the music stops some of the players will find themselves unseated.[39]

Large private power blocs do not behave like private citizens, yet democracy is not necessarily ruled out in a society in which blocs and individuals mingle and compete. The theory of "compensatory democracy" starts by assuming that direct

[36] *The Power Elite* (New York: Oxford University Press, 1959), p. 293.
[37] J. A. Livingston, *The American Stockholder* (New York: Collier, 1963), p. 137. Livingston is financial editor of the Philadelphia *Bulletin*.
[38] *Idem.*
[39] *The General Theory of Employment, Interest, and Money* (New York: Harcourt, Brace & World, 1962), p. 156.

representative democracy is impossible in a complex industrial society, but goes on to suggest that we profit greatly from the "pluralistic interplay" of countervailing forces themselves organized along democratic lines. The evidence, however, is impressive that Americans will sacrifice democracy within organizations in favor of other benefits. Public support for managerial short-circuiting of some of the democratic features of their organizations often appears to check the efforts we have made through legislation and regulatory measures to secure democracy in corporations and unions. American businessmen understandably favor organizational structures that respond to their initiatives; democracy is a time-consuming process and no business leader needs to be reminded that time is money.

In sum, our concern with organizational exigencies and the benefits allegedly flowing from hierarchial principles is sufficiently great that we frequently resolve conflicts between equity and efficiency in favor of the latter.[40] Our ambivalence on this score hardly coincides with the democratic ideals embodied in the laws of the land. Businessmen understandably prefer arrangements that do not upset the already delicate balances in the complex machinery of an industrial system, but it is well to remember that a price is exacted each time democratic principles are sacrificed to the requirements of industrial efficiency.

Industrial Democracy

Proof that we do sacrifice democratic principles under the pressure of industrial requirements is provided—with a regularity that would be downright horrifying to more rigidly committed democrats—by press reports on industrial conflict. These reports are often—even typically—accompanied by editorial commentary that is preachy and self-righteous in its condemnations of democratic impulses, even as it extols the virtue of efficiency and order. It would be fatuous to deny the degree to which the restiveness of managers has become part of the American value system in this regard.

When human discontent in a union serves to slow down our four-wheeled economy, when it inhibits the flow of entertainment by unionized actors and announcers on our TV screens, or when the picket signs of musicians offend the sensibilities of opera and symphony patrons, indignation is supposedly justified. Increasingly we are given to see that the private interests of intractable union members are trivial compared with the interests of the defenseless public; if a service to the public seems likely to be affected, then unions are clearly obliged to confine their action to civilized discussions with employers and to keep these, in turn, to a minimum. Above all, it has become a part of the conventional wisdom that strikes are extremely costly, and the fewer we have the better.

These are the lessons that countless pundits, editorialists, and reporters are teaching us in the 1960's: our society is, after all, confronted with so many threats and wracked by such uncertainty that we cannot afford irresponsible inter-

---

[40] For specific, if qualitative, analysis—where quantitative analysis is impossible—of the role of arbitrators in extending the reach of democracy in industry, see Eli Ginzberg and Ivar Berg, *Democratic Values and the Rights of Management* (New York: Columbia University Press, 1963).

ference with orderly economic processes and growth. We need not, or so it would seem, analyze the issues or the complexities of union organization—not to say the selfish interests of uninformed trade unionists who imperil both defense *and* economy—in order to invest our sympathies appropriately, for we are all aware of the imperatives of our times.

This grand chorus has an impressive unity. Occasionally, however, a theme is introduced that sounds slightly off-key. This is the principle of union democracy. When milk deliverers in Cincinnati voted themselves out of the Teamsters in 1961, for example, there was no little joy in the press.[41] Dissident drivers were interviewed and their reactions were reported as hopeful signs that even James R. Hoffa could not violate minimum democratic requirements forever without paying a price. Yet when some of Walter Reuther's striking auto workers voted down a hard-won settlement at the American Motors works at Kenosha, Wisconsin, a number of newspapers inveighed against prolongation of a strike that seriously and needlessly hampered the manufacture and sales of The Automobile.

Proponents of democracy—including, we may suppose, the Kenosha auto workers and their unlikely brothers the New York Philharmonic musicians, who also stubbornly resisted newspaper suggestions that their rewards in this world need not include an improved salary—may be forgiven possible consternation in the face of journalistic equivocations and the confused values of our business society itself. The press, after all, campaigned almost unanimously for passage of the Taft-Hartley Act and more recently for the Landrum-Griffin Act, both of which sought among other things to curb the power of autocratic union leaders through the cultivation of democracy in unions. This campaign, needless to say, enjoyed the public support of the business community. But there are few businessmen who would deny the advantages in dealing with "pros" in unions over dealing with politically insecure local union leaders. Favoring "grass roots democracy" is easy; bargaining with democrats is quite another matter.

Whether it is inconsistent to do so or not, we will in America continue both to fear "too much democracy" and become indignant about "not enough democracy," as though it were an object with quantitative attributes. When a union is demonstrably responsive to its constituents, we will continue to question the sense of responsibility of the blue-collar members to the larger public. When the organization of a union seems not to be democratic, we will worry about the morality and political ambitions of its white-collar leaders and seek through editorial exhortation and legislative pontification to bring democracy to the union hall and assembly line. But when a strike vote is announced, we will find some aspect of prior union procedures open to criticism in terms of some conception of democratic practice.

Our tendency to advance propositions about democracy in opposing strikes shows little sign of weakening, but that is hardly a sufficient justification for it. We do our democratic ideals a disservice by pretending that any strike, or threat of one, is *prima facie* evidence that democracy has broken down in one way or another. It is by no means clear that our society is entirely ill-served by striking

[41] For a fuller discussion of these and related cases, see the author's "The Nice Kind of Union Democracy," in *Columbia University Forum*, Vol. 5 (Spring, 1962), pp. 18–32. This essay contains relevant citations and dates that need not detain us here.

unionists; the price of lost production due to strikes may be significant to a given firm, but how infinitely greater must be the price paid, in totalitarian societies, for the orderly and strike-free economies they boast.

The press, of course, is not America, but it is entirely reasonable to impute to many citizens the editorial attitudes on which this discussion is based and to conclude that we do have some serious reservations about what was earlier referred to as "compensatory democracy" in practice.

BUSINESS AND THE INDIVIDUAL

While our system of business may have an impact upon capitalism and democracy that is sufficiently great to suggest the need for significant revisions in the economic and political theories that have currency in America, this is not one of its effects that reaches most deeply into the lives of most Americans. The fact that corporations do not have the status in the main body of formal theory that they have achieved in the economy is of intermittent interest to most citizens. A few of the complicated issues involved become somewhat crystalized, to be sure, in public debates during presidential election campaigns, over such vexing matters as "public spending" or "economic growth." Civil rights and civil liberties groups will be concerned about the inability of one or another public agency to ensure access to jobs or housing on a non-discriminatory basis. And unionists bent upon eliminating "sweetheart contracts" between corrupt union leaders and unscrupulous employers will resent the failure of legislators, prosecutors, and courts to assure them protection against repressive and coercive measures calculated to weaken and disarm union reformers. However, the public often believes, with the press and many corporate leaders, that a little democracy goes a long way and that the nice kind of democracy is the kind that does not interfere with the public convenience.

But if most Americans are only occasionally or selectively preoccupied with the modifications corporate reality has wrought upon "capitalism" and "democracy," they are regularly confronted with business in their efforts to earn their livings. In their workaday lives, they are constantly affected by the corporation; problems of size, power, and the imperatives of order and efficiency that remain abstract in their overall political and economic implications can and do become of great significance to them through their influence on the terms of employment contracts, the dimensions of the relationship between boss and worker, and the structure of employment opportunities. Every American is affected in these ways by our business system, but the men and women who actually work for one or another of our giant corporations are clearly affected most. The number of these citizens is great and growing. Employment is heavily concentrated in a handful of our largest corporations: 25 of the largest firms employed one-quarter of all persons working in manufacturing in 1965. In place of the yeomanry and the self-employed of an earlier day have appeared the workers, technicians, clerks, and managers whose livelihoods are inextricably bound up with the fortunes of large national corporations.

Certain aspects of this process of "bureaucratization" of work have received a good deal of attention in recent years. A number of studies, most of which have been classified and reviewed in Arthur Shostak's essay in this volume, have shown a solicitous concern, albeit on different grounds, for the psychological well-being of employed Americans. Some writers, and most especially Professor Daniel Bell,[42] have examined the limitations on meaningful work experience within large organizations in which skill hierarchies have been leveled and in which traditional crafts are converted into specialized jobs. Others, like Chris Argyris,[43] have explored the illogics of the organizational constraints upon the opportunity for members to "self-actualize." Apart from such psychological effects, the American system of business—particularly the large corporations that are such an important element of it—strongly influences the objective success and failure of countless individuals. Effects of this sort, which usually can be characterized not simply as good or bad, but as just or unjust, will be examined first; only then will the somewhat more shadowy psychological problems of industrial employees be considered.

Justice in the Relations Between Corporations and Individuals

The fact that Americans in growing numbers work in large privately owned corporations is obviously significant to any assessment of justice in the workplace. The comparative success of labor unions in protecting the rank and file of blue-collar workers should not blind us to the fact that three-quarters of all employed Americans negotiate with employers on the strength of their individual bargaining position in a formally free labor market. That the market does not always support their rights, as envisioned in the classical theory of the liberal state, is increasingly clear.

Many instances can be cited in which an individual's political rights have been infringed by his employer. In the contribution to this volume by Rogers and Zimet we may read of the unhappy fate of a steel executive in Alabama who dared to join an association seeking to assist in the desegregation of housing.

In another, less publicized, area engineers and scientists are beginning to note that their mobility in the labor force—their opportunities to exploit the investments they have made in their educations and training by responding to attractive job offers—is hardly absolute. In one celebrated case an engineer was enjoined from moving into a more responsible and better-paying job in his area of special competence (space-suit technology) because his employer, and eventually the court, felt he could not make such a change without taking with him precious company secrets. In this and other cases[44] the marketplace does not afford the

---

[42] "Work and Its Discontents," in *The End of Ideology* (New York: The Free Press, 1961), pp. 227–72.
[43] *Personality and Organization: The Conflict Between System and the Individual* (New York: Harper & Row, 1957).
[44] These and related cases are discussed in Ivar Berg and James Kuhn, "The Corporation and Civil Liberties," Business and Labor Committee, American Civil Liberties Union, April, 1966, mimeographed.

individual much help; employers can "freeze" an employee out of a particular technical niche if he insists on leaving. Even when the corporation's legal position does not appear very strong, a professional employee may hesitate to pursue a better job opportunity without some assurance that his new employer will offer legal and financial aid if he finds himself entangled with expensive suits or injunctions, while the employer to whom he might apply is likely to show a similar reluctance to become involved in litigation by hiring him.

With the increasing significance of complex technical operations in firms, with the growth of research and development or R&D and the increasing numbers of scientists, engineers, and technicians in the work force, this kind of proprietary power of corporations over the specialized skills acquired by employees looms as an important one. It is indeed ironic that the greater the investment made by individuals in their technical training and the greater their specialized knowledge, the greater the chance that the nebulous notion of "trade secrets" will limit their economic opportunities.

The interests of the corporations in these cases seem to be fairly clear; they have investments to protect and positions in their respective markets to consolidate and hopefully to expand. Journalists have accepted the companies' arguments for continued and increased protection of these interests. Writers in both *Fortune* and the professional journal *Chemical and Engineering News* have concluded over the years that the cases pose an ethical issue for employees, the recognition of which purportedly suggests an answer. The issue, as they size it up, is the conflict between an employee's obligation to his former employer not to divulge trade secrets and his duty to give his best to the new employer.

Such a formulation of the issue strongly implies that if the issue gives rise to any public interest, this interest is in restricting competition in the product and labor market and in distorting the utilization and allocation of technically competent manpower. Such is obviously not the case. While "trade secrets" are undoubtedly valuable to an employer, the public interest requires a careful balancing of the benefits of restricting information and employees against the losses caused by restraint of trade and possible curbing of labor mobility. Unquestionably many employers are honorably concerned about the well-being of their firms, but an uncritical acceptance of their arguments and actions may be dangerous to business firms generally, to the individual, and to the economy.

The corporations pleading in trade-secret cases against former employees tend to be confident of the nobility of their cause, whereas they make ambitious employees out to be exploitive, economic mercenaries whose loyalties are limited by their narrow definitions of self-interest and whose minds they sometimes regard as part of a corporation's inventory. The following characterization, in support of the thesis that "moral and ethical principles have now become secondary to achieving status among the worshippers of the bitch goddess 'Success',"[45] would not be out of place in such legal presentations:

[45] Philip Sporn, "Dimensions of the Ethical Problem," in Courtney Brown, ed., *The Ethics of Business: Corporate Behavior in the Market Place,* Columbia Business School Series No. 2 (New York, 1963), p. 5.

A bright young professional graduate is employed and receives some preliminary training. He is then enrolled in a special program at his employer's initiative and expense that may involve a full year's study at an outstanding school of nuclear technology. During the course of this study, not only his own salary, but his expenses, including those of his family, are taken care of fully. The consequent cost to the employer may be as much as $15,000, possibly even $20,000. Shortly after finishing his course, however, the employee exploits the skills acquired in the previous year's study to obtain a position with another employer. His justification is that it gives him wider opportunities he cannot see with his first employer. When the question of his moral responsibility in having permitted himself to be the beneficiary of such a special educational program, with the large expense which was incurred, is brought before him, his reaction is almost entirely as if he did not comprehend either the question or the issue.

Further, one is tempted to ask what about the moral responsibility of those who knew of his background, knew that he had been the beneficiary of this kind of training, and yet had no hesitation in negotiating with him to come to a new post, even though he had barely had time to say "thank you" for what he had received at the old.[46]

Few if any of the employees subjected to injunctions by former employers tried to leave in the first year after receiving expensive training; on the contrary, it is sometimes unclear whether the employer or the employee contributed more to the trade secrets that are the subject of the suit. Furthermore, some of the companies claiming the right to protect their investments, even at the expense of an individual's personal opportunity, accumulated their technical know-how with substantial public assistance in the form of government contracts. Thus taxpayers may unwittingly subsidize these restrictions on competition and individual mobility. It is also worth noting the possibility that in some instances patent applications do not contain full information on processes and devices. By limiting the mobility of knowledgeable technical personnel, under the guise of "trade secrets," employers may further safeguard the unreported portions of their patents, thus evading the spirit of patent laws.

The Remedies Available to the Injured

Since the public has an interest in the freedom of individuals to exploit their economic advantages and an interest in fostering product competition, some will question the assumptions made by employers who believe their position is legally and morally unchallengeable. To do so is not to doubt the good faith of company

---

[46] *Ibid,* p. 6. This formulation may be contrasted with a somewhat different position recorded a few pages later in the same work: "A society is good or ethical when it is organized in terms of the maximum development of the individual and the greatest good for the greatest number; and when it is organized to strive continually toward the improvement of these standards by bringing into play all the resources within that society, provided this does not deprive any of its individuals of their right to the *four freedoms.*" (p. 11.)

managers. That they have a legitimate concern for their company's good name, its efficiency, its community relations, and its hard-won technical triumphs cannot be gainsaid.[47]

In the trade-secrets cases that have reached the courts, employers typically prefer, as stated above, to bypass the demands and requirements of the market. Rather than offer improved conditions and wages to employees who have received attractive alternative employment proposals, they take the men to court. The bargaining relationship between employer and employee is redefined; the *individual* person becomes a litigant, contesting with a *corporate* person whose superior resources and ability to engage in long continued legal battles force him into an inferior bargaining position.

If the corporation wins, the individual may be denied effective choice in the marketplace for his labor, the implications of which are as serious as they are numerous. It is true that the number of jobs for professional managers and technical personnel has never been greater, and it is increasing rapidly, for the proliferation of large organizations creates these new jobs and positions faster than any other kind. The quantity of positions in existence should not be confused with the number of alternate job opportunities open to any one individual, however.

The bargaining power of white-collar employees does not necessarily increase as the number of white-collar jobs increases. The fact that only large organizations can provide the laboratories, engineering shops, experimental facilities, statistical records, computers, and capital equipment needed in many industries and occupations undermines the bargaining power of professional employees, technicians, and many middle-level white-collar personnel. They can find employment only among the large organizations—business, government, or non-profit corporations—that provide the opportunities for the specialization to which many of them have restricted their area of high competence. Their dependence is made greater by the tendency of larger firms to acquire smaller firms in which professionals and managers do have bargaining powers sufficient to avoid most constraints on their social behavior, political expressions, and job mobility. Finally, rapid technological change assures that the problem will become greater and that the number of people facing the problem will grow.

Encroachments on individual rights by the large organizations may, of course, contribute, in the long run, to collective action by professional employees, and by others in the growing army of white-collar workers as well, to gain more influence over their job rights and working conditions. There are, in theoretical terms, no reasons to believe that these newer masses will be blind to the relationship among their employment conditions, their opportunities, and their rights. Managers of large corporations probably would prefer not to contemplate such a development. If individuals do not enjoy the protection of "due process" within their employing organization and if at the same time they are denied escape from their situation through the market, however, they will not long suffer their bondage. Nor do they

---

[47] This discussion is adapted from Berg and Kuhn, "The Corporation and Civil Liberties," *op. cit.*

need to submit to it. The employees now being affected are articulate and educated and already have available professional associations that can become their militant defenders.

For the professionals and technicians to use their own associations as means to protect their rights and collectively bargain for them may not be necessary, if they are fully aware of the risks they run when accepting employment. Perhaps too few of the professionals presently realize the restrictions an employing company can later impose should they seek a job elsewhere; forewarned, they might be in a better position to discuss their rights and the limits to them before they accept employment and to demand compensation for any rights given up or limited. But there is no promise either in law or in the realities of contemporary American life that such "forewarning" will be offered them in any systematic way; corporate interests in the matter are still too complex to suggest the long-range position managers might take in respect to revisions in their present practice.

Since corporations and other large organizations deserve rewards for technological development, for innovation, and for inventive ways of advertising and distributing their wares, we may be able to devise ways to protect their interests along with those of the individuals. More consideration may, in time, be given to procedures for requiring, after a period of exclusive use, licensing of competitive firms to use secret processes and techniques in exchange for a royalty fee. Such a policy commends itself because the individuals would be free to seek job opportunities most advantageous to them, the originating company's interests would be respected, and the public would gain from increased competition in the product market as well as from increased freedom for individuals.

Other possible solutions and remedies may occur to the reader. Given the fact that large numbers of people are at least potentially affected by the decisions and precedents now being established, the issues involved deserve systematic attention. Surely unfavorable aspects of the general impact of business on individuals will grow to significant proportions if all the economic interests of large employing organizations are interpreted as property rights. Ironically, the property rights that liberal theory once regarded as absolutely necessary for the protection of individual rights now threaten to extinguish them in several respects.

Individuals in Corporations and Groups Outside Corporations

If there are grounds for concern about some of the ways in which growing numbers of unorganized Americans are coming to confront the "system" as employees and citizens, there also appear to be psychological problems in the experiences many individuals have as *members* of America's sprawling enterprises. Since the 1950's, a booming trade has developed in books and articles dealing with the psychic well-being of men and women who are seen to be, at one and the same time, too often the object of indulgent managerial succorance and too rarely recognized by managers to be other than "economic-men." One need only choose one's school of interpretation.

While many of the implications of this growing interest in the psychological health of a "bureaucratized" work force are explored here in the essays by Arthur Shostak on the meaning of work and by the editor on American ideology, it is worth making two points at the outset about the substitutability of (a) psychological for monetary rewards and of (b) psychological well-being for social concern.

Managerial efforts to introduce (one school of researchers) or expand (another school) the use of psychological strategies to foster good human relations, reduce "anomie," and improve employee morale rarely draw attention to the fact that the managers themselves are to a very considerable extent also part of the work force in business organizations. Human relations programs may thus sometimes represent an artful use of what critic Jacques Barzun has not altogether inappropriately described as "the misbehavioral sciences" to legitimatize, in a relatively inexpensive way, the power of managers over lower-echelon personnel. A search for legitimating characteristics is hardly surprising in the face of the separation of managers from property that once justified authority. Programs instituted for this reason do not appear to hold much promise, however. In the first place, they underestimate the intelligence of America's workforce, especially of the increasingly more sophisticated young people now entering the white-collar workforce for the first time. Second, group therapy and other psychological gimmicks seem unlikely to overcome the understandable anxieties generated by the mergers and acquisitions that regularly play havoc with job security, the computers that deprive middle-managers of the authority they once exercised over billing and tabulating clerks, or the "mystique of technique" of operations researchers that is offered as a replacement for the "hunches of the bunches" of personnel who once made inventory, marketing, and production decisions in committee meetings. While class conflict is of course not likely to break out in our large corporations,[48] neither is it likely that the behavioral scientist will be able to test his way through a population to locate employees or managers without personal interests or to obscure these interests in jobs, salary, and occupational security with ink blots or to deflect attention from conflicting interests by Freudian excursions into unresolved personality conflicts.

While the substitutability of psychological and more tangible rewards is evidently less than perfect, managerial concern for the psychological problems of personnel has sometimes completely displaced concern with wider social problems. Specifically, personnel managers and their consultants on human relations programs have often slighted the problems of individuals belonging to groups that have been excluded from our great enterprises and so been damaged far more deeply than the tender souls of men already at work. From the very beginning the civil rights movement drew much strength from the fact that individuals outside our business system are driven by it to form groups, no less than the employees within

---

[48] Riots in urban centers in the 1960's are, however, clearly as much class as caste efforts to attack an alien structure of which such corporations are an important part.

the system who organize for collective action. And while management may find employee groups irritating and unnecessary, groups of outsiders organized against a firm may sometimes have an even greater impact on its operations and balance sheet. The contribution by Rogers and Zimet describes the distressing results experienced by the management of one corporation that decided to locate a new plant in Selma, Alabama, completely unmindful of Negro efforts to secure their rights there. Similar individual cases abound, and the possibility of a wholesale reaction against managerial obliviousness to social problems has been forced upon the consciousness of the nation by urban riots on an unprecedented scale.

Although speeches by business leaders frequently claim that the opportunities for deserving individuals are as golden in the modern American business world as ever they were in the imaginary world of Horatio Alger, the fact is clearly otherwise: our corporations have not consistently lived by the philosophy that individuals should be promoted on the basis of their accomplishments and abilities alone. Every available study of the social composition of America's top-level business leaders discloses that selection procedures have participated in a more general social bias favoring the sons of white, middle-class, Protestant America.[49] To an important degree the characteristics, real or perceived, of other groups to which an individual may belong still weigh more heavily than his individual merit in corporate America. With respect to corporate discrimination against Negroes in particular, if one were to measure the progress of the United States in realizing its democratic ideals pertaining to employment since the early 1950's, when the Swedish economist Gunnar Myrdal documented the extent of discrimination in *An American Dilemma*, the result would be severely disappointing. Unions must share part of the responsibility that this situation exists, of course, but for most occupations management has primary responsibility for deciding whether discriminatory standards will continue to be observed. American corporations must be counted among the most powerful contributors to this persistent drag on our economy; to their credit, they are increasingly acknowledging that this is so.

Work remains to be done in America in respect to the full liberation of the individual. The benefits that can accrue to a corporation from manipulating employees and attempting to make chattels of highly specialized technicians or from discriminating against the less educated, the black, the Spanish-speaking, or the person whose age does not match some arbitrary requirement are limited in amount and offset by a host of disadvantages that seem certain to follow if corporate policies are not changed. If managers will scrupulously root out their

[49] Tight labor markets and the restlessness of minority groups in the 1960's may, however, modify slightly the portraits of corporate leaders drawn by William Miller, *Men in Business* (Cambridge, Mass.: Harvard University Press, 1952); Mabel Newcomber, *The Big Business Executive* (New York: Columbia University Press, 1955); W. Lloyd Warner and James C. Ablegglen, *Occupational Mobility in American Business and Industry, 1928–1952* (Minneapolis: University of Minnesota Press, 1955); Suzanne Keller, *The Social Origins and Career Lines of Three Generations of American Business Leaders* (Ph.D. Dissertation, Columbia University, 1953); and Reinhard Bendix, *Work and Authority in Industry* (New York: John Wiley, 1956), Ch. 4.

conscious and unconscious prejudices, act loyally to the best interests of their corporations, and strive for genuine efficiency in corporate operations, their firms will undoubtedly reap far greater rewards.

CONCLUSION

In the early pages of this introduction the task of attempting to assess the general impact of business on American society was postponed in favor of an examination of three questions that crosscut those around which the contributors organized their essays. The discussion of these three questions has suggested certain general propositions that the editor has found, in the course of his collaboration with the individual contributors, to hold true for the essays that follow.

The reader will sense an implicit warning that detailed examination of a particular aspect of American life will support few easy generalizations. Attractive as it may be to credit or to blame business for the quality of one or another facet of "life in these United States," the evidence is entirely too contradictory and incomplete to support more than a few tentative conclusions. The fact that many of the observations made about what was then a predominantly rural America by such nineteenth-century commentators as Alexis de Tocqueville and Harriet Martineau are still repeated in most modern efforts to locate "the American character" would seem to indicate that the business system has reinforced rather than initiated secular trends in America's development as a social system. Where the business system has initiated novel structural arrangements in industry, fostered new clusters of attitudes and motives, and introduced forces that generate seemingly unique social and political institutional complexes, it has done so in ways that were sufficiently continuous with American traditions, practices, and beliefs to make precise demarcations and delineations of its contributions exceedingly difficult. A pluralistic society given to the idea that conflict should be institutionalized, that pragmatism should govern as a philosophical principle in the weighing of social alternatives, and that the concept of private property should be seen, flexibly, as an adaptable value, would seem to be what the distinguished sociologist Talcott Parsons regards as a "moving equilibrium," capable of modifying and absorbing the impact of business.

While each author documents some one-to-one relationship between business and a particular aspect of the polity, economy, or society in America, none has found an unambiguous pattern in the data he assays. A slight modification of one of Professor Walton's observations concerning the impact of business on American political life would thus seem appropriate: different corporations and business leaders respond differently, at least at the margins, to each of a bewildering variety of issues. To the extent that the business community is differentiated according to the personalities of important leaders, corporate personalities, regional differences, and a host of other factors, there will continue to be shifts in alliances and contradictions in the attitudes and behavior of business, especially as it contemplates the state of the economy, the actions of government, the behavior of "countervailing" forces, and the greater issues of war and peace.

But while the business community represents no monolithic body of opinion or power,[50] we need not deny that the managers of corporations share an unquantifiable but qualitatively significant core of commitments as well as a quantifiable but qualitatively elusive degree of political, economic, and social power. Indeed, if the character of the impact of business on certain aspects of our society is not altogether clear, it may be less because the impact has been exaggerated by its army of critics than because all the data are not in. Business has a considerable impact on every other feature of our society, and, like any other influence of comparable dimensions, this impact involves costs as well as benefits.

One is left with the feeling that it is easier to document the benefits than the costs of America's institutional arrangements, which is certainly a result some will be pleased to discover. More than a few of the authors have been unwilling to make categorical statements in their essays even about developments that cause them considerable concern. Professor Bjork points out that our small business stratum has lost much to integrated industries, but he draws no unambiguous moral judgments and launches no accusations on the basis of this fact. Professor Eichner is restive about the by-products of the "megacorp," but he carefully notes the extent of oligopoly in our economy during the years that constitute the historical base period for scholars concerned with trends in economic concentration and qualifies his conclusions about modern practice accordingly. Professors Rogers and Zimet are concerned with the potentially self-serving consequences of corporate programs developed to better educate workers and citizens to their political responsibilities, but they also record widespread charges against business for its political lethargy. Dr. Freedman is at least tentatively troubled by the business-like approach of businessmen who have discovered education as an area of entrepreneurial derring-do, but she also demonstrates clearly a number of America's debts to corporations for the obligations they have voluntarily assumed in respect to education. One could go on; from whatever point of view the influence of business on America is approached, it appears to have much about it that is praiseworthy and certain aspects that we may hope the business leaders of the future will be able to improve.

Two particular themes emerge in almost every essay and so apparently are of a very general character. The first is the growth of technicalism in American life; the second, social differentiation on the basis of status. Increasingly, we are told, there is a concern in America and especially in American business operations with technical means to problem solving. Organic to such a concern, the arguments imply, is a significant commitment to positivist and empiricist standards of judgment, a widely shared preoccupation with numbers, plans, and apparatuses—

[50] This is also the judgment of Professor Arnold M. Rose in *The Power Structure: Political Process in American Society* (New York: Oxford University Press, 1967), pp. 89–133 and 483–93.

both mechanical and institutional—that will make more "rational" the process of selecting and implementing actions appropriate to needs that are perceived and evaluated largely on the basis of hard "evidence." Even the evaluations of business in this volume are frequently left, for lack of data, less complete than they would be if some emergency had forced the authors to spell out everything they believe to be true on the basis of their skilled intuition. One danger inherent in technicalism is that when things are not as they should be—when social change seems "too rapid," when discontinuities appear in the development of our democracy, or when too much personal dissatisfaction and alienation is discovered at work—the fault may be found in technique and technology rather than in the acts of people.

We may thus predict a continuation of the stream of books that identify events with things rather than with people by focusing on apparatuses, like the "technostructure," rather than on men and their values.[51] To the degree that such writings encourage our already exaggerated hesitancy to make qualitative and intuitional judgments in areas where no other kinds of judgment are currently feasible, we will persist in many programs and policies—public and private—that are radically wasteful, misdirected, inadequate, or, as in the case of segregation downright immoral.

The second general theme that appears in most of the essays can be discerned between, as well as in, the lines written. It would seem that we are undergoing, as a consequence of the interplay between historical commitments, the imperatives of continuing industrialization, and the exigencies of our business system, a process of progressively greater differentiation on the basis of status rather than class criteria. Indeed, one is tempted to suggest that the earlier "separation of the worker from the means of production" that so preoccupied Karl Marx and the later "separation of management from ownership" that still preoccupies modern students of capitalism are both special cases of a more general process of structural differentiation, the precise nature of which has yet to be defined.

Clues to this deeper-going process may perhaps be found in a fuller understanding of the problem of "creeping technicalism" and of the bureaucratic character of the basic ways by which labor and management (or "capital," to use a Marxian term) are divided in America. It is remarkable that the effects of bureaucracy appear with greatest clarity not in the essays on the political and economic effects of our business system but in Professor Wilson's essay on the impact of modern business on art. Apart from the author's wisdom on the matters before him, it may be that the technocratic-bureaucratic differentiation of the main elements of our society stands out most clearly in the relations of these elements with the least organized group of Americans, our creative artists.

It is in keeping with the editor's reading of his authors' works—for he feels, after so much discussion, a proprietary interest in them—to issue anew a plea for "more research." We need not fear what further investigation will reveal, for the

---

[51] There is a little of such technological determinism in John Kenneth Galbraith's *The New Industrial State* (Boston: Houghton Mifflin, 1967).

standards that condemn our failings are largely our own. America looks considerably better as a society when there is a comparison of America with most other countries in the world than when particular arrangements are measured against that cluster of ideals that inform our aspirations as a people. It is in the many interstices between our vaguely formed but numerous objectives as a people and the considerable attainments we have achieved, thanks in no small part to the character of our business system, where the greatest challenges lie for the future progress of the real business of America.

part 2

BUSINESS AND THE POLITY

In the industrial nations of western Europe, with their aristocratic traditions, careers in public service have until very recently been among those favored by individuals free to choose their occupations. Some of the most capable men in Europe, accordingly, chose to be civil servants or politicians, and government officials generally enjoyed high status and significant rewards. Men of commerce and industry were no exception in looking upon government officials with considerable respect, if not affection.

In America the case has been to a large extent different. "Politicians" have been the object of more than a little scorn, while the "American way" has typically been employed as a term in approbation of our economic system rather than of our political institutions. The balance of power between businessmen and politicians has similarly been interpreted as leaning in different directions in America and Europe; the swings in the fortunes of Americans (and to some degree the fortunes of people abroad) have been associated at least as often with the determinations of American business leaders as with those of the men who govern in Washington, in our state capitals, and in our city halls.

In this section the contributions attempt to estimate the impact of business on political arrangements in the United States. They review a wide range of studies and opinions and should afford the reader an opportunity to reach tentative conclusions about a problem posed by the title of an earlier book, Robert A. Brady's *Business as a System of Power*. Many critics at home and abroad have suggested that the power of business to shape the course of American politics is very great indeed, not simply in areas of policy where the interests of business are particularly visible and direct, but in all areas, including foreign affairs and political ideology. Other critics have denied these allegations and have pictured corporations as victims or at least as passive responders to the initiatives of politicians. Most scholars, it seems safe to say, entertain intermediate opinions, but they disagree over important details and degrees of emphasis. Quite apart from the issue of how much power American business has exercised historically are the two related questions, how much political power *should* it exercise, and how much *will* it exercise in the future unless restrictions against it are tightened.

The four essays that follow examine distinct aspects of the interplay between business and politics in the United States. The first three describe the interests, activities, and influence of business in, respectively, local politics, national politics, and American foreign relations. The section concludes with an estimate of the effect of business on the character of our contemporary political debate and ideology.

chapter 2

BUSINESS AND THE
LOCAL COMMUNITY

DAVID ROGERS AND MELVIN ZIMET *are associated with the Graduate School of Business Administration, New York University. Professor Rogers has published widely on political-sociological problems and has completed a major study of urban educational developments; both have interests in the political activities of business. In their essay, they discuss the historical and current participation of corporations in community affairs, the impact of business decisions on community institutions, and the principal social forces that are shaping the trend of corporate community relations for the future.*

American cities show extensive variations in social, political, and economic structure, and reliable statements about "local politics" or "community affairs" in general must accordingly be quite abstract. To avoid the meaninglessness that results from excessive abstraction, the authors have explicitly reviewed a wide range of evidence and have included a dramatic array of concrete examples in support of their analysis. Community relations represent a problem for national corporations largely because these concrete differences exist; familiarity with them is clearly a prerequisite for the foundation of an effective community-relations policy.

The evidence reviewed by the authors is basically of two kinds: evidence about individual communities and evidence pertaining to corporations and business leaders. The community study may well be the most significant contribution that American sociologists have made to their diffuse science; it provides a way to come to grips with the texture of American life in all its detail and diversity. On the other hand, these studies have given rise to radically different conclusions about the nature and direction of change of business activities, family life, work, play, and values in the United States. The safest generalization would seem to be that no city or town "is America," despite occasional suggestions to the contrary.

American corporations are hardly less numerous than our communities. To assess their community-relations policies the authors examine particular policies of particular corporations in action, the opinions and recommendations of business leaders, and some of the action literature produced by national business "peak associations" like the National Association of Manufacturers. They find correlations between the policies of certain national corporations and the characteristics of particular communities, but typically the relationship between business and community life is more abstract. Nearly all our communities are influenced in a similar and general way by the recruiting, marketing, investment, and building programs of corporations and by the membership of these corporations in peak organizations. But for the present, at least, considerable diversity in the details of community social, political, and economic life seems assured by the simple fact that the number of our national corporations (and unions) is so large. Many corporations are now moving toward a more active involvement in politics at both the local and the national levels, however, and the picture of community diversity in America may change. This possibility suggests a number of questions the reader may wish to keep in mind as he examines the essay:

1. In what kinds of community decision-making does the participation of corporations seem most clearly helpful and necessary? On what basis can a government official compare and weigh the opinion of a corporation and the contradictory opinion of a number of citizens?

2. What conflict of interest may occur when an officer of a corporation is also a member of a community agency responsible for levying taxes? Is this conflict greater than when the owner of a large home, an office building, or some other real estate is a member? What can be done to avoid such conflicts or their potentially undesirable consequences?

3. How can the interests of corporations in a community of 500,000 citizens be systematically taken into account by community decision-makers? Could this be accomplished without corporate officers above the foreman level participating formally in government, and if so, how?

4. In the fact of the increasing involvement of corporations in community political life, what measures are necessary to protect the community? On what grounds do we think that "the people"— many of them poorly educated and most only sporadically active in community affairs—will not be misled by political propaganda, whether sponsored by corporations, unions, or anyone else? Why is propaganda sponsored by corporations particularly dangerous?

DAVID ROGERS
AND MELVIN ZIMET

THE CORPORATION AND THE
COMMUNITY: PERSPECTIVES
AND RECENT DEVELOPMENTS

Among the most significant publics faced by the large corporation in America are the local communities or cities in which its headquarters and its branch plants are located. Corporate spokesmen often express the view that American business has "social responsibilities" to serve local communities in ways that go well beyond the performance of its narrowly defined economic functions. There are obligations of citizenship, so the argument goes, that American business, with all its resources, organization, and talent should meet.[1] Yet there are different schools of thought both on the issue of what the corporation's role should be and on the question of how much involvement and power it actually has in community affairs.

CORPORATE INVOLVEMENT: INTERPRETATIONS AND PROBLEMS

Both conservative and liberal business spokesmen argue vigorously for greater business involvement in the local community, though for understandably different reasons. Conservatives want to increase business involvement in municipal problems largely to prevent any more federal intervention, which they regard as ineffective and in conflict with basic American values. Liberal business leaders and many analysts of American business urge increased involvement as a matter of social conscience.[2] Sol Linowitz, the liberal former chairman of the Xerox Corporation, has recommended that the corporation make "social goals as central to its decisions as economic goals" and has even proposed that companies grant leaves of absence to employees wishing to serve in the antipoverty program.[3]

Arguments against business involvement in community and other non-profit activities may also be heard, however. Some American business leaders urge a posture of neutralism on controversial social issues. They feel it would be against their economic self-interest to become involved and that businessmen should simply not meddle in social affairs except as private citizens.[4] They are joined by

[1] See, for example, the two collections of readings from *Fortune*, *The Regulated Businessman* (Part 5) and *The Responsible Businessman* (Part 2), both edited by John A. Larsen (New York: Holt, Rinehart and Winston, 1966).
[2] Michael D. Reagan, *The Managed Economy* (New York: Oxford University Press, 1963), Ch. 7.
[3] *Business Week* (April 30, 1966), p. 102.
[4] Roger Blough, chairman of the board of U.S. Steel, for example, has often taken this position. See the discussion below on his role in civil rights controversies in Birmingham, Alabama, in 1963.

many critics of American business who fear that if national corporations get too involved in local politics, this might lead to a pattern of neo-feudalism with the corporation expanding its already substantial social and political power.[5] Their concern is that political pluralism in many medium-sized and large cities would be replaced by monolithic business control, as oppressive as in the old company towns of the nineteenth and early twentieth centuries.[6]

General Descriptions of Local Corporation Involvement

While it is essential that the debate continue as to what the corporation's appropriate community role should be, this debate will be more informed if it takes account of the evidence on the roles that corporations have in fact played in communities—for what reasons, and with what consequences.

There are sharp differences of opinion on whether American cities are generally ruled by a small power elite of big business interests or whether business plays a relatively minor role in influencing key community decisions, along with many other interest groups in a pluralistic and indeed politically fragmented setting.[7] This second view, emphasizing the "pluralistic" structure of community power, has generally prevailed. The thesis is that with the growth of the national corporation, a concomitant increase in the size and scope of its markets, and the separation of ownership control, there has been a progressive withdrawal of big business from any involvement in local affairs.

The best single example of this point of view is the compendium of city politics reports of the Joint Center for Urban Studies of MIT and Harvard. Joint Center researchers and staff have gathered the most comprehensive collection of data now available on governmental forms and interest group politics in American cities. Two general monographs, *City Politics*, by Edward Banfield and James Q. Wilson, and *Big City Politics*, by Banfield, summarize their major hypotheses with regard to the role of different segments of the business community in local politics.[8]

One such hypothesis, supposedly corroborated in city after city, is that of a dichotomy of interest between local business and absentee-owned corporations. Banfield and Wilson suggest a deep involvement in community affairs by local businessmen—for example, bankers, realtors, and managers of utilities and department stores. These businessmen are rooted in the community, are a major economic and political elite, and participate in making key decisions on such issues as downtown redevelopment, urban renewal, school bond issues, air and water

---

[5] Reagan, *op. cit.*, Ch. 7. The term "neo-feudalism" is used to refer to an extension of managerial authority from its legitimate sphere of producing goods to an essentially illegitimate sphere of non-economic activities. The term "corporate totalitarianism" is also used.

[6] *Ibid.*, Chs. 5–7.

[7] Nelson Polsby, *Community Power and Political Theory* (New Haven, Conn.: Yale University Press, 1963).

[8] *City Politics* (Cambridge, Mass.: Harvard University Press and MIT Press, 1963); *Big City Politics* (New York: Random House, 1965).

pollution, charter revision, and annexation. The impetus for programs on these matters is seen to stem mainly from the local business group, in alliance with politicians and some middle-class liberal interests, while national corporations are supposedly not involved.[9]

Yet, there are some inconsistencies and contradictions in the Joint Center's evidence that suggest qualifications to their generalizations about the non-involvement of national corporations. Their own data in fact indicate that in many cities the involvement of national corporations is a major factor in determining the degree to which projects and reforms get underway. We will give many examples below. Indeed, the evidence that the Joint Center's description of the national corporation's role in civic affairs is true generally rather than a reflection of corporate behavior in a few special cities is not substantial. A bias in favor of pluralism, moreover, informs much of the social science research on which the findings are based and should be taken into account in interpreting and evaluating their validity.[10] Neo-Marxist and populist critics of big business reject the pluralism view altogether. They argue that the non-involvement of corporations in community affairs is more apparent than real and that executives of large corporations still "call the tune" in major community decisions.

Local, Temporal, and Individual Variations

Social scientists writing about corporate involvement in community affairs are often subject to such characterizations as "pluralist," "neo-Marxist," or "populist" in part because conditions vary widely in the different cities they study, even in the same city at different times. Furthermore, there are differences among corporations in their community involvement, and even the same corporation may assume a different posture in different cities depending, for example, on whether its headquarters or branch plants are located there. This essay will report and interpret variations in the nature and extent of business participation in city politics as a function of (1) local conditions and (2) corporate imperatives. Both factors are viewed in a comparative and historical context, with special emphasis placed on social, economic, and political changes of the past few decades. We trace, in addition, (3) the effects of membership in national "peak associations" on the local political participation of large corporations. This political participation seems to have become highly organized and centrally directed and encouraged in recent years.

The essay concludes that the degree of involvement in community affairs now thought to be desirable by the policy makers of most national corporations falls somewhere between the views of the pluralists and those of the populists and the

---

[9] Banfield and Wilson, *ibid.,* Ch. 18.

[10] One of the few social scientists who has expressed skepticism about the thesis of national corporation withdrawal from involvement in community affairs is Marshall N. Goldstein. See his "Absentee Ownership and Monolithic Power Structures: Two Questions for Community Studies," in Bert Swanson, ed., *Current Trends in Comparative Community Studies* (Kansas City, Mo.: Community Studies, 1962), pp. 49–60.

neo-Marxists. In most communities, big business does not pretend to dictate the course of local affairs as it did in many nineteenth-century company towns. Yet, the view that national corporations are largely uninvolved in local politics is no longer valid. As we shall see, national corporations have changed their community-relations policies over the last two decades.

Purpose

The purposes of this essay are to survey what is known about the nature and extent of corporate participation in the civic affairs of communities, to assess the impact—both intended and unintended—of the economic decisions of business on community institutions, and to interpret recent trends in corporate participation, suggesting what social and political forces bear on corporate-community relations.

Several different sources are relevant to such an undertaking. First, there are studies dealing with community power structures and city politics. They focus on the role of so-called economic dominants at the local level. Some recent National Industrial Conference Board surveys on the public affairs activities of large corporations are also available. We need not limit the evidence to be examined, however, to completed studies. Some of our best data come from sources that community studies specialists rarely use—for example, business publications. Many articles in the *Harvard Business Review, Fortune*, and *Business Week* are suggestive of corporate policies and actions in the community affairs field. The *Wall Street Journal* also contains articles that illustrate trends in corporate-community relations. Among the best sources of information are the many pamphlets and bulletins of business associations directly involved in stimulating participation in community affairs.

This paper attempts to codify findings and case study reports from these sources. The well-known political scientists, Edward Banfield and James Q. Wilson, doubt the utility of such a codification at this time, since so few systematic studies have accumulated on the political participation of business in local communities.[11] Yet, when the scattered investigations and case materials are brought together, they in fact do suggest some hypotheses about historical trends and about conditions related to variations in the nature and degree of corporate involvement.

Corporate involvement in local affairs has a political significance that more than merits an interpretive study with whatever data one can find. As Charles Silberman has noted in another context: "Life cannot wait until all the evidence is in." The actions and inactions of corporations have long affected the viability of democratic institutions and the quality of life in American cities. Furthermore, corporate involvement in civic affairs is not restricted to the community level. A new "public affairs movement" among the managers of large corporations has been sponsored and directed through a few nationwide peak associations like the Effective Citizens Organization.[12] The implications of the movement are also national.

[11] Banfield and Wilson, *op. cit.*, p. 276.
[12] For an earlier discussion of this peak association phenomenon, see Robert A. Brady, *Business as a System of Power* (New York: Columbia University Press, 1943).

CHANGING CORPORATE POLICIES OVER TIME: FROM CONTROL TO NON-INVOLVEMENT

A number of community studies document the decline of the company town—a town in which the control of business was monolithic—that flourished in the nineteenth and early twentieth centuries. Such towns were characteristic of an early stage of industrialization and urbanization.[13] Robert O. Schultze described the bifurcation of power in Ypsilanti, Michigan, between branch plant managers who increasingly withdraw from active participation and local business and political leaders. Harry Scoble noted that none of the managers and executives of nationally known plants in Bennington, Vermont, were seen as involved in key civic controversies. Robert A. Dahl described the decline in power of local entrepreneurs in New Haven and their replacement by politicians representing a newly arrived and organized immigrant population. Thus, while two-thirds of the 30 New Haven aldermen were businessmen in the period 1875–1900, by 1900 the majority were neither businessmen nor patricians from old, "mainline" families.

The old company towns tended to be dominated by a few and often only one major business enterprise, usually local and family-owned. An old, middle-class, small business stratum that controlled local industrial, financial, and real estate enterprises was thus the ruling elite. With the important exception of the fierce labor-management struggles that sometimes occurred in factory and mining towns, local businessmen dominated the political and social life of most of these communities.

A traditional, paternalistic, and almost feudal relationship thus existed between the company and the community, paralleling that of the company and its employees. Community groups became as rigidly stratified as employees in the company. When dissent against the dictates of the ruling elite arose, it was generally quite visible and could be easily discouraged by direct sanctions—among them, the threat by the company to leave town.[14]

For the most part, the owners of major local business firms felt a sense of

[13] Robert O. Schultze, "The Bifurcation of Power in a Satellite City," in Morris Janowitz, ed., *Community Political Systems* (New York: The Free Press, 1961), pp. 19–80; Lloyd Warner, *The Social System of the Modern Factory* (New Haven, Conn.: Yale University Press, 1947); Robert A. Dahl, *Who Governs?* (New Haven, Conn.: Yale University Press, 1961), Ch. 6; Banfield and Wilson, *op. cit.*, Ch. 18; William H. Form and Delbert C. Miller, *Industry, Labor, and Community* (New York: Harper & Row, 1960), Chs. 13 and 14; Harry Scoble, "Leadership Hierarchies and Community Issues in a New England Town," in Janowitz, *op. cit.*, pp. 117–45; Norton Long, "The Corporation, Its Satellites, and the Local Community," in Edward S. Mason, ed., *The Corporation in Modern Society* (Cambridge, Mass.: Harvard University Press, 1959), pp. 202–18; and Peter H. Rossi, "Theory and Method in the Study of Power in the Local Community," in Charles F. Adrian, ed., *Social Science and Community Action* (East Lansing: Michigan State University Press, 1960).

[14] David Rogers, "Community Political Systems: A Framework and Hypotheses for Comparative Studies," in Swanson, *op. cit.*, for an earlier summary of company town studies.

personal responsibility toward the community and its welfare. There is some evidence that some company towns may have had a higher level of civic welfare than cities dominated by absentee-owned national corporations.[15] This civic feeling of the small businessman was undoubtedly tempered by a well-developed sense of responsibility for his private interests. However, this too was often translated into service to the community because, as a major employer, the enterprise and its economic health were closely identified with the economic health of the community, even if only over the short run.[16] Thus a closely knit, symbiotic relationship existed between the businessman and the community.

With the advent of the large, modern corporation and the proliferation of its branch plants throughout the nation, radical changes took place in the political structure of many local communities. One of the most significant of these changes was the rise of managers of absentee-owned plants to positions of potential influence and power and the concurrent decline of the former local business influentials who withdrew not only from active participation in the economic life of the community but also from its political life. In some cases where local businessmen did continue to participate in important civic activities, they may have been "fronts" for national corporation interests.[17]

The plant managers of branches of national corporations—the "new influentials"—were reluctant to step into the positions that had been vacated by the old elite group. For one thing, they thought of themselves as transients. Their advancement opportunities were with their companies and not with the community. Furthermore, many of them lived outside the town if it was a middle-sized city or larger. What civic identification they did feel was for their residential suburb. Finally, such managers and the corporations they represented were reluctant to become involved in local controversies. The purely economic stakes of a national corporation in any one community are limited, yet in an age of rapid communications, local difficulties can have serious national repercussions. Branch plant managers feared that extensive involvement in community affairs might have repercussions detrimental to the parent corporation's image and therefore to their own careers. They could point to the example of the middle-management executive fired by Bethlehem Steel in 1964 for becoming involved in fair housing and school desegregation groups.[18] Branch managers thus typically got involved only in "safe" issues where the corporation's public image and economic interests did

---

[15] C. Wright Mills and Melville J. Ullmer, "Small Business and Civic Welfare," Senate Document No. 135, 79th Cong., 2nd Sess. (Washington, D.C.: 1946); and Irving Fowler, *Community Power, Industrial Structures, and Civic Welfare* (Englewood, N. J.: Bedminster Press, 1965). Fowler's findings contradict those of Mills and Ullmer.

[16] Most of the company town studies mentioned above document this point.

[17] Mills suggested this pattern in his study in the 1940's, "The Middle Classes in Middle-Sized Cities," in Reinhard Bendix and Seymour Martin Lipset, eds., *Class, Status, and Power* (New York: The Free Press, 1953), pp. 203–13. Mills's work is often viewed as a prototype of the "conspiracy" view of ruling classes, yet trends in the 1950's and 1960's seem to have borne out his point about big business power in cities.

[18] Joseph A. Loftus, "Bethlehem Puzzled by Dismissal of Steel Aide over Racial Stand," *New York Times,* March 22, 1964, p. 51.

not seem likely to be damaged. Conspicuous community participation was limited to supporting the Community Chest, the Red Cross, and Little League baseball.

More business involvement may have existed in headquarters cities where corporations have larger economic stakes than in the communities where branch operations predominate, but the pattern of non-participation in civic affairs was nevertheless quite general. One consequence was a dispersion of power and influence in many American cities and a corresponding dearth of innovation on major civic problems. Those with the highest status and the most political resources no longer participated in the life of the community. The leadership for change that they could have supplied was conspicuously absent. The "new influentials" deposed the "old order" from its position of community leadership but put nothing in its place.

This did not mean that national corporations did not act in their own interests if the local situation required. They certainly did, though generally in a covert and status quo oriented way. Most community power studies, in concentrating so heavily on openly contested issues, seem to have overlooked the negative veto power of corporations responsible to absentee stockholders. A veto of this kind was exercised in Ypsilanti, according to Schultze, when national corporations located there refused to get involved in attempts to revise the city charter and to merge with a neighboring township, thus helping to defeat both proposals. Schultze believes that the veto is probably used quite frequently. The failure of many urban redevelopment projects can be traced to the neutralism or covert rejection of large corporations. Conversely, the success of some other projects appears to be a result, in part, of corporate support.[19]

From Non-involvement to Involvement

Corporate non-involvement was reported in cities throughout the nation. The pattern, however, was a transitional one. Many national corporations realized that their previous aloofness from local affairs had unwittingly contributed to the political power of other interests—labor unions, minority groups, entrenched political machines, and small local business—to push through community decisions detrimental to the corporation. Furthermore, such groups might lend their support to liberal state and federal legislators in opposing big business interests.

Many corporate managements expressed concern that this kind of liberal coalition might keep expanding the role of the federal government in regulating business and municipal life and began to encourage their branch plant managers and employees to participate in local politics. This was to counter the drift toward "federal coercion" and to restore such basic American values and institutions as "self-reliance," "free, private enterprise," and "local autonomy."

Thus, during the 1950's and 1960's, national corporations changed their community relations policies in response to a number of actual and perceived social changes—especially the assumed increase in labor power. Even though this

[19] Schultze, *op. cit.*, pp. 66–73.

assumption of labor's increased power may be incorrect, as many students of the labor movement believe, it affects business politics. As sociologist W. I. Thomas said, "If men define situations as real, they are real in their consequences." Many of the political education programs and efforts at grass roots involvement of large corporations are discussed quite frankly in American business circles as a move to counter the increased power of liberal interests, especially of COPE (Committee on Political Education), the political arm of the AFL–CIO.[20]

The new interest of national corporations in local politics has come to be known as the "public affairs" movement. In *Government and Industry*, a community-relations manual published by the Manufacturing Chemists Association, Thomas J. Diviney, civic affairs manager of Monsanto Chemical Company, defines "public affairs" as a management function "aimed at developing employee effectiveness in politics and government. Usually it is divided into three parts: political education and action; government information and action; and economic education." Though corporate spokesmen characterize the public affairs movement as a non-partisan one, they occasionally will acknowledge that conservative political candidates stand to gain much more than do the liberals since, for the most part, those trained in political action in company courses are drawn from the ranks of management. As the public affairs officer of one company told the authors, "We are not interested in training people who might work against us."

The increased organization and militancy of the civil rights movement was another development that affected business involvement in local affairs. American business leaders tried, at first, to assume a posture of neutralism on race relations issues.[21] They increasingly found that this was simply not possible and were forced to take public positions in civil rights controversies at both the local and national levels.

Automation and changing manpower needs have also forced greater business involvement. A mixture of concerns—for their corporations' images, their economic self-interests, and their responsibilities to the public—have provoked a heightened interest in the adequacy of public education, job retraining projects, and similar local matters.

Other types of local involvement by national corporations tend to be even more directly related to economic self-interest. Participation in the discussion of a school bond issue, for example, paid off handsomely for one of the more enthusiastic sponsors of public affairs programs, the Olin Mathieson Chemical Company. Shortly after Olin Mathieson built a new plant in the town of Hannibal, Ohio, a twenty-two year–$3.5 million school bond issue was proposed. Olin argued in newspaper advertisements that interest on the bonds would push the total cost to taxpayers to $6 million. The voters rejected the bond issue and later approved the $1.9 million pay-as-you-go program that Olin supported. Since Olin's plant accounted for 90 per cent of the real estate taxes assessed in Hannibal, more than $3.6 million of the over $4 million tax saving went to Olin.[22]

[20] "Corporations Make Politics Their Business," *Fortune* (December, 1959), pp. 100 ff.
[21] See our discussion below on this point.
[22] George Melloan, "Playing Politics," *Wall Street Journal*, February 17, 1964, p. 1.

Actions of this type are not new, but their frequency seems likely to increase as corporations become more sophisticated in the workings of local politics. "Neutralism" and non-involvement do not constitute a satisfactory basis for a corporation's community-relations policy. A more activist, interventionist posture is essential for the economic self-interest of absentee-owned corporations, and in recent years many have assumed one.

Changed patterns of industrial and business locations—the exodus of industry from inner cities and the location of branch plants in suburban and rural areas—have also increased the local involvement of corporations. They want to ensure that communities have adequate educational, cultural, recreational, and leisure facilities as inducements in the recruitment and retention of technical and managerial employees.

Finally, the worsening socio-economic problems and unrest of metropolitan areas have caused national corporations to foresee more federal intervention in municipal decision-making and in urban and regional development programs. Many business spokesmen have called for immediate action on these problems, partly to forestall the federal government's playing a larger role, partly because they believe that business can deal with such social problems as poverty and unemployment much more efficiently than can the federal government. The National Association of Manufacturers has itself undertaken a social welfare program—including projects on literacy training for underprivileged teenagers, consumer education, and the trading of information among companies on employment problems.[23] The NAM has held key caucuses, as have the U.S. Chamber of Commerce and the Committee on Economic Development, to discuss business strategy for dealing with the so-called crisis of the cities.

In sum, the social changes of the past two decades have imposed a new set of imperatives on national corporations. Since they cannot insulate themselves from major social and political controversies, one of their many accommodations has been to increase the level of their involvement in local affairs.

THE RANGE OF CORPORATE INVOLVEMENT IN SPECIFIC COMMUNITIES

The contemporary shift in the community-relations policies of national corporations in the direction of increased involvement can be seen in many community studies. Thus, Peter H. Rossi points out in his 1957 study of American Telephone and Telegraph managers in a Midwestern city that these men participate actively in community affairs. Doing so helped them gain access to one another and to community leaders. It also helped them relate to the local populace and provided a means of gaining prestige in the community to an extent that they would not otherwise have enjoyed as "outsiders."[24]

Robert Presthus, in his analysis of the power structure of two upstate New

[23] Frank J. Prial, "A 'New' NAM?", *Wall Street Journal,* May 31, 1966, p. 1.
[24] "The Organizational Structure of an American Community," in Amitai Etzioni, ed., *Complex Organizations* (New York: Holt, Rinehart and Winston, 1961), pp. 301–12.

York communities, suggests that some national corporations encourage their executives to participate in local affairs only so the company will not be regarded as an alien intruder.[25] And Banfield and Wilson suggest that branch plant managers occasionally participate quite actively in local affairs—sometimes as an escape from the boredom and tensions of their corporate existence and sometimes as training for later politicking in the corporation.[26]

Numerous other studies, in addition to those of Rossi and Presthus, point up this pattern of increasing corporate involvement. They attribute the involvement to such factors as the type of business in which the corporation is engaged, characteristics of particular cities where it is located, and the nature of inter-business relations within cities. What follows is a series of case studies of business involvement in prototypic cities that differ in location (region), economic base, size, and stage of urban and economic development. Each city represents a particular pattern of corporate-community relations, and the sequence of cases presented is from the smallest and least urbanized and industrialized cities to the largest and most complex.

Small Towns

Though the pattern of monolithic control by local business in company towns has given way in the many cities where urbanization and industrialization have taken place, there has been a resurgence of the company town pattern in many smaller cities around the nation, especially when national corporation headquarters are located there. Examples of this are legion, predominating in the Midwest and South and among extractive and heavy industry towns in particular. The difference from the company town of the past is a pattern of absentee rather than local business.

A prototype is Bartlesville, Oklahoma, a town of 34,000 that has long been under the economic domination of Phillips Petroleum. An account in the *Wall Street Journal* recently suggested that Phillips strongly influences every aspect of Bartlesville's community life. The town's economy, cultural affairs, civic projects, social activities, and politics are benevolently guided by Phillips or its employees. The company's $55 million annual payroll makes up about half of the estimated "effective buying income" of Bartlesville and the county in which it is located. "When Phillips twitches," one local businessman told the *Journal* reporter, "Bartlesville jumps."[27]

Other communities are in similar circumstances, housing companies whose headquarters overshadow the town. They include, as examples, the A. P. Green Fire Brick Company in Mexico, Missouri; Champion Papers in Hamilton, Ohio; Armco Steel Corporation in Middletown, Ohio; Hershey Chocolate Corporation in Hershey, Pennsylvania; and Cannon Mills Company in Kannapolis, North Carolina. Some of these company towns are actually fair-sized cities. Hamilton has a population of close to 75,000, Middletown has 43,000, and Kannapolis has 35,000.

[25] *Men at the Top* (New York: Oxford University Press, 1964), pp. 127–39; 407–11.
[26] *Op. cit.,* Ch. 17.
[27] James C. Tanner, "One-Company Town," *Wall Street Journal,* August 4, 1966, p. 1ff.

They are large compared to the company towns of the past. Together they represent a sizable segment of the nation (perhaps 10 per cent to 15 per cent) whose community life is substantially shaped by large corporations.

Trends in corporate locations have, if anything, increased the number of such company towns. Although most major corporations, especially in the oil industry, have moved their headquarters from communities where they got their start to bigger cities, company towns still flourish. Steel mills still provide the principal means of livelihood for some smaller Pennsylvania cities. The economic well-being of many a Midwestern city depends on a few large automobile or automobile parts makers with headquarters elsewhere. In recent years, New England textile firms have moved many of their operations to small Southern towns; electronics companies have put plants in small towns in both the West and the Southwest.

The decline of some old-time company towns, then, seems to have been more than counterbalanced by the rise of others. The newer ones differ in that, while a single enterprise may still control most civic institutions and affairs, the locus of control is from outside the community. Many small communities have thus become satellites of large national corporations whose imperatives, as perceived by top management, figure to an increasing degree in local decisions.

One of the best-known cases is that of IBM in Poughkeepsie, New York, a community with a population of 37,000.[28] When it moved to Poughkeepsie in 1940, IBM touched off what has proved to be a population boom. With a payroll of 11,500, it was the county's largest employer. Since then, IBM's executives have taken the place of the landed gentry who once dominated the area. Its managers help set the standards for the community.

IBM's presence has not been an unmixed blessing for Poughkeepsie. Backed up against the Hudson River, the city has no room to grow and is slowly being strangled by the surrounding towns. At the same time, Dutchess County, where Poughkeepsie is located and which has, like all New York counties, the responsibility for providing the facilities needed to keep up with the county's growth, is hampered by an antiquated township structure and is unable to do so.

By 1960, the seriousness of Poughkeepsie's plight had gained recognition throughout the entire county. A drive to save the city through the Action Council for the Poughkeepsie Area, led by William J. Mair, IBM's resident vice president, was begun. This group promoted an urban renewal plan calling for the construction of new middle-income and low-income apartment houses. It also planned a civic center for Poughkeepsie. IBM was and continues to be active in Poughkeepsie in other ways and has supported fair housing and other civil rights measures.

Bigtown: An Extractive Center in the South

Monolithic business control in local politics is not confined to small cities alone. A dramatic case of such control was reported by Pellegrin and Coates over a decade ago in their study of "Bigtown," a city of about 200,000 population and

[28] Joseph Lelyveld, "IBM Expansion Strains Dutchess," *New York Times,* February 10, 1964.

the nucleus of a Southern metropolitan area.[29] The situation there was quite reminiscent of that in nineteenth-century company towns. In Bigtown, community projects were doomed unless they had the approval of the absentee-owned corporations that had their headquarters there. The employers not only dictated the terms of their employees' participation but also decided what values were to be served by the projects and policies in which their employees were involved.

The Bigtown leaders and their middle-management employees served on the most powerful civic committees. They generally stated their own opinions in such a manner as to discredit all others. Pellegrin and Coates quote one prominent, old-time business leader as follows:

> We freeze out these New Dealers and other Reds. When we appoint people to important committee posts, we look at their record. If an individual has gone all out on some crazy idea, his goose is cooked. If I am chairman of a group that is making appointments, I go stone deaf whenever someone suggests the name of one of these radicals. My hearing improves when a good reliable person is mentioned as a possibility.[30]

Participation in the power-wielding, civic organizations of the city by the absentee-owned corporation was limited to a carefully planned list of eligible executives who had demonstrated, through lengthy service, their dependability and familiarity with company policy. When Bigtown's business leaders spoke of the desirability of increasing participation in community affairs, they were referring to their wish for more followers, not more leaders.

Marshall Goldstein attributes the active participation of the absentee-owned corporations in Bigtown to the fact that they were engaged in extractive operations rather than manufacturing, as were the automotive parts firms in Ypsilanti, whose civic non-involvement was reported by Schultze. Goldstein's point is that the differences in policies stem from the immobility of extractive operations. If a local decision goes against a manufacturing company, it can move its plants (or threaten to). Extractive companies, however, must remain near their oil, lumber, or coal. They have no choice but to become involved in community decision-making.[31]

There are undoubtedly many medium-sized cities like Bigtown throughout the South where absentee-owned extractive corporations have their headquarters and control local politics. Bigtown, then, is not solely a single case study but is representative of a particular kind of Southern city whose main economic base is in the extractive field.

Big Cities: North and South

But what of the largest urban centers of the nation? How powerful can national corporations be in such cities as Atlanta, St. Louis, Detroit, Seattle, and New

---

[29] R. J. Pellegrin and C. H. Coates, "Absentee Owned Corporations and Community Power Structure," *American Journal of Sociology* (March, 1956), pp. 413–19.
[30] *Ibid.*, p. 417.
[31] Goldstein, *op. cit.*

York with their many well-organized pressure groups, powerful local businessmen, and other such interests that might seemingly negate the power of big business?

As we noted earlier, the same pattern of corporate withdrawal portrayed in such small- and medium-sized cities as Ypsilanti and New Haven is claimed by Banfield, Wilson, and other urban affairs specialists for the largest cities in the nation. The nation's largest cities are portrayed as controlled by all varieties of interest except large, national corporations. Yet, evidence accumulating in recent years suggests an increased corporation involvement even there, despite all the "countervailing interests" that exist.

Two recent examples, from studies and reports on Southern cities, are Atlanta and St. Louis. Both are headquarters cities, a factor that might contribute to some business involvement. But they are large and economically diversified enough to suggest a pattern of political pluralism and minimal business dominance. Yet, substantial business involvement and dominance were found, and this merits explanation.

Floyd Hunter reported, for example, that big business exerts strong controls over community decision-making in Atlanta. His findings were later confirmed by Kent Jennings who used a more sophisticated research procedure.[32]

The fact that Atlanta and St. Louis are both headquarters cities and located in the South, like Bigtown, partially accounts for this pattern. The large, old family firms in each city continue to recruit from within. A hereditary plutocracy exists, and it is supported by an authoritarian and conservative value system that is reflected in a rigid class structure and in a pattern of one-party politics. These conditions limit the formation of unions and other interest groups that might offset the power of the business elite, and they facilitate the retention of control by the old ruling classes.

Yet, national corporations, as well as old-line family firms, play a significant role in local affairs in Atlanta and St. Louis. Indeed, there appears to be a cohesiveness between national corporations and local business with the former having considerable power in affecting local, municipal decisions.[33]

The most powerful interests in Atlanta are the heads of the principal department stores, its three or four biggest real estate firms, utilities, manufacturing companies, and major banks, in alliance with national corporate interests who have headquarters or branch plants there. More specifically, these are the Citizens and Southern National Bank, the First National Bank, the Trust Company of Georgia, Scripto, Rich's Department Store, Oxford Manufacturing, Atlantic Steel, and the Southern Company, in alliance with Coca-Cola, General Motors, and Ford. Operating through a cohesive and aggressive Chamber of Commerce, these firms

[32] Hunter, *Community Power Structure* (Chapel Hill: University of North Carolina Press, 1953); and Jennings, *Community Influentials: The Elites of Atlanta* (New York: The Free Press, 1964).

[33] On Atlanta, see Vartanig G. Vartan, "Atlanta Rushes to National Role," in *New York Times*, November 16, 1964, pp. 49ff. The St. Louis experience is described in "St. Louis Snaps out of a Long Costly Lull," *Business Week* (September 18, 1965), pp. 193–204; and Robert L. Bartley, "Business Helps St. Louis Fight Decay," *Wall Street Journal*, May 26, 1966.

wield considerable influence. Thus, while the record is not too clear with respect to General Motors and Ford, Coca-Cola is one of the major power centers in the city. The Trust Company of Georgia is known as the "Coca-Cola Bank" and has played an active role in the city's rapid growth. Thanks to it and other banks, as well as to a complex of insurance and financial institutions, Atlanta regards itself as "the Wall Street of the South."

Local business interests, working closely with national corporations, then, have contributed substantially to Atlanta's rise to prominence and to its increasing national role. Furthermore, Atlanta's claims of progress in race relations before the riots of September, 1966, may have been well founded. The cohesion and influence of its national business interests probably contributed to this development.

The case of St. Louis is even clearer in illustrating the role played by national corporations in urban development. There, a long trend of decay was reversed by an alliance between the city's political and business leadership. The alliance, first formalized in a civic redevelopment group called Civic Progress, began in 1953 and is now starting to show results. The leadership group included former Mayor Raymond R. Tucker, local business leaders, and the chiefs of a number of prominent corporations with headquarters in the city.

Interest in downtown development is easy enough to understand among department store heads and local financial interests, and a group of them furnished most of the eight originators of Civic Progress. They were almost immediately joined, however, by such others as August A. Busch, Jr., of Anheuser-Busch, William A. McDonnel of McDonnel Aircraft, Edgar M. Wueeny of Monsanto Chemical, and Donald Danforth of Ralston Purina.

Such national business leaders were apparently attracted to Civic Progress not only by local pride but also by the competitive needs of their companies, a familiar theme. Emerson Electric's W. R. Persons explains, "If you expect to have first-class people working for you, you've got to have a first-class place for them to live. I'm sure that this has been the underlying factor in everyone's mind."[34]

The cases of Atlanta and St. Louis parallel those of many other large headquarters cities throughout the nation, including Boston, Detroit, El Paso, Los Angeles, Miami, Philadelphia, and Seattle.[35] In a Joint Center report on Los Angeles, for example, James Q. Wilson notes that national corporations work in alliance with local business and political leaders on major civic projects.[36]

A Joint Center study of Detroit suggests that auto companies were large contributors to local projects.[37] Though many projects were enthusiastically initiated by newspapers and other essentially local business firms, national corporation personnel and money were significant factors in the implementation of projects. There was every indication that without such cooperation, many projects would not have been undertaken. In fact, there was reason to doubt whether local businessmen would initiate a project where there was a possibility that the large

[34] Quoted in Bartley, *op. cit.*
[35] Joint Center for Urban Studies at Harvard and MIT, Reports on City Politics.
[36] *Report of Politics in Los Angeles,* Joint Center for Urban Studies, 1959.
[37] David Greenstone, *Politics in Detroit,* Joint Center for Urban Studies, 1961.

manufacturers would balk. This was unlikely in view of the cohesiveness of the Detroit business community. The report indicates that one of the most important bases for the influence of Detroit big businessmen is this relative cohesion, and considerable evidence in the report supports the conclusion that these leaders often act cooperatively.

Another example of national corporation involvement is Seattle.[38] This city has a group of leading businessmen referred to as the Big Ten, an informal group of downtown financiers, real estate men, and industrialists. As Ross Cunningham, political editor of the Seattle *Times,* says, "If you want to get anything done in Seattle, you get about six members of the Big Ten together and tell them it's a good project." In Seattle, as well as in Detroit, there is a seeming cohesion within the business community, uniting "locals" with executives of national corporations. Rather than opposing each other, as suggested by Schultze's research and in similar studies, they have an identity of interests.

One generalization suggested by these cases is that national corporation involvement may well have a profound effect on the quality of life and effectiveness of municipal government in the nation's largest cities. Many urban affairs specialists note that a leadership vacuum has existed in most large, inner cities of the nation. This has accounted in part for the ineffectiveness of local civic and governmental efforts to reverse the trend toward decay, deterioration in quality of vital services, and a consequent exodus of business and residents to suburban and rural areas. All too often, municipal leaders do not have—or do not believe they have—the power to lead. The result can be described as government by power-bloc vote. Each special interest, including "reformers" who mainly want the right litany performed, has the power to sway uncertain leaders. Any movement from the status quo is a threat to some interest or other, and progress becomes impossible.[39]

The increased participation of national corporations in big city affairs can change the balance of power and counter such a fragmentation of special interest groups and power blocs. It already has in Atlanta, St. Louis, Detroit, and elsewhere, thereby contributing to their revival.

The case that further substantiates this thesis is New York City. While its problems are often considered idiosyncratic and *sui generis,* given New York City's size, geographical spread, heterogeneous population, massive ghettos, and entrenched governmental bureaucracies, its recent experience is, nevertheless, of general significance. Coincident with its decay is a complete withdrawal of national corporations, so many of which have their headquarters there, from any civic involvement whatsoever. Unlike the situation in other big cities, New York's corporate elite cannot be located for help on civic projects. Until very recently, it has been all but viewed as absurdity even to approach them.

Many of New York City's business leaders have, of course, become suburbanized and participate more in the local affairs of their residential communities—in Westchester County, in Fairfield County, Connecticut, in many New Jersey suburbs, and on Long Island's North Shore—than in those of the city. Many spend

[38] Banfield, *op. cit.,* p. 141.
[39] Robert L. Bartley, "Crisis for Cities is One of Leadership," *Wall Street Journal,* June 27, 1966, p. 16. The same point is made in Banfield and Wilson, *op. cit.*

much of their time traveling abroad. However, this is so on an increasing scale for corporate elites in almost all major cities of the nation. And yet, they are much more involved civically in the affairs of their headquarters cities.

The fact is that New York City is almost a special case of complete withdrawal by big business. The extent of urban decay and the degree to which entrenched interests have become solidified (the labor movement, local real estate and construction firms, civil service professionals and the Democratic Party) have discouraged corporate leaders from any civic participation.

The remarks of two executives to a *Fortune* reporter who was recording and interpreting New York City's decay reveal some other sources of this non-involvement there. As one commented:

> This is a violent, noisy, dirty city, the dirtiest I've ever seen. If you want to live comfortably here, you've got to insulate yourself as much as possible.

Still another noted:

> In Cincinnati I felt some peripheral responsibility as a businessman to get involved in civic affairs. In the company here in New York nobody has the slightest interest in my personal life. In the small city one's personal and business lives got all mixed up. Here, my wife and I are freer.[40]

The remarks of both of these men reveal some of New York's most basic difficulties. The first executive who talked of the importance of insulating himself was laying bare a kind of "self-fulfilling" prophecy that may have contributed to the city's decline. The very deterioration he so bemoaned and insulated himself from was, in part, a consequence of the insulated posture that he and other business leaders of the city had assumed for so long.

Yet even in New York City the isolation of the national corporation may be decreasing, as is strongly indicated by the recent cooptation of executives from six major companies to a new Management Advisory Council. Mayor John Lindsay has just appointed top executives of IBM, General Electric, the New York Central Railroad, Union Carbide, American Express, and the Metropolitan Life Insurance Company to work with city officials in infusing "high efficiency management methods" into the municipal government. In making the appointments, Mayor Lindsay declared:

> Their commitment to serve the city in this way means that, at long last, the city government is tapping the vast pool of management talent that exists in New York.[41]

Non-partisan Cities

A further development in American cities that has relevance for the degree and significance of corporation involvement is the trend toward non-partisan political

[40] Richard J. Whalen, *A City Destroying Itself* (New York: William Morrow, 1966), pp. 112–19. The quotes are from pp. 117 and 119.
[41] Charles G. Bennett, "Top Businessmen to Help Improve City Management," *New York Times,* October 21, 1966, p. 1.

organization. This trend is related to the decline of immigration of ethnic minorities (with the exception of the Negro, Puerto Rican, and Mexican) into the city; the upward mobility, assimilation, and acculturation of older ethnic minorities, and the emergence of new urban problems whose solutions depend on the imagination and political skills of urban affairs experts. Such problems as the physical and economic deterioration in downtown areas, the flight to the suburbs, the overloading of public facilities, the clamor for better schools, have all given new importance to technicians, professional administrators, and professional politicians trying to build viable coalitions out of diverse ethnic groups and social strata. "Machine" and "class" politics often have less relevance in such settings, and they have been gradually replaced by non-partisan political organizations.[42]

The relevance of these developments for the involvement and influence of corporations is fairly obvious. Non-partisanship inevitably results in the weakening of political party organizations. Professional politicians and city administrators are forced to mobilize coalitions without the help of pre-existing political structures. A leadership vacuum is created that can readily be filled by such elite groups as national corporations, with such substantial political resources as money, executive talent, and political and administrative skills.

These effects of non-partisanship can be seen in a number of cities. In Boston, elections have been non-partisan since the adoption of a reform charter in 1909. As a result, candidates now lack both patronage and party support. To conduct an election campaign, they must depend upon business contributors for financing. In Seattle, elections have been non-partisan since 1910 when, during a wave of reform, a charter amendment was placed on the ballot by petition. The result of this charter, which distributes authority so widely that neither a mayor nor anyone else can take charge, is a sort of do-it-by-citizen-committee style of government. If the system were partisan, the elected officials would have to show leadership in some matters, at least, in order to win election.

In Detroit as well, charter reforms, enacted in 1918, increased business influence over day-to-day government decisions. When the reformers eliminated ward representatives, they also eliminated the possibility of draining off ethnic and class antagonism through the small favors and perquisites typically provided in ward-based politics. When they removed political parties from the local scene they removed a mediating institution that might have intervened between lower-class groups and the State of Michigan.[43]

Elections in El Paso, to take another example, have been non-partisan since 1959. As already noted, without job patronage and with no party loyalty to hold an organization together, the only organization with funds for a campaign is that consisting of business groups. Elective officials in El Paso, as a result, do pretty much as business wants, usually without even being asked.[44]

Manifestly, the potential for interest group fragmentation, pluralism, and governmental ineffectiveness is very high in non-partisan cities. There are no

[42] Dahl, *op. cit.*, Ch. 5.
[43] Banfield, *Politics in Boston*, 1960; Charles W. Bender, *Politics in Seattle*; and Greenstone, *op. cit.*; all are Joint Center monographs.
[44] Banfield, *Big City Politics,* p. 73.

formalized means (machines and party organizations) for political integration. Political power resources are dispersed among many groups, with each able to veto the plans of others. One way out is for a strong mayor to mobilize a coalition strong enough to move a city off dead center. In city after city where urban re-development has been successful, or has at least gotten under way, national corporations became actively involved in such a coalition.

The cooptation of big business, however, is not without potential costs. There is always the danger that corporations that have contributed so much to particular municipal projects will also want to have some control over them and to influence the social goals and values that they may further.

Summary: Factors That Affect Corporate Involvement

Each city we have discussed illustrates the trend toward increased corporate in-volvement, contrary to the traditional view of many social scientists portraying national corporations as having withdrawn from active participation in local affairs. Accumulating evidence thus suggests that the traditional view is no longer valid—if, indeed, it ever was to the extent that its proponents claimed. The cases were selected for purposes of suggesting how the economic, social, and political changes of the past few decades have contributed to the trend. They also provide a specification and elaboration of our main thesis regarding increased corporate involvement. The following tabular presentation summarizes the studies reviewed above:

Table 1.

MORE INVOLVEMENT	LESS INVOLVEMENT
Type of Business	
Family	Absentee-owned
Local markets	Regional or national markets
Extractive or distributive	Manufacturing
Inter-Business Relations	
Centralization of influence	Fragmentation
Cohesion of interests	Factionalism
City Characteristics	
Small- or medium-sized	Large
Limited industrialization	Highly industrialized
Economically undiversified	Diversified
Minimal heterogeneity of population	High degree of heterogeneity
Limited unionization of blue-collar workers	Extensive unionization
One-party predominance	Two or more vigorous parties
Non-partisan politics	Partisan politics
Limited differentiation of polity from family and economic interests	High degree of differentiation
Limited organization of interests counter-vailing those of business	High degree countervailing organiza-tion
South, Southwest, or Midwest	East or Northeast

Many national corporations are more deeply involved in community affairs today than previously in large part because their earlier policy of neutralism began to have unfortunate consequences. The serious results that can follow from a neutral position were vividly illustrated by the experience of U.S. Steel in Birmingham, Alabama, when racial controversies exploded there in 1963.

The Civil Rights Movement: U.S. Steel in Birmingham

U.S. Steel had a large plant in Birmingham. Under the guidance of Roger Blough, its board chairman and a political and economic conservative, U.S. Steel resolutely held out against taking any positive public action in the racial controversy. On November 2, 1963, Blough wrote to the *New York Times*:

> I believe that while government—through the proper exercise of its legislative and administrative powers—may seek to compel social reforms, any attempt by a private organization, like U.S. Steel, to impose its views, its beliefs, and its will upon the community by resorting to economic compulsion or coercion would be repugnant to our American constitutional concepts, and that appropriate steps to correct this abuse of corporate power would be universally demanded by public opinion, by government, and by the *New York Times*. I believe that U.S. Steel management people as citizens should use their influence personally to help resolve the problems wherever they may be—and that they are doing so in Birmingham.[45]

This stance of corporate neutrality had numerous repercussions. In May, 1966, a lawsuit was filed in the Federal Court of Birmingham charging U.S. Steel with discrimination in having failed to promote two Negro mill hands and refusing to train them for promotion. By June, 1966, the National Association for the Advancement of Colored People had filed 200 complaints with the Equal Employment Opportunities Commission charging U.S. Steel with specific violations of the 1964 Civil Rights Act.

Demonstrations were staged outside the U.S. Steel headquarters in Pittsburgh and at the big U.S. Steel plant in Fairfield, Alabama. The NAACP asked the federal government to withhold its contracts from U.S. Steel on the grounds that it discriminated against Negro employees.

Despite the difficulties experienced by his firm, Roger Blough continued to believe that the corporation has no moral right to dictate to the community and that the way to right social wrongs "lies not in the issuance of mere laws and regulations, but that a great deal will depend on the attitude of individual communities."[46] Other business leaders disagree. A giant corporation like U.S. Steel

---

[45] November 2, 1963.
[46] Cited from *Company Experience with Negro Employment*, National Industrial Conference Board, Studies in Personnel Policy, Vol. 2, No. 201, p. 87.

is an especially visible and inviting target. Furthermore, what it does or does not do influences the attitudes of other firms in the industry, those of the communities in which its plants are located, and those in which the plants of its competitors are located. This means that no position it takes can really be neutral in its effects.

The implications of a decision to be neutral are all the more obvious if, like U.S. Steel, the corporation issues pronouncements on a great variety of other public issues.[47] In this case, choosing to be silent is not a neutral act. If business leaders cling to a set of essentially conservative values in a society in which there is continuing change in social conditions and in the balance of political forces, the label of "neutralism" will not be enough to protect them from costly harassment.

Hammermill in Selma

About a year after the difficulties of U.S. Steel in Birmingham came to national attention, the Hammermill Paper Company made what appeared to be a non-controversial decision to build a $30 million pulp plant in Selma, Alabama. Hammermill certainly had no thought of social pioneering. The decision was guided solely by traditional business considerations. Company officials worked with representatives from Selma and the State of Alabama on problems of financing, waste disposal, roads, and taxes. The racial question was never considered and was assumed to be irrelevant. Hammermill's president, John Devitt, stated, "The discussions were confined to economic issues; we were relieved that the race question was not involved." Whatever advice was received by Hammermill executives came from "knowledgeable Southerners." The advice of Negro leaders who might have given Hammermill a more realistic picture was not sought.[48]

The consequences of Hammermill's social neutralism were dramatic and violent. When the financial and other arrangements were completed in January, 1965, plans were made to announce the construction of the new plant with appropriate fanfare on February 3 in the state capital at Montgomery. On February 1, however, a discordant note was sounded when Dr. Martin Luther King informed the press, "We're going to turn Selma upside down and inside out in order to make it right side up." On February 2, King and 270 fellow demonstrators were jailed during a voter registration protest. On February 3, while the Mayor and other political and business leaders of Selma were in Montgomery to hear Hammermill announce its new plant, another 500 Negroes were jailed in Selma.

At the February 3 news conference, Hammermill Chairman James C. Leslie was quoted as saying that one of the deciding factors in the company's decision to locate in Selma was "the character of the community and its people." With reference to Governor Wallace, he said, "We appreciate the fine job you are doing for your state." President Devitt, in turn, was quoted as saying, "We think Selma—and Alabama—offer everything an industry could want."

[47] Ivar Berg, "The Confidence Game," *Columbia University Forum,* Vol. 6 (Winter, 1963), pp. 34–40.
[48] Peter R. Kann, "Lesson From Selma," *Wall Street Journal,* April 9, 1965.

Hammermill officials later contended that the statements were intended in a purely economic context and that they were most decidedly not directed at the mores of the society or meant as sociological implications or facts about the community. This explanation seemed less and less satisfactory to the company's critics as the violence against civil rights marchers in Selma grew.

Dr. Robert W. Pike, executive director of the National Council of Churches' Commission on Religion and Race, called the statements "either the height of naïveté or the depth of racism." He said he would urge some 30 national church groups to "reexamine their purchasing policies in relation to Hammermill products." Rev. Andrew Young, executive director of the Southern Christian Leadership Conference, warned that his organization would put pressure on Hammermill through union and college boycotts of Hammermill products and by staging demonstrations in front of Hammermill's Northern plants. On March 9, the day after Selma marchers were dispersed by police using tear gas and clubs, Roy Wilkins, executive director of the NAACP, wired Hammermill, "Are you not proud that Hammermill Paper Company, by building a new plant in Selma, will be helping to support the Wallace storm trooper kind of government?"

Neutrality was no longer a tenable position for Hammermill. In a statement issued on March 17, 1965, the company expressed its "deep concern with the denial of basic rights to Negroes in Alabama and the Selma community," and specifically promised training programs open equally to Negroes and whites. Had this statement been issued on February 3, it might have averted some of the bitterness that followed.

The Selma demonstrations, like those in Birmingham, were critical in the civil rights revolution of the 1950's and 1960's. Many Northern liberals and sympathizers with the civil rights cause flew to Selma to march in protest. The actions of Hammermill and of U.S. Steel illustrate the close relationship between the two major social changes of the South—its industrialization and the civil rights movement. To some observers, it suddenly became quite obvious that that industrialization could not proceed in the South if it came into conflict with the civil rights movement.

Hammermill's failure to foresee the social consequences of what they had considered a purely economic decision is understandable. American business leaders rate economic efficiency high in their scale of values and generally resist the warping effect of political pressure on economic affairs. Judging from what happened in Selma, however, major corporations cannot afford to be myopic about social conditions, for they have economic consequences, and these consequences are subject to at least partial control if business decisions are wisely made. Business' policy of non-involvement helped to trigger off the civil rights movement, much of which has to do with job discrimination. Any economic damage that results from civil rights protests should be considered in evaluating that policy.

Birmingham and Selma were dramatic episodes, but the experience of business there can be extrapolated to many other situations and issues. The posture of neutrality is difficult to maintain. Civic controversies on major issues frequently reflect underlying economic and political instabilities in communities that threaten the welfare of corporations located there. Their economic self-interest dictates that they must either become involved or move. The benefits of moving are often limited, however, since many of the community issues are, in fact, reflections of national developments. Indeed, boycotts by national civil rights organizations and federal sanctions against discrimination make relocation an almost irrelevant accommodation.

Education

While corporations were forced by outside pressures to take action in such controversial issues as civil rights, they involved themselves quite spontaneously in some other social matters. Even a brief review of the areas of community activity in which national corporations have become involved is sufficient to indicate that once they do become involved, they cannot limit their participation to a single issue. Employment is tied to desegregation; desegregation is tied to schooling; schooling is tied to taxes; and taxes are tied to politics.

The quality of public education is seen by big business leaders as a key to the problems of unemployment and of desegregation. It is becoming a significant factor in the determination of plant location. As a result, those actions of the community that center around the educational process are increasingly guided by the imperatives of the corporation.

In Louisville, Kentucky, for example, one of the leaders in attempts to bring about better tax support for the schools there and in surrounding Jefferson County was General Electric, which maintains its giant factory complex, Appliance Park, in Louisville. General Electric's management in Louisville, along wtih 200 local GE employees, worked actively to obtain passage of a tax referendum that would have provided new financing for schools.[49]

When the referendum failed, efforts shifted to the Kentucky legislature where a bill was passed providing for emergency financing for Louisville and Jefferson County schools. The success of the bill was partly due to the lobbying of GE and other major Louisville companies. It should be noted, however, that while these companies were major employers, they were not necessarily major taxpayers.

The importance of a good school system is gaining recognition from both major corporations and local communities. From the corporation's point of view, a good school system provides a superior work force. From the community's point of view, recognition and accreditation of its schools are significant factors in attracting new plants and business. Thus, when accreditation was withdrawn from 15 Duval County (Jacksonville) schools in Florida, the county's ability to bring in new industry was impaired.

In a number of instances, the corporation not only requires that the schools be good, it also has specific criteria by which it measures the school system's

[49] Melloan, "School Scrutiny," *Wall Street Journal*, September 23, 1965.

quality. They are usually quite similar to those used by education researchers and include such items as teachers' salaries, the ratio of pupils to teachers, the training of teachers, the relation of teachers and the community, school plant facilities, and the quality and scope of the curriculum. The criteria just listed, incidentally, are used by General Electric. Some of them, such as determining the quality and scope of the curriculum, are obviously a focus of much political controversy and raise questions about the many threats to democratic institutions of too much corporate involvement in community affairs. This issue is discussed below.

Another matter of concern to corporations is the accessibility and adequacy of colleges and universities in an area where they open a branch plant. This is of especially great concern to corporations such as IBM, DuPont, and Celanese that employ many scientific personnel. Sprague Electric Company of North Adams, Massachusetts, for example, recently decided to build a plant in Worcester, Massachusetts, rather than buy an existing plant in a more remote area. Said an unidentified company spokesman, "In Worcester, Clark University, with a strong physics department, and Worcester Polytechnic Institute offer our people a chance to continue work on their PhD's."[50]

In some communities, corporations do more than set standards. They make major contributions to raise the quality of public schools. The International Paper Company Foundation has budgeted $385,000 in 1966 for aid to 26 school systems throughout the nation where International Paper Company plants are located. The money is used to provide advanced training for teachers and to finance programs that the schools themselves have devised. The amount spent in 1966 is double the amount spent ten years ago.

Richard C. Millet, vice president of the Foundation, proudly reports that one school receiving Foundation aid became the first consolidated school in South Carolina to receive accreditation. The school cut its dropout rate to 3 per cent, quite low for a predominantly Negro school in the South, and has installed language laboratories and other facilities that are not common in rural Southern schools.[51]

Other industry foundations, such as the Corning Glass Works Foundation, perform similar functions. Their new interest in public education, while laudable, raises several questions. How can adequate safeguards be instituted against corporate control over what is taught if a corporation becomes a significant donor? What implications do the ideological commitments of business donors have for the balance of political power between more conservative and progressive forces in the nation? And aren't the corporate contributions to public education, like those of the federal government, a mere pittance relative to the problem? Do they actually help upgrade quality or do they merely raise expectations without really altering the substance and level of public education? (Some of these questions are

[50] "Podunk, Anyone?", *Wall Street Journal,* February 23, 1966, p. 8.
[51] Melloan, "School Scrutiny," *op. cit.*

treated at length in this volume by Marcia Freedman and Richard Eells.) Traditionally, local business has been somewhat niggardly in its attitude toward school appropriations. Real estate interests in particular have tended to oppose school spending. This pattern is slowly giving way to the new imperatives of national corporations that cannot afford to locate their plants in towns where schools and universities are of inferior quality.

Urban Renewal

Urban renewal is fast becoming another local issue in which national corporations are taking an interest. It has always involved local business interests, particularly downtown department stores, and real estate firms. National corporation involvement is becoming more and more prevalent. It may be more characteristic of non-manufacturing than of manufacturing firms, but the latter as well are involved. A few case studies are helpful in describing and interpreting such involvement. They are of Sears, General Electric, and U.S. Gypsum.[52]

Once committed to mail order business exclusively, three-quarters of Sears' business is now conducted in urban retail outlets. Conditions in the localities where Sears stores are located make it a matter of self-interest, if nothing else, to become involved. This self-interest has two aspects. The first is the threat to the Sears investment in these stores posed by the deterioration of the neighborhoods in which their stores are located. Prospective customers are hesitant about entering these neighborhoods, and shoplifting exacts a heavy toll on profit. Second, an urban renewal program could contribute to an increase in sales if residents in blighted areas could be engaged in a "clean up, fix up, paint up" type of program, since Sears carried all the necessary supplies.

Sears took a number of steps to promote such a program through its stores in communities throughout the nation. First, it prepared and published a booklet, *The ABC's of Urban Renewal,* to acquaint its own personnel with the urban renewal program. Professionally prepared, this booklet was so well received that over 100,000 copies were distributed, despite the fact that it was originally intended for Sears employees only. Then a second booklet, *Citizens in Urban Renewal,* designed to develop citizen interest and organization was also well received; 300,000 copies were distributed in just a few months.

To overcome one problem of urban renewal programs, the shortage of qualified planners, the Sears Foundation provided several graduate fellowships in planning. Sears also published the *Urban Renewal Observer,* a company house organ that described what Sears employees had been doing in urban renewal. This increased the visibility of their activities to top management, giving an added inducement to employee participation.

Sears program can be contrasted with General Electric's. GE has given more limited support for urban renewal. While Roy Johnson of GE is one of the moving spirits of ACTION (American Council to Improve our Neighborhoods),

---

[52] The Sears and General Electric cases are discussed in Webb S. Fiser, *Mastery of the Metropolis* (Englewood Cliffs, N. J.: Prentice-Hall, 1962), pp. 43–48.

there are countercurrents in the GE policy that tend to confuse and obstruct the program.

Sears' sole concern was to find solutions to pressing urban problems. It carefully avoided ideological detours into "free enterprise," "the evils of subsidies," or the "excessive power of labor unions." This was not the case with GE.

GE's policies toward labor made it difficult for the company to exercise political leadership in communities with strong unions. In addition, GE's orthodoxy required adherence to the "free-enterprise" creed. If a question involving urban renewal or middle-income housing carried with it implications of federal subsidy, no GE executive would participate, because in GE's creed such subsidies sap the vitality of local communities.

Webb Fiser suggests that the differences in perspective shown by GE and Sears may be attributed to differences in the nature of their business. Sears' primary customers are the local customers of its stores. GE's customers are drawn from a national market, including other industries.[53] This difference may be more general. The NICB study indicates, for example, that there is more public affairs activity among non-manufacturing (88 per cent) than among manufacturing firms (75 per cent). Given the size of their sample (1,033), this is a significant difference.[54]

Nevertheless, manufacturing firms are much more involved in urban renewal affairs than ever before, and GE's reluctance is largely a reflection of the top management's political and economic philosophy. IBM, for example, is a leader in urban renewal activity in Poughkeepsie, as we noted earlier. And U.S. Gypsum Company has undertaken an unusual new venture into slum rehabilitation in Harlem that may well reflect some future developments.[55]

U.S. Gypsum has undertaken to demonstrate that private enterprise can profitably undertake slum renovation. At a cost of $1.25 million, the company bought and is rebuilding six old bulidings in the heart of Harlem. Its self-interest lies in the theory that if it works in Harlem, it should work anywhere. As a maker of building materials, U.S. Gypsum wants to open a market it estimates to be more than $20 billion. Its management feels it can make sizable profits and emerge with honors for public service and private enterprise. If middle-class intellectuals can make money running, studying, and evaluating poverty programs, there would seem to be little reason why private enterprise should act differently.

The implications of the U.S. Gypsum venture are quite far-reaching, and they are increasingly recognized in the business community. The more it gets involved in such urban development activities, the more profits it can make while improving its image by demonstrating a concern for the "public interest." At the same time, it can hopefully keep the federal government out.[56]

[53] *Ibid.*, p. 47.
[54] *Business in Public Affairs Today,* reprint from Conference Board Record, National Industrial Conference Board, May, 1966.
[55] Bowen Northrup, "Profit in Rehabilitation," *Wall Street Journal,* April 11, 1966.
[56] Stanford N. Sesser, "Profits and Public Service," *Wall Street Journal,* September 5, 1966.

NATIONAL CORPORATIONS AND POLITICAL ACTION: THE ATTITUDES OF INDIVIDUAL LEADERS

Before a large corporation adopts a new policy, a great many officials have to believe that the policy is necessary. For this reason surveys of individual business leaders are sometimes valuable in forecasting future corporate behavior. In 1959, the *Harvard Business Review* conducted a survey to ascertain the attitudes of its subscribers toward participation in politics.[57]

Among those subscribers were far more executives from large national corporations than would be found in an equal sample of the general business population, so that the survey results may be taken as an indication of the attitudes of big business in particular. Out of a cross section of 10,000 subscribers, 27 per cent responded to the questionnaire. Almost to a man, the executives declared that businessmen should be more active in politics and that the maintenance of good relations with elected officials was important to their companies.

When it came to personal participation and, in a lesser degree, to company participation, however, the picture was quite different. Nearly one-half of the respondents indicated that their firms were not involved in political affairs in any way and only one-quarter had personally participated in the 1958 election campaign.

In 1964, the *Harvard Business Review* again conducted a survey, very similar to the one conducted in 1959.[58] There was a 31 per cent response to the 1964 survey. By a wide margin (78 per cent to 14 per cent), business executives believed that improvement in the political climate toward business would necessitate more political activity by business itself. While a large majority (80 per cent to 16 per cent) still felt that most businesses were afraid to get involved in political activities, an almost equally large majority (79 per cent to 15 per cent) disagreed with the idea that company activity in politics can only hurt business. There is little reason to doubt, in light of the cases already reviewed, that the political actions of large business will tend increasingly to substantiate the opinion expressed in response to this questionnaire that political participation is important.

Most of the businessmen who responded to the second survey believed that the influence of business in political affairs and on elected officials had increased since 1960. Significantly, more of today's executives believe that the political influence of business had increased since 1960 than did their counterparts of five years earlier in responding to a similar question on the trend in political influence of business from 1950 to 1959. The responses to this series of questions are shown in Table 2. Note that in 1959, 52 per cent of the respondents perceived the influence of business on political affairs since 1950 as having increased (18 per cent by a lot and 34 per cent by a little). At the same time, 35 per cent of respondents perceived the influence of business on political affairs since 1950 as

[57] Daniel H. Fenn, Jr., "Business and Politics," *Harvard Business Review,* Vol. 37 (May–June, 1959), p. 6.
[58] Stephen A. Greyser, "Business and Politics, 1964," *Harvard Business Review,* Vol. 42 (September–October, 1964), p. 23.

having decreased (18 per cent by a little and 17 per cent by a lot). In 1964, on the other hand, 60 per cent of the respondents perceived the influence of business on political affairs as having increased since 1960, and only 18 per cent perceived this influence as having decreased.

Similarly, in 1959, 43 per cent of the respondents perceived the influence of business on elected officials as having increased since 1950, while 39 per cent perceived this influence as having decreased. In 1964, however, 49 per cent of the respondents perceived the influence of business on elected officials as having increased since 1960, and only 19 per cent perceived this influence as having decreased during the same period of time.

The executives were aware that their political efforts in the past had not been

Table 2.   Perception of Business' Influence in Politics

YEAR OF SURVEY	ISSUE	INCREASED		REMAINED THE SAME	DECREASED	
		CONSIDER-ABLY	A LITTLE		A LITTLE	CONSIDER-ABLY
1959	The Influence of Business on Political Affairs Since 1950 Has	18%	34%	13%	18%	17%
1964	The Influence of Business on Political Affairs Since 1960 Has	15%	45%	22%	12%	6%
1959	The Influence of Business on Elected Officials Since 1950 Has	14%	29%	18%	21%	18%
1964	The Influence of Business on Elected Officials Since 1960 Has	10%	39%	31%	13%	6%

[59] Source: Stephen A. Greyser, "Business and Politics, 1964 (Problems in Review," *Harvard Business Review* (September-October, 1964), page 26. Reprinted by permission of the *Harvard Business Review*.

Table 3.   Businessmen View the Extent and Effectiveness of Business' Political Activity

EXTENT OF BUSINESS POLITICAL ACTIVITY	IN PAST	SHOULD BE	EFFECTIVENESS OF PAST ACTIVITY	
Very extensive	2%	19%	Very effective	2%
Fairly extensive	11%	41%	Fairly effective	24%
Moderately extensive	31%	29%	About 50-50	29%
Somewhat limited	34%	6%	Fairly ineffective	36%
Very limited	22%	5%	Very ineffective	9%

[60] Source: Adapted from Stephen A. Greyser, "Business and Politics, 1964 (Problems in Review)," *Harvard Business Review* (September-October, 1964), page 28. Reprinted by permission of the *Harvard Business Review*.

particularly effective. They were also aware, however, that business' political activity in the past had been rather limited. In the future, they indicated, such activity would be far more extensive. The data are summarized in Table 3. A total of 72 per cent of the businessmen queried believed that political activity should increase, and only about 8 per cent felt otherwise.

Official Policies

National corporations have become acutely aware of the need for official company policies regarding involvement in community affairs, partly as a result of political developments on the national level.

In 1962, Norton Long noted:

> Shocked at the Republican weakness at the polls, corporations such as General Electric have gone out to educate their middle and lower managements for political action. The revelation of corporate weakness in the local communities has been startling. . . . The reintegration of economic dominants into the local social structure is one of the main problems of our civic life.[61]

An article in *Fortune,* written in 1959, described in detail what was then a new and intensified interest of large corporations in practical politics, evidenced by direct encouragement and many positive inducements for employees to participate in local affairs.[62] It went on to report that corporations were trying to develop an ideology on which many of them could agree and in so doing were more openly declaring their positions on controversial issues than they had in the past. Hundreds of companies were already said to be giving bipartisan training courses in the area of practical politics for middle-management people. Such corporate giants as Gulf Oil, American Can, Monsanto Chemical, Republic Steel, and Borg-Warner had set up departments of government and political affairs; and some national associations of business (e.g., the Effective Citizens Organization) had become involved as consultants, conducting practical-politics seminars that were well attended by middle-management personnel from large, national corporations.

The increased involvement in politics for some large corporations like Ford, General Electric, Johnson & Johnson, and Gulf Oil actually began in the late 1940's and early 1950's. General Electric took the position that the businessman who says he is not involved in politics is kidding himself, and dangerously so; the company issued a pamphlet, "Political Helplessness of Business Hurts Everybody," that was distributed among 400,000 of its stockholders and management personnel in 1956. The company deplored the fact that union officials are thought to be important politically while businessmen are seen as impotent because politicians figure union officials can and do influence votes while businessmen can't and don't.[63]

[61] *The Polity* (Chicago: Rand-McNally, 1962), p. 135.
[62] "Corporations Make Politics Their Business," *Fortune* (December, 1959), p. 100ff.
[63] "Businessmen in Politics," *Time* (August 27, 1956), p. 64.

In 1958, when Gulf Oil's senior vice president, Archie D. Gray, announced that his company intended to take an active part in politics, he enunciated a philosophy that was to become more and more prevalent:

> Whether we want to be or not, Gulf and every other American corporation is in politics—up to its neck in politics—and we must either start swimming or drown. . . . If we are to survive, labor's political power must now be opposed by a matching force, and there is no place in the United States where such force can be generated except among the corporations that make up American business.[64]

What was a trickle of such corporate political activity was to become much more prevalent and more rationalized in the mid-1960's. In 1964, Xerox, IBM, Sears Roebuck, Kaiser Industries, Zenith Radio, and Inland Steel, among others, made sizable donations to President Johnson's campaign—the first time in many years that big business had supported a Democratic Presidential candidate. These and other corporations have also participated in local efforts on such significant problems as urban development and discrimination against Negroes.[65]

The interest of corporations and business leaders in increased political participation pertains to all levels of government, but its primary focus is on local or "grass roots" activity. As one business spokesman advised:

> Awareness of government must be advanced in community after community, through education in the art of government and in the process of practical politics. It means direct participation by business-oriented people in "grass roots" political activity.[66]

A recent survey on the public affairs activities of United States corporations conducted by the National Industrial Conference Board also indicates that participation has become widespread.[67] In an effort to determine how many companies are in public affairs, the Board asked cooperating companies, "What are you doing?" and "What have you done?". Of the 1,033 companies surveyed, 815 had a public affairs function at or about the local level. This, according to the Board, represents a tremendous increase from the number of companies with formal programs in the 1950's.

Two of the most significant kinds of public affairs programs mentioned were political and economic education of employees and contributions to and participation in community affairs. More than half of the companies surveyed (572) offered some form of what they called "bipartisan" political education to employees on a more or less continuing basis. Formal instruction through meetings and seminar courses was offered by 278 companies, while 294 addressed employees through

---

[64] Horace E. Shelden, "Businessmen Must Get into Politics," *Harvard Business Review*, Vol. 37 (March–April, 1959), p. 37.
[65] David T. Bazelon, "Big Business and the Democrats," *Commentary* (May, 1965), pp. 39–47.
[66] David Galligan, *Politics and the Businessman* (New York: Pitman, 1964), p. 126.
[67] *Business in Public Affairs Today, op. cit.*

company house organs and related means. The most common practice among the companies that used "courses in practical politics" was to make such instruction available to all employees.

Other findings are just as indicative of involvement. For example, over 90 per cent of the companies in the survey made financial contributions; 83 per cent lent personnel and space and made other gifts in kind to community activities. Of considerable importance is the fact that two-thirds of the companies in the study thought enough of their employees' non-job-related community activities to accord them some form of recognition. More than 75 per cent of the companies said that they encouraged employees to serve on local school boards, law enforcement commissions, and similar agencies.

The Ford Motor Company illustrates how large corporations have become involved in local affairs. The political arm of Ford's public relations effort is its Civic and Governmental Affairs Office (CGAO). CGAO maintains a Washington branch office and operates through eight regional managers across the country. It is also responsible for the Ford Community Relations Committees made up of local top management in each company city. The Committees are supposed to encourage Ford employee and company participation in civic affairs and at the same time seek favorable local conditions for the company. CGAO is headed by Thomas R. Reid, to whom we shall return shortly.

A Joint Center monograph on Detroit politics points out that the most significant activity of CGAO is its newest function—the Effective Citizenship Program.[68] This program is open to all supervisory employees who volunteer to participate. While sometimes represented as a bipartisan effort, the program does in fact have broad political objectives that place the company, like its president, among political moderates and, in some instances, just to the right of center. As Henry Ford II himself has put it:

> It seems to me that the best hope for stopping the present political drift toward a government controlled economy . . . lies in the political activation of a large, moderate, politically inactive middle-income group in our society. If it can be mobilized, it would provide a solid and wholesome buffer to extremes of either right or left.[69]

COMBINED POLITICAL ACTIVITY BY NATIONAL CORPORATIONS

Many of the business leaders and corporations active in politics on an individual basis are also interested in promoting political involvement throughout the entire business community. This interest is reflected in the public affairs movement. Certain business peak associations have initiated extensive programs to convert this interest into an efficient political force. One consequence of this development has been to increase electoral support for conservative politicians.

[68] Greenstone, *op. cit.*, pp. v–21.
[69] *Ibid.*, p. v–23.

Republican Interest in the Public Affairs Movement

In a 1965 address at a National Industrial Conference Board meeting on public affairs, former Vice President Richard M. Nixon strongly supported many of the social welfare programs of the National Association of Manufacturers and went on to urge the business community to increase its public affairs participation:

> It is my conviction that if the private business community, the power represented in this room and by your colleagues around the country, does not step in and take responsibility to find in the people's sector and in the private sector solutions for public problems, there isn't any question but that government will step in with massive solutions and those solutions inevitably are going to encroach on the private sector in a way that certainly will not be in the interest of your stockholders. . . . I know that when you chip away a little area of freedom in any particular institution or any particular activity that begins to snowball.[70]

The former vice president was suggesting that business could rally many local and national groups in formulating local, self-help solutions to problems of poverty, unemployment, public education, and other crises of the city. He thought that a moderate, middle-income coalition might be formed:

> In addition to our commercial sector and our government sector, there has always been a third sector, independent of either—a "people's sector"—that proudly took public responsibility before government could claim it. What is this independent sector? It is an endless variety of unique American institutions that are neither, on the one hand, commercial nor, on the other, governmental. The Conference Board is a perfect example. . . . To list even the major categories of such institutions in America would take the rest of the evening: hospitals, garden clubs, universities, lodges, private welfare agencies, churches, trade associations, national health organizations, labor unions, foundations, research institutes, private schools. They add up to a mighty force.

This is really what the public affairs movement of national corporations was all about in the 1960's. It was an attempt by big business, in alliance with and perhaps courted by such national political leaders as Nixon and Romney, to mobilize a large coalition of moderates or just to the right-of-center interests to restore conservative values and institutions. Though Southern Democrats are supported by corporations that are parties to the public affairs movement, the movement may be of much more benefit to the Republican Party than to the Democrats. The congressional elections of 1966 indicated that big business had become disenchanted with its role in President Johnson's broad centrist coalition of 1964. A look at the activities of the most political of the major business associations tends to confirm this impression.

Peak Association: The Effective Citizens Organization

The term "peak association" as used by Robert Brady in his seminal work *Business as a System of Power* refers to groupings of large corporations and trade associa-

[70] *Broadening the Dimensions of Public Affairs,* National Industrial Conference Board, Public Affairs Conference Report No. 3, 1965, p. 91.

tions for the purpose of coordinating business practices and policies.[71] The Effective Citizens Organization (ECO) is an excellent example.

ECO has been closely identified with the business-in-politics movement and with the political education of employees. It was founded in 1954, inspired by President Eisenhower's concern for involving businessmen in public affairs. A group of men led by Bruce Palmer, president of the National Industrial Conference Board, were the original founders. Both Willard Merrihue of General Electric and Thomas Reid of Ford's Civic and Governmental Affairs Office represent their respective companies on the board of directors of this organization, which is designed to enhance the political effectiveness of the middle-income, middle-management employee at the community level.

ECO's public relations statements describe it as having spearheaded the drive to "educate both management and employees in the American political system." It conducts top-level management seminars dealing with tactics and strategy for getting started in public affairs. In addition, it conducts workshops for local plant managers, representatives of trade associations, and often works in conjunction with local Chambers of Commerce in developing such programs.[72]

ECO can point to between 450 and 500 major companies now conducting active public affairs programs as a result of their seminars and training programs, as compared with only 53 in 1960. When an ECO spokesman comments that "politics is becoming a vital part of corporate affairs," he is referring to just such an increase in ECO membership.

Many of the companies ECO has serviced are quite large. Among those adopting its programs recently, for example, are American Airlines, Bethlehem Steel, Burlington Industries, and General Mills. A look at its board reads like a "blue-book" of American industry studded with names like U.S. Steel, General Electric, Ford, Gulf Oil, Standard Oil of Indiana and New Jersey, Chrysler, Phillips Petroleum, Aluminum Company of America, American Can, Dow Chemical, and Allis Chalmers, among others. Sixty-four per cent of its board members (34 of 53) are among the Fortune 500, with most of them (28) among the top 100 industrials. Four more are among the top 50 commercial banks and utilities.[73] Since the total membership of ECO consists of close to 500 firms of this type, this is a considerable amount of wealth and power.

Just how effective is the Effective Citizens Organization? The following data, a sample of results achieved by ECO programs in several different companies, would seem to indicate that it has achieved something more than a token success.

American Cyanamid conducted a survey in 1963 of its executives before and after they had completed a political action course developed by ECO. It found that 37 per cent of the political action course graduates have written to public officials about issues, an increase of 77 per cent; 51 per cent attended rallies, an increase of 98 per cent; and 195 helped in some way to formulate strategy

---

[71] *Op. cit.,* p. 3.
[72] *Let's Look at ECO,* Effective Citizens Organizations (Washington, D.C.), p. 6.
[73] This analysis was done from a list of board members provided by ECO. See also James C. Tanner, "A Double Life," *Wall Street Journal,* August 1, 1966, p. 1.

for party candidates, an increase of 141 per cent. The base year against which these percentage increases were tallied was just prior to the company's instituting a formal public affairs program.[74]

American Can Company has put 3,000 employees through its training courses, and its spokesmen estimate that 600 have gone into party work. Some have even become office holders.[75]

Monsanto Chemical, with an extremely active public affairs program, recently counted 300 employees who held part-time public office.[76] In 1962, 87 per cent of Ford's "management role" employees contributed to a party or to a candidate in Michigan.[77] In the fall of 1964, Aerojet-General Corporation, a California-based subsidiary of General Tire and Rubber Company, turned over more than $138,000 that had been contributed by employees to the parties and individual candidates during the election campaign. This was the largest amount Aerojet had raised since its first drive in 1958.[78] Every one of these corporations was active in ECO.

The effectiveness of ECO's programs is further indicated in its relationships with local business associations—e.g., Chambers of Commerce and trade associations. Illustrative of a grass roots, community level, political action program is one developed by the Manufacturers' Association of Syracuse, with ECO's assistance. The original impetus for the Syracuse program (General Electric was one of the leading firms in this program) was provided by a report of a subcommittee of the association. Contending that high, government-imposed costs were a serious deterrent to business activity, it issued the following call to action:

> The subcommittee recommends that the Manufacturers' Association of Syracuse, as a matter of policy, acknowledge a basic weakness in the political situation of industry and commerce generally. Bricks and mortar do not vote. The big weakness is that management's concern does not extend to the place where political candidates are measured, trained, groomed and eventually selected. Therefore, your committee recommends that the starting place for correction in connection with the state business climate . . . is fundamentally in political party participation at all levels and particularly at ward and precinct levels.[79]

Based on these recommendations, the following program was developed: (1) A "political primer" was published for management "to take the mystery out of the workings of the political party, and to give practical tips on how to become effective politically in one's own community"; (2) Top executives in Syracuse firms heard a one-hour presentation, and each was asked to designate one "upper-middle management" representative of his firm to follow through on; (3) Giving middle-management representatives a two-day concentrated dose of practical

---

[74] Galligan, *op. cit.,* p. 35.

[75] Melloan, "Playing Politics," *op. cit.,* p. 1.

[76] *Idem.*

[77] Ted Turpin, "More Companies Prod Employees to Donate to Political Parties," *Wall Street Journal,* October 13, 1964, p. 1.

[78] *Idem.*

[79] Shelden, *op. cit.,* p. 40.

politics, with political leaders of both major parties participating. Finally, (4) companies that were represented in the two-day seminars then set up plant seminars for their own management personnel.

The Syracuse workshops were in operation from 1957 through mid-1962. A survey conducted by Cornell in the fall of 1960 indicates that 73 per cent of those who had participated in some political activity after having taken the course had done nothing before their exposure to the course material. The report concluded, "It can be definitely stated that the Practical Politics Seminars generated a good deal of political activity in the Syracuse area."[80]

Trade associations, too, serve as a channel for the diffusion within the business community at large of ECO's programs and views. Many of the industries represented in ECO—steel, petroleum, chemicals—have developed separate public affairs programs through ECO's assistance. A pattern of interlocking directorates exists with industry and trade association leaders also serving as directors of ECO. As business leaders from so many industries periodically get together in ECO, they find common political and economic interests, with a classic "resonance effect" taking place.

The Manufacturing Chemists Association is a case in point. General G. H. Decker (USA, Ret.), president of the association, describes the renewed interest being taken by industry in public affairs as a "renaissance" in government relations.

> Today, there seems to be a new awakening to the fact that government is a part of the business of business, that a government which is ignored will, in turn, ignore. In short there are signs of a renaissance. More and more businessmen are turning politician. More and more companies are encouraging their employees to participate in the political processes. A new lexicon of terms—Public Affairs and Civic Affairs and Political Action and Practical Politics—is being braided into industry's way of life.[81]

General Decker describes the responsibilities of the chemical industry to interpret to government the problems and positions of the chemical industry, to foster grass roots support for industry-wide positions, and to support and to assist state and local government in matters on which these governments have cognizance. On the last point, he emphasizes the importance of dealing with many economic and social problems at lower levels of government so that the federal government will not move in.

The Association describes its community-relations manual as "an anthology of philosophy and advice which explores the juxtaposition of industrial affairs and government affairs." Its contents are revealing. The lead article, "Is the Chemical Industry Doing Enough?", deals with the question of whether the American chemical industry has concerned itself sufficiently with politics and government.[82]

---

[80] Galligan, *op. cit.*, p. 70.
[81] General G. H. Decker (USA, Ret.), "Renaissance in Government Relations," in *Government and Industry*, Manufacturing Chemists Association (Washington, D.C.). This is a community relations manual the association publishes for its members.
[82] *Government and Industry*, *op. cit.*, p. 6.

Its author, Thomas J. Diviney, was a former manager of Civic Affairs for Monsanto Chemical Company. He is also a director of ECO and is now an executive in the Division of Public Affairs Research of the National Industrial Conference Board. Diviney is a co-author of the Conference Board's recent study, *Business in Public Affairs Today.*

The Diviney article is followed by a public affairs symposium "Voices of Experience," in which Thomas Reid, director of Civic and Governmental Affairs of Ford, describes "Ford's Approach." Willard Merrihue, mentioned previously, and William G. White, vice president of U.S. Steel, outline those of General Electric and U.S. Steel. Both Reid and Merrihue are directors of ECO, and U.S. Steel is a member.[83]

A few pages later on, we come to a case study, "The Day P. A. Paid Dividends," by Stanley De J. Osborne, chairman of the board of Olin Mathieson Chemical Company. This is an account of Olin's successful public affairs campaign in Hannibal, Ohio, discussed above.[84] An Olin Mathieson executive is vice president of ECO.

Finally, there is a panel discussion of "The Industrial Editor's Role in Government Relations." The participants are Republican Congressman Robert Wilson, Walter B. Petravage, manager of the Public Affairs Department of the U.S. Chamber of Commerce, and Byron De Haan of the Caterpillar Tractor Company. De Haan, the only industrial member on the panel, is a director of ECO.[85]

ECO is not even mentioned in the entire manual, a curious fact, considering that its members played a major role in the preparation of the material. The point is this: the influence of ECO as an organization ranges far beyond individual actions of companies whose names appear on the roster and in ways that suggest some significant trends for the future of local, state, and national politics.

The pattern of interlocking directorates extends well beyond ECO and specific industry associations, to include the National Association of Manufacturers as well. Thus, 14 of the 53 companies represented on the ECO board of directors are also represented on NAM's board. Another 20 are represented in various NAM committees. That this is a group of firms with conservative and right-of-center views is indicated by both their substantial representation in NAM and their much-limited representation in the more progressive Committee for Economic Development. Only seven of ECO's board member firms are also members of the board of the Committee for Economic Development.[86] While the CED could hardly be said to stand for a consistently "liberal" position on many political and economic policy issues, it is certainly to the left of NAM, and considerably so on some matters.

The conservative tendencies of ECO members, meanwhile, are clear, as indicated by evidence on the contributions of its member companies to the Goldwater and Johnson Presidential campaigns in 1964. As is well-known, President Johnson

---

[83] *Ibid.,* p. 8.
[84] *Ibid.,* p. 19.
[85] *Ibid.,* p. 20.
[86] Data for this analysis come from lists of ECO, NAM, and CED boards of directors.

had a lot of big business support, and some of the Republican Party's complaints about the sizable contributions to the Democrats through the President's Club reflect this.[87] These contributions, however, did not come primarily from the big corporations belonging to Effective Citizens Organizations. Data from published lists of business contributors in the 1964 election campaign indicate that only six member companies of ECO supported Johnson, while 16 publicly supported Goldwater. While one might well assume that some, perhaps many companies, would have supported both candidates, it didn't work this way at all. Only two ECO members did—Ford and Olin Mathieson. What is most significant is that three of the six Johnson contributors among ECO members gave very modest support ($200 or under). Much of Mr. Goldwater's big business support, then, came from ECO member firms.[88]

National Association of Manufacturers

NAM is the oldest, the largest, and probably the best-known of the national business associations. Long symbolic of hard-core conservatism, it is now struggling, and with much conflict, for a new position.[89]

Prior to 1961, NAM was basically a national lobby for industry. Organized in 1895, it played a significant role in the establishment of the Department of Commerce and in the development of the parcel post system. During the pre-New Deal era, it was successful in its campaign to preserve high protective tariffs and in defeating child labor legislation.

The New Deal period and the years that followed were a succession of disasters for NAM. Between 1933 and 1941, it fought 31 campaigns to block New Deal social legislation, including the Wagner Act and the Social Security Act, and lost every one. Between 1957 and 1963, its membership declined from 21,000 to 14,000.

Recognizing the extent and severity of its decline, NAM hired Warner P. Gullander away from the General Dynamics Corporation at a salary in excess of $100,000 to become its first full-time president. Prior to that, NAM had been led by unpaid presidents, mostly small businessmen, elected for one-year terms.

Gullander in turn hired Richard C. Cornuelle as NAM executive vice president. Cornuelle saw the necessity for NAM to adopt a community action approach. It was his contention that the "independent sector"—unions, service clubs, churches, lodges, and community organizations—should band together with organizations like the NAM to cure social ills. His point of view is literally identical with that expressed by Richard Nixon in the latter's Conference Board speech. As NAM has started to modify its traditional views on business-government and

[87] Founded in 1961 by former Democratic national treasurer, Richard Maguire, the President's Club is a major source of campaign funds for the Democratic National Committee. Members contribute $1,000 or more. Membership in 1964 was about 5,000. *Congressional Quarterly* (September 9, 1966), p. 1,967.

[88] These data are from a study by David Rogers on the characteristics of business supporters of Goldwater and Johnson, as yet unpublished.

[89] Much of this discussion follows Frank J. Prial, "A 'New' NAM?", *Wall Street Journal,* May 31, 1966, p. 1.

business-labor relations and as it has developed a number of community action programs, it has gained greater respectability among businessmen and perhaps among other groups as well. It has become a part of a centrist and right-of-center coalition that is now mobilized by the Republican Party in elections.

Among the programs NAM has devised to put its community action concept into practice are MIND (Methods for Intellectual Development), STEP (Solutions to Employment Problems), and TIPS (Techniques in Product Selection). All are major departures from former programs, while serving many of the NAM's traditional goals, e.g., keeping the federal government out of business,[90] preserving local autonomy in government, and fostering self-help and economic individualism.

MIND is an experiment in training school dropouts for productive jobs. Several groups of deprived young Negroes have been already trained in basic stenographic and arithmetic skills by NAM and placed in industry. NAM is now urging its member companies to start similar programs. Corn Products Company, an NAM member, started such a program in the summer of 1966 at its Argo, Illinois, food processing plant near Chicago. This is, in part, an attempt to show that private industry can do the job more efficiently than the federal government.

STEP is a program through which NAM members trade information on employment problems. An example of how STEP assists NAM members at the local level is the experience of Diamond Alkali Company. Diamond Alkali was unable to train a small group of employees at its Houston plant for better jobs because of their illiteracy. The company set up a basic literacy program with the help of the Board of Fundamental Education. Workers can now move into Diamond Alkali's regular training program upon graduation from this program.

TIPS' director, Dawn Aurell, describes its community relations function in these terms, "Industry has done a magnificent job in consumer education, but no one has ever collected it or merchandized it properly." To overcome this problem, TIPS' staff will distribute information on new products, packaging, distribution, and credit through schools, clubs, civic organizations, and women's pages of newspapers and magazines.

NAM has also worked in the civil rights field. Months before the Civil Rights Act of 1964 was passed by Congress, NAM worked to prepare businessmen to comply with its provisions. Seminars were arranged all over the country. NAM labor relations specialists, representatives from the Justice Department, and members of the Urban League explained to industry personnel men Title VII, which forbids discrimination by race or sex in hiring.

Business-Industry Political Action Committee

Still another major industry association involved in the public affairs program is an NAM off-shoot, the Business-Industry Political Action Committee (BIPAC).

[90] NAM's objection to "government" does not necessarily extend to federal defense contracts and related expenditures. Indeed, Mr. Gullander's former firm, General Dynamics, has long benefited from its extensive collaboration with the Department of Defense.

The function of BIPAC is to help the political campaigns of congressional candidates whose platforms "reaffirm sound fiscal policies and who uphold the free, private and competitive enterprise system," acceptable to NAM and its membership.[91] Although there is no formal administrative connection between the two organizations, NAM founded BIPAC and is its chief financial backer.

An earlier NAM political action program, described as one of the most inflexible of such programs ever offered to businessmen, was abandoned in 1962.[92] BIPAC appears to have risen from the ashes of that earlier venture. It was founded in August, 1963, to provide financial aid to congressional candidates who "support the principles of constitutional government" and to encourage citizens to be more active and effective in the political party of their choice.[93] Its officers are Kenton R. Cravens, a St. Louis banker, chairman; Arthur H. Motley, president of Parade Publications and a former president of the U.S. Chamber of Commerce, vice chairman; and Joseph B. Lanterman, president of Armsted Industries, secretary-treasurer. Mr. Motley is also a director of ECO.

BIPAC's literature reveals an extremely close adherence to the most conservative aspects of the American business creed, and, understandably, to the views of NAM. It claims to represent the "competitive, free-enterprise" viewpoint and decries the "increasing trend toward centralization of our government and domination of the economy and the individual."[94]

The avowed enemy of BIPAC is COPE, the AFL–CIO's Committee on Political Education, whose effectiveness BIPAC officials continually emphasize. The 1964 congressional campaign was BIPAC's maiden effort and a total of $200,000 was spent in direct support of congressional candidates. BIPAC-supported candidates won in 34 House contests—40 per cent of the 86 House contests in which it had given financial assistance. Of the winning candidates, 10 were Democrats and 24 were Republicans; 9 of the 10 Democrats were Southerners.[95]

The overlaps in membership between BIPAC and ECO are just as marked as with BIPAC and NAM. BIPAC companies were virtually unanimous in their support of Goldwater, whose views on economic matters clearly paralleled their own.

It would certainly appear, then, that discussions of whether or not large corporations have any place in politics are somewhat academic. They are in politics, somewhat hesitantly and perhaps fumbling at first, but they are there. What is more important, they are in politics not just at the national level and not just for fund-raising. They are in politics at the community level and that is where the major political battle lines appear to be forming. Nor will these battle lines

---

[91] *The New Force in Politics* (Business-Industry Political Action Committee, New York, n.d.), a pamphlet addressed to "American Management," p. 2.
[92] Galligan, *op. cit.,* p. 72.
[93] Leonard Ingalls, "Business Group Enters Politics," *New York Times,* August 5, 1963, p. 1. The *Times* actually announced the birth of BIPAC.
[94] *The New Force in Politics,* p. 2.
[95] Robert L. Humphrey, "Executive Director's Report," *BIPAC Newsletter,* No. 5, December, 1964, p. 1.

be confined to the election of congressional candidates. Says Republic Steel's vice president, H. C. Lamb, one of the founders and a member of the board of directors of BIPAC:

> The publc affairs movement has yet to make a real impact on the schools—particularly on curricula and textbooks. Here we should work cooperatively with curriculum committees to see that our viewpoint is represented. For example, the Educational Research Council of Cleveland is presently revising the entire social science curriculum for about 40 school districts, and we're cooperating to see that this job is well done.[96]

CONCLUSION: THE SHIFTING BALANCE OF POWER

In the thirties, forties, and early fifties, the power of large corporations may well have been balanced by that of organized labor and various segments of the white-collar middle class. Signs of change, however, are becoming more and more evident, and the substance of the change may well pose a threat to such a balance of power and to pluralism. One such sign appears to be a decline in the strength of the labor movement. Another is the acceleration in growth and increasing conservatism of the new white-collar middle class. Still another is the concept of corporate citizenship as a substitute for community citizenship. All these signs point to greater power and influence for the corporation at national, state, and community levels. And the public affairs movement, the specifics of which we have already discussed, epitomizes the change.

While we will not review here recent developments in the labor movement, the evidence that unions have declined in power and influence appears to be quite compelling. Automation and shifting patterns of employment (the decline of hourly paid production jobs and the continued increase in technical, white-collar positions), shifts in industrial location from the East and from the Midwest (where unions have always been strong) to the South and smaller, rural communities (where unions have never had more than limited influence), the perpetuation in leadership positions of an older generation within the labor movement, and the disenchantment of a middle-class public and of middle-class intellectuals are some of the many social forces that may well indicate a decline in union power.[97]

Corporate spokesmen in the public affairs movement do, of course, claim the opposite—that labor has increased in power. Many of them, though they don't like to be quoted too often as saying so, report that their increased role in politics is to counter labor's power.[98] Some, working in such organizations as BIPAC and NAM, are very explicit in their political motivations, to support conservative political candidates who are usually antilabor. Yet, they are concerned that if their antilabor interest becomes too visible, the movement may fail. Many there-

[96] Melloan, "Playing Politics," *op. cit.*
[97] Solomon Barkin, *The Decline of the Labor Movement,* A Report for the Center for the Study of Democratic Institutions, 1961.
[98] "Corporations Make Politics Their Business," *Fortune, op. cit.*

fore represent it as a "bipartisan" effort to get executives involved in local politics, regardless of what candidates and economic philosophy they support. But it is bipartisan in the sense that only conservative (usually Southern) Democrats and Republicans are supported. And executives involved in the public affairs program acknowledge that if they get more and more managers and middle-income employees involved in local politics, this will more often than not help conservative, antilabor candidates and causes. The political strategy of public affairs spokesmen has been to play this down, resulting at times in a kind of obscurantism in public statements as to their actual goals. Many may well be like Ed Stone, Monsanto's manager of civic affairs and in 1966 a candidate for State Senator from Missouri's 26th District in the metropolitan St. Louis area. Friends and well-wishers accurately viewed Stone's campaign as a labor versus management battle, since his views on labor were well known. Yet, when asked for his position on the right-to-work issue, a most controversial one in Missouri, Stone suggested that he would take a scientific poll of his constituents and refused to state his own views.[99]

We would suggest that the public affairs movement has many more leaders like Mr. Stone who would line up against labor interests on many key issues. The result of their intervention in local politics would be a further decline in an already declining labor movement. Again, it must be remembered that one of the main peak associations in the movement, ECO, has close ties with two avowedly antilabor groups, NAM and BIPAC.

The continued expansion of professional, technical, and managerial positions has created a large white-collar class whose members, if anything, tend to identify more with management than with labor. They are the community leaders who dominate suburban politics. At the same time that labor unions as a countervailing force to "big business" may be in a period of decline, a conservatively oriented white-collar middle class led by a young, professional, technical, and managerial group is in the ascendancy. Alert corporate leaders have been quick to recognize the political potential of this situation. Their political education programs are aimed, to a large extent, at gaining the support of just this group. One aspect of what may well be a growing rapport between the large corporation and its white-collar employees is the concept of corporate citizenship—a concept that might aptly be termed "neo-paternalism."

This new white-collar class is, as many political observers have pointed out, a class without property and therefore without any "real interest." Politics are meaningless to such a class because they have no traditional interests to defend in the political arena. Corporate interests, as Andrew Hacker notes, become the interests of many in this class. The corporation gives its middle-class employees a community with which to identify and an immunity from politics. As this takes place, the corporation is itself obtaining even more direct access to the higher reaches of political parties and government.[100]

[99] James C. Tanner, "A Double Life," *Wall Street Journal*, August 1, 1966, p. 1ff.
[100] "Politics and the Corporation," in Andrew Hacker, ed., *The Corporation Take-over* (Garden City, N. Y.: Doubleday, 1965), Ch. 12.

One of the clearest statements of the substance and implications of this corporate citizenship concept is given by Horace Shelden, a director of the Industrial Relations Department of the New York Commerce and Industry Association. Commenting on General Electric's community relations program, Shelden notes:

> For many years General Electric has maintained an especially vigorous program of community relations stressing good corporate citizenship. It has communicated to the hilt in all directions. It does not hesitate to let the world know what it is. It does not believe in surrendering the allegiance of its employees to the unions that represent them.[101]

A New Coalition

A coalition of corporate management and a professional, technical, and managerial middle class seems to be well in the process of formation. Its ideological commitments may be somewhat to the right of center, opposing a continued expansion of the federal government in business and municipal affairs. Big business opposition to federal intervention is, to be sure, selective; large corporations rarely object to federal projects, subsidies, and defense contracts that contribute to corporate and local well-being. But, overall, business tends to oppose new social ventures by the government.

The coalition that is forming presents the corporation with an opportunity and a responsibility. The opportunity is to provide government with fresh and vigorous leadership, a function that, by virtue of the caliber of its personnel, the corporation is well qualified to fulfill. The responsibility is to see that the new leaders distinguish between corporate interest and community interest, that they participate in our pluralistic system rather than attempt neo-paternalistic manipulation, and that they do not neglect the many unsolved problems of our society, especially those of our cities.

SELECTED READINGS

EDWARD C. BANFIELD AND JAMES Q. WILSON, *City Politics* (Cambridge, Mass.: Harvard University Press and MIT Press, 1963). The first of a series of general works from the Joint Center for Urban Studies of MIT and Harvard on the power structures, political forms and styles, and interest group politics of American cities. One of the authors' many contributions is an analysis of the strengths and weaknesses of both old-style "machine" politics and "good government" reform administrations. Their data are drawn from studies of various cities, especially from some 30-odd case studies of the politics of particular cities written by Joint Center researchers. A pioneering work. The case studies on which it is based are also worth reading.

[101] Shelden, *op. cit.*, p. 41.

EDWARD C. BANFIELD, *Big City Politics* (New York: Random House, 1965). Draws on materials similar to those in *City Politics*. The same conceptual scheme is used in reporting and interpreting the politics of nine large American cities—Atlanta, Boston, Detroit, El Paso, Los Angeles, Miami, Philadelphia, St. Louis, and Seattle.

JOHN A. LARSON, ED., *The Responsible Businessman: Business and Society,* readings from "Fortune," (New York: Holt, Rinehart and Winston, 1966), *The Regulated Businessman: Business and Government,* readings from *Fortune,* (New York: Holt, Rinehart and Winston, 1966). Two useful compendia of articles and case reports of business-government relations. Numerous pieces study the relationship of business practices to other institutions in American society.

WILLIAM H. FORM AND DELBERT C. MILLER, *Industry, Labor, and Community* (New York: Harper & Row, 1960). An encyclopedic work by two industrial sociologists who have conducted numerous community power studies. Though some materials in the book appear somewhat dated in view of the many research studies since 1960, its discussions of conceptual and methodological problems in community research are still relevant for investigators and community action leaders.

DAVID GALLIGAN, *Politics and the Businessman* (New York: Pitman, 1964). The best book available on the public affairs movement of American business, by a historian and political scientist. Better as a discussion of how and why businessmen have become involved in local affairs than as an analysis of the implications of such involvement.

BERT SWANSON, ED., *Current Trends in Comparative Community Studies* (Kansas City, Mo.: Community Studies, 1962). A neglected but seminal collection of essays on research in comparative city politics. Many of the controversies among social scientists regarding research procedures and regarding their views on the nature of community power structures are cogently reviewed and summarized.

ROBERT A. BRADY, *Business as a System of Power* (New York: Columbia University Press, 1943). This is a well-known Marxist analysis of the "peak association" phenomenon in "advanced capitalist nations." The book is marked by clear biases that must be discounted, but it is also full of genuine insights.

chapter 3

BUSINESS AND THE
FEDERAL GOVERNMENT

CLARENCE C. WALTON, *Dean of the School of General Studies and Professor of Business in the Graduate School of Business at Columbia University, is a political scientist who has shown an enduring interest in exploring the relationship between the modern corporation and its political, economic, and social environment. He pioneered in the development of courses of study dealing with these relations and has served as a consultant to numerous corporations that felt a need for clearer policies defining their true interests in many areas of social action and concern. He writes therefore not only as a student of business' role in the democratic process but with the authority of a participant who was able to sense some of the changes described here while they were still in their formative stages.*

Dean Walton begins his essay by reviewing three interpretations of the significance of bigness in business and government institutions. Then he examines several aspects of public policy that have a direct impact on the business community. Turning to the impact of business policy on the government, he points out that business has many legitimate interests that are periodically challenged by other groups, and he outlines defensive strategies that the business community has used to maintain its position in the interplay of interests foreseen and provided for by the Founding Fathers. Finally, he describes the interaction of public policy and business strategy in three particular cases.

Among the most interesting developments described is the changing balance between "campaign" and "cameralist" techniques employed by business strategists in their positive dealings with the government. Businessmen have sufficiently overcome the political losses of the Great Depression to exercise once again an important influence on big government using old-fashioned campaign efforts

81

to tip the balance in elections and to influence office holders. At the same time, however, the center of interest in the relations between business and government has tended to shift from issues where campaign techniques are particularly effective to a new arena of highly technical negotiations where the cameralist techniques of sophisticated bargainers and experts are far more relevant. In the future, cameralism will increase even more as government becomes more complex and as the old ideological issues are subjected to a systematic application of legal, scientific, and organizational analysis. This trend toward expertise, combined with the increasing readiness of businessmen to discharge what they consciously regard as their "social responsibility," holds the promise that business activities in the public sphere will be more vigorous than ever but largely on an extra-political level.

The theme of increasing technicalism in American society appears in several of the essays in this volume, and it will therefore be useful for the reader to consider here under what conditions an issue of interest to the public at large and the business community is a technical rather than a political matter.

1. What are some of the public policies that seem to be shaped mainly by technical considerations? What public policies raise largely political questions?

2. Decide whether the basis for accepting or rejecting the following legislative proposals should be primarily technical or political: a tax increase during a prolonged period of full employment; a tax decrease during a recession already marked by substantial federal government budget deficits; a statutory prohibition against the use of radio or television for cigarette advertising.

3. Specify the principles by which one may determine whether an issue will raise mainly technical or mainly political questions.

4. On what fundamentally political questions is there now enough of a consensus among Americans that we may regard technical considerations as the governing considerations? What procedures are relevant for distinguishing between issues on which there is "consensus" and issues toward which large numbers of the population are simply apathetic?

CLARENCE C. WALTON

BIG GOVERNMENT,
BIG BUSINESS,
AND THE PUBLIC INTEREST

Like the folklore of capitalism, the folklore of politics abounds with its own peculiar brand of images and icons, shibboleths and slogans, rituals and rationalizations. These encumbrances hamper attempts to make clean and clear analyses of the relationship between government and business in the United States and lead instead to results that are both inconclusive and inadequate. Wherever there is an abundance of half-truths, there is also a danger not of their being rejected because they are partial but of their being believed too completely because they shed at least some light on problems obscured by shadows of uncertainty. Often we seem perilously close to incorporating into the national litany of beliefs and values certain propositions whose limited measure of truth makes them dubious candidates for entry. One thinks immediately of "splendid isolationism," social Darwinism, manifest destiny, laissez faire capitalism, and the like. Too often ideas are subordinated to idols that become ponderous obstacles to objective analysis.[1]

INTERPRETATION OF BIGNESS

If we live and operate in a confused milieu of idols and slogans, pertinent questions can spark irrelevant answers. For example, was it idolatry or intellect that led Americans to accept the proposition that a government is best which governs least? Is it still true? If the response is affirmative, then a clear corollary is that big government is monstrous! Questions asked of the form of government may also be asked of the form of our economy. Is a market society of small businesses the ideal? Or would we become a nation of peevish and petty shopkeepers? Are great businesses essential to a great society? Or do they forge a fiefdom dominated by a new breed of robber barons?

Informed men give vehemently contradictory answers to questions about the implications of size. In his speech at the Yale University commencement in 1962 the late John F. Kennedy defended his Administration against charges of big government by declaring that:

> If we leave defense and space expenditures aside, the federal government since the second world war has expanded less than any other major section of our national life; less than industry; less than commerce; less than agriculture; less than higher education; and very much less than the noise about big government.

[1] This was the complaint registered recently by Jacques Soustelle, *A New Road for France* (New York: R. Speller, 1965).

The truth about big government is the truth about any great activity: it is complex. Certainly it is true that size brings dangers, but it is also true that size can bring benefits.

Yet one of Kennedy's ablest advisors, Richard Goodwin (who assisted in the preparation of the President's major speeches), recently expressed the conviction that the "most painful and troubling condition of political life is the swift growth in importance of governmental power coupled with the steady diminution of the significance of the individual, inexorably transforming him from a wielder to an object of power."[2]

We are reminded constantly that Washington is crammed with the largest number of federal employees in all our history, even more than during World War II, that the federal payroll of $21.2 billion in 1966 was nearly twice what it was only a decade earlier, and that in California there are 265,130 federal employees, or 80,337 more than work for the state government. To the fearful there is so much of the "big brother" bureaucracy in current reality that George Orwell's chilling prophecy in *Nineteen Eighty-four* seems destined for fulfillment. The present motives for power may not be rooted in sadism, as in Orwell's state, but certainly the existence of governmental power in an amplitude approximating the Orwellian nightmare seems all too evident. The contemporary critic of federal expansion insists that we have gone far beyond the wildest speculations of Tacitus or Machiavelli, Hobbes or Nietzsche, philosophers remembered for having constructed an extensive domain for rule and control.[3]

Fear of the political leviathan is no longer confined to arch-conservatives, as the example of Richard Goodwin suggests. Arguing the necessity for returning power over local affairs to local groups, Goodwin would have California, not Washington bureaucrats from AID, run the agricultural programs in Chile; he would foster a Marshall Plan approach toward American cities and hand over antipoverty and job retraining programs to community associations. The significant point here is not the validity of Goodwin's suggestion but rather that one who had access to the inner sanctums of government would explicitly admit that the centralization of power has gone too far, too fast, and too easily.

The power of business elicits a similar range of reactions and feelings of uncertainty. Is big business a clear and present danger to the public welfare? The catalogue of affirmative answers can conveniently begin with the observation of the late C. Wright Mills on the great American corporations today:

> [They seem] more like states within states than simply private businesses. The economy of America has been largely incorporated and within their incorporation the corporate chiefs have captured the technological innovation, accumulated the existing great fortunes as well as much lesser, scattered wealth, and capitalized

[2] Mimeograph Paper, Arden House speech to the Institute of Life Insurance, Harriman, N.Y., November 30, 1966.
[3] Isaac Deutscher, "1984—The Mysticism of Cruelty," in *Heretics and Renegades, and Other Essays* (London: Hamish Hamilton, 1955), pp. 46–47, and George Kateb, "The Road to 1984," *Political Science Quarterly,* Vol. 81 (December, 1966), pp. 564–80.

the future. . . . Their private decisions, responsibly made in the interests of the feudal-like world of private property and income, determine the size and shape of the national economy, the level of employment, the purchasing power of the consumer, the prices that are advertised, the investments that are channeled. Not Wall Street financiers or bankers, but large owners or executives in their self-financing corporations hold the keys of economic power. Not the politicians of the visible government, but the chief executives who sit in the political directorate, by fact and proxy, hold the power and the means of defending the privileges of their corporate world.[4]

What makes a bad situation worse, according to Mills, is the fact that the power of large business is deployed to deny small businessmen their old entrepreneurial functions.[5] When Mills was rebuked by scholars like Talcott Parsons and Paul Lazarsfeld for making wide-ranging and unsubstantiated indictments, other critics rushed in to document Mills's charges. A typical view was that of Edward Zeigler, who argued that corporations represent the primary vested interest in this society: the corporate giants successfully seek high rates of return on investment, promote the view that theirs is the mandate to define the public interest, insist that business behavior be cloaked with immunity from government control, and identify commerce and commonwealth. Conversely, these corporate interests seek to avoid high labor costs, social welfare programs, and restrictions by any regulatory agencies.[6] From manufacturing and commerce come the greatest threats to society, Zeigler argues, but he also sees a new menace forming in the advertising sector.

The anxieties of the fearful and the misgivings of the skeptics are not allayed by better knowledge of how large and how rapidly growing our most successful corporations really are. Thomas J. Watson, Jr., chief executive of IBM, has described the spectacular rise of IBM from 1,200 employees and 800 stockholders in 1914 to more than 125,000 workers and 225,000 stockholders in 1961. The Cinderella-like quality of this corporation's growth was captured by Watson when he wrote that "if an individual had bought 100 shares of IBM in 1914 it would have cost him $2,750; if he had left these shares untouched, they would have been worth $5,455,000 by September 30, 1962; . . . all of this occurred in forty-eight years, about the working life of most businessmen."[7] *Fortune* magazine reported that General Motors' net operating revenues in 1965 exceeded the 1964 gross national product of all but nine nations of the free world. The corporation's 1965 federal income tax represented 1.87 per cent of the federal government's receipts for the year and 6.83 per cent of all corporation income taxes paid during that period.[8]

In many ways—size, organization, resources—IBM and General Motors epitomize the world of big business and become principal power centers outside the

[4] *The Power Elite* (New York: Oxford University Press, 1956), pp. 124–25.

[5] *White Collar* (New York: Oxford University Press, 1956), pp. 6–7 and 51–98.

[6] *The Vested Interests: Their Origins, Development and Behavior* (New York: Macmillan, 1964), pp. 36 and 263–64.

[7] *Business and Its Beliefs: The Ideas That Helped Build IBM* (New York: McGraw-Hill, 1963), p. 9.

[8] "The Mass of Statistics of General Motors," *Fortune*, Vol. 74 (July 15, 1966), p. 298.

government itself, capable of challenging the political sovereigns on many issues. If a single company is richer than many nations of the world, what then, asks the critic, is business power over the destinies of the nation likely to seem when the incomes and revenues of the corporate giants are aggregated?[9] Is an American President dealing with shadow or substance when he reacts violently and negatively to an announced price rise in steel or aluminum? Many critics believe that Supreme Court Justice Douglas was on firm ground when he argued, in a dissenting opinion, that the lessons of bigness "should by now have been burned into our memory by Brandeis":

> The curse of *bigness* shows how size can become a menace—both industrial and social. It can be an industrial menace because it creates gross inequalities against existing or putative competitors. It can become a social menace—because of its control of prices. . . . Size in steel is a measure of the power of a handful of men over our economy. That power can be utilized with lightning speed. It can be benign or it can be dangerous.[10]

His consistently expressed philosophy suggests that the evils of great concentrations of power outweigh the gains.

Or is a truer verdict rendered by former public servant—now corporate executive—David E. Lilienthal? He warns against the widespread and, to him, frankly emotional antagonism to business, and suggests instead that "size is our greatest functional asset and we should seek to capitalize rather than inhibit it, because only by such efforts will we establish a climate for growth."[11]

While Justice Douglas condemns size, and David Lilienthal praises it, a more common reaction is to accept bigness as a fact of life and to focus on its use. Andrew Hacker, for example, warns us that when big business moves into politics, when "General Electric, American Telephone and Telegraph, and Standard Oil of New Jersey enter the pluralist areas . . . we have elephants dancing among the chickens."[12] Other critics are unwilling to admit that big business has used its power effectively in the political arena. One frank estimate was given by Republican Congressman Edward Derwinski to a group of business leaders gathered under the aegis of the Chamber of Commerce in 1964:

---

[9] Howard Zinn's remark is not untypical of those who see the need to curb corporate powers: "Today, the great corporations—150 of them own half our total manufacturing assets—so affect the public interest that they need no longer be treated as private enclaves." "The Grateful Society," *Columbia University Forum,* Vol. 10 (Spring, 1967), p. 33. See also Andrew Hacker's comment that it is not a personal but an organizational elite that presides over corporate America: "A Country Called Corporate America," *New York Times Magazine,* July 3, 1966.

[10] United States v. Columbia Steel Company, 334 U.S. 495, 535–36 (1948). In 1911 Brandeis testified before a Senate Committee and said that the inherent ills of huge power outweigh the advantages coming from increased efficiency.

[11] *Big Business: A New Era* (New York: Harper & Row, 1952), p. 4. See also pp. 33–36 and 143–44.

[12] Hacker's introduction in Andrew Hacker and Joel Auerbach, "Businessmen and Politics," *Law and Contemporary Problems,* Vol. 27 (Spring, 1962), pp. 7–8.

Your political action programs are typical of the foolish Chamber activities in this field. Foolish, since you emphasize non-partisanship, while union organizers and socialistic groups direct their activities through the Democratic party. . . . The greatest danger to our free enterprise system is the gutless behavior of American businessmen, especially the national and the various state Chambers of Commerce.[13]

The trouble with business is its proclivity for talking too much and doing so little!

From such quotations one might conclude (a) that big business is a pervasive threat to the society and to the free economy itself; (b) that it is a system that has, in Robert Hilkert's words, "so succeeded in raising the living standards of 80 per cent of the people to present levels [that it] deserves some sort of medal of merit";[14] (c) that, like fire, it is a neutral force that may be used for good or evil; or (d) that it is an inert mass.

Social Science Investigations

Have public and private powers reached dangerous extremes? If so, does the threat follow from the interlocking of public and private power elites, as envisaged by Mills? Or does crisis confront us because of internecine warfare waged by the two Goliaths, each concerned only with maintaining its own position? Presumably the objectivity of scholars should enable them to reach the same conclusions about these questions, yet apparently contradictory findings continue to come from sociologists and political scientists who examine the problem of power. Generally, it seems that the sociologically oriented researcher tends to discover that power is highly concentrated, whereas the political scientist finds that power is quite diffused.[15] Sociologists, who start with the assumption that persons holding economic power are key wielders of influence and control, have been remarkably successful in producing empirical data in support of this premise.[16] Political

[13] Quoted by David J. Galligan, *Politics and the Businessman* (New York: Pitman, 1964), p. 63.

[14] "The Responsibility of Business and Industry for Social Welfare in Today's World," *Business Review of the Federal Reserve Bank of Philadelphia* (July, 1966), p. 3.

[15] Contrast the findings of Roland J. Pellegrin and Charles H. Coates, "Absentee-Owned Corporations in Community Power Structure," *American Journal of Sociology,* Vol. 61 (March, 1956), pp. 413–19, and George Belknap and Ralph Smuckler, "Political Power Relations in a Mid-West City," *Public Opinion Quarterly,* Vol. 20 (Spring, 1956), pp. 73–81, with the conclusions by political scientists like Robert Dahl, *Who Governs?* (New Haven, Conn.: Yale University Press, 1961), and Nelson W. Polsby, *Community Power and Political Theory* (New Haven, Conn.: Yale University Press, 1963).

[16] R. E. Agger, "Power Attributions of the Local Community," *Social Forces,* Vol. 34, pp. 322–31. After having completed a sociological analysis of Dallas, Professor Carol E. Thometz concluded that the city had an aristocracy of merit. See *The Decision-Makers: The Power Structure of Dallas* (Dallas: Southern Methodist University, 1963). Better known are Lloyd Hunter's two studies of power dealing with a single city and, later, with the nation: *Community Power Structure* (Chapel Hill: University of North Carolina Press, 1953), and *Top Leadership, U.S.A.* (Chapel Hill: University of North Carolina Press, 1959).

scientists, on the other hand, impressed as they are by the complexities of a pluralistic society, generally concentrate on concrete *issues* rather than social *classes*. Because different people respond to different issues in different ways, power appears to them to be fragmented. A pattern of decision-making by small minorities who are specialists within a given issue area, for example, has been found by political scientists to exist in small cities like New Haven[17] and large ones like Chicago and New York.[18] A similar fragmentation of decision-making was reported by three other political scientists to have existed among businessmen who engaged in activities related to urban renewal on the south side of Chicago. Despite power, prestige, and recognized administrative skills, most Chicago big businessmen were relatively ineffective in community decision-making, whereas a relatively obscure Negro dining-car waiter named Victor Towns was singularly successful in pressing his views of the needs of his block before city planners.[19]

The remarkable congruence between theoretical assumptions and empirically derived conclusions in sociology and political science respectively introduces a jarring note. With what degree of certitude can we rely on the findings of social scientists who study power relationships in society? Does the premise control the conclusions? Are scholars no different than jurists like Rufus W. Peckham, the adversary Justice Holmes described in 1905 as a judge whose "major premise was Goddamn it, meaning thereby that emotional predications somewhat governed him on social theories"?[20]

The immediate temptation is to seek a way to take into account both the elitism discovered by the sociologists and the pluralism discovered by the political scientists. One might assume, for example, that decision-making is concentrated in the hands of the few but that no single all-purpose elite is involved in all decisions at all times. An awareness that in our society some people and some groups "get their way" more frequently and more consistently than others is not the same as knowing what is the nature of their power or of being able to predict when they will be victorious and when they will not. As one moves from local to state, to national, and to international affairs, the range of political and economic constituencies and interests involved enlarges and changes the decision-making process dramatically. If this is so, it could be hypothesized that any issue that touches the

---

[17] Dahl, *op. cit.* See esp. Book II and Book V. The tendency for local elites to be self-limiting has been noted by a large number of investigators. See Arthur J. Vidich and Joseph Bensman, *Small Town and Mass Society* (Princeton, N.J.: Princeton University Press, 1955), esp. pp. 90–100.

[18] Herbert Kaufman, "Metropolitan Leadership: The Snark of the Social Sciences," Paper presented to the Social Science Research Council Conference on Metropolitan Leadership, Evanston, Illinois, April 1–3, 1960. This conclusion was amplified in the larger study conducted by Wallace S. Sayre and Herbert Kaufman, *Governing New York City* (New York: Russell Sage Foundation, 1960).

[19] Peter B. Clark, *The Chicago Big Businessman as a Civic Leader* (New Haven, Conn.: Mimeographed Study, September, 1959), and Peter H. Rossi and Robert Dentler, *The Politics of Urban Renewal* (New York: The Free Press, 1961).

[20] Quoted in A. M. Bickel, *Unpublished Opinions of Mr. Justice Brandeis* (Cambridge, Mass.: Harvard University Press, 1957), p. 64.

vital interests of many groups will tend to be resolved pluralistically through bargaining and counter-bargaining by the elite elements in these groups. The granting of a TV franchise by the FCC is not likely to stir as lively a struggle as a proposal to raise taxes, because the latter evokes participation by greater numbers and different kinds of groups. When a corporation and the Defense Department enter into long and detailed negotiations regarding provisions in a cost-plus contract, the issue may violently stir the two protagonists without creating a ripple on the surface of public opinion. When, however, an issue like the Taft-Hartley Bill involves three parties (business, unions, and government) the simple fact of triangulating the debate may precipitate a public stir. In short, elitism does exist in the United States, but it tends to shift in composition or in power potential at different levels of the system simply because the higher the position held by a given issue, the larger the number of claimants. Hence, a greater variety of forces begins to play on the contenders. In this interplay the existence of a common economic goal can give a greater capacity for power to the economic elite than to the non-economic organizations that so often appear incapable of inspiring the sustained interests of their members.[21] If economic unity is lacking as it was, for example, in the famous TFX controversy, then the assumption of ascendancy for the economic interests, all other things being equal, appears to be questionable.

This cursory review suggests clearly that the relationship between government and business in America is anything but simple. Our governmental system and our business community are each enormously complex, and the relationships between the two could hardly be characterized accurately in some brief and elegant new theoretical formulation. The present inquiry, of necessity, must be sharply delimited and will attempt to accomplish three objectives:

(a) To indicate briefly the formal constitutional ground rules that affect government-business relationships and, more importantly, the nature of the active interplay between politicians and businessmen in selected areas of public policy. This aspect of the analysis is designed to illustrate the emergence of policy in Washington from one of limited intervention to one of active and broad espousal of a great society—and with consequent modifications of certain philosophical premises;

(b) To suggest the different kinds of tactics available to business when it confronts government in pursuit of its private interest and in its definition of the public good;

(c) To provide a few illustrations that reveal the practical applications of business power to adversary relationships. It should be noted forthrightly that the illustrations employed herein do not embrace the important relationships between business and the executive branch—including, of course, the Department of Defense. Interest in the "military-industrial complex" was heightened by the warning given in a valedictory statement by President Eisenhower, but a deft probing into this area by Grant McConnell suggests that here the power elite

---

[21] Robert Presthus, *Men at the Top: A Study in Community Power* (New York: Oxford University Press, 1964), p. 406.

suffers "from internal disarray. It lacks the organization and unity necessary to give it the capacities which are feared from it."[22] The purpose of this essay is better served by focusing on the strategies available to business and the likely payoffs therefrom when it confronts the government. Regulatory agencies, the courts, and the Congress provide effective ways to illustrate such strategies.

THE CONSTITUTION, PUBLIC POLICY, AND BUSINESS

The highly malleable American Constitution seems to be a kind of catalyst that is able to unite economic and political elements into a durable compound. This quality was built into the Constitution by the framers themselves. Long before western Europe thought seriously of a common market, Americans sensed the enormous utility for a virgin country of an economic organization that would permit commerce to flow uninterruptedly from the Great Lakes to the Gulf and from the Atlantic to the Pacific. The intoxicating dream so stirred imaginations that the founding fathers introduced concrete institutional mechanisms of a unique sort. Territories that achieved a measure of economic and political maturity were not to be held in thralldom, as was the practice under mercantilism, but were to be admitted to the Union as free and equal states. Before England or France granted equality to all members of their respective empires, the Americans proclaimed a new doctrine of equality for all. It was a masterful demonstration of political innovation, because it opened and enlarged the areas for competing economic and sectional interest and, as a consequence, made flexibility a necessary and important characteristic for the basic law of the land. To view the Constitution, therefore, in a purely formalistic fashion, while a useful way to start, is insufficient.

Article IV of the Constitution requires that "Full Faith and Credit shall be given in each State to the public Acts, Records, and judicial Proceedings of every other State." This provision is of fundamental importance to the business community. Judgments on debts in one state can be executed in another state where the defendant has property. The records of mortgages, deeds, charters, and contracts must be given, when properly authenticated, the same force and effect by all states as they have in the state where these originated. A uniform medium of exchange and standards for settlement of accounts facilitated the orderly transfer of goods. Two famous decisions of the Supreme Court in 1819, McCulloch v. Maryland and Dartmouth College v. Woodward, laid the constitutional foundation for a national banking system and a "sanctity-of-contract" doctrine that was to be further developed by the Court into a pillar of support for business interests.

The way constitutional references to the economy were interpreted was influ-

---

[22] *Private Power and American Democracy* (New York: Knopf, 1966), p. 337. See also Ch. 8 in its entirety. Compare these views to those of Michael Reagan, "Business and the Defense Department," *The Western Political Science Quarterly,* Vol. 14 (June, 1961), pp. 569–87.

enced by the famous "midnight judges" incident of 1801. The Federalists, having lost the Presidency to Jefferson and Congress to the Republicans, before going out of office created new courts and staffed them with judges basically in sympathy with Hamilton's mercantilistic biases in favor of business. A month before, President Adams had appointed John Marshall as Chief Justice of the United States. The interpretation of various constitutional provisions relating to economic matters was thus securely placed in the hands of men predisposed to favor business during the formative period of the Union.

Important as these legal arrangements are as a framework for the interplay between the government and the economy, the focus of this essay must be on the interplay itself and on the policies to which government and business adhere in dealing with each other. Government policy with regard to business seems to have five distinct and identifiable aspects. These include (1) support of a market competition, (2) regulation of "natural" monopolies where market mechanisms are assumed to be inadequate, (3) protection of infant industries and promotion of all business, (4) establishment of minimum standards of social welfare, and (5) taking responsibility for economic stability and full employment. Each aspect relates to an area of intimate and intricate interplay between the public and private sectors that is covered by a separate set of ground rules and that makes the use of special strategies necessary. The five parts will be examined in turn.

Market Competition

Our antitrust policies flow from the Sherman Act of 1890. While this act and its statutory successors have been pilloried for their ambiguities, the original law was hailed by Chief Justice Hughes for a "generality and adaptability comparable to that found to be desirable in constitutional provisions."[23] Because the "generality" of the Sherman Act accords to the Supreme Court a crucial role in setting the course for American business, one of its effects has been to impose on business, particularly the large corporations, an obligation to seek out and employ the ablest legal talent available. Here is an area of interplay between big government and big business where power is less dependent on numbers and more on the ability to command professional resources that can develop and sustain a logic appropriate to the situation. The tendency of all great social and economic issues to become judicial belies Hamilton's prediction in *The Federalist,* Number 78, that the judiciary would always be the "weakest" and "least dangerous" branch of government. Decisions of the Marshall Court, the Taney Court, and the Warren Court testify to the power of the jurists.

Even when the Court congratulates itself on judicial restraint, the businessman senses its power. Justice Black, speaking in 1963 for a unanimous Court in Ferguson v. Skrupa, observed that the Court would not employ "due process" to "strike down state laws regulatory of business and industrial conditions because they may

[23] Appalachian Coals, Inc. v. U.S., 288 U.S. 344, 360 (1933).

be unwise, improvident, or out of harmony with a particular school of thought. . . . Whether the legislature takes for its textbook Adam Smith, Herbert Spencer, Lord Keynes, or some other is no concern to us." A certain irony characterizes this form of judicial self-restraint. If it keeps the courts from interfering with innovative laws regulating business, it is scarcely the variety of governmental self-restraint that business is anxious to see! Conscious of the vigilance of the Justice Department and concerned that a liberal court is certain to be "tough" on business, executives sometimes complain ruefully of the power of the judiciary. Yet it is safe to suggest that while some wounds have been inflicted, the corporate system has received no serious maiming at the hands of the judges. In short, since 1890 the power of business vis-à-vis the government has declined in the courts, but it has not withered.

Regulation

The second clear aspect of the government's policy toward business involves regulation, which became the typical, albeit not exclusive, American approach for handling problems created by monopolistic or quasi-monopolistic conditions in certain industries. Regulation of railroads and utilities and of banking and insurance was instituted to forestall exploitation of the community. In these fields the course of an individual business is now often more profoundly influenced by judgments of such agencies as the Securities Exchange Commission, the Federal Trade Commission, and the Interstate Commerce Commission than by formal statutes and court decisions. It is a large arena wherein the strengths and the mettle of business and government are daily tested in cases that receive little public attention but have substantial import. Legal talent is not enough here; it must be reinforced by economic expertise and a special skill in coping with bureaucracies.

Consider the effect of a decision by the Civil Aeronautics Board on the Flying Tiger Lines. A CAB decision (later sustained by the Supreme Court) that granted to cargo airlines the right to sell "blocked space" (a specified amount of space sold at discount to volume shippers on certain regular flights) gave the Flying Tiger competitive advantages over cargo-carrying passenger lines. Within three years, the company—helped by the war in Vietnam and by the CAB ruling—moved from a 1963 deficit in operations to a 1966 net profit of nearly $12 million and a $24 million gain in cash flow.

The truly "big" cases in the regulatory area are troublesome in several ways, not the least important being that they absorb enormous time and energies. A single case may require the presence of lawyers for months in a district court, and years may pass between the original grand jury action and final disposition. One complaint, initiated on September 29, 1939, by the Federal Trade Commission against the major oil companies in the Detroit market, resulted in proceedings lasting nearly six years before the FTC finally issued a cease-and-desist order against Standard of Indiana. The company then took the case into the regular courts in a fight that ended only in 1958 when the Supreme Court upheld the corporation. Eighteen years of bitter conflict ended with a victory for the corporation![24]

Promotional Activities

The promotion of industry represents a third major area of government policy affecting the business community. Despite its ideology stressing laissez faire, the American commonwealth has always been quick to support important public works such as canal and railroad building, improving harbors and river navigation, irrigation projects, and power generating facilities.[25] When business either lacks the resources for, or shows no interest in, a given project, these promotional activities by government are carried on with a minimum of criticism. When, however, the government undertakes projects that bring it—actually or potentially— into conflict with private business, hue and cry arise. Thus the country witnessed an intense struggle over the role of the Tennessee Valley Authority.

More recently there have been sharp thrusts by privately run electrical utilities against alleged government favoritism extended to the rural electric cooperatives. Clyde T. Ellis, the general manager of the National Rural Electric Cooperative Association (NRECA) since its founding in 1942, reported that a fierce struggle took place during the Eisenhower Administration between the private utilities and his own group. According to Ellis, the new administrator of the Rural Electrification Administration, David Hamil, had outraged the private power companies by policies favorable to the cooperatives; in 1957, to calm the private utilities, the Capehart-Hiestand Bill was introduced with administration support to "curb the co-ops." The proposal was quickly labeled the "Wall Street Financing Bill" and a battle began in which, in Ellis' own words, the Administration and the NRECA leadership "fought with every weapon at our command for the next two years."[26]

Despite President Eisenhower's popularity, and despite the allegedly wide support from private business for the Administration's bill, the cooperatives gained the victory. In this case, big business joined big government in what seemed an unbeatable coalition, but the effort proved ineffectual against the resistance of a group with seemingly far fewer resources. The co-ops' success was due in large measure to their ability to politicize a technical issue between the Federal Power Commission and the REA. Normally, when the subject matter of regulation is more technical, the discretion of the government agency is broader and less reviewable. Charles Reich of the Yale Law School noted the ability of different agency powers to augment the other to a point where private interests appear to

---

[24] Joseph C. Palamountain, *The Federal Trade Commission and the Indiana Standard Case* (University, Ala.: University of Alabama Press, 1964).
[25] See, for example, Walter Adams and Horace Gray, *Monopoly in America: The Government as Promoter* (New York: Macmillan, 1955), and Carter Goodrich, *Government Promotion of American Canals and Railroads: 1800–1890* (New York: Columbia University Press, 1960).
[26] *A Giant Step* (New York: Random House, 1966), p. 112.

be helpless: when New York's Channel 13 was up for sale, the Federal Communication Commission wanted the transferee to be an educational television station. Although expressly denied by Congress the authority to judge the comparative merits of would-be transferees, the seller was given reason to fear that a time-consuming, expensive investigation would be recommended unless it sold to the lower bidder, and an educational group. The seller bowed, and the FCC exercised a power denied it by Congress.[27]

The conclusion seems inescapable that in dealing with regulatory bodies no single tactic or resource can guarantee business a victory. Generally, however, extensive technical knowledge and the capacity to sustain the high costs of protracted hearings are necessary, and in each of these areas big business seems particularly well armed.

Formulating Minimum Welfare Standards

A fourth area of public policy affecting business relates to the establishment of a minimum of well-being for each citizen through unemployment insurance, crop insurance, Medicare, public-housing programs, workmen's compensation, old-age and survivors' insurance, and the like. Again, the outcry by business against government activity is limited to cases in which actual or potential business activity may be displaced. When the insurance industry (which had repeatedly insisted that it could not make money on medical insurance for people over 65) perceived the government moving in to fill the gap, it began to backpeddle and to deny the need for this kind of public coverage. Too tardy in making adjustments to stop the proposed legislation altogether, the insurance industry moved to accommodate itself to the inevitable by working to modify the statute in ways that would bring it some gains. When the bill finally emerged, the government's medical plan included an option to cover doctors' bills that would yield insurance companies $36 per registrant—yet involved little detailed regulation of doctors' fees.

Once any regulatory-type law has been approved, the result is another administrative agency. Coping with such bureaucracies, which are, in the words of one observer, "part elephant, part jack rabbit, and part field lark,"[28] becomes a major challenge to corporate executives.

Economic Stability

A fifth area of government policy affecting business, and one that is difficult to define and label accurately, involves the government's use of its expenditures, its tax power, and its borrowing capacity to promote stability and prevent depression or inflation. Policy of this type is heavily dependent on the formulations of John

---

[27] "The New Property," *The Public Interest*, Vol. 3 (Spring, 1966), p. 68.
[28] The words were attributed to Judge Prettyman in a lecture delivered at the University of Virginia by George Bookman, "Regulation by Elephants, Rabbits and Lark," in *Fortune*, Vol. 63 (June, 1961), pp. 137–39, 232, and 237.

Maynard Keynes whose view, now widely accepted, was that depression and unemployment resulted from inadequate total demand, and could therefore be fought by enlarging the total national income available for expenditures. This increment in total national income could be achieved through an increase in governmental expenditures, the effect of which would be multiplied because the dollars distributed are spent several times over by others.

In this new and sensitive policy domain the tendency of business associations like the National Association of Manufacturers and the Chamber of Commerce was to take a very cautious view, favor balanced budgets, and oppose government spending. A major area for conflict appeared to be developing when, quite dramatically, the Committee for Economic Development, an organization that is representative of many segments of business leadership, came out in 1954 in favor of the selective use by the government of fiscal and monetary devices to fight the threat of depression.[29] Despite the historic significance of the CED's action no one has yet fully traced this fascinating story of rejection by one influential segment of business of its pre-World War II conventional wisdom. The old stress on high interest rates, balanced budgets, tight reins on government initiative, and on circumscribing trade union ambitions suddenly modified by the activity of a single "business" association.

Governmental compensatory policy took a new turn when Walter Heller, chairman of the Council of Economic Advisers under both President Kennedy and President Johnson, engineered the famous 1964 tax cut, a watershed in the history of government policy. How the projected tax-cut figure of $10.5 billion was arrived at is a highly technical matter comprehensible only to experts. On the basis of long-observed stable relationships among income, consumption, and investment, a conclusion was made on the figure necessary to close the gap between the actual level of the Gross National Product and its potential level at full employment. Rather precise estimates indicated that the projected tax cut would produce a $36 billion increase in the GNP, with $26 billion resulting from personal income tax reduction and $10 billion from the corporation tax cut. The spectacular sequence to the tax cut was to be sustained growth plus a balanced budget! Conservatives were thrown into a maelstrom of doubt by the so-called new economics. Whether we have witnessed a cause-and-effect demonstration or an antecedent-and-result event is for experts to determine. It is significant that a business elite, speaking through the CED, was credited by Walter Heller himself for getting the tax cut adopted as national policy.

THE PERMANENCE OF CONFLICT

The 1964 tax cut illustrates how the interactions between government and business in a few policy areas have increasingly involved issues that are too complex

[29] See the report prepared by the Research and Policy Committee, *Defense Against Recession: Policy for Greater Economic Stability* (New York: Committee for Economic Development, 1954).

technically for more than relatively few to comprehend; hence influencing the electorate or lobbying before Congress—traditional tactics for exercising power— have become relatively less important in business attempts to shape technical, fiscal, and monetary policies during recent years.

Yet this change cannot blind us to the enduring and constant quality of economic conflict in a pluralistic society. Sections compete; industries compete; firms compete; classes compete. James Madison wrote in *The Federalist*, Number 10, that while "the most common and durable source of factions has been the various and unequal distribution of property," other causes could also be identified; he referred to a zeal people had

> for different opinions concerning religion, concerning government, and many other points, as well of speculation as of practice; an attachment to different leaders ambitiously contending for pre-eminence and power; or to persons of other descriptions whose fortunes have been interesting to the human passions all of which had divided mankind into parties. . . .[30]

Madison took note of *class* interests (in the conflict between rich and poor) and of *functional* or group interests such as landed interests, the manufacturing interests, the mercantilist interest, and the money interest. His perceptions proved sharper than many of the other Founding Fathers who had spent much time in the Convention of 1787 trying to reconcile only the *sectional* interests between North and South, East and West.

Since Madison's time, theorists have continued to watch these conflicts at work and from time to time have thought one or another of the interests to be particularly important. For example, in 1924 Arthur N. Holcombe of Harvard declared that national politics is inseparable from sectional politics.[31] A decade later, Holcombe was impressed by the fact that old sectional interests were giving way to greater emphasis on class politics, with middle-class habits of thought and middle-class objectives being in a position of pre-eminence.[32] Modern industrialization has brought such specialization within sections that if Holcombe were to review the question today he might find that the old presumed unities of sectional interests no longer exist at all.

Special economic interests are linked in organizations that cross many sections. Farmers in the cotton and corn belts work together in the American Farm Bureau; manufacturers find a measure of unity in the National Association of Manufacturers. In the words of Emmette S. Redford:

> [There is] an overlaying of functional interest on sectional interest, and of class interest on both. All three are significant. Sectionalism is revealed as South opposes North on minimum wages; classism as dividend receivers oppose wage earners on tax reduction; groupism as powerful sections of the petroleum industry contend with others over reduction in oil imports. The demands of people on government

[30] *The Federalist*, No. 10.
[31] *The Political Parties of Today* (New York: Harper & Row, 1924), p. 40.
[32] *The New Party Politics* (New York: W. W. Norton, 1933), p. 15.

are made by section, by class, and by functional grouping. The national parties must seek durable combinations of *sectional, class* and *functional* interests.[33]

In this maze, political and business leaders walk uneasily. Because they share a common interest in the long-term goals of stability and growth, yet often differ sharply over means and short-term advantages, the more sophisticated leaders in both camps constantly are involved in shrewd calculations of interest coalitions. Public opinion polls, analyses of voter reactions, and market surveys become stock-in-trade when the contending forces see proposed legislation that vitally affects their position. No longer is this a society where business can confidently chart a desired course for public policy and then rationally choose tactics to get the course adopted. Since the great crash of 1929, American business leadership has had to appraise two fundamental probabilities: What broad social trends threaten business? Which assure to business security and reasonable power to shape society's future? What can be done to check the first and encourage the second? To meet mounting criticisms, business turned inward to put its own house in order through a series of actions and policies designed to vindicate the role of free enterprise in a pluralistic economy. To encourage greater business influence on the American future, corporations adopted a more positive strategy. Each approach will now be briefly described.

DEFENSIVE STRATEGIES

Business entered the twentieth century supremely self-confident. The eighteenth-century promise of an American common market had achieved a spectacular fulfillment between the Civil War and the opening of the present century. In little more than a generation the United States moved from a niche behind England and France in industrial capacity to unchallenged world leadership. Despite periodic attacks on business by muckrakers, the political climate was benign: labor was weak, the power of southern planters was broken by the Civil War, and the western farmers were difficult to organize.

In Washington the judiciary was benevolent toward business, the Senate was a rich man's club, and the executive branch was made secure and safe by a succession of pro-business Presidents from Grant to McKinley. The Supreme Court's friendliness toward the commercial commonwealth stood in marked contrast to its hostility toward working men who sought to exercise their right of free association. And if the courts ever wavered the Senate stood ready to exercise appropriate pressures on behalf of business; there is a noteworthy symbolism in the fact that when popular discontent induced Congress to pass the Sherman Antitrust Act in 1890 the law was loosely worded in the hope that the problem would be tossed into the laps of the courts.

[33] Emmette S. Redford, *American Government and the Economy* (New York: Macmillan, 1965), p. 44.

The pro-business bias of government was natural enough to an acquisitive society that always tolerated and often respected the Vanderbilts and Goulds in New York, the Armours and Hannas in Chicago and Cleveland, the Carnegies in Pittsburgh, and the Pillsburys in Minneapolis. Many of these men, building fortunes at fantastic rates, knew how to employ wealth to achieve political strength. But a few observers began to ask whether the political mechanisms so useful to big business might not be turned to serve the needs of labor and the farmer. By the close of the nineteenth century, in fact, the country was well launched on its "organizational revolution"[34] and, although corporations were in the vanguard, it was to be only a matter of time until other claimants would join business in pressing their special interests on the national government.

The Challenge to Business Efficiency

The dramatic change in the comfortably dominant position of business came with the depression in 1929. The nature of this tortuous event can be suggested through metaphor: as the stock market plunged downward the intensity of claims from other groups shot upward. Almost overnight the overriding power of the Republican Party was broken. Even the Supreme Court was eventually moved to sustain a series of statutes such as the National Labor Relations Act and a state minimum-wage law. In 1937 the conservative Justice McReynolds cried out in alarm, "The Constitution is gone." In a sense, it was!

The struggles among three branches of government under a check-and-balance system seemed to give way in the 1930's to a new contest between a reasonably united government against a seemingly disarrayed business community. It was puerile for businessmen to boast of a nation that possessed the greatest industrial capacity in the world at a time when 12 million American workers were idle and when faith in the efficacy of a free-enterprise system was at ebb tide. Nearly a century of uninterrupted success had seemingly dulled the businessman's political acumen. Access to politically hostile government decision-makers, entrée before regulatory bodies in Washington that were falling increasingly under the influence of New Dealers, effective representation in the political process, prestige and influence over public opinion—all suddenly became matters of transcendent importance.

Rather clumsily, business undertook a massive campaign to sell Americans the ideal of "free enterprise" and allegedly poured over a $100 million into this unsuccessful venture.[35] One result, undesired and possibly unanticipated, was a toughened position by business opponents who saw in this move yet another crass attempt to resurrect in the public mind an identity between pecuniary power and moral goodness; to exploit what one critic averred was the "national tradition of exaggerated respect for production and producers and the equivalent neglect of

[34] Kenneth Boulding, *The Organizational Revolution* (New York: Harper & Row, 1953). He coined the phrase and described the process.
[35] William H. Whyte, Jr., *Is Anybody Listening?* (New York: Simon & Schuster, 1952), p. 6.

consumption and consumers. . . . This order of preferment has all but enshrined production and producers, and has permitted these groups and their basic motives to attain enormous scope."[36] The very fact that business felt obliged to "sell" an ideology in what had been historically a seller's market was measure of the change in the political and social climate.

The Legitimation of Business Leadership

The outbreak of World War II silenced one wave of criticism against business when still another began to emerge after 1945. The thirties questioned the efficiency of the business community; the late forties questioned its legitimacy. Attention was drawn to the fact that the managers of large corporations no longer owned what they effectively controlled. In the view of many, the rupture between ownership and control meant the dissolution of any real legal basis for management's existence. In reviewing these developments, Ernest Dale recently asked, "What real claims will management have to its position unless it owns the company it manages or represents the owners?"[37]

Business executives sought to demonstrate the legitimacy of their leadership by insisting that the functions they performed were essential to the healthy growth of a free society. Furthermore, if highly concentrated political powers existed in the federal government, sufficient powers of counterbalance were needed in the private sector to prevent the collapse of our pluralistic society. But the force of these arguments depended on the corporation's having its own house in order and demonstrating that it was using its large powers justly. The most obvious test of the large corporation's behavior was its treatment of its own employees. Some critics would hold that few large corporations passed this test in the 1950's, but two recent developments have greatly altered the picture.

Industrial democracy. The first development was, in a sense, imposed on the corporation. In a 1960 landmark decision (Warrior and Gulf Navigation Company v. U.S. Steelworkers), the Supreme Court declared that arbitration "is the fulcrum of collective bargaining on which rests the entire system of industrial self-government."[38] Since that time, arbitration has become recognized as a major new social instrument for the resolution of conflicts arising during the life of a labor contract and as the necessary supplement to collective bargaining; arbitrators' decisions are becoming what Justice Douglas has called "the common law of the shop." After having carefully studied the implications of the Warrior decision, Eli Ginzberg and Ivar Berg of Columbia University have concluded that because

[36] Edward Zeigler, *op. cit.,* p. 143. Zeigler asserts that "a peculiar kind of thought distinguishes our vested interest and [that] the consequences of that thought are noxious to the health of the nation," p. 6. It seems rather doubtful that Americans honor "productivity" exclusively because an ideology has been "sold" to them by predatory businessmen.

[37] "Management Must Be Made Accountable," *Harvard Business Review,* Vol. 38 (March–April, 1960), p. 49.

[38] Eli Ginzberg, Ivar Berg *et al., Democratic Values and the Rights of Management* (New York: Columbia University Press, 1963), p. 17.

of the great discretion allocated to the arbitrator, and because the courts have been loathe to enter conflicts involving substantive issues—or even the reasoning underlying arbitrators' decisions—the arbitrator is "unwittingly the instrument for expanding the reach of democracy at the workplace. He helps to extend and deepen the area within which democratic values find expression. In this process, he makes a significant contribution to the strengthening of industry and to the expansion of democracy."[39]

The second development was the widespread introduction of what has been frequently called "constitutionalism" or due process in the personnel process of large corporations.[40] With the coming of unions, blue-collar workers were often better protected against arbitrary action by top management than were the middle levels of management. White-collar employees have no union to defend them in conflicts with their superiors and no recourse when these confrontations lead to demotions, discipline, or dismissal. Since many variations of due process exist in corporate organizations, generalizations regarding the effectiveness of various procedures designed to protect the manager are unwarranted here. It seems fair to suggest, however, that unilateral systems of discipline and discharge often fail the criteria of justice because they do not assure objectivity in the quest for evidence, do not allow for appeal, or do not provide a petitionary system that verifies and vindicates a superior's decisions. The trend to constitutionalism, however, has led to voluntary changes in other practices. Bilateral grievance systems, for example, have been undertaken to provide more adequate fact-collecting and greater impartiality.[41]

The importance of constitutionalism is not the effectiveness of the system per se at this stage of early development but the fact that corporations have moved voluntarily to adopt systems of equity and justice that have proved feasible in the political realm. What was deemed essential to an individual's right as part of the public interest in the public domain is moving into the private sector.

Corporate social responsibility. By the 1960's, American business was no longer dealing with a society content to accept the market as the sole arbitrator of its destinies. Housing was inadequate, educational opportunities limited, health services restricted, urban centers deteriorated. Each inadequacy was a standing invitation for government intervention and enlargement of the public bureaucracy. Business had essentially two options: to respond by producing goods and services at maximum profit or to respond by providing goods and services where necessary —even if it meant the heresy of selective non-profit ventures by profit-oriented enterprises. To take the former option meant turning over to government many important areas of activity and a consequent increase in taxes. To pursue the second alternative involved risks but afforded business a precious opportunity to help contribute to the shaping and direction of the Great Society.

---

[39] *Ibid.,* p. 205.

[40] William G. Scott, *The Management of Conflict* (Homewood, Ill.: Richard D. Irwin, 1965). Also relevant is the essay by Wendell French, "The Nature and Problems of Organizational Justice," in E. B. Flippo, ed., *Evolving Concepts of Management* (Chicago: Academy of Management, 1965).

[41] Stephen R. Michael, *How Managers Are Fired* (New York: Columbia University, 1967). Unpublished Ph.D. dissertation.

For the most part, the second alternative has been seized by the larger corpora-tions. Simply stated, the large corporation now feels called upon to show concern for, and make contributions to, the public interest in ways substantially alien to the earlier model of what was considered "good" corporate behavior. Earlier, businessmen generally followed John Locke and Adam Smith in believing that the public interest is automatically achieved when the various private interests are permitted to compete as equals. Contrary to Greek and Christian views of public order, Locke thought that the political community was founded not on what is common to men but on what is individual to man. Civil society existed for the sake of private utility, and the political order operated above all for the protection of property and "to promote for men's acquisitive appetites a greater degree of satisfaction than would be possible under conditions of anarchy."[42] Adam Smith carried Locke's idea of a society built on individual interest to a higher theoretical level; according to his conception of the "invisible hand," the individual acquisitive interest was itself a source of order and provided the standard of judgment for good government and efficient economy.

The new response by business has been to adopt a strategy described by the term "corporate social responsibility." Despite the *ad hoc* character and improvi-sations that were the mark of many early exercises in "social responsibility," despite evidences that some companies were simply jumping on a bandwagon without knowing where it was headed, and, finally, despite the public relations "hoopla" that surrounded even modest ventures in pursuit of the public good, a conviction emerged among many businessmen that there is a "public interest" that transcends the immediate and private interest. In a speech at Westminster College in Fulton, Missouri, on November 16, 1965, Joseph C. Wilson, president of the Xerox Corporation, alluded to indications "of maturing thought that gain is no longer thought to be the sole motivating force of businessmen. . . . The kind of escape from responsibility prescribed by Adam Smith is now considered by many businessmen as unrealistic, a concept of utmost sterility."[43]

A willingness to help in the creation of a more humane and more civilized society prompts many executives to employ corporate resources of large enter-prises in ways that promise no measurable and immediate payoffs and to take steps that stockholders would have found easy to block under stricter definitions of corporate interest and property rights.[44] But the executive is caught in an unhappy position. Demands for socially responsible action are accompanied by expressions of fear that this will bring him too directly into the political arena where he will use his power and employ his pressure for himself first and for the community second.[45] These fears probably exaggerate the cohesiveness of the business com-munity. Except for the Business Advisory Council, relationships among corporate

[42] *Second Treatise on Government.*
[43] *The Conscience of Business* (Fulton, Mo.: Westminster College, 1965), p. 1.
[44] Clarence C. Walton, *Corporate Social Responsibilities* (Belmont, Calif.: Wadsworth, 1967).
[45] Theodore Levitt, "The Dangers of Social Responsibility," *Harvard Business Review,* Vol. 28 (September–October, 1950), pp. 46–47. See also the essay by Professor Rogers and Zimet in this volume, p. 39.

presidents suggest no enduring organizational ties; reactions among them tend to be irregular and informal; their responses seem more concerned with the particular company than with the business community as a whole.[46]

Has the strategy represented by the corporate–social-responsibility ideology really worked? While a decade or two provide insufficient evidence for a definitive answer, it is worth noting that the debate over "legitimacy" is waged more hotly by academicians than by those who really count—stockholders, judges, and lawmakers. The government shows signs of wanting more business initiative and more business cooperation in building a great society. Some of the leadership of the disadvantaged groups themselves, like Whitney Young of the Urban League, welcome business help in alleviating the economic pressures on the American Negro. Finally, it should be noted that the new "face" of corporations as they move to discharge their social responsibilities has received the approval of several state judiciaries and has put the corporation itself nearer the mainstream of contemporary ideology, which rejects as too simplistic the old "Wilson maxim" that what was good for the country was good for General Motors and vice versa.[47]

POSITIVE STRATEGIES: CAMERALISM AND CAMPAIGN

The direct dealings of businessmen with the national government are primarily of two types. One type consists of the exchanges between government bureaucrats and business specialists (lawyers, economists, market analysts) on matters of a *technical* nature. These relationships can be described as cameralism. The name has been taken over from a nineteenth-century German school of economists who stressed sophisticated management of public finances as a key to public policy; the present use of the term, while unconventional, can be defended on the grounds that it is less pejorative than "bureaucracy," "politics," or "expertise."[48]

The second type of interchanges between businessmen and the national government are *political* in a more old-fashioned sense, involving business efforts to sway elections and influence influential people by organizing pressure groups, lobbying, making donations, and providing speech writers to favorites. These methods can be described as part of a strategy of campaign. Business campaigners engage in a variety of maneuvers designed to promote a "business" conception of the good society. Unlike many of our traditional political wardheelers, who reflect the interests of party bosses and political organizations, business campaigners speak for private interests that operate openly under the law and that assume

[46] Hacker, in Hacker and Auerbach, *op. cit.*

[47] Lynn H. Peters, "The Paradoxical Fate of the Business Ideology," *Business and Society,* Vol. 7 (Spring, 1967), pp. 33–40. Peters argues that a more sophisticated kind of pragmatism is introducing a new relativistic value structure more in keeping with contemporary pluralism.

[48] Alfred Cobbin declared that political theory as affected by eighteenth-century cameralism was a theory "of bureaucrats, about bureaucrats, for bureaucrats." "The Decline of Political Theory," *Political Science Quarterly,* Vol. 68 (1953), p. 335.

there is no necessary conflict between their private good and the community's general welfare.

Because ours is a technological society and because the delicate mechanisms of the economy have responded well to monetary and fiscal controls, it has been suggested that this is the season for experts only and that old-fashioned politics should be abandoned. The battles between the White House and business over prices in the early 1960's and other evidence suggest that political dialogue and moral persuasion are still vital enough to make a complete abandonment of the campaign strategy in favor of cameralism inadvisable. However, a growing dependence by business on cameralism is probably inevitable. The technical problems of an industrialized, urbanized, scientific society have increased enormously to a point where the Jeffersonian faith in the ability of the common man to make appropriate decisions is questioned as never before. Most Americans are accordingly resigned to seeing more decisions pass from the campaign arena to the inner chambers of the cameralists, and it is here that business probably has a distinct advantage. When decisions are worked out by specialists, high-priced talent is often determinative of success, and corporations can clearly buy such talent. The more complex the matter under discussion, the less control the politicians dealing with business are likely to retain. Corporations can, therefore, partially offset the decline in naked political strength suffered in the 1930's by increasing the number of specialists they employ and the number of operations where these specialists can be put to work.

Cameralism and the Regulatory Agencies

It has been noted that business operations are vitally affected by the policies and definitions of such agencies as the Federal Trade Commission, the Civil Aviation Board, the Securities and Exchange Commission, and their counterparts. For them the skilled cameralist becomes a primary instrument for policy.

The relationships between some of our largest corporations and the regulatory agencies are often quite close, and this suggests another great attraction to the cameralist approach for big business. The government group to be convinced is relatively small, commonly possesses shared technical knowledge in its field of jurisdiction, is usually in regular contact with colleagues from the private sector, and cannot itself afford to create too dramatic a hue and cry in the constituency it affects. Indeed, without support from the regulated, the regulator's efforts may be frustrated—as was illustrated in Joseph B. Eastman's abortive efforts as Coordinator of Transportation under the New Deal to induce management and unions to nationalize the railroads.

The success of a cameralist strategy depends on the willingness of a corporation to be guided by the same "fair-shares concept" that determines government operations themselves in their efforts to get adequate slices of federal funds.[49] The

[49] Aaron B. Wildavsky, *The Politics of the Budgetary Process* (Boston: Little, Brown, 1964), esp. pp. 128–38.

fair-shares concept could easily be violated if, for example, an airline such as TWA, which has east-west connecting points, sought from the CAB permission for the New York-Miami routes now dominated by such lines as Eastern and National. That business has moved with effective restraint in this area tends to be borne out by commentators who best know the regulatory field. Experts like Henry Friendly have noted a tendency for commissions to identify themselves with the interest of the regulated.[50] The Bureau of Mines, for example, has created a very complicated federal-state quasi-conservation system designed to keep certain mineral prices above the production costs of relatively inefficient producers by tailoring supply to demand.[51] Not every businessman would agree that the important regulatory agencies are sympathetic to business, of course; some insist that agencies like the Federal Trade Commission, the SEC, and the Antitrust Division of the Justice Department are "hard" on business interests. Since these agencies exercise great control, the complaints of businessmen are persistent and loud.[52] On balance, however, we can say that business has learned how to cope with and deal with the regulatory agencies.

Cameralism also extends to the relationship between business and the judiciary because legal issues arise from technical aspects of the market and the statutes. In the 1950's and 1960's the Supreme Court sometimes seemed rather exclusively concerned with personal liberties and procedural problems especially compared to its preoccupation in the 1930's with economic matters; but in fact that Court has continued to handle important cases that affect the business community quite directly. Prior to the Alcoa decision in 1945, it was generally assumed that the exclusion of competition under the Sherman Antitrust Act, actual or potential, was a necessary element to the "offensive monopoly" section under Section II of that Act. But the Court held that the intention of Congress was to avert the power to monopolize, however achieved.[53] In subsequent cases the Court held that the mere position of the power to monopolize, coupled with the intent to exercise or preserve it—even if the power has not actually been used—is alone sufficient to constitute a violation of the Sherman Act.[54] On March 28, 1955, in a decision written by the late Justice Frankfurter, the Court held unanimously that the National Labor Relations Act preempted the right of the Missouri Supreme Court to bar by injunction a strike against the Anheuser-Busch brewing company in St. Louis. In another unanimous decision the following May, the Court held that

[50] "A Look at the Federal Administrative Agencies," *Columbia Law Review,* Vol. 60 (April, 1960), pp. 429–46. Critics have often felt that the regulatory agencies tend to follow a Darwinian law where survival of regulators depends on adaptation to the regulated. One of the earliest and severest critics was Walton Hamilton, *The Politics of Industry* (New York: Knopf, 1957).

[51] Bernard D. Nossiter, *The Mythmakers: An Essay on Power and Wealth* (Boston: Houghton Mifflin, 1964), pp. 127–28.

[52] The cleavages between the FTC and the Antitrust Division of the Justice Department have not consistently resulted in a standoff between the two. Rather than stalemate, we have witnessed a tendency by one or the other to move aggressively against business.

[53] United States v. Aluminum Company of America, 148 F. 2D and 416 (2DCIR. 1954).

[54] The American Tobacco Company v. United States, 328 U.S. 781 (1946).

the provision of the Railway Labor Act that permits a carrier and a union to sign a union-shop contract, notwithstanding the law of any state, prevailed over the right-to-work provision of the Nebraska Constitution.[55] Such decisions as these seem to reflect a willingness on the part of the Supreme Court to move against so-called economic rights. William T. Gosset, president of the American Bar Association, observed recently: "The right to freedom of contract; the right to operate an unorganized shop; the right to employ child labor; the right to free speech and advertising a product for sale; the right to the unrestricted use of one's private property—all of these individual claims, once assumed to be rights, and many more, have been substantially curtailed by statute or by judicial decision."[56]

The foregoing should not suggest that, in its cameralist techniques, business has been enormously successful before the various regulatory bodies and singularly unsuccessful before the courts. On the contrary, business showed a high degree of sophistication in using the judiciary to enlarge the areas where corporations might voluntarily embark on programs allowing them to define the public good and to contribute quite directly toward it. A case in point is the modest beginning in this direction represented by the Smith Manufacturing v. Barlow case of 1953.[57]

Campaign Techniques

When business moves directly to influence the selection of office holders or the course of specific pieces of legislation, it enters directly into the political process and becomes involved in a campaigner's strategy. Here the object is to elect members in the legislature and executive branches who are believed to be hospitable to business interests. The campaign strategy is costly, highly visible, involves third parties, and, as a consequence, riskier than the cameralist approach. It can be exercised in a variety of ways, especially in grass roots political participation and lobbying.

Grass roots participation. The Worthington Corporation of New Jersey, which employs about 20,000 persons all over the world, carries on enough political activities to justify its claim that "companies like ours breed responsible citizens. Employees are encouraged to participate in the activities of their communities, and hundreds of employees do serve, in every capacity from volunteer firemen to mayor, contributing their knowledge, time and ability to their fellow men and our free society."[58] Not the least important aspect of Worthington's political activities

---

[55] Railway Employees Department v. Hanson, 351 U.S. 225 (1956).
[56] "The Law: Leader or Laggard in Our Society," *The American Bar Association Journal* (December, 1965), p. 3.
[57] See A. P. Smith Manufacturing Company v. Barlow *et al.* (May, 1953). New Jersey SP CT Chancery Division, Atlantic Reporter 97, pp. 186–96, and Clarence C. Walton, "The Changing Face of a Business Corporation's Responsibilities," *Temple University Economic and Business Bulletin,* Vol. 17 (September, 1964), pp. 3–14. See also Walton, *Corporate Social Responsibilities,* pp. 42–52. In his essay in this volume, Professor Eells considers this case and its implications for corporate "donative" powers.
[58] *A Report to Henry* (1966), p. 3.

is its use of key personnel to develop close informal relationships with members of the New Jersey legislature so that its voice might be heard on matters of crucial public policy. In a little-publicized effort, the corporation supported a state sales tax and worked diligently to assure that revenues therefrom would be employed to support higher education in that state.

The Caterpillar Tractor Company of Joliet, Illinois, declares quite forthrightly that its public relations efforts go far beyond the usual plant receptions and tours. The company analyzes political issues and maintains legislative contacts—though it does not employ full-time professionals in either Springfield or Washington. Caterpillar's public affairs manager, Bryon DeHan, declared that his company took straightforward positions on local, state, and national issues. In Joliet, the company worked in behalf of retention of the council-manager form of government; at the State House in Springfield, it argued in favor of tightening the Illinois workmen's compensation law (a law that cost the company about $750,000 a year) and in opposition to a proposed state income tax fund. In Washington the company supported the McClellan Bill of 1963 to curb union power and a proposal by the Administration to reduce taxes; it opposed the Medicare Program.[59]

Caterpillar maintains the same sort of contacts with politicians as the Worthington Corporation. The company has plants, offices, and parts depots in 22 places and 19 different congressional districts. In each, according to Mr. DeHan:

> [There are] one to four people with whom we regularly communicate . . . and whom we ask to communicate, in turn, with legislators on specific issues in terms of the specific effect of such issues on our ability to make sales and employ people. In this fashion, we get participation on legislative matters from engineers, accountants, from manufacturing people and others . . . and their opinions go to Washington in terms of political constituencies and hometown votes.[60]

A more conservative approach has been adopted by the Chase Manhattan Bank of New York, an institution that employs approximately 14,000 persons—all in the white-collar category. In 1959 the bank inaugurated a "public affairs program" that was intended

> to encourage all of us to study, think, and act as effective responsible citizens. This is not a program to endorse particular measures, or men of particular parties. It is not an attempt to organize a pressure group in favor of banking. It is purely an effort to increase your individual participation in electing capable men and women—in supporting measures for the general welfare.[61]

How effective such "grass roots" approaches are remains to be seen. A study of a midwestern city found that a number of executives had responded to company importunities to make political friends for the corporation in that community

---

[59] Byron DeHan, "The Caterpillar Public Affairs Program," Speech given at the Conference on Vocational and Adult Education in American Liberties. Arden House, Harriman, N.Y. (March 11–13, 1966), pp. 2 and 7–8.

[60] *Ibid.*, pp. 8–9.

[61] Quoted by James J. Maher, vice president in charge of public affairs, in a speech to the Arden House Conference, 1966, noted above.

mainly with a growing skepticism. One executive stated flatly to an investigator that it must be remembered that "what I do doesn't affect us just here. The guy who represents our company in this area could affect our reputation in a lot of other places as well. . . . Why, if I went out and got myself involved in local politics, you'd see a new boy in these shoes so damn fast it'd make your head swim."[62]

Pressure groups and lobbying techniques. Organization of a pressure group for lobbying is a traditional and effective way to exert continuing influence on national, state, and local politicians. The state statutes designed to control lobbying, which came in at the turn of the century, have weaknesses that persist even in the more recent legislation enacted in such states as California, Michigan, and North Carolina.[63] Non-compliance with the law is encouraged by non-enforcement. The lack of news value when breaches do occur suggests strongly that the state system of control over lobbies is fundamentally defective.

Lobbyists working at the national level also appear to have avoided strict controls and to have been successful. Some critics charge that their influence, always potent, is even greater in an economic structure that has been transformed into a "managed economy."[64] Business lobbyists, for example, and specifically the United States Chamber of Commerce, have been credited with stopping the federal aid-to-education bill in 1957; lobbyists for the oil industry were held to have turned back repeated attempts to repeal the 2.7 per cent depletion allowance in tax benefits for the oil companies. However, the charge needs qualification. The oil depletion issue represents one of those problems that do not elicit independent public interest, and in the face of such apathy an organized group can be effective. As for the 1957 education bill, at best the lobbyists achieved only a short delay.

One way pressure groups can influence legislation is to influence public opinion. However, the scale of operation necessary to make much of an impact in this way is well beyond the resources of most groups. Thus every private group seeks a multiplier effect by entering into an alliance with a political party. This leads to the eventual (albeit at times reluctant) involvement of businessmen in campaigning to elect officials regarded as "sensible" toward business interests. How readily voters are "manipulated" or "enlightened" by any of the participants in a campaign is, of course, an extraordinarily murky subject. Analyses of voter partici-

---

[62] Robert O. Schulze, "The Role of Economic Determinants in Community Power Structure," *American Sociological Review,* Vol. 23 (February, 1958). Bobbs-Merrill reprint, No. 22, p. 8.
[63] Edgar Lane, *Lobbying and the Law* (Berkeley: University of California Press, 1964).
[64] Michael Reagan, *The Managed Economy* (New York: Oxford University Press, 1962), p. 208; W. Milbrath, *The Washington Lobbyist* (Chicago: Rand-McNally, 1963). According to Douglas Cater, "managed economy" results in "managed news." The American people, he holds, are in danger of constantly being led away from truth by journalists—the very people on whom they should surely be able to rely. Cater further argues that the compelling pressure "comes from basic economic trends in the communications business. News is big business. News is a commodity that must be purveyed to an ever expanding audience by increasingly monopolistic distributors." *The Fourth Branch of Government,* (New York: Random House, 1965), p. 17.

pation and voter behavior have only too frequently yielded contradictory results.[65] Despite the uncertainties of political theorists, however, the practical businessman, no less than the practical politician, knows that campaigns are important and that the winners substantially influence the fortunes of both government and business.

In the late nineteenth century business went into politics with a vengeance. Mark Hanna introduced the systematic assessment plan whereby a company was expected to contribute to the Republican Party according to a formula related to its prosperity and to its special interest in a given region.[66] Although Congress passed laws in 1907 and again in 1925 that forbade corporations to contribute to campaigns in federal elections, business has consistently found ways to support partisan candidates. In 1936 the Duponts were active in seeking to defeat Franklin D. Roosevelt,[67] and, later, Eisenhower and Nixon received substantial support from the business community. The real spur to more intensive political activity came at the very end of the 1950's; the 1958 congressional elections were a stinging defeat for Republicans, and the pro-labor bias of the new Congress led executives like Archie D. Gray of Gulf Oil Corporation, Thomas R. Reid of Ford Motor Company, and Lemuel R. Boulware of General Electric to expressions of alarm and to summonses to the corporate community to become active politically. The *New York Times* (January 30, 1959) quoted Arthur Motley of the U.S. Chamber of Commerce as saying that business campaign tactics are ineffectual because too "much effort to enact sound legislation takes place after the legislators are elected." The 1958 theme was set by the Manufacturers Association of Syracuse, which sought to have corporations encourage middle-management personnel to become part-time politicians. The practical results were generally disappointing if the criterion of success was the number of young business executives elected to state and national legislature. But both the House of Representatives and most state legislatures tend to remain sensitive to the needs of the business community.

If involvement in politics is a "constant" in a democracy, the form participation actually takes varies with issue and circumstance. After World War II corporations exhibited a tendency to go-it-alone by reducing their reliance on trade and business associations and by not following policies developed by the NAM or Chambers of Commerce. This new independence was attributable both to the negativism of the standard trade associations and to the growing numbers of a new type of professional managers who showed increasing signs of wide tolerances toward social programs that once would have been labeled as radical.[68]

The split between the business associations and the modern managers is a clear

[65] Bernard Berelson, Paul Lazarsfeld, and W. N. McPhee, *Voting* (Chicago: University of Chicago Press, 1954), pp. 311, and G. Almond and S. Verba, *The Civic Culture* (Princeton, N.J.: Princeton University Press, 1963), esp. pp. 474–81.

[66] Louise Overacker, *Money and Elections* (New York: Macmillan, 1932) pp. 112–13.

[67] Overacker, *Presidential Campaign Funds* (Boston: Boston University Press, 1946), pp. 16–18.

[68] *Fortune* noted this in explaining the business world's preference for Johnson over Goldwater in "The Switch in Campaign Giving." Vol. 72 (November, 1965).

indication that the business community is not behaving as a monolithic giant. Even if the power of the business community is fragmented, the costs of electioneering have risen to such staggering heights that skeptics fear the financial power of our large corporations. While it is impossible to estimate the amount of money contributed in terms of goods and services (the use of billboards or the loan of an advertising man or a public relations executive to a party committee) the election cost of Presidential years may well be approaching the $200 million mark. Money counts, and corporations have money. One critic has noted that the "long-run dollar increase appears no greater than the rises in price-level and the national income and therefore should not necessarily be looked upon as a source of danger,"[69] but the politician, the average citizen, labor unionists, and small businessmen are not likely to find much comfort in such an assurance.

Statutes do exist, of course, that at least on the surface tend to restrict the political maneuverability of corporations. Under a section of the Federal Corrupt Practices Act, corporations organized under the authority of Congress are forbidden to make expenditures in connection with any election to political office or in connection with a political convention or caucus held to select candidates for political office. Corporations are also prohibited from making contributions in federal elections. Because the restrictions are unrealistic, there is much covert activity by business. In view of this activity, and since the Supreme Court has intimated that the restrictive statutes may violate the First Amendment,[70] Congress may eventually conclude that it would be wiser to give business and all other interest groups legitimate access to important decision-making points and then to insist simply that all such political action be part of the public record.

At present the restrictive laws remain, however. In 1966, Congress passed the Tax Adjustment Act, prohibiting the deduction of cost for political advertisement as a business expense; the same law imposed a limitation on the purchase of admission tickets for fund-raising events if the proceeds go, directly or indirectly, toward a political party or a political candidate. (Despite the laws a contribution of $1,000 still gets a businessman into President Johnson's inner club with a dinner visit to Washington.)

Such laws force business corporations to express their interest in campaigning in oblique ways. Normally, campaign drives are organized on a "bipartisanship" basis in order to avoid legal entanglements. But financial contributions may take the form of direct contributions to advertisements, subsidizing fund-raising dinners, the use of company facilities, providing costs of expensive advertisements in national publications, and the like.

How effectively businessmen feel they are responding in the public arena is open to debate. Apparently businessmen were more optimistic about their political influence in 1964, during the Democratic Administration, than were their counterparts five years earlier during the Eisenhower Administration. A survey by Stephen A. Greyser suggested that businessmen believed "that the trend in business'

[69] Alexander Heard, *The Costs of Democracy* (Chapel Hill: University of North Carolina Press, 1960).
[70] United States v. The Congress of Industrial Organizations, 355 U.S. 106, 129 (1948).

influence is growing with respect both to political affairs in general and to elected officials in particular. In fact, fewer than 20 per cent of the respondents believe that business' influence is on the wane.[71]

BUSINESS IN ACTION: OIL, TARIFFS, AND LABOR

How business moves within the political arena and the varying degrees of effectiveness that characterize these efforts have been illuminated in two recent books— one by Robert Engler on the politics of oil and another by Raymond A. Bauer on the politics of foreign trade. Engler concluded that the "petroleum politicos" are extremely effective in the exercise "of a socially irresponsible system of power" and that they "mock the ideals of responsible government, a just society, and a peaceful world."[72] Bauer, on the other hand, concluded that in the politics of tariff, business pressure groups were ineffective: "its lobbies were, on the whole, poorly financed, ill-managed, out of contact with Congress and, at best, only marginally effective in supporting tendencies and measures which already had behind them considerable congressional impetus from other sources."[73] A review of the evidence in the two studies can suggest some of the reasons for such different results of corporate political activity.

The Politics of Oil

The oil industry is a vital element in the American economy, and its international operations are of critical importance to many other nations. Oil and gas together supply 70 per cent of total U.S. fuel-energy requirements. The output of oil has grown from half a million tons in 1859 to over 2.5 billion tons a century later.

America's international oil business is dominated by five companies (Standard of New Jersey, Socony Mobil, Gulf, Texas, and Standard of California), who control nearly two-thirds of the reserves of the Middle East and 70 per cent of Canada's output.[74] The economies of scale in the industry are such that huge investment, large markets, and a kind of long-range planning appear to be needed; the impact of the invisible hand of the free market is difficult to discern. Cemented together in a close bond, the "top five" of the industry have used cameralist political techniques with great success. Generally speaking, they have operated under benevolent government regulators. Despite various antitrust investigations over the years, they have been able to ward off any serious judgments. During the Eisenhower Administration, five of the major American producers were accused

---

[71] "Business and Politics, 1964," *Harvard Business Review* (September, 1964). The earlier study was made by Dan H. Fenn, Jr., "Business and Politics," *Harvard Business Review* (May–June, 1959). See also William H. Baumer and Donald Herzberg, *Politics is Your Business* (New York: Dial, 1960).

[72] *The Politics of Oil* (New York: Macmillan, 1961) p. 485.

[73] *American Business and Public Policy: The Politics of Foreign Trade* (New York: Atherton, 1963) p. 324.

[74] Engler, *op. cit.*, pp. 35–53 and 66–68.

of violating the Sherman Act and certain tariff regulations by conspiring to divide and control foreign production and distribution while fixing prices and limiting competition. The suit petered out and a consent decree in 1960 ended the case with Jersey and Gulf by forbidding them to engage in cartel practices. No substantial injury was sustained.

The big international oil companies have also conducted an active campaign strategy by successfully retaining the image established by John D. Rockefeller, Sr., of the small businessman endowed with boldness and courage and representing the best in the American tradition of free enterprise.[75] Moreover, the industry has managed to create in the public mind a link between the national welfare and the industry's welfare.

In foreign affairs the oil companies have been charged by Engler with having created a system of private treaties that carve out protective domains for themselves and with making foreign policy through their ability to organize international boycotts against unfriendly governments and their capacity to cut prices until competition is destroyed.

Because Robert Engler's value structures seem tinged with a kind of ideological "progressivism," is his conclusion about the oil industry's power thereby suspect? Are we, in fact, suffering under a corporate tyranny? The industries have power. The power is being used. Public opinion is undisturbed. The government is accommodating. Have, therefore, the nation's vital international interests and the domestic public interest been injured—or protected—in the process?

The Politics of the Tariff

A totally different picture emerges from Bauer's study of the politics of the tariff. Historically, the tariff was viewed as a defense against the evils of European cartels and monopolists; consequently, it enjoyed a substantial measure of public support. Although enacted originally as a source of revenue rather than as a tool for protection, the tariff became as early as 1789 a device to protect the infant steel industry. Protectionism was sharpened and extended after the War of 1812, and several times again in the nineteenth and early twentieth centuries. The Reciprocal Trade Agreements Act of 1934 reversed the current.

In 1953, President Eisenhower asked a new Republican Congress to extend the life of the Trade Agreements Act. A bill started its odyssey in the Committee on Ways and Means, in which two ardent protectionists (Reed and Simpson) acted as chairman and third-ranking majority member respectively. Congressman Simpson, representing Pennsylvania coal interests, advocated oil-import quotas to protect his state's mining operations. Oil producing states and the small local independents rallied to Simpson's support. But the big oil interests campaigned energetically against the Simpson bill and defeated it. Had the oil interests walked off with a handsome victory? And, if so, was the public interest hobbled or promoted? As a matter of record, the protectionists, though unsuccessful in

[75] *Ibid.,* p. 430.

securing approval of the Simpson bill, introduced into the law a proviso that made the imposition of quotas an administrative act to be taken whenever findings of fact showed injury to an American industry.[76]

The election of a Democratic majority to Congress in 1954 seemed to open the way for a possibly stunning defeat for the protectionists, but the old-school southern congressmen, forgetting two centuries of southern trade liberalism, desirous of protecting new southern textile manufacturing installations, and worried by rising unemployment in their districts, did little to change the law.

The American business community seemed to be as incapable of bringing any power to bear on the problem of tariff revision in 1954 as the southern congressman. Large multiproduct firms found it difficult to adopt a consistent policy toward tariffs because some products had an export market whereas others were subject to stiff foreign competition. One division of a firm could favor or remain indifferent to tariff reduction while another could be unremittingly hostile.

The political weakness of big business in the matter of tariff reduction, therefore, was due to the fact that a conflict of interests existed not only among businesses but often within the same company. What hurts one industry may help another. The unity of objectives so apparent in the international oil industry's dealings with the government is singularly lacking when business approaches the tariff problem.

Labor and the Landrum-Griffin Act

In seeking to influence national oil and tariff policies big business faced no major adversary. When public policy that significantly affects labor-management relations comes under review, however, big business is directly confronted by the big unions. The story of the passage of the Landrum-Griffin Act in 1959 illustrates the kind of business behavior that results when a united front becomes imperative against a strong adversary. A sketch of the background helps to sharpen understanding of the issue.

The Wagner Act of 1935 (a) forbade employers to interfere with, coerce, or restrain employees who wanted to engage in coordinated activities, (b) outlawed discriminatory treatment or discharge of union-minded employees, and (c) required an employer to bargain in good faith with the union that represented the majority of its employees in an appropriate unit. While from the very beginning the National Labor Relations Board and the Supreme Court emphasized this "duty to bargain" requirement, criticisms were raised in many quarters. In 1961, for example, the CED issued a report (prepared by a committee of scholars headed by Dr. Clark Kerr) that declared that it was unrealistic to expect that good faith could be legislated; indeed, provisions designated to promote "good faith have become a tactical weapon used in many situations as a means of harassment."[77]

---

[76] Bauer, op. cit., p. 35.
[77] The Public Interest and National Labor Policy (1961), p. 82.

The power of the NLRB to order a company to hold elections to determine whether the unions had a legitimate claim to represent the employees of a given plant seemed particularly obnoxious to business, and in 1939 a movement was begun to change the law. The National Association of Manufacturers enlarged its staff, and NAM officers began to visit government officials. The Chamber of Commerce also intensified its activities; it was said to have held 27 simultaneous steak dinners at which 300 Congressmen were entertained by delegates of the Chamber from the Congressmen's home states.[78] The results of the movement were disappointing, however, and the matter was dropped with the outbreak of World War II.

The advent of a Republican Congress in 1946, the first in 14 years, gave business a major opportunity to move aggressively in the field of labor-management policy. All Congressmen were given a leather-bound copy of a booklet entitled *Knowledge Built America*, which contained the legislative ideals set out by the 51st Annual Congress of American Industry, a group aligned closely to the NAM. The NAM increased its radio broadcasts and sponsored programs for teachers, clergymen, and other professional groups to publicize business' grievances with the Wagner Act. Partly as the result of such business activities as these Congress overrode, in 1947, a Presidential veto to pass the Taft-Hartley Act. The Act ruled out the closed shop, outlawed secondary boycotts, regulated political activities of unions, and revived government injunctions. Significant, too, was the fact that the Act gave priority to state right-to-work acts over the Taft-Hartley provisions allowing the union shop. Labor leaders were outraged by the new law. The triumph of business seemed complete.[79]

Despite its victory business soon again became restive. While the Taft-Hartley Act had outlawed secondary boycotts and the so-called hot-cargo agreements, the prohibitions were not effective. A "hot-cargo" agreement is a provision in a labor contract whereby management agrees not to require its workers to use materials produced in a non-union shop. Union lawyers found a loophole when they discovered that unions could persuade employers to agree "voluntarily" not to require the use of non-union materials.

The 1950's were years of management-union tensions. Business grew eager to have enacted several revisions in national labor law, but the outlook for favorable government action dimmed as the decade drew to an end. The Senate, which had been almost evenly split with 50 Democrats and 46 Republicans in 1958, was transformed into a 64–34 Democratic stronghold by the fall elections of that year. In the House, a slender Democratic majority of 231–200 was transformed into an overwhelming majority, 283–158. Democrats now controlled both the Committee on Labor and Public Works and the Subcommittee on Labor and Public

[78] R. E. Lane, J. D. Barber, and F. I. Grenstein, *An Introduction to Political Analysis* (Englewood Cliffs, N. J.: Prentice-Hall, 1962) pp. 90–95.
[79] Gerard D. Reilly, "The Legislative History of the Taft-Hartley Act," *The George Washington Law Review,* Vol. 29 (December, 1960), p. 297. See also Harry S. Millis and Emily Clark Brown, *From the Wagner Act to Taft-Hartley: A Study of National Labor Policy and Labor Relations* (Chicago: University of Chicago Press, 1950).

Welfare in the Senate. In the House, the Committee on Education and Labor consisted of 20 Democrats and 10 Republicans. Seventy per cent of the candidates backed by the unions in congressional contests were elected. Perhaps even more discouraging for business was the crushing defeat suffered in California by the conservative Republican Senator, William Knowland, who had run for the governorship as a stepping-stone to the Republican Presidential nomination in 1960 and who had firmly supported a right-to-work law for his state. Right-to-work laws were defeated in almost a score of states, whereas only one was passed.

The political atmosphere thus seemed unusually hostile to business in 1959, yet in that year Congress passed the Landrum-Griffin Act. This action led Professor Alan McAdams to raise the central question: "How could a law so out of character with what was expected have emerged from the 86th Congress?"[80] Part of the answer is that the business community developed and carried out a reinvigorated campaign strategy. The first concern of business was to obtain an effective law against the secondary boycott, but instead of seeking to achieve that objective directly the business strategists chose to focus their publicity on the nominal issue of corruption in labor unions. Corruption required extensive investigation and business felt that if jurisdiction in these investigations was given to the Senate Committee on Labor and Public Welfare a whitewash would result. Yet labor was equally opposed to investigative jurisdiction being given to the Government Operations Committee.

As a compromise there was created a select Committee on Improper Activities in Labor-Management Affairs consisting of four Democratic Senators (John McClellan, Sam Ervin, Jr., John Kennedy, and Pat McNamara) and four Republican Senators (Joseph McCarthy, Karl Mundt, Irving Ives, and Barry Goldwater). Robert Kennedy was appointed chief counsel. The business strategists managed to form a conservative coalition by getting on the select committee the two Southern Democrats, McClellan and Ervin, along with Republicans McCarthy, Mundt, and Goldwater. The McClellan Committee's investigation served basically to link the public image of John L. Lewis in 1947 to that of Jimmy Hoffa in 1959. The former had come to be identified in the public mind as one so committed to workers' interest that the public interest became secondary; it was Lewis' image that had sparked demands for the Taft-Hartley Act. Now Hoffa became the symbol of the need for reform that helped to bring about the Landrum-Griffin Act.[81]

Of equal importance with the McClellan hearings to the success of the business program was the fact that four of President Eisenhower's key assistants (William Persons, Gerald Morgan, Bruce Harlow, and Edward McCabe) were all conservatives who pushed Congress toward a pro-business bill. Another major step was to win President Eisenhower's public support for new labor legislation, something he had never given. On August 6th, 1959, in one of his most political speeches, President Eisenhower addressed the American people over all major

[80] Alan K. McAdams, *Power Politics and Labor Legislation* (New York: Columbia University Press, 1964), p. 5.
[81] *Ibid.*, p. 136.

radio and television networks on labor problems. The response was an inundation of mail requesting strong labor legislation; swept under was the original and milder bill sponsored by Senators Kennedy and Ives.

Business strategists were also busy arousing constituents to flood congressmen with mail favoring the Landrum-Griffin Act. A television program on the Armstrong Cork Company's Circle Theatre, "Sound of Violence," which portrayed union hoodlums in the jukebox field and ended with an appeal by Senator McClellan for reform, was singularly effective. Incidentally, Henry J. Marshall, director of employee relations at Armstrong, was a member of the Secondary Boycott Committee of the United States Chamber of Commerce.

Many factors were responsible for the passage of the Landrum-Griffin Act. The coordinated efforts of the Chamber of Commerce, the National Association of Manufacturers, and the effective exploitation of a labor "scandal" and its nationwide dissemination through the televised McClellan hearings all provided stimuli for the avalanche of mail that influenced congressmen. The findings of the McClellan rackets committee and the direct intervention of President Eisenhower were obviously important as well. Political maneuvering in the Senate in anticipation of the Presidential nominations of 1960 was another imponderable factor. The Democratic leadership was well aware that Senator Kennedy, who had been an author of a milder version of the bill, was seeking the prestige that goes with sponsorship of a major law in his quest for the Presidential nomination. His rival, Senator Lyndon Johnson, had written a letter to management recalling his support of Taft-Hartley over Truman's veto and of his conviction that much of the Landrum-Griffin Bill made sense. The Administration's role in coordinating much of the work of the management groups themselves was also a factor. Yet with all caveats enjoined there is no doubt that in this instance business moved effectively and well to outmaneuver labor in the initial stage when the select committee was to be formed to carry on the investigation of labor corruption and in the enlisting of White House support on a national issue.

Faced by a powerful and united adversary on an issue judged vital to the entire economic community, business showed a capacity to campaign effectively to arouse public opinion, to secure conservative appointees to the select Senate committee that was created to spotlight alleged union power and corruption, to draw out a hitherto reluctant president to make a major policy speech, and to influence the nature of the legislation itself.

SUMMARY AND CONCLUSION

Having reviewed selected portions of the literature, as well as three concrete issues bearing on government-business interactions, can one conclude that large private corporations now exercise such vast powers that business is, in fact, a dangerous leviathan? And that these developments have substantially reduced the nation's ability to promote the public interest? When definitive answers are sought the record proves disappointingly inadequate. Nevertheless, the inconclusive results emerging from this survey do reveal interesting position points from which valid insights, value judgments, and further research possibilities may be achieved. A summary of these points would include the following:

(1) The American Constitution envisioned a vast common market in which competitions would emerge not simply from class conflicts but from sectional and other interests.

(2) The framers tended to accept the philosophical premises of Locke, who thought that the public interest was the summing up of valid private interests; hence the general welfare would occur when legitimate private concerns could seek to advance their causes under "fair rules" of competition.

(3) These "fair rules" were generally developed during the first century and a half of our national existence by both Congress and the courts in ways favorable to private interests, so the position of business was secure.

(4) Industry's security was threatened in the twentieth century by three developments: (a) the 1929 depression, which generated doubts about the *efficiency* of business; (b) the separation of ownership from effective control over the enterprise, which challenged the *legitimacy* of corporate leadership; and (c) the undertaking by government of extended public programs (full employment, aid to education, Medicare), which questioned the *primacy* of business as the main pillar of a prosperous economy and a free society.

(5) Private industry vindicated its role as an efficient production machine during World War II.

(6) Corporate enterprise sought to reestablish its legitimacy internally by adopting procedures akin to due process for white-collar employees and, externally, by exercising social responsibilities designed to permit the private sector to voice its views on what a future "great society" should become.

(7) The "great society" thrusts of government and business in the 1960's represent a gradual shifting in philosophical premises from the Lockean toward the Aristotelian view that the general welfare must be deliberately and carefully promoted by those in power and in ways that transcend mere private utilities.

(8) This new direction, plus the growth of technology, has resulted in a spreading public bureaucracy that, contrary to much business criticism, has not seriously disadvantaged private business; on the contrary, using its cameralist techniques, business can look forward to a profitable cooperative and, at times, competitive relationship with the public sector.

(9) Large corporations no longer depend as heavily as they once did on national "business" associations like the NAM or the Chamber of Commerce to develop a consistent business approach to political issues. Rather, the large firm makes its calculations as it perceives a given issue affecting its own interest. While this development tends to fragment business power on a range of specific issues, business has shown resiliency and imagination in moving to protect interests that are common to the business community as a whole.

(10) The analysis of selected issues relating to the oil industry, to tariff policy, and to labor laws suggests that, in those instances where big business was singularly

successful, the public was either unconcerned on a point where industry had clear and unified objectives or that the public and business shared the same views.

(11) The relationship of big government and big business today is a far cry from what it was in the past when legislators were bought and sold, when the dominant Republican Party was a shield for business, and when the courts were its great ally. In a sense, there is more rather than less competition today among the three great sectors of public life: government, labor, and business.

(12) Since the competition is among organizations, the Jeffersonian dream of power of the solitary citizen has been shattered with, of course, attendant dissipation of the cherished myth of American individualism.

SELECTED READINGS

HARLAN CLEVELAND AND HAROLD D. LASSWELL, EDS., *Ethics and Bigness* (New York: Harper & Row, 1961). The essays are uneven but add up to a substantial contribution. Practicing politicians and business executives join theologians, philosophers, and social scientists in probing the "value" problem of bigness in American society. One of the themes running through the book is caught in David Truman's observation that "the immediate American problem is more fundamental than governmental structure. It is the deeply moral problem of a political society that is strongly antipolitical and thus antigovernmental, one in which the obligations of political leadership are avoided and in which, partly as a consequence, the often tragic dilemmas of public responsibility are not understood."

BERTRAND DEJOUVENAL, *The Pure Theory of Politics* (New Haven, Conn.: Yale University Press, 1963). A brilliant French scholar suggests that modern society breeds mediocrity in positions of great power, that society is necessarily host to both entrepreneur and rentier, and that it will always be the scene of conflict between the "attentive" statesman seeking to forestall trouble and the "intending" administrator who sets out to get what he wants.

RICHARD EELLS, *The Government of Corporations* (New York: The Free Press, 1962). Presents an interesting thesis that corporations are political as well as economic organizations and hence must "constitutionalize" themselves—that is, curb their own powers over the individual. Geared to a theoretical level that suggests need for supporting empirical data.

CARL J. FRIEDRICH, ED., *The Public Interest* (New York: Atherton, 1966). These essays provide an effective entrée to the literature—including conflicting viewpoints—on the concept of the public interest. The pieces by Gerhart Niemeyer, Harold Lasswell, Glendon Schubert, and Frank J. Sorauf are especially useful.

GRANT MCCONNELL, *Private Power and American Democracy* (New York: Knopf, 1966). A persuasive argument that the American quest to fragment political power has really not limited power; rather it has thrust authority on local governments and private groups. The result is conformity, elitism, and the flight of public values from effective public consideration.

NELSON W. POLSBY, *Community Power and Political Theory* (New Haven, Conn.: Yale University Press, 1963). A perceptive reappraisal of the current state of social science theory about power and policy making. The locale studied is New Haven, but the scholarly results are quite general.

ARNOLD ROSE, *The Power Structure: Political Process in American Society* (New York: Oxford University Press, 1967). A scathing critique of the findings of sociologists such as C. Wright Mills (*The Power Elite*) and Floyd Hunter (*Community Power Structure*) who have depicted power as concentrated in elites at the national and at the local levels, respectively. Chapters 3, on "Elites," and 12, on Medicare, are particularly valuable.

FRANK J. SORAUF, *Political Parties in the American System* (Boston: Little, Brown, 1964). A relatively small introduction to party politics, eclectic but very well done—including some original interpretations for a functional approach to politics.

CLARENCE C. WALTON, *Corporate Social Responsibilities* (Belmont, Calif.: Wadsworth, 1967). Shows how corporations have responded—and are responding—to the problem of contributing to the public interest. Develops models to demonstrate the differences among concepts of social responsibility and the dangers of simplistic definitions.

chapter 4

BUSINESS AND AMERICAN
FOREIGN RELATIONS

CHARLES F. STEWART *teaches economics and international business at the Columbia Graduate School of Business. Author of a history of Morocco's economy, he has co-authored an encyclopedic inventory of reference material bearing on international business and is active in several programs and institutes dealing with problems in comparative economics.*

The detailed character of the network of our post-war economic relationships is too often obscured by news headlines dealing with chronic deficits in our balance of payments (the "gold problem"), the seizure of American properties by foreign states (the case of Fidel Castro is illustrative), the pros and cons of trade with communist countries, and the nagging problems associated, each year, with America's foreign-aid program. The shock experienced by most of the hundreds of thousands of Americans who travel abroad for the first time each year and find themselves surrounded by familiar gasoline signs, tall buildings bearing familiar corporate names, and diminutive versions of Ford and GM autos bearing down upon them reflects the gap between headlines and the reality of American involvements in the economics of other nations. The fact that such presences are increasingly taken in stride by the host nations may indicate some changes in attitude toward what after World War II was referred to as American "coca-colonialism."

Professor Stewart begins his essay by reviewing the historical overseas trade and investment activities of Western businessmen, giving special attention to the way these activities were affected by the shift from the colonial to the post-colonial era. Then he describes a typical modern multinational business corporation having its headquarters in the United States and subsidiaries in several foreign countries. He analyzes the internal politics of such a cor-

poration, its relations with the United States and foreign govern-
ments, and its impact on the society and economy of the countries
where its subsidiaries are located. He concludes that the modern
businessman is as much of a cultural catalyst and social "revolu-
tionary" as ever, but that his destabilizing impact may be offset by
the multinational corporation, a new instrument that if used wisely
can be a powerful force for achieving greater prosperity and unity
throughout the world.

Implicit in Professor Stewart's portrait of American businessmen
abroad is the idea that they have been able to share, to no small
degree, responsibilities for economic development with foreign
governments and to avoid political showdowns like those that take
place at home, with foreign leaders.

1. What conditions have militated against the emergence of an
equivalently benign attitude among those same businessmen toward
government activities in the U.S.?

2. The Logan Act makes it unlawful for American businessmen
to practice foreign relations on their own. Suppose a corporation
with mineral interests in a particular country is contractually obli-
gated to pay royalties to the government there and that the govern-
ment is currently undergoing a "succession crisis" in which two
groups are vying with each other for recognition by the United
States. How might the executives of the company meet their obli-
gations?

3. In an earlier "colonial" time, according to Professor Stewart's
analysis, there were instances in which foreign policy often reflected
the private interests in the major industrial countries. At present it
may be more common for private U.S. corporations to be utilized
by the government in pursuit of its policy objectives. Thus, Ameri-
can executives have occasionally been asked to report on foreign
business associates to Federal agencies. And IBM was prevented
from selling a new computer system to France in the 1960's in
order to deny President DeGaulle access to it for military use. What
consequences for America's economic development inhere in ar-
rangements whereby corporations may become instruments of
foreign policy?

4. The Hickenlooper Amendment to the Foreign Assistance Act
requires that aid to a country be discontinued if its government
expropriates American-owned assets without "prompt, adequate,
and just compensation." Compare and contrast this institutionalized
arrangement with what Professor Stewart refers to as the "gunboat
diplomacy" of an earlier era. What implications for the politics of
American businessmen are there in such an arrangement? Under
what conditions are the owners and managers of corporate assets

overseas "caught in the middle" and under what conditions do they gain (by the reduction of risks, for example) through such arrangements?

CHARLES F. STEWART \ ## THE BUSINESS
OF AMERICA ABROAD

Unlike soldiers and statesmen, the businessman, for whatever reasons, has largely made his contribution to history quietly. Perhaps "busyness" has left the man of affairs little time to develop and demonstrate articulateness; perhaps, along with William Durant, most have felt that "nothing is often a good thing to say, and always a clever thing to say," especially in environments hostile to business. More likely, however, the nature of the businessman's contribution is such that it fails to attract the attention of most recorders of man's activities. While soldiers and statesmen alter landscapes and boundaries and introduce other changes that can be identified, dated, and sometimes quantified, the businessman's role is largely faceless and timeless. This is not to say that the businessman is historically unimportant; his activities help sustain a measure of continuity and evolution in human affairs without which perpetuation of the race would be impossible. On the pages of history, the businessman is seldom seen but is always there.[1]

In his anonymity, the businessman, even in his most coolly rational decisions based on the profit calculus, is probably still the world's leading subversive of the status quo. While money can certainly be made in a static situation, there is often more to be made by introducing a calculated change—technological, social, or economic. Henry Ford's reach for "the other 95 per cent" of the potential automobile market changed American life as fundamentally as Lenin's "soviets plus electricity" changed Russia. Consciously or unconsciously, businessmen become agents of change in their pursuit of profit.

The capability of the businessman to bring change has been greatly increased in the twentieth century. The widespread adoption of the corporation in its modern form has resulted in the pooling of vast amounts of resources—natural, capital, and human—that can be rallied to the cause of change at the most strategic junctures. A significant proportion of these resources is being devoted to reducing the costs of distance; goods, people, and above all ideas are being transported

---

[1] Of course there are historians who labor in the field of business history, and the businessman also has his critics, going back at least as far as Karl Marx. For sheer popularity, however, the memoirs of General Motors' Alfred P. Sloan, Jr., hardly compared with those of Dwight D. Eisenhower. For a general view of the businessman's role over the centuries, see the durable book by Miriam Beard, *A History of Business,* Vol. 2 (Ann Arbor: University of Michigan Press, 1938).

farther and faster at a steadily increasing rate. Thus, our "subversive" business-man now has the world for his territory. Pushed by increasing economies of plant scale and attracted by the widening opportunities for sales on a global basis, many businessmen have burst from the confines of markets—the U.S. market among them—that were coextensive with political boundaries. While political boundaries still inhibit the businessman's freedom to roam, his new world-mindedness makes them appear far less formidable than they seemed when his thinking was focused by the prospects and problems of national markets.

THE HISTORICAL CONTEXT

Of course the roaming businessman is not a new phenomenon, nor is his role as an agent of change or as a subversive of the status quo. Venetian and Yankee traders, although far apart in time, were both incidentally the brokers of culture while they pursued the ducat and dollar. The technology available to them, how-ever, limited their brokerage function, and governments, for whatever reasons, added further constraints. What makes the role of the contemporary businessman in world affairs different in kind from that of his predecessors is the modern technological revolution. On the one hand, this revolution has increased the magnitude and duration of culture contact possible through the business broker; on the other hand, it has tended to bend the will of government officials every-where in a direction often favorable to business, because to eschew the fruits of technology today would be, sooner or later, to die politically.

The cultural influence of our Venetian and Yankee traders was largely reflected in changing consumption patterns. The investment of these traders abroad was usually limited to the working capital they committed to inventories of goods; physically they penetrated foreign nations but little beyond their maritime periph-eries. Consequently, their influence on local production functions was almost nil, although the trade they brought did cause local businessmen to deepen their own investment in production facilities for the goods exchanged.

The pace of cultural contact quickened in the nineteenth century; more im-portant, its nature changed. The Industrial Revolution shifted the emphasis of western businessmen from trade and commerce to the creation of large-scale aggregations of capital sunk in production facilities and corporate organizations to match. The resulting pressure of high overheads required a large and con-tinuous flow of raw materials, as well as large markets to absorb the output. In order to ensure both sources of supply and markets, even more capital was required to integrate backward and forward. Geographically, the industrializing countries —most notably Great Britain, with the United States as an exception—found their own territories much too restricted and turned their eyes to the wide realms as yet untouched by the force of the machine. Thus with large companies there arose large empires.[2]

[2] The shortfall of capital in the United States was met by large inflows from Europe. Colonial territories actually received a small amount of the total movement, but in

The rush toward empire was not accompanied by unanimous approval on the colonizing side. The debate whether colonies were profitable was loud and vociferous. Karl Marx argued that investments in colonies were certainly profitable to stockholders, since the balance sheets of the companies set up there did not reflect the most important cost involved in their operations, namely the expenses of troops and public administrators to provide security and stability. Since these expenses were invariably borne by the taxpayers in the mother country, and since, in addition, these same taxpayers were often obliged to buy colonial products at higher prices than they would have had to pay for goods from other sources, there was a certain logic in the Marxian contention that colonies were an ill-disguised means of redistributing income at home.[3] Objections to empire building were also heard from critics who were regarded as respectable, at least in some circles, among them Clemenceau, who characterized the French military occupation of Tunis after a default in payments on French-held bonds as a *"coup de bourse."*

Others took a more favorable view of the participation of business in colonial operations, arguing that enterprise was a substitute for force. The maxim of Cecil Rhodes that "rails cost less than bullets and carry farther" was widely quoted and later even translated by the French Marshal Lyautey into *"un chantier vaut un bataillon"* (a construction project is worth a battalion). Those who lobbied for empire in terms of the "white man's burden" naturally also wanted business to help hold it up; among them were missionaries who, in some instances, went abroad to do good and did well.

Investment Abroad

The merits of the argument were lost as events unfolded, however, and our first global businessmen in the modern sense preceded, followed, and sometimes accompanied their flag abroad. The continued presence of the familiar Union Jack or Tricolor soon persuaded many traders that it would be present in their colony forever, and they abandoned the near-liquidity resulting from their concentration on trade goods for the possibility of a long-term capital gain from direct investment.

---

terms of impact on the present world scene, its influence has been much more than proportionate. For a review of international capital movements in the last century, see Ragnar Nurkse, "International Investment Today in the Light of Nineteenth-Century Experience," in Barry E. Supple, ed., *The Experience of Economic Growth* (New York: Random House, 1963), p. 129.

[3] In some areas not under direct colonial domination, the repayment problem was simplified by default on obligations owing European investors. Certain Latin American countries and the United States are examples. For details see Raymond Vernon, "Saints and Sinners in Foreign Investment," *Harvard Business Review*, Vol. 41 (May–June, 1963), pp. 146–55. The various studies by J. Fred Rippy of British experience in Latin America further suggest that all was not bonanza. See, for example, *British Investments in Latin America: 1822–1949* (Minneapolis: University of Minnesota Press, 1959). The more recent Cuban case is described in Theodore Draper, *Castro's Revolution: Myths and Realities* (New York: Praeger, 1962).

The character of the operations in which capital was usually invested abroad reflected the need of the empire builders for raw materials and markets. Much investment found its way into plantation agriculture and associated marketing facilities or into extractive industries. Another area of investment was transportation and other public utilities designed to support agriculture and mining. These developments in the colonies' capacity to supply the mother countries led to the creation of new demand. As the colonies became increasingly lopsided economically in their concentration on the production of one or a very few products for export, they were ripe for vastly increased imports of relatively cheap machine-made products. The subsequent inward flow not only provided the basis and terms of trade—raw materials for manufactured goods—but also destroyed the local handicraft groups. The Indian weaver, for example, could not compete successfully with the looms of Lancashire.

The bargain struck between the colonizers and colonized was quite clear. The businessman, with home government guarantees of stability and security, provided capital and active management in overseas dependencies, even though the new production technology ranked alongside democracy on the banned list. The dependents supplied raw materials, markets, and a labor force that grew all the more rapidly as a result of medical and sanitary practices imported from the industrializing countries. In essence, the function of the colonized was to be hewers of wood and drawers of water for the mother country, to live as an appendage on the margin of the Industrial Revolution. The relative power positions of the parties were also clear, as manifested by various treaties and "contracts" signed in the nineteenth century among military, political, and economic unequals.

The changed relationships between the haves and the have-nots since the second world war are symbolized by the one country-one vote rule in the General Assembly of the United Nations and by the rapid dismantling of empires. The simple yet powerful idea that there is no scientific reason why *all* men cannot share in the fruits of technology is now held worldwide. This dynamic version of the idea of progress has replaced the static philosophy of resignation to perpetual poverty in the poor countries.

The American Experience

While the nineteenth century and the years before 1914 largely belonged to the European powers, the Americans were not idle. Sheltered by the British navy, which gave real effect to Monroe's brash proposal that Europe keep its hands off the Americas, the United States was able to get on with its own version of empire. Expansion across the continent to the Pacific uncovered what appeared to be limitless opportunities to absorb limited energies. Since opposition by the Indian tribes was weak numerically and culturally, extermination often took the place of the "contract" imposed by European powers upon more numerous and culturally significant peoples elsewhere. There was little resemblance between the functions of the Indian Bureau and the Colonial Office.

Although the share of foreign trade in America's gross national product declined during the century, the orderly development of domestic empire demanded stability in our part of the hemisphere.[4] The final dissolution of the Spanish empire to the south, however, had left many new countries that were (and still are) unstable by U.S. measurement. Since most important decisions affecting the Spanish colonies had always been made either in Spain itself or by a colonial administration whose members were recruited exclusively in the mother country, after the wars of independence no local civil service remained that was trained to handle problems of the kind that faced the new nations. Among these problems were the many national ethnic and cultural differences that had to be resolved before any political and social consensus on national goals could be achieved. Instead of consensus, meaningful evolution, and stability, the countries to the south of the United States experienced a series of revolutions. All too often an unstable equilibrium, rather than any attempt at social reform, was restored by a military dictatorship. The daily newspapers suggest that the search for consensus still goes on.

Sometimes, in the judgment of the "colossus of the north," the efforts of a southern country's military establishment to restore stability were inadequate, and outside help was imperative, wanted or not. Intervention in Cuba in the Spanish-American War set a precedent for further operations in the Caribbean region. American troops became well known in Nicaragua, Cuba, Haiti, and the Dominican Republic (where recently they appeared anew) during occupations of varying lengths. Their presence along the Panama Canal, on the other hand, was continuous, since for many products the eastern and western seaboards of the United States could be linked more cheaply by a voyage through the canal than by shipment overland, even though the land route was considerably shorter. In the view of the United States, the advantages of the canal had to be protected.

The military operations of the United States were of course not confined to Latin America or the Caribbean. Operations by the fledgling U.S. Navy in 1801 against the Barbary pirates to eliminate their interference with Yankee shipping established an American presence in the Mediterranean that is perpetuated today by the ever steaming Sixth Fleet. In the Far East, Perry's arrival in Japan had commercial overtones; so did America's participation with the European powers in putting down the Boxer Rebellion in China. The presence these established is maintained today in the western Pacific by the Seventh Fleet.

Landing the Marines was an extreme step; naturally, many diplomatic activities of a less drastic kind were also conducted during the period. The United States stood to lose a great deal if the European powers extended the *pacte colonial*— the system of tying dependencies to the mother country through closely controlled exchanges of raw materials for manufactured goods—for it meant a drastic reduction in trade between the dependencies and third parties. In countries where the interests of several powers were great, outright annexation by any one of them would have been a threat to the peace. The result in these cases was diplomatic

[4] For a broad view of the period, see Douglass C. North, "The United States in the International Economy," in Seymour E. Harris, ed., *American Economic History* (New York: McGraw-Hill, 1961), pp. 181–206.

rather than military maneuver. China was a good example in the Pacific. American trading interests in China were significant and long standing, and when the European powers threatened to divide the country into a few exclusive commercial spheres, the United States supported an "open door" policy and participated in its administration. Closer examination of this famous policy suggests that it should be qualified as "inward swinging"; although the United States demanded that the European powers grant its businessmen equal access to Chinese markets in the spirit of free competition, there was no parallel demand that the Chinese be granted reciprocity in American and European markets. (Negotiation by the powers was *over* China, not *with* China.)

On the other side of the world, much the same history was written in Morocco, where negotiations were so delicate and the positions of the powers were so rigid that Europe was on the brink of war over the issue at least twice before 1914. While the eventual outcome was a French protectorate, France's freedom of action in Morocco was severely restricted by international agreements that, as in the case of China, gave all the powers equal and very favorable access to the Moroccan market, again without reciprocity.[5] From practically the very beginning, treaties between Morocco and its trading partners were concerned with two sets of rights—economic and extraterritorial. Put another way, the treaty provisions were guarantes by the Moroccan government of (1) the commercial rights of its trading parners and (2) the personal safety of the traders and protection of their possessions. Foreigners were exempt from paying internal taxes as were their Moroccan employees, otherwise known as protégés. Import duties, regardless of the product, were a flat 10 per cent. Disputes between foreigners and disputes between a foreigner and a Moroccan were adjudicated by consular courts; in these cases, foreign laws were applied on Moroccan soil. While the initiative to establish these provisions was taken by European powers, the United States did not shrink from insisting on equal treatment. Not until 1956, many years after the other powers had relinquished their privileges, did the United States finally give up these rights, including its special consular courts.

The Decline of Colonialism

Colonialism by annexation was no longer fashionable after World War I, but colonialism through international agreement tended to replace it. The mandates of the League of Nations were really international recognition of *faits accompli,* the control by Britain and France over the Near Eastern areas of the defunct Ottoman Empire. More than trade was involved in these areas; oil seepages in what is now Iraq had been noticed, and this aroused the interest of a great many countries, including the United States, which was rapidly becoming a nation on wheels. Intervention by the State Department helped secure participation by American companies in the development of the oil in British-mandated Iraq and other countries in the area.

[5] A summary of the events leading to the agreements can be found in Charles F. Stewart, *The Economy of Morocco: 1912–1962* (Cambridge, Mass.: Harvard University Press, 1964), pp. 39–53.

The history of empire since 1945 has been one of dissolution. Perhaps the British left India more willingly (or less unwillingly) than the French left Indo-China or Algeria, but both left. Naked force in diplomacy was no longer in vogue either. Operations by British and French forces at Suez in 1956 met with widespread disapproval and caused the fall of the Eden government in Britain. When the U.S. marines landed in strife-torn Lebanon two years later, oil was obviously as much involved as previously in the diplomacy of the Near East; the military operation itself, however, was carried out with considerable official embarrassment. If it is ever possible to conduct "gunboat diplomacy" with circumspection, then the United States involvement in Lebanon is a classic example.[6]

Perhaps it can be said that both political and commercial colonialism burnt themselves out. The obvious possibilities for profit were quickly seized upon; the marginal possibilities that might have been utilized later were forgotten as the costs of colonialism rose. The hewers of wood and drawers of water had observed benefits reserved to others under the *pacte colonial* and wanted to share them; they provided the proletarian muscle for independence movements, while restless local intellectuals provided the ideology. The fusion of revolutionary ideas with mass discontent meant that no amount of force could maintain the peace; as Marshal Bugeaud observed in the Algeria of the 1840's, "You can defeat an army, but you cannot defeat a people in arms." Marx would doubtless have agreed.

THE POST-COLONIAL ERA

The colonial past inevitably weighs on the relationships between ex-masters and ex-subjects, but life must go on. The continuing need of developed and under-developed countries to trade with each other may allow the durable businessman to play his timeless role of supplier of the material things of life and, as innovator, the role of subversive of the status quo. Innovation, of course, implies the introduction of disequilibrium into an otherwise static system, in this case an economic and social system, that is calculated to reflect favorably in a firm's profit and loss statement. But societies also have such accounting in a welfare sense, and it stands to reason that any change introduced by an individual businessman, if it is to be durable, must likewise show a positive effect on the receiving society's "profit and loss" statement. For this reason, the businessman investing abroad today should heed Jean Cocteau's caveat of "knowing how far to go without going too far".[7] One might add "too soon," for the past is filled with the failures of those

---

[6] It is also testimony that a watered-down policy produces watered-down results since, during the occupation, a pro-American government gave way to a neutral regime. Even more circumspection, of course, is represented by Guatemala in 1954 where apparently the Central Intelligence Agency was substituted for troops. The Dominican Republic of Juan Bosch represented the use of both.

[7] Quoted by David Rockefeller, "What Private Enterprise Means to Latin America," *Foreign Affairs*, Vol. 44 (April, 1966), p. 413. Accommodation of the firm to an "alien" environment is the subject of an excellent treatise by Richard D. Robinson, *International Business Policy* (New York: Holt, Rinehart and Winston, 1964).

who went too far too soon. Successful transition of a new idea to reality requires a keen sense of timing.

The Implications of Sovereignty and the Need for the West

The really crucial difference between the colonial era and the present one is that former dependencies are now sovereignties, albeit often shaky. While the implications of sovereignty are many for the foreign investor (some will be dealt with subsequently), the most fundamental is that change must now be accepted voluntarily by the host people.[8] No longer can a plan for innovation be rammed through at the point of a foreign bayonet. Negotiation must be substituted for force, even though the history of force always remains as a factor coloring the course negotiations follow.

While the legacies of the colonial past—overpopulation, illiteracy, and undernourishment—provide continuity between the past era of colonization and the decolonization of the present and future, difference between rule by a mother country and home rule represents a discontinuity. The problems may remain essentially the same, but the differences in purposes, actions, and aspirations between colonial administrators and nationalist leaders fundamentally alter the way the problems are viewed.

The bitter aftertaste of colonialism has found its way into the nationalist ideology of many countries, and a suspicion of neocolonialism runs through many of their contacts with the more developed western powers. At the same time, unstable but sovereign governments are caught up in the difficult search for consensus on national goals. These factors lead not to the calculable risks that businessmen can usually tolerate and often welcome but to uncertainties that they (as do we all) abhor.

The situation in the new nations is further complicated, but perhaps brightened, by the insistent demand of the poor—who usually constitute the majority of the population—for a better life. The intensity of this demand is unlikely to diminish soon, for the disparity between the rich and poor nations is widening rather than narrowing. The western businessman has the technology and capital to help, and it is clearly in the interest of the western powers (especially the United States) that he give it, for the world is not likely to achieve lasting stability while it remains one-third affluent and two-thirds destitute.

The transfer of capital and know-how from the haves to the have-nots is imperative, but how to achieve the transfer is not so evident. Foreign-aid programs represent one philosophy or approach to the problem. Coincidental in many new nations with the departure of the last troops to the motherland has been the arrival of an American foreign-aid mission. Although the emphasis of our foreign aid has varied over the years and among countries, its fundamental focus has been on providing infrastructure—dams, roads, and education—that will improve

---

[8] Conrad M. Arensberg and Arthur H. Niehoff, *Introducing Social Change* (Chicago: Aldine, 1964), p. 2.

the climate for both local and foreign private investment. If the public sector leads in a meaningful way, then private interests, motivated by profit, will naturally follow, or so the argument goes. Yet, if one compares the volume and direction of our foreign aid on the one hand and of direct investment abroad by U.S. firms on the other, it is not difficult to detect a divergence. While government aid is concentrated in the developing countries, the bulk of private investment is flowing to Canada and western Europe. If investment in petroleum facilities is excluded from the total picture, then the divergence is even more striking.

No doubt the reasons for the divergence are multiple, but one is especially to the point here. The old colonial arrangements provided that the western business-man, under the aegis of his own government, would supply management, capital, and know-how, while the colonial country would provide natural resources, labor, and markets. The businessman's investment would be long term, and he would himself be *active* in its management. However, governments jealous of their newly won sovereignty clearly prefer that the investor be *passive* in the matter of management, although they would welcome long-term capital and know-how. The difference lies in the degree of control the businessman is to exercise over his investment. The less control he can exercise, the less willing he is to invest; ac-cordingly, in many countries the volume of investment forthcoming has become a function of the terms offered concerning control.

The new countries would have powerful competitors for foreign investment funds even if they were to grant very liberal terms concerning control. The rapid economic growth of Europe—spurred by the formation of the supranational European Economic Community—has created a very attractive investment situa-tion where payout periods are reasonably clear. Fast-rising incomes, a rapidly developing middle class with tastes similar to those in the United States, and statistics that allow meaningful forecasts are present in Europe and woefully absent in the developing countries.

Attractive investment possibilities are not lacking in the developing countries; they are only more difficult to ferret out. "Differences in languages, cultures, currencies, and economic and political ideologies all present insuperable problems for the timid and unseeing, and at least formidable problems for the determined and discerning. To the latter, of course, go the rewards for problem solving. . . ."[9]

THE BUSINESSMAN AS A CULTURAL CATALYST

In the last analysis, the fundamental difference among the peoples of the world is cultural. But culture is not immutable, and man has always borrowed "new things, ideas, and techniques from his neighbor, whether this neighbor is of his own kind or from another culture."[10] The remainder of this essay will focus primarily, though not exclusively, on the international businessman as conveyor

[9] Charles F. Stewart, ed., *The Global Businessman: Readings from Fortune* (New York: Holt, Rinehart and Winston, 1966), p. iii.
[10] Arensberg and Niehoff, *op. cit.*, p. 2.

of culture. For the businessman clearly is a conveyor of culture, or a cultural catalyst: he lends his own culture and borrows the culture of others.

The context in which the international businessman enters as a catalyst is schematized in Table 1. The diagram indicates that a hypothetical American firm, Intercontinental Products, Inc., of New York, has committed investment funds to an alien environment (which, borrowing from the field of ecology, we have called the "habitat") by incorporating a subsidiary, Intercontinental Products, S.A., under the laws of the host country to manufacture and to sell a line of consumer porducts. Sharing the habitat with the subsidiary are the most important elements to which the company must relate in carrying on its business—the host government, competitors, suppliers, and consumers. Outside the habitat per se, but having an influence on it, are the U.S. government and the stateside parent of the subsidiary.

Table 1.

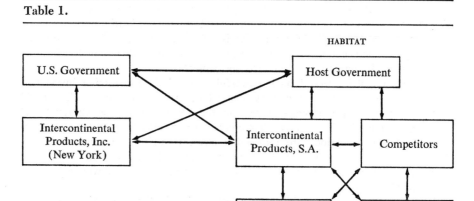

HABITAT

No society is ever completely static, but, for the sake of illustration, the elements of the habitat are assumed, before the incorporation of the U.S. subsidiary, to be in approximate equilibrium; their character is unchanging. The insertion of the American subsidiary upsets the equilibrium of the habitat, thereby unleashing a series of interactions among the elements. This interactive process, depicted by the arrows, represents a search for a new equilibrium among the elements, hopefully one that will include the new American firm. The new equilibrium will be reached through accommodating cultural changes in the character of each element; the final result for each changed element will be a new habitat.[11]

[11] In the case of the American firm as one element, there would also be an internal equilibrium in the matter of organization. With the environment (other elements) also in equilibrium, problems and decisions would be routine within the organization,

The relationships among the elements in Table 1 are simultaneous, but it is necessary to examine them one by one. First we shall look at parent-subsidiary relations and then U.S. government relations with the parent and the host government. Later the relations wholly within the box will be discussed.

Parent-Subsidiary Relations

Intercontinental Products, Inc., is set up as a multinational company, an increasingly popular form of organization for firms with significant overseas business.[12] The organizational chart for the company is shown in Table 2.

In contrast to the traditional company, which has an international division responsible for all the company's overseas business, Intercontinental has organized its headquarters on a worldwide geographical basis. All the operations of company subsidiaries in a particular region of the world are controlled by a unit for that region. (In Table 2, only the subsidiaries for Latin America are shown.) The regional units are headed by vice presidents at headquarters with co-equal status who report directly to the president. U.S. domestic operations are controlled by the North American unit.

Conflict between global and national interests. Theoretically at least, the president and staff have divested themselves of their former preoccupation with the U.S. domestic market or some other national market and are constantly on the alert for sales and investment opportunities wherever they may arise in the world. All headquarters decisions are reached through weighing multinational alternatives; all thinking, in essence, is "anational." The aim of the headquarters personnel is to effect an optimum worldwide allocation of all the company's capital, people, and other resources in order to maximize the company's near-and-long-term advantage.[13] It would be difficult, ruling out business opportunities in outer space, to think any bigger.

While the global businessman did not invent the concept of one world, he is perhaps its chief supporter today. Yet he lives in a world of nations, and this gives rise to a conflict. Nationalism is evident on the organization chart in the form of

the ideal setting for the bureaucrat. It would be more correct to say that there would be a *tendency* toward equilibrium within the habitat and each element, since it is a function of leadership (our global businessman) ". . . to galvanize an organization and to prevent the equilibrium from becoming an end in itself." Henry A. Kissinger, *Nuclear Weapons and Foreign Policy* (Garden City, N.Y.: Doubleday, 1958), pp. 248–49.

[12] There is a growing literature on the multinational company. One of the pioneering articles is Gilbert H. Clee and Alfred di Scipio, "Creating a World Enterprise," *Harvard Business Review,* Vol. 37 (November–December, 1959), pp. 77–89. There is also a growing number of companies that are moving toward organization along multinational lines. See Enid B. Lovell, *The Changing Role of the International Executive* (New York: National Industrial Conference Board, 1966). An insight into the problems involved can be found in Richard D. Robinson, *International Management* (New York: Holt, Rinehart and Winston, 1967).

[13] For details, see Dennis J. O'Connell and John J. Benson, " 'Sourcing' Abroad for Domestic Profit," *Harvard Business Review,* Vol. 41 (March–April, 1963), pp. 87–94.

Table 2.

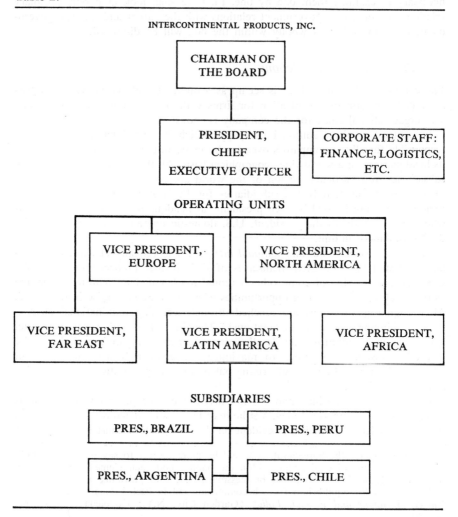

INTERCONTINENTAL PRODUCTS, INC.

the subsidiaries organized by country, often incorporated under the host country's laws. It is naturally even more evident in the daily operations of the company. Take the matter of investment opportunity. It might well be, for example, that earnings arising in the Argentine subsidiary could earn a greater profit if they were used to expand plants in Chile, or even South Korea, rather than being plowed back into the Argentine subsidiary itself. To the parent company, the shift of capital would be good business; to the Argentine government, however, it would represent a drain of investment funds and a foreign exchange burden. At best hostile politicians would call the shift of funds a "capital drain" and at worst imperialist exploitation of the country.

Similar conflicts can arise in the allocation of people. It may make good business sense to center all research and development in one or a very few countries, with a consequent concentration of scientific talent. Politicians in the excluded countries would characterize the company policy as a "brain drain," however, while they watched some of their relatively few scientific people, most probably educated at government expense, emigrate to the favored countries.[14]

Finally, it is quite conceivable that the raw material sources and potential consumers for the company's products are distributed around the world in such a fashion that the company would prefer to concentrate certain phases of the production process in particular countries. Thus, Saudi Arabia has extensive petroleum resources but a very small market for refined petroleum products. Rather than refining any oil in Saudi Arabia, the multinational company might prefer to export crude oil, refine it in another country, and return the small quantity of refined products needed by the few consumers in Arabia. To local opinion makers, however, a policy of this sort rings unmistakably of the *pacte colonial*.[15] In all of these cases, there is an apparent divergence between what is good for the multinational company and what is good for the individual nations in which it operates.

The conflict between the interests of the host country and the multinational company is likely to be fought out within the ranks of the company itself if local businessmen or the host government are allowed to participate in the ownership of the subsidiary, whether on a majority or a minority basis. Local participants in a joint venture with a multinational corporation are likely to look with considerable disfavor on the corporation's export of its share of dividends when opportunities for local expansion appear very attractive. (Note that the local participants are making their calculations in absolute terms, while the parent management is thinking relatively in terms of alternative opportunities elsewhere.) The local participants would also reflect the host country's position in our example of deciding where to locate research and refining facilities. One result of the divided loyalties of the local participants in a joint venture may be that company secrecy, often highly valued by multinational management, is lost.[16]

[14] Between 1949 and 1961, approximately 43,000 scientists and engineers entered the United States, and many came from the less developed countries. At the same time, over 90 per cent of the Asian students in the United States did not intend to return home. See "Education and Economic Growth," *World Business*, No. 3 (November, 1966), p. 15.

[15] For a treatment of the Mexican reaction to such a policy, see Wendell C. Gordon, *The Expropriation of Foreign-Owned Property in Mexico* (Washington: American Council on Public Affairs, 1941).

[16] This is true particularly when government is the partner. See David E. Lilienthal, *The Multinational Corporation* (New York: Development and Resources Corporation, 1960). For a survey of business opinion about joint ventures, see Karen K. Bivens and Edith B. Lovell, *Joint Ventures with Foreign Partners* (New York: National Ind strial Conference Board, 1966).

Communication and control. Since time immemorial, the businessman has been concerned with effective control over supplies and markets, both actual and potential. The ability of the global corporation to control these aspects of its operations is attenuated by the world's fragmentation into national parts, each with a sovereign government able to exert great pressure on that fragment of the corporation within its jurisdiction. This sharing of control over the company's operations may frequently benefit one nation or another, but to the extent that corporate welfare multinationally is coextensive with world social welfare, global sub-optimization is probably the result.[17]

Even if a subsidiary is 100 per cent owned and controlled by the parent company, there is still plenty of room left for conflict between headquarters personnel and those in the field. The head of the subsidiary company, for example, seems to be in a naturally equivocal position. He seems to have a great deal of authority; he heads a distinct legal entity, the subsidiary corporation, and very often he is charged with profit responsibility for his operations. Unlike the usual corporate president, however, the president of a subsidiary often has little or no control over several strategic factors that can greatly affect his profit record. Transfer pricing is a case in point. Overall company policy may determine the prices at which he buys from and sells to other units of the enterprise, and the policy adopted can either so widen or narrow his gross margin that his own efforts to improve his profit-and-loss statement in other aspects of his operation seem futile. Even if a fair transfer-pricing policy is adopted, the president is not responsible for it, and he is denied a chance to do better on the open market. Cost allocation among the subsidiaries of technical services supplied by the parent or distribution of research and development expenditures can also be a bone of contention. While accountants may claim that these problems are theirs, human relations are deeply involved as well.

Interference by the parent does not stop with the determination of the subsidiary's buying prices for materials and selling prices for finished products; it can also extend to cost performance within the firm. Many a subsidiary, for example, has been slowed down by incompetent personnel forced upon it by headquarters management that, locked in by a self-imposed no-discharge policy, has assigned its misfits (by definition expensive) to the Siberia of the foreign subsidiaries.

The primary problem in parent-subsidiary relations is one of communication. On the one hand, how can headquarters personnel be made to appreciate the real and subtle problems encountered by subsidiary management in its particular habitat? On the other hand, how can those in the subsidiary be persuaded to think globally when their responsibility is encompassed by national frontiers? Improvement in communication is surely the answer, but saying this does not lessen the difficulty of achieving it.

[17] This notion is merely an extension of the argument applied to tariffs that restrictive action by one country can enhance that country's welfare at the expense of the rest of the world. The classic article is by Tibor Scitovsky, "A Reconsideration of the Theory of Tariffs," in Howard S. Ellis and Lloyd A. Metzler, eds., *Readings in the Theory of International Trade* (Philadelphia: Blakiston, 1949), pp. 358–89.

The Role of the U. S. Government

Since the time of the Pilgrims, the international operations of American businessmen have been a subject of governmental interest.[18] Government measures have
been passed both to help and to hinder business in pursuit of its international objectives. We saw earlier in this essay that during the nineteenth century the
government intervened militarily in several instances where its citizens' commercial interests and personal security were threatened abroad and, in other
instances, engaged in international negotiations and treaties to safeguard the ability
of American businessmen to compete.[19] With the Roosevelt era and the New
Deal, a great deal of domestic legislation was passed that restricted the businessman in his activities, but the Reciprocal Trade Agreements Act, by providing a
basis for bargaining down tariffs and other barriers with trading partners throughout the world, served to increase his scope for international action.[20] The successor
Trade Expansion Act of 1962 went further in the same direction. The participation of an American delegation in negotiations with the members of the General
Agreement on Tariffs and Trade, although without the official sanction of the
Congress, has also contributed to a freer climate for trade.

As government promotion of greater participation by Americans in world
trade is not a new phenomenon, neither is the long and inhibiting reach of the
antitrust laws. While only a limited number of cases involving the antitrust laws
and international operations has ever come to trial, the very dearth of relevant
court opinions adds to the uncertainties in making international business arrangements, among them licensing agreements that, by their very nature, have some
element of restricting access to a process or product. The test of whether a particular arrangement or act violates the antitrust laws appears to be whether or not
it affects the course of domestic commerce or impairs the ability of other U.S. firms
to compete abroad with the offending company.[21] The test is too imprecise,
however, to be much help in weighing the possible antitrust implications of most
arrangements.

The uncertainty of the global businessman is compounded when he must
operate in countries that have compulsory cartel membership or less formal ar-

---

[18] For a comparative view of several western countries, including the United States,
see Andrew Schonfeld, *Modern Capitalism* (London: Oxford University Press, 1965).
[19] Many concessions granted by governments to foreign firms contain the so-called
Calvo Clause, however, which provides that, in case of dispute, the firm will not appeal
to its own government for diplomatic intervention. See Roy Blough, *International
Business: Environment and Adaptation* (New York: McGraw-Hill, 1966), p. 262.
[20] The U.S. negotiators were in a position to offer extensive tariff reductions in return for
similar favors, since the Hawley-Smoot Act of 1930 had set the highest level of tariffs
in the history of the country. An account of the politics of foreign trade in recent years
can be found in Raymond A. Bauer *et al., American Business and Public Policy* (New
York: Atherton, 1964).
[21] The classic study on international application of the antitrust laws is Kingman
Brewster, Jr., *Antitrust and American Business Abroad* (New York: McGraw-Hill,
1958). Ludwig Erhard made the case for competition rather than a return to Germany's
prewar cartelization in *Prosperity Through Competition* (New York: Macmillan, 1958).

rangements of the sort prohibited by the U.S. laws. The multinational firm is then caught in a conflict of laws. At the opposite extreme, uncertainty is not eased when American-type laws are adopted in areas where nothing very similar existed before, because precedents are lacking to show the businessman how the new laws will be applied. Articles 85 and 86 of the Treaty of Rome (which established the European Economic Community) are an example; they prohibit the establishment of some new cartels, but their application to older national cartels is not clear. The disinterested patriot may cheer that the American ideology of promoting competition is being grafted on foreign roots, but the operating executive who must live with its development may be forgiven if he takes a dimmer view of the process.

Contemporary measures. Trade negotiations and antitrust applications have a long history in America; recently they have been complemented by a variety of government measures meant to influence the size and location of direct investment abroad, among them the investment guarantee program and tax provisions providing advantageous treatment for income from certain foreign sources. Under the terms of the investment guarantee program, the U.S. government will, for a premium, protect the foreign investments of America firms against losses due to nationalization, expropriation, inconvertibility of earnings, and certain other risks. The federal tax law grants American corporate taxpayers a credit—which they may use to offset tax liabilities incurred in the U.S.—for any taxes they have had to pay to other governments and in the case of the developing countries allows the corporation to defer paying its taxes until earnings are repatriated to the United States. Finally, the government has entered into bilateral treaties with several countries to avoid double taxation of the same income by the signatories.

The investment guarantee program is for the modern investor a substitute for the military force of the prewar years and is certainly more benign from the viewpoint of public policy. The deferral of taxes on earnings from investments in developing countries, while perhaps a discrimination against investments in developed nations where U.S. taxes are due when profits are earned, is really a commendable attempt to make private investment follow the lead of our aid programs.

The U.S. government has brought other forms of legislation and "moral suasion" to bear to direct and control the volume of American trade and investment abroad. Perhaps the clearest example of the direction of trade consists in the government's embargoes on commercial dealings with mainland China, North Korea, and North Vietnam, which have been in effect for many years. This firm policy was extended in at least one instance to another nation when an American automobile manufacturer was "advised" by Washington to forbid its Canadian subsidiary to export trucks to China, even though Canada maintained no similar embargo. The sale of strategic materials to other communist countries has also been restricted, although the definition of what is "strategic" has varied in the light of such circumstances as the changing East-West trade policy of political allies who are also competitors and oscillations of temperature in the Cold War. Probably trade direction of this type will diminish in the future. Despite the U.S. involvement in

Vietnam, a warming trend in relations with eastern Europe and the Soviet Union has been discernible, which leads one to suspect that, once the war is concluded, East-West commercial relations will considerably improve. They may also extend far beyond mere trade, as is already evidenced by a new type of East-West commercial partnership or joint venture.

Called "co-production," the new system works as follows. A western capitalist enterprise brings to the partnership technical assistance, machinery, and world markets while the eastern state-owned enterprise contributes relatively cheap skilled labor, local capital needs, raw materials, and local markets. The output of the new factory is subsequently distributed between the partners according to an agreed formula for sale in their particular markets.[22] The arrangement permits a mutually beneficial combination of complementary resources from East and West and, at the same time, permits the two partners to maintain their separate ideologies. A real clash between the two would come, not in the plant where technology knows no ideology, but in distribution and marketing. But the division of output between the partners eliminates the possibility of conflict.

Government attempts to control international capital flows have resulted from the serious balance-of-payments difficulties evidenced by our loss of gold in every year since 1957. The government has concentrated on both short- and long-term investment with the goal of slowing down the capital flow rate of increase. The so-called Interest Equalization Tax is designed to narrow the gap between interest rates in the United States and the higher rates abroad; American investors are thereby discouraged from placing their funds in foreign securities. The flow of direct investment overseas was reduced sharply in 1965 by the introduction of a "voluntary" program administered by the Department of Commerce, which asked firms to help improve the balance of payments by (1) slowing the increase in investment abroad and (2) stepping up repatriation of earnings. Both requests led U.S. firms to enter the already overcrowded capital markets abroad to obtain funds needed for expansion and thus caused a rise in foreign interest rates, much to the displeasure of local firms also pressed for funds. Generally speaking, American companies have far greater financial capacity than foreign firms, so their loan applications look better to foreign bankers than those of their own compatriots. For world businessmen, there is only a little consolation in the oft-repeated official statements that these American measures are only temporary and will be removed once payments are brought into balance.

These latter-day measures, with their overtones of an earlier mercantilism, make it difficult for an American multinational manager to be simultaneously a good businessman and a good U.S. citizen. At times he is clearly forced to choose. For example, in 1961 the management of the Ford Motor Company decided

---

[22] For details on this and other forms of technological exchange, see Emile Benoit "East-West Business Corporation," *The New Republic* (February 18, 1967). Confined largely to European companies thus far, increasing American interst in co-production ventures is demonstrated by the pooling of efforts by the International Basic Economy Corporation (Rockefeller-controlled) and the Tower Corporation (Eaton-controlled) of Cleveland to seek similar arrangements in eastern Europe.

for good, sufficient, and urgent business reasons that it ought to propose to buy the minority interests of Ford of England; Washington, for good, sufficient, and urgent balance-of-payments reasons, asked the Company not to take the step. In this dilemma, Ford management chose to follow its business instincts.[23]

The example of Ford is probably the exception rather than the rule; most American companies, willingly or not, become instruments of American foreign, political, and economic policy. As such, they cannot always buy, sell, and invest in the best market on the best possible terms. Competition is thereby impaired, and the longer the measures restricting competition remain in effect, the more likely it is that permanent changes in structure will result. Short-term measures have a way of producing long-term effects, often other than those intended. If the elements of contemporary American foreign economic policy are consistent and rational, they have these characteristics not within the context of an economic ideology but of expediency.

United States–Host Government Relationships

Relationships between the governments of the United States and the host country are of course fundamentally political, but they have economic aspects. Although altruism and a sense of obligation to the poorer two-thirds of the world undoubtedly play some part in American foreign-aid programs, members of Congress are much more likely to be swayed in hearings on foreign economic aid by arguments that claim that foreign aid makes a positive contribution to the political aims of our foreign policy.[24] Furthermore, except in the cases of the United Arab Republic and India where the Soviet Union and the United States have competed in giving aid, the promised political results of aid seem to have been fully realized. The new nations often take a neutralist stance, but true independence in political affairs must be based on economic independence. Economic independence means, in turn, "that market ties of any country with the outside world are ideally so numerous that no single tie can inhibit freedom and flexibility of economic and political action."[25] Few of the developing countries come even remotely close to qualifying as economically independent, particularly those whose balance of payments are shored up and whose planned long-term growth rates are partly sustained by U.S. aid programs. The practice of tying aid whenever

[23] For an elaboration of this story, see "Ford Buys a Subsidiary," in James M. Kuhn and Ivar Berg, *Values in a Business Society: Issues and Analyses* (New York: Harcourt, Brace & World, 1968), pp. 87–92. A striking example of how the actions of one firm can affect a nation's balance of payments arose in Australia a number of years ago, when the Holden Company proposed to remit dividends to its U.S. parent, General Motors. If the Australian government had allowed the transfers (which it did not), stringent measures to conserve foreign exchange would have been necessary. See Edith T. Penrose, "Foreign Investment and the Growth of the Firm," *Economic Journal,* Vol. 66 (June, 1958), pp. 220–35.

[24] Congressional debates today are much more sophisticated than the one in 1951 over whether to send surplus stocks of agricultural products to a starving India while Nehru was pursuing a neutralist course in the Cold War.

[25] Stewart, *The Economy of Morocco,* p. 163.

possible to American exports in itself pulls the country into the dollar orbit. While tying may produce a desired neutral effect on our balance of payments, aid recipients are often extremely reluctant to accept it. The explanation of their attitude is probably that more attractive sources of supply are to be found elsewhere. To the extent that the country receiving financial help cannot expend the funds in the best market wherever in the world that may be, then the U.S. taxpayer has received less return per aid dollar.[26]

Perhaps paradoxically, the uncertain nature of American aid from one year to the next serves as a further binding on the recipients. Congress, always jealous of its prerogative to make the annual appropriations for annual expenditures, refuses to make commitments beyond the magic fiscal year, but economic development is by definition long term. Consequently, uncertainties as to the size of aid over several years lead to a caution by aid administrators in recipient countries that is akin to the bankers' caveat against borrowing short-term and lending long. The leverage exercised by Congress thereby is undoubted, but whether it is good for either party to an aid agreement from an economic viewpoint can be seriously questioned, again in terms of return per aid dollar.

That Congress looks beyond economic, through the aid program, to political and social development as well is evidenced by the adoption of Title IX of the Foreign Assistance Act of 1961, as amended, which concerns the "Utilization of Democratic Institutions in Development":

> In carrying out programs authorized in this chapter, emphasis shall be placed on assuring maximum participation in the task of economic development on the part of the people of the developing countries, through the encouragement of democratic private and local governmental institutions.

To the extent that the Agency for International Development is successful in promoting democratic institutions, the subsidiary is likely to be affected in those ways that are well known to management in the United States.

Host Government–Subsidiary Relationships

While the headquarters of the multinational corporation and the United States government push for change abroad (in ways that do not always indicate a mutuality of purpose) the real impetus for change comes from elements within the habitat (see Table 1). The interaction between the host government and the subsidiary is particularly crucial.

As part of a national policy to reduce dependence on other countries through diversification of their own economies, many governments have encouraged multinational corporations to establish local enterprises that will provide substitutes for imports, especially imported consumer products. Examples of the projects desired include the local manufacture of textiles, drugs, certain chemicals, and even the

[26] The same holds true for the requirement that aid cargoes be moved in American ships that have to charge considerably higher freight rates than their foreign competitors do over the same routes, even though they are beneficiaries of building and operating subsidies.

local assembly of autos. In order to convince the multinational corporation to come in, the host government must offset the disadvantages of small markets and the uncertainties associated with political instability by making concessions, i.e., by surrendering a portion of its sovereignty over the foreign enterprise. High tariffs, import quotas or embargoes, tax relief, and prohibition of competing enterprises are favorite devices used to attract foreign capital; they all relate to the fundamental fact that markets in the new nations are narrow. While the United States' domestic market may be large enough to permit several firms to operate efficiently in the same industry, the relatively narrow market of the developing country may mean that, given the same technology, only a single firm can operate there efficiently. In such a case the single firm would have a "natural monopoly" in the developing country such as is ordinarily associated with public utilities in the United States.[27]

What the sovereign power gives, however, it also can take away. Many of the concessions offered by developing countries today are not dissimilar to those granted in the United States during the nineteenth century to what turned out to be public utilities, particularly the railroads. Ultimately, as history shows, reciprocity for concessions appeared in the form of regulation of rates and service. It is just possible that this history might repeat itself elsewhere.

A side effect of the establishment of a subsidiary in a new nation is that it constitutes one more independent organization to serve as a buffer between the state and individual or family. In highly developed industrial societies, between the family and the state there lies a host of intermediate organizations of which the corporation and the labor union would represent but two instances. In the less developed countries the number and variety of such organizations is quite limited. The effective use of modern technology requires intermediate organizations, however, since the family is too small to operate every form of business and the regular government is inappropriate. Recognition of the inappropriateness of the government as a business manager is found in the establishment in many countries of state-owned corporations with separate identities and a responsibility to show a profit, and in Soviet Union's increasing decentralization of decision-making in industry since the death of Stalin. Another virtue of intermediate organizations is that they encourage the growth of a substantial middle class, a potent force for economic, political, and social stability.[28]

[27] Technically, a natural monopoly is a situation where average unit costs of production of a single firm are still falling when the limits of the *entire* market are reached. If two firms are in the market, then average unit costs of production for each would be higher than in the case of the single enterprise.

[28] A great deal of instability, however, can occur in this process. The elimination or downgrading of old organizational forms incident to the establishment of new ones is bound to result in shifts of the power positions of countless individual citizens. Though the society as a whole may gain from the change, old power positions are not surrendered easily. For opposing views of this process, see Paul A. Baran, *The Political Economy of Growth* (New York: Monthly Review Press, 1957), and Clark Kerr *et al., Industrialism and Industrial Man* (Cambridge, Mass.: Harvard University Press, 1960).

By simply being a good citizen, a subsidiary also has beneficial effects on the host country. American bankers abroad have in many cases set informal standards of behavior and performance adopted via the "demonstration effect" by local bankers. In several cases, these same bankers have helped governments write new national banking laws, while resisting the temptation to add provisions favorable to themselves.[29]

Other Relationships

The foreign subsidiary must necessarily relate to other elements in the habitat, among them its raw materials suppliers, labor representatives, competing firms, and above all consumers.

Suppliers. As part of a policy of corporate good citizenship, as well as a desire to increase productivity, many subsidiary managements rely as much as possible on local suppliers for their needs, including their needs for labor and management itself. Implicit in this policy is a rejection of the economics of "what is" and the conscious creation of "what can be." For a technically advanced multinational firm, there are few external economies in many developing countries—no labor force already trained in modern skills, no suppliers of intermediate products capable of meeting quality and delivery standards so necessary to effective mass production, and no really reliable services such as good rail transportation. The gap caused by these missing external economies can be bridged by the foreign firm itself, however.

Upgrading of labor skills occupies a first priority, particularly for industries with advanced and complex technologies. An outstanding example is the IBM-World Trade Corporation, whose demand for highly skilled manpower appears insatiable. The limited supply of such manpower abroad therefore looms as the ultimate constraint on IBM-World Trade's expansion abroad. In order to circumvent it, the company has established training schools at strategic places around the world, including one in Nigeria.[30] Add to this training the company policy of using local nationals wherever and whenever possible at the highest levels of management, and IBM-World Trade becomes a very attractive addition to any national economy. Any lingering doubts about the company are likely to disappear before the attractiveness of its product. A good argument can be made—and this company has made it—that the computer is a most productive substitute for the missing labor skills. The only negative aspect in the IBM "package," from the host country's point of view, is the company's insistence on 100 per cent ownership of its subsidiaries; but the other positive elements more than outweigh this defect.

The establishment of a new subsidiary in an underdeveloped country may also lead to the creation of new independent enterprises there or to the expansion of

---

[29] Perhaps the oil companies have had less success on this score, at least in Argentina and Libya, where the petroleum laws that they helped establish have been drastically revised in directions highly favorable to the governments.

[30] See Bartlett Harvey, "The World Impact of American Technology," *Annals of the American Academy of Political and Social Science,* Vol. 366 (July, 1966), pp. 41–50.

existing ones. An oil company's policy to restrict itself as much as possible to the extraction and transportation of petroleum, for example, led its management to aid in the development of local entrepreneurs to supply auxiliary services on a contract basis. The aid was not only financial but also took the form of assistance in setting up accounting procedures, personnel policies, and other elements associated with modern management. The company, in lending capital and know-how, helped to assure itself of quality products or services delivered on schedule, while the country gained in terms of increased incomes and productivity.[31]

A subsidiary need not be in the industrial sector to disseminate modern management techniques via its supply needs. Sears, Roebuck has had considerable success in Latin America in developing local suppliers of most of the products it sells. With a program reminiscent of the putting-out system employed in England before the Industrial Revolution, Sears has reached back to suppliers with financial and technical assistance. Unlike those English merchants, however, Sears has not insisted that the company be the sole buyer of their output. On the contrary, Sears' management has encouraged its suppliers to develop other customers and, coincidentally, has opened up sources of quality products for retail competitors.[32]

Competition. The biggest impact of the U.S. subsidiary on its local competitors does not come vertically through suppliers but horizontally in the marketplace. Sears is again an example. Locally owned department stores were forced to adopt modern merchandising methods in order to survive, yet the arrival of Sears did not spell the demise of small shops with a limited product line. Clustered around Sears in Mexico City, for example, are a number of little stores, each specializing in products for which Sears has a department. The Mexican shopper, then, has a choice of suppliers not unlike that of his counterpart in the contemporary large shopping centers in the United States.

Many U.S. subsidiaries choose not to wage unlimited competition with local companies. Backed by what appear locally to be the huge financial and technological resources of its North American parent, the subsidiary is seen as having the awesome potential of sweeping all competitors from the market. This "technology gap," a phrase heard as often in Europe as in the developing countries, can fuel the chauvinism of the host country's government, whether it is headed by a DeGaulle or by a Nasser. Under these circumstances, management may find "soft competition" the better part of wisdom.

Consumers. In many developing countries the majority of consumers are possessed, to use Adlai Stevenson's famous phrase, with "rising expectations," but these expectations are usually unmatched by as rapidly rising incomes. The

[31] For a study of the impact of the Arabian-American Oil Company on the economy of Saudi Arabia, see Carleton S. Coon, "Operation Bultiste," in Peter Franck and Howard M. Teaf, eds., *Hands Across Frontiers* (Ithaca, N.Y.: Cornell University Press, 1955).

[32] An account of Sears' operations in Mexico can be found in Richardson Wood and Virginia Keyes, *Sears, Roebuck de Mexico, S.A.* (Washington: National Planning Association, 1953). For a broader view of contracting-out, see Felicia J. Deyrup, "Contract Production in Underdeveloped Countries," *Social Research*, Vol. 23 (July, 1956), pp. 171–85.

gap is at once a further source of political discontent and a challenge to the ingenuity of marketing people to offer quality products at prices people can afford to pay. Recognition of this general gap should not obscure the marketer's vision of finer distinctions, however. In most developing countries, most products have not just one market but three, composed of people who can be classified as traditional, transitional, and modern.[33] The "traditional" consumer is probably rural, poor, illiterate, and bound by customs that have prevailed for centuries. His principal means of communication is oral, and the marketer trying to reach him must struggle with all the inefficiencies and imperfections associated with transmittal of information by word-of-mouth. The "transitional" consumer is likely to be a city dweller but of rural origin, semi-skilled, and with a curious combination of traditional and new ways, the last often visually identifiable by a mixture of traditional and western dress. The "modern" consumer is relatively well-to-do, in a professional or the civil service, literate—often in two or more languages—and dependent on electronic media for information. The modern consumer sets the style for his compatriots (the "demonstration effect"), so producers tend to design their products for him.

While the proportions of the three groups of consumers vary from one developing country to the next, all three types are always present. Reaching each of the groups requires a different marketing strategy—the use of different channels of distribution (the supermarket and the bazaar), price policies (fixed and haggling), packaging (large expensive and small cheap sizes), and advertising media (magazines and movie films).[34] While economic development can be regarded partly as a process of changing everyone's dependence on an oral system of communication for dependence on a modern media system, it can also be seen as a change in patterns of consumption and an upgrading of products within the patterns.

The management of a subsidiary can alter consumption patterns through its selling efforts, and, through close attention to quality control, it can offer a better product. The poor, least of all, can afford shoddy products. American subsidiaries that process food and drugs have by and large a good record of offering quality products, adverse publicity to the contrary, even in countries with no equivalent of our Food and Drug Administration. The same holds for subsidiaries that produce consumer durables. In many languages, the word for sewing machine is Singer, and the product is a must item in the dowry of even the poorest girl.

The American enterprise in a foreign habitat, then, must try to satisfy the present needs of consumers with a better product and help meet his "rising expectations." If it can do this effectively, it will have established itself in the habitat, and its

[33] The development and use of this typology can be found in Daniel Lerner, *The Passing of Traditional Society: Modernizing the Middle East* (New York: The Free Press, 1958).

[34] Although the "traditional" person cannot read, he can see, and the groups interested in maintaining the status quo in the developing countries ". . . would be better advised to burn movie films than to burn the works of Marx and Lenin." Arthur Smithies, "The Effect Abroad of American Private Enterprise," *Annals of the American Academy of Political and Social Science,* Vol. 366 (July, 1966), p. 52.

future will depend in part on the growth of output and income in the habitat as a whole. An enthusiasm for growth of this type is not the least important cultural characteristic that an established subsidiary can help transmit to a developing nation.

CONCLUSION

Some philosophers believe that economic principles ultimately order the course of human events because the population of the world continuously expands and makes imperative a more rational use of our limited resources. Unfortunately, no such necessity seems to be present in the world; man often chooses folly over rationality, less of the good things of life rather than more, war instead of peace. Whether economic rationality on a world scale is inevitable or not, however, most men would agree that it is desirable, and the multinational corporation, with its almost limitless possibilities as a disseminator of products, capital, and technology does seem an ideal mechanism for increasing it.

The multinational corporation can be an instrument for welding together the fragments of a divided world. The largest schism, of course, is that between the have and have-not nations; it represents an international form of dualism that, with modern communications, can no longer be ignored. Both parties are aware of the division and how people live "on the other side of the traces"; the resentment of the poorer nations mingles with their natonalism. Taken together, the schism and nationalism mean that the multinational corporation must chart a tortuous course in an insecure world.

In a sense, the multinational corporation adds to the insecurity of the modern world because, through its subsidiary, it tends to increase the differences between the values of a dual economy—modern versus traditional—within a given country.[35] The firm can offset this effect to some extent by being a good citizen, paying taxes, and obeying the laws. It can strive to adapt its products, organization, and people to a changing habitat, but the other elements must do the same if dualism is to be overcome. While the multinational corporation can participate, it cannot unilaterally solve the basic problem of the new nations, which is to create a rapidly expanding economy, the best safeguard for the interests of all.

Nationalism was a noble idea born in another age; today it is an outmoded concept, and the world must pay an awesome and rising price for clinging to it. The multinational corporation, in having to answer to many national masters, is able to serve none well. Yet the day of a true international community, regulated by international law, is not yet here. The global businessman is ahead of his time and far ahead of the politicians and diplomats who still think in terms of national interests. Whether he is a harbinger of a better age will only be known when

[35] For an expanded treatment of the dangers of dualism, see Barbara Ward, "The Western Corporation and the Underdeveloped Areas," in Melvin Anshen and George L. Bach, *Management and Corporations, 1985* (New York: McGraw-Hill, 1960), pp. 159–82.

the future has become history. The global businessman's command of technololgy, however, certainly gives him unparalleled power to be a subversive of the status quo and to make a better future possible. How well he uses his power will depend on his own wisdom and that of the other elements in the habitat abroad that have power to constrain his decisions, most notably the host government. Perfect cooperation will forever remain an ideal, but even an approximation would be a large contribution in the worldwide struggle for a better life, an endeavor worthy of the dignity of man and a positive outcome of culture contact in a shrinking world.

SELECTED READINGS

CHARLES F. STEWART AND GEORGE B. SIMMONS, *A Bibliography of International Business* (New York: Columbia University Press, 1964). This bibliography comprises a listing of some 8,000 books and articles having to do with international business in its economic, political, and social dimensions and in all major areas of the world. Included are both historical and contemporary materials.

HERBERT FEIS, *Europe the World's Banker, 1870–1914* (New York: W. W. Norton, 1965); PARKER T. MOON, *Imperialism and World Politics* (New York: Macmillan, 1947). Both of these works are classics in their field and should be read by any serious student of international business history. The author of the first book deals in considerable detail with the intricacies of direct investment abroad by Europeans during the height of colonization, while Moon is more concerned with the political aspects of the colonial process. High finance and big power politics marked the last half of the nineteenth century, as a reading of these books will show.

JOHN FAYERWEATHER, *Facts and Fallacies of International Business* (New York: Holt, Rinehart and Winston, 1962); RICHARD N. FARMER AND BARRY M. RICHMAN, *Comparative Management and Economic Progress* (Homewood, Ill.: Richard D. Irwin, 1965). Professor Fayerweather provides a good descriptive overview of recent developments in international business, and the reader will need little or no background in business or economics. Theoretical underpinnings for much of what the author argues are found in the second book cited. The work of Professors Farmer and Richman represents an attempt to place the business enterprise in the process of economic development.

A. A. FATOUROS, *Government Guarantees to Foreign Investors* (New York: Columbia University Press, 1962); CONRAD M. ARENSBERG AND ARTHUR H. NIEHOFF, *Introducing Social Change* (Chicago: Aldine, 1964). Much more specific than either Fayerweather or Farmer and Richman, the authors of these two books focus on two crucial areas of contemporary international business—business-government relationships and the social impact of change. In both books there are recorded outstanding failures as well as successes, and there is much to be learned from both.

chapter 5

BUSINESS AND
AMERICAN IDEOLOGY

IVAR BERG *is Associate Professor at the Columbia University Graduate School of Business.*

Surely one of the important aspects of the genius of American businessmen is that they are capable of adapting themselves to the multitude of forces around them. In the introduction to this volume the point was made that they have tempered some of the most unsettling competitive facets of capitalism and, to a certain extent, some aspects of our democratic structure that might otherwise have served to increase social equity at the expense of efficiency. While businessmen have been relatively successful in achieving their political goals, they have sometimes seemed to fail in their search for ideas and arguments to support their position. According to a group of distinguished social scientists, the "American business creed" reflects a good deal less sophistication than may be found in business behavior. They see this creed to be constructed from oversimplifications about political, social, economic, and hence ethical issues, conjured by the businessman as a psychological means to help him cope with what is described as his role strains.[1] The fact that his ideology largely condemns government, while his behavior reflects his real interests in subsidies, in restricting cutthroat competition, in a variety of regulatory measures, and in specific protective tariffs, for example, is regarded as evidence of the confusion engendered in the businessman's mind by the many conflicts in his social roles.

The contradiction may be more apparent than real, however. It is conceivable that the "American business creed" serves another function than the distinctly psychological one indicated by Dr. Sutton and his colleagues, a function not hampered by the creed's

---

[1] Francis X. Sutton, Seymour Harris, Carl Kaysen, and James Tobin, *The American Business Creed* (Cambridge, Mass.: Harvard University Press, 1956).

*loose construction and somewhat contradictory content. The func-
tion of the creed may well be not to prevent institutional changes
and reforms but simply to slow them down, thus giving the established business order time to find ways of adapting these modifications to serve this order—or at least not twist it out of shape. When
the business community has had easy access to the political machine,
as it did from 1952 to 1960 during the two terms of President
Eisenhower, it has not gone on the offensive to gain some positive
advantage; rather, it has simply encouraged further slackening in
the pace of change.*

*The following questions should be considered in the light of
discussion of ideology in the essay:*

*1. How may one account for the limited contribution of Amer-
ica's labor leaders to political and ideological debate in our business
society?*

*2. In this essay pointed reference is made to the neglect of "wel-
fare economics" and to the difficulty of estimating "social costs."
Identify as many gross categories as you think would be necessary
for estimating the "costs" of unemployment. Remember to consider in your effort the "costs" of programs designed to reduce unemployment.*

*3. A reader commented, after reading the essay, that the author
was obviously an "anti-intellectual," as proven by his discussion of
education. Formulate an argument in defense of the author's position and against the reader's charge.*

*4. What characteristics of American society might be viewed as
safeguarding employees against manipulation by employers versed
in the modern "behavioral sciences" and the ideological commitments they are alleged, implicitly, to serve?*

IVAR BERG \ ## BUSINESS IDEOLOGY
AND AMERICAN SOCIETY

The great ideological debates that enlivened the American prewar era seem
slightly irrelevant today.[1] The 1964 Presidential election, in which the ideologically
inclined Senator Barry Goldwater lost so decisively; the surprisingly close partnership in the 1960's of Administration Democrats and business leaders, once such
vociferous foes; the continuing efforts of modern Republicans to dissociate them-

[1] This is a revised and expanded version of materials that originally appeared in "Of
Social Change and the Businessman," *Columbia Journal of World Business,* Vol. 1
(Summer, 1966), pp. 121–30.

selves from "extremist groups"—all these signs point to a new kind of ideological peace, or somnolence. Few in America now call for a repeal of the twentieth century, much less the nineteenth; many seem ready to ratify all the Deals— New, Fair, and possibly Fast—that have passed for reform since the 1930's.

IDEOLOGICAL QUIESCENCE

Editorialists in the American business press continue to preach laissez faire, of course, but columnists in the same papers report wide support for a host of government activities that benefit corporations, the "widows and orphans" who own them, and the "new breed of professionals" who manage them. Businessmen form part of the consensus; many view with increasing favor America's efforts to solve its nagging domestic problems, especially when their corporations stand to benefit from federal and state programs designed to achieve that end.[2]

The American political left is also making peace with its cherished devils. It is almost embarrassing to observe the efforts of old-line planning enthusiasts to justify the Soviet bloc's recent preoccupation with the basic principles of cost accounting—long ignored in the U.S.S.R.—and decentralized management. While the American right seeks to make room for "individualism" in large collectivist bureaucracies,[3] the left is struggling to give theoretical status to "socialist profit."

The preoccupation of informed Americans with economic growth, with productivity, and with inflation has pushed aside questions of equity and working conditions in political economic debate. Such highly charged issues from the past as income distribution, for example, capture little attention today. When the government attempted to impose wage "guideposts" in the early 1960's, the majority of Americans failed to respond in any way; essentially the same passivity greeted the government's efforts to define strikes as the consequences of failures in collective bargaining (rather than as organic parts of the bargaining process). This passivity may reasonably be interpreted as a signal that "class politics" are but vestigial elements in America and that the terms of political debate have been sharply redrawn. Even the civil rights "revolution" has been (relatively) free of a "class-conscious" mentality. The riots of Negroes in some urban centers, in which young people are conspicuous, are of course more than slightly tinged by class interests. But these are perhaps somewhat less fully supported by similarly situated Negroes who have supported civil rights leaders. The efforts to achieve integrated restaurants, swimming pools, hotels, and other public accommodations and to exercise voting and job rights can hardly be counted as revolutionary; rather,

[2] See "The New American Horizon," Securities Research Division, Merrill Lynch, Pierce, Fenner & Smith, New York (May, 1966), a lengthy pamphlet that reminded investors of "the lucrative markets created by . . . social programs" after it had extolled "the economic virtues of a free society."

[3] See James W. Kuhn and Ivar Berg, *Values in a Business Society* (New York: Harcourt, Brace & World, 1968), Section 4.

they are efforts on the part of a minority to join the majority in the enjoyment of the rights and amenities that follow from citizenship.

Reasons for the Present Status of Ideology

The question of whether ideology has in fact ended, as Professor Daniel Bell has phrased the matter, or has merely lost much of its significance is not vital; either way we have witnessed an important change in the meaning of belief systems that formed the subject matter of the *Kulturdebatte* of the recent past. Bell succinctly outlined the major modern "calamities and changes" that have caused the old ideologies "to lose their 'truth' and their power to persuade" many of their earlier protagonists:

> The Moscow Trials, the Nazi-Soviet pact, the concentration camps, the suppression of the Hungarian workers form one chain [of events]; the modification of capitalism, the use of the Welfare State, another. In philosophy, one can trace the decline of simplistic, rationalistic beliefs and the emergence of new stoic-theological images of man, e.g., Freud, Tillich, Jaspers, etc. . . .
> At the same time American culture has almost completely accepted the avant-garde, particularly in art, and the older academic styles have been driven out completely. The irony, further, for those who seek "causes" is that the workers, whose grievances were once the driving energy for social change, are more satisfied with the society than the intellectuals.[4]

It may well be that a thoughtful minority has been influenced by such chains of events; the increasing skepticism in intellectual circles about simple and sovereign ideological schema may indeed have been triggered by an existential concern with the sufficiency of rationalist approaches. The distinctively nihilistic behavior of some young Americans—reflected in their hostility toward the "old left" as well as toward "middle-class norms"—could also be taken as evidence of a growing disenchantment with the hardened categories of traditional political debate and disgust with the immoralities and perversions with which so many causes in modern history have been encumbered. But such a historical analysis leaves us vaguely dissatisfied in an age in which Lenin's colorful observation that "men do not ride the coattails of history" has become a commonplace. Sociological analysis is evidently required. Several attempts have already been made to supply it; we have had a spate of books about unions, for example, in which the authors—mostly disillusioned liberals—strain to arrange their selected facts to demonstrate that labor leaders have forsaken ideals in favor of bureaucratic outlooks and businesslike manipulation of the environment. In most instances, these studies exaggerate the ideological fervor and overlook the pragmatic character of the American labor movement of yesteryear.[5] It may be doubted that the historical left in America ever drew much of its vitality from the labor leaders now accused

---

[4] *The End of Ideology* (New York: The Free Press, 1960), p. 373.
[5] See the essay by James Kuhn, p. 284.

of selling their souls. The wasting away of that vitality, once formidable, though chaotic, is largely the fault of the left itself. Some leftist groups lost their interest in attacking the status quo and became part of it; others have persevered in advancing arguments addressed to yesterday's wrongs and couched in opaque and curiously antique verbiage. Those of the latter type have become little more than tired antibusinessmen.

The Role of Business Leaders

When attention is given to the role of business leaders in modifying the terms of ideological dispute, the focus is likely to fall on the small if militant group of ideologues among them who are preoccupied with advancing the fortunes of the so-called radical right, a group that contributes to the decline of ideology largely by making it disreputable. There are almost no analyses of the commitments of businessmen in general,[6] despite evidence that these are influential in the marketplace of ideas. If there were, very possibly they would show that businessmen, rather than resisting the liberalizing course of American history in this decade, have generally cooperated in setting that course, thus draining the ideological fervor (by weakening the credibility of their favorite scapegoat, the business tycoon) out of the social forces that nourished romantic faiths and utopian ideals. This has been particularly true in the past decade, during which business leaders in ever larger numbers have entered government service to preside over the implementation of reforms born of the Great Depression for which they were blamed.

A full appreciation of the businessman's crucial impact on ideas is made difficult by our overriding interest in his narrower function as an agent of economic process. While virtually ignoring his impact on ideology, we credit (or blame) the businessman for technological changes, overlooking the fact that he restricts as often as he facilitates technological advance. This oversimplification is a reverse image of our stereotype of the ideologically committed union leader. Such stereotypes—together with the facts that the businessman's impact on ideology has been subtle and unintentional and that he has a penchant for historical anonymity—largely explain why we have failed to see that business leaders have been instrumental in bringing about the eclipse of class politics in America.

In assessing the role of business leaders, it is important to distinguish between their motives on the one hand and their behavior on the other. American businessmen have not consciously rejected all the substance of their older political attitudes, and there have unquestionably been times when business leaders seemed determined

---

[6] There have, of course, been efforts to identify the beliefs of businessmen and to compare them with their actions. See Francis X. Sutton, Seymour E. Harris, Carl Kaysen, and James Tobin, *The American Business Creed* (Cambridge, Mass.: Harvard University Press, 1956). These authors, however, refer to the beliefs of business spokesmen who represent, as Robert Heilbroner suggests, "an ill-defined constituency" ["The View from the Top," in Earl Cheit, ed., *The Business Establishment* (New York: John Wiley, 1964), p. 3]. For a critique of Sutton *et al.*, see David Rogers and Ivar Berg, "Occupation and Ideology: The Case of the Small Businessman," in *Human Organization,* Vol. 20 (Fall, 1966), pp. 103–11.

to remind workers of what the unreconstructed left would call their "class interests." Thus, during the great steel strike of 1959, the steelworkers, who had become thoroughly accustomed to seeing their leaders strolling arm-in-arm through the mills with the captains of industry and to hearing their leaders speak at union conventions about "a new era of labor-management cooperation," were reminded that old conflicts over management rights and efficiency could be revived at will in corporate board rooms. As negotiations between management and the union proceeded, the vaguely scandalous issues of featherbedding and work rules that allegedly fostered wasteful practices were suddenly and surprisingly introduced by management. The steelworkers' union at once rose up to defend the rules that had been sanctified by long practice in the mills and hammered out in bargaining between shop representatives and front line supervisors. The union— which entered the negotiations riven by internal dissent, led by a man lacking full membership support, and weakened in its preliminary bargaining effort by widespread popular concern over inflation—was converted into a unified and powerful force on the initiative of managers.

This case, while perhaps indicative of deeper social strains, is an exception. The labor-management conflicts of recent times are less a reflection of class conciousness—at least between union leaders and employers—than of a growing chasm between unionists and their leaders. As the vice president for industrial relations of a major electrical products manufacturer told participants in a conference at Columbia University (on creativity in large organizations!): "We do better with Harry Bridges, however 'red' he is, and with Jimmy Hoffa, for all his cynicism, than with democratic union leaders, because their word is good; they don't have trouble keeping their members in line."

Thought, Word, and Deed

Business leaders have contributed to the increasingly apolitical character of present-day American life, however piously they may perform the litany of an older system of beliefs, and have contributed by their acts to the "politics of consensus" of the 1960's. If we identify the ideology of business leaders with their behavior rather than with the statements they pay professional ideologues to make or the responses they give to polls and surveys,[7] we find that their contribution to "consensus" constitutes the really significant impact of their beliefs. In several of their actions, some more fundamental than their handling of collective bargaining relationships, corporate leaders have influenced not only the substance of political life in America but the structure and functioning of American society as well.

Three of these actions will be explored further in order to illustrate the impact of American business leaders on American ideology. They are, first, the business community's adoption of the so-called New Economics; second, its cooperation with other parts of society in placing incredible emphasis on formal education; and,

[7] A similar suggestion is made by John R. Bunting, *The Hidden Face of Free Enterprise* (New York: McGraw-Hill, 1964).

third, its contribution to today's "creeping technicalism." Separately, any one of the three developments might have ignited the utopian polemics of the old left and the romantic rhetoric of the old right. Together, however, they have enveloped and extinguished the few flickers of the old ideologies that remained after totalitarians on the left and the right had removed their basic intellectual force.

THE BUSINESSMAN AND ECONOMIC POLICY

The liberal economics of past decades had two parts. One part was essentially Keynesian and consisted of the fiscal and monetary techniques necessary to control the extremes of the business cycle. The other part, technically unrefined, was an amalgamation of welfare with institutional economics. In accepting the first of these—with modifications in the details of its applications—the businessman left modern liberals in exclusive possession only of their welfare economics, the least-developed part of their analytical armament. A serious unevenness has resulted from business support for just half the liberal program. On the one hand, progress has been made in controlling the business cycle. On the other hand, welfare economics languishes. According to William K. Kapp:

> [Very] little if indeed anything has been done . . . to "humanize" economics and to broaden the scope of its investigations. . . . Certainly . . . there is as yet little evidence that social costs (and social returns) have found the recognition which they deserve. The implicit identification of entrepreneurial costs and returns with total costs and total benefits continues to govern the methodology of theoretical economics. . . . Fundamentally . . . the treatment of social costs [e.g., pollution] as a minor and exceptional disturbance rather than as a characteristic phenomenon of the market economy reflects the still very imperfect way in which these costs are taken into consideration in the economic calculus of the system of business enterprise.[8]

Old and New in the New Economics

That Keynesian economics should now command the loyalty of businessmen is easier to understand when we note how neatly its technical apparatus has been detached from the liberals' concern and preoccupation with the question of income redistribution that went along with it in earlier years. A review of programs and policies that give flesh to the formal structure of today's New Economics reveals what has taken the place of the discarded liberal elements: generous depreciation allowances, tax reductions—especially for corporations and middle-to-upper-income groups—subsidies and stockpiling programs that shelter innumerable firms from the chill winds of the marketplace, and similar components that could hardly fail to stir business enthusiasm.

Even the much-publicized initial "attacks" of the federal government on poverty

[8] *Social Costs of Business Enterprise*, rev. ed. (New York: Asia Publishing House, 1963), pp. 8–9.

in America earned a certain benevolent sympathy from the business community when it became clear that the government would avoid an all-out "war" on poverty and concentrate not on providing jobs but on correcting the educational inadequacies and other handicaps of the poor themselves. These minimal efforts were made still more attractive by Administration statements that the campaign must be waged with the help of businessmen rather than "Ivy League do-gooders" and by the inclusion in the program of a great variety of projects promising heavy profits to business subcontractors.[9]

While publicity about the war on poverty was at its height, the equanimity of businessmen was unmistakable. One journalist reported that a reference by Senate Minority Leader Everett Dirksen to the national debt drew hearty laughter at the 1966 convention of the National Association of Manufacturers—hardly the response of a class-conscious group terrified by the prospect of fiscal irresponsibility.[10] The impression was reinforced when the delegates at the convention reelected as the head of their organization a high executive of the General Dynamics Corporation, a company, as one columnist pointed out, that "was organized on the basis of confidence in the favor of government."

The New Economics is a logical means to achieve growth in an economy for which investment is a primary determinant and in which investment varies according to the degree that the climate of opinion in the business community encourages or discourages business confidence. America had such an economy; the problem was to find a way of securing a favorable climate. The New Economics, which nicely sidesteps questions of what we spend public funds for, has been the therapy chosen to keep our economy healthy, and no liberal can deny that it has worked in recent years. The debate over ends has been suspended, and our industrial production continues to mount. No conspiracy theory is needed to explain the behavior of modern businessmen; motives may be ignored.

Difficulties in Making a Case for Reform

Lord Keynes now belongs to his former critics, and this leaves the liberals in the tradition of the 1930's holding a bag of causes and arguments that seem almost completely ineffective in present-day debate. They argue, for example, and with considerable feeling, that crime, family instability, and a multitude of other costly forms of individual deviance and social pathology are a function of unemployment, underemployment, and maldistribution of income, but they have been unable to demonstrate satisfactory causal relationships or to rebut the argument that the attempt to eliminate the alleged roots of these evils might be more costly than the evils themselves, especially if it raised taxes to the point of weakening the incentive to invest.

[9] For a early and pessimistic—and ultimately correct—review of some of these programs, see Ivar Berg and Marcia Freedman, "The Jobs Corps: A Business Bonanza," *Christianity and Crisis* (May 31, 1965), pp. 115–19.
[10] The laughter was derisive of welfare spending that contributed to the debt; nevertheless, it was laughter and not an angry outburst followed by a time honored militancy on the part of conservative business critics of public policy.

The author is especially aware of these difficulties as a result of joining with two colleagues, Eli Ginzberg and Marcia Freedman, to write a chapter entitled "The Hidden Costs of Unemployment" for the President's 1966 report on manpower.[11] In the end we were unable to do more than discuss statistical associations that were *suggestive* of a link between income and deviance. The associations observed by researchers could usually be challenged on various grounds; in the case of juvenile delinquency, for example, the apparent connection with poverty could not be proved because of biases in police and court records favoring the children of middle- and high-income groups. The author encountered a similar problem in a report to the President's crime commission in 1967.[12]

Even when statistical associations can be established, the precise nature of the underlying causal relationships between socioeconomic status and social pathology is rarely clear enough to prevent a really vigorous public program, aimed at curbing the pathological conditions, from seeming like anything but social experimentation. Thus the expected gains from any public policies designed ultimately to redistribute income must be balanced against the costs of the crises of confidence engendered by them. Any new federal program is likely to cause a few critics of public policy to withdraw from the marketplace and to cut back on investments out of fear that incentives will be eroded by taxes and that inflation will accompany welfare spending. The number of businessmen who react this way must be expected to increase as the new social legislation promises to be more meaningful.

It is not likely that the hard-core iconography of past ideological debate will ever re-emerge in America. In adopting substantial portions of the liberals' programs and neatly detaching them from the traditional liberal cause, businessmen appear to have "done their part"; they can accuse manic progressives, perturbed by the phyrric quality of their victory, of being downright ungrateful in the face of a new spirit of doctrinal compromise. Americans will be obliged, therefore, to listen to a debate over who can best run programs and more sensitively select proper moments for adjusting policy to fit given circumstances to do what both groups now refer to as the fine tuning.

THE BUSINESSMAN AND EDUCATION

Though the ideologists of the left have seen their sails go limp as the need for economic planning and the feasibility of strong welfare measures were limited by the New Economics, they have also done much to cause their own obsolescence.

---

[11] See *Manpower Report of the President and A Report on Manpower Requirements, Resources, Utilization and Training by The United States Department of Labor,* transmitted to Congress, March, 1964 (Washington, D.C.: Government Printing Office), Ch. 4, pp. 49–65.

[12] See *The Economics of Delinquency and the Delinquency of Economics,* A Report to the President's Commission on Law Enforcement and the Administration of Justice (Washington, D.C.: Government Printing Office, 1967).

A case in point is their indiscriminate support of the value of education. American business also places tremendous emphasis on education, but by using it as a screening device and prerequisite for work, rather than handing the liberals an easy victory, it has discovered quite unintentionally a powerful weapon with which to silence its former critics or at least to dampen their ideological fervor.

This new emphasis seems all the more remarkable when we recall that businessmen in an earlier time were skeptical of the democratic implications of education. Even "management science" and its chief practicing philosopher, Frederick W. Taylor, were seen by many as threats to the status quo insofar as they implied that anyone could manage a business operation save for lack of technical skill and a capacity for applying measurement techniques to the production process. In 60 years, business leaders have changed their tune and joined in the chorus praising education as the way to individual economic salvation. Educational requirements for a great many jobs in the economy have gone up over the past decades.

The new attitude of business is partly a reflection of the fact that employers have for many years enjoyed a loose labor market. Stressing that education is a *sine qua non* is often simply a new way of suggesting that the unfortunate are fully responsible for their condition and so do not deserve any help. As long as opportunities for education expand faster than the numbers willing to respond to these opportunities, goes the argument, then individuals can only blame themselves for their circumstances, whether they be technicians who fail to become engineers or teenagers who fail to find employment because they are dropouts from school.

The Usefulness of Education

The virtues of a well-educated workforce are constantly held before a society preoccupied with work and economic growth. The economists who write of "human capital" have shown that there is a positive relationship between educational achievement and income[13] and between economic growth and education.[14] But they do not prove an *interesting* causal relationship between education and income in an economy in which educational requirements are specified for so many jobs; the resulting relationships are virtually tautological.

They have also failed to demonstrate that the qualities with which educational achievements are generally identified are actually exhibited in a measurably superior degree in educated people. While information on education is a staple requirement of most employment applications and is taken at face value as

[13] See Theodore W. Schultz, *The Economic Value of Education* (New York: Columbia University Press, 1963), and Gary Becker, "Investment in Human Beings," *Journal of Political Economy*, Vol. 52 (October, 1962), Part 2 (Supplement), p. 9.
[14] See Edward F. Denison, *The Sources of Economic Growth in the United States*, Supplementary Paper No. 13, Committee for Economic Development (January, 1962). See also Fritz Machlup, *The Production and Distribution of Knowledge in the United States* (Princeton, N. J.: Princeton University Press, 1962), Chs. 4 and 10. For a critical brief assessment see Bruno Frey, "A Critique of Economic Theories on Education, Research, and Technical Progress," *The MBA*, Vol. 1 (February, 1967), pp. 32–37.

critical evidence in the screening process, it is by no means clear that formal educational attainments are any proof of intelligence, ambition, energy, personal stability, and inventiveness. The facts that very large numbers of bright high school graduates do not go to college and that the I.Q. of high school dropouts is by no means uniformly low[15] are generally forgotten. Businessmen readily accept the economists' argument, and the voices of parents become more and more shrill as they drive their children on through the groves of academe.

Basic to this process is the widespread acceptance of the idea that jobs have so changed that applicants require vastly greater amounts of formal education to fill them. There is, however, good reason for wondering whether jobs have in fact changed as much as the educational requirements that come to define them.

In a study of the relationships between changes in technology and in educational requirements, Abraham Jaffe summarized some of his findings as follows:

> [Among] all workers, manual and white collar, there were increases in educational attainment between 1950 and 1960. Such changes, however, bear little, if any, relationship to changes in output per worker as among different industries. Furthermore, even in those industries which apparently were undergoing the most rapid technological changes (as measured by changes in output per worker) half or more of the male manual workers were "dropouts." Clearly, these data do not prove that modern advancing technology necessarily requires its workers to have more formal schooling.[16]

In several instances when employers have been brought to admit that an employee could perform well in a new job with fewer school hours than are now required, they have argued that the excessive requirements are maintained to insure "promotability" in the workforce. One may doubt that this explanation is true and, if it is true, question whether the excessive requirements are just.

The most persuasive explanation for the elevation in educational requirements is in two parts. First, the educational level of the average young person entering the workforce has been rising independently in every decade, much faster than actual requirements.[17] We may note, in passing, that large numbers of engineers are employed as technicians to fill shortages in that occupational category.[18] Second, as has already been noted, unemployment rates have been relatively high in the period during which the requirements have gone up.[19] The significance of this is suggested by a National Industrial Conference Board study of the labor market in New York's Monroe County, which shows that educational requirements go up each spring and then go down again, for the same jobs, as the calendar

---

[15] S. M. Miller, Betty L. Saleem, and Herrington Bryce, *School Dropouts: A Commentary and Annotated Bibliography* (Syracuse, N.Y.: Syracuse University Youth Development Center, 1964), pp. 52–57.

[16] Abraham J. Jaffe and Walter Adams, "Educational Attainment and Modern Technology, a Brief Note," *The Statistical News,* Vol. 16 (December, 1964).

[17] R. S. Eckaus, "Economic Criteria for Educational Training," *Review of Economics and Statistics,* Vol. 6 (May, 1964), pp. 181–90.

[18] C. S. Benson and P. R. Lohnes, "Skill Requirements and Industrial Training in Durable Goods Manufacturing," *Industrial and Labor Relations Review,* Vol. 12 (July, 1959), pp. 540–53.

[19] Eckaus, *op. cit.,* p. 182.

marks the days away from high school commencement exercises;[20] business seems to vary educational requirements to adjust to the supply of labor. The questionable logic behind such practices contributes a good deal more support to the wage demands of a "high quality" labor force than it does to assumptions, in the theory of the firm, about the rationality of the manager. If the labor market were suddenly to tighten, educational requirements might well begin to decline.

One might attempt to justify the emphasis of business on education by saying that other things being equal, more education in a worker is better than less. This principle may be erroneous, however; raising educational requirements may not be "good business" in every case. Dr. Lawrence Hinkle of the Cornell Medical School believes, on the basis of a study of employees in several large companies, that virtually all the physical and psychological illnesses (and therefore the absenteeism) encountered in each of several particular skill categories occurred among those with relatively more rather than those of relatively less formal educational achievement.[21] It was notable that employers were oblivious of these facts in their praise of the better-educated groups. A large-scale investigation by the author yielded evidence that points in the same direction. In working populations of heterogeneous educational backgrounds performing the same jobs, the better-educated personnel contribute disproportionately to work dissatisfaction, turnover, and other seemingly undesirable organizational statistics.[22]

Education and the Social Structure

Whatever its true relation to productivity, educational achievement has the advantage of seeming nicely neutral—more neutral than class and related considerations—as a criterion by which a society can become differentiated or, as the sociologists have it, "stratified." Even the most egalitarian of spokesmen have never denied that there is a hierarchy of ability in a democratic society and that ability should govern in such matters as employment. If one can assume that ability and educational achievement are intimately related, as nearly everyone does, a fair basis for the distribution of status and other social rewards would seem to have been found.

The trouble is that while educational achievement may indeed have a little to do with ability, it has more than a little to do with inherited social position and the values of the family into which one happens to be born. That a bright ghetto youngster has fewer long-run educational opportunities than the plodding son of a business or professional type is too obvious to require much comment. On the one hand, the child of poor parents may be excluded from good schools for financial

---

[20] "Measuring Job Vacancies: The Third Survey," The Conference Board Record, November, 1965, New York National Industrial Conference Board (pamphlet).

[21] Report by Dr. Hinkle to a seminar on "Creativity in Large Organizations" at Arden House, Harriman, N.Y., 1961, sponsored by the Wolfson Foundation.

[22] The report of the findings from this investigation by the Columbia University Conservation of Human Resources Project is to be published in 1968 in Eli Ginzberg, ed., *Manpower Strategy for the Metropolis* (New York: Columbia University Press).

reasons; on the other hand, the same child may be handicapped in school by the differences between the intellectual environment provided by his home and the environment experienced by the majority of children who grow up in middle-class families.[23] This is a fact that many liberal advocates of the educational criteria for social decisions too conveniently forget. In America it has become more difficult than in the past to accumulate and transmit real property to one's children. But it is possible to pass on intellectual and educational values, even as it is possible to provide opportunities for education that are almost as valuable as the older forms of property were to the beneficiaries of an apparently less democratic system. Rather than leading to a more democratic society in which all youngsters start out on an equal footing, the current emphasis on education in America may well represent a mechanism working to insure that the advantages of being born well are as great as ever.

This process tends to be accentuated by the habit of middle-class parents— including the liberals among them who are most ready to assist in the drive for integrated schools—to move to suburban school districts "for the children" or to sacrifice in order to send their children to private schools that protect "educational standards" against the day their youngsters will apply to "the leading colleges." The efforts of school systems in some of our largest cities to maintain adequate opportunities for educational growth are bound to suffer, at least in the short run, from such decisions; the problem of maintaining standards is obviously more serious when the vast majority of pupils in central-city schools come from low-income families that have less well-developed commitments to education.

If jobs depend upon inflated educational credentials, and these, in turn, are most easily acquired by the moneyed, the obvious effect is to freeze the economic and social status quo. When viewed in this light, the well-meaning liberal's toleration of increased educational requirements by employers belies his traditional hostility to privilege. Reluctant as he might be to believe it, the liberal may have become a servant to a social structure whose basic characteristics are not likely to change despite the enactment of hard-won reforms.

BUSINESSMEN AND THE BEHAVIORAL SCIENCES

The New Economics disarmed the businessman's traditional antagonists while his hiring practices have increasingly distracted them. The final blow to the liberals' position has been the businessman's new dedication to science, especially to the behavioral sciences. Liberals long saw in several of the behavioral sciences evidence to support their economic views on the "dehumanizing" effects of an industrial society arranged along the lines of private enterprise, with its emphasis on competition, profit, deferred gratification, and rugged individualism. Their shock at seeing the businessman turn these same sciences to the use of private enterprise was correspondingly profound.

[23] For detailed data see John Coleman, *Equality of Education Opportunity*, Office of Economic Opportunity (Washington, D.C.: Government Printing Office, 1966).

Creeping Technicalism

The modern businessman has, to an important degree, become an applied social scientist in his own right while acting as a patron of the social sciences. Many sociologists, psychologists, and anthropoligists used to remain scrupulously independent of business, but today men in these fields are joining operations researchers, statisticians, and economists in ever larger numbers in the nation's offices, laboratories, and factories. Social science research institutes are becoming increasingly dependent upon contracts from private business for research on worker morale, consumer spending patterns, and customer attitudes.

No program for business executives is complete without an introductory lecture on the applications of behavioral science to organizational problems; no big-company personnel installation is complete without Thematic Apperception Tests, Rorschach ink blots, and "depth counseling"; few upper-level, white-collar workers will for long be able to avoid "sensitivity training" in "T Groups" led in clinically sophisticated, non-directive fashion by a growing corps of human relationists. While clinical psychologists are busy helping executives in "T Groups" to see how their personal insecurities and "interpersonal incompetence" lead them to become dependent on "authoritarian" organizations in their dealings with subordinates, these same subordinates are studied by sociologists bent upon discovering their "norms," their "informal organizations," and their "interaction patterns." Just as systems analysts armed with differential calculus, computers, and probability theories are busily locating and easing bottlenecks in production and distribution, social psychologists equipped with "survey instruments" are conducting field investigations on everything from the beer-drinking habits of women and the erotic fantasies of automobile buyers to the "status anxieties" of employees confronted with "frustrated mobility aspirations."

Industrial Technicalism and the Focus of Research

This creeping technicalism, in which the sciences of man are put to practical use within the framework of an enterprise, is obviously not without consequences for our society and the sciences that study it. Although as recently as the late 1940's psychologists were concerned with discovering the prerequisite for the formation of an "integrated" and "autonomous" personality, they are becoming increasingly preoccupied today with the analysis of the individual's capacity to function at work. Where private property and other elements of capitalist society were once almost automatically taken to be the source of alienation, à la Marx, the emphasis is now on the disenchanting consequences of life in large, complex organizations, whether these be capitalist or Communist.[24]

This last development is particularly interesting because it corresponds to a fundamental shift by the scientific community in its view of the modern business leader and his power: the manner in which managerial authority is exercised rather

[24] For another view and a more extensive analysis of the developments discussed here in outline fashion, see the contribution by Arthur Shostak, p. 338.

than its legitimacy is now at issue. One result of this shift has been a simplification in the prevailing conception of the relationships between employers and employees. Increasingly these relationships are seen in organizational rather than, as in the past, in political terms. If there are conflicts between "status groups"—in classless bureaucracies—they are seen as the result of psychological irrationalities on the part of employees and technical weaknesses in the managers' uses of their organizations or professional shortcomings in managerial "styles." In the best known of these new and ideology-free characterizations of relationships at work, Chris Argyris cautions top managers to make more room for the "self-actualization" of workers and professional supervisors lest "the conflict between the system [i.e., the organization] and the individual" impede progress.[25] "Human beings," he writes, "are not simple and they deserve the consideration of not being manipulated by trick or specious methods." A new generation of social scientists has seized upon the challenge, presumably to find more scientifically reputable means to the same manipulative ends, so "that management [can] become more free to create bigger organizations, newer products, more effective distribution schemes, and so on."

Prescriptions have changed along with analysis and description. An earlier concern with democracy in society is rapidly giving way to a preoccupation with the individual's participation in decision-making and with ways to modify organizational elements, such as the command hierarchy, in order to permit the "inherent tendency [of the human personality] to maintain itself."[26] The world of power relationships and group conflicts that Madison, in *The Federalist,* considered basic to our political system is being scaled down to research size, while the twin bases upon which power so often lawfully rests in our democracy—property and contract —are made to seem increasingly irrelevant.

The political consequences of the increasing expertise of business in the social sciences are important. The American left, historically given to proving its case "scientifically" and strengthened by a virtual monopoly over the use of the behavioral disciplines and methodologies in political debate through a long period of anti-intellectualism in business and conservative quarters, has seen its monopoly disappear.

CONCLUSION

A 1965 report entitled *The Concept of Poverty,* published by the U.S. Chamber of Commerce, begins with a passage from the writings of Wesley C. Mitchell, the great researcher into business cycles:

> Our best hope for the future lies in the extension to social organization of the methods that we already employ in our most progressive fields of effort. In

[25] Chris Argyris, *Personality and Organization* (New York: Harper & Row, 1957).
[26] *Ibid.,* p. 23.

science and industry . . . we do not wait for catastrophe to force new ways upon us. . . . We rely, and with success, upon quantitative analysis to point the way; and we advance because we are constantly improving and applying such analysis.[27]

Commenting on the passage, former Assistant Secretary of Labor Moynihan pointed out that it is "as succinct a case for social planning as could be made [and] is not the product of either the thought or the institutions of the liberal-left."[28]

As Moynihan's comment suggests, many of the standing proposals of liberal ideology have been accepted today, but rather than being honored for its loyal service, ideology itself has fallen into disrepute. Certain difficulties plague liberal ideology in particular, of course. On the one hand, even its fringe recommendations are being taken over and advocated by representatives of the business world; at the 1966 convention of the National Association of Manufacturers, for example, Laurance Rockefeller used part of a morning session to lecture the audience on the evils of polluting the nation's waterways. During the same year, a few leading businessmen could also be found in the front ranks of the movements favoring the extension of civil rights and a limitation on America's participation in Vietnam. On the other hand, both liberal ideology itself and its chief advocates have been swallowed up in the politics of consensus; they have become part of the establishment. Detached criticism has given way to opportunism and what the left itself, in former times, deplored as vulgar pragmatism. It was frequently reported in the press, for example, that critics of the Administration's War on Poverty were rewarded by invitations to come to Washington to "put up or shut up," as one academic entrepreneur explained upon his appointment to a management job in the Office of Economic Opportunity. A battle over the kinds of strategy appropriate to a war on poverty is thereby turned into a debate over tactics by the device of converting those who propose alternative strategies into bureaucrats with a stake in prevailing policies.

But quite apart from the difficulties that are special to liberalism, ideology as such has come under increasing attack. One of the best formal statements in support of the proposition that ideology is no longer relevant—directed at the left as much as to the right—appeared in President Kennedy's 1962 commencement day speech at Yale; he claimed that the issues before the American people are essentially technical issues that make traditional ideas "obsolete" and that they require the attention of trained specialists who tinker at the margins of complex problems. Homelier formulations abound; in the first issue of *The Public Interest*, for example, the new editors announced that "it is in the nature of ideology to preconceive reality; and it is exactly such preconceptions that are the worst hindrances to knowing-what-one-is-talking-about" and that theirs would be a

middle-aged magazine for middle-aged readers. . . . [Young] people tend to be enchanted by glittering generalities; older people are inclined to remember rather

[27] Cited in Daniel P. Moynihan, "The Professionalization of Reform," *The Public Interest*, Vol. 1 (Fall, 1965), p. 6.
[28] *Idem.*

than to think; middle-aged people, seasoned by life but still open to the future, do seem to us—in our middle years—to be the best of all political generations.[29]

As if to drive the point home, the lead article in the same magazine was entitled "The Professionalization of Reform," a favorable view of the process by a liberal who had taken his turn as a public servant.

America in the 1960's experienced a progressive substitution of discussion of means for debate over ends. Ideologists, however, are not the only people who "preconceive" reality. The "scientific" decision-maker is all too likely to disregard the existence of competing national power groups, whose conflicts are not amenable to technical but rather to political solutions.

It may be a piece of dangerous folly to cover over the interstices of actual disagreement with the rhetoric of consensus. In times gone by the business leader's reservations about education and his slightly anti-intellectual attitude toward Keynesian economics and the behavioral sciences contributed, almost perversely, to the quality and vitality of democratic institutions. These institutions thrive in American society, it may be suggested, to the degree that there is a debate over ends and to the degree that choices are vividly presented for an informed population of citizens. Insofar as their behavior contributes to the "end of ideology," business leaders add to the pressures on these institutions at a time when they are already seriously threatened by the nationalistic imperatives of international politics and the restless preoccupation at home with order and efficiency.

It may not yet be time to dispense with ideology. We need ideologists, not for their "prefabricated interpretations" of reality, but for their sharp challenge to basic belief systems and for their conflicting views on such fundamental issues as the aims of our foreign policy, the proper role of government, and the rights and responsibilities of individuals. If we get these things, a few "prefabricated interpretations" are perhaps a small price to pay.

SELECTED READINGS

RALF DAHRENDORF, *Class and Class Conflict in Industrial Society* (Stanford, Calif.: Stanford University Press, 1959). A synthesis of earlier perspectives on social conflict with more recent perspectives on social order, the book offers an illuminating theory of social change in industrialized societies. The author's review of theories and relevant findings is sufficiently complete for the book to serve as a useful guide to the literature in this field.

SEYMOUR MARTIN LIPSET, *Political Man: Where, How and Why Democracy Works in the Modern World* (New York: Doubleday, 1960). A collection of essays on "the causes and consequences of political behavior" by one of America's most prominent political scientists, it touches effectively on a variety of ideological

[29] Daniel Bell and Irving Kristol, "What Is the Public Interest?" *The Public Interest*, Vol. 1 (Fall, 1965), p. 3.

issues relating to the structure and function of democratic institutions both public and private.

FRANCIS X. SUTTON, SEYMOUR HARRIS, CARL KAYSEN, AND JAMES TOBIN, *The American Business Creed* (Cambridge, Mass.: Harvard University Press, 1956). An intriguing analysis of the statements about social, political, and economic issues made by professional business ideologues on behalf of American business leaders, interesting not because the authors' analysis is completely persuasive but because of the detailed material it contains on the productions of trade and other business associations. The analysis of businessmen's "role strains," while probably not adequate to explain their ideologies, is highly suggestive in respect to other apects of businessmen's performance.

REINHARD BENDIX, *Work and Authority in Industry*: *Ideologies of Management in the Course of Industrialization* (New York: John Wiley, 1956), published in paperback by Harper & Row. A rewarding discussion of materials relevant to an understanding of the dynamic character of "business ideology," it uses the comparative method to isolate the evolution of managerial beliefs with special emphasis upon those having to do with managers' authority in the work place. Much weight is given to the process of "bureaucratization" in turning managers away from class-consciousness and toward "managerial ideology."

B. J. WIDICK, *Labor Today: The Triumphs and Failures of Unionism in the United States* (Boston: Houghton Mifflin, 1964). While the author of this volume probably romanticizes the early commitments of America's labor unions, he has nevertheless written a lively journalistic account of the character of these unions and their ideological stances in the period of the 1960's.

part 3

BUSINESS AND THE ECONOMY

The frequent statement that America's is a "mixed economy" is a sufficiently accurate appraisal of the facts of our industrial society to cause one to wonder whether the effort to discriminate the "economy" from the "polity" is not merely futile. But if the two elements we are attempting to distinguish lack any precisely identifiable counterparts in the empirical world, the distinction is nevertheless a useful analytical one. Most businessmen are convinced, perhaps rightly, that that the entrepreneurship and free-enterprise principles of our private sector are largely responsible for our considerable industrial success. And social scientists, mindful as they are of the necessary governmental role in man's drive to alleviate the problems of scarcity that militate most seriously against political stability, give considerable weight to the free-enterprise system in appraisals of the preconditions for the maintenance of democratic political insitutions.

In this section the first two contributors examine the role of business in the development of America's economy, the consequences to the economy of the paths this developmental process has followed, and the organizational forms that the process has helped produce—most notably our most successful larger corporations. Curiously, the growth-engendering diffusions of technical advances that take place in a non-integrated, non-concentrated economy have contributed in dramatic ways to integration and concentration. According to both authors, America has experienced a succession of waves of growth based on innovations that are organizational and commercial rather than technical in nature, a process that has created political problems even as it has appeared to solve traditional economic ones.

The section's third essay reports on the accelerating evolution of technology and technological research in which the public, through its political bureaucracy, provides much of the "venture capital," the bureaucratized scientific community the ideas and techniques, and the businessman the management and productive skills in a system that bears at best an ambiguous resemblance to the past.

chapter **6**

BUSINESS AND THE
MARKET MECHANISM

ALFRED S. EICHNER *teaches economics at Columbia University and has specialized in the study of oligipoly. Business concentration and monopoly power have been subjects of concern to businessmen and economists at least since the days of Adam Smith, and they have elicited a vast body of literature ranging in character from the apocalyptic visions of Karl Marx to abstruse disquisitions on statistical methodology in the scholarly journals. Praise for competition and condemnation of monopoly are voiced by most Americans, not least by the businessmen whose fondest dream is to gain a decisive and lasting advantage over their rivals. But once we have come out thus squarely for virtue and against vice, the question remains whether the problem of monopoly power in America is actually one that requires any remedial action to be taken, now, by business itself or by the government. What is the actual balance between competition and monopoly power in the United States today? This is an extraordinarily difficult question to answer, but Professor Eichner, who has engaged in research on problems of economic history as well as patterns of resource allocation, is particularly qualified to review the outstanding studies of the problem and to offer some conclusions of his own.*

Professor Eichner begins his essay with a discussion of industrial concentration ratios and then provides an assessment of the somewhat more familiar institutional dimensions of "business as a system of power." He traces the historical progress of consolidation in the United States, examines the giant corporations or "megacorps" that have emerged, and finally considers the problem of interlocking corporate relationships. He reports little evidence that would confirm the fears of the late 1930's that the concentration of economic power in America is constantly increasing; it is clear, however, that the economic power of a relatively small handful of corporations is more than sufficient to justify the concern and attention of thoughtful citizens. It is his judgment that the concentration we do have has helped to temper the swings of the business cycle and otherwise to dampen the effects of price competition on "rational" resource allocation; it has also contributed to a seemingly intractable inflationary pressure and a skewing of national financial activity away from "social investments." His concern about the distorted uses to which great economic power could be put—especially if it were to be exercised in response to a community of special private interests—is matched by some confidence that the power of business is at least partially limited by the power of our "big government," which is, as he sees it, alert to the potential threats of unfettered oligopolistic industrial might.

These questions should be kept in mind by the reader as he proceeds through the essay:

1. How is an "industry" to be defined? Imagine a country with poor land, a large population that eats only bread and milk, and (besides its electronic and textile complexes producing products for export) none but the following firms: 1,000 wheat farms, 5 dairy farms, 50 mills, 50 bakers, 2 pasteurizing plants, 1 trucking operation, 25 insecticide companies, 20 supermarkets, and 1 farm-machinery company. How concentrated is the food industry? How concentrated are farming, food processing, distribution, the chemical industry, and the farm-machinery industry?

2. Compared to the mythical economy described in the first question, the American economy is incredibly complex. In what American industry would you locate (a) the billion dollar, multiproduct Studebaker Corporation now that it no longer produces cars, and (b) the exclusive manufacturer of a unique, patented drug that is a complete cure for cancer?

3. In distinguishing an "industry" in the United States, which is more practical: first to define an industry and then gauge monopoly power within it, or first to look for monopoly power and then attempt to discover the range of firms affected by it? What would be the values and limitations of concentration ratios for "industries" delimited on the basis of traditional behavior as recorded by conventional wisdom?

4. What responsibility has the top management in a giant "mega-corp" to exercise "managerial restraint" similar to the "judicial restraint" of the Supreme Court? How often and how much is such managerial restraint in fact exercised today?

ALFRED S. EICHNER \ BUSINESS CONCENTRATION
AND ITS SIGNIFICANCE

During the 1930's the fear was often expressed that the American economy was rapidly losing its competitive character. In 1936, for example, Professor Arthur R. Burns of Columbia University wrote in *The Decline of Competition* that "an industrial organization which was in the broad sense competitive has become diminishingly so during the past half century." He added, "Elements of monopoly have always been interwoven with competition but the monopoly elements have increased in importance. They can no longer be regarded as occasional and relatively unimportant aberrations from competition."[1]

Several years earlier Adolph A. Berle and Gardiner C. Means had called attention to a similar trend. "Economic power, in terms of control over physical assets," they wrote in *The Modern Corporation and Private Property*, "is apparently responding to a centripetal force, tending more and more to concentrate in the hands of a few corporate managements." Noting that the assets of the 200 largest corporations had grown at an annual rate of 5.4 per cent a year between 1909 and 1928, while the assets of all corporations taken together had increased at an annual rate of 3.6 per cent a year, they pointed out that if these same rates of growth were to continue, the 200 largest corporations would control all economic activity by 1970. "In conclusion, then," they said, "the huge corporation, the corporation with $90,000,000 of assets or more, has come to dominate most major industries if not all industry in the United States. . . . There is apparently no immediate limit to its increase. It is coming more and more to be the industrial unit with which American economic, social and political life must deal."[2]

In order to determine how valid were the fears expressed by Berle and Means, Burns, and others, Congress in 1936 created the Temporary National Economic Committee. In a special message urging the formation of such a study group, President Franklin D. Roosevelt declared, "Among us today a concentration of private power without equal in history is growing. This concentration is seriously impairing the effectiveness of private enterprise. . . ."[3] Before World War II brought a premature end to its work, the TNEC published a number of studies that gave added impetus to the fears that untoward developments were occurring in the economy.

It is this question of concentrated economic power that will be considered here. The approach will be, first, to examine what empirical evidence exists that can

---

[1] (New York: McGraw-Hill), pp. 3 and 40.
[2] (Chicago: Commerce Clearing House, 1932), pp. 9, 35, 40–41, and 44.
[3] U.S. Temporary National Economic Committee, *Final Report and Recommendations* (Washington: Government Printing Office, 1941), p. 11.

throw light on the historical trend and current extent of business concentration and, second, to offer an interpretation of that evidence. It will be seen that the structure of the American economy cannot be viewed simply in terms of the dichotomy between competition and monopoly traditional to our political discourse and that to a significant degree the important market structure in the non-government-controlled sectors today is oligopoly, characterized by a few large corporations exercising limited discretion as to what prices shall prevail. This type of market structure, not being amenable to traditional forms of social control, presents a serious problem for public policy.

THE TREND OF CONCENTRATION: EMPIRICAL STUDIES

If the fears expressed by Burns, Berle and Means, and others are less frequently heard today, at least part of the reason is that several empirical studies have by now been made of the actual extent to which the American economy has become more concentrated since the turn of the century. Two distinctly different issues are involved: one, the extent to which individual markets or industries have become more concentrated; the other, the extent to which the economy as a whole has become more concentrated.

G. Warren Nutter

Perhaps the most important of the various studies pertaining to the first issue is one by G. Warren Nutter, *The Extent of Enterprise Monopoly in the United States, 1899–1939*,[4] which covers not only a larger portion of the economy but also a longer period of time than any of the similar studies. Professor Nutter used what is known as a concentration ratio to determine whether individual industries should be classified as "effectively monopolistic" or "workably competitive." A concentration ratio is a measure of the percentage of an industry's output produced by the largest four, eight, twenty, or whatever other number of firms is considered to be relevant to the purpose at hand.[5] In his study, Nutter used a concentration ratio of 50 per cent for the four largest firms—that is, if the four largest firms in an industry accounted for 50 per cent or more of that industry's output, it was classified as "effectively monopolistic." Otherwise, it was considered to be "workably competitive."[6]

[4] (Chicago: University of Chicago Press, 1951.)
[5] Concentration ratios are usually based on data obtained from the *U.S. Census of Manufacturing,* conducted periodically by the Department of Commerce. To preserve the anonymity of the firms replying to the census' questionnaires, the market shares of individual companies are not published. Instead, the census merely lists the percentage of the various specified markets accounted for by the largest four, eight, and twenty firms. This same convention is generally followed by economists as well.
[6] Nutter, *op. cit.,* p. 38. The term "workably competitive" had no significance other than the strictly statistical one.

The concentration ratios that Nutter thereby derived showed the extent of concentration in individual industries only. In combining these ratios to obtain a measure of concentration for the economy as a whole, each industry had to be weighted according to its relative importance. The reason for this can be seen from a relatively simple example. Let us suppose that industry A were "effectively monopolistic," industry B were "workably competitive," and that these two industries comprised the entire economy. If this were the case, it might be inferred that only 50 per cent of the economy was concentrated. However, if industry A produced 95 per cent of total output and industry B only 5 per cent, this would be a misleading inference.

Nutter chose as the measure of the relative importance of the industries surveyed the percentage of the national product originating in them. This figure, obtained by subtracting the market price of all material inputs from the market price of all output, avoids giving undue weight to those industries that add little value of their own to the products they purchase from other industries but nevertheless have a high volume of sales. Using this measure as his weight, Nutter was able to make a comparison between 1899 and 1937, excluding that portion of the national product originating either in government or in government-regulated industries, which we may summarize in the following table:[7]

Table 1. Percentage of Non-Government and Government-Regulated Production Accounted for by Effectively Monopolistic and Workably Competitive Industries, 1899–1937.

	EFFECTIVELY MONOPOLISTIC	WORKABLY COMPETITIVE
1899	18.6	81.4
1937	14.7	85.3

To meet possible criticism that his criterion for classifying an industry as "effectively monopolistic" was too narrow, Nutter employed a second, somewhat broader definition. In addition to those industries selected under his first criterion, he classified as effectively monopolistic those industries that separate, individually focused studies had shown to be "monopolistic" in nature, even if the industries did not have concentration ratios of 50 per cent or more for the four largest

[7] See *ibid.*, pp. 38–39. Nutter actually classified the national product according to three sources, effectively monopolistic industries, workably competitive industries, and government and government-regulated industries. He was then able to make a comparison between 1899 and 1937, in terms of the share of the national product originating in each of the three categories of industries. The figures presented here have been adjusted to exclude the effect of the government and government-regulated category.

firms.[8] He also classified as effectively monopolistic those sub-groups of major industries in which the four largest firms accounted for three-fourths of the output of any particular product line.[9] Since the necessary data was available only for 1937, not for 1899, this broader criterion could not be applied to both years. Nonetheless, even though it resulted in an upwardly biased estimate, Nutter recalculated the figure for the extent of effectively monopolistic industries in 1937, using the second definition, with the result that effectively monopolistic industries were found to account for 25.8 per cent of non-government and government-regulated production.

Nutter interpreted this larger figure as an upper limit of the extents of "effective monopoly" in 1937, taking the previous figure of 14.7 per cent as a lower limit. He also suggested that the actual figure probably lay halfway between the two extremes.[10] Following this suggestion, we can revise the previous table as follows:

Table 2. Percentage of Non-Government and Government-Regulated Production Accounted for by Effectively Monopolistic and Workably Competitive Industries, 1899–1937.

		EFFECTIVELY MONOPOLISTIC		WORKABLY COMPETITIVE	
1899			18.6		81.4
1937	Upper Limit	25.8		74.2	
	Average		20.25		79.75
	Lower Limit	14.7		85.3	

Because of the many gaps in data and the various statistical difficulties Nutter encountered in his investigation, these results need to be interpreted with care, as Nutter himself stressed. Still, it seems reasonable to conclude from his study that the extent of "effective monopoly," so defined, probably did not change appreciably between 1899 and 1939.

[8] Nutter relied for his information on a study by Clair Wilcox for the U.S. Temporary National Economic Committee, which sought to summarize the available evidence of monopoly in the American economy from prior individual industry studies. Clair Wilcox, *Competition and Monopoly in the American Economy,* U.S. Temporary National Economic Committee Monograph No. 21 (Washington: Government Printing Office, 1940).

[9] An industry might produce any number of major product lines. When the four largest firms in an industry accounted for at least 75 per cent of the output of any such product line, that portion of total industry output represented by the product in question was included as part of the "effectively monopolistic" industries.

[10] Nutter, *op. cit.,* pp. 38–39.

Henry A. Einhorn

Henry A. Einhorn, in a later study,[11] extended Nutter's work to a more recent period, covering the years from 1939 to 1958. Employing substantially the same criteria as in Nutter's second, and broader, definition, Einhorn found that with only one major exception the extent of "effective monopoly" in the American economy had remained virtually unchanged during the years he surveyed. The one exception was the contract construction sector of the economy, consisting of two major industries. Nutter had classified this sector as effectively monopolistic primarily because earlier studies had shown that the two industries involved were controlled, on a regional basis, by cartel-like arrangements. But Einhorn, relying on a more recent investigation, concluded that the same conditions no longer held; he therefore reclassified the contract construction sector as workably competitive.[12]

Clearly, no major change in the structure of the contract construction sector occurred. The most that can be said to have happened is that regional cartel-like arrangements previously in effect had broken down. Perhaps it would be even more accurate to say that the contract construction sector should not have been classified as effectively monopolistic in 1939. Following this line of reasoning, we can revise Nutter's findings slightly as follows:

Table 3. Percentage of Non-Government and Government-Regulated Production Accounted for by Effectively Monopolistic and Workably Competitive Industries, 1899–1937.

		EFFECTIVELY MONOPOLISTIC		WORKABLY COMPETITIVE	
1899			18.6		81.4
1937	Upper Limit	22.3		77.7	
	Average		18.5		81.5
	Lower Limit	14.7		85.3	

This revised estimate merely reinforces the previous conclusion, that between 1899 and 1937 the extent of "effective monopoly" remained essentially unchanged.

Unfortunately, because the basis of computing national product originating in various industries changed after 1937,[13] Einhorn's results for the later period

[11] *Enterprise Monopoly and the Concentration of Domestic Industrial Output, 1939–1958,* unpublished doctoral dissertation, Columbia University, 1963.
[12] *Ibid.,* pp. 17, 202–05. Nutter had relied on Wilcox, *op. cit.*; Einhorn drew on Carl Brehm, "The Residential Construction Industry," in Walter Adams, ed., *The Structure of American Industry,* 3rd ed. (New York: Macmillan, 1961).
[13] Nutter, *op. cit.,* p. 37.

cannot be compared directly with Nutter's findings for the earlier years. The reader having thus been warned, we shall present Einhorn's results in a slightly revised form:[14]

Table 4. Percentage of Non-Government and Government-Regulated Production Accounted for by Effectively Monopolistic and Workably Competitive Industries, 1939–58.

	EFFECTIVELY MONOPOLISTIC	WORKABLY COMPETITIVE
1939	21.69	77.91
1954	20.41	78.92
1958	17.90	81.39

The slight decrease in the extent of effective monopoly between 1939 and 1958 reported by Einhorn probably reflects the decline of manufacturing relative to services over the period covered, the latter sector tending to be far less concentrated. Still, the decline is so slight that, considering the inherent shortcomings of such statistical investigations, one might safely conclude that the extent of effective monopoly has not changed significantly since 1939, or even over the entire period from 1899 to 1958. At the least, the Nutter and Einhorn studies should put to rest the fears that major American markets or industries are rapidly becoming more concentrated.

Morris A. Adelman

A study by Morris A. Adelman of the economy as a whole is equally reassuring on this point. In an article written for the *Review of Economics and Statistics* in 1951, Adelman took a second look at Berle and Means' survey of the 200 largest non-financial corporations and concluded that the trend toward increased concentration of assets that it had shown was questionable. "For what they are worth," Adelman wrote, "[Berle and Means'] 1909–24 figures do show increasing concentration. . . . But the data seem far too weak to support much in the way of inference."[15]

Far more reliable, Adelman said, were the data underlying a later study by

[14] Cf. Einhorn, *op. cit.*, pp. 13–14. In revising Einhorn's table, the government and government-regulated category has been omitted, and the contract construction sector, accounting for 3.90 per cent of non-government and government-regulated production, has been shifted from the effectively monopolistic to the workably competitive category in 1939.

[15] "The Measurement of Industrial Concentration," Vol. 33 (November, 1951), pp. 269–96.

Means alone, covering the years from 1929 to 1933, since these data were taken directly from income-tax records. The later Means study showed the following:[16]

Table 5.   Assets of Large Corporations as a Per Cent of Total Assets of Respective Groups, 1929 and 1933.

		1929	1933
200	Large Non-financial Corporations	47.9	54.8
75	Large Manufacturing Corporations	36.2	40.2
85	Large Transportation and Other		
	Public Utility Corporations	79.0	86.1
25	Large "Other" Corporations	10.9	14.8

Still, though the data underlying the study were more reliable, Adelman found that the study itself presented a somewhat misleading picture. "A rough calculation," Adelman wrote, "suggests that from one-third to one-half of the 1929–33 increase in concentration [shown by Means] is a statistical mirage." And a significant portion of the rest, he added, might simply reflect the onset of the Great Depression.

To test this hypothesis, Adelman examined the change in the share of total assets held by the 139 largest manufacturing corporations between 1931 and 1947. He found that whereas they held 49.6 per cent of the assets of all manufacturing corporations in 1931, they held 45.0 per cent in 1947. Adelman therefore concluded, "If there has been any strong and continuing tendency since 1931 to greater concentration in manufacturing, it must be detectable in the corporate balance-sheet statistics for this period. These statistics do not show it. Therefore the tendency probably does not exist."[17]

Adelman's conclusions are supported by a more recent study showing that the percentage of total corporate industrial assets held by the 100 largest non-financial corporations had not increased significantly between 1929, the first year for which satisfactory data are available, and 1958. The 100 largest non-financial corporations held 25.5 per cent of all corporate industrial assets in 1929, 28.0 per cent in 1935, 26.7 per cent in 1948, and 29.8 per cent in 1958.[18] These relatively small changes from one benchmark year to the next can be explained largely on the basis of the different cyclical conditions in those years.

Thus it would appear that the extent of economic concentration, whether viewed

[16] National Resources Committee, *The Structure of the American Economy*, Vol. 1 (Washington: Government Printing Office, 1939), Appendix II, Tables iv, v, cited in Adelman, *op. cit.*, p. 286.
[17] Adelman, *op. cit.*, pp. 289–90.
[18] Norman R. Collins and Lee E. Preston, "The Size Structure of the Largest Industrial Firms," *American Economic Review*, Vol. 51 (December, 1961), p. 989.

from the point of individual industries or from the point of the economy as a whole, has not perceptibly increased since the turn of the century. However, we should be careful not to jump to a further and quite different conclusion: that the extent of economic concentration was, and still remains, insignificant. It may well be that while the extent of concentration has not changed, it is nonetheless sufficiently great to warrant concern. But before we turn to the question of its current extent, we had best discuss the meaning and importance of undue economic concentration.

THE SIGNIFICANCE OF CONCENTRATION

From the point of view of the economy as a whole, undue concentration of economic power implies that the control of the economy is in the hands of a small group in a strategic position to effect its will over that of other social and economic forces. The supposed danger of such concentration lies in the possible threat it poses to the nation's democratic political institutions and to the citizen's individual freedoms. Historically, the alleged existence of undue concentration of economic power has been a potent political rallying cry, from the time of the Jacksonian Democrats' attack on the Second United States Bank on down through the Progressive movement's assault on the "trusts." Whether such concentration as exists today constitutes that type of threat to the nation's institutions we shall take up at a later point.

Economists have generally been more concerned about a second type of undue concentration: economic concentration within individual industries. Such concentration, they have argued, vitiates the working of the market mechanism, resulting in misallocation of resources, maldistribution of income, and impairment of technical efficiency. In a somewhat oversimplified view of things, some economists tend to regard all industries in either/or categories: those industries characterized by large numbers of firms, none of which has a disproportionate share of the total market, and in which, as a result, the market mechanism is thought to function effectively are classified as competitive; all other industries are classified as monopolistic. Both the Nutter and Einhorn studies are within this tradition.

Oligopoly

Such a two-fold taxonomy ignores the most important aspect of the structure of the American economy—the widespread existence of industries that are neither competitive nor monopolistic. They cannot be called competitive because they are characterized by having only a few firms or, what is essentially the same, a few firms of disproportionate size. Being only a handful or more in number, these firms recognize the interdependence of their actions; as a result, they scrupulously avoid price competition, often through the expedient of following the pricing actions of one of their own, usually the largest firm in the industry. Price competition being eschewed, even if it may occasionally reassert itself during periods of severe depression, the market mechanism becomes less effective in performing its essential task of allocating resources, distributing income, and promoting efficiency, at least in the short run.

Yet, neither can these industries be called monopolistic. Aside from the obvious linguistic inaccuracy, such a classification implies a much greater unity of action and degree of control than can actually be said to exist when a handful or more of large firms coexist in a state of uneasy truce. Such a classification also ignores the many important forms of competition that do take place, even if price competition is not one of them.[19]

These industries fall in the category of oligopoly, which literally means "few sellers." Unfortunately, it is not as easy to define what is meant by few sellers as it is to define what is meant by either one seller or many sellers. How many firms, in fact, do constitute a "few"—two, four, eight, twenty? The answer, apparently, depends on the circumstances and characteristics of the individual industry, for the essence of oligopoly is not structural but behavioral—the recognition by the firms in an industry of their interdependence and the resulting efforts by those firms to avoid price competition. The study in depth of an individual industry will usually disclose whether, by its behavior, it should be classified as oligopolistic or competitive; a brief glance at the industry's concentration ratio by itself may be inadequate.

Still, a look at the concentration ratio for selected industries can provide a useful overall impression of the extent of oligopoly, especially if the concentration ratio is realistically defined and carefully applied. The Nutter and Einhorn studies can, in fact, serve such a purpose—if their category of effectively monopolistic industries is reinterpreted to mean oligopolistic industries. However, the concentration ratio that they employ, 50 per cent of output by the four largest firms, probably excludes many industries in which the recognized interdependence among firms is sufficiently great to warrant the industry's being classified as oligopolistic. At most, the Nutter and Einhorn studies may be interpreted as indicating the lower limits of the extent of oligopoly in the American economy.

Carl Kaysen

A study that probably comes closer to identifying the true extent of oligopoly in the American economy is the one by Carl Kaysen in *Antitrust Policy*, a book coauthored by Donald F. Turner.[20] Kaysen made a more careful and detailed investigation of what were the economically meaningful markets than did earlier

---

[19] These forms of non-price competition include, e.g., sales promotion, such as advertising and dealership systems, product development, and technological improvement of the production process.

[20] *Antitrust Policy, An Economic and Legal Analysis* (Cambridge, Mass.: Harvard University Press, 1959).

Table 6. Extent of Oligopoly in Manufacturing, 1958.

	NUMBER OF INDUSTRIES	PER CENT OF INDUSTRIES	VALUE ADDED ($1,000,000)	PER CENT OF VALUE ADDED
Type I Oligopoly	63	33.0	30,765	22.2
Type II Oligopoly	57	29.8	48,534	35.1
Others	71	37.2	59,163	42.7
Totals	191	100.0	138,462	100.0

students.[21] Instead of using the Bureau of the Census three-digit industry classification as Nutter and Einhorn did, he used the four-digit classification, which consists of sub-categories within the three-digit system. He then combined these four-digit industry groups into larger ones when he felt the circumstances so warranted.[22] As Kaysen himself explained, "We have reduced the 440 four-digit product class groups [as defined by the Bureau of the Census for the manufacturing sector] to 191 industries, of which 83 represent combinations of two or more four-digit product classes. Of these, 173 are put forward as economically meaningful markets, while 18 are the inevitable statistical catch-all, a 'miscellaneous industry.' The number of consolidations is sizable, which reflects a willingness to define markets broadly and accept a low value for the substitution coefficient in separating markets."[23] Kaysen also took the trouble to distinguish between industries that were national in scope and industries that were either regional or local in character.

Besides the greater care with which he delineated his industries, Kaysen also used a broader structural measure of oligopoly than had Nutter and Einhorn. He defined two types of oligopoly: Type I consisted of industries in which the 8 largest firms accounted for at least 50 per cent of all output, while the 20 largest firms accounted for at least 75 per cent of all output. Type II, an even broader category, consisted of all industries in which the 8 largest firms accounted for at least 33 per cent of all output, regardless of what proportion the 20 largest firms accounted for.[24] These criteria, like all concentration ratios, are undoubtedly arbitrary; still, they probably come as close to defining oligopoly structurally as is possible, and the criterion for Type I oligopoly, in particular, seems quite sound.

[21] Deciding what is the meaningful market area is another of the subjective factors that enters into the computation of a concentration ratio. The more broadly the market is defined, the lower will be the concentration ratio. Thus, the question of what is the meaningful market area is an important one, as can be seen from the several important antitrust cases that have hinged on this issue. Cf. U.S. v. Columbia Steel Co., 334 U.S. 495 (1948); U.S. v. Bethlehem Steel Co. and Youngstown Sheet and Tube Co., 168 Fed. Sup. 576 (1958); and U.S. v. Brown Shoe Co., 370 U.S. 294 (1962).
[22] For example, the three-digit industry, construction, mining and drilling machinery, 353, includes the four-digit industries, construction and mining machinery, 3,531, and oilfield machinery and tools, 3,532.
[23] Kaysen and Turner, op. cit., p. 29. See the Methodological Appendix, pp. 295–99.
[24] Kaysen and Turner, op. cit., p. 30.

As Kaysen pointed out, "In Type I oligopoly, recognition of interdependence by the leading firms is extremely likely, and the 75 per cent share of the first 20 sellers makes it likely that the response of the smaller sellers will not limit the behavior of the larger firms."[25]

Using Kaysen's delineation of economically meaningful markets and his criterion of oligopoly, we can present the figures in Table 6 on the extent of oligopoly in American manufacturing as of 1958.[26]

As Kaysen pointed out, the value added (or share of national income originating in an industry) is but one aspect of an industry's importance. "The simple addition of markets by some quantitative weight," he wrote, "such as the national income originating in each market, ignores the fact that certain markets, apart from their size, by their strategic location in the economic process are especially important. . . . The most obvious example is furnished by the markets for capital goods, whose market variables influence investment decisions throughout the economy."[27] For this reason Kaysen consulted an input-output table[28] to determine which of the 191 industries delineated produced primarily consumers' goods and which produced primarily producers' goods, either investment items or material inputs.[29] The extent of oligopoly in each of these separate types of industry, based on 1958 value added, can be summarized as in Table 7.[30]

The table suggests that oligopoly is most prevalent in the industries that supply investment goods and least prevalent in the industries that supply consumer goods,

---

Table 7. Extent of Oligopoly Among Consumers' Goods, Material Inputs, and Investment Goods Industries (as a Percent of Value Added by Those Types of Industries).

	CONSUMERS' GOODS	MATERIAL INPUTS	INVESTMENT GOODS
Type I Oligopoly	24.6	18.7	27.3
Type II Oligopoly	29.0	42.0	39.6
Unconcentrated	46.4	39.3	33.1
	100.0	100.0	100.0

---

[25] *Ibid.,* p. 27.

[26] See Kaysen and Turner's Statistical and Methodological Appendices, *op. cit.,* pp. 295 ff. Since Kaysen presented figures only for the value of shipments from the industries he delineated, the figures for value added have been taken from the *Census of Manufacturing,* 1958. See especially, Appendix C, pt. 2.

[27] Kaysen and Turner, *op. cit.,* p. 24.

[28] These are tables that show how much of each industry's output is purchased by various other industries and how much, in turn, various other industries supply to that same industry.

[29] Kaysen and Turner, Methodological Appendix, *op. cit.,* pp. 322 ff.

[30] Six of the industries—typewriters; coke and by-products; heating and cooking equipment; cutlery, hand tools, and general hardware; miscellaneous electrical products; and miscellaneous manufacturing products—could not be classified under any of the categories and so have been omitted from the analysis.

with the material inputs industries falling between the other two categories. The historical reasons for this situation will be discussed presently, but first several words of caution need to be entered. Kaysen's data were derived from the 1954 Census of Manufacturing, and this suggests that they might be somewhat outdated. However, as the Nutter and Einhorn studies indicate, concentration data tend to be stable over time, so this does not appear to be an important qualification. Far more serious is the fact that several of Kaysen's industry classifications appear challengeable. It seems strange, for example, that the china and earthenware food-utensils industry should be classified as Type II oligopolistic, especially when one considers the effect of foreign imports on the industry. Similarly, it seems strange that the bread and related products industry should be classified as unconcentrated, especially in light of testimony before the Senate Antitrust and Monopoly Subcommittee that disclosed typical oligopolistic pricing behavior.[31] These reservations merely emphasize the point made earlier, that evidence on industry structure must be supplemented by evidence of actual behavior for a true picture of the extent of oligopoly.

Turning from manufacturing to other sectors of the economy, one discovers that in many cases control by the market has been superseded by government regulation, at least where prices are concerned. This is true of agriculture, transportation, public utilities, and commercial banking and insurance. Together, these various sectors accounted for 23.6 per cent of national income in 1958. Government enterprise and imports, meanwhile, accounted for another 13.2 per cent of national income. Since manufacturing accounted for 28.3 per cent, there remain sectors accounting for only 34.9 per cent of national income still to be analyzed.[32]

Of this 34.9 per cent, 1.5 per cent is accounted for by mineral extraction industries. Kaysen attempted to develop the same type of analysis for this sector of the economy as he did for manufacturing, but he was handicapped by the fact that data on mineral extraction industries were neither as recent nor as comprehensive.[33] With this qualification in mind, we can recast Kaysen's findings:

Table 8. Extent of Oligopoly in Mineral Extraction Sector, 1939.

	NUMBER OF INDUSTRIES	PER CENT	VALUE OF PRODUCT ($1,000)	PER CENT
Type I Oligopoly	25	40.3	417,287	21.4
Type II Oligopoly	3	4.9	154,906	7.9
Unconcentrated	10	16.1	1,298,886	66.5
Unclassified	24	38.7	81,901	4.2
Totals	62	100.0	1,952,980	100.0

[31] U.S. Congress, Senate, Committee on the Judiciary, Subcommittee on Antitrust and Monopoly, *Hearings on Administered Prices*, "The Bread Industry," pt. 12, 1959.
[32] *Statistical Abstract of the United States: 1958*, p. 327.
[33] Kaysen and Turner, *op. cit.*, pp. 37–38 and 39.

It should be noted, first, that the relative importance of the various industries is measured by the value of their final product rather than simply by the value added and, second, that the data are from 1939. Lack of better data, unfortunately, dictated both choices.

The above table would seem to indicate that oligopoly is less extensive among mineral extraction industries than among manufacturing industries. To put this observation in its proper context, however, it is important to point out that over half the value of the unconcentrated industries in the above table is accounted for by a single industry, bituminous coal. Were it not for this one industry, the mineral extraction sector would closely parallel manufacturing in the extent to which it is characterized by oligopoly.

This leaves the wholesale and retail trade, the construction, and the service sectors to be analyzed. Concentration data for these three sectors are even more difficult to obtain than for the mineral extraction industries; were they available, they would probably show oligopoly to be of negligible proportions. This does not mean, however, that these sectors are competitive, at least in a formal economic sense. To a large extent—impossible to determine precisely—the firms in these sectors all possess some degree of protection against price competition, whether it derives from the unique service they provide, the unique geographical location they occupy, or some other special characteristic that distinguishes their product, however defined, from all others. These sectors, then, are characterized by what economists call monopolistic competition rather than by perfect competition or even oligopoly. Yet, while the existence of monopolistic competition may lead to certain socially undesirable results, undue concentration of market power is not one of them.[34]

Summary

In summary, it seems that more than a third of the national product is supplied by the government itself or by government-regulated sectors of the economy, while fully another third is supplied by sectors that can perhaps best be described as monopolistically competitive. This leaves less than a third supplied by sectors in which concentration of market power in the form of oligopoly is at all widespread, and even within those sectors oligopoly is to be found in no more than a bare majority of the industries involved.

Nonetheless, the concentration of economic power in the form of oligopoly may be of far greater significance than these figures alone would seem to indicate. Manufacturing, the sector in which oligopoly is most often found, occupies a strategic position within the American economy. It is the sector to which the

---

[34] According to economic theory, monopolistic competition leads to inefficient-sized firms. This, however, can be considered as simply the cost that society assumes for having a wide variety of products and services, conveniently located in a number of separate locations. One could, for example, obtain gasoline more cheaply at retail if motorists were willing to go to a single central pumping station within each of our metropolitan centers. The same is true of drugs and drugstores.

primary industries, such as those engaged in agriculture and mining, must generally sell their products, and it is the sector from which the tertiary industries, such as those engaged in wholesale or retail trade, must generally obtain their supply of goods. If the effect of oligopoly is to create control over prices, then the ultimate result of oligopoly in the manufacturing sector may well be—as it is in the case of monopoly—a redistribution of income, a loss of efficiency, and, perhaps most important, a misallocation of resources. This last possibility seems especially likely in view of the fact that oligopoly is more widespread among those industries that supply goods to other industries than among those industries that supply goods to consumers and is most widespread of all among those industries that supply goods for investment purposes.

We are thus confronted by the fact that in the most strategic of all sectors, manufacturing, oligopoly is so common as to be characteristic of more than half of all industries. We also know, however, that the extent of oligopoly in manufacturing has probably not increased to any significant degree during the last sixty years. How, then, are we to explain these facts?

THE NINETEENTH-CENTURY CORPORATE REVOLUTION

In the years just before the turn of the century the American economy underwent a radical transformation, so profound in its effects that it has been called by some the American Corporate Revolution.[35] In fact, it was not until this revolution began to create widespread public concern that economists and government officials began collecting the data that now make possible the analysis of concentration patterns and trends. As a result, however, most studies take as their jumping-off point the years following the turn of the century, when the American economy had already begun to settle in its present pattern. Thus they fail to cover the period of greatest change. To understand the nature of the American economy today, it is essential to have in perspective the events that occurred earlier.

Consolidation, 1865–1904

Joseph Schumpeter, in his classic defense of an untrammeled capitalist economy, ridiculed the notion of an earlier "golden age of perfect competition." In his view, capitalism had always included significant elements of monopoly.[36] But if in this country there ever was such a golden age of competition, it was in the years immediately after the Civil War. For by then most of American industry, stimulated by the rapidly growing domestic market, among other things, had emerged from its rudimentary state. Most industries during this time, at least those engaged in manufacturing, displayed all the characteristics of perfect competition. The

[35] See, for example, the essay by Gardiner C. Means in the book of that title (New York: Collier, 1964).
[36] Joseph Schumpeter, *Capitalism, Socialism and Democracy* (New York: Harper & Row, 1942), p. 81.

number of firms was large, entry into and exit therefrom was relatively easy, and products were becoming more and more standardized. Yet, by the time the depression of 1873 began to give way to a new wave of prosperity, many American businessmen had already become disenchanted with a regime of perfect competition.

As one journal, reflecting the widespread feeling of contemporary businessmen, later put it:

> The effect of competition in regulating the prices of manufactured articles is not, at best, wholly satisfactory. It may prevent them from being too high or too low, but it does not prevent wide fluctuations from year to year which involve loss to both the producers and to the public. In fact, in the present workings it makes them inevitable. A man will not go into business unless prices are so high as to give him what he thinks a good prospect of interest on his investment after paying all other charges, but when he has once invested his money, he will not be able to withdraw it without loss. This plant, once established, must be kept in operation, even though the returns do not pay interest or full cover maintenance charges. It then becomes a life and death struggle with him to maintain his position in the trade. He will compete all the more actively while prices are below cost, as long as his financial resources will stand the strain.
>
> Instead of establishing one natural or normal standard of prices, competition then furnishes two distinct ones. One, which includes all elements of cost, determines when new capital will come in; another, which only includes operating expenses in the very narrowest sense, determines when old capital will be driven out. One of these points may be very much higher than the other. The standard of prices in pig iron in a time of inflation is two or three times as high as in the period of depression which follows. For the concerns which have lived through the depression have a temporary monopoly in the "boom" which enables them to command the highest returns, while those which have afterwards been tempted to come in by these specially high prices throw their stock on the market just when it is not needed, and intensify the downward reaction.[37]

In other words, the coexistence of large-scale enterprise requiring substantial fixed investment and a regime of perfect competition led to results that businessmen found intolerable. This was especially true of capital goods industries, subject as they are to more severe fluctuations in demand than other industries. While academic economists might applaud the tendency of prices to decline over the long run, businessmen were appalled by the prospect of having their capital "expropriated" in the process. The next two decades were to witness the struggle of these businessmen to overthrow, in a parody of the Marxian prophecy, the regime of perfect competition.[38]

---

[37] *Commercial and Financial Chronical,* July 28, 1888.

[38] It is not meant to suggest that the acts of these businessmen were in line with a pre-conceived view of how the economic system should be reconstructed. Rather, they were no more than the pragmatic response to existing conditions, the working out through trial and error of the problems with which the businessmen of that day found themselves faced.

This is not the place to present the complex details of that struggle.[39] Suffice it to say that by 1895 American businessmen had learned that by consolidating the great majority of firms in an industry and reorganizing them as a holding company chartered by one of the states—most commonly New Jersey—they could avoid the worst consequences of unbridled competition. This was particularly true if, at the same time, they placed barriers to the entry of other firms.

The movement reached its peak when, in the decade between 1895 and 1904, an average of 301 firms a year disappeared, absorbed either by competitors or by newly chartered holding companies.[40] Altogether, 318 industrial consolidations, involving 5,300 separate plants and more than $7 billion in new stock issues, came into being.[41] As one student of the period has written, "Combination on this scale has never been closely approximated, even when the later merger activity is estimated in terms of depreciated currency."[42]

Reasons For and Reactions Against Consolidation

Despite a conventional view to the contrary, this radical transformation of the American economy cannot be explained by the desire of businessmen to exploit potential economies of scale, though this thought was not entirely absent from their minds. In most cases, whatever economies of scale were possible could be achieved within the firm itself or, at most, through a slight expansion of the firm. It was not necessary to consolidate virtually an entire industry.[43] Nor can this radical transformation be explained simply by the desire of businessmen to reap unusually large profits. Though this element was not entirely absent, such a prospect would not have been sufficient by itself to induce these men, so jealous of their freedom to do as they might please in their economic pursuits, to give up their independence in the large numbers they did. The corporate revolution can best be explained by the desire of these businessmen to achieve some degree of control over prices, to rule the market rather than to be ruled by it. This can be seen in the actual results. In 60 per cent of the 1895–1904 mergers, as measured by capitalization, a single large corporation succeeded in gaining control of at least 62.5 per cent of its industry's market; and in another 10 per cent of the mergers a single large corporation succeeded in gaining control of between 42.5

---

[39] This history is presented, though with primary attention to a single industry, in the author's *The Emergence of Oligopoly: Sugar Refining as a Case Study,* unpublished doctoral dissertation, Columbia University, 1966. For an earlier outline of the same history, see Henry R. Seager and Charles A. Gulick, Jr., *Trust and Corporation Problems* (New York: Harper & Row, 1929).

[40] Ralph L. Nelson, *Merger Movements in American Industry, 1895–1956* (Princeton, N. J.: Princeton University Press, 1959), p. 34.

[41] John Moody, *The Truth About the Trusts,* quoted by Donald Dewey, *Monopoly in Economics and Law* (Chicago: Rand-McNally, 1959), p. 50.

[42] Dewey, *op. cit.,* p. 50.

[43] What is meant here are only technical economies of scale, that is, those economies associated with actual increased efficiency, whether in direct or overhead costs. Pecuniary economies of scale, those associated with increased market power, are another matter.

per cent and 62.5 per cent of its industry's market.[44] If economies of scale or unusually large profits were also achieved, this was merely ancillary to the main objective.[45]

It was not long, however, before the inevitable reaction set in. The American people, historically distrustful of monopoly in any form,[46] would not tolerate a situation in which numerous industries, many of them supplying the necessities of life, were controlled or dominated by a single large corporation. As part of a broad-based movement for reform known as Progressivism, they demanded that the consolidations be broken up.

To a certain extent, they had their way. In a series of precedent-setting decisions, breathing new life into the moribund Sherman Antitrust Act, the Supreme Court ordered the Standard Oil Company of New Jersey broken up into more than 30 separate companies, the American Tobacco Company's assets divided among 16 enterprises, and the E. I. du Pont de Nemours Company split into three autonomous concerns. Taking a cue, the United States Steel Company voluntarily reduced its share of the market to less than 50 per cent, and was rewarded for its preemptive act when the Supreme Court refused to uphold a similar dissolution decree against the giant of the steel industry.[47] Thus the principle of law was established that while no one large corporation could supply virtually the entire output of an industry, several such large corporations could—provided they did not act too ruthlessly to eliminate their competitors.

But it was oligopoly, not perfect competition, that emerged as a result of the courts' endeavors, for competition, having once been destroyed, proved impossible to recreate. Firms had disappeared, entrepreneurs had entered other lines of business, plants in many cases had even been dismantled.[48] Moreover, the courts were reluctant to press the campaign of "trust-busting" too vigorously, for fear of penalizing innocent stockholders who had invested in the consolidations long after they had been organized and for fear of causing the loss of possible economies of scale.[49] Though many of the Progressives had hoped for a return to the golden age of perfect competition, they had to settle for something considerably less.[50]

[44] Nelson, op. cit., p. 102.

[45] Those who engineered the various consolidations were not uninterested in profit maximization. The purpose of the consolidation was to assure a profit of some sort, whatever its actual size. The distinction between what is or is not a fair profit is an illusive one, and economists have as much trouble answering that question as psychiatrists have in determining whether a defendant in a criminal case is legally sane or not. In neither case do the terms lend themselves to precise scientific definition, being essentially ethical in nature.

[46] Cf. Arthur P. Dudden, Antimonopolism, 1865–1890, unpublished doctoral dissertation, University of Michigan, 1950.

[47] U.S. v. Standard Oil Co. of N. J., 173 Fed. 177 (1909), 221 U.S. 1 (1911); U.S. v. E. I. du Pont de Nemours & Co., 188 Fed 127 (1911); U.S. v. American Tobacco Co., 221 U.S. 106 (1911); U.S. v. United States Steel Corp., 251 U.S. 417 (1919).

[48] Eichner, op. cit., pp. 639 ff.

[49] Cf. Dewey, op. cit., pp. 246 ff.

[50] There were, of course, those who realized that the old competitive order could never be reestablished and who therefore supported a program of regulation and control, as distinct from a program of antitrust prosecution.

Oligopoly as a Compromise

As far as the businessmen themselves were concerned, oligopoly was a tolerable compromise. Control over prices could still be achieved, though with less certainty than when a single large corporation dominated the industry. The recognition that any attempt to increase one's market share by cutting prices might provoke a destructive price war was usually sufficient, by itself, to persuade a firm to eschew that method. And if it were not sufficient, the actual experience of a price war always brought the lesson painfully home. The problem was that with several large corporations coordination of pricing decisions within an industry was extremely difficult—even if absolutely essential. Each concern was large and powerful in its own right, free to take whatever actions it felt were to its own best interests, and there was no reason to believe that the actions would be beneficial for all members of the industry without some overall direction. Consultation among the various parties, the most obvious solution to the problem, was prohibited by law. Nonetheless, through trial and error, the various oligopolistic firms gradually learned to overcome the problem of coordination, whether through a system of price leadership, basing points, market sharing, or even collusion.[51] This coordination of pricing decisions, making possible some degree of control over prices, continues even to this day, and it represents the historical legacy of the corporate revolution and the subsequent Progressive reaction.[52]

Schumpeter on Oligopoly and Growth

But should one conclude that because prices are, to a certain extent, controlled and resource allocation thereby distorted that the rate of economic growth in the United States has been adversely affected?

Schumpeter was inclined to dismiss such a suggestion as absurd on the face of it:

> It is necessary to point out that the rate of increase in output did not decrease from the nineties from which, I suppose, the prevalence of the largest sized concerns, at least in manufacturing industry, would have to be dated; that there is nothing in the behavior of the time series of total output to suggest a "break

---

[51] Price leadership is the system whereby one firm in an oligopolistic industry initiates all price changes, these changes then being matched by all other firms in the industry. Basing points enable oligopolistic firms in industries where transportation costs are significant to charge the same price regardless of the locality in which the product is being sold. All firms charge the same base price, plus the published freight rate from the base point, usually the nearest plant location, to the point of sale. Market sharing is a system whereby different firms agree to sell in different areas, thereby avoiding competition with each other. Collusion is the system whereby officials of the oligopolistic firms simply meet secretly to agree on a common schedule of prices. Cf. Burns, *op. cit.;* George W. Stocking and Myron W. Watkins, *Monopoly and Free Enterprise,* (New York: The Twentieth Century Fund, 1951), Chs. 6–8.

[52] That collusion may continue to be an important means of coordinating price policies is shown by the large number of such cases that have been prosecuted by the government in recent years. For an analysis of one such case, see the author's "Trial by Myth," *The Second Coming,* Vol. 1 (1962), pp. 46–50.

in trend"; and, most important of all, that the modern standard of life of the masses evolved during the period of relatively unfettered "big business." . . . Nor is this all. As soon as we go into details and inquire into the individual items in which progress has been most conspicuous, the trail leads not to the doors of those firms that work under conditions of comparatively free competition but precisely to the doors of the large concerns—which, as in the case of agricultural machinery, also account for much of the progress in the competitive sector—and a shocking suspicion dawns upon us that big business may have had more to do with creating that standard of life than with keeping it down.[53]

Schumpeter suggested that price competition was perhaps the least important of the various forms of competition that might prevail. "In capitalist reality, as distinguished from its textbook picture," he wrote, "it is not [price] competition which counts but the competition from the new commodity, the new technology, the new source of supply, the new type of organization (the largest scale unit of control for instance)—competition which commands a decisive cost or quality advantage and which strikes not at the margins of the profits and the outputs of the existing firms but at their foundations and their very lives." Schumpeter called this type of competition "the Process of Creative Destruction."[54]

Schumpeter's explanation for the discrepancy between the empirical findings of non-competitive behavior and what one might have expected to result on the basis of economic theory appears to be only a partial one.[55] Another important factor was a unique social institution spawned by the corporate revolution, the megacorp. Once the nature of that institution has been surveyed, it will be possible to examine the effect of industrial concentration on economic growth with greater insight.

[53] Schumpeter, op. cit., pp. 81–82. This point, that larger size firms tend to be more progressive, was later picked up and elaborated on by John K. Galbraith, American Capitalism: The Theory of Countervailing Power (Boston: Houghton Mifflin, 1952). It has since become a point of considerable controversy among economists. Cf. Henry H. Villard, "Competition, Oligopoly and Research," Journal of Political Economy, Vol. 66 (1958), pp. 483–97; Jacob Schmookler, "Bigness, Fewness and Research," and Villard, "Reply," Journal of Political Economy, Vol. 67 (1959), pp. 628–35. A reasonable synthesis of the conflicting views on this question is that in proportion to their numbers, larger firms tend to be more progressive than smaller firms and that, more important, larger firms, because of their greater resources, are better able to exploit a new technological development once its commercial possibilities have been recognized; however, a technological breakthrough is more likely to come from a smaller firm because of the large absolute number of such firms and also because of the greater freedom of action they have—they can better afford to take risks, since the consequences of failure, at least for the individuals involved, is so much less. Cf. Aaron W. Warner, Dean Morse, and Alfred S. Eichner, eds., The Impact of Science on Technology (New York: Columbia University Press, 1965), pp. 84–142. For a review of recent statistical work on this question, see Jesse Markham, "Market Structure, Business Conduct and Innovation," American Economic Review, Vol. 55 (May, 1965), pp. 323–32.
[54] Schumpeter, op. cit., p. 84.
[55] Critics of the Schumpeterian view have pointed out that the Process of Creative Destruction, if operable at all, works very imperfectly, since the list of America's largest corporations shows little change from year to year. Cf. Collins and Preston, op. cit.

THE MEGACORP

The English language, usually so inventive, has so far failed to produce an adequate name for the institutional offspring of the corporate revolution. "Corporation" covers too broad a group, from General Motors and General Electric to the small, individually owned proprietorship that has been incorporated for business convenience. On the other hand, the terms "large corporation" and "modern corporation" suggested by some fail to convey a clear distinction. Perhaps such a word as "megacorp" may prove more useful.

A megacorp means a corporation that is, first, sufficient in size to be included among the country's 500 largest non-financial corporations as measured by either sales or assets—though this characteristic alone is not enough. The corporation must also be a multi-plant enterprise, and it must possess some degree of market power—that is, it must constitute a significant share of a relatively important industry into which the entry of new firms is made difficult by the existence of substantial market barriers. These barriers may take the form of control over raw materials, patented technological process, the large initial capital outlay required to build an efficient-sized plant, or the substantial sales expense necessary to penetrate a market in which advertising outlays have created intense brand loyalty. In other words, the megacorp must be a large oligopolist.

Origins and Characteristics

Most likely, such a megacorp can trace its origins to the corporate revolution. Ralph Nelson, for example, found that of the 100 largest manufacturing corporations in 1955—all of which under the above definition would be classified as megacorps—20 were born as a result of consolidations between 1895 and 1904, while another 8 resulted from court-ordered divisions of three other consolidations dating from the same period—the Standard Oil Company of New Jersey, the American Tobacco Company, and the E. I. du Pont de Nemours Company. In addition, many of the other 100 largest corporations began as mergers promoted as counterweights to the industrial giants born in the corporate revolution.

Perhaps the most important characteristic of the megacorp for our purposes is its separation of management from ownership, a phenomenon the quantitative significance of which was first pointed out by Berle and Means in *The Modern Corporation and Private Property*.[56] This historical development, in retrospect, appears as the inevitable consequence of allowing the creation of a business

---

[56] *Op. cit.* There are, of course, some firms that by every criterion except the separation of management from ownership would be classified as megacorps. Such family-held enterprises are best regarded as cultural relics that over time will tend to conform to the general pattern. Recent developments in regard to the Ford Motor Company—its decision to go "public," that is, to list its shares on the stock exchange—and in regard to Trans-World Airlines—the forced removal of Howard Hughes from his position

organization, the corporation, whose life lasts well beyond that of any individual. The fact that impersonal bureaucracies, governed by self-perpetuating oligarchies only nominally responsible to vast numbers of poorly organized stockholders, have gained control over the business life of the nation[57] has had profound social and economic effects, not the least of which is the change it has brought about in business motivations and incentives.

The megacorp characterized by the separation of ownership from control has a quite different time orientation from the small proprietorship in which both those attributes reside in the same individual or group of individuals. Protected some-what against the buffeting of market forces, the megacorp can afford to take a longer view of things. Instead of being forced to maximize profits in the short run, it can opt for maximizing profits in the long run, eschewing those actions that, while perhaps immediately remunerative, might impair its future prospects.[58] This reflects, in part, the fact that the megacorp has the requisite resources to tide it over any short-run difficulty and the fact that it can expect to be on hand for any long-run payoff. But it also reflects the fact that the first loyalty of the megacorp's management is to the megacorp itself rather than to its putative owners. In fact, the stockholders comprise only one of several "constituencies" to which the megacorp management feels responsible. (Others include suppliers, dealers, and employees; each of these groups has its own way of pressing its claims.) Since the management does not directly benefit from any short-run increase in profits, it tends to place a lower value on this type of windfall than would the stockholders if they themselves were making the choice; this is particularly true if the short-run increase in profits seems likely to come at the expense of the megacorp's long-term position. While the existence of stock-option plans has led management to identify its interests more closely with those of the stockholders than would otherwise be the case, the essential divergence in goals and outlook nonetheless remains.

Some of Its Effects

By concentrating on the long rather than the short run, the megacorp tends to act as a stabilizing force within the economy. It will, for example, avoid price changes unless it expects them to continue in effect for a considerable time, that is, for

---

of sole control by a group of large insurance companies—illustrate the tendency. For a study that brings the Berle and Means findings up to date, see Robert J. Larner, "Ownership and Control in the 200 Largest Non-financial Corporations, 1929–1963," *American Economic Review*, Vol. 56 (September, 1966), pp. 777–87.

[57] This view is challenged in Don Villarejo, "Stock Ownership and the Control of Corporations," Parts 1 and 2, *New University Thought*, Vol. 2 (Winter, 1962), pp. 54–55, but not successfully in this author's opinion. For a study that supports the Berle and Means thesis, see R. A. Gordon, *Business Leadership in the Large Corporation* (Washington: Brookings Institution, 1945).

[58] Cf. Gordon, *op. cit.,* pp. 331 ff. as well as other studies. For a British view of the same phenomenon, see Roy Lewis and Rosemary Steward, *The Managers* (New York: New American Library, 1961).

at least several months.[59] This is partially because of the difficulty the megacorp has coordinating its pricing decisions with its fellow oligopolists, but the emphasis on long-run goals is probably even more important. Whatever the precise reasons, the result is that the megacorp's pricing actions tend to dampen rather than accentuate cyclical fluctuations in price.[60] This should not be surprising, since the initial impetus that gave rise to the megacorp was the desire on the part of businessmen to cope with the untoward effects of cyclical fluctuations.

In the areas of investment and employment, too—though here the evidence is much less clear—the megacorp seems to act as a stabilizing force. Production— and with it, employment—appears to be geared to a time horizon that makes it possible to ignore seasonal and even, to some extent, cyclical fluctuations. Changes in inventory take up the slack created, bringing production and sales into balance.[61] Investment, meanwhile, is geared to an even longer time horizon, in some cases apparently extending as much as twenty years into the future. A cyclical downturn in demand seems to be recognized as just that, a temporary departure from the secular trend; some megacorps have even begun to accelerate their investment during these periods of minor recession in order to take advantage of the lower prices that then prevail.[62]

Because of the control it has over prices, limited though that control may be, the megacorp is better able to finance its long-run objectives and in so doing to contribute to a higher growth rate for the American economy. On the one hand, its larger size and more secure market position give the megacorp greater access to the capital markets, at lower interest rates, than other business enterprises. On the other hand, American manufacturing corporations typically finance only about two-fifths of their total investment from outside sources; the other three-

[59] For overwhelming evidence on this point, see the various hearings conducted by the Kefauver committee on administered prices. U.S. Congress, Senate, Committee on the Judiciary, Subcommittee on Antitrust and Monopoly, *Hearings on Administered Prices, 1957–1963.* Some economists, most notably Professor George Stigler of the University of Chicago, have pointed out that while list prices may remain unchanged for relatively long periods of time, the actual prices tend to fluctuate. It is questionable, however, whether this phenomenon of "shaded" prices is of significant proportions except during periods of unusually slack demand.

[60] John K. Galbraith, "Market Structure and Stabilization Policy," *Review of Economics and Statistics,* Vol. 37 (May, 1957), pp. 124–33. See also the testimony of Gardiner C. Means before the Kefauver committee, *op. cit.,* Part 1, pp. 74–90.

[61] Because its production schedule is geared to a longer time horizon, the megacorp is less likely to cut back on its output in the face of a fall in demand, and this tendency avoids, at least temporarily, the layoffs that might accentuate the fall in aggregate demand. Also, employment tends to be more stable, both over the year and over the business cycle, in an oligopolistic industry such as automobiles and steel than a competitive industry such as the garment trades.

[62] See, for example, the advertisement by the McGraw-Hill Book Company in the *New York Times,* November 22, 1960, announcing the results of the McGraw-Hill investment survey. For a contrary view, see Robert Lindsay, "The Stability of Business Capital Outlays," *Review of Economics and Statistics,* Vol. 40 (May, 1958), pp. 159–63, and Ernest H. Weinrum, "Is There a Trend Toward Increasing Stability of Capital Outlay?" *ibid.,* Vol. 41 (February, 1959), pp. 80–81.

fifths is financed internally, from retained earnings and depreciation.[63] Retained earnings may, in a certain sense, be considered a levy on the consumer, similar in its effect on the income stream of households to the indirect taxes that government uses to finance its own activities. But whereas government can rely on its police powers to enforce its levies, the corporation must rely solely on its market power. It is here that the megacorp has a special advantage, for its market power is considerable. As one of several oligopolists that together control the output of their industry, it can obtain additional investment funds by raising its prices— subject only to the fear that it may lose markets to substitute products, that it may provoke government intervention in the form of antitrust prosecution, or that it may create such a wide margin between prices and costs that outside firms may be encouraged to enter the industry despite the high barriers that exist. While at times these considerations may be effective restraints on megacorp pricing power, they nonetheless allow a considerable margin for discretion in raising prices and thereby increasing retained earnings. Moreover, they are only distantly related to the traditional notion of the competitive forces at work governing private pricing actions. Viewed in this light, the megacorp appears as an extremely effective social instrument for mobilizing investment funds through a system of forced savings, doing this in such a way that, at least for the megacorp itself, the real cost of capital is reduced.

THE MEGACORP AND ECONOMIC GROWTH

It is against these advantages—its stabilizing influence on the economy and its encouragement to capital formation—that the megacorp's possibly deleterious effect on resource allocation must be weighed. Peter Wiles has suggested that while economic systems based on free markets may allocate resources more efficiently, economic systems based on central planning may actually lead to greater economic growth, for whatever losses may result from poor allocation will more than be offset by the increased ability to mobilize total resources.[64] Wiles' point was not that total welfare would be maximized by central planning but only that economic growth per se would be maximized.

Wiles used the United States and the Soviet Union as prototypes of the two economic systems in an effort to explain, during a period when there was considerable concern on that point, why the Soviet economy was growing at a more rapid rate than that of the United States. Actually, however, it is misleading to view the United States as a pure example of a market type of economy, as Adolph A. Berle and Eli Ginzberg and others have recently pointed out.[65] Even leaving

[63] "Financing the Expansion of Business," *Survey of Current Business,* Vol. 37 (September, 1957), p. 8.
[64] Peter J. D. Wiles, "Growth Versus Choice," *Economic Journal,* Vol. 66 (June, 1956), pp. 244–55.
[65] Adolph A. Berle, *The American Economic Republic* (New York: Harcourt, Brace & World, 1963); Eli Ginzberg, Dale Hiestand, and Beatrice Reubens, *The Pluralistic Economy* (New York: McGraw-Hill, 1965).

aside those sectors that are either government-operated or government-controlled, the American economy fails to conform to such a description. The widespread existence of oligopoly in the crucial manufacturing sector suggests instead a mixture of free markets and planning. Within the megacorp itself, the allocation of resources is accomplished by discretionary command,[66] just as it is in the Soviet economy as a whole. (In fact, the Soviet economy can in some ways be thought of as a single megacorp encompassing the entire nation.) Within the oligopolistic industry to which the megacorp belongs, allocation is also made primarily by discretionary command. Though prices exist, determining what quantities of the final product will be sold, these prices are, as a practical matter, set by the discretionary actions of the oligopolists themselves rather than by the market. It is for this reason that Gardiner Means and others refer to them as "administered prices."[67] Market influences are not entirely absent, of course. Any megacorp can, for example, force its fellow oligopolists to reduce their profit margins by unilaterally cutting its own prices, even though the reverse is not true: no single megacorp, acting alone, can force its fellow oligopolists to increase their profit margins. But such market influences merely determine the limits within which the megacorp has direct command over the allocation of resources; they do not govern the actual allocation.

Allocation Within the Economy as a Whole

Only within the economy as a whole, that is, among oligopolistic industries, is allocation made principally by the market, for it is only on this scale that the market becomes sufficiently impersonal to function effectively. As Schumpeter pointed out long ago, the most important sources of competition are inter-, not intra-industry. This point is all the more pertinent to the extent that purely competitive industries are satellites of oligopolistic industries; that is, they sell (or buy) almost entirely to (or from) megacorp-dominated industries. The automobile parts industry, for example, which is highly competitive, sells a large proportion of its output to the four major automobile producers, while the aluminum fabrication industry, which is also highly competitive, obtains its principal input from one of the five major aluminum producers. In either case, the highly competitive industry must take its pricing cue from the oligopolistic industry to which it is satellite.

In effect, then, the American economy constitutes a system of decentralized planning, with decisions at the firm and even, to a large extent, at the industry level being made by discretionary command—these decisions then being coordinated for the economy as a whole through the market mechanism. In this way

---

[66] "Discretionary command" is the ability to allocate resources outside of a market mechanism. Cf. Robert L. Heilbroner, *The Making of Economic Society* (Englewood Cliffs, N.J.: Prentice-Hall, 1962), pp. 12–14, and J. R. Commons, *Institutional Economics* (New York: Macmillan, 1934), pp. 64–69. Heilbroner uses the term "command" to describe extra-market allocation, while Commons speaks of both "managerial" and "rationing" transactions, the former referring to unilateral extra-market allocation and the latter to multi-person extra-market allocation.

[67] Means, *The Corporate Revolution,* pp. 77 ff.

there is at least some overall control over the efficient allocation of resources, at the same time that individual components, viz., the various megacorps, are allowed considerable flexibility in mobilizing resources. The fact that the American economy has outperformed other economic systems over the past sixty years may to some extent be related to the balance that has been struck between direct planning and market allocation.[68]

What has just been said, however, should not be taken to mean that the American economy is the best of all possible economic systems, that it cannot be further improved. The nation's inability to control wage-price spirals, its relative neglect of social needs, and even its balance-of-payments difficulties can be traced to flaws in the system of decentralized planning that characterizes the American economy.

Social Controls over Megacorp Decisions

As already noted, the megacorp is an extremely effective mechanism for mobilizing resources, but once those resources have been mobilized, there are at best only tenuous social controls over how they will be allocated among various ends. Most important, the megacorp management must choose between increasing the incomes of the megacorp's several constituencies and increasing the megacorp's rate of investment. This is the familiar conflict between present and future consumption, but in making this choice (in conjunction with its fellow oligopolists), the megacorp is to but a limited extent subject to the disciplining force of the market rate of interest. This is because, as already noted, the megacorp under normal circumstances obtains its investment funds internally, that is, by setting prices at a level sufficient to bring a return over costs adequate to finance planned investment in the next period.

If the matter were entirely its own to decide, the megacorp management would probably prefer to hold the income of its constituencies constant, applying to investment projects whatever funds remain after satisfying those claims. This is because its primary interest is in enhancing the importance of its own corporate entity. But as a practical matter, the various constituencies have powers they can bring to bear on the megacorp management, forcing it to increase their incomes. Perhaps the most familiar of these powers is the right of the stockholders to vote for the election of new megacorp officers. This is more of an implicit than an actual threat, since it is extremely difficult for so disparate and disorganized a group as the stockholders to exercise such a power. Still, there are always persons ready to solicit proxies and wage battle in the stockholders' behalf;[69] thus, even if

[65] In this same connection, campaigns by Soviet leaders to introduce a system of more rational prices into their economy should be interpreted as efforts on their part to strike a better balance between direct command and market allocation.

[69] Cf. "The Raiders, Challenge to Management," *Time* (July 25, 1955), pp. 80–81; "Proxy Fights: Here's How . . . They're Won," *Newsweek* (April 23, 1956), pp. 78–80. See also David Karr, *Fight for Control* (New York: Ballantine, 1956), and Robin Morris, *The Economic Theory of "Managerial Capitalism"* (New York: The Free Press, 1964), Ch. 1.

it were not already predisposed to do so for other reasons,[70] the megacorp management would find itself under constant pressure to increase the rate of dividends.

In the 1920's, only the stockholders among the megacorp's several constituencies had effective bargaining power, with the result that their income alone among those of the several constituencies tended to rise as a result of the large increases in productivity that were achieved in the twenties.[71] This unbalanced income distribution pattern, together with certain institutional weaknesses, triggered the stock market speculation that led, in turn, to the Great Crash of 1929.[72]

By the early 1950's, the institutional pattern had been altered so that the megacorp's employees also had effective bargaining power, largely as the result of trade-union organization. This bargaining power was used to obtain increases in wages similar to the increases in dividends that stockholders had obtained in the 1920's and still continued to obtain in the 1950's. Since wages accounted for approximately 74 per cent of all non-material costs in manufacturing compared with 5 per cent for dividends,[73] it was impossible both to maintain desired levels of investment and to hold prices steady, especially since the growth in productivity had fallen off from the high rate of the 1920's.[74] Confronted with this dilemma, the megacorp management quite naturally opted for higher prices, but the result was what came to be known as "cost-push" inflation, the steady 1 per cent to 1.5 per cent annual decline in the purchasing power of the dollar, even aside from whatever other inflationary pressures might exist.

What is being suggested here is the possibility that the "cost-push" inflation of the 1950's had the same basic cause as the stock market speculation of the 1920's and that this basic cause was the lack of effective social control—such as the various factor markets, according to traditional economic theory, are supposed to provide—over how the megacorp's resources were to be allocated, first between investment and an increase in the income of its several constituencies, and then among the several constituencies themselves.

Domestic and International Investment Imbalance

The megacorp's very effectiveness in mobilizing resources also leads to social imbalance, for it gives the megacorp a considerable advantage over other social

---

[70] On the one hand, because of its own close identification with the property-owning classes and, on the other, because of the continuing allegiance to the somewhat anachronistic notion that the stockholders are, in some metaphysical sense, the "real" owners, the managers of megacorps may be inclined to distribute more of the megacorp's claims over resources to stockholders than the stockholders' bargaining power alone would dictate.

[71] John W. Kendrick, *Productivity Trends in the United States* (New York: National Bureau of Economic Research, 1961), p. 136.

[72] Cf. John K. Galbraith, *The Great Crash* (Boston: Houghton Mifflin, 1954), and George Soule, *Prosperity Decade, From War to Depression, 1917–1929* (New York: Holt, Rinehart and Winston, 1947), Ch. 15.

[73] National Industrial Conference Board, *The Economic Almanac*, 1964, p. 232. The figures are based on the years 1950–54.

[74] Kendrick, *op. cit.*, p. 136.

institutions, most importantly the government. The latter, before it can act to meet a demonstrated social need for a particular type of investment, must first obtain approval from an elected legislative body to raise taxes—to pay the interest on the money to be borrowed if not to pay the full amount of the investment itself. The megacorp, on the other hand, can obtain the funds it needs—subject to the limitations noted above—by adding to the prices it charges for its products, thus effecting its own levy on the consumer but without having first to obtain approval from any legislative body. This is perhaps the way it should be, at least for those goods that are best supplied through a private market mechanism. But there are certain other goods that a private market mechanism cannot supply; these public goods, such as education, transportation, and pollution-control facilities, can only be supplied by government.[75]

This is not to say that the megacorp has unlimited power to finance its investment projects by raising its prices,[76] nor that other factors are not also important in explaining social imbalance. But the greater ease with which the megacorp can gain command over resources is perhaps one reason why, in the American type of economic system, private needs tend to be met more quickly and more assuredly than purely public ones. Fortunately, this imbalance seems on the way toward being corrected as a result of a recent social innovation that demonstrates at once the value of the American pragmatic tradition and the adaptability of the megacorp. This social innovation is the government contract system, by which the megacorp is hired by the government to carry out those functions considered necessary for meeting social needs.[77]

Finally, the megacorp's ability to accumulate a continuing high level of capital funds through the price mechanism may lead to the employment of those funds overseas when sufficiently attractive investment opportunities cannot be found in this country. The alternative, either a price reduction or an increase in financial liquidity, is not likely to appeal to the management of a megacorp interested in the perpetuation and enhancement of its own company as a going concern. A rise in megacorp investment abroad has, in fact, been observed in recent years.[78] This is hardly a trend to be deplored in a world that requires, as part of the solution to its long-term ills, the massive movement of capital from the richer to the poorer lands.[79] But it has led to certain short-run economic and political problems.

Unfortunately, most of the flow of megacorp funds has been not to the least developed parts of the world but primarily to the rich, industrialized nations of

[75] The existence of social imbalance, as first argued by John K. Galbraith, in *The Affluent Society* (Boston: Houghton Mifflin, 1958), has, it should be noted, been challenged by other economists. Cf. F. A. Hayak, "The Non-Sequitor of the 'Dependence Effect,' " *Southern Economic Journal*, Vol. 27 (April, 1961), pp. 346–48, and Henry C. Wallich, *The Cost of Freedom* (New York: Harper & Row, 1960), pp. 165–72.
[76] See above, pp. 190–91.
[77] Ginzberg *et al., op. cit.,* pp. 147 ff.
[78] *International Commerce,* September 2, 1963, p. 8. It is assumed that most direct foreign investment by U.S. firms is made by megacorps.
[79] Gunnar Myrdal, *Beyond the Welfare State* (New Haven, Conn.: Yale University Press, 1960), Ch. 13.

western Europe and to Japan and Canada.[80] Together with the enormous expense of maintaining an American military presence in those same countries, it has overtaxed the monetary mechanism created after World War II to handle the quite different international relationships of that earlier period, leading in turn to the current United States balance-of-payments "problem."[81] Of the several possible solutions to this problem—elimination of American megacorp investment abroad, reduction in United States military commitments abroad, and reform of the international monetary mechanism—the last, while perhaps most desirable, is blocked by the political difficulties created by American megacorp investment abroad. These political difficulties are the fears held by some foreigners—many Frenchmen, among others—of an American take-over of their local economies. Those who hold such fears have therefore blocked reform of the international monetary mechanism in the hope that continuing pressure on the American balance of payments would lead to measures in this country to restrict megacorp investment abroad. (It is interesting that the other possible course of action, a reduction in United States military commitments in Europe, has been openly predicted by these same foreign groups.)

INTERLOCKING CORPORATE RELATIONSHIPS

It is possible that the power of the megacorp as an institution is limited to a single industry, yet the power of the officials that control it extends throughout the economy as a whole, thereby giving rise to a different type of concentrated power. There are two reasons why such concentrated power would be a matter for serious concern. The first is that through their control of the economic system certain groups in society might be able to seize control of the political system as well, thus endangering our system of democratic government. The second reason is that once in control, the groups that hold the reins of power might manipulate the economic system to their own advantage, against the interests of society as a whole. Of course, these two possibilities go hand-in-hand.

From what has previously been said, one might very well expect to find a dangerous degree of concentrated power within the American economy. Indeed, when one looks at the same set of statistics Berle and Means first called attention to, it shows, if not the degree of concentrated corporate wealth Berle and Means predicted would occur by this time, at least a degree of concentrated corporate

[80] Approximately two-thirds of America's net private direct foreign investment in 1963 and 1964 went to western Europe, Canada, and Japan. Evelyn M. Parrish, "The U.S. Balance of Payments in 1964," *Survey of Current Business* (March, 1965), pp. 12–13.

[81] Robert Triffin, *Gold and the Dollar Crisis* (New Haven, Conn.: Yale University Press, 1961); U.S. Congress, Joint Economic Committee, *Factors Affecting the United States Balance of Payments*, 87th Cong., 2nd Sess., 1962, see esp. the papers by Seymour Harris, "The U.S. Balance of Payments: The Problem and Its Solution," pp. 1–26, and by Philip W. Bell, "Private Capital Movements and the U.S. Balance of Payments Position," pp. 395–482.

wealth that is still significantly high. In 1962, the 200 largest industrial corporations controlled 49.5 per cent of all non-financial corporate assets, though they
comprised only .0016 per cent of all corporations. The next 300 largest corporations, meanwhile, controlled another 10.8 per cent of all non-financial corporate
assets.[82]

The concentration of economic power may even be greater than the above
figures suggest. The substantial number of directors that many of the nation's
largest corporations have in common, the close ties these corporations have to a
relatively small number of banking and other financial institutions, and the "communities of interest" thereby created have often been cited. A recent study, for
example, focused on a group of 232 companies chosen from among the nation's
250 largest industrial corporations, found that while these 232 companies had a
total of 3,196 directorships, the directorships were held by only 2,784 individuals.
Thus, 303 persons held more than one directorship in the companies studied, 221
of them occupying a seat on two separate boards of directors, 56 occupying a seat
on three separate boards of directors, and 23 occupying a seat on four or more
separate boards of directors. In addition to the 303 individuals who held more
than one corporate directorship, there were another 149 persons who, while not
simultaneously a director of another large corporation, were nonetheless an executive of one. Finally, the study found that of the 2,784 directors, 258 were the
representatives of important commercial banks, investment banking firms, or large
insurance companies, with 53 of them holding more than one directorship in the
232 large corporations studied.[83] Studies by the federal government disclose a
similar pattern of interlocking corporate relationships.[84]

Various inferences are possible. Might it be that certain individuals, because
of their imputed knowledgeability and keenness of judgment, are more in demand
to serve as directors of megacorps than others? Or might it be that certain individuals are chosen to serve as directors of two or more corporations in order to
forestall competition among them? This is a much more ominous possibility—
though not as ominous as might at first appear, since competition among megacorps in the same industry is usually quite limited even when there are no
common directors.

Finally, might it be that the system of interlocking directorates has arisen as a
means of uniting the megacorpic business community, welding it into a cohesive
force capable of imposing its own policies on the rest of society? This is a most
ominous possibility but one that seems, upon serious reflection, somewhat
implausible, for it presupposes that there are particular policies that those in

---

[82] *Statistical Abstract of the United States: 1965*, pp. 490 and 494–95.

[83] Villarejo, *op. cit.*, Part 3, pp. 54–55.

[84] U.S. Federal Trade Commission, *Report on Interlocking Directorates,* Washington,
1951; U.S. Congress, House of Representatives, Select Committee on Small Business,
*Interlocking Directors and Officials of 135 Large Financial Companies of the United
States*, 85th Cong., 1st Sess., 1958; U.S. Congress, House of Representatives, Committee
on the Judiciary, *Interlock in Corporate Management* 89th Cong., 1st Sess., 1965.
Mention should also be made of the pioneering study by the U.S. National Resources
Council, *Structure of the American Economy,* Washington, 1939.

control of the nation's megacorps, with all their diversity of interests, would find mutually acceptable. In fact, it would seem that the only policies that could win such a broad range of agreement would be policies that are so clearly in line with the overall group interest that they would be acceptable even without any interlocking relationships. One need not raise the specter of some controlling business elite, held together by a system of interlocking directorates, to explain the unanimity of businessmen on issues.

Of course, one need accept none of the three interpretations. In fact, the most probable explanation of the great number of interlocking corporate relationships is the desire to give a voice in management affairs to men representing important constituencies—stockholders who happen to have equity interests in other mega-corps, representatives of large financial institutions who are important suppliers of credit, and executives of other megacorps that are either major suppliers of inputs other than capital and labor or purchasers of outputs.

Even if one still holds to the view that there exists a cohesive, coordinated community of interest among the nation's largest corporations that is antagonistic to the general public interest, one would still take cognizance of what has been perhaps the much more important development during the last thirty years, the increasing role of the government in the economy. It is this factor that has made the question of concentrated private economic power so much less important than it once seemed. Today, through the proper application of monetary and fiscal policy, the federal government can effectively regulate the aggregate level of economic activity. It can determine which geographical regions are to be stimulated, which industries encouraged, and which interest groups favored. It can do this, irrespective of what the megacorpic business community may wish—though this community, as one of the more important interest groups, can undoubtedly make its influence felt in such matters. The historical solution to the problem of concentrated private economic power has been an increase in the role and powers of the federal government, and this solution is still capable of being applied.

Conglomerate Expansion

Only one last point need be made here in regard to the problem of concentrated economic power. It relates to the growing trend toward conglomerate expansion, that is, the tendency of many megacorps to move into entirely new industries, totally unrelated to those in which they are already situated.[85] To a certain extent, this trend is but a new phase in the historical evolution of the megacorp, enabling such a company to diversify its activities and become less dependent on the shifting fortunes of a single industry. This type of expansion is often accompanied by the disappearance of some existing corporation either through merger or outright purchase. For this reason, some persons have urged that the antitrust laws

[85] Cf. U.S. Congress, Senate Committee on the Judiciary, Subcommittee on Antitrust and Monopoly, *Hearings on Economic Concentration,* Part 1, "Overall and Conglomerate Aspects," 88th Cong., 2nd Sess., 1964.

be amended to prohibit conglomerate expansion, on the ground that it leads to the further concentration of economic power.[86]

Rather than being prohibited, however, it might be better if this type of expansion were encouraged. No matter how many industries a megacorp may become involved in, they would represent but a small proportion of the total economy. On the other hand, conglomerate expansion may have certain positive features to recommend it. Insofar as the nation's oligopolistic industries are concerned, it may represent the best means of introducing an element of competition into them, for it is much easier for a corporation already established in one industry to breach the barriers of another than for a new corporation starting from scratch. It is entirely possible that some of our less dynamic industries, suffering from the stifled development that sometimes comes from having a too well-protected market position, may well be revitalized in the process, while capital that would otherwise flow overseas may then be able to find profitable outlets here at home.

Of course, one cannot predict with any certainty that these would be the actual results. But such a pattern of intermegacorp competition, transcending existing industry boundaries yet mitigated by the system of interlocking corporate relationships, may well be the next logical step in the development of that peculiar mixture of discretionary planning and market allocation that characterizes the American economy.

SELECTED READINGS

EDWARD S. MASON, *The Corporation in Modern Society* (Cambridge, Mass.: Harvard University Press, 1959). A collection of stimulating essays by economists, lawyers, and political scientists discussing the problem of social control posed by the megacorp.

ADOLF A. BERLE AND GARDINER C. MEANS, *The Modern Corporation and Private Property* (Chicago: Commerce Clearing House, 1932). The classical treatment of the problems arising from the separation of management from ownership.

JOSEPH SCHUMPETER, *Capitalism, Socialism and Democracy* (New York: Harper & Row, 1942). The summary statement of the Schumpeterian analysis of capitalism.

CARL KAYSEN AND DONALD F. TURNER, *Antitrust Policy, An Economic and Legal Analysis* (Cambridge, Mass.: Harvard University Press, 1959). Both a sophisticated analysis of the extent of oligopoly in America and an interesting proposal for revising the antitrust laws.

C. WRIGHT MILLS, *The Power Elite* (New York: Oxford University Press, 1959). Perhaps the most persuasive argument that concentrated economic power exists within American society.

[86] Corwin D. Edwards, "Conglomerate Bigness as a Source of Power," Universities-National Bureau for Economic Research, *Business Concentration and Public Policy* (Princeton, N. J.: Princeton University Press, 1955), pp. 331–51.

GARDINER C. MEANS, *Pricing Power and the Public Interest* (New York: Harper & Row, 1962). An analysis and suggestion of remedies for pricing power in the steel industry.

JOHN M. CLARK, *Competition as a Dynamic Process* (Washington: Brookings Institution, 1961). A full-length treatment of the concept of workable competition offering a dynamic analysis of oligopoly.

WILLIAM J. BAUMOL, *Business Behavior, Value and Growth*, rev. ed. (New York: Harcourt, Brace & World, 1967). Some contributions to oligopoly theory, a persuasive demonstration that business motives other than profit maximization can be rationally and consistently implemented, and comment on the relationship of these motives and economic growth.

chapter 7

BUSINESS AND
ECONOMIC GROWTH

GORDON C. BJORK, *who combines the technical equipment of the economist with the broader perspective of the historian, has dedicated his essay to an examination of American economic development as a function of the interplay of political-legal institutional arrangements, socioeconomic attitudes and values, and the responsive adaptations of businessmen.*

The more recent efforts of newly developing countries to take their place in the community of industrialized nations and the struggles of nations already industrialized to increase their rates of economic growth have inspired many attempts to determine the relative contribution of various factors in producing the "wealth of nations." While the influence of institutional arrangements, cultural values, and historical patterns on economic activities has by no means been ignored, most of the exciting intellectual undertakings of economists and policy makers pursuing this interest have focused on the empirical associations between growth rates and variations in such factors as investment, tax rates, aggregate demand, interest rates, the changing educational achievements of the labor force, technological changes, and many other dimensions of social and economic life that lend themselves to quantification and statistical manipulation.

The role of businessmen who competently adjust and redesign their organizations, successfully negotiate new and complex legal arrangements with unions, distributors, and government contractors, and who imaginatively pursue modifications in the attitudes and tastes of consumers tends to be bypassed in such studies. The measures by which such economic performance is gauged no doubt reflect but certainly do not single out the creative acts of managers who expertly incorporate the discoveries of scientists, the handi-

craft of computer wizards, the arcane arts of the advertising agency, and the sometimes quixotic behavior of federal regulators into their calculations and decisions in respect to corporate planning, production, and distribution.

Professor Bjork's essay attempts to isolate the impact on American development of the kinds of institutional and entrepreneurial factors so often excluded from consideration by the social scientist's ceteris paribus. *After considering several qualitative dimensions as well as the more measurable aspects of American economic development, especially as they are reflected in the development of three key industries, he concludes that our economic achievements are attributable to the fact that "the structure of economic activity has permitted, encouraged, and indeed necessitated the proper responses from individuals." Policies, laws, and values have been significant elements in the evolution of this "structure" while the innovations of businessmen in organization and distribution have facilitated the fruitful exploitation of resources and technological advances.*

Among the beneficially potent variables Professor Bjork identifies is the creative tension between integration and disintegration in the structures of firms, industries, and the economy generally. To this tension he attributes costs as well as benefits, however, among them the "passing of small business in the wholesale and retail trades." His discussion suggests a number of interesting questions:

1. What qualitative standards might be applied in weighing the benefits of an economically healthy small business stratum to the economy? To the society?

2. Some critics might claim that Professor Bjork has over-emphasized the benefits of rationalized distribution systems and modern advertising practices and underestimated their costs. What have been some of consequences of increased organizational size for entrepreneurial daring, the availability of credit for various kinds of research, and the general efficiency of American business?

3. Professor Bjork, not less than most observers, has specifically identified "political stability" as a factor influencing the favorable "responses" of businessmen in American history. Upon reading this essay, one of the editor's students commented that there is more political stability in American history books than in American history and that America's political instabilities have contributed a great deal to business opportunities. Comment on this observation. (Keep England in mind in assessing the point in contention while disregarding any nations whose politics have been especially chaotic.)

GORDON C. BJORK \ ## BUSINESS AND ECONOMIC GROWTH: A LONG-RUN PERSPECTIVE

In the late 1950's and the early 1960's the goal of economic growth assumed over-riding importance in America. During the Presidential campaign of 1960, the late John F. Kennedy articulated a widely held feeling when he charged that the recent economic performance of the United States had not been satisfactory and when he said that it was "time to get America moving again." Progress has been an integral part of the American perspective. For many decades it had been assumed that economic growth was an inherent feature of the American free-enterprise system and that apart from providing a stable social and political frame-work with fiscal and monetary stability there was no need for collective action through government to alter economic performance. Private enterprise was be-lieved to be sufficient unto itself. The sluggish performance of the American economy in the 1950's, coupled with Khrushchev's challenge that capitalism would be "buried" by the superior economic performance of a communist economy, caused many Americans to think seriously about the continuing potential of the American free-enterprise system to provide an acceptable rate of economic growth.

CAPITAL FORMATION, INNOVATION, AND THE AMERICAN ECONOMIC SYSTEM

The most meaningful standard of performance for evaluation of the free-enterprise system is the rate of growth in per capita producton of goods and services. Eco-nomic growth is often discussed in aggregate terms. However, unless one is interested in a country's military potential (and aggregate output is not the only important aspect even here), aggregate figures are misleading as to the real im-provement in the productive performance of an economy because they fail to take account of the influence of population growth. Per capita output in real terms and its rate of increase are the most meaningful measures of economic performance.

There are only two ways in which real per capita output can be increased: either the quantity and quality of productive inputs contributed by a population of a given size must increase or the efficiency with which those productive inputs are organized must be improved by technological or organizational innovations. This essay is addressed primarily to an examination of the latter—the way in which the American economy has grown over the past 150 years by increasing the ef-ficiency with which production is organized.

Traditionally, economists have emphasized the overriding importance of capital formation in economic growth. Insofar as capital accumulation is governed by factors largely beyond the control of businessmen, the adoption of this view would relegate the businessman to a relatively minor role in the process of economic growth. In his widely read books on the historical process of economic growth, W. W. Rostow has hypothesized that it is a precipitous rise in capital formation at some point in time that allows an economy to "take off into sustained economic growth."[1] "Orthodox" economic theory has always emphasized that capital deepening was the primary way in which increases in output per worker were achieved.

The businessman, in the orthodox economist's scheme of reference, was the decision-maker who would substitute capital for labor in response to changes in relative prices of the two factors of production when it was economically rational to do so. The role of the businessman was essentially that of a human computer— to estimate the relative costs of producing a specified article, given a certain technology and set of factor prices, and to direct the productive process. This implied that the function of the businessman could be performed by any competent administrator. The private-ownership and free-market characteristics of the American economic system were not necessary characteristics for good performance.

In the last few years the empirical study of economic growth has led to a shift away from the view that capital formation is the all-important factor. A trail-blazing article published by Robert Solow of MIT in 1957 indicated that it had not been capital deepening but technological change embodied in improved capital equipment and productive processes that had been responsible for most of the economic growth in the United States during the first part of the twentieth century.[2]

Solow's findings were confirmed in a study undertaken by Edward F. Denison for the Committee on Economic Development.[3] Without discussing the assumptions underlying the measurement methods of Solow and Dension or the biases introduced by them, it is interesting to note that they arrived at similar conclusions about the importance of technological change. Denison's estimate was that between 1909 and 1957 improvements in technology and in the organization of production accounted for some 58 per cent of the measured growth in per worker output. Some 42 per cent of the measured growth was due to improvements in the quality of the labor force resulting from education and increases in the quantity of capital.

What implications are there for economic growth in the American business system of private ownership of the means of production and the freedom of the marketplace? Would collective ownership of the means of production or state control of economic activity produce a higher rate of growth than the "free-enterprise system"? One cannot give a definitive answer to these questions by theorizing or by looking at the available evidence because of the multitude of differences among societies at different points in time.

[1] *The Process of Economic Growth* (Oxford: Clarendon Press, 1953); *The Stages of Economic Growth* (Cambridge: Cambridge University Press, 1960).
[2] "Technical Change and the Aggregate Production Function," *Review of Economics and Statistics,* Vol. 39 (August, 1957).
[3] *The Sources of Economic Growth in the United States and the Alternatives Before Us* (New York: Committee on Economic Development, 1962).

The sources of economic growth in a society are very complex. Many of the "answers" that observers have found in studying the historical record are inevitable only because of the conceptual framework that was used to structure the "questions." It is not possible to isolate some fraction of economic growth as attributable to "business" or "government" or "labor" or "investment in education." All are inextricable threads in the fabric of American economic activity.

The empirical evidence on the sources of economic growth has necessitated a shift in emphasis by students of the process of economic growth from capital formation to the forces affecting innovation in productive techniques. If innovation in productive processes is more important than capital intensification and efficient use of existing techniques, then the structure and character of economic organization as it affects, permits, rewards, and necessitates innovation becomes of paramount importance.

Insofar as the American free-enterprise business system is characterized by flexibility and offers strong incentives for innovation it becomes a very important factor in the rate of economic growth. Observers of the American scene have noted different things in the record of business performance. In the last analysis, all disputes must center on an evaluation of the historical evidence. And, unfortunately, if the study of history reveals anything, it does not reveal the same things to all people.

The term "free enterprise" is a convenient way to distinguish the American economic system from other types of economic organization, but it tells very little about the complexity of the system or its underlying values. There are two essential features of the system that deserve emphasis. The first is its general reliance on the economic forces operating in free markets to set prices and guide decisions about production and investment. The second is the important role it gives to private property, which is broadly defined, widely distributed, and subject to few restrictions on its use. Neither of these characteristics of the American free-enterprise system is unique to that system. Furthermore, a significant proportion of economic activity in the United States is either carried on or regulated by the various levels of government. The use of private property has been subjected to increasing restrictions as the society has become more complex and interdependent, and the use of property by one individual affects the value of property of others. Still, in comparison with the rest of the world, the individual citizen in the United States has a large degree of freedom to engage in economic activity as he pleases and as he is able, and relatively more reliance is placed on free markets in the United States than in other societies.

THE HISTORICAL BACKGROUND: 1776–1870

In testimony before the congressional Joint Economic Committee in 1959, Raymond Goldsmith estimated that sometime around 1840 a secular rise in productivity began in the United States and has continued at a reasonably stable long-term rate to the present.[4] This date for the beginning of steady growth in the United States agrees generally with what economic historians know about the changes that were taking place in the national economy at the beginning of the nineteenth century.

When Britain's 13 American colonies declared their political independence in 1776, they also sought freedom from the British mercantile policies that had tied them to the economy of the metropolitan country as producers of raw materials and as consumers of British manufactures. When the American Constitution was ratified in 1789, the immediate prospects for economic growth were not encouraging. The largest part of the population was engaged in subsistence agriculture, as is the case in underdeveloped countries today. The market-oriented agricultural sector found that there was little prospect for growth because of the lack of expanding demand for its major products. Before the Revolution, over half of total exports had been of tobacco, but European demand was stagnant. More tobacco was shipped from the United States in 1790 than would be again until 1840. The West Indies had also been a profitable market for American provisions, which were used to feed the slaves on the sugar plantations, but the Caribbean sugar plantations reached the peak of their development toward the end of the eighteenth century, and they provided no prospects for the expansion of trade. The rising population in Europe was a potential market of great importance for American grain and lumber, but transportation costs were still too high to make the export of these bulky goods a profitable large-scale activity. Finally, the American merchant marine was restricted by the mercantile policies of the European nations, which were trying to build up their navies and improve their balance of payments. These policies reduced demand for the output of the American shipbuilding industry, which had been the colonies' most important industrial activity before the Revolution.

Contemporary observers were optimistic, however, as the new nation started its independent political life. One American wrote to a Philadelphia newspaper in 1789:

> There is a spirit of emulation, of industry, of improvement, of patriotism, raised throughout the states. . . . In no period have they made a more rapid progress than within this year or two; . . . Every nerve and sinew seems to be at its utmost stretch, and this is not by the interposition of the legislative; but by the patriotic or interested and enterprising spirit of the individuals; perhaps, even by the want of an effectve government, I might almost have added, and, as in most similar cases, might have marred.[5]

But the real problem for America had never been the absence of resources or initiative. Before enterprising individuals could have unlimited opportunities for economic advancement, certain changes had to take place that would allow the

[4] U.S. Congress, Joint Economic Committee, Hearings, *Historical and Comparative Rates of Production, Productivity, and Prices,* 86th Cong., 1st Sess., 1959, pp. 277–78.
[5] Letter reprinted in *The American Museum,* a periodical published in Philadelphia by Matthew Carey, 1787–93, Vol. 6, pp. 236–38.

transformation of the United States from an underdeveloped nation to a developed one.

Hamilton's Report

No one understood the problem of industrialization more clearly than Alexander Hamilton, the first Secretary of the Treasury. In his famous *Report on Manufactures* of 1791, he pointed out that industrial growth would be slow and difficult in the United States because of the advantages possessed by foreign competitors.[6] He advocated the use of tariffs to give American manufacturers a protected home market and the judicious use of subsidies to get them started. These measures were to be coupled with internal improvements to open up the areas outside the few seaport cities to internal trade. Hamilton also favored a land policy limiting rapid westward expansion, since this might spread the population too thinly and force manufacturers to pay high wages to prevent laborers from leaving industrial employment to become small farmers.

Hamilton saw clearly what was needed to make industrialization possible; he was aware of the need to use governmental powers to establish certain preconditions for expansion by the business community. He was, however, ahead of his time; Jeffersonian policies more suited to a nation of small farmers than to businessmen generally were followed during the first 50 years of the new nation's existence. Still, before 1840, significant progress was made in establishing conditions favorable to rapid industrial growth in the latter half of the century.

War, "King Cotton," and Early Development

Between the beginnings of the Napoleonic Wars in Europe (1792) and the outbreak of the second war with Britain (the War of 1812), the American economy received a temporary fillip because of the neutral status of the United States. This was a period of unprecedented prosperity for Boston, New York, Philadelphia, and the smaller seaport towns as American ships were employed in the carrying trade of both France and England. Manufacturers benefited from the temporary prosperity and from the removal of competition by imports from Europe. The wars were as efficacious in encouraging industrialization as was Hamilton's policy of protection and subsidies. Robert F. Martin's figures for per capita income in 1799, the period of peak prosperity during the Napoleonic Wars, suggest a higher standard of living than was reached again until 1840.[7] With the return to peace

[6] *Report on Manufactures,* Dec. 5, 1791. Reprinted in *The Reports of Alexander Hamilton,* Jacob E. Cooke, ed., (New York: Harper & Row, 1964), pp. 115–204.
[7] Robert F. Martin, *National Income in the United States, 1799–1938,* National Industrial Conference Board, Study No. 241 (New York, 1939). These estimates are open to a great deal of criticism. Cf. William N. Parker and Franklee Whartenby, "The Growth of Output Before 1840," *Trends in the American Economy in the Nineteenth Century,* Vol. 24 of *Studies in Income and Wealth* (New York: National Bureau of Economic Research, 1960).

in 1815, income per capita—especially in the commercial and manufacturing areas—fell, and the United States had to face once again the problems of building an industrial economy from an undeveloped structure geared to subsistence agriculture and the export of staple raw materials.

However, not all the advances made since 1790 were eliminated by the return of peace. In New England and the middle Atlantic region, the manufacturing that had been established during the European wars, although buffeted by the winds of foreign competition, readjusted and retrenched to resume gradual progress. In Massachusetts, the mercantile and shipping interests invested capital in textile factories,[8] and from the need for textile machinery came the beginnings of the machine-tool industry that, in turn, later produced equipment for a variety of industrial uses, including railroads.

More importantly, the prospects for the South and the West had been changed by "King Cotton." The invention of the cotton gin by Eli Whitney had been a major technological breakthrough. It gave American cotton production a decisive cost advantage that—coupled with a rising demand for the fiber from the expanding industry in England and New England—stimulated the rapid geographic expansion of cotton production across the South. In 1790, the declining profitability of tobacco, rice, and indigo—the principal colonial staples—had been forcing the South into diversified agriculture. By 1820, the booming demand for cotton had altered the social and economic history of the nation by concentrating investment in the southern states on the production and export of one commodity —cotton.

Unfortunately for the South, the cotton boom did not lead to industrial development but only to the extension of cotton culture. The revenues from the export of the commodity did not stay in the region for reinvestment in manufacturing or commerce or the provision of "social overhead capital" in transportation improvements and urbanization. Newspapers of the ante-bellum South were full of laments that the revenues generated by cotton production did not stay in the South but went to pay for northern manufactures and the shipping, insurance, and financial services of mercantile houses in Boston, New York, and Philadelphia. In per capita income, the South dropped behind the rest of the nation and has remained there to this day.[9]

The development of large-scale cotton production in the South had an important impact on the other sections of the country. It generated and financed interregional trade that made possible later industrialization in the middlewest and northeast. Until the 1820's, the area west of the Alleghenies was a frontier region with little possibility of integration into the economy of the Atlantic seaboard. The profitability of cotton culture in the South created a market for the foodstuffs of farms accessible to the Ohio-Mississippi river system. This, in turn, spurred canal build-

---

[8] Lance Davis, "Stock Ownership in the Early New England Textile Industry," *Business History Review*, Vol. 32 (1959).

[9] Richard A. Easterlin, "Inter-regional Differences in per capita Income, Income, Population, and Total Income, 1840–1950," in Parker and Whartenby, *op. cit.*, pp. 73–140.

ing to bring into production for southern markets those areas lying away from the cheap transport furnished by the rivers.

The completion of the Erie Canal in 1826 connected the western states and New York City, providing cheap transportation for bulky commodities. By the start of the Civil War, railroads had largely completed the integration of the economy east of the Mississippi. Meanwhile, the northeastern states had developed manufacturing, financial, and commercial facilities to serve the needs of the West and the South. Cotton had played a leading role in the process of regional specialization and, additionally, had provided export revenues to finance a significant volume of foreign investment in railroads and municipal developments.

Businessmen, Local Government, and Transportation Improvements

Douglass North, who has focused attention on the importance of international and interregional trade during the period prior to the Civil War, has argued that during this period there was little need to consider the contribution of the entrepreneurial abilities of particular businessmen.[10] In an acquisitive society, where the forces of the market were allowed to operate freely, economic progress would be inevitable. His emphasis on the macroeconomic forces at work during the period has had a very salutary effect on the writing of American economic history. Yet, it is also pertinent to note that individual businessmen shaped the social institutions and that their economic and political entrepreneurship was vital to the provision of publicly financed investments in transportation facilities and other forms of social overhead capital.

Prior to the middle of the nineteenth century, the important businessmen were not those engaged in manufacturing. With the exception of textiles and a few firms engaged in the production of transportation equipment, manufacturing was carried on by small-scale firms operating in limited local markets. The first listing of an industrial concern on the New York Stock Exchange was in 1836, and 20 years later there were only some 20-odd firms listed. Of course, there were firms with considerable capital whose securities were not traded, but, by and large, manufacturing was carried on by small local firms operating with primitive production techniques.

The businessmen responsible for the conduct and finance of international and interregional trade were crucial to economic growth during this period. The exploitation of the static comparative advantages of different regions of the country became possible as internal transportation improvements created an integrated national market. The fact that New England could buy cheap cotton from the South and cheap food from the middlewest enabled it to sell cheap textiles and other goods and services to the other regions. Of importance for future growth was the construction of a transportation network to carry on interregional trade.

In this period before the Civil War the federal government did not play an active role in transportation improvements. Local governments, however, did,

[10] *The Economic Growth of the United States, 1790–1860* (Englewood Cliffs, N. J.: Prentice-Hall, 1961).

especially in building canals and railroads to the cities and areas they served. The impact of the Erie Canal on the trade of New York City and the economic development it brought through the Mohawk Valley was a powerful demonstration to other states of the importance of transportation facilities. Local governments were important in the provision of transportation investment for two principal reasons. The first was the factor of high risk. Government guarantees of interest and principal on bonds used to finance internal transportation improvements made them salable at home and abroad where they would otherwise have been unacceptable to private investors. The second was the factor of social returns. Promoters of many of the transportation improvements were less interested in direct returns on capital invested than in the effect on land values and the level of economic activity in areas integrated into the market by the transportation improvements. Social returns exceeded the realizable private returns from railroad and canal operations, and consequently public investment was considered by the business community both necessary and appropriate.

Foreign investors, persuaded by government guarantees and lured by the high profitability of the Erie Canal, poured large amounts of capital into improvements in the 1830's, only to lose everything in the Panic of 1837. Investors lost their capital, but the physical capital—in the form of canals and railway roadbeds— was there to be used in the expansion of trade and commerce. While the merchants who promoted these internal improvements ventured little of their own capital, they furnished the entrepreneurship and stimulus to government that was of crucial importance in laying the foundations for economic development. Although we are accustomed to think of the mid-nineteenth century in the United States as a period of laissez faire, much recent historical writing supports the view that government (especially local government) was the willing servant of the business community. Businessmen of the period realized that economic development depended upon the existence of capital investment, which could only be made collectively, and they mobilized collective action to deal with it.

THE HISTORICAL BACKGROUND: 1870–1960

By the middle of the nineteenth century certain necessary preconditions for rapid economic growth in the United States had been achieved. Domestic markets had been enlarged by the provision of cheap transport for goods and materials. Agricultural productivity was rising with the opening of the fertile lands of the great midcontinent area and with improved agricultural implements and techniques. Although it has been thought traditionally that industrialization and rapid economic growth were triggered by the Civil War, recent reexaminations of the evidence have tended to show that the Civil War disrupted the economy and slowed its rate of progress. The war's effects on the South were catastrophic, but it has been argued that even the North experienced adverse effects.[11]

[11] Thomas C. Cochran, "Did the Civil War Retard Industrialization?" *Mississippi Valley Historical Review,* Vol. 48 (September, 1961).

Without going into the contributing economic causes of the Civil War, it seems reasonable to generalize that one of its effects was to transfer political power in the federal government. The agrarian coalition of the South and West, which had controlled the nation since the end of the eighteenth century, was replaced by a Republican Party imbued with a Hamiltonian philosophy that sanctioned the use of the federal government to make possible rapid industrialization. Federally sponsored railroads were built to the Pacific coast. Tariffs on manufactured goods were raised at the beginning of the war and were not significantly lowered until recently.

Economists and historians have argued interminably over the effects of tariff protection on industrialization, and perhaps no final answer can be reached on that subject. It is worth recording, however, that specific groups of manufacturers *thought* tariffs were important, and to the extent that the existence of tariffs created greater optimism and security they may have stimulated entrepreneurs to "give hostage to fortune" by investing in plants and fixed capital assets.

The economic growth of the United States since the Civil War is compared in Table 1 to that of several European nations and Canada.

Table 1.   Percentage Rate of Growth in Output Per Capita for Selected Western Nations.[12]

	1870–1913	1913–50	1950–60
Belgium	1.7	0.7	2.3
Denmark	2.1	1.1	2.6
France	1.4	0.7	3.5
Germany	1.8	0.4	6.5
Italy	0.7	0.6	5.3
Netherlands	0.8	0.7	3.6
Norway	1.4	1.9	2.6
Sweden	2.3	1.6	2.6
Switzerland	1.3	1.5	3.7
United Kingdom	1.3	1.3	2.2
Canada	2.0	1.3	1.2
United States	2.2	1.7	1.6

Rapid Growth: 1870–1913

Between 1870 and 1913, economic growth in the United States outstripped the performance of every western nation except Sweden. It was not only a period of rapid growth in per capita incomes but also a period of accelerated population growth as millions of Europeans emigrated to share in the bounties of the new

[12] Angus Maddison, *Economic Growth in the West* (New York: The Twentieth Century Fund, 1964), p. 30.

world. This was the fabled period of the business tycoon in the United States. Today, the average American might not remember the names of such Presidents as Garfield, Arthur, or Cleveland, but he would recognize names like Rockefeller, Carnegie, Morgan, and Vanderbilt, for their effect on the country was far greater than that of the Presidents. Contemporary opinion of business leaders ranged from the adulation of Horatio Alger to the censure of the "muckrakers," who called the great industrial tycoons the "robber barons." Unfortunately, most of the biographies of the business leaders of the period furnish precious little information that can be used to evaluate their and their businesses' impact on the rate of economic growth. Such an evaluation can really only be accomplished by going back to such primary evidence as the records of individual firms and the trade journals of various industries. By and large, this work is yet to be done; one can hope that it will be done with the same care as has been lavished by other historians on their materials.

The shift from agriculture. The period from 1870 to 1913 was one of transition from a predominantly agricultural economy to an economy in which the manufacturing and service sectors were of primary importance. This transition was connected to the growth of productivity in America. Productivity did increase in agriculture itself, although most of this increase came about because of the industrial production of improved agricultural equipment. Productivity also increased as a result of a shift of the labor force from agriculture to manufacturing. The agricultural labor force increased in absolute terms all during the period, but it steadily declined as a relative proportion of the population. Since productivity was higher in industry than in agriculture, this shift in the composition of the labor force was responsible for a good deal of the measured increase in per capita output. Average per capita output would have risen if labor had been shifted from a sector where marginal productivity was low to a sector where it was high, even though there was no productivity increase within either sector.

Two comments need to be made about the shift of labor from agriculture. First, because farmers raise some of their own food, and for a number of other reasons too detailed to state here, the measured increase in output that results from a transfer of labor from the farm to the city may substantially overstate the increase in "real" per capita income. Second, economic growth resulting from intersectoral shifts from agriculture to industry is a "once over" gain for a country. After the productivity increase resulting from contracting the agricultural labor force from 50 per cent to 10 per cent of the population has been registered, it cannot be duplicated in a subsequent period; even a further contraction from 10 per cent to 2 per cent would not yield the same results.

Population growth. A second characteristic of the period from 1870 to 1913 that sets it apart from later periods is that it was a time of very rapid population growth as a result of extensive immigration from Europe to the United States. The structural adjustments that accompany economic growth are much easier to accommodate during a period of rapid population growth. Demand for all goods and all types of labor increases in absolute terms even though there are relative declines in some sectors. This means that it is not necessary for many firms to contract production or employment absolutely. Under these conditions a society's response to economic change is likely to be flexible. It is easier for a man's son to leave an occupation that is declining in relative importance because of technological change than it is for the older man to leave because the occupation no longer affords him a living. Overall growth imparts a certain fluidity to structural change in the economy. The absolute decline of the agricultural sector after the first world war created some problems of readjustment that have not yet been solved by our economy.

Another favorable effect of the influx of immigrants was a change in the age structure of the population over a short period of time. The proportion of the population active in the labor force increased, with a consequent increase in the average input of labor per person of the total population. The economy also benefited from the fact that these immigrants had been educated and trained at considerable expense by their countries of origin; the returns from this investment accrued to the United States.

With the conditions that existed between 1870 and 1913, there would have been economic growth even if there had been *no* capital accumulation, organizational innovation, or technological change in the business enterprises of the United States. The fact that there was a good performance in the industrial sectors enhanced and accelerated the growth that occurred as a result of these other factors.

Temporal classifications inevitably do violence to the continuity of economic development. 1913 serves as the end of an era in the United States only because it marked the end of a century of comparative peace in Europe. However, 1913 could also be said to mark the achievement of a certain stage of development in the economy. A transportation system had been completed that linked the sections of the country together and allowed the economy to benefit from economies of scale and the exploitation of the comparative advantage in the production of the different regions. Financial markets had been developed to allow the effective mobilization of capital. Steel production had been rationalized and brought to a high level of economic efficiency, thus providing a basic input in the nation's economy at a lower cost. Developments in coal mining and petroleum production and refining made available a supply of cheap energy. A machine-tool industry with a high degree of technical competence and adaptability stood ready to provide the tools for consumer-goods industries. Progress in the processing and distribution of food had reduced its price to the consumer. In making provision for the necessities of life, the American business system had made possible a high standard of living for the masses.

From 1913 to 1950

Between 1913 and 1950 the forward thrust in the American economy came in the provision of consumer durables—goods that yield a stream of services over a period of time. The existence of a large sector of the population with incomes significantly above the amount necessary to provide for food, clothing, and shelter, coupled with the existence of the prerequisites for low cost production, made possible a tremendous boom in the production of such goods as automobiles, washing machines, refrigerators, radios, modern kitchen stoves, and, at the end of the period, television sets. The establishment of consumer finance companies was another necessary development to volume production of consumer durables, since most families had to purchase items over a period of time, and retailers needed credit for the large inventories they required. These consumer durables made life more pleasant for the average American, and enormous increases in productivity were achieved in their fabricaion.

Continuous-flow production, or the assembly line, was not new to America. A continuous-flow flour mill had been constructed by Oliver Evans in 1785. However, it is Henry Ford to whom credit must go for putting the concept into operation in the fabrication of consumer durables. Two other production concepts were necessary to the high-level operation of the assembly line. One was product standardization; there had to be a mass market willing to accept a standardized model of the product. Prior to Ford, automobile makers had chosen to produce highly differentiated products and to sell them at high prices; Ford standardized his product and found a market for it. The second necessity for assembly-line production was the "scientific management" concept popularized by Frederick W. Taylor. The idea of training workers for the performance of specific jobs antedated Taylor in several industries, but he introduced methodical observation to the diagnosis of processes and reorganized plant layouts and job specifications to eliminate all possible time and motion loss. There were, of course, objections from labor that increased productivity through scientific management would merely make the working man work harder. Much of the objection was due to resistance to any kind of change, and most of it was overcome with a minimum of difficulty. Ford introduced scientific management in his automobile plants and made it more acceptable to his workers by paying each one a wage of $5 a day.

While productivity increases in the consumer-goods industries during the period from 1913 to 1950 were spectacular and readily apparent because of the products' familiarity to the householder, an equally important revolution was taking place in the basic industries that depended on scientific advance and its technological embodiment. Chemists discovered a wide range of materials that could be obtained from hydrocarbons. Chemical engineers constructed petroleum refineries capable of "cracking" crude petroleum into constituent particles that could then be converted into a wide spectrum of products ranging from fuels and fertilizers to plastics and pharmaceuticals. A great variety of products was similarly found to be obtainable from coal.

Improvements in the use of both coal and petroleum for fuel greatly increased thermal efficiency in the conversion of energy. Between 1900 and 1950, the amount of electricity that could be generated from a pound of coal increased about seven-fold. While scientific advances that reduce the cost of energy and raw materials are not readily observable by the individual consumer, they are a major contributor to the growth in economic well-being.

The spur to developments in chemical transformation of coal, petroleum, and a wide range of other materials was largely pressure on large corporations to diversify. For example, the DuPont company found itself at the end of the first world war with liquid assets, skilled manpower, and a greatly curtailed market for the company's traditionally most important product—explosives. The company's response was diversification into a wide range of chemicals and other products. Petroleum producers also felt the need to diversify. Despite the great increase in demand for gasoline and lubricating oil between the wars, production of crude oil and refining capacity increased at an even greater pace. Competition among petroleum producers forced them to search for economic utilization of by-products; the result was diversification into petrochemicals and products made from them.

American agriculture did not share in the prosperity of the 1920's. The postwar collapse of European markets for American food exports took away a source of expanding demand that had absorbed a large percentage of the increases in American production in the 30 years preceding the world war. In the United States increased income was not being spent on food. The stagnation of demand for food was accompanied by increases in agricultural productivity resulting from such innovations as tractors and chemical fertilizers. The result was an excess supply of labor in the agricultural sector. Part of the excess labor in agriculture was absorbed into the expanding manufacturing sector, but the economy was plagued with increasing rigidities as the aggregate demand for goods and services was dragged down by the depression in agriculture.

The adjustment problems of agriculture in the 1920's were considerable and were exacerbated by the large amount of agricultural debt incurred by farmers during the years of agricultural prosperity and high prices preceding 1920. However, this bad situation grew even worse in 1930 when the bottom fell out of the market for agricultural commodities. Prices plummeted, and in 1932 net farm income was less than one-third of what it had been in 1929. Agricultural prices began to rise slowly after 1933, but prosperity did not really return to agriculture until the second world war. In 1948, after three years of high postwar demand for American agricultural exports in Europe, the fortunes of the agricultural community once again took a turn for the worse; this time the government stepped in to prevent price declines through the use of price supports.

The record of American productivity growth between 1913 and 1950 looks very satisfactory in terms of what European nations were able to attain during that period. Yet, the European nations had to survive the physical destruction of two wars and the breakdown of international trade that took place in the interwar period. Furthermore, their populations did not have the high incomes at the turn of the twentieth century that would have given them prosperous domestic markets for mass production of consumer goods. The United States had unparalleled advantages for economic growth during this period, and individual industries revolutionized production techniques and rationalized the organization and distribution of production. Yet the economy as a whole was frustrated in the 1920's and 1930's by chronic unemployment of men and capital. There was no notion of collective responsibility for the maintenance of full employment and the easing of the burdens of transition that are made necessary by economic growth. The New Deal of Franklin D. Roosevelt was a disaster operation necessitated by the breakdown of the economy. The passing of the Full Employment Act of 1946 was a statement of collective intention that the breakdown would not be allowed to occur a second time and that to prevent it the government was directed to use the means at its disposal to keep aggregate demand expanding at a rate sufficient to compensate for population growth and productivity increases.

The Decade of the 1950's

The economic performance of the United States during the decade of the 1950's was sluggish in comparison to Europe's. (Table 1.) There are, of course, a number of factors that combined to give some European countries advantages in competitive "growthmanship." Many of these countries were rebuilding their economies from the ground up, and part of the growth represented a recovery of lost ground. In Germany, large numbers of highly skilled workers fled from behind the Iron Curtain to increase and improve greatly that nation's quantity and quality of "human capital." In Italy and in France, the shift of population from subsistence peasant agriculture to industry gave both countries a large increase in productivity due to the intersectoral shift. The beginnings of a "mass consumption" society gave European producers the high demand for consumer durables experienced in this country between 1913 and 1950.

In the United States, several factors contributed to the lower rate of growth in measured per capita output. There was relatively little movement out of agricultural employment, because the agricultural sector was small in 1950. The most important increases in employment were in the service sector, which renders personal services rather than producing products and includes government employees, teachers, doctors, lawyers, beauticians, etc. It is difficult to measure the economic output of the service sector; output is arbitrarily measured at factor cost, which omits any increases in quality or quantity of services that might have occurred through improved training or organization of labor. Between 1950 and 1960, consumer expenditures for services rose from 33 per cent to 40 per cent of total spending. This meant a progressively larger part of the economy was being concentrated in a sector where productivity increase was difficult to measure.

Apart from biases in the measurement of per capita income growth in the 1950's, two real factors contributed to a slowdown in the increase of per capita output. Because of changes in the age structure of the population, there was a declining percentage of people in the 18–60 age group from which the majority of the work force is drawn. And there was persistently high unemployment during the 1950's. The economic impact of this unemployment was to keep output significantly below what it could have been, given the United States' supply of labor, capital, and technology.

It should be obvious that the factors contributing to a relatively low growth rate in the United States during the 1950's did not have much to do with the performance of particular industries. The shift in the pattern of consumer expenditures from goods to services reflected the needs and wants of an affluent society, not the structure of the business system. Business organization obviously has nothing to do with changes in the age structure of the population. If the unemployment is caused by lack of aggregate demand, then the solution lies with the judicious use of monetary and fiscal policy in bringing expenditures up to the production capabilities of an economy operating at full employment.

Much of the unemployment and underemployment that occurred during the 1950's resulted from the failure of the labor force to adjust to the different pattern of skills that were necessary. The investment in relocation and the retraining of workers displaced by economic growth and technological change are not the responsibility of individual business firms. And since the benefits of economic growth are enjoyed by society collectively, the human costs of unemployment should not be borne by individual workers who are the unwitting victims of economic change. It should be an acknowledged public responsibility to finance the retraining and relocation of the labor force made redundant in particular industries and locales. Private enterprises should not be asked to finance retraining, because they cannot be sure that they will be able to retain workers in whose training or retraining they may have made considerable investment. It is interesting to note that in the federal government's current large-scale campaign to upgrade the labor force the education and training is being financed by the federal government but is being carried out by many private business concerns on contract. Cooperation between business and government in education and in the financing of research and development will expand steadily in the future because of the desirability of rapid growth and the impact that it has on society.

INDUSTRIAL STRUCTURE AND TECHNOLOGICAL CHANGE

Economic growth has thus far been treated largely in aggregate terms as a social process, yet the technological and organizational innovations that are responsible for a large part of economic growth are implemented by individual men in individual firms in particular industries. The process of economic growth occurs in individual economic units when output per unit of input is increased. In order to gain an insight into the way the American business system has operated in particular industries, three very different ones will be examined—the steel, textile, and machine-tool industries.

The Steel Industry

The American iron and steel industry was technologically backward in comparison to its European counterparts at the close of the American Civil War. Production was widely dispersed geographically and most of the smelting of iron ore was done in inefficient charcoal or anthracite furnaces. In the period between 1870 and 1913, there was rapid technological change in the industry. The low costs of production in new furnaces resulted in continuing expansion of capacity more rapid than expansion of effective demand. There were some attempts by the industry to create "pools" to divide existing markets, limit production, and curtail the building of new capacity in order to keep prices up, but these were of little avail. The relentless expansion of new capacity forced prices down and closed down the older, less efficient producers.

After the Civil War, change came rapidly in iron and steel production. The rapid increase in domestic demand, coupled with tariff protection, made expansion of new, efficient capacity profitable for those who had the foresight to undertake it. Modern furnaces were more efficient than the old, and their lower costs of production quickly eliminated older producers who could not compete with the new, lower-cost furnaces. A period of rapid technological change within an industry inevitably brings cries of distress from those producers who fail to modernize to avoid the cost-price squeeze. The fierce competition in the steel industry stimulated economic growth by necessitating the adoption of new methods and abandonment of the old. Thus, it had a salutary effect on the improvement of productivity for the industry and the economy as a whole.

In 1870, the United States' output of pig iron was less than one-third that of Great Britain's. In 1874, an American metallurgist claimed that English producers of pig iron had an advantage of $5 per ton on labor costs over American producers and that they had further advantages stemming from larger scale, technically superior facilities that were better managed.[13]

By 1891, an Englishman noted that the tables had been reversed by American improvements on ideas that had originated in Britain. The Americans had improved on British layouts and had profited from British errors by not repeating them. As the Englishman noted:

> Their blast furnaces are more capacious than ours, their engines are more powerful, their rolling mills are of new improved construction. The high standard of education, and especially of the technical education of the people in America, is undoubtedly much to their advantage.[14]

The early realization of the importance of education of the labor force for improved productivity in the United States is a suggestive piece of corroborative evidence for the current emphasis on the importance of education and training for economic growth. The evidence on relative prices supports the view that the American industry was rapidly outstripping its European counterparts during the period.

It is interesting to make some international comparisons of the American iron and steel industry with European competitors at the close of the nineteenth century, because the technological knowledge of steelmaking was available to all.[15] The higher cost of capital and labor in the United States, along with lower fuel

---

[13] Victor S. Clark, *History of Manufacturers in the United States*, Vol. 2 (3 vols.; New York: Dover, 1963), p. 310.

[14] Quoted in American Iron and Steel Association, *Bulletin*, Vol. 15 (February 16, 1881). Quoted in Clark, *op. cit.*, Vol. 2, p. 311.

[15] Statistics collected from Clark, *op. cit.*, Vol. 3.

costs, stimulated the adoption of a different set of techniques. Still, the differences in labor productivity were notable. While pig iron output per worker in Germany in 1900 was about 400 tons per week, it was 1,300 tons at the Carnegie works in Pittsburgh. Some idea of the scale and productivity of American furnaces in 1907 can be gained by noting that the average yearly output of American furnaces was 77,000 tons. This compared with averages in Germany of 43,000 tons, in Belgium of 36,000 tons, in England of 27,000 tons, and in France of 25,000 tons. The difference seems even more remarkable when we recall that cheap wood in the United States allowed the continuing production of some old charcoal furnaces of very small size.

Some idea of the temporal progress of the American steel industry can be gained from the following indications of maximum output of the best furnaces:

1850	10 tons per day
1875	100 tons per day
1894	400 tons per day
1905	918 tons per day

A great deal of attention has been given to the impact of the great merger of 1900 that created U.S. Steel and of the concentration and mergers that preceded it. It would seem probable that the vertical and horizontal integration that took place in the steel industry from 1875 to 1900 played a part in the drastic lowering of the real costs of production. Economies of scale were one result, and the integration of the industry allowed savings in better planning, better heat utilization, smaller inventories, and lower administrative overhead. The mergers were spurred on by downward pressure on prices resulting from the continuing introduction of more and more efficient production methods. The firms that survived were those that could scrap obsolete facilities and build newer ones.

The U.S. Steel Corporation, when created in 1900, controlled over 50 per cent of finished steel output and 43 per cent of pig iron output in the U.S. The capital assets of the firm were valued at $1.4 billion. Many observers feared that the new giant would try to stifle competition, but during the first decade of its existence it lost considerable ground to its major competitors, particularly Bethlehem, Jones and Laughlin, and Youngstown Sheet and Tube. Part of the firm's relatively disappointing performance may be explained in terms of the difficulties of integrating and managing such a large complex of activities. Part of it may also be explained in terms of the high proportion of Bessemer capacity possessed by U.S. Steel during a period in which the open-hearth process used by competitors gave them an advantage. Obsolescence is not redeemed by size. The U.S. Steel Corporation did not stifle technological change in the early period of its existence, although the steel industry has subsequently been criticized by many for oligopolistic policies designed to preserve the status quo.

Given the spectacular growth in iron and steel production between the Civil War and World War I, one is still left with the difficult question of whether American businessmen accelerated the process of technical innovation or whether it was the natural result of rapidly expanding demand and keen competition.

In a recent article, Peter Temin argued persuasively that the most important factor explaining differential rates of growth in productivity among the United States, Britain, and Germany was the different rates of growth in demand for iron and steel in those countries.[16] Rapid increase in demand led to construction of new facilities embodying the most advanced production techniques. Differences in productivity in the three countries could be easily explained in terms of the more rapid increase in domestic demand in Germany and the United States, coupled with tariffs that kept Britain from selling in those markets. American and German steelmakers had an advantageous position for the exercise of their entrepreneurial abilities.

During the period after the Civil War, there is some evidence that the U.S. industry was lacking in scientific expertise as compared with British and German steelmakers. The Bessemer and Siemens-Martin (open-hearth furnace) processes were developed in Britain and Germany and were only slowly adopted in the United States. Andrew Carnegie, for example, was criticized for being slow to adopt the Bessemer process, but his defense that the process was still too experimental to be an economic gamble worth taking was probably a shrewd guess at the time, the early 1870's.

Between 1870 and 1890 the success of Carnegie in the steel industry was in large part a result of his willingness to innovate and to pay high salaries to obtain technically competent steelmakers. He minimized capital costs by replacing obsolete equipment during the troughs of depressions when construction and financing costs were low. Charles Schwab said in 1896, in a memorandum intended for private circulation within the Carnegie Steel Company, "The great success with which we have always met in our business has been largely due to the fact that we have anticipated our competitors in manufacturing better and cheaper than they do."[17]

When Andrew Carnegie withdrew from a pool of beam producers because he knew he could undersell the rest of the industry, the head of Jones and Laughlin commented that Carnegie had improved "the art, science, and practice of steel making [and had] increased tonnage and reduced costs years before it would otherwise have been brought about, [but his] unreasonable competition was childish and against public policy."[18] The equation of the public interest with higher prices and restricted output is an interesting piece of "doublethink," unless the preservation of high-cost producers in an industry is considered to be in the public interest (as is often argued in a roundabout way).

Apart from its financial aspects, the formation of the United States Steel Corporation was an attempt to decrease competition and to raise profits by raising prices. It has had some success in doing this up until the present day, but it has also progressively lost its share of the market to other producers who have ex-

---

[16] "The Relative Decline of the British Steel Industry, 1880–1913," in H. Rosovsky, ed., *Industrialization in Two Systems* (New York: John Wiley, 1966).
[17] Quoted in W. Paul Strassman, *Risk and Technological Change* (Ithaca, N.Y.: Cornell University Press, 1959), p. 43.
[18] Quoted in Clark, *op. cit.*, Vol. 2, p. 302.

ploited geographical advantages and technological advances in the production of particular kinds of steel. The industry as a whole has increased its productivity at a rate well above the average for American manufacturing.

The Textile Industry

The textile industry provides an illustration of an industry in which productivity growth generally has been well below the average of manufacturing industry. At the end of the nineteenth century, value added in the manufacture of textiles was approximately equal to that in iron and steel production. The two industries, however, were very different in their performance, structure, and history. Textile manufacturing was the first large-scale industrial enterprise in the United States and dated from the beginning of the nineteenth century, when the Napoleonic wars gave it an initial impetus. At a time when most ironworks were still very small operations, textile mills were built that employed large quantities of capital and labor and used advanced techniques for spinning and weaving.

Until the middle of the century, American firms were considered fairly progressive and efficient compared to their English competitors. This was attributed partially to the high price of labor in the United States, which acted as a spur to technological and organizational innovation to economize on wages. In England the abundance of labor for employment in textile production not only reduced the incentive to increase labor productivity but may have acted as an important deterrent by creating social attitudes hostile to changes that threatened textile workers with loss of employment. In the 1830's, the so-called Luddites roamed the textile districts in England smashing looms because they saw that machinery was reducing the demand for their labor. The United States was never subject to a similar phenomenon. In New England, the shortage of labor was such that the mills were operated largely by women who planned to work for a few years in order to accumulate a dowry.

Contemporary observers thought that English looms were superior to American ones, but they also noted that the American labor force was utilized more effectively. In evidence given before a British parliamentary committee in 1854, it was stated that an American worker would ordinarily tend four looms while his British counterpart would operate two. American employers actually gave training to their workers to enable them to handle more looms.[19] Management attention to efficient labor utilization thus occurred in the textile industry years before the "scientific management" movement was pioneered by Frederick W. Taylor.

Another advantage that the textile industry had in raising productivity in the United States during the nineteenth century was the character of market demand. The American consumer was ready to buy cheap, standardized textiles, and the textile producer was ready to buy stock models of textile machinery. This willingness of both producers and consumers to standardize products gave the American

---

[19] H. J. Habakkuk, *British and American Technology in the 19th Century* (Cambridge: Cambridge University Press, 1962), pp. 47–48.

producers an advantage over their foreign competitors. As one English observer stated, "The willingness on the part of the American public to buy what is offered them, if it in any way answers the purpose, has given a great advantage to the North American manufacturer over his European competitor who has to contend with habits and prejudices of centuries' standing. . . ."[20]

Some observers have charged that the American textile industry tended to stagnate during the latter half of the nineteenth century. W. Paul Strassman characterized the period after 1835 as one of "technological conservatism."[21] He argued that the increasing capital requirement for mills limited the entry of new competitors, and the old firms preferred to protect their financial position rather than take risks with new equipment. "The inertia and prejudices of the mill owners, the buyers of textile machinery after 1840, appear to have been a greater obstacle to innovation than the prejudices of cloth and yarn buyers. In the case of old mills, the desire for uniformity discouraged major changes even in replacements for worn-out machines."[22]

Naturally, it was not a period completely without progress. Industry journals in 1876 recorded that for two large New England textile corporations, output per operative had increased 300 per cent between 1838 and 1876.[23] After 1880, there was considerable labor unrest in New England. This unrest, attributable to dissatisfaction with wages, and the fact that the industry began to move to the South after this period, suggest that the New England industry was not able to make productivity increases at a rate sufficient to stay in a high wage area. When an industry is unable to compete in labor markets, it is an indication that its rate of growth in efficiency is lagging behind that of other industries. The movement of the textile industry to the South is suggestive evidence of Strassman's charge of conservatism.

The charge that the managers of New England textile mills were irrationally conservative has been explored at great length by Irwin Feller.[24] He examined the faster rate of adoption of the Northrop automatic loom between 1894 and 1914 by southern mills and concluded that this was not a result of conservatism but of an economically rational calculation, by both northern and southern managers, based on different costs of labor and the more limited labor savings of the Draper loom in the North in weaving with fine warp thread. The New England mills could not have obtained a rate of profit on the operation of the new looms sufficient to cover their cost of capital, while the southern mills could. Thus, the traditional emphasis on "managerial conservatism" as an explanation for the decline of the New England textile industry is not denied, but cost factors are selected as the more important causal explanation.

[20] D. L. Burn, "American Engineering Competition," *Economic History,* Vol. 2 (January, 1931), p. 306.
[21] *Ibid.,* p. 88.
[22] *Ibid.,* p. 98.
[23] Clark, *op. cit.,* Vol. 2, p. 388.
[24] "The Draper Loan in New England Textiles," *Journal of Economic History,* Vol. 26 (September, 1966).

Another explanation of the technological conservatism of the textile industry in the period up to the end of the second world war is the close relationship between textile producers and the makers of textile machinery. Mills tended to become tied to particular machinery producers, and the result was often the making of minor changes in existing models of machines rather than the adoption of new devices. Mill owners preferred to keep one type of machine to reduce maintenance costs and to simplify the training of operatives. This tended to result in indivisibilities in substitution in the individual mill, and progressive replacement of old looms with new, more efficient types was resisted.

The relationship between the textile machinery manufacturers and the mills tended to persist until after World War II, when the established producers were unable to fill the flood of new orders. General machine shops without experience in the production of specialized textile equipment were given orders, and they tended to be more adventurous in introducing innovations. Textile firms, faced with rapidly rising wages, were more receptive even to radical changes and high-priced machinery as long as the savings in labor cost promised relief from the cost-price squeeze. The completion of the industry's migration from New England to the South also speeded innovation. The new plants and work force in the South were not tied to an existing set of techniques. Modern plants designed for the use of electrically driven spindles and looms replaced plants originally designed in the nineteenth century for the use of water power and steam.

The mere survival to the present of the textile industry in the United States is a measure of its adaptability. Tariffs and quotas have given the American industry a measure of relief from foreign competition. Even so, low transportation costs, wide international diffusion of textile technology, low foreign wages, and a high, rapidly rising domestic-wage level have forced continuing innovation by the American industry. Nevertheless, the textile industry is not a sector of the economy where American entrepreneurs have been in the vanguard of change.

The Machine-Tool Industry

Like iron and steel, the machinery and machine-tool producing sector of American industry occupies a very strategic place in the process of industrialization, because its products largely serve as inputs for the producers of consumer goods. Machine tools are power-driven devices used to shape metal by cutting and include such tools as lathes, drill presses, planers, and grinders. Reductions in the cost of producing steel or machinery make possible further cost reductions in the cost of capital goods and consumer goods. As capital goods fall in price, there is both an "income effect" and a "substitution effect." The decrease in the cost of producing capital goods means an increase in real income for society. But the lowered cost of capital goods causes an increased substitution of machinery for labor. In terms of economic theory, innovations in the machinery producing sector of the economy increase the marginal efficiency of capital. This is the essential character of technological change. Increased prodution is possible with a given amount of labor and capital only with improvement in the productivity of capital goods.

It is difficult to date the emergence of an American machine-tool industry because early manufacturers had to devise their own tools to make parts for machinery they used in production. As noted above, textile manufacturers in the early nineteenth century started machine shops to produce their own textile machinery. This led to developments in the production of machine tools that made possible the "American system" of manufacture—the manufacture of products with interchangeable parts. The development of machine tools that could produce parts to small tolerances was absolutely necessary to this type of mass production. Traditionally, Eli Whitney has been given credit for being the first entrepreneur to attempt mass production and the use of interchangeable parts. He adopted the practice of mass production of identical parts in the production of firearms. It is interesting to note that the source of this momentous innovation was a government contract. Whitney introduced this technique because of a large order for standardized goods that had to be produced in a short period of time.

Nathan Rosenberg has suggested that the machine-tool industry played an extremely important part in the process of economic growth in this country because of what he calls "technological convergence"—the tendency for certain types of process innovations to become applicable to a wide range of production problems in different consumer-goods industries.[25] Basically, the argument is that solutions of problems such as friction reduction, power transmission, or automatic stamping and shaping that are solved in one industry make possible solutions in other industries. Technological innovations in production processes may occur in a specific industry, but they are embodied by the capital goods producing sector, which acts as a center for the diffusion of technical knowledge and technological devices.

Ever since the late Joseph A. Schumpeter focused attention on the importance of the entrepreneur in innovation,[26] there has been a tendency on the part of students of business and economic history to concentrate on innovation as it appears in particular firms. Rosenberg's research into the machine-tool industry in the United States calls attention to the transmission of technical knowledge that makes innovation in certain productive processes possible and transferable by the agency of the machine-tool industry. The structure of the machine-tool industry is of crucial importance because it is the means by which technological innovation is embodied and diffused throughout a wide range of industries in the economy. The structure of the machine-tool industry in the United States has been particularly favorable for the rapid transmission of technological change. It has been characterized by a high degree of functional specialization rather than by specialization in the production of capital goods for particular industries. Numerous small firms have produced components or machines for particular processes and have not been tied to particular customers.

In an article incorporating Adam Smith's famous dictum about specialization,

[25] "Technological Change in the Machine Tool Industry, 1840–1910," *Journal of Economic History*, Vol. 23 (December, 1963).
[26] *Capitalism, Socialism and Democracy*, 3rd ed. (London: George Allen and Unwin 1950).

George A. Stigler argued that productivity growth increases with specialization in production.[27] Costs are reduced as firms are able to accomplish every stage of the production process at the least possible cost, and this is only possible when there is sufficient volume in a specific process to allow it to be carried out with maximum economies of scale. To illustrate by example, an individual textile producer would be very inefficient in the production of looms if he only had to make the limited number required for his own use. By purchasing the looms from a machine shop specializing in loom fabrication, he reaps some of the economies of large-scale production. The process continues through successive stages of production—if the loom manufacturer can buy electric motors from a firm specializing in their production, they can be obtained far more cheaply than if the firm had to produce the few necessary for its own use. The large number of firms in the machine-tool industry, each specialized in particular processes, is important in the achievement of the economies of scale. It may seem paradoxical but it is true that a large number of small firms buying and selling to each other may enjoy more economies of scale than a large, vertically integrated company that produces goods to satisfy all its own needs.

Specialization by process is advantageous not only in a static sense; it is important also in a dynamic sense, because firms specialized by process rather than by final product transmit technological innovation from one industry to another. Rosenberg points out that the spectacular growth in the automobile industry after the turn of the century was possible only because technical problems in the production of precision gears and strong, lightweight wheels and in precision grinding had been solved by the machine-tool industry for the bicycle producers.[28] As bicycle production declined, automobile production rose, and the firms that formerly produced bicycle parts shifted easily into the production of auto parts. In this connection, it is interesting to note tht General Motors rose to preeminence in the automobile industry as a company whose many divisions bought a wide variety of parts and components from numerous specialized producers. It is equally instructive to remember that the technological conservatism of the textile industry prior to the second world war was blamed by industry observers on the tendency for mills and textile machinery manufacturers to become mutually dependent.

The American machine-tool industry has always consisted of a large number of small firms specialized by process. The lack of vertical integration by producers of final products has been conducive to the rapid transmission of technological change from one firm to another *within* an industry, and it has also resulted in solutions for technical problems in one industry being utilized in another. The "American system" of interchangeable parts has been widely diffused in manu-

---

[27] "The Division of Labor Is Limited by the Extent of the Market," *Journal of Political Economy*, Vol. 59 (June, 1951). Smith stated, in *The Wealth of Nations* (1775): "The greatest improvement in the productive powers of labour, and the greater part of the skill, dexterity, and judgement with which it is any where directed, or applied, seem to have been the effects of the division of labour."
[28] Rosenberg, *op. cit.*

facturing because the structure of the American machine-tool industry has permitted the use of interchangeable solutions to technical production problems.

The logic of the American business system imposes a system of "natural selection" on business firms; those best able to stand competitive pressures in the factor and product markets survive. The assumption that underlies the treatment of the relationship of the American business system to the process of economic growth in this essay is that the function of businessmen is the adaptation of production to new market situations and technological possibilities. The adaptability of businessmen depends, to a large degree, on the structure of economic activity and the rate of growth of demand. The American steel industry was very quick to adopt new techniques during its period of most rapid growth. Technological innovation was a matter of survival in a fiercely competitive market, and entrepreneurs in the steel industry were quick to respond. In the textile industry, the slow and stable growth of demand, coupled with only modest improvements in production processes, earned the industry a "conservative" reputation for what was eminently rational behavior. In the machine-tool industry, competition within the industry not only enforced growth but also led to the rapid diffusion of technological change from one industry to another. These three industries suggest that the economic growth of the United States has been able to occur at a high rate because the structure of economic activity has permitted, encouraged, and, indeed, necessitated the proper responses from individuals.

ORGANIZATIONAL INNOVATION AND ECONOMIC PROGRESS

Alfred D. Chandler, Jr., has argued that the greatest innovation in American business in the period between the Civil War and the present was the modern business corporation.[29] The essence of the modern corporation that emerged was its size, and the impact of size on the character of business created a need for new methods of control. Leaving aside questions of size relative to markets, it is undeniable that modern business enterprises are large in absolute terms and are growing steadily larger. What significance does size have for economic efficiency? Traditionally, academic economists have argued that while there might be decreasing real costs of production for an expanding firm in a given industry because of the possibilities of specialization, economies of scale are limited in the last analysis by the difficulties of efficient control when an organization grows too large. If, as Chandler suggests, significant organizational innovations make possible an increasing span of control, the effect would be favorable to productivity by making possible further technological economies without having them offset by organizational dis-economies. A recent study by Joe S. Bain indicated that while there were no significant technological economies in U.S. industries that would dictate oligopolistic control of markets by a few firms, there were definite economies of scale in marketing, distribution, and finance that favored bigness.[30] One

[29] "The Beginnings of Big Business in American Industry," *Business History Review,* Vol. 33 (Spring, 1959).
[30] *Barriers to New Competition* (Cambridge, Mass.: Harvard University Press, 1956).

only has to look at a firm such as General Foods to see the importance of economies of scale in marketing and distribution in a highly competitive industry where technological economies of scale are not present. From the standpoint of the economy as a whole, these economies of distribution and control made possible by organizational innovation are an important source of economic growth. If big corporations can reduce the number of sales and supervisory personnel *per unit of output,* then this manpower is available for work elsewhere to increase net output. There is evidence that large firms do have lower administrative costs per unit of output than do smaller firms.[31]

An important contribution to economic growth in the period 1870–1930 came about in the rationalization of distribution systems. This was, in turn, dependent upon the increase in the size of markets that resulted from earlier technological improvements. At the end of the Civil War, for example, fresh meat was relatively expensive in eastern cities because it could only be supplied by small packing houses in close geographic proximity. Improvements in railroads, and especially the introduction of the refrigerated car, made it possible to supply the eastern urban areas with animals raised in the West, where they could be produced far more cheaply. This expansion of the market led to the development of big meat-packing companies, which introduced production line methods to the slaughtering process and utilized the whole animal.

Another effect of the integration of the economy was to speed up the elimination of middlemen. This process began toward the end of the century and has continued to the present. In the nineteenth century, the general store was the source of supply to the consumer of a wide range of products. The general store, in turn, was supplied by independent "general" wholesale houses that carried a wide range of goods and specialized in a certain geographic area. Both the small general store and the independent wholesaler are now very much less consequence in the economy than they were a hundred years ago. Wholesaling has been progressively taken over by the manufacturers of products, and small retailers have been replaced by retail chains. The marketing functions formerly performed by small wholesale and retail merchants have been supplanted by advertising.

While the passing of small businesses in the wholesale and retail trades may be mourned, rationalization of distribution by the elimination of wholesalers and the closing down of many small retailers has made manpower available for more efficient utilization elsewhere in the economy. To the extent that reorganization has reduced the size of inventories per final sales dollar, it has also freed capital for investment to increase output elsewhere.

Advertising has played an important part in the process. The wholesaler and retailer used to serve the function of evaluating the merits of goods for their customers. The establishment of the quality of certain products in the mind of the consumer by brand differentiation has eliminated the function of evaluation formerly performed by the merchant in his selective buying. Further, innovations

[31] Seymour S. Melman, "The Rise of Administrative Overhead in the Manufacturing Industries of the United States, 1899–1947," *Oxford Economic Papers*, Vol. 3 (February, 1951).

in packaging have made possible self-service, which has greatly increased the sales per salesperson.

THE BUSINESS SYSTEM AND CAPITAL ACCUMULATION AND ALLOCATION

What impact did the American system of business have on capital formation during the period from the end of the Civil War to 1913? First, it is necessary to remember that the volume of total domestic-capital formation cannot exceed the volume of real saving, and real saving is determined by a complex of social factors. The presence of a large number of entrepreneurs, both farm and non-farm, is a partial explanation of the high rate of saving that obtained during the period. It is an observed characteristic of the self-employed that they save a large part of the income received—a habit reinforced in the United States by emphasis on the Protestant ethic of thrift. The character of a business system obviously conditions the willingness of the population to save. One could also take the mechanistic view that the opportunities for profitable investment determine social attitudes toward saving and institutional characteristics of business organizaton.

Veblen on the Misallocation of Capital

Whereas the American system encouraged the accumulation of capital, critics have charged that it allocated the capital collected in less than an ideal way. Major misallocations of investment took place, for example, in railroads. Large financial gains were possible in both the initial flotation of securities and road construction and later in the reorganization of competing or bankrupt roads. The activities of Jay Gould, Daniel Drew, Cornelius Vanderbilt, and others in railroad finance were notorious. Large amounts of capital were taken from the government and from private investors for expenditure, at best, on physical assets that never earned near the social rate of return and, at worst, on the corruption of legislators and the conspicuous consumption of "the robber barons." The economic evil of such activities is that capital misspent on railways might have been more productively spent elsewhere.

Thorstein Veblen[32] was one of the foremost critics of the results of financial manipulations that had no productive consequences for the economy. He saw in much of the merger movement that occurred just prior to the turn of the century an attempt to restrict production rather than to expand it. Capital was being mobilized to *decrease* the volume of production by buying up capacity and shutting it down.

Veblen argued that on balance the private-enterprise system contributed nothing to economic growth. Balanced against the gains in efficiency brought by rationalization of production in some fields were cases where rationalization was prevented for pecuniary advantage and where a costly duplication of facilities was fostered

---

[32] *The Theory of Business Enterprise* (New York: Charles Scribner's Sons, 1904). Reprinted by New American Library (New York) as a Mentor Book, 1958.

by competition. The favorable effects of pecuniary incentives of personal productivity were offset by the losses to society as a whole from socially unproductive expenditures on advertising and from duplication of sales and administrative expense.

The fault of the American system, as Veblen saw it, was the lack of coincidence between pecuniary gain and improvements in productivity. This resulted in a great deal of business activity that merely reallocated income rather than creating "utility" and made the social consequences of production problematic.

Veblen acknowledged that the businessman was "responsible" for much of the innovation that was socially desirable, but, he generalized:

> The period between the time of earliest practicability and the effectual completion of a given consolidation in industry marks the interval by which the businessman retards the advance of industry. Against this are to be set the cases, comparatively slight and infrequent, where the businessmen in control push the advance of industry into new fields. . . .[33]

Veblen's conclusion is in sharp contrast to Schumpeter's emphasis on the contribution of businessmen to economic growth through continual innovation.

Weakness of Financial Structure

A further aspect of the organization of the American economic system during the nineteenth and early twentieth centuries deserves mention: the unstable character of the banking and financial structure. A money market developed in New York because of the large volume of commercial bills created by international and interregional trade going through the port of New York. This in turn led to the dominance of the New York Stock Exchange over other stock exchanges in the country. As the nineteenth century progressed, New York banks increasingly attracted short-term deposits from banks in the rest of the country. In turn, they would use this liquid cash to buy short-term paper and place it in "call loans" to finance speculation by member firms of the exchange and their customers. Periodic liquidity crises occurred when country banks called back their deposits from New York banks, which in turn would "call in" their loans to securities dealers. The results were financial panics of increasing severity that led to the reluctant acceptance by the banking system of the Federal Reserve System in 1913.

In the period after 1913, the Federal Reserve left a great deal to be desired in its structure and policy, but at least it had the potential to limit the chronic instability of a financial structure that periodically liquidated a large number of firms with consequent disorganization and loss of production in the economy. Responsibility for the character of the financial system did not lie exclusively with the banking and financial community, for there was a widespread public fear of centralizing financial power in the hands of a lender of last resort. Insofar as businessmen were the dominant social and political group during the period, they

---

[33] *Ibid.*, Mentor Book edition, p. 27.

must bear partial responsibility for the failure to institute rational reform of the system they operated.

CONCLUSION

A hundred years ago Karl Marx wrote of the achievements of a capitalist society:

> The bourgeoisie during its rule of scarce one hundred years, has created more massive and more colossal productive forces than have all preceding generations together. Subjection of nature's forces to man, machinery, application of chemistry to industry and agriculture, steam navigation, railways, electric telegraphs, clearing of whole continents for cultivation, canalization of rivers, whole populations conjured out of the ground—what earlier century had even a presentiment that such productive forces slumbered in the lap of social labor?[34]

While Marx's paean of praise was made about Britain in the throes of the Industrial Revolution, a change in terminology would make it applicable to twentieth-century America.

The success of a private-enterprise system in the United States during the last century has depended importantly on a set of social and economic conditions that have provided the framework within which business enterprise could function. A set of political institutions favorable to economic growth was of great importance, and federal and local government in America has always been sensitive and responsive to the needs of business. One of the strongest arguments made for independence from Britain was the desirability of throwing off the shackles imposed on manufacturing and trade by the British Navigation Acts in order to secure a government favorable to American business interests. A strong federal union was advocated and was embodied in the Constitution to foster interstate commerce and to provide favorable conditions for business enterprise. In the nineteenth-century ante-bellum period, local governments were eager to participate in the provision of the transportation facilities necessary to the expansion of markets. One of the principles for which the Union fought the Civil War was the desirability of using the federal government to foster domestic manufacturing and commerce by the use of tariffs, which would secure the domestic markets for U.S. producers and would expand those markets by federally supported transportation improvements.

American social and legal mores have traditionally emphasized the sanctity of contract and the importance of property rights and personal liberty. Property rights and contractual rights, as opposed to relationships based on status or privilege, were guaranteed by the Constitution to individuals. These traditions have provided both the security necessary for business and the fluidity of social and economic relationships necessary to accommodate the impact of economic growth and technological change on the population. As Professor Kuhn points out (p. 284),

[34] *The Communist Manifesto,* reprinted in *Capital,* Max Eastman, ed. (New York: The Modern Library, 1932), p. 326.

the willingness of American labor to treat its relationship to management as a contractual relation subject to bargaining has contributed to economic growth by making technological change easier.

The quality of the labor force, the most important productive input in the economy, has been high and improving in the United States for a long period of time. It has long been a part of our social philosophy that education equalized opportunity and that it was necessary to the preservation of democratic government. Progressive business leaders in colonial New England realized, in addition, that voting taxes on themselves for the support of public education was "good business" because it provided them with a superior labor force. Given the relative shortage of labor in the United States, and especially the shortage of technically skilled labor, the practice of upgrading the skills of the labor force on the job began well back in the nineteenth century.

Turning to the character of American capitalism itself, there are a number of features of the behavior of American businessmen that have had a favorable effect on economic growth. First, there has always been a spirited response to the profit incentive. It has never been eschewed as immoral in this country, by any but a very small group of people, to make money in business. In this respect, the United States has differed markedly from some European countries where it has been socially acceptable to "have" money but not to "make" it. Further, Veblen and "conspicuous consumption" to the contrary, American businessmen have by and large re-invested profits rather than expending them on consumption. In recent years this practice has been further enforced by the internal financing methods of major U.S. corporations.

Second, business in the United States has certainly "used" government to promote its objectives in expanding markets, but it has never had much help from government in restricting them.[35] Certainly, there has been tariff protection, and patent protection has given some firms technical monopolies. But, for the most part, the American political tradition has always resisted concentrations of power and has refused to give them legal sanction. Prior to the passing of the Sherman Antitrust Act in 1890, there was widespread concern about the growth of "pools" and "trusts." The Sherman Act and succeeding legislation came out of an ancient common law tradition that conspiracies to control production or fix prices were per se against the public interest. In the face of this prevailing social philosophy, output restriction and price-fixing have been the exception rather than the rule in American business; even firms that possessed monopoly power have been very sparing in its use. This has not been a case of social conscience; it has been a shrewd observation by large firms that it was better to "run scared" than be challenged in court by the government.

Third, the structure of American business has evolved in a way that has been

---

[35] A contrary point of view has been put forward in Gabriel Kolko, *The Triumph of Conservatism* (New York: The Free Press, 1963). Kolko argues (not very successfully in this writer's opinion) that government regulation and control of monopolies was used by large corporations to *restrict* competition and preserve a status quo in several industries.

favorable to growth. Where there have been technological advantages to monopoly in particular markets such as electric power, telephones, or railroads, private monopolies have been permitted but have been controlled. Where there have been market conditions and scale considerations that allowed for only a few firms, oligopoly has developed but has behaved reasonably well; the electrical manufacturers' conspiracy and the price-fixing by the producers of carbon steel are examples to the contrary. There has been a growing feeling that bargaining between oligopsonistic customers and oligopolistic suppliers produces results that approximate what would result in the long run if perfect competition existed. Few Americans have been doctrinaire about accepting only perfect competition in the economy.

Much of American industry is still characterized by small units. It was argued in the body of the paper that this characteristic of the machine-tool industry was very conducive to the transmission of technological innovation. Industrial production in the United States has always been characterized by a considerable degree of vertical non-integration. Firms have purchased and sold components of final products with other firms. This has allowed specialization of production, and the economies of scale are truly achieved by the existence of a number of small firms specialized in the provision of one particular product or service.

A discussion of the relation of American business to economic growth is difficult because structure and performance are all bound up with one another. Particular firms and particular men have been responsible for significant contributions to aggregate growth through their innovations in technology and organization. At the same time, these men and firms operate within a social framework that makes their activities possible and rewarding. American businessmen have made an important contribution to economic growth—but so have American farmers, teachers, lawyers, and mechanics.

The real task of businessmen in promoting the commonweal is in doing their job to the best of their ability—cutting costs through investment and innovation and expanding output. The pace at which this can be done depends on the provision of a high rate of effective demand, scientific advance, and improvement of the productivity of the labor force. All of these things depend on collective action. If the historical record of American economic growth shows anything, it is the importance of collective action to provide the prerequisites for a high and expanding level of economic activity and the importance of entrepreneurial skills in carrying out ever more efficient organization of production.

SELECTED READINGS

Victor S. Clark, *History of Manufactures in the United States* (3 vols.; New York: Dover, 1963). An encyclopedic work that covers the development of various American industries from colonial times to the first world war.

Stuart Bruchey, *The Roots of American Economic Growth, 1607–1861* (New York: Harper & Row, 1965). An attempt to relate the process of economic growth to political and cultural factors. This book contains an excellent bibliography on business, economic, and general history for the pre-Civil War period.

EDWARD F. DENISON, *The Sources of Economic Growth in the United States and the Alternatives Before Us* (New York: Committee for Economic Development, 1962). A detailed statistical analysis of the impact of education, capital formation, labor force change, technology, and other factors on the growth of the American economy from 1909 to 1957.

ROBERT W. FOGEL AND STANLEY L. ENGERMAN, EDS., *The Reinterpretation of American Economic History* (New York: Harper & Row, 1967). A collection of controversial and incisive essays that seeks to measure quantitatively the importance of various factors in the performance of the American economy in the nineteenth and early twentieth centuries.

DOUGLASS C. NORTH, *Growth and Welfare in the American Past: A New Economic History* (Englewood Cliffs, N. J.: Prentice-Hall, 1966). This book is an attempt to "debunk" many of the views held by previous generations of historians about the importance of government, railroads, monopoly, and agricultural discontent. It is controversial and well-written.

ROSS M. ROBERTSON, *History of the American Economy*, 2nd ed. (New York: Harcourt, Brace & World, 1964). One of the best "standard" texts on American economic history. Especially good on banking and monetary institutions.

W. PAUL STRASSMAN, *Risk and Technological Innovation* (Ithaca, N.Y.: Cornell University Press, 1959). A well-organized and perceptive account of factors affecting performance of the iron and steel, textile, machine-tool, and electric power industries. Suggestive evidence is presented on the role of the entrepreneur.

chapter 8

BUSINESS AND SCIENCE

KARL B. HILL *is Special Assistant for Research and Technology, U.S. Department of Housing and Urban Development. His experience as a business consultant, anthropologist, lawyer, and member of Associates for International Research—a consulting organization that has sought to apply the skills of scientists and their disciplines to problems in business and government—has exposed him to many facets of the issues he discusses in this chapter. The essay begins with a survey of the history of business and science and then turns to two critical aspects of their relationship in the United States today—the role of federal government in funding research and development and the consequences of technological advances for the growth of the nation, regions, industries, and particular firms. Finally, Hill considers business and science as interrelated subcultures that influence each other and the social mores of the entire country.*

In a celebrated analysis written in 1919, Thorstein Veblen concluded that "technology—the joint creation of the artisan, the technician, the engineer, and later the scientist all brought together by the captains of industry and of finance—[had] an inner logic and dynamism somewhat separate from that of the system of private enterprise of the West under which the technology evolved";[1] he predicted that "modern technology would come into conflict with the business enterprise system in America and mold it to its own deep-seated and overriding requirements."[2]

Veblen was right to stress the importance of technology; according to a recent study by Jay M. Gould, the "continued exponential growth in the technical labor force has brought the total number of scientists and engineers in the United States to 1.4 million in 1965, and government agencies predict that by 1970 nearly one out of

[1] Jay M. Gould, *The Technical Elite* (New York: Augustus M. Kelly, 1966), p. 15.
[2] *Ibid.*, p. 13.

*every 20 members of the labor force will be an engineer, a scientist,
a technician, or a teacher of technology.*"[3] *Veblen's forecasting was
not as acute as his analysis, however; according to Hill's analysis,
he would seem to have underestimated the free-enterprise system's
capacity to move away from its "inner logic" (organized rather
strictly, in Veblen's judgment, around its financial interest in restricting production) and to incorporate new technology and technologists without experiencing any fundamental alteration. This is
not to say that business has victimized or swallowed up science.
Contrary to a common opinion, Hill suggests that science has
benefited at least as much as business from their industrial partnership and that business values and interests have at crucial junctures
in our development rubbed off on the scientific establishment.
Shared commitments to pragmatism are not the least important
components of the partnership he describes.*

*The pace of technological innovation in the United States will
quite likely continue to quicken as new developments occur. The
reader, in this connection, may keep the following questions in
mind in reading the essay:*

*1. Why do we sometimes seem to find it easier in the U.S. to
adapt ourselves to technological innovation than to the agents of
these changes? The citizens of New York City, for example, found
it easier to adapt to electric power, with all the changes it brought,
than to Consolidated Edison, the locally controversial utility company that serves New York and incidentally pollutes its air. Should
the soot from steam-generating plants be regarded as an aspect of
the advance we call electrification?*

*2. Hill shows that the direct costs of many innovations have been
"socialized" through federal support for research and development
financed by tax monies. Compare the advantages and disadvantages,
to a* democratic business system, *of the various ways in which the
human costs of dislocations caused by technological change can be
borne.*

*3. Hill argues that despite the significance of government support
for R&D, there is some protection against the evils of "government
planning" in the fact that innumerable agencies of government are
involved, each of which allocates only a fraction of the total sum of
federal investments. In what ways does this multiplicity of agency
investors, all spending tax monies, parallel the multiplicity of investors in a private market, who draw a good part of their funds
from retained earnings? Why will a particular agency be influenced
by the operations of other agencies the way one private investor is
influenced by other investors?*

[3] *Ibid.*, p. 48.

KARL B. HILL \ BUSINESS, SCIENCE, AND
THE GOVERNMENT: TECHNOLOGY
IN A PLURALISTIC SOCIETY

The relationship between business and science is as momentous for Americans in the twentieth century as were the associations of autocratic dynasty and priestly prophecy for the ancient Egyptians, aristocratic family tradition and popular demagoguery for the citizens of the Greek city-states, and commercial wealth and ecclesiastical loyalties for the residents of the Renaissance city-states in Italy. "Industrialism" is the best single word for the modern union of science with business. We shall see that this union transforms both of the partners and that business contributes as much vitality and creativity to science as it takes from it. The crucible of industrial science in America has been the source of many of our most striking triumphs, as well as some of our most baffling social problems.

This essay surveys the background, nature, and consequences of industrial science in the United States. It begins with a review of the history of business and science. Then it turns to an important factor in the evolving relationships of the business and scientific communities today, the activities of the federal government in funding research and development, and also to some of the important reasons behind these activities—the economic consequences that technological innovation has for national economic growth and the prosperity of regions, industries, firms, and individuals. Finally, it examines business and science as two interrelated sub-cultures and attempts to assess the overall significance of the interplay between them.

THE HISTORY OF BUSINESS AND SCIENCE

Popular histories that trace science back to elevated intellectual origins, while assigning to business a background of acquisitiveness and haggling if not actual piracy, are either mythical or one-sided. The truth is that the earliest times present no close analogues to modern science and the contemporary business corporation, leaving us wide degrees of freedom in defining which activities of pre-literate man to consider "business" or "science" or something else altogether. The origins of business can with equal validity be found in productive fishing, hunting, and agriculture; in primitive forms of social power over material allocations within a group; or in the earliest systems of commerce and exchange, which usually had religious and familial meanings as well as an acquisitive one. The origins of science, in turn, were found by Bronislaw Malinowski in the handicraft and manu-facturing activities of early man, but another celebrated social scientist, Robert Redfield, thought they lay in the superstitious and academic attempts of priestly scribes to find written symbolisms relating astronomical to dynastic events. Our historical conclusions are bound to differ depending on whether we stress the instrumental or the symbolic side of science, the productive and innovative side of business or the side that accumulates the means and products of production.

Only in recent times has the philosophy of science demonstrated that instrumentalism is essential to symbolism and to knowledge itself and has economics demonstrated that acquisitiveness operating in a marketplace contributes very essentially to productivity. Some mathematical conceptions originated among Egyptian priestly scribes to whom innovation and invention were actually enemies; others were formulated by early Middle-Eastern civil servants who were charged with counting and recording quantities of grain in order to collect their ruler's taxes. Even among most modern nations, organized science had its beginnings in efforts to support and extend government control: coastal and geological surveys, censuses of population, military engineering, determinations of the weights and measures needed for the minting of money, and the like. Today, as in the past, most scientists are not great innovators but scholars and conservators who explicate and pass on traditional symbolic formulae.

The modern tendency to view business and science as polarized forces—often united in an uneasy alliance but sometimes coming into direct conflict—has its roots in the Classical era. The Greeks were the first people to achieve a clear conception of objective, non-theological "knowledge." They distinguished knowledge not only from superstition and belief but from efficacious practical activities, as we can see best in Aristotle's famous division of all human faculties into the three realms of knowing, doing, and making.

Our thinking about science and industry has also been influenced by the supposed contrast, within the Classical world, between the superiority of the Greeks in pure science and the superiority of the Romans in applied engineering. An economist, discussing the possibility of conflicts between basic science and applied technology, recently wrote:

> This possibility is suggested by the broad historical generalization that, at least until modern times, human societies have been distinguished by superior attainment either in pure science or in technology, but not in both together. Even now it is frequently argued (for example, in recent discussions of British science policy) that concentration on basic research detracts from technological progress and the development of applications, by depriving applied science of the prestige necessary to attract able and ambitious minds.[1]

Whatever their differences of emphasis and accomplishment, both Greek and Roman technology assumed slave labor for the support of the basic scientist's life and leisure as well as for the motive power to drive machines invented by engineers. This assumption of the permanence of slave labor, by demeaning productive and commercial activity, prevented the conception of any close relationship

[1] Harry G. Johnson, "Federal Support of Basic Research: Some Economic Issues," in *Basic Research and National Goals* (Washington: Government Printing Office, 1965), pp. 129–30.

between commerce and science, thus depriving ancient science of many potential experiments and discoveries in the area of motive powers and natural forces.

It was during the European Middle Ages, which we often depict as both dark and inhumane, that both business and science emerged in a recognizably "modern" form. Business progress required a definitive advance beyond slave (unvalued) labor and equally required serious attention to theories of pricing. A theology was developed that dignified rather than demeaned labor and that introduced the highest conceptions of justice into the commercial realm of exchanges and prices. The famous scholastic doctrines regarding "just price," "usury," and closed "guilds" should not be viewed as reactionary, but rather as part of the progressive "new economics" of that time.

These theological and corporate developments favorable to business progress were joined by engineering advances. Lynn White's classic article of 1940 concludes:

> The chief glory of the later Middle Ages was not its cathedrals or its epics or its scholasticism: it was the building for the first time in history of a complex civilization which rested not on the backs of sweating slaves or coolies but primarily on non-human power.[2]

By the tenth century, medieval Europeans had achieved three inventions that had eluded the Romans in exploiting the power of the horse. They invented a horse collar resting upon the animal's shoulders that would not choke him when he exerted great traction; nailed horse shoes, without which his hooves soon broke or split; and a tandem harness by which to utilize teams of horses for large jobs. Medieval Europeans also made important advances in the use of water power. The Romans had placed vertical waterwheels in running water and had set at least one in a natural waterfall, but the Europeans were the first systematically to exploit the water's head or height, a source of much greater power than the normal surface flow of a stream or river. The first windmills appeared in the twelfth century, and they were successively improved as the motor force for grinding grain, pumping water, and other operations. The great medieval harnessing of non-human power led to many other inventions in the channeling of that power by the use of pumps, gears, and cranks.

These advances in wind, water, and horse power had been accomplished by the fourteenth century. No further significant improvement in power took place until the steam engine, itself an offshoot from medieval pumps, came into limited use early in the eighteenth century. The Renaissance and Enlightenment brought not an acceleration of engineering inventions but much philosophical and scientific thought about *why* things work as they do and many imaginative programs for futuristic engineering projects, such as we find in Leonardo da Vinci's notebooks and the many utopias of the period. The process of generalizing inventions and relating them to social objectives was beginning. It remained for our own time to fulfill many of the futuristic projections, both engineering and sociopolitical, set

[2] Lynn White, "Technology and Invention in the Middle Ages," *Speculum,* Vol. 15 (1940), pp. 141–59.

forth by da Vinci, Condorcet, Leibnitz, and other prophets of the post-medieval period. In the sphere of business and commerce, the fifteenth through seventeenth centuries witnessed the beginnings of a factory system, a patent system, and more systematic as well as extensive international trade. The untitled commercial classes gained increasing rights and influence with their affluence in most European countries, a development that both stimulated industry and democratized government.

The eighteenth century saw a revival of practical inventiveness and the application of science to industrial problems in Europe, interests that soon spread to America. James Watt perfected a vastly improved steam engine in Scotland at about the same time that Benjamin Franklin, in America, experimented with natural lightning by flying kites in thunder storms, making fundamental contributions to the theory of electricity and putting this knowledge to practical use by his invention of the protective lightning rod.

Background in America

In colonial America, science had closer connections with theology and government than with business. Many early American scientists were religious ministers, seeking a truth that would be both "Scriptural and Rational Doctrine," as their quest was expressed in one of Jonathan Edwards' sermon titles. In the decades before the Revolution, deism became popular because it offered a bridge between revealed religion and experimental science. Several natural philosophers and scientists held public office, partly as a result of a general opinion that science was more closely related to government than to business.[3] These associations led up to the establishment of the United States Coast Survey by the Treasury Department in 1807 and to other government actions at about the same time in regard to weights and measures, interior mapping, and the census.

Early American scientists tended to be many-sided in their interests and to maintain closer connections with Europe than did American engineers and inventors. Thomas Jefferson pursued researches in agronomy, meteorology, paleontology, engineering, and architecture in addition to his statesmanship. Jefferson and Franklin were frequent travelers to Europe for scientific exchanges as well as for missions of state. Three successive John Winthrops were members of the British Royal Society, the first having been a charter member of the Society as well as Governor of Connecticut.[4] One of the most eminent scientists produced by colonial America, Benjamin Thompson, Count Rumford, of Woburn, Massachusetts, developed such strong European connections that he became a Tory agent during the Revolution and afterwards resided in various European capitals. This scientific activity, however, while lively, was carried on more in the spirit of the Enlightenment than in the new practical inventive spirit making itself felt in England. Early America had scientists and craftsmen, but few engineers to bridge

[3] See Don Price's discussion in his *Government and Science* (New York: New York University Press, 1954), p. 3.
[4] Dirk J. Struik, *Yankee Science in the Making* (New York: Collier, 1962), pp. 48–49.

the gap between them, and fewer businessmen capable of putting new technologies to work. As late as 1803, there seem to have been only six steam engines in the entire country, all of them long-obsolete Newcomen models.[5] Robert Fulton introduced the first Watt-type steam engines in America, a step in some ways more remarkable than his development of the first commercially practical steamboat. American business was often no quicker to adopt homegrown improvements than the latest European technology. Oliver Evans of Wilmington and Philadelphia had been inventing and sketching a whole series of high-pressure steam engines, more advanced in design than the Watt model itself, long before Fulton belatedly introduced Watt engines from Europe.[6]

Benjamin Franklin was a unique prototype for the learned yet practical industrial scientists that America needed in large numbers. Not only did he combine science with statesmanship, as did so many other leaders of the Revolution and writers of the Constitution, but he translated a great deal of his science into craftsmanship and then profitable production. Franklin followed up his electrical discoveries by inventing the lightning rod and marketing it, his heat transfer experiments by developing the Franklin stove, and his optical researches by inventing bifocal spectacles. When in 1743 he founded the American Philosophical Society in Philadelphia, it was "for the promotion of useful knowledge." Monetary profit was clearly within his definition of the "useful"; he remarked, when founding Philadelphia's first hospital, that it gave him more pleasure than any getting of money had ever done. Franklin's work presaged the union between science and business, freed from religious dogma, that has come to full fruition in the America of today. His achievements and many of his maxims express a philosophy, in his time unnamed, that has done much to facilitate the interplay of business and science in America—pragmatism.

The Nineteenth Century

During the nineteenth century in the United States, a growing corps of engineers began to mediate between its basic scientists and its industrial craftsmen, national business corporations developed that were alert to new technologies and capable of quickly disseminating better ways of doing things, and the national climate of opinion evolved in the direction of increasingly secular practicality. These changes had such an impact upon science in this country that eighteenth-century American science and twentieth-century American science seem products of different nations and peoples as well as different times. Eighteenth-century American science seems Hellenistic in its purity, its philosophic bent, its frequent relations with political theory, and its haphazard relations to industrial practice. Twentieth-century American science, despite its extraordinary world leadership in basic research, seems hauntingly Roman—magnificent in engineering, closely linked to corporate developments, frequently serving urban agglomerations of peoples, often a leading edge of foreign influence or technological invasion, and sometimes directly military.

[5] *Ibid.,* p. 304.
[6] *Idem.*

During the nineteenth century, the emphasis in American science shifted from medicine, agronomy, and astronomy toward geology and biology, then still later toward chemistry. These shifts were accompanied by a growing popular interest in science. No one did more to kindle this enthusiasm than the Swiss immigrant Louis Agassiz, whose public lectures drew hundreds and were much talked about, even in frontier cities. Agassiz was also one of the last great defenders of theology in science, dedicating his great name and last years to the struggle against Darwin's theory of evolution.

A less publicized but more important event in the late nineteenth century occurred in Cambridge, Massachusetts: Charles Sanders Peirce and several friends developed the philosophy of pragmatism, once and for all achieving the reconciliation of scripture with reason that had so worried Jonathan Edwards. Benjamin Franklin had made an end run around religious and philosophical questions, which few could hope to follow. Peirce delineated a new kind of scientific philosophy, that later pragmatists like John Dewey would export to the whole world. Peirce analyzed any "scripture" into the practical consequences of its words. For him, "heavy" meant "if let go, it would fall." He coined the word "pragmatism" for this doctrine. Invented to clear up metaphysics and to make philosophy and metaphysics compatible with experimental science, it tended to free science from religious and other dogma and transform it into an activity very compatible with industry and business. Pragmatism completed the long evolution of "science" from a division of scholastic religious philosophy to a partner of business in the secular world.[7]

Industrial research began to expand out of the back rooms late in the nineteenth century. The obscurity of its earlier operations did not result from a lack of appreciation for the effectiveness and results of research but rather from businessmen's fear of losing trade secrets to competitors and their wish to protect the morale of their employees, who were often violently opposed to inventions and innovations.[8]

A pioneering commercial research laboratory, Arthur D. Little Co., sprang up in 1886. It specialized in research conducted for others, for a fee. About a decade

[7] Pragmatism had similar effects in American law, largely due to the brilliance of Oliver Wendell Holmes, with C. S. Peirce a member of the Cambridge group that founded the doctrine. Holmes' belief that a law's full meaning is found in its practical consequences is reflected in his most important court opinions, such as this famous sentence from Schenck v. United States, 249 U.S. 52 (1919): "The most stringent protection of free speech would not protect a man in falsely shouting fire in a theater and causing a panic." Justice Louis Brandeis went even further in reshaping our legal system as a kind of science or pragmatism, writing in his dissenting opinion in New State Ice Co. v. Liebmann, 285 U.S. 311 (1932): "It is one of the happy incidents of the Federal system that a single courageous state may, if its citizens choose, serve as a laboratory; and try novel social and economic experiments without risk to the rest of the country."

[8] A close connection between inventions and unemployment occurred to the minds of many, long before the "automation" of our own day. Soon after inventing his cotton gin on a plantation near Savannah in 1793 Eli Whitney wrote home to his father in the north, "It makes the labor fifty times less, without throwing any class of People out of business." See Dirk J. Struik, *op. cit.*

later, larger corporations began establishing their own laboratories. In 1900, Willis R. Whitney organized the General Electric Laboratory at Schenectady, New York. In 1902, Charles L. Reese organized for the DuPont Company the first of the many laboratories it now maintains, the Eastern Laboratory. Frank B. Jewett began his telephone research in 1904, shortly thereafter organizing Bell Telephone Laboratories. In 1913 came the Eastman Kodak research organization, set up by C. E. K. Mees. Trade association laboratories followed, and then non-profit institutions such as Armour Institute and Battelle Memorial Institute, which make their research results available only to the company or government agency paying for it.

The Evolving Role of the Federal Government

During the nineteenth century the U.S. government came to view itself as an economic arbiter and regulator but never as an economic planner. This outlook resulted in the creation of a host of "regulatory" agencies. Many governmental science bodies were established in the United States, but these generally regarded their mission as specific, limited, and unrelated to research of commercial value. The professional organizations of American scientists themselves have followed the pattern of the British Royal Society, a loose, non-governmental confederation, rather than the pattern of the French Académie des Sciences, founded for the express purpose of administering research and solving problems facing various government agencies. The American Philosophical Society in the eighteenth century, the American Association for the Advancement of Science and the National Academy of Sciences in the nineteenth century, and the many societies of chemists, engineers, and other specialists in this century were all formed to promote communication among like-minded specialists, later becoming protective and lobbying organizations to represent the members' collective interests in dealings with industry or government. The federal government's National Science Foundation was created only after the last world war and is still a hybrid organization controlled in part by the President and in part by professional scientific societies.

It is through contracts and grants rather than administrative organization or planning that the U.S. government has entered science in a massive way in the twentieth century—with the largest contracts occurring in defense, space, and atomic energy. The government behaves like a business dealing with businesses; it purchases, through contracts and grants, specified research products or research activities. The contracting by the federal government for research and development is portentous for relationships between business and science in America, because these federal funds account for well over half of all R&D expenditures in the country and thus set research objectives for most of the nation's scientists and engineers.[9] Government becomes both a competitor of corporations and univer-

[9] See Appendix B in *Basic Research and National Goals, op. cit.* In 1961–62, about two-thirds of all U.S. investments in R&D were made by the federal government. About nine-tenths of all federal expenditures for R&D were accounted for by three agencies:

sities, in the hiring of scientists and the determination of their research objectives, and the principal customer for a special group of corporations.

Since the government's R&D contracts are let by a bewildering variety of government agencies—according to the appropriations Congress allocates to each of them and their particular programs—and since there is no general federal agency in the field of science (the National Science Foundation is significant chiefly as a keeper of valuable statistics on all these contracts, grants, programs, and recipients), the business ideal of competition among many small entities tends to be repeated within the federal government itself, where hundreds of agencies' research budgets and programs overlap, compete, or go their own way in splendid isolation.

Because of the impact that federal research expenditures have upon science education and progress in the different fields of science, however, the rationale of their allocation is beginning to receive increasing attention in Congress. In January, 1966, the Research and Technical Programs Subcommittee of the Committee on Government Operations of the House held hearings on "The Federal Research and Development Programs: The Decision-Making Process." After Dr. Donald F. Hornig, Director of the Office of Science and Technology, Executive Office of the President, had testified on the Administration's allocative procedures, Congressman Benjamin S. Rosenthal of New York stated:

> It seems to me that a very basic inconsistency shows through in your statement. You say: "I do not believe that any single mechanism within the Executive Office of the President, for example, or even within the office of the head of each department and agency, could be relied upon to blueprint the nature of research and development needed to satisfy our needs."
>
> Then two paragraphs later you say: "I do not believe our biggest problem is how to allocate our research, it is how to concentrate the right kind of effort on a variety of problems on which great progress is possible."
>
> In one sentence you say someone should be responsible for coordinating the program, and then you say you do not believe any single mechanism is at hand. I do not believe anyone has an overview of the situation, and you seem to substantiate those fears.[10]

It can be argued, as Dr. Hornig seemed to argue before the Subcommittee, that the overall allocation of federal funds to research disciplines and research missions is less important than the effective selection of objectives, programs, and contractors within each mission-oriented government agency. After all, it is specific agencies and programs, not overall statistics, that achieve results. The weakness of this argument is that any sponsor of two-thirds of the nation's scientific and engineering activities will have the effect of allocating and planning,

---

Department of Defense, National Aeronautics and Space Administration, and Atomic Energy Commission.

[10] Benjamin S. Rosenthal, in *The Federal Research and Development Programs: The Decision-Making Process*, Hearings before a Subcommittee of the Committee on Government Operations of the House of Representatives (Washington: Government Printing Office, 1966), p. 8. (The remarks quoted were made on January 7, 1966.)

whether it wants to or not. In the long run, students will be attracted to, and discoveries will be made in, the areas of research upon which research institutes and universities concentrate. This concentration of education and effort is shaped by federal expenditures for contract research, whether that shaping is planned or unplanned. It could be argued in support of the present pattern that an unplanned impact of federal R&D expenditures upon science, scientists, and ultimately upon a free-enterprise system is preferable to any science planning the government is in fact capable of executing. This argument gathers strength from the enormous difficulty of foreseeing which specialties and objectives of science will be in demand a few years hence. There has been a significant time lag in all nations between the according of priority to certain fields of science and engineering and the training of technological cadres in these critical fields. The gap between priorities and fields of training must usually be closed by career changes and shifts between specialties, which depend upon the breadth of education and the intellectual flexibility of the scientists making such shifts and the adaptation of employers in government, business, and educational centers.

THE DOMINANT ROLE OF THE FEDERAL GOVERNMENT IN FUNDING R&D TODAY

The roles of government, industry, the foundations, and the universities are quite different in making possible the complex technological activities of our pluralistic society. The universities and foundations keep alive the purest traditions of basic science and what might be called "the ethic of objective investigation." The federal government now leads in the funding, as industry leads in the management or "housing" of R&D projects. Both the proportion of the nation's R&D that should be financed by the federal government and the appropriateness of public or private funding for particular R&D objectives are debatable. There are areas of R&D, such as medical research, for which large sums of money would probably be forthcoming from charitable foundations and private philanthropists were the federal government not already lavishly funding these particular areas. There are other areas, such as defense and space R&D, in which expenditures can be justified only by the federal government. In most areas of science and engineering it is rather uncertain whether R&D funds would be allocated more wisely by government or by private industrial and non-profit organizations. The current strategy of the federal government is usually to fund and thus allocate, but not to manage and conduct, the greater part of U.S. R&D activity.

Total U.S. expenditures for R&D climbed slowly but steadily during the 1950's and 1960's, both in dollar amount and as percentage of gross national product. In 1953, total R&D absorbed $5.2 billion, which was 1.5 per cent of the $364.6 billion GNP of that year.[11] A decade later, in 1963, total R&D funds had more

---

[11] "National Patterns of R&D Resources: Funds and Manpower in the United States, 1953–68," National Science Foundation Publication 67–7 (Washington: Government Printing Office, 1967). This publication is the source of other statistics in the same paragraph of the text. See esp. pp. 22, 23, and 26.

than tripled to reach a figure of $17.3 billion, which was 2.9 per cent of the 1963 GNP of $590.5 billion. In the last few years, there has been a slower rate of increase in R&D expenditures and their percentage of GNP, primarily due to the leveling-off (but not decline) in federal financing of costly development projects. Total R&D expenditures in 1966 are estimated to have been $22.2 billion, which would have been 3.0 per cent of the $739.5 billion GNP for 1966. The projection of GNP for future years would be uncertain as well as brave, but the National Science Foundation has estimated that total R&D expenditures will reach approximately $25 billion in 1968, a relatively modest increase over the 1966 level. If the rate of increase in the nation's R&D expenditures continues to slow down, both absolutely and as a percentage of GNP, this development will accentuate the importance of wise allocative and management procedures in our use of the funds that are expended upon R&D.

Is the federal government the best arbiter among the nation's many problem areas that compete for R&D attention? This question is forced upon us by the dominance of the federal government as the principal source of R&D funds: 53 per cent of total national R&D expenditures in 1953 and 63 per cent of these expenditures in 1963.[12] Furthermore, the agencies that account for most of the federal funds flowing into both in-house and contract R&D—the Department of Defense, NASA, and the AEC—pour large additional funds into technological activities of prototype production and series production, undertakings that are expensive in both dollars and technical manpower but are not counted as R&D expenditures.

Since 1953, federal funding of R&D has increased about twice as rapidly as industrial funding of R&D, as shown by the National Science Foundation figures presented in Table 1. The increase in the federal financing of *non-defense* R&D, shown as a percentage of total national R&D expenditure in the last column of Table 1, increased even more dramatically, in part because the dominance of defense expenditures within the total national expenditures for R&D peaked in the late 1950's and declined thereafter without any similar peaking and decline of total federal R&D funding (both defense and non-defense).

When we turn from the funding of R&D to the National Science Foundation's figures on its management, a very different picture of the research involvements of the different sectors of society presents itself. Table 2 shows that industry actually houses and manages most R&D, including that which is federally funded. It also shows that R&D becomes progressively more expensive as ideas are translated into hardware, moving along the continuum from basic research, to applied research, and finally to development. In spite of industry's national dominance as the performer of R&D, universities and colleges have managed to retain their traditional dominance over basic research, both in actual dollar expenditures and in growth rate of expenditures. (Some of this phenomenon may be accounted for by the tendency of record-keepers to categorize research projects as "basic" because they are being performed in universities and as "applied" or "development"

---

[12] *Ibid.*, pp. 22–23.

Table 1. Sources of R&D Funds, by Sector and Broad Purpose, 1953–66.[13]
(Millions of dollars)

| | SOURCES BY SECTOR | | | | | | NON-DEFENSE FINANCING | | |
YEAR	TOTAL R&D FUNDS	FEDERAL GOVERNMENT	INDUSTRY	UNIVERSITIES AND COLLEGES	OTHER NON-PROFIT INSTITUTIONS	DEFENSE FINANCING AS PER CENT OF TOTAL R&D	TOTAL AS PER CENT OF TOTAL R&D	NON-FEDERAL AS PER CENT OF TOTAL	FEDERAL AS PER CENT OF TOTAL
1953	5,210	2,750	2,240	150	70	48.0	52.0	47.1	4.9
1954	5,730	3,125	2,365	170	70	48.0	52.0	45.5	6.5
1955	6,270	3,490	2,510	190	80	47.3	52.7	44.2	8.5
1956	8,470	4,840	3,340	200	90	48.5	51.5	42.9	8.6
1957	9,900	6,100	3,460	230	110	52.1	47.9	38.4	9.5
1958	10,850	6,765	3,700	260	125	51.9	48.1	37.6	10.5
1959	12,520	8,035	4,055	290	140	53.5	46.7	35.9	10.8
1960	13,710	8,720	4,510	330	150	51.5	48.5	36.3	12.2
1961	14,500	9,215	4,750	370	165	49.2	50.8	36.4	14.4
1962	15,610	9,885	5,115	420	190	44.6	55.4	36.7	18.7
1963	17,350	11,220	5,445	490	195	40.2	59.8	35.3	24.5
1964	19,180	12,530	5,880	560	210	36.0	64.0	34.7	29.3
1965(prel.)	20,470	13,070	6,530	640	230	32.1	67.9	36.2	31.7
1966(est.)	22,220	14,070	7,210	700	240	—	—	—	—

13 *Ibid.*, Table B–1b, p. 23 and Table B–3b, p. 26.

Table 2. Rates of Increase in R&D and Basic Research Expenditures, by Performing Sectors, 1953–65, and 1965 Dollar Levels.[14]

	ANNUAL GROWTH RATE [a] (PER CENT)			1965 DOLLAR LEVEL (IN
SECTOR	1953–65	1953–58	1958–65	MILLIONS)
Research and Development				
Total	12.1	15.8	9.5	$20,470
Federal government	9.8	6.3	12.3	3,090
Industry [b]	12.0	18.2	7.8	14,200
Universities and colleges [b]	15.2	14.1	16.0	2,510
Other non-profit institutions [b]	16.2	12.7	18.9	670
Basic Research				
Total	16.1	14.8	17.0	2,926
Federal government	12.7	4.4	19.1	424
Industry [b]	12.3	15.1	10.3	607
Universities and colleges [b]	19.2	17.8	20.0	1,690
Other non-profit institutions [b]	17.4	20.7	15.0	205

[a]Compound rates.
[b]Includes funds from the federal government for research centers administered by organizations under contract with federal agencies.

because they are the subject of industrial contracts.) Both educational institutions and other non-profit institutions have grown faster than industry as performers of even the total category "R&D" (which is overwhelmingly composed of development expenditures) in recent years, except for the middle and late 1950's, when the rapid growth period of defense and space systems projects peaked.

Tables 3 and 4 bring together sources of funding with sectors of performance, first for R&D, then for basic research alone. This allows us to see clearly the directions of intersectoral transfers of funds. For example, the federal government transfers into non-governmental sectors, for their management and performance, about 75 per cent of the total federal funds for R&D. Industry not only absorbs most of these federal-transfer R&D funds (5 or 6 times the amount of these transferred funds that colleges and universities absorb), but actually spends considerably more of the government's money than its own money upon R&D.

In basic research, shown in Table 4, the federal government transfers a somewhat lower proportion of its funds to non-governmental sectors, and the relative absorption of these transfers by industry and by universities is the reverse of that for total R&D transfers. Industry uses only about a fifth as much federal money for basic research as do the colleges and universities. Since industry conducts or manages a considerable effort in basic research ($650 million in 1966), and since

[14] *Ibid.*, Table 1, p. 7.

industry has been so successful in gaining intersectoral transfers of R&D funds from the government, it is surprising that the transfers of federal funds to industry for the conduct of basic research are so small ($200 million in 1966), in comparison with either industry's self-funded basic research ($450 billion in 1966) or federal transfers to colleges and universities for performance of basic research ($1,063 million in 1966). Part of the explanation may lie in the motivation of profit-making businesses to maintain ownership control over the patents and trade secrets that can flow from the conduct of basic research. Another part of the explanation lies in the ingrained tendency of the keepers of statistics and records to polarize "business" and "science" (assigning one to industry and the other to universities in the statistics), even though production and knowledge are thoroughly interlaced in our modern society.

The relatively small funding of basic science, in relation to applied science and development, exhibited in Table 2, is not necessarily a subject for particular concern, since basic research is less dependent upon expensive equipment and since the number of persons with genuine talent for basic science is quite limited. No useful purpose would be served by expanding the funding of basic science to the point that the new research posts could only be filled by men of very little talent. On the other hand, an excessive funding of applied R&D could damage basic research by drawing away those best qualified to conduct it. Whether the

Table 3. Sources and Users of R&D Funds, 1966 (National Science Foundation Estimates) [15] (Millions of dollars)

SOURCES OF FUNDS	USERS OF FUNDS (PERFORMERS)					TOTAL FUNDS SUPPLIED	
	Federal Government	Industry	Colleges & Universities		Other non-profit institutions		
			Proper	Federally Controlled Research Centers		$	%
Federal Government	$3,260	$ 8,300	$1,340	$650	$520	14,070	63
Industry	—	7,100	50	—	60	7,210	33
Colleges & universities	—	—	700	—	—	700	03
Other non-profit institutions	—	—	90	—	150	240	01
TOTAL FUNDS USED $	3,260	15,400	2,180	650	730	22,220	100
%	15	69	10	03	03	100	

Table 4. Sources and Users of Basic Research Funds, 1966 (National Science Foundation Estimates)[16] (Millions of dollars)

SOURCES OF FUNDS	USERS OF FUNDS (PERFORMERS)					TOTAL FUNDS SUPPLIED	
	Federal Government	Industry	Colleges & Universities		Other non-profit institutions		
			Proper	Federally Controlled Research Centers		$	%
Federal Government	$459	$200	$1,063	$202	$125	2,049	64
Industry	—	450	27	—	20	497	15
Colleges & universities	—	—	530	—	—	530	16
Other non-profit institutions	—	—	77	—	80	157	05
TOTAL FUNDS USED $	459	650	1,697	202	225	3,233	100
USED %	14	20	53	06	07	100	

distribution of money between types of research is optimal cannot be determined on the basis of the data given in Tables 1 to 4.

Some 52 per cent of the nation's basic research was performed in the universities and colleges in 1966—without counting basic research in such university-administered federal contract research centers as the Lincoln Laboratory and the Argonne National Laboratories. This high concentration of fundamental studies in universities is fortunate. Teaching gives basic research scientists a traditional and stimulating activity for which they nominally receive their salaries. It is important that teaching is a "product-oriented" activity, focused on the end result of well-educated adults, rather than a "process-oriented" activity, devoted to promoting and securing ever more funds for the process of teaching itself. Research may also be "product-oriented," focused on the end results of new discoveries, better mathematical formulae, more economical theoretical explanations, or superior devices and hardware. But today, when $10 billion or more is annually transferred by the federal government to non-government sectors for the conduct of R&D, "research" is under strong pressure to orient itself toward securing ever greater financial support for the *process* of research itself. "Research" is close to becoming a prestigious and fund-worthy process, *independent of its demonstrable results*. The researcher who is also a teacher is likely to carry over into his research activities the "product-orientation" of teaching. He may also carry over into his research an expectation of sharp criticism—graduate students are inquisitive and discerning critics.

Agency Sources and Program Distribution of Federal R&D Funds

When we turn our attention to the distribution of federal R&D funds by source agency and by research use, we find that the various defense and space agencies spend the most R&D money and that physical science and engineering receive most of the money spent. When development is included in the totals along with pure and applied research, the percentage of R&D expenditure devoted to the non-physical sciences is small to the point of insignificance. Probably for this reason, the National Science Foundation, while it releases statistics on government-supported basic research and applied research by field and discipline, issues no such figures for total governmental R&D expenditures.

Richard J. Barber has attempted to fill this gap by working up a table from Bureau of the Budget estimates supplemented by his own estimates; his conclusions are shown in Table 5.

Table 5.   Federal R&D Expenditure, Fiscal 1965, by Program Area.[17]

PROGRAM AREA		ESTIMATED EXPENDITURES (IN MILLIONS)
Space research		$6,700
Military research		5,200
Medical research		1,300
Nuclear research		1,200
Agricultural research		179
Oceanographic research		138
Meteorological research		108
Water research		73
Transportation research		
Aviation	46	
Maritime	9	
Surface	0	
General	1	
Total		56
Educational research		24
Vocational rehabilitation research		19
Welfare administration research		7
Other (not allocated)		87
		$15,287

[17] Program estimates by Bureau of the Budget, 1965 Federal Budget. Other estimates from Richard J. Barber, *The Politics of Research* (Washington: Public Affairs Press, 1966), p. 79.

The imbalances of government R&D expenditures—they are mainly authorized by the defense and space agencies, concentrated in the physical and engineering sciences, and paid to a small number of chief industrial systems contractors— have an even greater effect on corporate activities than their absolute size would suggest. Corporate funding of in-house or self-funded research is overwhelmingly devoted to areas of clear governmental interest, in anticipation of large governmental development contracts, or devoted to incremental improvements in meeting the demands of existing commercial markets.[18] The area of oceanography and underseas research is typical. *Forbes* magazine recently estimated present annual "wet-space" research expenditures at $7.5 billion, of which $4 billion are for defense, $3 billion for oil and gas exploration, only $250 million for mining and chemical (which are newer than offshore oil and gas, but offer at least equal potentials), and only another $250 million for *all other* non-military research (governmental, corporate, and academic).[19]

Justification for Governmental R&D Expenditures

"Technological transfer" (also called "spin-off" or "fall-out") is sometimes argued by defense and space spokesmen as an important justification for their employing or funding the great majority of the nation's scientists and engineers. In time, real and significant transfers from space technology to civilian technology will undoubtedly occur. But with the same R&D investments in basic science and *directly* in applied civilian technology, how much greater and earlier would be the benefits for our cities, our transportation, our consumer products, our quality of air and water, and our public and private utilities? I find it difficult to take seriously the argument of technical transfer as a justification for R&D expenditures on the scale of our space program, since the argument amounts to saying that it is better to take a circuitous route than a direct one—and the circuitous routes are not selected for their probable scientific harvest so much as for their human drama, e.g., putting a man on the moon. In any case, we can be sure that those who are happy with and rationalize the employment of most of the nation's scientists and engineers in defense and space projects would advance some other justification for this allocation of scientific manpower if civilian benefits from such research failed to materialize.

The reason for being of all the largest federally funded R&D programs is not their indirect effect on civilian technology but their direct contribution to our foreign policy. Defense R&D for security and deterrence, space R&D for international prestige, supersonic transport R&D for the protection of future balance-of-payments accounts—not even a small fraction of the money spent on these programs can be justified on the basis of foreseeable technological transfers. The R&D and civilian sector areas usually mentioned as possible beneficiaries of tech-

[18] T. S. Eliot noted in his *Choruses from "The Rock"* that all men are ready to invest their money but most expect dividends.
[19] "The Big 'Wet-Space' Scramble," *Forbes,* May 15, 1966.

nological transfers have a far greater need for their own funds and their own mission-oriented R&D.

There is one possible rational goal for extremely complex and expensive Big Science projects, independent of foreign relations. This is the goal of extending the state of the arts of what is technologically possible—without regard to the utility of the particular project and without regard to what other nations are doing. Project Mohole, designed to drill a deep shaft into the earth's mantle, was justified in just these terms—to extend the technological state of the arts. An important side effect of complex projects chosen solely for their difficulty would be the absorption of systems development engineers into non-military projects, something which will be vitally needed in the event of relaxed foreign affairs. It is not unreasonable to fear that idle physicists and systems development engineers would naturally gravitate to the designing of new and more destructive weapons systems if left bereft of sufficiently complex and challenging projects. This has been the trend throughout the history of physics and engineering.

If objectives of complexity, difficulty, and challenge were explicitly recognized for a small number of federal engineering projects, we would have a better chance to achieve the widest and most interesting extensions of engineering ability, for the smallest cost. As science is challenged by the unknown, so engineering is challenged by the construction project no one has yet accomplished. This challenge should be encouraged and channeled, through rational comparisons of alternative projects.

Pure science is usually inexpensive enough to be financed by foundations and universities or even by the scientists themselves; but "pure engineering" is very expensive and must be financed by the government, whether for pressing needs of defense and foreign relations or explicitly for the challenge presented. The engineering challenges presented by the conquest of space are not necessarily more stimulating than the engineering challenges presented by under-earth, under-water, or urban engineering projects. Urban betterment would perhaps be the most complex systems development project of them all, since it would involve property law, administrative law, intergovernmental relations, social psychology, sociology, economics, architecture, and medicine as well as systems engineering. Such a close partnership of systems engineering with the older humane sciences and their different perspectives would probably be highly beneficial.

The reasons for government expenditure on R&D so far examined are insufficient to justify the actual, dominating proportion of federal funding in our national R&D. Since federal allocative behavior in the R&D field seriously and often adversely affects the balances of scientific endeavors, regional economic activities, federal budgeting, and the choice of fields by graduate students, it is necessary to ask the basic question of whether the federal government should finance R&D at all, outside of the most strictly essential defense projects. The answer is "Yes," and the essential reason was stated succinctly in July, 1965, in the first report of the Committee on the Economic Impact of Defense and Disarmament (the "Ackley Committee"): ". . . the nation has a collective stake in a national expenditure on civilian R&D that is higher than a competitive market economy finds it profitable to undertake."

The government is the only consumer of some R&D results, as in defense and space. Other R&D projects, such as the development of a supersonic aircraft, demand outlays too massive for any private firm to bear. The resulting products of still other R&D undertakings—such as the development of radical new systems of urban transportation—may be marketable only in conjunction with far-reaching changes in property laws, zoning and condemnation procedures, traffic control systems, or municipal finance—matters beyond the effective influence of private firms. Finally, applied research may achieve benefits to the community that are not marketable to individuals, e.g., the reduction of smog and air pollution. These are *applied* researches that require government support.

In regard to *basic* research, a solution to a fundamental problem represents an addition to social capital; once the discovery is made, it benefits a wide range of individual, business, and public users. Yet basic research, when it requires elaborate equipment or requires many professionals working over an extended period, may cost too much for any one business firm to support, especially in view of the uncertainty of success. The patent system attempts to remedy the disproportion between the high cost of research and the small profits a firm could earn from a new invention under free market conditions. By giving to the person or organization paying for research a monopoly for a time over the disposition (or profit) of its results, the patent system stimulates inventive activity. If the cost of a research project is greater than the potential returns to any private interest but is less than the potential return to our society at large, then the financial risks of the project ought to be socialized in the general interest. In many cases the patent system is insufficient to achieve this result.

It does not follow that the only or best way to socialize the financial risk of big research is to be found in cost-plus and incentive contracts, such as those used for the great majority of defense and space R&D projects. Other types of contracts, new types of grants and loans, new forms of tax incentives, revisions of the patent system, and institutional changes within the federal government itself should all be considered.

THE ECONOMIC CONSEQUENCES OF TECHNOLOGICAL INNOVATION FOR NATIONAL ECONOMIC GROWTH

Among our articles of faith today are the propositions that economic growth is powered by the profit motive of free-enterprise competition, is stabilized by government fiscal and monetary policies, and actually takes place through technological innovation. A shift in American beliefs about economic growth occurred in the 1950's. In 1955, the eminent economist Alvin H. Hansen, long an advocate of deficit financing and fiscal solutions to cyclical problems, told the Congressional Joint Committee on the Economic Report that scientific and technological research provided a sounder basis for long-term growth than capital accumulation.[20] Our

[20] Alvin H. Hansen, "Federal Tax Policy for Economic Growth and Stability," paper submitted to the Subcommittee on Tax Policy, Joint Committee on the Economic Report, U.S. Congress, November 9, 1955, pp. 15–16.

great wartime research efforts in radar and atomic energy helped convince many congressmen that Hansen was right. More adherents to the technological view of economic growth swung into line when the Russians orbited Sputnik I, a technological achievement by a capital-poor society that had an effect of Billy Graham megatonnage in converting capital accumulation pagans into technological innovation believers. Between 1953 and 1960, American industry doubled the amount it spent on R&D from its own funds, and more than quadrupled the R&D it conducted using federal funds. This tremendous expansion of R&D within a brief period, only a small part of which is attributable to better reporting of R&D expenditures, took place during a period of relatively slow growth in the GNP, as we shall see.

The popularity of faith in technological innovation bounded further ahead in the 1960's. Firmly ensconced as the imputed cause of economic growth, technological innovation—in the guise of "productivity increase"—became in addition the political measure of allowable price and wage increases in an inflation-conscious society.

Attempts to Demonstrate That R&D and Growth Are Related

Neither technological innovation nor its economic impact is new. The medieval invention of non-human power sources and the seventeenth-century innovation of the factory system had economic consequences of comparable magnitude to the consequences of today's electronic and business machine revolutions. Newer are the systematic encouragement of innovation and the existence of organized markets for the rapid dissemination of newer technologies, developments that led Schumpeter to conclude that twentieth-century capitalism had institutionalized the apparently maverick phenomena of invention and change. Newest of all is the popular and even political character of our fervent belief in the economic efficacy of technological innovation. The following summary statement by an OECD panel is typical of current faith:

> Most attempts to assess the influence of changes in the principal factors of production on economic growth in mature industrial countries show that the rise in capital/labor ratio accounts for only a small part of the long-term increase in productivity, while the traditionally exogenous variables, usually grouped together under the heading of "technical progress," account for up to 90 per cent of increases in real product per person employed.[21]

The difficulty is that the "exogenous" variables—those outside the formal or closed system of the economic calculus—are a catch-all category, defined negatively by what they are not. They are left-overs, like the sociologist Pareto's "residues," and perhaps just as mystical. We have wide degrees of freedom to call the economic residues "free enterprise," "wise government," "national vigor," "technological innovation," or what we like. The economic efficacy of R&D is

---

[21] Christopher Freeman, with Raymond Poignant and Ingvar Svennilson, in *Ministers Talk About Science* (Paris: OECD, 1965), p. 96.

like a ghost we all believe in but no one can claim to have seen. The same OECD panel states the empirical difficulty:

> Most countries have more reliable data on poultry and egg production than on numbers of research scientists or on output of discoveries and inventions. Even such statistics as are available usually cover only a part of the R&D effort. In most cases they exclude research in the social sciences, operational research, research on management techniques, scientific information and documentation services, data collection, geological survey work, and quality control activities. As in the case of education, the available R&D statistics are limited to input, so that productivity or quality of output are not reflected.[22]

The causative role of technological innovation in economic growth could only be established by demonstrating correlations over time between indices of invention or technological innovation on the one hand and indices of economic growth on the other hand. Such correlations are incredibly difficult to demonstrate in any objective way because of the large number of uncontrolled variables that characterize economic growth in different countries and in the same countries at different times. No one has claimed to have established a definitive correlation between technological and economic processes. Thus, the popular and political faith in technological innovation has become ascendent at just the time that professional economists are having second thoughts about the nature, measurement, and extent of technological innovation's contributions to real economic growth.

Let us examine a few of the measurements and reasonings that have been adduced to argue that technological innovation does or does not account for economic growth. Causation is inferred from the fact that as R&D expenditures have increased in the U.S., gross national product (GNP) has increased, as shown in Table 6.

Table 6.   Total U.S. Expenditures for R&D in Relation to GNP, 1953–60. (Dollar amounts in millions, at current prices.)[23]

YEAR	GNP	R&D FUNDS (REVISED)	R&D FUNDS AS PER CENT OF GNP
1953–54	$365,385	$5,150	1.41
1954–55	363,112	5,620	1.55
1955–56	397,469	6,390	1.61
1956–57	419,180	8,610	2.05
1957–58	442,769	10,030	2.26
1958–59	444,546	11,070	2.49
1959–60	482,783	12,620	2.61
1960–61	504,448	14,040	2.78

[22] *Ibid.,* p. 97.
[23] *Reviews of Data,* No. 33, NSF 62–9 (Washington: National Science Foundation, 1962), Table 7, p. 7. GNP totals refer to calendar years; the first figure is for 1953. R&D totals refer to fiscal years beginning July 1.

Upon close examination, these figures reveal only that R&D funds have increased, both absolutely and as a percentage of GNP, steadily and without regard to rises and dips in economic output. Strong R&D expenditure increases are shown for 1954–55 and 1958–59, periods of slowdown in economic growth. And for the entire period 1947–60, total national R&D expenditures tripled, while in the same period the rate of economic growth actually dropped from 3.7 per cent to 3 per cent per annum.[24]

One of the most thorough studies of economic growth in the U.S., Edward F. Denison's *The Sources of Economic Growth in the United States and the Alternatives Before Us*, raises serious questions as to whether investments in R&D stimulate any more economic growth than would be stimulated by any other reasonable investments as such.[25] Denison's calculations of different sources that contributed to economic growth, probably the most detailed calculations of this kind that have been attempted, indicate that the national rate of return on organized R&D is about the same as on investment in general non-residential capital. As Harry G. Johnson has pointed out, the calculated rate of return on R&D might be much higher if improvements in product quality were given consideration, if it were true that R&D yielded its benefits only with a substantial time lag, and if only the more efficiently managed R&D were considered.[26] Despite these limitations, Denison's calculations are the best we have relating economic growth to investment in R&D. For the period 1929–57, about 32 per cent of U.S. economic growth is ascribed to the increase in output per unit of input; somewhat over half of the increase in output per unit of input is in turn ascribed to the category "Advance of Knowledge"; and something like 20 per cent of "Advance of Knowledge" is attributed to organized research and development during the period. Thus, about 3 per cent to 4 per cent of U.S. economic growth from 1929 to 1957 is ascribed to organized R&D by these calculations. While this may underestimate the contribution of R&D for reasons already mentioned, it may also overestimate the economic contribution of R&D, since Denison's "Advance of Knowledge" category is in reality a residual category left over when more measurable economic factors have been accounted for—and as a residual category can be expected to include errors of measurement together with political, cultural, and other less known contributors to economic growth.

[24] Herbert J. Hollomon, "Science, Technology and Economic Growth," in *Physics Today*, Vol. 16 (1963), p. 38.

[25] (New York: Committee for Economic Development, 1962).

[26] Harry G. Johnson, "Federal Support of Basic Research: Some Economic Issues," in *Basic Research and National Goals*, Washington, 1965, pp. 134, 135, and 141. Johnson remarks in his footnote (7): "Denison relates the contribution to growth to current research and development expenditures; since research and development expenditure has been growing rapidly, the rate of return would be higher if calculated on the basis of earlier (smaller) expenditures." Johnson refers to other comments on the Denison book in Moses Abramovitz' "Economic Growth in the United States," a review article, in *American Economic Review*, Vol. 52 (September, 1962), pp. 762–82.

International Comparisons

Another way to attempt the demonstration of a relationship between technological innovation and economic growth is to measure the inventions and discoveries that result from research rather than the funds devoted to research. While expenditures can be compared meaningfully from year to year, relative quantities of inventions and discoveries tend to be capricious for particular years—so those interested in this approach have usually compared national performances against each other rather than particular years of performance within the same country. When the immediate products of research, scientific discoveries and engineering inventions, have been quantified for different countries over considerable periods of time, then the national rates of economic growth are compared with the respective performances in discovery and invention. Nobel Prizes have commonly been used as a measure of scientific discoveries (Table 7), and patentable inventions as a measure of engineering innovation (Table 8).

Tables 7 and 8 both show a growing predominance of the United States, particularly in engineering, but even in scientific discovery in recent years. Table 7 shows that the U.S. share of Nobel Prizes in science increased dramatically from the period 1901–30 to the period 1931–60. (Actually, the major part of the increase came after World War II, when European societies were temporarily disorganized and many of the best European scientists had even immigrated to the United States, a distinction of prewar and postwar periods not made in the table.) Whatever the causes of increased U.S. leadership in scientific discovery, as

Table 7. Nobel Prizes in Science by Countries, 1901–30 and 1931–60.[27]

| | NOBEL PRIZES IN SCIENCE | |
COUNTRY	1901–30	1931–60
United States	6	33
England	15	18
Germany	27	14
Switzerland	3	5
Austria	3	4
Sweden	6	2
Italy	2	2
U.S.S.R.	2	2
France	11	Less than 2
Holland	6	Less than 2
Denmark	4	Less than 2

[27] Hendrick W. Bode, "Reflections on the Relation Between Science and Technology," in *Basic Research and National Goals* (Washington: Government Printing Office, 1965), Tables 5 and 7, pp. 52 and 54. Two tables in the source are combined into one table here.

Table 8. Invention Rates in Various Countries.[28]

COUNTRY	A TOTAL ON SELECTED LIST 1600–PRESENT	B AVERAGE ANNUAL RATE 1930–39
United States	203	38,300
Great Britain	58	9,050
Germany	32	14,600
France	29	9,550
Italy	14	3,900
Switzerland	0	3,130
Sweden	4	1,030

measured in Nobel Prizes, this leadership does show a correlation with long-term trends in U.S. economic growth.

The type of evidence presented in Tables 7 and 8 does suggest that the United States has achieved world technological leadership during the same decades that its economy has become the most prosperous in the world. On the other hand, countries credited with a much lower proportion of the world's scientific discoveries and engineering inventions, such as the U.S.S.R. and Japan, have shown extraordinarily rapid economic growth during these same decades. This raises the question whether national leadership in technological innovation confers greater benefits upon the country maintaining such leadership or upon other countries that use the R&D results without themselves sustaining such high expenditures for R&D.

Difficulties in Correlating R&D and Growth Series

It can of course be argued that R&D expenditures require some years to achieve their effect upon the economy, and that the rapid economic growth rate of the United States in the 1960's is attributable to the rising R&D expenditures of the 1950's. But this reasoning is uncertain; one could always find some later period of prosperity and rapid economic growth to nominate as the beneficiary of earlier R&D expenditures.

The lack of a closer correlation between R&D expenditures and economic growth in the U.S. during the last 20 years can be plausibly explained, while still saving the hypothesis that R&D causes economic growth, by maintaining that too much of the R&D increases went into military and space projects. For instance, in 1962, 71 per cent of the $15 billion expended upon R&D in the U.S. was spent by the government for defense and space related projects. And of the 400,000 scientists and engineers employed in R&D in 1962, 280,000 were employed in

[28] *Ibid.,* Table 6, p. 53.

defense and space projects.[29] We have already discussed the possibility of technological transfers from defense and NASA research to civilian industry; they may happen but obviously not quickly or uniformly enough to show up in our figures in a recognizable way. The GNP's rate of growth was probably less influenced by large R&D expenditures in defense and space than by much smaller company-financed R&D expenditures in agricultural fertilizers, agricultural machinery, oxygen-process steelmaking, polymer chemistry, electrostatic copying, television research, and electronic data processing, to mention but a few productive fields of civilian R&D.

Innovation Supply Inelasticities

The argument that recent economic growth results in part from earlier (and smaller) R&D investments and that therefore far greater future economic growth can be expected to ensue from recent and larger R&D investment must be weighed in light of the possibility that the supply of first-rate technological innovation is relatively inelastic. If this is true, then no substantial increase in economic growth could be expected from recent large increases in R&D investment, even assuming what cannot easily be demonstrated, that R&D results bear some recognizable connection to economic growth. In his article entitled "The Supply of Inventors and Inventions,"[30] Fritz Machlup examined the elasticity of four factors, and summarized his findings thus:

> First, we discussed the supply of inventive labor, regardless of quality, and found it to be subject to increasing supply prices. Second, we looked into the supply of inventive labor capacity and were impressed with the possibility that additions to the inventive personnel will be of inferior quality. Third, we analyzed the supply of new (raw) inventions and concluded that, beyond a point, the law of diminishing returns will be operative. And fourth, we inquired into the supply of inventions selected for actual use and discovered a tendency toward a diminishing ratio of exploitation.
> . . . The cumulative loss in the efficiency of incremental compensation for inventive work may be very serious.[31]

Depending on just how sharp these inelasticities really are, a large increase in R&D investment might accomplish little but to raise the salaries of first-rate scientists and engineers for inventing what they would have invented anyway and of inferior men for inventing nothing. Naturally, education eases the inelasticity Machlup noted in inventive labor capacity, but the contribution to economic growth of such an increase would be impossible to measure, since education also contributes to economic growth in so many other ways. As Denison's investiga-

[29] Hollomon, *op. cit.*, pp. 42 and 44.
[30] In *The Rate and Direction of Inventive Activity: Economic and Social Factors,* Report of the National Bureau of Economic Research, New York (Princeton, N. J.: Princeton University Press, copyright 1962), pp. 143–67.
[31] *Ibid.*, p. 166.

tions raise a question whether the economic benefits of R&D investment would not be duplicated by any reasonable investments—so Machlup's investigations suggest that the economic benefits of technological education may be duplicated by investment in any reasonable education program.

Government Policy

The theoretical question of relationships between economic growth and R&D investment is inseparable from the policy question of whether the federal government should devote increased financial support to science and engineering. Some of the conditions and assumptions for arriving at any rational answer to this question have been clarified by the economist Harry G. Johnson in a report to a congressional committee:

> . . . there is no disputing that basic research has played a significant part in the growth of the U.S. economy. This fact by itself, however, does not constitute a case for Government support of basic scientific research, though scientists frequently write as if it did; the argument that it does is equivalent to arguing that, because part of the growth of output is attributable to population growth, the Government should subsidize births and immigration. In order to establish a case for Government support, it must be shown that basic research yields a social return over its cost that exceeds the return on alternative types of investment of resources. Alternatively, it must be shown that the amount of basic research that would be carried on in the absence of Government support would be less than what would be economically optimal.[32]

As we have seen, social scientists have not been able to demonstrate whether or not economic growth receives greater stimulation from R&D investment than from ordinary capital investments, public welfare investments, and investments in general education. This does not release the government from the task of choosing between alternative investment opportunities; it simply means that the choice may have to be made partly on grounds less convincing than those proposed by Professor Johnson. Surely one of the most important considerations is what kind of society we wish to create. The choice of means by which to stimulate and maintain economic growth should not be a purely economic question, much less a purely technological question. We should select some mix of R&D investments, other capital investments, social welfare investments, and educational investments with not only economic but also political and social consequences in mind.

In the midst of the Great Depression, Franklin Roosevelt appealed to the nation to support his proposed minimum wage and minimum hour laws; his strongest argument for benefiting our needy classes was this: "American industry has searched the outside world to find new markets, but it can create on its very doorstep the biggest and most permanent market it has ever had." The need for new social legislation is not likely to disappear as the greater productivity following from technological innovation creates new requirements for ever larger markets and more employment opportunities.

[32] *Op. cit.,* pp. 135–36.

THE ECONOMIC CONSEQUENCES OF TECHNOLOGICAL INNOVATION FOR REGIONS, INDUSTRIES, AND FIRMS

Among the beneficiaries when the federal government allocates R&D funds—in ways other than would the private decision-makers of the marketplace—are particular firms, industries, classes of professionals, and geographical regions of the country.

The individual degree-holders and professionals who earn most as a result of the government funding of R&D (and usually work under grants or contracts in the defense and space industries) are not always the same persons who would earn most if the main funding of R&D were the responsibility of the private sector and the monetary values of individuals' efforts were measured by the industrial yardstick of patentable inventions and product innovations or by the university yardstick of widely reviewed journal articles. Government sponsorship of R&D can sometimes be as conducive to make-work projects and contract-extension maneuvers as the self-funding of industrial R&D is conducive to actual product introduction, and as conducive to secrecy as a university salary is conducive to publication. Very little of the government-funded research work is kept secret for military or national security reasons.[33] Some of it is kept secret from competitive firms during the time that the secretive firm can develop commercial products or proposals for further government research. Much of it is kept secret from Congress or from administrative agencies other than the funding agency. Much of it goes unpublished for the very good reason that its scientific and scholarly quality is so low that it would be ridiculed if published in a scholarly journal, especially were its cost revealed.

Differences in Impact Among Regions

The regions of the country benefiting most from government-funded R&D have consistently been Southern California, the Middle Atlantic or New York and New Jersey area, and the New England area centering around Boston with its universities and its electronic industries on Route 128. The Southwest and Southeast have been coming up fast, and because of the prevailing low levels of income in the Southeast, government R&D expenditures may be having a greater total impact there than in any other section of the country. The traditional industrial regions around the Great Lakes have felt neglected in the parcelling out of government R&D funds, and with some reason. Middlewestern universities and state industrial commissions have banded together in pursuit of many substantial pending R&D awards, however; and in 1967 they landed one of the richest prizes, the Atomic Energy Commission's expensive new accelerator.

For fiscal 1963, ten states carried away 75.5 per cent of the federal government's R&D awards, as shown in Table 9.

[33] See the chapter entitled "Information Restrictions" in Richard J. Barber, *op. cit.*, pp. 91–108.

Table 9. Allocation of Federal R&D Awards by Leading States, Fiscal 1963.[34]

STATE	PER CENT OF TOTAL
California	38.9
New York	9.4
Massachusetts	4.6
Maryland and the District of Columbia	4.5
Pennsylvania	3.6
Texas	3.4
Washington	3.3
New Jersey	2.9
Florida	2.5
Missouri	2.4
Sub-total for 10 states	75.5

Except for a few sizable government R&D facilities located in low-income regions, such as Huntsville and Oak Ridge in the Southeast, most federal R&D funds seem to have made the rich regions richer and the poor poorer. Certainly this has been the general effect of government R&D contract awards to private industrial firms; those R&D funds that have reached low-income regions have chiefly done so as part of the federal government's own in-house research. Our nation's poorest region, Appalachia, has benefited from very few R&D contracts and facilities. It is difficult for regions lacking science-based industries to gain R&D contracts and difficult for them to attract science-based industries since universities and other supporting institutions for technological creativity are lacking.

One reason why R&D is regionally concentrated is that, for optimal immediate performance and economy, perhaps it *should* be. It does help an electronics firm to be near Harvard and MIT or an aerospace firm to be in the aerospace complex of Southern California, where professional scientists, service facilities, and technical traditions are located. Another reason is that the bureaucrats of Defense and NASA stand to lose far more by a bad contract award than they can ever gain by a good award to a new contractor, so they are naturally prone to keep going back to the same tried contractors in California, Massachusetts, and New York, unless there are exceptionally convincing reasons to award R&D work elsewhere. But bureaucratic safety and actual short-run performance advantages should be weighed, at some level of government, against the social and economic consequences of concentrating the most technological and rapidly growing industries in

[34] *Report on Geographic Distribution of Federal Research and Development Funds,* House Subcommittee on Science, Research, and Development, 88th Cong., 2nd Sess., 1964, p. 7. (This is discussed in Barber's book, where I learned of it.) Included in the total are prime contracts and grants awarded by the eight federal agencies that fund the most R&D, which together accounted for 99.2 per cent of the $9.9 billion federal funds for R&D in fiscal 1963.

a few selected regions of the country. From the standpoint of regional balance and the fight against poverty, it is precisely these fast-growing and educative R&D industries that should be located in such depressed regions as Appalachia.

Differences Among Industries

Turning from geographic to industrial concentration of government-funded R&D, we may see in Table 10 an indication of how selected industries fared in securing federal R&D funds in 1961. The proportion of sales dollars spent upon R&D

Table 10.   R&D Funds in Selected U.S. Industries, 1961. [35]

INDUSTRY	SALES IN BILLIONS OF DOLLARS	R&D IN MILLIONS OF DOLLARS			R&D AS PER CENT OF SALES
		FEDERAL	COMPANY	TOTAL	
All manufactur-ing industry	246.0	6,313	4,480	10,872	4.4
Aircraft and missiles	16.4	3,537	385	3,957	24.2
Electrical equip-ment and com-munications	23.1	1,533	861	2,404	10.4
Machinery	20.0	292	600	896	4.4
Chemicals	23.4	224	845	1,073	4.6
Motor vehicles and trans-portation	28.0	191	609	802	2.9
Scientific instruments	5.3	176	208	384	7.2
Primary metals	20.0	16	143	160	0.8
Food	35.0	4	101	105	0.3

differs about 80-to-1 between the aerospace and food industries, the extreme industries in this respect. The R&D expenditures of any industry are a product of both its in-house and government-funded research. Those that receive large government grants for R&D invariably spend a considerable portion of their own funds on R&D as well, often in anticipation of winning further government contracts or in adaptation of government products for commercial uses. But those industries that spend large amounts of their own funds on R&D do not invariably receive substantial R&D funds from the government; the chemical and primary metals industries, for example, spend very substantial in-house sums on R&D, while receiving comparatively modest funding from the government.

[25] NSF 64–9 (Washington: National Science Foundation). The R&D "Total" includes minor amounts from other sources.

When measured as per cent of sales, total R&D is far higher in three industries —aerospace, electrical equipment, and scientific instruments—than in any others. Among these three highly research-oriented industries, it is interesting that there is an inverse relationship between government funds and company funds for R&D. The aerospace industry is first among these three in absolute amount of federal R&D funds but spends only one-ninth as much company funds as federal funds on R&D. The scientific instrument industry is last among these three in federal funds received but actually spends considerably more company funds than federal funds upon R&D.

In surveying the economics of R&D at the national level, we noted that if federal funds were withdrawn from R&D there would still be very large sums devoted to R&D; probably much more than in the past, since science is more fashionable today. It is quite possible, at the national level, that individuals and corporations contribute fewer dollars to non-profit R&D than they would in the absence of federal R&D expenditures. In the same vein, we can note at the industry level the possibility that some of the high-research industries might continue to devote a high proportion of sales dollars to R&D by increasing self-funded R&D, even were federal transfers of funds for industrial R&D withdrawn or reduced.

The question "How much systems development could and would private industry undertake without federal funding?" will never receive a concensus answer, since the vested interests in opposite answers are so strong. Businessmen in those industries that receive relatively few and small federal R&D contracts, while paying high federal corporate income taxes (and perhaps experiencing sharp competition in the hiring of engineers, the hiring of executives, and the marketing of products from those industries and firms that have a greater participation in the federal R&D largesse) will be fiscally conservative, believing that the federal government should reduce taxes, in part by leaving industry to self-fund its own R&D projects. On the other hand, businessmen in what President Eisenhower termed "the military industrial complex"—those companies that collectively account for the majority of federal R&D dollars and individually depend upon the federal government as their chief customer—must argue that private industry cannot afford the R&D expenditures the nation needs. This argument is being extended by analogy from the defense and space industries to such civilian public sector industries as urban transportation, air and water pollution control, the desalinization of sea water, and undersea exploration.

Federal funds may stimulate industrial R&D directly, by paying for the actual cost of developing a nuclear reactor or a supersonic aircraft, or indirectly, by supporting a market for the products of R&D. This market may consist only of the federal government itself, as in the case of military aircraft and missiles, or may consist of widely distributed local governments and individual citizens, as in the cases of improved subway cars sold to municipalities that receive federal grants for urban mass transportation and improved diagnostic medical equipment sold to hospitals that service Medicare patients. In a broad range of such cases, federal expenditures for products or services bolster up an area of technology within which the actual R&D projects are governed by market competition rather than direct federal grants and contracts.

The aircraft industry provides particularly clear examples of every kind of federal stimulation of industrial R&D. Boeing's C97 military cargo plane and KC97 military tanker version of the same basic aircraft, propeller aircraft developed during World War II with Air Force financial backing, provided prototypes for the relatively rapid and inexpensive development of the commercial Stratocruiser aircraft. On the other hand, the Boeing 707 series of commercial jet aircraft evolved most immediately from a company-funded prototype, the "dash 80" four-jet military tanker aircraft. Boeing felt that the B52 bomber system required a jet tanker element, a tanker of higher altitude and faster capabilities than the KC97 propeller tanker, and when the Air Force failed to fund the design and development of such a jet tanker, Boeing did so on company funds. However, this self-funding decision was undoubtedly influenced by know-how in jet aircraft design gained during the federally funded B47 and B52 jet bomber projects and by the prospect of a large federal market for the products of this self-funded systems development. The marketable products were the KC135 jet tanker and the 707 series commercial jets, the tankers directly purchased by the Air Force, and the civilian 707's purchased by commercial airlines, all of whom receive substantial federal support through mail subsidies, airport programs, etc.

Two other Boeing aircraft development projects, the 747 and the SST, provide examples of the least direct and the most direct federal support for commercial R&D projects. When Boeing lost out to Lockheed in the federal design competition for development and production of a very large military transport plane, the C5— which Lockheed will both sell directly to the military and use as the prototype for closely related commercial passenger and cargo aircraft—Boeing decided to proceed ahead entirely on company funds with the development of a larger commercial aircraft, the 747 series, intermediate in size between the 707 series and Lockheed's C5. Here the only apparent federal influence is very generalized— federal regulation of air lanes and support of airports to be used by the 747 and various forms of federal assistance to the airlines that will purchase the 747. But federal assistance has been quite direct in the case of the SST, for the development of which Boeing won a federal design competition. Federal dollars are paying for the actual R&D process of designing the American SST, though the complete development costs are not defrayed by the federal government, and for this reason the customer airlines have contributed funds to Boeing far in advance of the delivery or even testing of planes.

We can learn from these events in the aircraft industry how complex and varied the channels of federal support for R&D are likely to be in other industries that become, in their turn, the beneficiaries of public policy and federal funds. Uncertainty is high regarding the appropriate level as well as the most efficacious and appropriate channels for federal assistance to R&D in different industries. Should we praise the aerospace and electrical equipment industries as "progressive" for their high proportions of sales dollars expended upon R&D, or should we compliment the food and primary metals industries as "efficient" for the high multiples of sales they derive from relatively small expenditures upon R&D? There are even difficulties in identifying the R&D that should be treated as conducted by a particular industry. National Science Foundation statistics depict the food industry at the bottom of the ladder in per cent of sales dollars spent upon R&D—but should we classify R&D in insecticides, fertilizers, cryogenics, soil analysis, many fields of chemistry, and even marketing methods as "food industry R&D"? There is no single "right" proportion of sales dollars for R&D in any industry, and the variations among firms within an industry support this conclusion. Lear Jet did well for a time in the aircraft industry with a relatively small R&D budget, almost all of it company-funded. Mead Johnson did very well in specialized sectors of the food and dietary industry, with a much higher R&D budget than is customary in that industry. It is also clear that whatever the appropriate investments in R&D may be for each individual industry, the actual per cents of sales dollars devoted to R&D are heavily influenced by the federal allocative patterns—patterns from which exceptional firms may isolate themselves but entire industries cannot escape.

Differences Among Firms

Within industries, R&D tends to be strongly concentrated within the few largest firms. The National Science Foundation has developed the statistical concept of the "large performer firm" from findings that R&D tends to be concentrated in firms with two characteristics: (1) large size, having more than 1,000 employees, and (2) organized departments and programs for the performance of R&D. Such "large performer companies" score higher on both government-funded and company-funded R&D, regardless of whether R&D emphasis is measured as per cent of payroll, per cent of value added, or per cent of new capital expenditures (Table 11).

Table 11.   1958 R&D Funds (Total and Company): All Companies in "Census of Manufacturers" vs. Large Companies with R&D Programs.[36]

ITEM	TOTAL R&D FUNDS AS PER CENT OF—			COMPANY R&D FUNDS AS PER CENT OF—		
	VALUE ADDED	NEW CAPITAL EXPENDITURES	PAY-ROLL	VALUE ADDED	NEW CAPITAL EXPENDITURES	PAY-ROLL
All manufacturing companies	5.5	62.9	9.6	2.4	27.2	4.1
Manufacturing companies having 1,000 or more employees and R&D programs	9.6	90.5	16.7	4.1	38.7	7.1

[36] *Industrial R&D Funds in Relation to Other Economic Variables*, NSF 64–25 (Washington: National Science Foundation, 1964), Table S–2, p. ix.

In the year 1958, the average total R&D funds (company-generated funds plus transferred funds from government contracts and other sources) per company was $29,000 for *all* companies in the "1958 Census of Manufacturers," but $7.2 million for manufacturing companies with organized R&D programs and more than 1,000 employees.[37]

Some indication of the industrial concentration of federally funded R&D is given by the facts that in 1961, 32 per cent of all federally financed R&D went to four companies, and 96 per cent of all federally financed R&D went to 200 companies. (A more detailed picture is presented in Table 12.) It is true that industrial activity in general is concentrated in a limited number of large firms, quite apart from either R&D expenditures or federal funding, but federal funds for R&D are very much more concentrated in fewer firms than either employment or manufacturing sales are concentrated. In other words, the concentration of industrial activity is being increased as a result of federal R&D allocative practices. The right hand of the Justice Department's Antitrust Division would seem not to know, or for policy reasons not to disturb, what the other hand of defense and space R&D procurement is doing to increase industrial concentration in the nation.

Table 12. Percentage of R&D Performed by Manufacturers, Ranked by Their Total Funds for R&D, in Comparison with Their Percentage of Sales and Employment, in 1961.[38]

COMPANIES RANKED BY TOTAL FUNDS FOR R&D	PER CENT OF TOTAL FOR ALL MANUFACTURING COMPANIES PERFORMING R&D				
	NET SALES	EMPLOY- MENT	TOTAL FUNDS FOR R&D	FEDERAL FUNDS FOR R&D	COMPANY AND OTHER FUNDS FOR R&D
First 4	4	5	22	32	9
First 8	10	11	34	45	20
First 20	17	19	54	66	38
First 40	24	26	69	83	50
First 100	40	40	81	92	66
First 200	52	50	88	96	78
First 300	60	57	91	97	84

A different indication of the concentration of R&D in larger firms, correlations between size of firm and the speed of adopting technical innovations, suggests that quite apart from federal funding influence there is a tendency for larger firms

[37] *Ibid.,* p. x.
[38] National Science Foundation, but reproduced here from Barber, *op. cit.,* p. 73. The "Net Sales" in 1961 of all manufacturing companies performing R&D were $242 billion.

to benefit most from R&D advances. Edwin Mansfield investigated 14 technological innovations in four industries and found statistically reliable correlations between size of firm and the speed at which innovations are adopted.[39] The innovations he examined included the continuous mining machine, the continuous wide-strip mill, the pallet-leading machine in the brewing industry, and the diesel locomotive. The National Science Foundation speculates as follows on why larger firms adopt technological innovations faster than do smaller firms:

> First, since larger firms have greater financial resources, more extensive engineering departments, better experimental facilities, and closer ties with equipment manufacturers, they can pioneer more cheaply and with less risk. Second, innovations are more adaptable to larger firms because they have a wider range of operating conditions. Third, since large firms have more units of a particular type of equipment, they are more likely to have at any one period of time some units which need replacement.[40]

In other words, sufficiently large firms are self-insurers against the uncertainties and risks of technological change. On the other hand, size can also bring inertia. Although the average small firm is slow in adopting innovations, alert, technologically oriented small firms may be fastest of all in adopting or pioneering change.

Apart from size of firm, Mansfield investigated but found no statistically significant relationship between speed in adopting innovations and such factors as youth of top management, profit level of the firm, and growth rate of the firm. His investigations leave us free to guess and follow our own prejudices as to whether firms with falling profit trends innovate out of necessity—or whether firms with rising profit trends innovate out of ebullience and affluence. We are only foreclosed from believing that the average small firm adopts technological innovations as rapidly as the average large firm.

BUSINESS AND SCIENCE AS OPPOSED YET ALLIED SUBCULTURES

Let us turn from the impact of federal policies upon the interplay between business and science to an examination of the characteristics of business and science themselves. There are several marked differences between business values and the values of science, but at least an equal number of similarities join these subcultures together in an alliance of objectivity, efficiency, and profound social change. The individuals who practice business and science tend to share an above-average emotional stability, considerable repression and sublimation of impulses (such as dependence and aggression), and high intelligence; though scientists usually avoid situations of interpersonal conflict, while businessmen often seek opportunities to express interpersonal dominance. Often the same persons are both businessmen and scientists or perhaps are technical professionals first and

---

[39] Several papers summarized in *Reviews of Data on Research and Development*, NSF 62–16 (Washington: National Science Foundation, 1962).
[40] *Ibid.*, p. 2.

later become business executives. For example, at least 27 new enterprises have been started since 1950 by former employees of the MIT Instrumentation Laboratory, and more than 50 companies have been founded by former members of the Lincoln Laboratory of MIT.[41] The progression of engineers' careers up into the executive ranks of business, within the same business firm, is even more frequent.

The widest differences between business and science appear when pure or basic science is contrasted with the most directly consumer-oriented categories of business activity such as advertising and retailing—Madison Avenue, Hollywood, and the smaller Fifth Avenue shops in New York. In this comparison, science seems oriented to knowledge and business to profit, science set in a world of ideas and business set in a world of people. But our famous retailing and advertising establishments stand out as quite distinctive even within the world of business—they are so much warmer, zanier, and unencumbered with system than the typical large business corporation; similarly, our purists of science engaged in theoretical research are hardly typical of the scientific community as a whole. The values of the basic research scientist have been described by W. O. Baker, vice president for research, Bell Telephone Laboratories:

> The paradox of choice for the research scientist is, of course, the choice between doing what his interests impel him to do and doing what some large part of society might seek to have done. . . . those having the ablest and most creative minds will prefer to use them in basic research by following up the undirected, uncontrolled, unspecified, unprogrammed, and certainly unknown courses revealed as the work itself goes ahead. . . . Therefore, we have somehow to present to the gifted researcher situations in which he will feel little or no inhibition of the free travel of the pathways of his mind.[42]

This absolute independence from the desires of others and total absorption in one's own ideas can be as narcissistic as the exhibitionism found in Hollywood or on Madison Avenue. (On the other hand, the most self-oriented activities are frequently the most beneficial to society in the final results, in both science and business.) "Applied" scientists and "organization" businessmen are close to each other in values and thoughtways, if only because both are seeking to realize external objectives and satisfy the expectations of others.

Science currently seems oriented to the exotic, business toward satisfying simpler and humbler consumer needs—but perhaps this impression is a matter of changing fashions. Before the atomic bomb, television, and space flight, science probably seemed more sedate than business to most Americans. Not too long ago, the genial and harmless physics professor was our popular image of the scientist, whereas flamboyant business tycoons of the sort described by Theodore Dreiser and F. Scott Fitzgerald seemed to embody the quintessence of business. Perhaps

[41] *Annual Report: Research Program of the Management of Science and Technology, 1964–1965* (Cambridge, Mass.: Alfred P. Sloan School of Management, MIT, 1965). Prepared by Donald G. Marquis and others, p. 27.
[42] "The Paradox of Choice," in *Symposium on Basic Research*, (Washington: AAAS Pub. No. 56, Copyright 1959 by the American Association for the Advancement of Science), pp. 41, 44.

the pendulum will swing again in the future; operations research, input-output analysis, the computer, and other genuine applications of scientific method to business operations have created an atmosphere of intellectual challenge as well as personal adventure in the business world of today and tomorrow.

A more substantial difference between the worlds of science and business than the popular stereotypes we may hold of them is the extent of their dependence on competition and cooperation. Private-enterprise business is essentially competitive; it is still governed in the main by reliance upon "arm's length" negotiation and fear of the "dead hand" of monopoly. Although science has its own competitions among individual scientists and among nations, it is an essentially cooperative endeavor in the sense that the new knowledge published by one scientist or discovered in one nation becomes available to all others. C. P. Snow has said that science is "easy," in that once anyone has done something scientific or technological anyone else can do it too. The principal exceptions to the cooperatively shared utility of scientific results occur when discoveries are kept secret for military reasons and when inventions are patented for commercial reasons. The case of secrecy has nothing to do with the inner nature of science as such (and rarely avails for long). The case of patents is clearly an imposition of advantage-seeking business values upon cooperative scientific values, curtailing the free operation of scientific communication and sharing.

Business accomplishments are also shared in that successful techniques are emulated when unprotected by patent or copyright. But the essential business product—from the point of view of the businessman—title of ownership to assets, is by its very nature incapable of being shared. (Ownership interests can of course be divided, into millions of shares if needed, but such divided parts cannot be equally utilized or enjoyed by more than one person. Title of ownership is essentially exclusive.) Knowledge can be shared without becoming less true for the discoverer, but bank accounts cannot be shared without diminishing in their value to the depositor. While ownership must be exclusive, scientific knowledge must be demonstrable and at least potentially shared to be scientific at all. The patent system in an organized business society is an attempt to make of an object of knowledge an object of ownership with the policy objective of thus stimulating the discovery of further useful knowledge.

Similarities Between Business and Science

Turning from the differences to the many similarities of our business and scientific subcultures, we can note that some of these similarities are traditional, while others are of relatively recent origin and reflect the common response of business and science to such pervasive contemporary forces as professionalization and the increase in the scale of almost everything.

Quantification. Scientific equations and profit-loss statements are both quantitative. Business and science share a commitment to numbers and quantification of the qualitative. One result is undoubtedly an increase of man's power to control some of the forces of nature; another result, a psychological one, is that the colorful and the concrete are on the defensive in our culture today.

Objectivity is closely related to quantification. The existence of objective yardsticks of success is essential in both science and business. The replicable laboratory experiment is a chief source of objectivity in science, while the judgment of the market encourages objectivity in business. The laboratory experiment is objective in ways that the market is not, since it pits the scientist against non-human nature, even if a human element enters into the interpretation and evaluation of how well the scientist has predicted or controlled the forces of nature. The market consists of people—buyers and sellers. Ideally it is objective in that the sellers and buyers with whom a businessman deals are so numerous, and the businessmen who compete with each other so numerous, that no one can rig the market—but all real markets are imperfect and in varying degrees manipulable. Subjective errors of business judgment are not always exposed by the market test, and qualities of dominance and leadership may bring great success in business. Furthermore, many businessmen and firms are motivated by a whole variety of sentiments other than the pure profitability that a perfect marketplace could judge with objectivity. As firms become larger and more bureaucratic, the objectivity of market forces may reach only weakly into the lives and interpersonal relationships of employees within the firm—interrelated as they are by seniority, compatibilities and incompatibilities, and other non-economic forces still less understood.

Instrumentalism, a means-end view of ideas and activities, is shared by business and applied science—some would say by pure science as well. Instrumentalism is not only opposed to doctrines and ideas defended for their own sake, it is also opposed to idleness and the absence of any ends. Even in popular language, "business" and "busy" are opposites of "leisure." The instrumentalism common to business institutions and most science and engineering is producing profound effects upon our psychological dispositions and our uses of leisure time. It is quite possible that the gains in leisure time attributable to increases in productivity of work are less significant for our quality of life than the inner changes wrought in us by our ever more efficient instrumentalism. Many executives and professionals simply cannot stop "optimizing," efficiently achieving instrumental objectives, however far they are from their office in time or space. Europeans generally take a dimmer view of this situation than do Americans. Jacques Ellul writes:

> Technique has become the new and specific *milieu* in which man is required to exist, one which has supplanted the old *milieu,* viz., that of nature. . . . It is formed by an accumulation of means which have established primacy over ends. . . . in every domain, technique has established stricter and stricter domination over the human being. . . . We conceive all problems in their technical aspect, and think that solutions to them can only appear by means of further perfecting techniques.[43]

[43] "The Technological Order," in Carl F. Stover, ed., *The Encyclopaedia Britannica Conference on the Technological Order* (Detroit: Wayne State University Press, 1962), pp. 394, 409, and 414.

Instrumentalism produces other problems for the clerical or production line worker, which are commented upon as follows in a UNESCO study:

> Many workers and employees doing routine high speed jobs not involving any responsibility find that their free time is ruined by fatigue, more mental than physical, so intense as to make them totally unable to enjoy themselves, or even to recuperate their strength. Other reports, on the contrary, speak of the pursuit of extreme forms of compensation for the distintegrating effects of piecemeal factory jobs on the personality.[44]

American views tend to be more optimistic about industrial life than the views just quoted, and to express fear of unemployment rather than overemployment. There has been more agitation in America for the educational and productive use of leisure time than for gaining release and psychological distance from instrumentalism. J. K. Galbraith has depicted what he senses to be a "new class" of American executives and professionals, who engage only in what they enjoy doing and grow through doing—in effect, spending all of their working time as leisure, and all of their leisure in productive ways.

Accumulation and Progress. Science and business further share a belief in the cumulativeness of results, the scientific brick in the cathedral of knowledge, and the business profit transferred to undistributed surplus or re-invested. The nineteenth-century historian Henry Thomas Buckle thought that scientific advances were uniquely *cumulative* while changes in religion, art, style, and manners were merely *replacive*. Scientific discoveries undergo reinterpretation and business assets undergo reinvestment, but so long as things go well their quintessential value grows cumulatively in each case. Of course, faith in accumulation implies a belief in progress, which is yet another important value that links together the cultures of science and business. Vannevar Bush expressed the common viewpoint of the worlds of science and business when he advised President Franklin D. Roosevelt that basic research "leads to new knowledge. It provides scientific capital."[45]

Internationalism is shared by business and science, often going beyond a resemblance to an operational linkage. Science became international at the point in time that it was objectively true and universally replicable. Commerce had always reached across national borders, but it has become even more international as technology has improved communications and transportation. Technology, in the forms of machines, patents, and even engineers, has become a prime export. To appreciate the internationality of science and business, it is only necessary to contrast their passage across national borders with the passage of religious beliefs, styles of dress, language, or ways of life. Money and scientific knowledge are peculiarly effective invaders among nations, far faster and more effective in their invasions than cultural beliefs or armies. A speeding up of migration is another

[44] Georges Friedmann, "Leisure and Technological Civilization," in *Sociological Aspects of Leisure,* Paris: UNESCO International Social Science Journal, Vol. 12 (1960), p. 513.

[45] *Science, The Endless Frontier*, Report to the President on a Program for Postwar Scientific Research, by Vannevar Bush, Director of OSRD (Washington: Government Printing Office, 1945), p. 13.

of the international effects of business and science. Alex Inkeles has demonstrated a tendency to the international standardization of occupations among industrial nations, which facilitates the movement of occupational specialists across national borders.

Largeness of scale and professionalization of individuals are common trends in business and science today, as they are in most other sectors of our society. In the business sphere, the chief economist of the Federal Trade Commission estimated in May, 1966, that 200 corporations would hold 75 per cent of the nation's manufacturing assets by 1975. In science, some areas of high-energy physics, nuclear science, and aerospace engineering have become so complex and so dependent upon massive equipment that only a few large institutes or industrial centers provide the conditions necessary to fruitful work in these fields. The phrase "critical density," originally a reference to the quantity and compression of radioactive atoms requisite for a self-sustaining nuclear chain reaction, has assumed another meaning in the everyday language of the world of big science: the number of scientists and engineers requisite to create a stimulating environment within which great discoveries and "breakthroughs" are likely to occur. The phenomenon was first observed in the pioneering scale of R&D successfully undertaken in the Lincoln Laboratory radar project and the Manhattan Project for the control of nuclear fission.

The largeness of scale that has become typical in both business and science by no means eliminates the small organization and the individual practitioner in either field. If anything, scale and professionalization or bureaucratization tend to confer upon the independent operator greater freedom, eccentricity, and effectiveness than ever before. Even within the large organizations, professionalization is consistent with individual identity. Some large organizations cultivate individuality and dissent. All of them expend more effort than ever seeking the right men for the right jobs. In science, a researcher needing a particular item of specialized information still thinks first of going to another individual scientist he believes is most likely to already have the information. This human situation will not necessarily be changed by the development of automatic systems for the retrieval of technical information. One of the more advanced efforts in scientific data retrieval is that being conducted by Dr. Myer Kessler at MIT, and he has made the names of individual scientists the key elements in his computer's memory storage.

New Intermediaries Between Business and Science

These numerous similarities and points of contact between science and business are accentuated today by specialized sub-cultures that have sprung into being specifically to mediate between the equally complex and dominating forces of science and business. Management consultants have proliferated in numbers and gained in technical expertise—the good ones no longer rely upon out-simpling or out-complexing the baffled client. Consultants provide small businesses with experience and knowledge (often gained in working for or consulting with larger businesses) in many specialized areas that the smaller firm cannot hope to cover with its own internal staff: electronic data processing, newer marketing techniques, product development, the preparation of complex public stock issues or loan applications, etc.

There is a fermentation of technology and management perspectives within many university departments. Business schools offer advanced management training to engineers and welcome their own business graduates back to the campus for refresher courses in the management of technology. Engineering schools offer degrees in management or even in the economic and social relationships of science. In the money markets, the legions of bright young security analysts constitute another kind of university, complete with its separate faculties specializing in the major industries. Most of the analysts preach a gospel of technological innovation to those raising capital and those investing capital alike. They are teachers as well as missionaries, conveying to even the most conservative managements some understanding of the importance and sources of corporate growth rates.

In established universities, professors of business, engineering, and related subjects perform a wide-ranging task in the cross-fertilization of ideas, as they move between their teaching and writing, their supervision of innovative graduate students, and their consulting assignments to the most varied clients. Symposia, summer conferences, and other variations of the "think tank" are staged by the universities to bring technologists and business managers into close if brief contact.

At a lower level of sophistication, but reaching a wider audience, are the trade magazines of the research industry that appeal to both businessmen and scientists. They are proliferating almost weekly, with such descriptive titles as: *Laboratory Management, Aerospace Management, Missiles and Rockets, Industrial Research, Research Management,* and *R/D.* They seem to devote most of their articles to substantive science and engineering, some articles to the R&D environment (including federal procurement actions), and the smallest number of articles to actual techniques and issues in the management of technological research. The "management" articles promised by the titles are gradually increasing in number and pertinence.

THE SIGNIFICANCE OF THE RELATIONSHIP BETWEEN BUSINESS AND SCIENCE TODAY

Our most potent national resources and practical capabilities have their sources in both business and science—particularly in those areas of technology and transformation where business and science are not just coordinated but integrated. Business and science are spiritual as well as material forces. Many of our norms of judgment and behavioral mores are informed by considerations of profitability or the logic of discovery.

The productive association of business and science explains some of the most dramatic statistical changes in our society. In the single year of 1964, IBM advanced from eighteenth to ninth among American corporations in annual sales volume. A decade earlier, IBM had been a small company, dwarfed in size and in technological resources by such giants as GE and Westinghouse, but still it was a dwarf willing to risk its future in commitments to a meeting point of business and science, computerized business machines. In the same year of 1964, McDonnell Aircraft advanced from 101 to 65, Celanese from 159 to 82, Litton Industries from 102 to 85, and Xerox from 294 to 227 among American corporations in annual sales volume. Signal Oil and Gas, which during the year acquired the aerospace research firm of Garrett, advanced from 149 to 105.[46]

Such economic changes produced changes in thinking. The stock market noted these crucibles of intense interaction between business efficiency and technological imagination by according exceptionally high price-earnings ratios to such technologically oriented firms. But this bidding up of the prices of technologically oriented companies was fully justified. The enthusiasm of money managers for IBM and Xerox has not, in the event, proved so excessive as many conservatives judged at the time. All of these firms have continued to grow, since 1964, much faster than the economy as a whole. Those investors who bought their common stocks at high price-earnings ratios have been richly rewarded. Money managers in the mutual funds and investment banking houses have generalized such investment experiences, bringing to bear upon every publicly owned business in America a new standard of investment evaluation that substantially affects the flow of even the most conservative funds. Our stock and bond markets are the vital heart of our allocative system; through them every corporate businessman feels technological innovation breathing down his neck.

On the international scene, America itself may be likened to a giant technological business. In the five year period from 1961 through 1965, the United States added more real production to its gross national product than the combined *total* gross national products of France and West Germany in 1965.[47] This American productivity supports a "technological invasion" of Europe by American firms. It increases American ownership interests in both Europe and the underdeveloped world, bringing increased resentments with increased participation. It acts as a powerful magnet of salaries and opportunities, attracting migrant scientists, engineers, teachers, and medical doctors to the U.S. from most parts of the world— including the backward nations most in need of holding their few well-trained technologists. This same productive union of business and science in the U.S. pays the bill for our foreign economic aid, our military assistance programs, our

---

[46] "Directory of the 500 Largest U.S. Industrial Corporations," *Fortune* (July, 1965). It is true that some of the growth of technological firms has come through mergers rather than been generated internally. Of the companies mentioned in the text, two have made significant acquisitions since 1964. McDonnell Aircraft has acquired Douglas Aircraft through an exchange of securities, and Signal Oil and Gas has recently been acquired by the Mack Truck Corporation. Such growth by merger or acquisition does not detract from the truth that technology generates growth. There is here a self-fulfilling prophecy. Corporate acquisitions are facilitated by the acquiring companies' high price-earnings ratios, attributable in large part to the management skills and technological innovations of "growth companies."

[47] Economists of the Morgan Guaranty Trust Company, as reported in the Washington *Star*, April 3, 1966.

national luxury of space competition with Russia, and our leadership position in the armaments race. The benefits of this union may be counted among the factors that have led America's chief competitor in the field of technology to a limited emulation of our free-enterprise system. The fact that the Soviets have injected competitive forces and market prices into their own technocratic system of engineer-managed economics is by now well known.

At the base of this component of America's power structure, so much felt on the international scene, is our American "knowledge industry." This industry, including publications and education as well as engineering, now accounts for about a third of our gross national product[48] and is widely believed to account for the rate of growth in the other two-thirds of our national product. Within the knowledge industry, applied research and development has grown more than 15-fold since 1930 and now represents an expenditure of over $20 billion per year. We spend much less upon pure scientific research, but the amount is still enough to account for over half of the world total. This international leadership produced by the creative partnership of business and science in America can be quantified and documented: by numbers of missiles produced, numbers of Nobel Prizes received, the dollar value of foreign business acquisitions and equity investments, and the rates of increase in the productivity of labor.

Impact on Social Mores and Structure

Some less quantifiable aspects of the relationship between business and science are equally important for the quality of life in our society. As two of the more dynamic and innovative forces on our society, science and business combine to transform our working lives, our recreations, our educational system, our social issues, and our problems of government and politics. As prestigious and richly rewarded activities, science and business often set the pace for other national goals and personal objectives, thus becoming ends as well as means. Generally they are secularizing forces. Traditional values based upon scripture, custom, or sentiment tend to be modified if not undermined by the combined impacts of business and science. For this reason, some cultural conservatives may perceive natural science as unnatural, social science as unsocial, and highly productive business as unproductive—for our quality of life. But for those who are meaningfully engaged in business or science, these are intensely interesting activities, in and of themselves.

Many of the founders of modern science were leisure-class amateurs, attracted to research by its inherent fascination. Business similarly attracts or retains many energetic and imaginative persons who have a genuine choice among activities, who either inherited or have long since earned sufficient means to free them from "work." Neither science nor business is "work" to the more proficient practitioner, and least of all are these pursuits "work" to those who operate in the exciting boundary areas linking commercial profitability to our expanding knowledge of nature and machines.

[48] Fritz Machlup, "Knowledge—the Growth Industry," *Fortune* (November, 1964).

CONCLUSION

Industrial science is significant for the problems it creates as well as for the successes it achieves. Too much power may become concentrated in those firms, government agencies, universities, and research institutes that achieve a critical density of technological expertise and corresponding funds. Our current allocation of resources and talents to technological endeavors rather than to education, social welfare, consumer goods, and other competing needs may be excessive. Even if the national level of investment in science and technology as a whole is appropriate, our sub-allocations to the different special sciences and to different R&D objectives may suffer from imbalance. While for most branches of science and technology today is a period of unparalleled opulence, some branches of research still subsist on starvation diets. By aerospace and defense industry standards, we devote only small pittances of talent to such obviously important objectives of applied R&D as improved urban transportation, purification of our air and water, modernized methods of housing construction, and the development of inexpensive (and perhaps labor-intensive) manufacturing techniques for underdeveloped societies. Below the national level, allocative decisions in the utilization of engineering capabilities are crucial for the prosperity of regions, business firms, and graduate training centers.

But uncertainties need not be disturbing. Entrepreneurial risk-taking is the essence of business activity, while the purest flame of scientific discovery thrives on the mysterious. The dynamic integration of business with science that has evolved in modern America equips us to approach with greater optimism many perplexing uncertainties, including even those of the relationships among business, science, and government.

SELECTED READINGS

Basic Research and National Goals (Washington: Government Printing Office, 1965). A symposium by eminent economists, physicists, chemists, administrators, and others. In general, the essays by scientists provide narrower and rosier perspectives than the essays by economists. Most of the articles are useful in clarifying the various, and often conflicting, national goals that can be served by investments in science. Harry G. Johnson's economic discussion is as clearly written as it is logically incisive and should be essential reading for all those who uncritically support each and every investment in research.

RICHARD J. BARBER, *The Politics of Research* (Washington: Public Affairs Press, 1966). This book is essential reading for all who are interested in the extent and nature of federal influence upon the nation's R&D establishment. Among the disturbing tendencies explored, and in some cases well documented, are (1) favoritism, which results in a relatively few large corporations receiving an increasing slice of federal R&D expenditures; (2) the dominance of federal expenditures, particularly defense expenditures, in determining the specialties and research objectives of all the nation's scientists and engineers; (3) the decline of meaningful competition in many areas of federally supported R&D; (4) the institutionalization of optimistic cost estimates for federally supported R&D projects, which in the event cost substantially more than estimated, often by thousands of per cent; (5) government absorption of the development cost for valuable patents and technological designs that may then be controlled by profitable businesses; and (6) informational restrictions on the free dissemination of scientific results obtained at the public expense, most of which restrictions appear to have no connection with the national security. The book is inquisitive and contentious without becoming polemical.

Federal Research and Development Programs: The Decision-making Process, Hearings before the Research and Technical Programs Subcommittee of the Committee on Government Operations of the House of Representatives, 89th Cong. (Washington: Government Printing Office, 1966). The testimony of eminent university, industrial, government, and foundation scientists strongly suggests that federal funding policies may have induced a "brain drain" into the defense and aerospace fields, contributing to the sparsity of university programs and the generally poor results of the industrial projects in many non-defense areas of R&D that are critical to urban development, public health, quality of environment, and other civilian "public sector" goals.

JOHN KENNETH GALBRAITH, *The New Industrial State* (Boston: Houghton Mifflin Company, 1967). This book shows the close relationship of technological progress to organizational integration on a national scale. The Bell Telephone System is introduced as a positive example, and the fragmented local transit systems are offered as examples of a piteously backward technology. Relationships between business and science are explored particularly in the chapters entitled "The Imperatives of Technology," "The Technostructure," and "The Educational and Scientific Estate."

KARL B. HILL, ED., *The Management of Scientists* (Boston: Beacon Press, 1964). This is a report on an "action-oriented" symposium focused on how organizations can be directed to improve the usable output of R&D projects. Two chapters by a historian and a psychologist provide background pictures of science as an institution and scientists as individuals. The central chapters by a corporation president and by a federal executive who has held high posts in the Department of Health, Education, and Welfare and in NASA offer prescriptions for the motivation, management, and direction of scientists and engineers working within industrial organizations.

CHARLES D. ORTH III, JOSEPH C. BAILEY, AND FRANCIS W. WOLEK, EDS., *Administering Research and Development* (Homewood, Ill.: Richard D. Irwin and Dorsey, 1964). This substantial and useful volume is a combination casebook and collection of essays and studies. The relationships of business management and businessmen to scientists and engineers are focused upon throughout. The essays by Renato Tagiuri, Louis B. Barnes, Tom Burns, Charles D. Orth III, and Herbert

A. Shepard provide a representative sampling of industrial corporations, while other essays offer psychological and sociological studies of value to the specialist. The case material is extensive. General readers may find the shorter cases most instructive.

Don K. Price, *The Scientific Estate* (Cambridge, Mass.: Harvard University Press, 1965). The best recent general treatment of relationships between science and the federal government. The posture is broader and less critical of the federal government than that of Barber's book. The historical reviews of nuclear secrecy in the 1940's and 1950's, of the impact of Sputnik upon federal research activities, and of the origin of the National Science Foundation are particularly stimulating. Many current dilemmas of federal R&D policy are traced to their historical origins.

The Rate and Direction of Inventive Activity: Economic and Social Factors, Report of the National Bureau of Economic Research, New York (Princeton, N.J.: Princeton University Press, 1962). A thick volume of scholarly essays, most of them by economists, few of them light and all of them accompanied by independent comment from other scholars. The subject is technological innovation, as in Schon's book mentioned below, but here the authors' approach is that of technical economic analysis rather than intuition and social study. Problems are equally covered at the level of the national economy and at the level of the business firm.

Donald A. Schon, *Technology and Change: The New Heraclitus* (New York: Delacorte, 1967). One of the first books to concentrate upon processes of innovation as such, whether the innovations are scientific, technological, organizational, or social and cultural. The close relationships among these different kinds of innovation are exhibited. The obstacles to innovation within large organizations are thoroughly explored, while the positive role of large scale organization in promoting technological rationalization and progress receives less emphasis than in Galbraith's book, mentioned above.

Technology and the American Economy, Report of the National Commission on Technology, Automation, and Economic Progress (Washington: Government Printing Office, 1966). This distinguished group of economists, industrialists, labor union heads, social scientists, and federal executives was assembled primarily to evaluate the impact of automation upon employment, but its wide-ranging report provides both insights and statistics regarding national economic growth, industrial concentration, manpower retraining, and public sector needs, as well as trends in employment and unemployment. General readers will be interested in the summary volume, which contains both Commission recommendations and the dissenting views of some members. Specialists will find the lengthy appendix volumes a rich mine of data.

part 4

BUSINESS AND SOCIAL STRUCTURE

The business system influences the lives and the associations of all Americans in uncounted and probably uncountable ways. Religious groups, for example, have historically been favored or disadvantaged as wealthy businessmen have reinforced first one and then another of the preferences, prejudices, and preoccupations of the larger society. Even among the dominant Protestant groups there is a prestige hierarchy in which the denominations favored by businessmen stand high. Other voluntary associations are similarly influenced by the facts of a business society. The frustration of campaign workers for a dizzying number of charities who continually hear the excuse "I gave at the office," points (if somewhat humorously) to the fact that the whole concept of private charity—dear to critics of organized welfare—has been organized and rationalized by businessmen who advise, direct, and manage enormous funds and large staffs of American "do-gooders."

The American social structure is enormously complex, and up-to-date information on many aspects of it is lacking. The contributions in this section focus on three aspects of our social organization and behavior that have been rather thoroughly studied. They also represent assessments of the impact of business at successive removes along the span of organizations stretching from the business system to the individual citizen. American unions, the first contribution makes clear, are in many ways a specialized part of the business system itself. The family, the second contribution suggests, is shaped and reshaped in important ways according to the changing needs of both the business system and the individual family members. The third essay in the section considers how the social structure is reflected in individual minds and traces the evolving significance that working in the American business system has for the individual. Together, these three measurements of our social structure and social behavior suggest that the values, demands, opportunities, and requirements of business exert a pervasive and substantial influence throughout American society.

chapter **9**

BUSINESS AND UNIONS

JAMES W. KUHN *is Professor of Industrial Relations at Columbia University and the author of numerous monographs on collective bargaining and other aspects of labor-management relations. Like the majority of informed students of American unions, he believes that these organizations have become inextricably merged with the market system. Interpretations of the significance of the fact vary according to the beliefs and preferences of the observer, but the fact itself provokes little argument: unions have largely eschewed whatever modest "ideological" preoccupations might have informed their practice earlier in favor of a highly pragmatic adaptation of ends and means to the realities of our business system.*

Professor Kuhn regards the rationalism and middle-class bent of unions as the almost inevitable by-products of the commitment of most Americans to private property, to technical rather than political solutions to problems, and to evolution rather than revolution as a useful principle of social change. They are also by-products of the organizational imperatives flowing from the obligation to negotiate on a daily basis with professional managers.

To some observers these qualities of American unions are a cause for concern and restiveness. Hope is increasingly expressed that unions will become "more political," that they will strive to mobilize popular support for federal planning to facilitate the achievement of "full production, full distribution, and full employment." Doubts have also been expressed about the way we turn over to a decentralized system of collective bargaining many social and economic problems that, in the democratic countries of western Europe, are objects of national political concern and centralized action.

Other students of the labor scene in America are more optimistic. It has been argued that by concentrating on workers' rights in the workplace and that by organizing to utilize the law as well as a highly sophisticated apparatus for bargaining and for handling grievances unions have increased the prospects for orderly and efficient industrial democracy. Reform politics and class-conscious partisanship, some conclude, might distract union leaders from the important intra-organizational political and technical functions they now perform.

One may wonder what implications for management and a business society flow from the tendencies Professor Kuhn describes. Thus, the reader may puzzle over the use, by both managers and unions, of the courts in the adjudication of disputes, since this appears to be a move away from bargaining efforts by the parties to an agreement. The following specific questions will also guide the reader of this essay:

1. The principle that unions should be democratic is enshrined in law; managers of unions and corporations increasingly recognize the need for competent experts. What logic might be employed to identify an optimal balance in unions between democratic values and bureaucratic organizational principles?

2. According to Professor Kuhn, many of the characteristics of unions stem from the specifics of bargaining relationships with corporations. What specific characteristics may develop in unions as a result of growing unionization among employees in public service?

3. Much is made here of the proprietary interests of union members in their jobs and of the imaginative use by unions of litigation in an effort to husband the workers' resources. What advantages accrue from these two developments to managers? To union leaders?

4. It has been argued that as union leaders achieve significant roles in industry they become more "conservative" in their attitudes and that business leaders become more "liberal" as they achieve higher levels of education. If these trends are correctly noted and if they continue, what institutional mechanisms would support some of the older commitments of unions and employers, respectively, on such vital issues as income distribution and the role of government?

JAMES W. KUHN \ **BUSINESS UNIONISM IN A LABORISTIC SOCIETY**

After studying the American labor scene at first hand in the mid-1960's, a Soviet labor scholar concluded, "American unions are like businesses. Business production, wages—that is all I hear anybody in labor talk about. I think they are not so much different from business as a part of it." He was not the first foreign observer to decide that labor in America is business-minded and pro-capitalist. Sixty years ago, when union membership accounted for barely 9 per cent of the non-agricultural work force in America, the German scholar Werner Sombart wrote:

> Indeed I believe that the relation of the American laborer to capitalism is even more intimate than even [his] friendly declarations and testimonials of respect really express. I believe he enters into it with all his heart: I believe he loves it. . . . The greater intensity of American labor is nothing more than the expression of the laborer's fundamentally capitalist mental attitude.[1]

Other kinds of unionism might have developed in America, of course; several have gotten a foothold at one time or another only to fade away.

TYPES OF UNIONISM IN AMERICA

In 1917 Robert F. Hoxie, one of the earliest and most perceptive American students of labor, identified several types of unionism, of which one was business unionism. This type was oriented toward trade or industry interests, he said, not toward those of the working class as a whole. Its practitioners were parochial in viewpoint, limiting their concern to immediate and local affairs. Hoxie also described another type, the predatory union, which is a variation of business unionism in the way that racketeering in the United States is an illegal variation of business.[2]

A third type that Hoxie found, revolutionary or radical unionism, was illustrated by the IWW (Industrial Workers of the World, or "Wobblies") and the Western Federation of Mine Workers. These two groups were still forceful enough in 1917 to send shivers down the spines of many patriotic Americans. Since then they have faded; their bold, anarchistic philosophy would seem as dated and quaint in the labor movement today as would old tintype photographs in split-level homes. Later, in the upsurge of union organizing in the thirties, communists became active and rose to leadership in a few unions, the most prominent of which were the Electrical Workers, the Mine and Smelter Workers, and the Furriers. While the communist rhetoric clanged with the urgency of a fire bell, alarming Americans, the activities of communist unions were seldom any more dramatic than those of non-communist business unions, though communist leaders were frequently more adept, harder-working bargainers. After World War II the national labor federations repudiated and rejected all unions with communist leadership. On the defensive within the movement and prosecuted by the government, the communists faded from the labor scene. A few still exist like a caste of untouchables on the fringes of the labor movement.

A fourth type of unionism described by Hoxie, uplift unionism, had almost disappeared by the time he wrote. It had appeared intermittently throughout the nineteenth century and had flourished briefly in the 1880's when the Knights

---

[1] "Study of the Historical Development and Evolution of the American Proletariat," *International Socialist Review*, Vol. 6 (September, 1905), pp. 135–36.
[2] *Trade Unionism in the United States*, Lucy Bennett Hoxie, ed. (New York: Appleton, 1921).

of Labor gathered a mixed group of workers, farmers, and small tradesmen to promote a program of reforming industrial America. At its peak, in 1886, the Knights of Labor enrolled nearly three-quarters of a million members, but within a few years it could claim no more than 100,000; by 1900 it was practically extinct. Uplift unionism appeared again in the 1930's as reformers rushed to the support of the new industrial unions in the mass-production industries. The enthusiasm of the reformers for industrial unionism was part of their enthusiasm for the New Deal in general; when that passed, the tincture of uplift unionism in the CIO went with it. The pallid ghost of reform still haunts union conventions, but it stirs delegates to no more action than to approve resolutions originally formulated in the 1930's in favor of higher minimum wages, shorter hours, extension of social security, and more health services. In 1967, Walter Reuther and the union over which he presides, the United Automobile Workers, challenged the labor movement to "become the vanguard of social progress" and to restore "the dynamic spirit of social responsibility." While the challenge enlivened the union scene, it did not seem much more likely than past declarations of social concern to provoke fundamental changes in the industrial system.

Of the major types of unionism described by Hoxie, modern scholars can find only one of any importance today. James J. Healy of Harvard has recently written:

> The outlook of unionism can best be characterized by the term "business unionism" . . . Successful labor leaders who have followed the business unionism philosophy are essentially businessmen elected to represent groups organized primarily to do business with employers—to bargain for the *sale* of the *product* which the union controls.[3]

Such a characterization of American labor is not derived from academic analyses but is based upon the opinions of trade union leaders themselves. Over 40 years ago John L. Lewis declared that "trade unionism is a phenomenon of capitalism quite smiliar to the corporation. One is essentially a pooling of labor for purposes of common action and sales. The other is a pooling of capital for exactly the same purposes. The economic aims of both are identical."[4] In 1940, Philip Murray, president of the steelworkers' union, noted that "the modern labor union has in many respects become a big business."[5] Other unionists have made the same point, using their own organizations as examples. A Carpenters' official in 1946 declared, "I think we will all agree that this [union] is big business";[6] and more recently a Teamster officer boasted of running the "union like a corporation. We deal in one commodity—labor."[6]

Some union leaders prefer not to be as explicit as the men quoted here, but the

[3] Healy, ed., *Creative Collective Bargaining* (Englewood Cliffs, N.J.: Prentice-Hall, 1965), p. 6. Italics added.
[4] *The Miners Fight for American Standards* (Indianapolis: Bell Publishing, 1925), p. 16. Quoted by B. J. Widick, *Labor Today* (Boston: Houghton Mifflin, 1964), pp. 168–69.
[5] Jack Barbash, *The Practice of Unionism* (New York: Harper & Row, 1956), p. 77.
[6] *Ibid.*, pp. 77 and 388.

structure and activities of their unions appear to reflect a labor movement that uses business as its model. A brief survey of the organization of unions, their functions, bureaucracy, and wealth, will indicate the degree to which unions resemble business.

THE BUSINESS LOOK OF AMERICAN UNIONS—THEIR ORGANIZATION AND WEALTH

Ranked by size, the distribution of unions is, as one might expect, like the distribution of business firms. (See Table 1.) The six largest unions (Teamsters, Auto Workers, Steelworkers, Machinists, Electrical Workers, and Carpenters) enroll about one-third of all union members. Thus, the largest number of unions is small (one-half have about 25,000 members or less), whereas a small number accounts for most of the membership. The 14 largest unions (each with 300,000 or more members) report more than half the total members.

Table 1.   Concentration In 189 Unions[a] and Among the 500 Largest Industrial Corporations,[b] 1964.

	UNIONS GROUPED BY MEMBERSHIP	PER CENT OF TOTAL	MEMBERSHIP (THOUSANDS)	PER CENT OF TOTAL
Largest	6	3.2	6,014	33.6
Next	15	7.9	4,907	27.4
Next	52	27.6	5,486	30.6
Next	53	28.0	1,341	7.5
Next	63	33.4	172	0.9
	189	100.0	17,920	100.0

	CORPORATIONS GROUPED BY SALES	PER CENT OF TOP 500	ASSETS (MILLIONS)	PER CENT OF TOTAL FOR TOP 500
Largest	25	5	$ 92,513	41.2
Next	75	15	57,796	25.7
Next	100	20	33,278	14.8
Next	100	20	19,359	8.6
Next	200	40	21,704	9.7
	500	100	$224,650	100.0

[a] Data from Bureau of Labor Statistics, *Directory of National and International Labor Unions*, 1965, Bulletin No. 1493, p. 53. Because of rounding, sums of individual items may not equal totals.
[b] Data from *Statistical Abstract of the United States: 1966*, No. 689, p. 492, and *The Fortune Directory*, August, 1965.

The distribution of members among unions is markedly similar to the distribution of assets among the 500 largest industrial corporations. Of the total assets owned by the 500 largest firms, the first six firms own over one-fifth, and the last two-thirds account for about another one-fifth. The bulk of corporate assets, that is to say, is held by a small number of firms; the two largest corporations, Standard Oil of New Jersey and General Motors, reported assets of nearly $24 billion in 1964, 10 per cent of all those owned by the nation's 500 largest industrial corporations.

Since unions are confronted by large companies—many of which employ tens of thousands of workers, while nearly a dozen have hundreds of thousands of employees—it is not surprising that they, too, are large. Even if the government were to limit union enrollment to only the employees of a single company, a General Motors union would have a potential membership of over 640,000, while Ford workers might hope for as many as 317,000 members, and at General Electric a union would have 263,000 possible members. Unionists would not want membership limited to a single company, of course. They seek to enroll members in many firms and in various industries to exploit fully the economies of size. In those industries such as trucking, construction, or garment manufacturing where firms are small, a union must organize employees in thousands of firms in order to be an effective bargaining agent. Unions such as the Teamsters, Carpenters, Mine Workers, Hotel Workers, and Ladies' Garment Workers have grown large in this way, counting members by the hundreds of thousands.

The Advantages of Size

The efficiencies that accompany large union size are not merely those of bargaining power. In fact, a larger membership does not necessarily increase bargaining strength; among other reasons, the more members there are, the greater is the chance that diversities of interests will lead to divisions within the organization. Large size more surely offers efficiencies in allowing the unions to use specialists and professionals to carry out their manifold activities.

There are 150,000 collective agreements in the United States, and unions must have men able to help administer their provisions or enforce their terms in thousands of garages, stores, schools, offices, and factories. They must also have men available to renegotiate these agreements, men who are knowledgeable about current business trends, familiar with the economies of the industry involved, and expert in the strategy of bargaining. Because the agreements directly affect almost every aspect of the production process and indirectly affect investment policy, pricing policy, and marketing, union negotiators must be well acquainted with all phases of business, up to date on current developments, and capable of analyzing the consequences of the policies they advocate. The affairs in which they are involved are so intimately a part of business operations that they must become expert about business themselves. Such expertness is not gained without experience and concentrated effort. Negotiators do not leave the assembly line to help write an agreement and then go back to their job in the plant. Full-time officials are needed who can become proficient enough in the intricacies of wage schedules, layoffs, overtime, job assignments, fringe benefits, and shop disciplinary procedures to meet managers on at least even terms.

In addition to the vital work of negotiating and administering agreements, unions have other functions that can be maintained most successfully and efficiently by specialists. Unions must constantly organize as new firms appear and plants are opened in new locations. Every union maintains a staff of organizers that seeks to win the votes of the unorganized in representational elections conducted by the National Labor Relations Board and to gain new members. Unions also provide advice and aid to new locals struggling with the unfamiliar problems of collective bargaining. Finally, the arbitration of grievances arising under existing agreements is a major and costly service almost all unions provide. An advocate before an important arbitrator (or arbitration board) needs to know what he is about, for even simple cases can easily cost the union as much as $500.

To help elected officers in the complex business of negotiating and administering agreements, unions employ a variety of professional experts. Industrial engineers and time-study or time-and-motion staff men provide aid in working out the details of wage-rate provisions; they may also act as consultants to managers of small firms, advising them about plant layout and the kind of equipment to install. Today most unions employ consultants to help in negotiations about complicated welfare, unemployment, and pension programs; they furnish advice to members, too, who may be unable easily to comprehend the rights and benefits to which they are entitled. In the area of antidiscrimination, many, though not all, unions have built up staffs to help make and guide union policy. Discrimination by sex, race, or color in hiring and union representation is now illegal, and unions seek to avoid infringement of the law as well as to offer support to workers on the job or looking for jobs.

Union officials at local as well as national levels need a continual flow of economic data and of the details of negotiations in other firms and industries; they employ research staffs to provide such information. Unions often maintain an educational department to prepare materials and programs that present the union point of view, primarily to inform their own members but also to win a favorable hearing from the public. Almost all unions publish a newspaper or bulletin, usually monthly. These publications are on the whole undistinguished but are probably useful to members, for they do present news of events at locals, describe the activities of the national office, and report speeches and opinions favorable to labor.

Unions actively promote their and their industry's interests through lobbying; for this work still another kind of specialist must be hired. Building-trade unions zealously protect and promote local construction codes that require labor of a kind they can provide. The Textile Workers union has appealed often and forcefully to Congress for restrictions on Japanese imports, and it has been in the forefront of those calling for higher minimum wages. At the same time it has promoted products made by its members.[7] The Teamsters have mobilized their political strength in Congress and before the Interstate Commerce Commission to fight "preferential financial treatment for railroads by government and discriminatory rate-fixing rules which would enable rail carriers to undercut the trucking industry." On the other side, the rail brotherhoods support government aid to rail companies and lobby for other kinds of favorable treatment. The United Mine Workers have urged Congress to stop "squandering" money on the development of atomic energy as a potential rival to coal; the American Federation of Musicians long lobbied for repeal of the 20 per cent cabaret tax, claiming that it destroyed 41,000 jobs for musicians and five times as many for cooks, waiters, and service help; the Machinists, who have many members in the airplane industry, propagandize the importance and "necessity" of a supersonic transport plane built with government funds. In order to assure success for their political lobbying, unions have to employ public relations experts, ex-Congressmen, lawyers, and other political specialists.

The Character, Pay, and Organization of Union Officers

In the administration of regular daily affairs, unions need able management. Joseph Bierne, president of the Communications Workers of America, has written of the variety of skills union leaders must now utilize in scrutinizing their substantial treasuries (extensive accounting reports must be sent periodically to the Department of Labor), managing "a headquarters adequate for the job, staff and a payroll to meet," and handling "legal problems, political activity in all its various forms, and finally international activities of ever increasing importance."[8] Any union leader who is such a man of affairs as Bierne describes naturally will resemble a busy business executive.

Some labor leaders seemed even more like businessmen when their large staffs of employees organized unions of their own to bargain with their union employers. Walter Reuther, president of the Auto Workers, cried out in chagrin, as have employers for years, "but my door is always open to anyone with a complaint," and David Dubinsky of the ILGWU angrily accused the organizers of his staff of being disloyal, divisive and subversive—terms employers have long applied to union organizers in their plants.

Though unions have created bureaucracies of some size and centralized many functions that can most efficiently be handled by full-time, expert personnel, they have not yet shown a willingness or the ability to attract and keep men and

---

[7] An advertising flyer put out by six TWUA locals reads: "Ride UNION all the way on TYREX tires. Only TYREX tires give you UNION-MADE tire cord. No other tire can make this claim. For that smooth (no nylon thump) ride, buy TYREX."

The Ladies' Garment Workers Union regularly promotes the union label. It asks the public, in full-page ads, to "look for it the next time you shop for women's or girls' apparel. It is your guarantee that the clothing you buy was made by skilled craftsmen in a shop reflecting the best American standards and traditions."

[8] *New Horizons for American Labor* (Washington: Public Affairs Press, 1962), p. 25.

women in the various staff positions who are the equal of those commonly found in management. They face two problems: the first is the need to find jobs with which the top officers can reward supporters and disarm opponents. Positions in the union bureaucracy, in the time-study department, on the research staff, or in the Washington office are easily and often filled with such appointees. The second problem is that union pay is not particularly attractive compared with salaries offered by business firms. Salaries for the lower-rank union positions usually are not far below comparable positions in business but the progression to the top salary is short indeed. For their experts and specialists unions depend upon men so devoted to the cause of unionism that they will sacrifice income and opportunity elsewhere, or they limp along with those who are not apt to find opportunity for better employment elsewhere.

Some of the chief officers of a few of the largest unions receive pay that must look very rewarding, indeed, to the union members and lowly paid staffmen. For example, in 1962, James R. Hoffa, president of the Teamsters, received a salary of $62,096 and an expense allowance of $10,906. Vice president Harold Gibbons' salary was $34,582, and expenses came to $23,646. David McDonald, then president of the United Steelworkers, collected a salary of $50,000 in 1962 and was provided $20,939 for expenses. The president of the Plumbers union was given a salary of $31,500 in 1961 and an expense allowance of $24,174. The Musicians paid their president $35,000 plus expenses.

The payments made to these exceptionally well-paid officers are no match for business, however. The Teamsters union paid its president only one-seventh as much as the $516,000 in salary and bonuses (exclusive of stock options) the Ford Motor Company paid its president. The lowest paid of eight top Ford executives, the vice president of Product Planning and Styling, received $101,000, more than twice the salary of the Steelworkers' president. Yet the Teamsters, the Steelworkers, the Plumbers, and the Musicians are among the few unions that reward their elected officials generously, while Ford's salaries are not at all unusual in the business world. Further, business firms also allow ample expense accounting, stock options, and many other fringe benefits to add to basic salaries and bonuses.

The median salary of international union officers in 1950 was a bit over $12,000, according to a study by Philip Taft.[9] The typical salary of full-time local officers fell in the $5,000–$6,000 class. Even if one were to assume that in the years since 1950 these salaries have doubled, they would still be more comparable to those paid in the Civil Service than to those in the business world. Taft commented that the "salaries of union officers appear on the whole to be quite modest . . . even the chief executives do not on the whole receive salaries which, even on the basis of austere standards, can be regarded as excessive."[10]

In form and management of their activities, unions have obviously borrowed business practices and approaches. Insofar as they resemble business, however, unions are smaller, truncated versions, not replicas. In 1961, for example, the

[9] *The Structure and Government of Labor Unions* (Cambridge, Mass.: Harvard University Press, 1954), pp. 102–03.
[10] *Ibid.*, p. 110.

UAW employed a staff of 31 professionals exclusive of its 43-man education department. Such a group may be sizable, but for the second largest union in the country, enrolling over a million members in almost every state and bargaining with the largest corporations, it can hardly be called large. Any one of the smaller automobile companies undoubtedly employs a professional staff many times larger.

By forming large units and developing bureaucracies in the pursuit of effective, efficient organizations, unions may not necessarily be patterning themselves after business; rather they may be responding, as business firms do, to the opportunities and requirements of any organization in an expanding, interdependent society. After all, unions in most industrial countries display many of the same organizational traits and activities that American unions do. In one feature American unions are unique, though. Their income and wealth are far larger than those enjoyed by unions anywhere else in the world. In their bulging treasuries, fat investment portfolios, ostentatious marble and glass headquarters, high salaries and lavish expense accounts, American unions are most businesslike, according to foreign observers and American commentators.

The Assets of Unions

The amassed assets of the unions and the total flow of their revenues are impressive. In late 1962 *Fortune* estimated that "in one way or another unions have a say in the management of assets totaling about $4.5 billion. . . ."[11] General funds, cash, union office buildings, and strike reserves assets that belong solely to the union organization exceed $1.5 billion;[12] the rest is made up of welfare and pension funds, the management of which unions must legally share with management. The National Industrial Conference Board estimated in 1955 that the dues collected by all unions might come to roughly $460 million annually.[13] Dues have increased since then, and membership is the same, so the figure would be a bit higher today; a guess that unions have an income of somewhat above half a billion would prabably not be far from wrong.

Some unions individually report sizable assets, too; the uses to which these assets are put vary from union to union. Many are like careful, cautious bankers. The International Ladies' Garment Workers Union, for example, with net assets of over $84 million in 1964 in addition to $399 million in funds,[14] has invested heavily in housing developments and conservative, low-risk securities. Like other unions, it holds a large share of its general funds in easily marketable government bonds. Few unions are willing to risk discovering that their strike funds have evaporated in a bear market, and so they generally do not invest in common stock. The practice of the Teamsters, in this as in several other matters, is ex-

---

[11] "Labor's Capitalists," *Fortune*, Vol. 66 (November, 1962), p. 153.
[12] H. Robert Bartell, Jr., "National Union Assets, 1959–1961," *Industrial and Labor Relations Review*, Vol. 19 (October, 1965), p. 81.
[13] National Industrial Conference Board Reports, *Handbook of Union Government Structure and Procedures*, Studies in Personnel Policy, No. 150 (1955), pp. 30–33.
[14] *New York Times*, May 17, 1965.

ceptional and more entrepreneurial. In 1960, the national union held 61 per cent of its over $38 million assets in marketable securities and only 19 per cent in government bonds.[15] In 1955 the Teamsters officers found an advantageous use of stock purchases for their pension fund when they invested more than a million dollars in Montgomery Ward. An outside group was trying to wrest control from the incumbent management, and in what appeared to be a deal, or at least a recognition of common interests, the management broke company tradition and policy to recognize the Teamsters as bargaining agent for its workers in Chicago, while the union swung its stockholder votes to management, defeating the outsiders.

The Teamsters union also urges a bolder investment policy upon the trustees of its pension funds than do most unions. They have invested heavily in mortgages of luxury resorts in Georgia, Las Vegas gambling casinos, and real estate in Los Angeles. The result in 1961 was a 12 per cent higher yield (4.6 per cent) than the average yield on all union pension funds (4.1 per cent). But other unions have learned the art of earning income through profitable investments. The International Brotherhood of Electrical Workers in 1961 earned about 5 per cent on its portfolio of government-insured home mortgages (50 per cent of the total), corporate bonds (20 per cent), and common stock (20 per cent). One of the large districts of the Retail and Wholesale Department Store Union received yields of 4.7 per cent to 5.8 per cent on its pension funds in the period 1957–62.[16]

A few unions, most notably the United Mine Workers, have invested outright in business. The UMW bought stock in two large banks in Washington, D.C., and it also bought 10 per cent of the stock of the West Kentucky Coal Company, 50,000 preferred shares. In 1960 it also owned 33,590 shares, worth $3.3 million, of American Coal Shipping, a company backed by the UMW to carry coal abroad and to expand markets for American coal. The union has loaned money at various times to businessmen, such as the industrialist Cyrus Eaton who holds large investments in coal. The Amalgamated Clothing Workers has long been noted for its banks in New York and Chicago and for the insurance company it owns. The Amalgamated banks, which make loans both to members and to clothing employers, gained a reputation for sound, conservative management when they easily weathered the bank crisis of 1933.

Presenting a financial record of union income, assets, and salaries in terms of grand totals and outstanding examples from among the largest unions—as has been done here, and typically is done by the public press—can be misleading. Since union wealth is neither held nor controlled by a single organization or even a few leaders, its significance can best be understood by analyzing the amounts of money available to the individual unions. In 1957 average annual dues were about $34; today, they may be $10 to $15 higher. The national offices typically receive less than half of the dues collected; the rest stays with locals and intermediate bodies. Probably not more than a dozen national unions have incomes over $10 million a year. The national office of the 440,000 member ILGWU, for example,

[15] *Business Week* (June 4, 1960), pp. 82–83.
[16] *Fortune*, Vol. 66 (November, 1962), p. 172.

averaged less than $15 million annually for the period 1962–64, and the national office of the 160,000 member Rubber Workers received only a bit more than $4 million in 1964.

The larger part of the unions' income stays with, and is divided among, the more than 40,000 locals and 2,500 regional councils, joint boards, and other intermediate bodies. The result is a drastic thinning of union resources; however impressive they may appear in balance sheet totals, they are not deployed so as to give any overwhelming show of strength. In 1959 the average local had about $16,000 in its treasury and the average intermediate body had $41,000; the general funds of the six largest unions amounted to about $368 million, the remaining 248 unions (national unions, various joint unions and AFL-CIO organizations) shared about $32 million.[17] A single long strike for any one of the unions, even one of the big six, could quickly deplete its funds.

Compared to unions in other countries and even to American unions of thirty years ago, the American union of today has large financial resources and appears to be capitalistic, wealthy, and businesslike. Should we shift the basis of comparison to modern business firms, however, the wealth of unions appears in a dramatically different light. The management of the American Telephone and Telegraph Company controls an employee trust fund of $4.7 billion—equal to *all* the assets in whose management union leaders have *some* say. The company's *profit* of $2.1 billion in 1965 was about four times the *revenues* of all union combined. In 1963 General Motors and Standard Oil of New Jersey each reported assets more than twice those of all unions, and another five companies had assets as large or larger than the combined union assets. One may conclude that if American unions practice business unionism, they model themselves on small, not big, business.

Unions resemble business in the size of their membership, in the functional specialization of their bureaucracies, and—a little—in their accumulated assets. Of course the same characteristics are also shared by churches, fraternal clubs, universities, foundations, charities, and other organizations. What seems to constitute a more special link between unions and businesses is a matter of fundamental attitudes, and it is to an examination of these that we now turn.

THE BUSINESS IDEOLOGY OF UNIONS

When Robert Hoxie used the term business unionism nearly fifty years ago, unions were small, poor, and hardly bureaucratic. Nevertheless, he and later scholars perceived in their interests and activities an approach to the workers' problems and a dominating value system that clearly distinguished them from the socialistic, politically involved unions of Europe. To sum up the pragmatic, parochial, here-and-now concern unions showed for job rights, they used the term "business." They did not mean thereby to imply that unions were a new form of business organization—only that union members accepted society as it was and sought their

[17] *Ibid.*, p. 153.

goals largely in non-political ways. Nevertheless, the scholars chose better than they knew, for American unionists did more than simply *accept* the business system and eschew deep involvement in politics. They tried to become part of the system as it was developing and changing with the rise of industrialism; accepting the wage system, they offered to sell their labor for a wage and to work according to the terms and conditions of labor agreements that they negotiated with employers. They came to recognize the job rights and working rules secured through bargaining as a kind of property. These were valuable, not only for the protection they provided unionists at the place of work, but also because they could be sold or traded or exchanged if any advantage was to be gained. The business values associated with selling for gain guided their approach to collective bargaining and labor relations.

With the exception of the radical unions, which were always a small minority, American unions have never been antibusiness. They differed and disputed with employers, to be sure, but they never hoped to displace them or by striking put them out of business. Some examples of union pronouncements show the attitudes of unionists in the early and mid-nineteenth century. In 1834 the General Trades Union, the first council of unions in New York City, publicly announced a policy that "it will always be governed by the maxim 'live and let live' and while it is willing that employers shall have a just and equitable profit from the labor of those they employ, it will always endeavor to obtain for those who labor a just remuneration for their services."[18] A declaration adopted by representatives of twelve hat-finishers unions in 1854 reads very much like union statements a hundred years later:

> We are fully alive to the fact that the interests of both employers and employees are identical and we declare and acknowledge their right to manage and control their business as they see fit, but at the same time claim for ourselves as a body the privilege of agreement upon any concerted action whereby our interests as mechanics shall not be injured.[19]

The employers, with whom these and the other unions of the time were ready to meet, typically managed small, family-sized firms, and they and their workers both existed within the setting of a predominantly agricultural society. The political and social ideal was still a nation of property owners—farmers and tradesmen—and the United States came remarkably close to fulfilling it. In 1840 more than two-thirds of the labor force followed agricultural pursuits; in 1860, at the start of the Civil War, almost 60 per cent; not until 1880 did more people find jobs outside agriculture than in it. In 1839 agriculture contributed almost 3.5 times as much to national income as did manufacturing; by 1859 it still accounted for more than 2.5 times as much; and from 1889 to 1912 the contribution to national income of each was roughly the same. Only after 1912 did manufacturing pull

[18] John R. Commons and Associates, *Documentary History of American Industrial Society* (Cleveland: Arthur H. Clark, 1910), Vol. 5, p. 308.
[19] Philip Taft, "On the Origins of Business Unionism," *Industrial and Labor Relations Review,* Vol. 17 (October, 1963), pp. 33–34.

ahead. By this time business had come to include many large corporations with millions of dollars of investments and factories employing thousands of workers.

That workers should want to share in the social ideal of a prosperous, developing nation of property owners is not surprising. Their problem was to claim something that the society would recognize as property. If they could but secure property, the full power of the government would protect their right to use it in their interests, and they could stand on an equal footing with farmers and the small firm employer. Many workers hoped, as the Iron Moulders did in 1859, at least to raise their position as journeymen and through unified action to avert the continuing decline in wage and work standards.[20] Others gave freer scope to their imaginations, and hoped, with the Hat Finishers, "for the day . . . not far distant when the just and honorable employers [would] see the necessity of obliterating the line of demarcation still existing between employers and employed. . . ."[21] The most visonary hope of labor in agrarian America was expressed by Terence V. Powderly, president of the Knights of Labor. He would have abolished the wage system, though not out of any anticapitalist pique or socialist bias. "The aim of the Knights of Labor—properly understood—" he declared, "is to make each man his own employer."[22]

The Knights proposed to further the democratic, individualistic ideal, as earlier national labor organizations had, by encouraging small producers in a cooperative society and by attacking the "aggressive accumulation of wealth" (the rising industrial business forming trusts and "monopolies"). They had no program for workers who might spend their whole life as employees, for they did not discern the true shape of the emerging industrial world. They knew and honored the agrarian values of the past.

Hopeful workers joined the Knights of Labor by the hundreds of thousands in the late 1880's to help Powderly establish cooperatives, reform the wage system, and gain for themselves the protection of life and livelihood that American society promised those who owned property. They quickly discovered, of course, that the Knights espoused a dream of the past. Its leaders and program were looking back to a nation that once was but would never be again. "Each man his own employer" made little sense in the burgeoning industrial world of large firms and sprawling empires of mills, mines, and rails. Most workers could no longer realistically expect to emulate the farmer or the tradesman. Increasingly they realized that they would not rise from their position as employees. If they were to be a part of society, sharing its protections and rewards, they would have to find an appropriate property within their industrial setting.

Services to Supplement Ideals

A number of the craft unions had been experimenting along lines different from the Knights. In the first half of the 1800's the shoemakers, carpenters, coopers,

[20] *Ibid.*, pp. 32–33.
[21] *Ibid.*, p. 26.
[22] Quoted in Gerald M. Grob, *Workers and Utopia* (Evanston, Ill.: Northwestern University Press, 1961), p. 38.

and printers, among others, sought to find a place for themselves within the wage system. They accepted their position as employees and tried to maintain and if possible to increase wages. In good times they succeeded in raising them but failed in depressions to hold them. In either case, workers showed only a sporadic loyalty to the union: on the one hand, when the union could not provide benefits, workers saw little point to membership. On the other hand, once the union secured a raise, "the immediate aim of the society [trades union] having been accomplished, members gradually lost interest and many ceased to pay dues or withdrew altogether.[23] Unions had not discovered a service they could provide in good times and bad, before, along with, and after wage improvements.

Gradually, through trial and error, the leaders of the craft unions developed business-like activities that they carried on with increasingly professional competence. First, they began to offer continually available services and protection through the grievance process at the place of work that made membership worthwhile and dues a payment for something valuable. Second, and just as important, they discovered ways in which they could make themselves and their unions of great usefulness to employers. Until after 1900, when business managers began to recognize the value of Frederick W. Taylor's ideas of scientific management, they usually left management and direction of the work force to foremen or to the skilled workers themselves. In industries where shops were small, as in printing, or where work was irregular in amount and location, as in construction, confusion and inefficiency reigned in the labor market and often in the shop or at the work site as well.

Unionists took up the task of ordering both in a businesslike way. Through the closed shop they sought to regularize the hiring of workers, offering employers a supply of competent men and finding jobs for members who sought work. Through apprenticeship rules they of course tried to avoid an "oversupply" of labor; but they perhaps also helped to raise work standards, providing employers with better quality workmen than they otherwise might have hired through the prevailing casual methods. The craft unions acted as employment and training agencies, and their officers assumed many of what we now call managerial functions at the place of work as well. They developed job rules to guide the work force and to safeguard work conditions on the job. Either unilaterally, through by-laws as in the Printers' case, or bilaterally, in negotiations with employers as carried out by the Bricklayers or Stove Moulders, unions established rules for assignment of job, layoff, recall, shift hours, pay rates, promotion, and discipline. Local officers and sometimes unionized foremen then policed the shop to enforce the rules and to assure workers that their job claims would not be arbitrarily disregarded.

While the unions designed work rules primarily for the benefit of their members, employers gained as well. The often untrained, inadequate, uninformed selection and supervision of workers before the unions appeared could hardly have been better than "management" by union rules and probably was much worse. The

---

[23] George E. Barnett, *The Printers* (Cambridge, Mass.: American Economic Association, 1909), p. 9.

business-minded workers strongly supported their unions, appreciating the valuable, continuing services their dues "bought" them. Of course, unions continued to promise and to work for higher wages, but the shop services for workers and union benefits for employees provided the basis for strong, stable craft unionism.

In the context of American social and legal thought, union job rules and agreements with employers implied claims that were not yet property but that were, to the worker, a property-like substitute for the real property of the farmer and the financial property of the businessman. If unionists could gain from employers at least a modicum of recognition for their job claims, they would be able to adapt the old American ideal of "every citizen a property holder" to a modern society dominated by giant industrial firms.

Union Attitudes to Business Size and Productivity

The craft unions founded the American Federation of Labor in 1886 under the leadership of Samuel Gompers and set a new tack for the American labor movement before the winds of industrial change. They proposed to move with industrialism rather than against it. Their leaders were now ready to accept the facts of industrial life. Gompers observed in 1888, "The fact is being fast forced upon the consciousness of the wage workers of this continent that they are a distinct and practically permanent class of modern society; and, consequently, have distinct and permanent common interests."[24]

The unionists in the Federation muted their earlier enthusiasm for trust-busting, and they made clear their willingness to deal with Big Business. In 1907 Samuel Gompers noted that "organized labor has less difficulty in dealing with large firms and corporations today than with many individual employers or small firms."[25] That large firms should have taken a more pro-union stand than small companies is not surprising. They were the most active experimenters in creating cartels, trusts, and other devices for stabilizing prices and taming the competitive market. Their managers could better appreciate the contribution of collective bargaining to wage stability or union-enforced price-fixing. Gompers himself suggested another explanation for a dampening of union enthusiasm for trust-busting. In his view, trusts and large corporations were successfully solving the problem of production, offering an ever increasing flood of goods to the nation, and steadily increasing their ability to raise wages. Size brought with it inherent advantages for the firm, and from those advantages unions could reap unprecedented benefits.[26]

As Lloyd Ulman has pointed out, the business unionism of the AFL was not

---

[24] Grob, *op. cit.*, p. 140.

[25] Lloyd Ulman, *The Rise of the National Trade Union* (Cambridge, Mass.: Harvard University Press, 1955), p. 37. Only eight years before, Gompers had written, "I have insisted, and do now insist, that the only power capable of coping with and (if necessary) smashing the trusts is that much abused and often ridiculed force known under the euphonious title of 'The Trade Union Movement' as understood and practiced by the A.F. of L." Quoted in Grob, *op. cit.*, p. 184.

[26] Grob, *op. cit.*, p. 183, quoting and paraphrasing Gompers in the *American Federationist*, 1899 and 1907, and in a speech to the AFL Convention, 1891.

known for a pessimistic, defensive, scarcity-conscious approach to collective bargaining. He quotes the expansive sentiment of Gompers in 1916:

> It [organized labor] won't stop at all at any particular point. . . . The working people will never stop in their efforts to obtain a better life for themselves, and for their wives and for their children and for humanity. . . . I would not want any man to believe that our movement is satisfied. There is not anything satisfying in what we have accomplished. It is gratifying but simply whets our appetite for better and better and still better things.[27]

With such an attitude, union leaders and their members easily came to appreciate the value of increasing productivity. By the 1920's the AFL was publicly calling for increased efficiencies in production, arguing that union help in raising productivity would generate additional revenues out of which higher wages could be paid. A number of unions sponsored programs to raise productivity as an offset to the higher wages they sought. The most prominent of these were the garment unions, the hosiery workers, the railroad shop craftsmen, the streetcar workers, and the printing pressmen.[28]

Later, after World War II, when managers were more reconciled to unions than they had been in the 1920's, they took up the old AFL call for higher wages from increased productivity. The unions responded eagerly. In 1950 General Motors proposed to increase wages by an "annual improvement factor" of 3.2 per cent, a figure estimated to be equal to the average rise of national productivity. The United Auto Workers readily agreed to the proposal and sought the same provision from other companies. In a number of major industries such as steel, electrical equipment, farm implements, and aluminum, unions and management agreed to similar provisions, recognizing the importance of increased efficiency and rising productivity to improve benefits for their members.

David McDonald, then president of the United Steelworkers union, pointed out the importance of efficient production to delegates at the union's convention in 1954. He declared:

> We are engaged in the operation of an economy which is a sort of mutual trusteeship. . . . There is a mutual trusteeship between one group of employees known as managers and another group of employees known as the working force. Both groups have obligations to the owners, the stockholders and to each other. The managers must give full consideration to the just claims of the workers [and] the working force must see to it that the steel properties are operated successfully, because if they are not operated successfully, they will have no jobs.[29]

Earlier, Sidney Hillman of the Clothing Workers had expressed the same sentiments, which are common and usual among American unionists: "There is no chance to bargain efficiently with an employer whose business is not prosperous: labor must be industry conscious." At another time, he remarked, "We help the

[27] Ulman, op. cit., pp. 587–88.
[28] Sumner H. Slichter, Union Policies and Industrial Management (Washington: Brookings Institution, 1941), pp. 370–559.
[29] Quoted in Barbash, op. cit., p. 380.

employers for one excellent reason. The clothing workers must make their living out of the clothing industry—just as their employers."[30]

Other unions and their leaders have encouraged technological change in the interests of higher wages or improved conditions of work through increased productivity. The United Mine Workers, for example, has approved the mechanization of coal mining and for the past twenty years has given management a free hand in making technological changes. Between 1950 and 1964 the average tons of coal mined per man per day more than doubled, rising from 6.77 tons to 16.84 tons.[31] From the rapid increase in productivity the miners have been able to secure wages much above those once commonly paid in the industry. Through its ownership of some mines, with its powerful political lobbying influence, and by means of its bargaining position, it has sought to rid the industry of the smaller, less efficient, and often unorganized mines. So effective has it been that the small companies have sued the UMW for promoting monopoly by conspiring with large producers.[32]

On the West Coast the longshoremen's union has provided another example of union interest in promoting productivity. Concerned with declining port business, which promised fewer jobs and perhaps lower pay in the future, the union offered to sell its restrictive work rules for $27 million over a period of five years. Managers of the shipping companies accepted and began to modernize their port and ship facilities. The union has since chided some of the companies for not moving faster in increasing productivity and has even offered to help finance some of the mechanization. The union president, Harry Bridges, a professed Marxist but an able practitioner of business unionism, has made clear that the union would welcome a reduction of the number of shipping companies. Such a development, he feels, would bring increased economies, greater profits to the industry, and better opportunity for higher wages.

Work Rules and Featherbedding

With few exceptions, unionists have shown themselves to be business-minded in their appreciation of increasing productivity since the 1920's; for even longer they have shown a businesslike approach in establishing and changing the terms under which they agree to work. An examination of union practices shows that only a very few have struck wage bargains or established work rules to restrain production; rather they have sought to insure workers a share of the industrial abundance that is generated by business firms.[33] Unions have not primarily aimed to conserve jobs

---

[30] *Ibid.*, p. 377.

[31] *Statistical Abstract of the United States: 1966,* Table No. 1050, p. 713.

[32] See United Mine Workers v. Pennington, 381 U.S. 949 (1965), 59 LRRM 2369.

[33] Sumner H. Slichter, James J. Healy, and E. Robert Livernash have concluded that "make-work rules do not usually begin as attempts by unions to force employers to hire excessive numbers of workers." These eminent labor scholars examined in detail the more troublesome rules, management's partial responsibilities for them, and efforts to change or to do away with them. See their monumental study, *The Impact of Collective Bargaining on Management* (Washington: Brookings Institution, 1960), pp. 317–41.

and make work, though their agreements may at times have accomplished these results. They were intent upon aggressively exploiting their situation, prepared to give and take as bargaining strength allowed.

A few unions have been accused of rigidly insisting upon notorious "featherbedding" rules. Though a person only casually acquainted with union activities may gain the impression that make-work and featherbedding are common union practices, the frequency with which the same few examples are cited suggest quite the opposite. The Musicians' union has sometimes required that theater managers hire a whole band when one trumpeter would have sufficed; the Locomotive Firemen tried to protect the jobs of their members long after there was no coal for them to shovel; and the Typographers have members reset "bogus" type for advertisements that have already been printed from mass-produced matrices. Painters in some cities have banned sprayguns.[34] Some local longshoremen's unions maintain work gangs larger than employers think efficient.

The unions regularly mentioned as featherbedders have had to contend with rapid technological change that threatened the livelihood of many of their members. Thousands of musicians in the twenties and early thirties lost their jobs as talking movies appeared, for example; as for the Firemen, the introduction of diesel locomotives in the forties and fifties displaced tens of thousands of their men. In their desperation, the unions involved have sometimes adamantly insisted upon rules and job rights that have seemed unreasonable to the public. With continued negotiations and hard bargaining, however, management has usually found that the union was willing to settle on a new rule. The unionists did not give up their old work rules or demands for job protection freely, of course, but almost always they would exchange them for high enough consideration. A few exceptions are noted below, but these simply emphasize another occasional aspect of union business-mindedness—the managerial pretensions of some union leaders.

PROPERTY RIGHTS FOR BUSINESS-MINDED UNIONISTS

The same commercial tradition that led American farmers to clear and cultivate land not so much to satisfy a desire for ownership as for the opportunity to market it or its products also influenced organized workers. They made job claims and helped establish work rules not so much to "own" them as to market them through the process of collective bargaining. Where technological change is as ever present as in American industry, "ownership" of a job provides only a fleeting security. The owner of an obsolete, threatened job possesses little of value if he simply clings to it. More sensibly, unionists seek to sell their job rights for as high a price as they can secure before they become worthless and out of date.

---

[34] The Painters have sometimes also won restrictions of the size of paintbrushes, but researchers conclude that this is not in fact a restrictive practice; see William Haber and Harold M. Levinson, *Labor Relations and Productivity in the Building Trades* (Ann Arbor: University of Michigan Press for the Bureau of Industrial Relations, 1956), p. 164.

For over half a century labor scholars have observed and reported the willingness of unionists to sell for compensating considerations work rules or other conditions of work, including wages, and to buy from employers certain terms of employment in exchange for existing rules and work conditions. One might even describe a negotiated bargain for a higher wage rate as a benefit purchased by the union in exchange for not exercising its right to engage in concerted activities unwelcomed by the employer. As early as 1912, George Barnett pointed out that unions often exchanged work rules, for which they had fought hard, for wage benefits. And in his detailed, perceptive study of union policies of 1941, Sumner Slichter noted that "if the union can get something in exchange for abandoning a burdensome rule, it will naturally do so. Likewise the best opportunity for employers to insist that a restrictive rule be dropped is when the union wants something—a wage increase, a reduction in hours, or something else."[35]

Two cases illustrate the way in which unions and managers have negotiated practical exchanges. In the 1930's the railroads accepted a variety of work rules, including the retention of firemen on diesels, in return for the rail unions' acceptance of lower wages than the workers might otherwise have expected. In the late 1950's and early 1960's the rail managers decided that the work rules and extra workers had to be eliminated. Forgetting that the workers had paid and were still paying for them in lower wages, the managers insisted that the rules and jobs be given up gratis. Only slowly did they come to realize that they would have to offer something in exchange for the various work rules the workers had won a quarter of a century earlier. Reluctantly and belatedly they recognized that the union members are as devoted to the market process of giving value for value received as any member of the business community.[36]

In the automobile industry a similar exchange had been agreed to in the 1940's, and the president of General Motors publicly admitted that "makework rules were purchased by lower wages than would otherwise be obtainable."[37] Moreover, such rules had originally helped management to "stockpile" and hold workers when the labor market was tight. Later, when workers were not in scarce supply, the auto companies found themselves burdened with work rules for which they had no use. To eliminate or modify them, management had to buy them back with wage increases or other beneficial conditions of work.

Union and Management Intransigence

Employers have found that at times some unions have refused to sell work rules that managers eventually have found to be restrictive or unrewarding. The International Typographers union, one of the country's oldest labor organizations and

[35] Slichter, *op. cit.*, p. 390.
[36] See James W. Kuhn and Ivar Berg, "Bargaining and Work Rules," *Social Research*, Vol. 31 (Winter, 1964), pp. 466–81.
[37] Lloyd Ulman, "Unionism and Collective Bargaining in the Modern Period," *American Economic History*, Seymour E. Harris, ed. (New York: McGraw-Hill, 1961), p. 447.

the parent of many of the printing trade unions, has often taken the stand that it does not bargain about certain matters. Many of the work rules it enforces have been incorporated into its bylaws. Once a work rule is made part of the basic charter, it is, according to union officers, solely a matter for union determination. Professor Barnett remarked many years ago that the ITU "takes the exalted ground that after they have passed a law it is as irrevocable as the laws of the Medes and Persians."[38]

The refusal to bargain over certain issues has been more typical of business spokesmen than union leaders, however. Arguing that they would not surrender their managerial prerogatives, employers have long objected to negotiating with union representatives over a variety of topics. They resisted bargaining over wages and hours in the early 1800's, and more recently they have objected to discussing pensions, stock-option plans, and subcontracting with union representatives. The resistance has not rested on any legal foundation, for an employment contract may include almost any provision that the employer is willing to offer and the employee to accept. Managers have defended their unwillingness to bargain on the basis of a claimed prerogative—an asserted exclusive right to fix employment terms that is not to be questioned or examined. The feudal implication of assigned status is obvious in such a prerogative, which is equally repugnant to democratic, contractual relationships whether managers or union leaders appeal to it.

Usually union members are in the position of challenging management's status and trying to participate in some of the shop decisions that affect them; in some industries, though, union leaders have assumed a number of the managerial functions themselves because employers abdicated supervision of production to concentrate on marketing or some other aspect of the business. In printing, for example, the ITU organized the foremen and all other personnel regularly on the press floor; through the closed shop it also controlled hiring and discharge. It was thus able to make and to enforce shop rules as well as to direct and to discipline the workers and their immediate supervisors. As the union accumulated managerial power it began to assume some of the same pretensions of managers. As manager of the printing shops it refused to bargain over some issues.

Other unions, usually craft organizations of skilled workers, have come to perform managerial functions and, like the ITU and business managers, have resented and resisted challenges to their decisions and authority.

Emerging View of Job Rights as Property

The willingness of unionists as representatives of employees (though not as managers) to sell job conditions and their reluctance in giving them up when nothing is offered as compensation are expressions of the workers' belief that a kind of property right inheres in the existing beneficial conditions of employment. That is, a job is valuable because it secures for the worker a return. As in the case of a commercial property, its value as an asset is largely determined by its earning

---

[38] Barnett, *op. cit.*, pp. 435, 437, and 440–41.

power. Anything that diminishes the earnings of an asset, of course, adversely affects its worth. Likewise, any diminution of wages or worsening of the conditions of employment makes a job less valuable. If managers unilaterally change conditions and so lessen or impair the return to the workers, workers and their union leaders feel that they have had something of value taken from them by arbitrary action. Depreciation of this kind, they argue, is unjust to the workers and moreover is not in character with our American tradition of protection for rights and property.

That unionists should come to view their job claims as a kind of property right is not surprising when one examines the course of court decisions defining property. As late as 1877, in Munn vs. Illinois, the Supreme Court held that only tangible goods were to be considered property. In dissent, Justice Fields argued, "All that is beneficial in property arises from its use, and the fruits of that use; and whatever deprives a person of them deprives him of all that is desirable or valuable in the title and possession."[39] Within a few years Fields' dissenting view became the majority opinion of the court. If a business cannot set the price of its products or services, the court decided, "it is deprived of the lawful use of its property, and thus, in substance and effect, of the property itself, without due process of law and in violation of the Constitution of the United States."[40] If the ability to fix a price or return from a business activity is a property right, workers might well argue by analogy that they too could claim a property right in the terms on which they held their jobs.

Businessmen in the late 1800's and early 1900's certainly were not prepared to accept any property claim of workers as to their jobs or wages. They maintained that they paid for labor service in hourly or daily wages and that neither party could legitimately make any further claims upon the other. Except for the craft unions that had been able to organize strong footholds in a few industries, the union movement did little to develop job claims as property rights until after World War II. Its major efforts in the 1920's, 1930's, and well into the 1940's were directed toward getting employer recognition and establishing collective bargaining. Until managers accepted unions and were willing to negotiate and to reach agreements with them, unions could hardly engage in businesslike conduct. As long as managers insisted upon setting the terms of employment unilaterally, defending their right to do so upon prerogatives derived from some alleged superiority of right, unions had little chance to show their loyalty to the American institutions of property or their willingness to engage in the business practices of give-and-take transactions.

Even before unions had organized extensively, management had begun to lay the basis for a development of work rules and conditions of employment into a property right. Undoubtedly it had not intended to prepare the way for new property rights for workers, but it responded to a traditional, deeply held, and

[39] 94 U.S. 113, 141 (1877).
[40] Chicago, Milwaukee and St. Paul Railway Company v. Minnesota, 134 U.S. 418, 458 (1890).

basic understanding of society that encourages Americans to extend property rights to all individuals.

When managers first began to assume centralized control of employees in the twenties, in the interests of efficiency they initiated such new programs as hiring and firing according to standards and rules established by a personnel office (rather than on the arbitrary authority of foremen), worker representation councils or grievance committees, paid vacations, seniority systems for layoff and recall, stock ownership plans, group insurance, pensions, and in a few cases guaranteed income or work. These were introduced and popularized *before* unions had organized much of industry. Though the programs were unilaterally administered and formally maintained solely at the pleasure of the managers, they began to change the earlier relationship between the worker and his job, as well as the relationship between workers and management.

No longer did a worker merely perform his work and receive his pay. Now managers were interested in reducing turnover, seeking from the worker loyalty and higher morale as well as his labor service. For this they offered benefits that did not end with the completion of the work day. If laid off, an unemployed man might still accumulate seniority or vacation rights for varying periods of time or might still receive pension or insurance benefits. If fired by a foreman, he might find that in fact his employment had not been terminated if he appealed to higher management. The safeguards received by a worker under the programs of the twenties may have been weak and the benefits received for his loyalty may have been minimal by today's standards, but "The Job" began to be less clear-cut as a concept than it had been formerly; work and pay had become more complex, and the relationship of worker and manager was clearly becoming more than a series of instantaneous, implicit contracts terminable at any time by either party. Each expected from the other considerations and benefits of value beyond the hourly work and hourly pay. The expectations that the mutual benefits would continue to be enjoyed were valuable and created for both parties a claim that became eligible for consideration as a property right. It was similar to the valuation of the expectation that a stream of revenue will continue.

After the thirties, when the labor movement organized most of the manufacturing sector of the economy with the encouragement and aid of the federal government, unions insisted on writing into collective agreements all the programs the managers of the twenties had introduced; thus they became joint programs. The mutual expectation arising from those programs, now introduced into almost every major industrial firm, was based, however, on a legally unenforceable document. Unions and workers were free to strike for better terms at any time they thought their bargaining position was better than it had been when the agreement was negotiated. Managers insisted that an agreement without the force of law was an anomaly in a country where most practices contracted in good faith are enforceable. Aware that in nearly a century and a half, court decisions had only intermittently expressed sympathy with union values, labor leaders were decidedly unenthusiastic with the proposal to make collective agreements legally enforceable.

It would subject the strike to more legal restrictions, they feared; they hardly considered how a legally binding agreement might be useful to them in protecting work rules, job claims, and contract provisions.

In 1947 business lobbyists succeeded in getting Congress to approve such a proposal, in Section 301 of the Taft-Hartley Act. Unwittingly, business had finally provided unions the legal foundations for increased property rights or, at least, job rights and work claims that could seek the protection and enforcement of the law.

THE FUTURE OF PROPERTY FOR WORKERS

How fast and how far the courts will develop the claims of workers under collective agreements into property rights remain to be seen. To date a number of court decisions have made clear that managers cannot unilaterally or arbitrarily disregard workers' job claims, work rules, or any of the terms and provisions of the agreement unless explicitly allowed to do so by the agreement. They must at least negotiate with union representatives before they take actions detrimental to the workers' interests as defined by the existing implied or written agreements.[41] In recent decisions the Supreme Court has required management to negotiate with designated union representatives where subcontracting might remove jobs[42] and has forbidden a company from closing a part of its operation to avoid negotiating with a union.[43] The National Labor Relations Board ordered, and a lower court upheld it, that an employer who had moved his plant to a new location to escape a union agreement had either to move the plant back or to move the union workers to the new location. Further, he had to pay employees any wages lost because of his actions.[44] The collective agreement has become a guarantee of jobs for the union workers in such a case, making them legally valuable property indeed.

In another case pregnant with possibilities for the further development of job claims into property rights, the Supreme Court declared that where a judge had to choose between injury to the property interests of a business firm and loss of jobs for workers who would be displaced by machines, equal rights were involved. The workers' interest in their jobs as a source of livelihood was equal with the interest of the firm in fully utilizing its property. The court stated:

> The dispute out of which the judicial controversy arose . . . involves the discharge
> of employees from positions long held and the dislocation of others from their

[41] Steelworkers v. American Navigation Co., 363 U.S. 564 (1960), 46 LRRM 2414. Steelworkers v. Warrior and Gulf Navigation Co., 363 U.S. 574 (1960), 46 LRRM 2416. Steelworkers v. Enterprise Wheel and Car Corporation, 363 U.S. 593 (1960), 46 LRRM 2423.

[42] Fiberboard Paper Products Corp. v. NLRB, 379 U.S. 203 (1964), 57 LRRM 2609.

[43] Textile Workers v. Darlington Manufacturing Co., 380 U.S. 263 (1965), 58 LRRM 2657.

[44] Sidele Fashions, Inc. et al. and Philadelphia Dress Joint Board, ILGWU, 133 NLRB 547 (1961), Philadelphia Dress Joint Board v. NLRB, 50 LRRM 2957 (1962).

homes. . . . It is true that preventing the Railroad from instituting the change imposed upon it the burden of maintaining what may be a less efficient and more costly operation. The balancing of *these competing claims* of irreparable hardship is, however, the traditional function of the equity court. . . .[45]

Surely here the Court has come close to declaring an interest in a job a property right.

Property and the American Heritage

While concentrating on immediate ends and solving day-to-day labor problems, business and the courts as well as unions have almost unwittingly been guided by community traditions and commonly accepted social patterns to create various kinds of property rights for workers in their jobs. According to the American heritage, the ownership of property defines one's individuality and insures one's liberty, offering a protective buffer against the competitive, self-seeking drives of others. The industrial technology that makes large organizations necessary made obsolete the old dream of the Knights of Labor that every man should be a property owner. The attractiveness of the doctrine has nevertheless led American workers, bereft of *real* property, to seek through unions protection for their job claims as if they were property. The traditional American identification of property with individual liberty has made law makers and even businessmen (whose intangible claims have already been redefined as property) recognize the legitimacy of the workers' aspirations. The courts have not recognized a definite title of property ownership for workers in their jobs as yet, but they may continue the drift of recent decisions and define job rights in more and more property-like terms.

As the labor agreement becomes clothed in the elaborate legal garments of the business contract and as job rights are increasingly invested with the honor and rank of property, the public will recognize more clearly that when union leaders negotiate agreements and bargain for the workers they are performing the same functions as businessmen. Unionists have a responsibility to preserve and enhance the assets of their organization and the workers they represent. They may buy, sell, trade, or manipulate those assets to increase the workers' income at the least possible cost, but they should not be expected to give up those assets for nothing in return or to allow an income flow to be cut off, diminished, or diverted without strenuous efforts to preserve it. Unionists in the main tradition of American labor have always performed these functions like the business-minded men they are.

Business Vices as Well as Business Virtues

Investing the labor agreement with the rights and obligations of property will no doubt raise problems. The business values of unionists should allay fears, however, that such a development will impose upon industry a rigid, unyielding approach by

[45] Locomotive Engineers v. Missouri-Kansas-Texas Railroad, 46 LRRM 2429, 2431–32 (italics added).

workers to change. They and their union leaders appear to be ready enough to sell or trade off rules and policies considered by managers to be restrictive; they value increasing productivity enough that they will work for it if they receive a share of its rewards. They do not, of course, expect to have to bear the full or major burden of technological change or adjustment instituted to increase output. As their claims to various job conditions, and even to a job itself, grow more secure, they may be expected to ask a higher price for giving them up when exploitation of technical advances requires that course to be followed. They will thus be asking for a greater share in expected productivity gains, perhaps a not unreasonable request on the part of men who in the past have sometimes suffered displacement or unemployment, or at least borne the cost of retraining and the expense of finding new employment.

Business-minded unionists may raise problems for the general membership and for the public if they negotiate and bargain over job rights with management at less than arm's length. Instead of joining management to raise productivity, to the eventual benefit of all, they may conspire with managers to exploit the public, as businessmen have been wont to do at least since the days of Adam Smith. The returns of conspiracy can often be as lucrative as those from increased efficiencies. Economic tradition says that businessmen need concern themselves only with self-interest, leaving the competitive market to restrain and guide their activities in the service of the public. Insofar as the market is weak or ineffective in the face of oligopolistic industries, other restraints and guidelines may be needed. Should unions add the power they possess, enhanced by stronger ownership of job conditions, to benefit the particular interests of the firms and the union, the public interest may certainly suffer. A further problem is that union leaders and managers may also be tempted to collude to further their own private interests by denying workers their full rights on the job and the wages that are their due. Assurance of democratic procedures within unions (and within corporations?) should lessen this last problem, but it by no means solves the more general problem posed by the possibility that unions will as readily acquire the oligopolistic vices of business as they have acquired its competitive virtues.

CONCLUSION

Business unionism in the United States has avoided a radical split between business and labor. It has helped teach the work force the benefits of increased productivity, and it has contributed to the development of *quid pro quo* collective bargaining that has facilitated adjustment to economic progress and encouraged workers to accept technological change. But the businesslike stance of unionists in a world of large industrial organizations and monopolistic markets does not always serve the public. It is not surprising that government officials sometimes call for market guideposts or other restraints for union and business activities. The irony in the development of business unionism is that though folklore insists that unions are antibusiness and that workers need to understand the business system better, experience indicates that they are pro-business and, to the chagrin of the business community, know all too well how to make the system work for them.

SELECTED READINGS

SAUL ALINSKY, *John L. Lewis, An Unauthorized Biography* (New York: G. P. Putman, 1949). This biography of America's most colorful, forceful labor leader may touch too lightly upon Lewis' faults and shortcomings for some readers, but it makes clear the business-mindedness and capitalist orientation of a man who was widely condemned in the thirties and forties as a dangerous radical.

NEIL W. CHAMBERLAIN, *A General Theory of Economic Process* (New York: Harper & Row, 1955). Chamberlain presents a general bargaining theory that explains why unions and management not only attempt to raise the cost of disagreement to force settlement of disputes but also are encouraged to induce each other to settle disputes by offering cooperative aid, *quid pro quo* exchanges, and mutually beneficial terms.

JOHN R. COMMONS, *Legal Foundations of Capitalism* (Madison: University of Wisconsin Press, 1957); see especially Chapters 2–5, 8, and 9. In this difficult book Commons brilliantly examines the American institution of property and its vital role in our business system. He suggests why unionists have long sought to transform their job claims into property rights; he also forecasts a new concept of "equity" to "protect the job as the older equity protected the business," making a job into a kind of business property.

ROBERT F. HOXIE, *Trade Unionism in the United States* (New York: Appleton, 1921). A posthumously published collection of lecture notes and articles, edited by Lucy Bennett Hoxie, that contains the original analysis of business unionism and other major types of unionism found in the United States.

WILLIAM M. LEISERSON, *American Trade Union Democracy* (New York: Columbia University Press, 1959). Leiserson was a knowledgeable labor scholar who perceptively examined the problems and opportunities of conducting free collective bargaining within the constraints of union democracy. Though he wrote of union experience before the government attempted to insure democratic procedures through the Landrum-Griffin Act of 1959, his analysis and judgments are still pertinent.

SELIG PERLMAN, *A History of Trade Unionism in the United States* (New York: Augustus M. Kelley, 1950). Perlman's short history examines American unions before the depression of the thirties and the rise of the large industrial unions of the CIO. Eschewing radical reform of society, workers built successful, enduring unions, he argues, by concentrating on job-centered benefits and by trying to protect themselves at their place of work from employers' arbitrary rule.

SELIG PERLMAN, *The Theory of the Labor Movement* (New York: Augustus M. Kelley, 1949). Perlman presents his theory of unionism in this study, comparing American labor experience with that of Great Britain, Russia, and Germany. Unionism in any industrial society, according to Perlman, is normally job-centered; intellectuals may from time to time entice unionists into political activity, thus taking attention from their main concern with work rules and job rights.

RICHARD E. WALTON AND ROBERT B. MCKERSIE, *A Behavioral Theory of Labor Negotiations* (New York: McGraw-Hill, 1965). Though the theory presented does not advance our understanding of labor negotiations very far, the analyses of bargaining situations and the wealth of empirical materials provide an excellent insight into the operations of contemporary collective bargaining.

chapter 10

BUSINESS AND THE FAMILY

HYMAN RODMAN AND CONSTANTINA SAFILIOS-ROTHSCHILD *view the impact of business on the American family largely in terms of the effect on the family of certain aspects of the urban-industrial character of American life for which the modern corporation bears considerable responsibility. This approach allows them to utilize in their essay important works from the rich social science literature dedicated to analyzing the influence of the process of industrialization on social structures and economic development. Among the crucial social changes that have been recurrently noted in these studies have been the separation of production from the household and the resulting alterations in family structure.*

Dr. Rodman and Dr. Safilios-Rothschild are the authors of numerous illuminating studies of family structure in America and elsewhere. The research that these Merrill-Palmer Institute investigators have conducted in Greece, the Caribbean area, and the United States has led them to employ the concept of the "occupational-earner role" to better trace the link between the world of business and the life of the family. In this essay they examine corporate influence upon the family as it is expressed in business policies that substantially affect employment, income distribution, consumer tastes, and other phenomena that in turn have consequences for family structure.

Some of the most provocative implications of the authors' discussion stem from the point that, while in what we regard as the "typical" American family only the husband holds the occupational-earner role, in reality more and more women are entering the work force and assuming roles that were historically regarded as appropriate only for men. This may alter the traditional allocation of instrumental and expressive roles within the American family, with important consequences for child-rearing practices, patterns of income distribution, and wage patterns. Concurrent with these changes in the roles of adults, American adolescents have come to constitute a new and enormously significant consumer group whose tastes, backed by their share of the "discretionary income" of family units and their own substantial earnings, have conspired to produce additional discontinuities in American society.

Parallel to the authors' consideration of the impact of business on the family is their examination of the impact of family mores on the character of the performance of managers and laborers at work. The relationships explored by the authors suggest a number of questions:

1. What effects might the increase in the number of multiple-earner families have on the mobility of labor in the American economy? How are the effects likely to differ in the short and the long runs?

2. What kinds of adjustments, if any, are necessary in a society in which managers may relocate their operations and in which their employees belong to multiple-earner families? Will these adjustments be more likely to facilitate economic growth or to hinder it?

3. What effects on American class structure may stem from the fact that the multiple earners in many families hold jobs in different occupations and with different incomes? What comparative social ranking would you expect to find among a family with a single income of $10,000, a family with two incomes of $7,500 each, a family with incomes of $10,000 and $5,000, and a family with two incomes of $10,000?

4. What relationship is there between the desire of employees for security at work and the breakdown of the traditional family structure? What changes may occur in our attitudes toward work as the new family mores gain increased acceptance? In what ways may we anticipate that the nature of family ties in America will affect the quality of American entrepreneurship?

5. Some observers argue that "status conscious" wives and employed women, whatever their marital status, are unsympathetic toward unions. Others claim that unions are strengthened in an economy in which there are multiple-earner families. What consequences for the labor movement are likely to develop from emerging family patterns?

HYMAN RODMAN
AND CONSTANTINA
SAFILIOS-ROTHSCHILD

BUSINESS AND
THE AMERICAN
FAMILY

Neither the business world nor the family world exists in a vacuum. Each is situated within a social and cultural context that contains the other, and, for a fuller understanding, each should be examined in relation to its total context. We will attempt to do so in this essay, but we will focus specifically upon the relationship of American business to the American family. Since both business and the family play so large a part in the life of most individuals, studying the way each influences and interacts with the other is especially important.[1]

THE OCCUPATIONAL-EARNER ROLE

Our basic frame of reference in this essay is the occupational-earner role as the major link between the "business" world—the total occupational world—and the family world. This refers to the two roles being performed by the same person—the occupational role in the work world and the earner role in the family. In the typical American case it is the man who plays these roles and who links together work and family. It is expected that the husband-father will work and that he will be the earner for the family; in this sense his joint occupational-earner role is a key link between the two organizations we are concerned with—the family organization and the work organization. Put more simply, the husband-father works at a job and earns money to support his family. This is generally expected within American society, and it is typically expected by the members of the family. The pattern of income distribution in the business world thus has a basic impact upon family structure. The family's status and style of living stem largely from the economic and social rewards of the man's job, and as a result the family may be organized to make it possible for the man to carry out his occupational role. For example, executives carry out some of their business outside of the office during social occasions, and several studies have pointed to the manner in which their wives must

[1] For other accounts of this topic see Theodore Caplow, *The Sociology of Work* (Minneapolis: University of Minnesota Press, 1954), pp. 248–80; Georges Friedmann, *The Anatomy of Work,* Wyatt Rawson, trans. (New York: The Free Press, 1961), pp. 103–04, 128–31; William G. Dyer, "The Interlocking of Work and Family Social Systems Among Lower Occupational Families," *Social Forces,* Vol. 34 (March, 1965), pp. 230–33; Rex A. Lucas and others, "Industry and the Family," A Report for the Canadian Conference on the Family, mimeographed, n.d.; Robert Rapoport and Rhona Rapoport, "Work and Family in Contemporary Society," *American Sociological Review,* Vol. 30 (June, 1965), pp. 381–94.

organize the household in order to be considered good executive wives.[2] Similarly, the time schedules of policemen, firemen, or railroad workers might require their families to celebrate Christmas or other holidays somewhat earlier or later than others. If a man is transferred by his company to another city, then the family as a whole must adapt to a new city and neighborhood and to new schools and friends.[3] The mutual interdependence of business and family is further underlined by transfer policies of business organizations, which are made to coincide with the school year so that the shift will be less disorganizing for families. Night work, Sunday work, and business travel all require adaptations on the part of the family to business requirements. As occupational roles have become more complex and more demanding they have come to exert a more pervasive influence upon all aspects of life, including the most intimate, one's circle of friends and one's family.

A number of questions follow from our view of the occupational-earner role of the male as the major link between work and family organization. How does the fact that the man plays this joint role affect the organization of the family? How does it affect his work life? What happens when a man's wife also plays an occupational-earner role or when any other member of the family does (e.g., an adolescent son)? These questions, all closely related to our model of the key occupational-earner role of the husband-father, will be dealt with here.

A HISTORICAL VIEW OF BUSINESS AND THE FAMILY

There has been some argument among social scientists and other commentators upon the contemporary American scene as to whether "the family" has become weaker or stronger. Some argue that the family has become less significant in the lives of its members, and others argue that it has become more significant. According to the former viewpoint, the historical rise in the divorce rate reflects the lesser significance of the family; according to the latter, it reflects the greater significance of the family.

To try to shed light upon this controversy and to evaluate the evidence on both sides of the question, we must look briefly at the historical background of the contemporary relationship between work and family. In this way we can put the controversy into a perspective that will enable us to get a better understanding of the nature of contemporary family life.

Decline in the Significance of the Family Farm

Up until the mid-nineteenth century the American family was usually a farming family, and as such it was both a productive work unit and a consuming unit. Farm-

[2] William H. Whyte, Jr. "The Wives of Management," *Fortune,* Vol. 44 (October, 1951), pp. 86ff; Margaret L. Helfrich, "The Generalized Role of the Executive's Wife," *Marriage and Family Living,* Vol. 23 (November, 1961), pp. 384–87.

[3] Clark E. Vincent, "Familia Spongia: The Adaptive Function," *Journal of Marriage and the Family,* Vol. 28 (February, 1966), pp. 29–36.

ing and living were synonymous,[4] and the occupational-earner role of the male was fused into the role of the farmer. The roles of farmer, father, and husband were carried out in the same spatial areas, and there was less separation between work and family roles than is true for a modern business executive or industrial worker. Of course, the spatial separation between the location of work and the family and the behavioral segregation between the work role and the family role are not the same thing. For instance, the business executive may work at a suburban branch office near his home, and the university professor may live in faculty housing within the university area, but their work and family roles are still segregated in comparison to the overlap of these roles in the farm family.

During the nineteenth and twentieth centuries the relative economic importance of the American family farm declined. Technological changes led to rapid increases in industrialization and urbanization that absorbed many who would otherwise have gone into farm occupations. Agricultural mechanization tended to render small family farms inefficient, and the management of large farms became a business undertaking, with the consequent decline of many of the differences between urban and rural residents. As small farms throughout the United States were bought and consolidated, and also as the Industrial Revolution enveloped the farming economy, many who were raised on farms migrated to the beckoning industries of the larger towns and cities. The farm population declined, and the farm family lost its position as the dominant family type. Not only did the proportion of farm families decrease, but the ideal image of the self-sufficient farm family faded from the American scene.

The farm population in 1965 was 6.4 per cent of the total United States population. This was a decrease from farm population percentages of 30.1 in 1920, 24.9 in 1930, 23.2 in 1940, 15.3 in 1950, and 8.7 in 1960.[5] Similarly, the relative share of the rural population of the United States (including both farm and non-farm population elements living in rural areas) has decreased from 94.9 per cent in 1790 to 84.7 per cent in 1850, 60.3 per cent in 1900, 36.0 per cent in 1950, and 30.1 per cent in 1960.[6]

Impact on Family Relationships

As work patterns have shifted from predominantly family labor on farms to wage labor in plants and offices, there have been many changes in the relationship between business and the family. If one considers the typical early American situation, the husband was the head of the family as a kinship group and the head of the family as a work group. As a consequence, a number of roles were played

[4] Howard W. Beers, "A Portrait of the Farm Family in Central New York State," *American Sociological Review,* Vol. 2 (October, 1937), pp. 591–600.
[5] *Statistical Abstract of the United States: 1966,* p. 616.
[6] Computed from U.S. Bureau of the Census, *Historical Statistics of the United States: Colonial Times to 1957* (Washington: Government Printing Office, 1960), p. 14; *Statistical Abstract of the United States: 1964,* p. 16. The figures for 1950 and 1960 are based upon new Bureau of the Census definitions of "urban" and "rural" areas.

by the farmer-husband-father that reinforced the dominant position he held within the family. According to James M. Williams:

> The parental control united in itself several lines of influence. The parents were the directors of the daily work in which all participated. And the family was not only an economic organization but also an educational organization. Until the establishment of the common school system, children got their education in the home. . . . The parents were also instructors in religion. . . .
>
> The father and mother made it a point to agree in all their beliefs, as well as in all requirements of the children, in order that the parental authority might not be weakened by disagreement. The wife was apt to yield to the husband in cases of a difference of opinion, not only because it was customary for the wife to yield to her husband, but also in order to set an example that would strengthen the father's authority over his children.[7]

Not only a patriarchal tradition but also the organization of work, family, and society supported the central position of the man. As Beers has commented, "Fathers were austerely dominant. Wives were obedient, faithful, subordinate in person and in law. Strict obedience was required of children."[8]

In the early stages of industrialization, employment in the home often became available for members of farm families who wanted to earn cash to purchase goods that were not available on the farm. This "putting out" system was the beginning of the process of differentiation between work and family, in which members of the family could contribute to the industrial production of goods while remaining within the household and while still carrying out farm tasks.[9] With increased mechanization, however, it became more efficient to bring the workers to a central factory and to concentrate production there. As a result, a shift was gradually made toward completely differentiated work roles, so that a worker was no longer a family worker subject to the authority of the head of the family but an industrial worker subject to the authority of the head of the factory. Under these changed conditions, the father's role as head of the family was no longer heightened by his role as head of a family work group. In addition, there was an opportunity for other members of the family to earn an independent livelihood, and this opened the way to possible changes in the authority structure of the family.

Wider Social Changes

The relationship between work and the family, as we have noted, takes place in a larger societal context. Work and family roles were not the only ones to undergo differentiation from the nineteenth to the twentieth centuries. The family was no longer the exclusive or major organization responsible for the education and welfare of its members; other organizations such as schools, churches, and various governmental agencies began to take on certain specialized jobs. Ogburn,

---

[7] *Our Rural Heritage* (New York: Alfred A. Knopf, 1925), pp. 65–66.
[8] *Op. cit.*, pp. 591–92.
[9] Wilbert E. Moore, *Industrial Relations and the Social Order*, rev. ed. (New York: Macmillan, 1951), pp. 22–24.

in an early paper, noted that the family was losing certain functions—economic, educational, recreational, and protective.[10] Many others have discussed this "loss of functions" by the family. In a summary, Ogburn and Nimkoff have stated:

> What has been happening during the last century or two is that we have lessened our dependence on the family for the satisfaction of our needs and wishes. Formerly the family was the principal locus of economic activity, and the source of many educational, recreational, religious, and protective services. At the present time, the economic activities are largely separated from the home and are carried on by industry, commerce, banking, transportation, and the like, while recreation is being increasingly commercialized also.[11]

Among the changes that have been noted over the past 150 years are the rising divorce rate (which has been stable since 1955), the falling (but fluctuating) birth rate, and the changing sexual mores (which are now less condemnatory of premarital or extramarital sexual relations).

Interpreting the Changes

The facts about changes in such matters as the birth rate or the divorce rate are well established, but the interpretation of them offers many difficulties.[12] Some critics have evaluated the changes as indicative of failure on the part of the family to maintain control over its members. Rather than being oriented toward the welfare of the family, individuals became oriented to their personal welfare; they were getting divorces at the first sign of disharmony in the marital relationship, were reluctant to take on the burdens of rearing children and of supporting aged parents, and were placing personal pleasure above the importance of the taboos on premarital and extramarital sexual behavior. Other observers, however, have evaluated these changes in terms of the structural requirements of a changing economic order.[13]

> In this view the declining birth rate was seen as an indication of the lesser utility of children—they were no longer needed for the family farm or the family firm. As a result, parents were beginning to have as many children as they "wanted" rather than as many as they "needed." Similarly, the rising (or high) divorce rate was seen as an indication of the greater mutuality in the relationship between husband and wife. No longer did they stay together because of social

[10] William F. Ogburn, "The Changing Family," *Publications of the American Sociological Society,* Vol. 23 (1928), pp. 124–33.

[11] Ogburn and M. F. Nimkoff, *Technology and the Changing Family* (Boston: Houghton Mifflin, 1955), p. 15.

[12] For additional details see Hyman Rodman, ed., *Marriage, Family, and Society: A Reader* (New York: Random House, 1965), pp. 251–54, 287–92; Crane Brinton, *A History of Western Morals* (New York: Harcourt, Brace & World, 1959), pp. 381–91; Pitirim A. Sorokin, "The Depth of the Crisis: American Sex Morality Today," *Christianity Today* (July 4, 1960), pp. 811–13.

[13] Moore, *op. cit.,* pp. 530–37; Talcott Parsons, "The American Family: Its Relations to Personality and to the Social Structure," in Parsons and Robert F. Bales, *Family, Socialization and Interaction Process* (New York: The Free Press, 1955), pp. 3–33.

pressures, regardless of the quality of their relationship; they now were staying together because of their mutual affection, because they "wanted" to and not because they "had" to. The fact that the birth rate did not continue its decline through the 1930's and 1940's and that the divorce rate did not continue its rise . . . suggests that a reasonably good adjustment has been made by the American family to its changed conditions. The more ominous predictions that the society would die out as a result of the lack of incentive to raise children, or that lawful marriage would become indistinguishable from non-marital sexual relationships, have proven to be exaggerated.[14]

The predominant view among social scientists at present is that the changes in family organization are permitting the family and its members to adapt to the changing circumstances of life in the work world and in the society at large. For many people it is no longer possible to maintain strong and enduring relationships with their neighbors, friends, colleagues, and kinsmen in a stable community. There is a great deal of mobility—often both geographic and social—on the part of the contemporary middle-class family. As a result, an individual is to a greater extent dependent upon the members of his immediate family for psychological and emotional support. According to this interpretation, marriage and the family are increasingly specializing in companionship and emotional functions, and where there is a lack of satisfaction with the relationship there is a greater likelihood of divorce. But the high divorce rate is matched by a rising marriage rate (the proportion of people who are marrying) and a high remarriage rate after divorce, an indication that there is no disillusionment with marriage as an institution but only with the relationship to a particular spouse. In this context a new marriage still represents the most potentially rewarding means of establishing a stable bond of affection. In other words, the high divorce rate is not regarded as an indication of a weaker family but as an indication of the greater emphasis upon affectional functions and mutual development in the marital relationship.

It should therefore be clear that it is not advisable to talk about the historical development of a "stronger" family or a "weaker" family; rather, attention should be focused on the changing functions that are being played by the family in a changing world.

MASCULINE AND FEMININE ROLES IN BUSINESS AND THE FAMILY

There is a great deal of controversy about the role of women in contemporary American life. According to some social commentators, women can only find satisfaction through pursuing a career on an equal footing with men. According to others, women can only find satisfaction in fulfilling their "natural" functions as wives and mothers. While such stark statements of the contrasting positions involve a considerable amount of simplification, they do highlight the issues centering on women's roles in the world of work and the world of the family.

The controversy about the different choices open to women implies a less dis-

[14] Hyman Rodman, ed., *op. cit.*, p. 252.

cussed but equally important controversy about the complementary masculine roles. Insofar as women play the traditional wife-mother role, men can continue to play the traditional occupational-earner role. But as feminine roles change and wives pursue careers, there is pressure upon the masculine role to assume substantial responsibility for various family and household tasks.

Role Differentiation in Small Groups

One area of research relevant to a discussion of the roles of men and women centers around the role differentiation process that has been observed in small-group studies. This research has shown that there is a tendency for two kinds of roles to differentiate: one is a task or instrumental role, and the other is a socio-emotional or expressive role.[15] Thus, there is a tendency for one member of the group to specialize in the role of instrumentally pushing the group along toward a particular solution and for another member to specialize in the expressive area and to enable the members of the group to let off steam and to remain in a harmonious relationship with each other.

The theories expressed by George C. Homans[16] and by Talcott Parsons[17] have recently helped to clarify the distinction between instrumental and expressive roles. They have distinguished, in the first place, between the external and internal problems of a social system. The external problem faced by all social systems is how it will manage to survive in its total environment. The instrumental role is one that is specifically geared to this functional problem—it is directed toward solving the problems that the environment poses for the group. The internal problem faced by all social systems is how it will maintain harmony among members of the group so that the group can continue to function as a unit. The expressive role is geared toward fulfilling this functional problem.

It is of particular interest that even in small-group research based on *ad hoc* groups one sees a tendency for the instrumental and expressive roles to differentiate. Zelditch, in addition, has indicated that the same kind of differentiation shows up when one looks at families cross-culturally—he is able to point to such role differentiation, in which it is the male who usually plays the instrumental role and the female who usually plays the expressive role.[18] That this is true on a widespread basis is a fact that is worth commenting upon from two points of view.

The first point is that the tendency for role differentiation seems to be well confirmed and suggests that a group may be able to function most efficiently when there is some differentiation between an expressive and an instrumental role. Of course, Bales showed that some of the experimental groups had a "great man"

[15] Robert F. Bales and Philip E. Slater, "Role Differentiation in Small Decision-Making Groups," in Parsons and Bales, *op. cit.,* pp. 259–306.
[16] *The Human Group* (New York: Harcourt, Brace & World, 1950).
[17] "General Theory in Sociology," in Robert K. Merton, Leonard Broom, and Leonard S. Cottrell, Jr., eds., *Sociology Today* (New York: Basic Books, 1959), pp. 3–38.
[18] Morris Zelditch, Jr., "Role Differentiation in the Nuclear Family: A Comparative Study," in Parsons and Bales, *op. cit.,* pp. 307–51.

leader in them—a leader who was able to combine within himself both the task and the socioemotional roles. But this was a rare occurrence, and the general tendency was for the roles to differentiate.

A second point of significance is that cross-culturally, in families, it is the male who usually plays the instrumental role and the female who usually plays the expressive role. Why should this be so? Clearly there is no biological difference that necessarily calls for this kind of distinction. The biological difference that involves the woman in childbearing is important, but it can be reacted to and elaborated upon in varying cultural forms. There are exceptional societies where women play the more instrumental roles and men the more expressive roles. Nevertheless, it may be that the major biological difference between men and women has been capitalized upon by many different societies as the basis for determining the direction in which role differentiation will go and thus explains the general uniformity noted.

We can see the result of such differentiation within the American family in that it is typically the husband-father who plays the occupational-earner role, thereby joining together the business firm and the family.

The Common Research Model of the Family, and Some Variations

The type of family in the U.S. upon which most research has been done is the middle-class, white, urban, Protestant family with two to four children, where the husband works at a "good" job, and the wife plays her role as wife-mother and perhaps does some voluntary social and civic work.

Since the father is working at some type of middle-class job, and since his salary is fairly good, it becomes possible for the members of the family to become organized about his occupational-earner role both in the kind of neighborhood that they live in and in the style of family life that they follow. The mother, as a result, usually does not work (or if she does, it is at some part-time job), and her major attention is on the upbringing of her children and the adequate performance of her role as wife-mother. The husband is absent from the home for a good period of time, so the major child-rearing function is placed upon the wife. The relationship between husband and wife is an affectionate one, which we can find symbolized by the vast number of idiosyncratic and pet names that spouses use toward each other.[19]

Naturally enough, not every family in America conforms to the dominant type, and even within "typical families" the relations of the several members with the world of business vary as functions of their age, sex, and other factors. One of the major variations from the model, which will not be dealt with in detail, occurs when the man in a family has difficulty with the occupational-earner role. Since the occupational-earner role is the major role a man is expected to play in American society, we would expect a variety of consequences for the family under

[19] David M. Schneider and George C. Homans, "Kinship Terminology and the American Kinship System," *American Anthropoligist,* Vol. 57 (December, 1955), pp. 1194–1208.

conditions such as unemployment, underemployment, poorly paid employment, physical disability, mental illness, or retirement from the work force. Under all of these circumstances the man is not able to carry out the occupational-earner role that is generally expected. The lower-class man, for example, plays an occupational-earner role that is severely damaged, and many of the problems written about lower-class families and much of the discussion about a "culture of poverty" stem from this basic fact.[20]

Two other alternatives to the dominant family type result from the occupational involvement of adolescents and married women. We shall therefore discuss the period of adolescence and the working woman from the perspective of the relationship between business and the American family.

BUSINESS, FAMILY, AND THE ADOLESCENT

The increasing automation of business in American society modifies the demand for manpower, especially at the unskilled levels. This has created a special problem for adolescents; many of them are entering the work force without special skills, and as a result their rate of unemployment is high. The problem is further complicated by the fact that a growing number of individuals is entering the labor force for the first time—a result of the "baby boom" that followed the second world war.

One factor that mitigates the problem of youth unemployment is the extension of the period of adolescence in the United States. Young people are attending school for longer periods of time and in this way are becoming better prepared for complex careers while their entry into the labor market is postponed. The suggestion is common now that the period of formal schooling be increased in order to provide a better education for all individuals and in order to alleviate further the problem of unemployed youth.

The Adolescent's Occupational-Earner Role and Morality

Adolescence has become a time in which participation in the occupational-earner role is often postponed because of formal schooling. But while this change has

[20] Hyman Rodman, "Middle-Class Misconceptions About Lower-Class Families," in Rodman, ed., *op. cit.*, pp. 219–30; Daniel Patrick Moynihan, "Employment, Income, and the Ordeal of the Negro Family," *Daedalus*, Vol. 94 (Fall, 1965), pp. 745–70; Oscar Lewis, *Five Families: Mexican Case Studies in the Culture of Poverty* (New York: Basic Books, 1959); Hylan Lewis, "Child-Rearing Among Low-Income Families," in Louis A. Ferman, Joyce L. Kornbluh, and Alan Haber, eds., *Poverty in America: A Book of Readings* (Ann Arbor: University of Michigan Press, 1965). It should be noted, by way of qualification, that in underdeveloped countries such as Greece, where the worth of a man is not measured in terms of his earning capacity, the lower-class male suffers little loss of esteem within his family, and he does not become a marginal member of the family; see Constantina Safilios-Rothschild, "A Comparison of Power Structure and Marital Satisfaction in Urban Greek and French Families," *Journal of Marriage and the Family*, Vol. 29 (May, 1967), pp. 345–52.

partly helped to relieve some of the pressures in the labor market, it has produced other problems. For example, according to traditional morality, marriage should be postponed until a man can support his wife, and sexual relations should be postponed until marriage takes place. As a result, there is a conflict for the physically mature adolescent who is biologically driven toward sexual relationships but who is not in a position to play the role that would entitle him to sexual relationships.

One solution to this conflict has been for individuals to play the occupational-earner role from a young age. This has been particularly true at the lower levels of the class structure; the data are quite clear that in the lower social classes children continue at school for a lesser period of time, and marriages take place earlier. But the rate of unemployment among lower-class youth is also higher and has consequences for the structure of the family.

Another solution to the potential conflict is one that involves a change in traditional values. Early marriage has become accepted even where a man cannot support a family through the occupational role. Parents, for example, will frequently provide help to the young couple that is still at school; in addition, the wife may work to put her husband through college. As a result, the age of marriage has been on the decline for a great many years, and the drop has been from a median age for men of 26.1 in 1890 to a median age of 22.8 in 1963, and from a median age for women of 22.0 in 1890 to a median age of 20.4 in 1963.[21]

A third solution, still to gain complete acceptance, involves an attenuation of the strong taboo against premarital sexual relationships. Such relationships now often provide a solution to the adolescent conflict between physical maturity and economic dependence. Particularly as contraceptives have come to provide more certain protection against pregnancy, and as sexual relationships prior to marriage have been confined to "love" relationships and to "going steady" relationships, the traditional ban on premarital sexual relationships has been relaxed.[22] In addition, now that divorce has become more acceptable, an early marriage may be broken later on in case of dissatisfaction; to some extent this relieves the pressure against early marriage and perhaps also against premarital sexual relationships that may lead to pregnancy and marriage but that may also subsequently lead to divorce. Perhaps the name of one of the sections of the Society for the Study of Social Problems—"Marriage, Family and Divorce"—is symptomatic of the greater expectation that this is a sequence not altogether unusual.

Certain special conflicts are faced by the female adolescent. Because of the double standard, a more conservative attitude toward premarital sexual relationships is expected of the female, by others and by herself. There is also a greater pressure upon the female to marry. At least one result of this is to be seen in the research findings that suggest that girls, in looking forward to a marriage, have a

[21] *Statistical Abstract: 1964, op. cit.,* p. 65, and Rodman, *Marriage, Family, and Society, op. cit.,* p. 293.
[22] Winston W. Ehrmann, *Premarital Dating Behavior* (New York: Holt, Rinehart and Winston, 1959); Ira L. Reiss, *Premarital Sexual Standards in America* (New York: The Free Press, 1960).

more open and flexible personality so that they might meet the needs of any prospective fiancé.[23] In other words, there is greater pressure upon the female to marry and, as a result, a reluctance on her part to develop strong career plans or even strong personality characteristics, because this might delimit the field of men from among whom she can find a husband.

Advertising and Parent-Youth Conflict

There are certain business practices that are relevant to the relationship between adolescents and their parents. Adolescents in the United States have consumer tastes that are different from other age groups. The extent to which business has intruded upon this situation and become a factor in promoting such tastes—and perhaps indirectly in furthering the split between adolescents and their parents— is an open question.

Adolescents have become a tremendously significant consumer group for a wide variety of products, such as automobiles, cosmetics, clothing, phonograph records, and movies. Business advertising practices have helped to cultivate this particular market. As a result, the huge advertising budgets of American business may have had a hand in furthering the split in consumer tastes between the adolescent and adult generations even while encouraging everyone to "think young."

Sherif and Sherif[24] point out that adolescents frequently have a very specific idea of the particular kind of car they would like to have—including the make, model, color, year, and engine type—while they infrequently have a specific idea about the occupation they would like to follow. Business has thus been highly influential in cultivating a refined sense of taste on the part of adolescents and in reaching them as consumers. Sherif and Sherif point out that almost all young men want to own cars and that many of them do own cars or have access to cars to drive; they go so far as to refer to a "car culture" as a common trait shared by American youth. Similar things could be said about youth's taste for music and for movies. Although there is a relationship between the youth culture and business practices, this does not tell us anything about whether one is the cause of the other.

It can be argued that the strain between youth and adults has been documented for many ages and precedes the existence of business advertising practices; therefore, business is not contributing to the generational split but is merely addressing itself to a separate youth culture already in existence in order to sell a particular market. The contrary argument is that there is a good deal of difference from society to society in the nature of the split, if any, that exists between youth and adults. This is even true within our own society, where varying groups of youths may be more or less closely tied to adult values and adult tastes. As Kingsley

[23] Elizabeth Douvan, "Sex Differences in Adolescent Character Process," *Merrill-Palmer Quarterly,* Vol. 6 (October, 1960), pp. 203–11.
[24] Muzafer Sherif and Carolyn W. Sherif, *Reference Groups* (New York: Harper & Row, 1964), pp. 203–07.

Davis has pointed out, there are, in addition to a number of universal features that tend to separate the generations, a number of variables that may or may not combine with the universal features in order to produce parent-youth conflict.[25] It can therefore be argued that the advertising practices of business have become an additional variable that helps to produce a greater amount of parent-youth conflict in American society.

THE WOMAN'S OCCUPATIONAL-EARNER ROLE

Despite the usual dilemma faced by American girls in their late teens and early twenties of whether to choose a career or marriage, it seems that a large and increasing number of women combine some kind of employment with marriage and also motherhood.

The employment of married women has increased considerably in the United States during the last two decades. In 1963, married women represented three-fifths of the female labor force. This upward trend is true even for the women whose working stirs up the most controversy, those who have children under six years old. In 1963, one-third of all married women whose husbands lived with them and almost one-fourth of mothers with children under six years old were employed.[26] This recent increase in the employment of married women on a full-time and a part-time basis is not restricted to the United States; it seems to be a definite global trend.[27] While more pronounced in some countries than in others, the tendency is evident in all parts of the world and appears to be common to countries in different stages of development.[28] In some countries a third or more of all married women are economically active, and more than half of all women in the labor force are married.

The nature of women's employment has changed at least as much as its extent. Married women probably always helped in the family farm or business, but they were not paid for their labor in the past. Presently, married women in significant numbers hold remunerative non-agricultural occupations, and they can use their earnings to live independently of their husbands or other relatives if they choose to do so.[29]

Meeting the Demands of Marriage and Work

The usual solution for the woman's "marriage versus career" dilemma once was to work until the birth of the first child and to return to work after the departure

---

[25] "The Sociology of Parent-Youth Conflict," *American Sociological Review*, Vol. 5 (August, 1940), pp. 523–35.

[26] Rodman, ed., *op. cit.*, p. 291.

[27] *Women Workers in a Changing World,* International Labor Conference, 48th Sess. (Geneva: International Labor Office, 1963), pp. 14–15.

[28] *Ibid.*, p. 15.

[29] William J. Goode, *World Revolution and Family Patterns* (New York: The Free Press, 1963), p. 21.

from home of the last child. The long interruption of employment was justified on the basis of the children's absolute need of the mother. The average period away from work has gradually been decreasing in recent years as more and more people learn that children of any age do not suffer detrimental effects when the mother is working, but this notion still has a serious effect on the work experience of women. In the sciences, for example, the peak of creative work is reached when the investigator is in her twenties and thirties; the pattern followed by many American women scientists of interrupting their employment at just this age decreases their contributions and puts them at a definite disadvantage.[30]

The intermittent character of female employment restricts women to occupations in which "employment is typically by short time, in which the gain in skill achieved by continuous experience is slight, in which interchangeability is very high, and in which the loss of skill during long periods of inactivity is relatively small."[31] The occupations in which women tend to concentrate—such as secretaries, salesladies, private household workers, teachers, waitresses, service workers, nurses, and social workers—all conform to the above criteria.[32] According to Caplow, "Well-organized occupations have usually been able to prevent the entry of women and have done so . . . . The occupations which women are able to enter freely are those which have low prestige and poor working conditions or are associated in some way with home and housework."[33]

Another solution to the conflict of demands of work and family that is commonly chosen by women in most of the economically developed countries—especially in the Scandinavian countries, the United Kingdom, Canada, and the United States—is to work part-time.[34] In the United States in 1958 about one-third of employed women worked part-time; one-third worked full-time but only for part of the year; and one-third worked full-time all year. Only one-third of the working women, then, could be regarded as having work commitments comparable to those of men.[35]

Part-time women workers in the United States are predominantly in non-industrial occupations, especially in private domestic work and the retail trades as saleswomen.[36] Part-time employment has generally been considered ideal for married women with family responsibilities who would like to combine a limited

[30] Alice S. Rossi, "Women in Science: Why So Few?" *Science*, Vol. 148 (May 28, 1965), p. 1199.
[31] Caplow, *op. cit.*, p. 245.
[32] *Ibid.*
[33]*Ibid.*, p. 246. Rossi (*op. cit.*, p. 1197) has pointed out that "women lost rather than gained ground in the sciences between 1950 and 1960, for although they appeared in greater absolute numbers in 1960, the rate of increase was much lower than that of men." In 1960, only 9 per cent of the employed natural scientists and less than 1 per cent of the engineers were women.
[34] "Part-time Employment for Women with Family Responsibilities," *International Labor Review,* Vol. 75 (January, 1957), p. 547.
[35] Richard C. Wilcock, "Women in the American Labor Force: Employment and Unemployment," in *Studies in Unemployment*, prepared for the Special Committee on Unemployment, U.S. Senate (Washington: Government Printing Office, 1960), p. 153.
[36] "Part-time Employment for Women with Family Responsibilities," *op. cit.*, p. 547.

amount of work with child-rearing and housekeeping duties. Such work offers the stimulation of activities outside the home while it requires a minimum amount of readjustment within the family. However, a woman's inability to work full-time places a number of restrictions upon the kinds of occupations she may enter. She is effectively barred from undertaking a responsible administrative or professional job, and her chances for promotion within the occupational hierarchy are inhibited. In addition, part-time workers have a limited commitment to their jobs, and they tend to be regarded as marginal employees. This affects their rate of pay and fringe benefits, and in the long run, since it influences the image of the working woman as such, it also affects the wages and employment conditions of women who work full-time.[37]

Attitudes Toward Women Working

Probably many women have followed either the part-time or the interrupted employment pattern because of societal pressures against married women with children committing themselves to full-time occupational roles. As societal attitudes toward the full-time employment of women change in the future, the popularity of part-time work, with all its attendant disadvantages and limited rewards, most likely will decline.

The fact that only women are asked why they work indicates the unconventionality of their act and often leads them to rationalize in order to "defend" themselves. Who asks men why they work? In the American culture, work is considered to be a basic responsibility of a man, the non-fulfillment of which is inexcusable. Not so for women. They must justify in socially acceptable terms their decision to work.[38]

Hoffman reports that when women are asked why they work "somewhere between 55 and 90 per cent of the answers will be in terms of money, depending upon the particular sample of women being interviewed, the phrasing of the question, whether it is part of a questionnaire or personal interview, etc."[39]

Even the most traditional of women seem to feel that it is all right for a married woman, with children of any age, to work in order to provide necessities and to help pay debts.[40] Economic "need" tends to legitimize a married woman's participation in the labor force, even if she has young children. But economic need, as well as all other needs, has a subjective component, and very different financial circumstances may be defined as requiring additional funds by women of different aspirations and personalities. Wives who have very high expectations for social

[37] *Ibid.*, pp. 548–51. However, it is possible that legislation requiring equal employment opportunities for women, as passed in the United States in the Civil Rights Act of 1964, may counteract this.

[38] Lois Wladis Hoffman, "The Decision to Work," in F. I. Nye and L. W. Hoffman, eds., *The Employed Mother in America* (Chicago: Rand McNally, 1963).

[39] *Ibid.*, p. 22.

[40] Hortense M. Glenn, "Attitudes of Women Regarding Gainful Employment of Married Women," Ph.D. dissertation, Florida State University, 1958, p. 35.

mobility and who are eager to acquire the material symbols of success may define their employment as a financial necessity. Any woman, whatever the income bracket of her husband, could easily rationalize her desire to work or her actual employment in terms of financial necessity; her work contributes to the welfare of the family by providing a better standard of living.

In the view of the continuous pressure upon women to legitimize their work, and because of the ease with which they can develop a ready justification hinging on some subjective definition of economic necessity, the data elicited by interviews of women concerning their reasons for working appear rather meaningless. If one were to ask men why they work, they would ordinarily also answer that they need the money; very few would give as a reason the utilization of their talents, intrinsic satisfaction, or feeling of accomplishment. Probably those few men would tend to be in professional, artistic, and administrative occupations. The reasons for working may well be related to the occupation and the satisfactions it can offer to the employee, rather than to the sex of the employee, but we are not likely to find out through the kinds of questions that have been asked.

The notions that a wife should work only when her family needs money and that generally a woman's salary is not a reliable or substantial part of the family's income are, according to Foote, results of "the assumption that women's pay was small and uncertain and not long-continuing."[41] When data are examined that group women according to their husbands' incomes and show the percentage that actually works in each group, we find that prior to World War II, "high rates of participation for married women were limited to low-income families and to non-white women. Today [1956], while the participation rate of wives still has an inverse relationship to the income of husbands, the relationship is becoming less pronounced, even for women under 45 years of age. . . ."[42] Shiffman's analysis of 1960 data (as compared to 1950 data) shows that "the participation rate of married women appears to have risen faster among those married to men in higher income brackets."[43] This suggests a current trend toward a declining influence of the husband's income upon the wife's labor force participation.[44]

Until now, high income and education exercised marked and opposing effects upon the wife's actual or intended participation in the labor force; a high family income tended to inhibit working, while a high level of education tended to promote working.[45] The recent trend toward increasing numbers of higher-income

[41] Nelson N. Foote, "New Roles for Men and Women," *Marriage and Family Living*, Vol. 23 (November, 1961), p. 329.

[42] Wilcock, *op. cit.*, p. 143.

[43] Jacob Shiffman, "Marital and Family Characteristics of Workers, March 1961," *Monthly Labor Review* (January, 1962), p. 13.

[44] Matilda White Riley, Marilyn E. Johnson, and Sarane S. Boocock, "Woman's Changing Occupational Role—A Research Report," *The American Behavioral Scientist*, Vol. 6 (May, 1963), p. 37; Jacob Mincer, "Labor Force Participation of Married Women: A Study of Labor Supply," in *Aspects of Labor Economics*, Report of the National Bureau of Economic Research (Princeton, N. J.: Princeton University Press, 1962), pp. 63–97.

[45] Riley *et al.*, *op. cit.*, p. 36; Wilcock, *op. cit.*, p. 146.

wives who work suggests that the conflicting influences of income and education are being resolved; a high educational level facilitates the labor-force participation of married women, while high family income is no longer inhibiting their participation (except at the very high income levels).[46]

Effects of Maternal Employment Upon the Husband-Wife Relationship and the Personality Development of Children

Although female employment in general is controversial, it is the employment of married women with husbands and children that attracts the most criticism and most of the speculative and evaluative commentary. The most fervent critics of mothers working come to their conclusions on the basis of a few selected cases rather than on the basis of systematic research findings. This procedure allows the values and personal biases of the critics to have freer play. Sussman has documented this and has pointed out some of the consequences that are presumed to result from a mother's working:

> Defeminization, family instability, rejection of children, creation of juvenile delinquents, loss of intimate emotional relationships with children, distorted personality development of children, and poor school performance by children are a few examples of perceived consequences of a mother's working away from home. Informed laymen, respected educators, clinically oriented psychologists, psychiatrists, and family life educators, among others, have most often voiced these consequences.[47]

Research on the effects of the employment of mothers upon their children or marital adjustment, however, has until recently been inconclusive and has yielded contradictory findings.

Hoffman, in discussing different studies comparing children of working mothers and children of non-working mothers, examines such intervening variables as social class, full-time versus part-time employment, age and sex of child, and mother's attitude toward employment to see whether they help to clarify the effects of a mother's working. For example, the studies by Nye, by Glueck and Glueck, and by Gold of the relation between the employment of mothers and juvenile delinquency can be better understood when the respondents' social-class background and corresponding values and attitudes are closely examined.[48] Similarly, the mother-child relationship is better understood when information is available on the mother's attitude toward her employment. Hoffman and Douvan found that when the mother's employment is gratifying to her, the mother-child relationship is a warm one—possibly a little too warm with younger children, suggesting that the mother may feel guilty under the prevailing social norms con-

[46] Riley *et al., op. cit.,* pp. 36–37; Seymour L. Wolfbein, *Employment and Unemployment in the United States* (Chicago: Science Research Associates, 1964), pp. 238–42.
[47] Marvin B. Sussman, "Needed Research on the Employed Mother," *Marriage and Family Living,* Vol. 23 (November, 1961), p. 368.
[48] These research studies are discussed in Hoffman, "Effects on Children," in Nye and Hoffman, eds., *op. cit.,* pp. 192–96.

cerning child-rearing practices. However, when the mother is dissatisfied with her employment, the mother-child relationship is not warm, and the children may be burdened with household tasks.[49]

Some changes are reported in the husband-wife relationship when the wife works (although these changes are not detrimental to the family, as was predicted by critics of mothers' employment). Hoffman found that working mothers participated less than non-working mothers in household tasks and made fewer decisions about routine household matters, while their husbands participated more and made more such decisions.[50]

With respect to the family power structure, Blood and Wolfe found that working wives tended to lower the husband's average authority score and to have a greater voice in decision-making.[51] In a later article, Blood modified this finding by stating that working wives tend to make fewer decisions about household tasks and to share more decisions with their husbands in the economic area (car, house, insurance, wife's employment), but there is no change in the total amount of power or influence they exert over their husbands.[52] Kligler's study also reports that middle-class working wives make significantly more decisions about "major purchases, loans, savings, and investments."[53] Hoffman found that although her total sample of working women did have more power than non-working women, when she matched the two samples for husband's occupation and age and number of children the difference disappeared.[54] It is only through more carefully controlled studies comparing working with non-working wives that we will be able to ascertain how the wife's employment affects decision-making.

Hoffman also found that the wife's acceptance or rejection of the ideology of male dominance plays an important role in the relationship between wife's employment and the relative amount of wife's power. She concludes that ". . . whereas working may exert a pressure toward her increased power in the family, the male dominance ideology might lead her to become actually less dominant than before in order to compensate for the threat offered by the sheer fact of her employment."[55] Hoffman's more sophisticated approach to the study of this problem suggests that the relationship between employment and authority within the family is quite complex, and for this reason the rather crude data that are available up to now seem contradictory and are inconclusive.

In the area of marital adjustment, Powell found that only working mothers of adolescents had lower marital adjustment than non-working mothers; there was

---

[49] *Ibid.*, p. 204.

[50] Lois Wladis Hoffman, "Parental Power Relations and the Division of Household Tasks," in Nye and Hoffman, eds., *op. cit.*, p. 229.

[51] Robert O. Blood, Jr., and Donald M. Wolfe, *Husbands and Wives* (New York: The Free Press, 1960), pp. 40–41.

[52] "The Husband-Wife Relationship," in Nye and Hoffman, eds., *op. cit.*, p. 294.

[53] Deborah H. Kligler, "The Effects of the Employment of Married Women on Husband and Wife Roles," Ph.D. dissertation, Yale University, 1954.

[54] Hoffman, "Parental Power Relations and the Division of Household Tasks," in Nye and Hoffman, eds., *op. cit.*, pp. 229–30.

[55] *Ibid.*, pp. 226–29.

no relationship between employment and marital adjustment among mothers in other stages of the life-cycle.[56] Since many mothers of adolescents enter (or return to) the labor force at that stage in their life-cycle, it may be that marital maladjustment existing prior to their employment was one of the factors motivating them to work. Locke found no difference in the proportion of happily married or divorced wives who were employed, and in Blood and Wolfe's study the average satisfaction scores of working and non-working wives were also similar.[57]

It seems, then, that the only clear consequence of wives' employment is a more equal allocation of household tasks to both spouses. Working women tend to do less of what is traditionally considered to be "woman's work," while their husbands tend to take up some of this work. In the families of working women sex ceases to be the only criterion for the distribution of household tasks and other activities, while ability and interest play a more important part.

When married women share in the performance of the instrumental role, it is possible that their husbands may have to share in the performance of the expressive role. There seems to be some evidence that fathers do tend to become more involved with child rearing and the socialization of their children when their wives work. This decrease in the segregation of masculine and feminine roles inside and outside the home may indicate "the emergence of many new forms of complementarity between husbands and wives."[58]

SOCIALIZATION FOR OCCUPATIONAL ROLES

When parents socialize their children they try to implant in them the values, skills, attitudes, and qualities that they judge necessary for the appropriate and successful performance of adult roles. The experiences of parents suggest to them the qualities that should prove valuable and helpful to their children. Since the occupational role is the most important one in the lives of American males, we would expect fathers to transmit to their sons those qualities, skills, and attitudes that they found most helpful in their own occupational experiences. Indeed, Aberle and Naegele found that middle-class fathers tend to prepare their sons to enter some kind of middle-class occupation—any professional or business career—while most of them prefer and expect their daughters to marry.[59]

The Choice of Values to Transmit

Since occupational positions are to a large extent achieved in our society and not inherited, middle-class fathers can best help their sons by equipping them with high educational and occupational aspirations and by developing in them the kinds

---

[56] Kathryn S. Powell, "Family Variables," in Nye and Hoffman, eds., *op. cit.*, pp. 232–33.
[57] Blood and Wolfe, *op. cit.*, p. 101.
[58] Foote, *op. cit.*, p. 329.
[59] David F. Aberle and Kaspar D. Naegele, "Middle-Class Fathers' Occupational Role and Attitudes toward Children," in Norman W. Bell and Ezra F. Vogel, eds., *A Modern Introduction to the Family* (New York: The Free Press, 1960), p. 130.

of skills and abilities that would be instrumental in their obtaining, retaining, and succeeding in middle-class occupations. In Aberle and Naegele's sample, the characteristics that middle-class fathers were concerned about and tried to foster and reinforce in their children were exactly those characteristics generally thought to be desirable for success in middle-class occupations.[60] According to Aberle and Naegele the "ideal typical successful adult male in the middle-class occupational role should be responsible, show initiative, be competent, be aggressive, be capable of meeting competition. He should be emotionally stable and capable of self-restraint."[61]

In comparing middle-class and working-class parents, Kohn found that "there are characteristic clusters of value choice in the two social classes: working-class parental values center on conformity to external proscriptions, middle-class parental values on self-direction."[62] In Kohn's sample, middle-class fathers tend more often to value consideration and self-control while working-class fathers tend more often to value obedience.[63] Similarly, Kohn points out that middle-class mothers more often value curiosity, happiness, consideration, and self-control, while working-class mothers more often emphasize obedience, neatness, and cleanliness in their children.[64]

Kohn explains the class differences in the values transmitted to children (especially sons) on the basis of the differential abilities and skills required by middle-class and working-class occupations. In order to make decisions, to assume responsibility, and to get ahead in middle-class occupations a person must be able to rely on himself, while in order to follow directions and to adapt to one's subordinate position in working-class occupations a person must be more amenable to direct supervision.[65] In brief, Kohn suggests that occupational differences contribute to different emphases in the middle class and the working class. Within the former there is a greater need for self-direction; within the latter there is a greater need for following rules. As a result, it may be more advantageous for a middle-class child to be trained in self-reliance and for a working-class child to be trained to follow externally imposed rules.

There are also indications that the values considered necessary by middle-class parents for their children's occupational success tend to adapt to changing requirements for such success. For example, it seems that even in positions of industrial leadership a shift in emphasis has recently occurred from managers notable for "individual risk, innovation, dominance and self-reliance" to men in tune with "the ideal image of the manager as the skillful organizer of cooperative efforts."[66]

[60] *Ibid.*, p. 132.
[61] *Ibid.*
[62] Melvin Kohn, "Social Class and Parent-Child Relationships: An Interpretation," *American Journal of Sociology,* Vol. 68 (January, 1963), p. 475.
[63] Melvin Kohn, "Social Class and Parental Values," *American Journal of Sociology,* Vol. 64 (January, 1959), p. 341.
[64] *Ibid.*, p. 345.
[65] Kohn, "Social Class and Parent-Child Relationships," *op. cit.*, p. 476.
[66] Reinhard Bendix, *Work and Authority in Industry* (New York: John Wiley, 1956), p. 441.

As Hughes writes, "there is plenty of evidence that the model businessman is seen as a team worker rather than as a person who goes it alone."[67] These trends seem to suggest that, in addition to self-reliance, such skills as interpersonal competence, ability to cooperate, and "getting along with others" would also be instrumental in obtaining, retaining, and succeeding in middle-class occupations. And, in fact, middle-class parents apparently train their children to develop such characteristics.[68]

While sons seem to be adequately prepared to play a middle-class or working-class occupational role, girls in both social classes are not usually socialized for occupational roles but rather for becoming more desirable in the marriage market-place.[69] As a result they do not usually develop the appropriate personality for successful performance in occupational roles; this perhaps helps to explain some of the difficulties girls often encounter in the occupational world. Daughters of working mothers, however, are better prepared to play an occupational role than daughters of non-working mothers. They are also likelier to consider combining an occupational role with their familial roles of wife and mother. This is probably the result of two main factors: their mothers give them a greater opportunity to develop such characteristics as responsibility, independence, self-reliance, and dominance;[70] and they can identify with their working mothers who act as models.[71]

Other evidence that underlines the importance of socialization experiences for the successful performance of adult work roles is provided by studies of manual workers who attempted to become businessmen. Mayer and Goldstein found that when blue-collar workers entered the world of business practically all either failed altogether within two years or failed to make their business a profitable undertaking.[72] Apparently neither their early socialization experiences nor their previous work experiences had equipped them with the motives and abilities needed to succeed in business: the ability to plan and decide "rationally," the ability to defer gratifications (to define business as a challenge to be met and not as a short-range satisfaction-granting enterprise), and high achievement motivation.[73]

[67] Everett C. Hughes, "The Making of a Physician," in *Men and Their Work* (New York: The Free Press, 1958), p. 124.

[68] Evelyn Duvall, "Conceptions of Parenthood," *American Journal of Sociology*, Vol. 52 (November, 1946), pp. 193–203.

[69] Kohn, "Social Class and Parental Values," *op. cit.*, p. 344; Aberle and Naegele, *op. cit.*, p. 132.

[70] Alberta E. Siegel, Lois M. Stolz, Ethel A. Hitchcock, and Jean Adamson, "Dependence and Independence in Children," in Nye and Hoffman, eds., *op. cit.*, pp. 67–81; Prodipto Roy, "Adolescent Roles: Rural-Urban Differentials," in *ibid.*, pp. 165–81.

[71] Lorraine Dittrich Eyde, *Work Values and Background Factors as Predictors of Women's Desire to Work*, Ohio State University, College of Commerce and Administration, Bureau of Business Research Monograph No. 108 (Columbus: Ohio State University, 1962), p. 47; Riley *et al.*, *op. cit.*, pp. 33–37.

[72] Kurt B. Mayer and Sidney Goldstein, "Manual Workers as Small Businessmen," in Arthur B. Shostak and William Gomberg, eds., *Blue-Collar World* (Englewood Cliffs, N.J.: Prentice-Hall, 1964), p. 547.

[73] *Ibid.*, p. 549.

The kinds of skills, abilities, and characteristics that are fostered in a child during socialization prepare him (or her) for a certain range of activities and occupations; unless some kind of unusual experiences and influences impinge upon the individual, he will find it difficult to function in those types of occupations for which he has not been socialized by his parents.

SUMMARY

In reviewing the relationship between business and the American family we have focused primarily upon the impact that business has had upon family structure. Since work sometimes flows over into social occasions, we have noted some of the pressures upon the wives and families of executives to make adjustments to certain business demands. In addition, such matters as work transfers, business travel, and night, weekend, or holiday work also require adjustments on the part of the workers' families.

At one time, within the American farm family, the roles of farmer, husband, and father were carried out by the man within the same spatial area and were closely interrelated. Technological advances, however, have led to extensive urbanization and have differentiated the role of worker and family member; work is now seldom carried out as a family enterprise in which the father is the head of the family and of the work team. It is almost always carried out within a separately organized business enterprise in which individual family members work apart from other members of the family.

Other changes of the past century have been a rising divorce rate and an increasing liberality in sexual mores. Some have regarded this as a sign of family breakdown and moral decay, but most social scientists interpret the evidence as a transition in family structure that relates to the changing structure of business and technology in the society as a whole.

Although women have increasingly been entering the work force—including married women with young children—their basic patterns of employment are still quite different from those of men. Many married women who work interrupt their careers for child rearing, and many others engage in part-time work. Precisely because of this continuing emphasis upon the marital and familial roles of women, they have not yet achieved equality in business.

According to popular conceptions, the employment of working mothers has deleterious effects upon the personality development of children and upon the husband-wife relationship. The research evidence, however, fails to confirm these conceptions. It is important to consider the influence of other variables, such as social class and attitudes of husband and wife toward the wife's employment, before we can begin to specify with greater confidence what the consequences of the woman's employment are.

We have also seen that the evolution of business demands for labor require the adolescent to postpone his entry into an occupational role. He is therefore often unable to enter into an earner role within the family. As a result, the traditional morality that calls for a man to be able to support his family before he marries and that forbids premarital sexual relations is challenged. Certain changes have resulted, including a greater acceptance of early marriage, even when the man is not playing the occupational-earner role, and a greater acceptance of premarital sexual relationships under certain conditions.

In examining business advertising practices geared toward the adolescent market, it is not clear whether business was furthering a split between adolescent and parental tastes or merely capitalizing upon differences. It may very well be that both are taking place. The impact of business advertising upon family structure, directly and indirectly, deserves closer study.

Two of the most basic elements of the relationship between business and the family are these: (1) the fundamental role played by business in income distribution has a pervasive influence upon the structure and style of living of the family and underlies a great deal of the discussion in the literature about social class differences; and (2) the fundamental role played by the family in the socialization of children has a pervasive influence upon the attitudes, interests, and motivations of those who are entering the business world and plays an important role in the career decisions made by individuals and in their relative success or failure in the work world.

SELECTED READINGS

THEODORE CAPLOW, *The Sociology of Work* (Minneapolis: University of Minnesota Press, 1954). McGraw-Hill published a paperback edition in 1963. This book focuses on such general questions as the development of separate occupational groupings, their prestige, and the consequences of membership in them. Chapters are included on "Occupations of Women" and "Occupation and Family."

MELVIN L. KOHN, "Social Class and Parent-Child Relationships: An Interpretation," *American Journal of Sociology*, Vol. 68 (January, 1963), pp. 471–80. An examination of the differences in values of middle-class and working-class parents, the origin of these differences, the consequences of such parental values upon the socialization of children for different types of occupational roles, and the consequences of these different parental values for the parent-child relationship among middle-class and working-class families. (Reprinted in *Marriage, Family, and Society, infra.*)

F. IVAN NYE AND LOIS WLADIS HOFFMAN, *The Employed Mother in America* (Chicago: Rand McNally, 1963); see especially the chapters by Hoffman, "Effects on Children: Summary and Discussion," and by Nye, "Adjustment of the Mother: Summary and a Frame of Reference." A summary and creative evaluation of ten research studies dealing with effects of maternal employment upon children. The findings are evaluated in the light of methodological and theoretical considerations and are summarized under four major variables: full-time versus part-time employment; age of child; sex of child; mother's attitude toward employment.

Nye's review of the adjustment of the working mother begins with the conclusions of the research articles in the book and attempts to formulate a sociological conceptualization of maternal employment.

TALCOTT PARSONS, "The American Family: Its Relations to Personality and to the Social Structure," in Parsons and Robert F. Bales, *Family, Socialization and Interaction Process* (New York: The Free Press, 1955). Parsons' chapter reviews some of the changes taking place in the American family, notes the differences of opinion among social scientists of the meanings of these changes, and discusses such issues as the "isolation" of the American nuclear family and the interdependence of the occupational system and the American kinship system.

HYMAN RODMAN, ED., *Marriage, Family, and Society: A Reader* (New York: Random House, 1965). The book contains some very clearly written and concise summaries of the sociological research on the family in several areas, including dating relations and sex roles, mate selection, husband-wife relations, and parent-child relations. The material it includes on the changing American family, the role of women, and the lower-class family is of special relevance to this essay.

CLARK E. VINCENT, "Family Spongia: The Adaptive Function," *Journal of Marriage and the Family*, Vol. 28 (February, 1966), pp. 29–36. This article emphasizes the extent to which the family must adapt to social changes associated with industrialization. Power to resist changes that might have a major impact upon families seems to be lacking. Internal adaptation to the needs of family members is discussed as well as external adaptation to the demands of other institutions.

chapter 11

BUSINESS AND THE MEANING OF WORK

ARTHUR B. SHOSTAK *is a noted young sociologist whose investigations in industry, including especially the world of blue-collar workers, have made him very sensitive to the complexities in popular, managerial, and academic views concerning the meaning of work. Two basic attitudes toward work were brought to the attention of Edward Kennedy while on tour through a Massachusetts factory during his campaign for a seat in the United States Senate. "I understand you've never worked a day in your life," a worker challenged Kennedy. While the startled candidate mumbled an inaudible reply the worker added, "Well, let me tell you, you haven't missed a thing." The anecdote nicely highlights the fact that work in America has many meanings and involves a great range of our fundamental values.*

After a careful review of both qualitative discussions and empirical research bearing upon the employment experience of Americans, Professor Shostak realistically concludes that the interplay of factors operating in the workplace is so complex that the impact of private employers on the meaning of work for employees is not subject to any simple and all-inclusive formulation of the type frequently offered in sensational, best-selling exposés. His thesis is that the meaning of work is relative: attitudes and responses to it vary over time with specific changes in economic circumstances and among particular categories of employees possessing varying personal characteristics, backgrounds, and experiences and according to changes in more general American values.

While employers are certainly not solely responsible for the meaning of work, Professor Shostak makes it plain that businessmen have not been attentive to the opportunity—through the design of organizations and particularly the pay, skill, and status hierarchies these involve—to modify their employees' outlook toward work.

A pervasive engineering outlook and a view of employees as "units of production" have blinded employers to the opportunity for restoring to work the significant rewards once characteristic of many of the crafts, callings, and occupations that have been lost in the course of advancing job specialization, levelled skill hierarchies, and meaningless titles. Human relations programs and sensitive supervisors, he writes, cannot compensate for faulty structures. The effects of low motivation and low job involvement among workers are therefore as consequential for managers concerned with productivity and quality as for workers concerned with self-esteem, dignity, and opportunities for meaningful advancement.

In reading Professor Shostak's essay, the student should consider how the rapid growth in public employment, already underway in the late 1960's, will provide different experiences for the millions of Americans in a "pluralistic economy." Other questions and considerations include the following:

1. What implications for the meaning of work will flow from the increasing educational achievements of managers, many of whom will have had sophisticated training in the behavioral sciences? What circumstances will determine whether the tools developed in these sciences will be used to manipulate workers or to improve opportunities for enhanced involvement in work?

2. In his historical overview, Professor Shostak indicates that the meaning of work for Americans has undergone a systematic, if slow, evolution. But he implies that managers' attitudes toward their work forces have remained fairly stable despite fad-like changes in personnel techniques adopted over time. How might we account for this stability in managerial perspectives?

3. Professor Kuhn, in his essay on labor, told us that, as a consequence of union policies and legal developments, workers are coming to enjoy proprietary rights in their jobs. What kinds of evidence might one consider in examining the effect of this development upon the worker's view of his job?

4. Imagine a time in the future when, according to many social critics, Americans will come to be more alike in their individual backgrounds and outlooks as a consequence of prolonged prosperity, integration, increasing orders of income equality, ethnic "homogenization," and related trends. Assume further that the view of employees as production units continues to be a characteristic one among employers. How, under these circumstances, would one modify Professor Shostak's analysis?

ARTHUR B. SHOSTAK   \   THE IMPACT OF BUSINESS
                            ON THE MEANING OF WORK

While men spend nearly half their waking hours at work, few appear to ponder the very significant impact work has on them or the impact business has on their work; in this essay both matters will be explored. Special attention will be paid to the efforts the American business community has made over time to shape the various meanings of work.

INTRODUCTION

Several elaborate ideologies already contain as principal elements definitions of what the meaning of work is or should be; Table 1 capsulizes ten such approaches.[1] One of the most influential ideologies is that of the Mayoists, followers of the sociologist Elton Mayo, father of the "human relations theory." Mayoists contend that the greatest value of work is its ability to promote both social harmony and the leadership of a rational business elite. Work does not always fulfill this promise, they say, because irrational notions popular with the masses keep workplace discontents alive, but business can still triumph over such discontent and assume its appropriate leadership in the political community if it will only convert the place of work into a vital center of interest for everyone, all day and every day.

Equally provocative is the ideology of the alienation theorists and the mass society critics. These analysts generally find nothing especially valuable about work; in fact, they condemn it as nearly or even completely meaningless. They hold businessmen responsible for a conscious elimination from work of most, if not of all, possibility for significant human growth. As for an ideal relationship between work and life, this school does refer cryptically to notions of self-actualization and ego integrity, but its main preoccupation is an attempt to show that ancient values are being lost, that the workplace suffers under a hierarchy of malevolent "power elite" types, and that the likelihood of reform or progress in these or any equally basic matters is limited.

Unfortunately, the Mayoists and those who decry mass society (or mass calamity), like the other schools outlined in Table 1, suffer three major short-

[1] Note that Table 1 contains only a sample of all the possibly relevant schools; the followers of Veblen who stress craftsmanship, those of Dewey who stress life training, and several other schools are absent. For related commentary on the ideologies of management in the course of industrialization, see Reinhard Bendix, *Work and Authority in Industry* (New York: Harper & Row, 1963). Writings of the chief exponents mentioned in the table are cited in succeeding footnotes.

Table 1. The Meaning of Work in Various Ideologies.

SCHOOLS (CHIEF EXPONENT)	WORK PROBLEMS	WORKER PROFILE	CHIEF VICTIM	CHIEF VILLAIN	REFORM PRESCRIPTION
Marxist (Engels)	Worker is cruelly exploited	Slave, angry or brutalized	Worker	Capitalist	Communism, through revolt
Socialists (Crosland)	Worker is subtly exploited	Prole, angry or coopted	Worker	Capitalist (individualist)	Socialism, through evolution
Mass society critics (Goodman)	Work has no meaning, robs man of manhood	Cipher, empty or disorganized	Society	Elite (patrician)	Humanistic revisionism, through education
Neo-Freudians (Fromm)	Work is boring, deadening, and emasculating	Puppet, sick or coopted	Society	Status quo oriented, opinion molder	Humanist industrialism, through education
Pro-laborites (Tannenbaum)	Work has been atomized	Lonely or retreatist	Worker	Production-obsessed managers	Union paternalism
Mayoists (Mayo)	Workers' social needs are overlooked	Man-child, stunted and lonely	Worker	"Economic man" champions among managers	Corporate paternalism
Organization analysts (Argyris)	Employees are treated as children, not adults	Man-child, stunted and cowed	Employees (entire labor force)	"Theory X" authoritarians among managers	"Theory Y"; co-determination; decentralization
Organization critics (Whyte, Jr.)	Social ethic has displaced the work ethic	Pawn, smiling and uncertain	Employees (entire labor force)	"Other-directed" types among managers	Covert fight from within; disguised resistance
Technocrats (Taylor)	Work has not been rationalized by "science"	Naïve, untutored, and adaptable	Employees (entire labor force)	Elitists of an antisocial persuasion	Adoption of scientific management; operations research
Conservatives (Buckley, Jr.)	Work lost its dignity, is now a racket	Child, misled and spoiled	Society	Misguided bureaucrat and labor union "bosses"	New respect for craftsmanship; repeal of labor legislation

comings. First, they exaggerate the real significance of a single facet of work, whether this be work's power to create harmony or its power to dehumanize. Critics of the Mayoists point out, for example, that loneliness may merely be a cost in the struggle toward rational self-development. Divided loyalties may be the surest guarantee against totalitarianism. And discontent may be the very price of progress itself.[2] Second, the ideological schools give business too much credit for shaping events. Business is less powerful, less purposeful, and less conscious of its impact on work (and on life) than they suggest. Third, the schools indulge in ideological excess. Many of their blanket judgments about work—that it is "entirely without positive meaning or psychic contribution" or "thoroughly banal and dehumanizing," for example—deserve considerable skepticism.

None of the ideological systems presented in Table 1 is likely to seem completely convincing to the modern student of work. While making use of them as guides to observation, it seems better to shift our attention to more concrete evidence concerning the reactions of men to their work and to proceed inductively. To this end, this essay is divided into four major parts. The first reviews the meaning work has had in the course of American history, and stresses the ability of men to make of work what they choose. The second discusses individual variations in the personal meaning of work. The third concentrates on the impact business has today on three major components of the meaning of work: job involvement, job satisfaction, and job motivation. The fourth part recommends alterations in conventional perspectives of work. Special attention is paid throughout to the many gaps in research that make tentativeness advisable and further exploration indispensable.

HISTORICAL MEANINGS OF WORK[3]

When asked what he considered life's most valuable activities, Sigmund Freud tersely recommended *"Lieben und Arbeiten"* (love and work).[4] The *Arbeit* in his formula, however, was something very special: it was ascetic, arduous, com-

[2] Clark Kerr and Lloyd H. Fisher, "Plant Sociology: The Elite and the Aborigines," in *Common Frontiers of the Social Sciences,* Mirra Komarovsky, ed. (New York: The Free Press, 1957), p. 309. A classic essay of model quality, the Kerr-Fisher discussion of the Mayoist school of human relations makes plain the extraordinary "vision" that underlies this managerial ideology, a vision that would have us remake society in the corporate image. For field reports on the vision realized, see Alan Harrington, *Life in the Crystal Palace* (New York: Knopf, 1959); W. H. Auden's short poem, "The Unknown Citizen," in *Collected Poems of W. H. Auden* (New York: Random House, 1945); Robert Graham, *The Annals of Logan* (New York: Holt, Rinehart and Winston, 1961).

[3] In this essay "work" refers to what Elliot Jacques calls "employment work," where an employer specifies the functions performed and pays a wage or salary for the services rendered. This excludes the "work" of housewives and of most people who are self-employed (independent lawyers, doctors, artists, and craftsmen, for example); it concentrates attention on blue- and white-collar members of formal industrial organizations. In keeping with the general absence of literature on shift workers, women workers, and

pulsive, and absolutely pleasureless activity. The French utopian Charles Fourier, on the other hand, regarded work as an aesthetic means of self-expression. Believing men by nature creative and active, he argued the need to match men and jobs, and to vary work content in such a way as to make work both attractive and pleasurable. The position of Karl Marx falls between those represented by Freud and Fourier. Marx, whose writings preceded those of Freud, held that work could be rewarding for the individual in the way that the work of a creative artist is rewarding, as a manifestation of human skill, determination, and power. However, even such liberating and educating work could not be regarded as an agreeable, spontaneous activity; the element of painful effort in work was undeniable. And so the controversy has raged. Down through the decades sages have wrestled with the "true" meaning of work—even as certain vested interests have strained to establish other meanings more appropriate to protecting their profits of the moment.

Adriano Tilgher, a distinguished pioneer in the study of work, has traced a fascinating history of change in the cultural meanings of the concept from Biblical times to the 1920's, the decade in which he wrote.[5] Tilgher's analysis suggests that the concept of work has undergone three major historical changes. It has lost its pre-Christian association with degradation and with the slavery of a subhuman species, a cultural meaning once common to the Greeks, tempered somewhat by the ancient Hebrews, and finally abandoned by Renaissance philosophers. It has also lost much of its religious significance, a quality stressed by medieval philosophers, tempered by the Calvinists, and abandoned by most contemporary commentators. Finally, work has lost most of its utopian significance, its key role in the formation of character and in the maintenance of an ideal society, whether of Marxian, Fourierian, or Comteian design. Currently, work is regarded as an activity in which man is free to find dignity or not, as he chooses, with his choice reflecting secular as well as sacred constraints. Work is no longer thought to

---

male Negro workers, the word workers should be understood as referring to male blue-collar Caucasian dayshift production workers of unskilled, semi-skilled, and skilled status. "Employees" refers to all full-time members of business enterprises, from the president to the workers, the stock clerks, and the janitors. "Meaning of work" refers both to the understanding of work encouraged by business and the understanding of work that exists as a common denominator in the minds of adults who work, children who pretend they are working, and retired persons capable of reviewing their work experience as a completed whole.

[4] As quoted in Sol W. Ginsburg, *A Psychiatrist's View on Social Issues* (New York: Columbia University Press, 1963), p. 191. See also Norman O. Brown, *Life Against Death* (New York: Modern Library, 1960); Philip Rieff, *Freud: The Mind of the Moralist* (New York: Viking Press, 1959). Of exceptional value is an essay by David Riesman entitled "The Themes of Work and Play in the Structure of Freud's Thought," in Riesman's *Individualism Reconsidered* (New York: The Free Press, 1954).

[5] *Homo Faber: Work Through the Ages* (Chicago: Henry Regnery, 1964). Edward Gross, in his introduction, notes that "the story of work is not one of constant and inevitable improvement." Also valuable for its historic perspective is Goetz A. Briefs, *The Proletarian: A Challenge to Western Civilization* (New York: McGraw-Hill, 1937).

be the only or even the best way to gain nourishment, to test one's character, or to attain happiness.

The Meaning of Work in America

The progressive democratization and the secularization of work form an important part of the background of the meaning of work in America. The current concept of work is better understood if we trace changes in its meaning through eight distinct periods in the nation's history; this evolution is summarized in Table 2. It is important to note in each period the character of the labor force at the time, the stage of the industrialization process, and the model of man endorsed by business leaders and their allies.[6] The dates in the table are approximate, since cultural meanings are particularly difficult to pinpoint in time. The shorter and shorter time spans covered by the successive periods attest to the heightened pace of change in America. Anachronisms, cultural lags, and occupational and workforce heterogeneity lead to a persistence of certain meanings across periods; primacy, rather than purity, guided the classification. Some notes on each of the periods in the table follow here.

Pre-Industrial Meanings. From 1630 to the beginning of our Industrial Revolution in 1840, work had the Malthusian meaning in America that it retains today in three-quarters of the world—it was believed to be a grim and natural necessity. The opprobrium directed at idlers by the governors of the energetic Jamestown Colony and the association between idleness and the devil traced by the fanatical Salem Puritans are characteristic. Relatively stable and secure, work reinforced mores, customs, and accepted habits. It was thoroughly integrated with prevailing life patterns: men entered the workforce early; birth determined class and status; life was short; and retirement from work was generally unknown. The operative model of man encouraged by the opinion-molders of the day was that of Subsistence Man, or man with good reason to believe that without work he might not survive.

Industrial Take-off. Other kinds of work soon became available in the new

---

[6] On the conscious use of business advertising to affect ideas about work, see John M. Blum, "Exegesis of the Gospel of Work: Success and Satisfaction in Recent American Culture," in *Trends in Modern Society*, Clarence Morris, ed. (Philadelphia: University of Pennsylvania Press, 1962), pp. 26, 27. See also Daniel J. Boorstein, *The Image, or What Happened to the American Dream* (New York: Atheneum, 1962), and Bendix, *op. cit.* Especially useful is Francis X. Sutton *et al., The American Business Creed* (New York: Schocken, 1962); on p. 297 the authors note ". . . the mass media are in the hands of big business, run by businessmen subject to the same ideology-producing forces as other businessmen, and thus, naturally, exponents of the same ideology." Nels Anderson's view is that "the real analyst of work and the changer of its character has been the engineer or the manager having responsibility for technological supervision. [They] have not been concerned about the social, psychological, or philosophical unit meanings. Their attention has been focused on performance, output, and unit costs. [In] the course of defining and refining tasks they have profoundly influenced life outside their workplaces." *Dimensions of Work* (New York: David McKay, 1965), p. 6.

Table 2. The Changing Meaning of Work in America.

PERIOD	MEANING OF WORK	MODEL OF MAN	BUSINESS GOAL	SPECIAL CIRCUMSTANCES
Pre-industrial: colonial to 1840	Grim necessity; religious obligation	Subsistence man	Creation of an agricultural surplus for trading	Pre-industrial; agricultural base; wars and want
Industrial take-off: 1840–60	Advancement opportunity	Ambitious man	Development of an industrial work-force; productivity highs	"The work ethic" plus the "rags-to-riches" ideology
Industrial take-hold: 1860–1900	Economic opportunity	Economic man	Control of labor force through wage manipulation	Civil War "boom" followed by recessions; triumph of industrial north over agrarian south
Industrial scientism: 1900–20	Exercise in applied logic; man as tool	Scientific man	Mastery of engineering applications, use of logic and science	Frederick Taylor's scientific management program; boom times
Industrial paternalism: 1920–35	Dependency opportunity; surfeit of rewards	Social man (lonely child)	New influence over worker as a social being	Company union movement; weakness of AFL; popularity of human relations approach
Industrial reconstruction: 1935–40	Self-esteem support (token of grace)	Anchor-seeking man	Economic survival	The Great Depression; collapse of company unions; upsurge of AFL and CIO
Industrial patriotism: 1940–45	Patriotic enlistment	Service-rendering patriotic man	Contribution to war effort; profits and productivity	Second world war; liberalization of employment practices
Industrial quietism: 1945 to present	Security insurance; "other-directed" image prop	Security-conscious materialistic man	Stabilization of market; introduction of advanced automation	Decline of organized labor's power, persistence of unemployment; teen-age and Negro pressure for jobs and for advancement possibilities

nation, work that did not rely on the subsistence agriculture of the colonial masses and the craft and self-employment of the more affluent urban residents. After 1840, the nation began to capitalize in earnest on its abundant natural resources, its abundant human resources (a surplus of immigrant labor, the genius of inventors like Whitney), and its ability to "borrow" technological innovations pioneered abroad. While work retained its close association with bare economic survival, the locus of action shifted more and more from the land to the city, and the tempo of life quickened.

Work gradually came to have a new meaning. By 1860 work in the United States was associated with personal opportunity, partly through the efforts of the business-allied "public relations" men of the day who proclaimed a "gospel of self-help" in which work was held up as a secular creed. Work gave the new immigrant his citizenship, his right to eat, and his identity. Indeed, the "work ethic," our secularized adaptation of Protestant and specifically Calvinist theology, assured the Ellis Island immigrant that industrial commitment and sacrifice were right and proper. The truly worthy, he was taught, were especially rewarded here on earth, while all could expect some measure of divine recompense for earthly anguish. The operative model of man encouraged by the business propagandists of the laissez faire economy was that of Ambitious Man, man freed from feudal caste bonds and challenged to improve his personal lot through hard work.

Industrial Take-hold. The late 1800's saw the establishment of giant corporations and new family fortunes, along with the conversion of the previously self-employed—some 80 per cent of the labor force in the early 1800's—into a proletariat of wage and low-salaried workers. Work lost the links it had had in colonial times to bare survival, and it also lost some of its associations with wishful and grandiose Horatio Alger-like ambition. Instead, for the grandchildren of the Ellis Island immigrants, work became closely associated with small-scale economic advancement and the quest for personal security.

Business first moved at this time into large-scale, blatant manipulation of the labor force. By focusing employee attention on economic conditions, it helped shape the predominant meaning of work at the time, much as various public figures with large business holdings—like the Jamestown governors, or the wealthier ministers of the self-help gospel persuasion—had done earlier. Aware of disunity in the world's largest industrial mass, business used pay scale variations both to tie the masses to the factory and to set men against one another: pay was divisively awarded in accordance with age, sex, and ethnic origin. The financier Jay Gould boasted at the time, possibly not incorrectly, that he could buy one half of the labor force to murder the other.

Industrial Scientism. Business was ripe in the early 1900's for Frederick Taylor's new gospel of scientific management. To be sure, certain business traditionalists grumbled and a critical congressional investigation resulted. But the initial resistance to Taylor's ideas, based partly on fears that the movement might mean a "democratization" of management (because of its emphasis on management as a service, one that could be learned by trainees), melted in the face of the gains allegedly possible if work were rationalized. The pro-engineering "progressive" branch of American business was quick to see in the scientific management of its work an answer to the perplexing problem of productivity plateaus, especially those based on surreptitious, employee-pegged, production norms. These business technocrats sought to have work now mean obedience to the dictates of logic and science; the slide rule and the stopwatch were to predominate.

Soon, work in large urban industrial complexes did come to mean systematization. The operative theoretic model of the worker, so sharply spoofed by Charlie Chaplin in "Modern Times," was that of Scientific Man, or man meshed with other instruments of production to maximize his total contribution to output. While workers were still recognizably concerned with wages (Henry Ford attracted as much attention by paying exceptionally high wages as he did by demonstrating the vast potential of part standardization and mass production), they were encouraged by business ideologists and their allies to be disciples to social physics, order, system, and "the one best way."

Industrial Paternalism. Most businessmen were soon disillusioned by the administrative complexities of scientific management; they were also perplexed by the ingenuity of workers at finding ways to deceive and escape the control of the managerial slide rule and stopwatch. In the late 1920's business began to experiment with new tactics in its uneasy campaign to make labor more efficient. Attention turned to vocational psychology, a new applied discipline that offered aid in matching the right employee to the job (the antithesis of Taylor's scientific management). Attention was also paid to the applied social psychology, or human relations theory, of Elton Mayo and his colleagues at the Harvard Business School, a subject that synthesized both psychological and management insights.

Guided especially by Mayo's insistence that men need to be positively associated in work with their fellows, business came to endorse still another model of man. Attention now focused on Social Man, man with a recognizable set of social and psychological as well as economic needs. With the aid of opinion-molders (columnists, speech-givers, and others), work for those in the employ of high-profit, well-established industrial giants came to mean "support" in a very paternalistic sense. Employer-employee relations reached a new degree of subtlety. Affluent in the "roaring twenties" as never before and intent on strengthening their new company unions, businesses enlarged the paternalistic functions of personnel departments and sought to foster the harmony emphasized by Mayo's school. At the (planted) request of company unions, personnel departments sought and often achieved the establishment by the company of showers and lockers, subsidized in-plant cafeterias, medical units, loan services, programs of after-hours sports and games, and, even in the early 1930's, counseling services!

Industrial Reconstruction. The Great Depression of the 1930's sharply curtailed corporate paternalism, even as the rivalry of the new CIO and the old AFL combined with a government ban on company unions to undo that once-elaborate movement. With more than 13 million Americans unemployed and unable to find a job, work took on meaning as a scarce cultural commodity. To avoid selling apples on street corners, masses of unemployed workers moved restlessly from city to city and from coast to coast, through "dust bowls" and ghost towns. Work came close to recapturing the meaning it had had before the Civil War, when the "work ethic" dominated. There was one important new variation, however; dreams of personal mobility and of self-made fortunes were now conspicuously absent. They had long since faded before business castes and cartel practices. The operative model of man was that of Anchor-seeker, man struggling to establish his moorings in a mad world he preferred to think he had not made. Reemployment was considered the only defense against a corrosive self-humiliation. Work was the key to self-esteem, to self-acceptance. While the song lyrics plaintively begged a "dime," the deepest-reaching cry of the day asked, "Hey Buddy, can you spare—a job?"[7]

Industrial Patriotism. The second world war ended the depression; boom times characterized the revitalized economy of our "arsenal of democracy." In a very few years workers, rather than work, became the scarce and indispensable "commodity." America needed production, and business and labor set out to provide it. Labor-management feuding was temporarily suspended, and both sides sought to control absenteeism, lateness, personnel turnover, and other threats to the war effort. Record-breaking workers explained publicly that "this is the least we can do for the boys at the front."

Although the patriotic motive for working hard was reinforced by the workers' post-depression pleasure at being wanted and valued, well paid from cost-plus contracts, and upgraded in skills and seniority, it was definitely the focus of attention as management attempted to shape the meaning of work to increase production even more. Work was carefully suffused with a patriotic appeal that went beyond anything previously known. The operative model of the worker fostered by business and government public relations specialists was that of the Service-rendering Patriot, man giving his all for a selfless cause larger than himself. Employee-pegged production norms fell by the wayside as productivity soared. The labor force took all the overtime offered. Technological advances followed one another with amazing speed. And a level of personal contribution and resource utilization was achieved that surpassed all previous standards.

Industrial Quietism. Since the end of the second world war, the predominant model of man encouraged by the business community has been that of Security-conscious Materialist. The widespread acceptance of this model is undoubtedly linked to the "invisible scar" of haunting depression memories, concern about the post-1954 recessions, and preoccupation with hard-core national and emergency levels of local unemployment. At present, work means especially material security. Business now wants to retain men in whom it has made a sizable training investment, and it supports what Arthur Ross has called "the new industrial feudalism." The contemporary worker in the United States is encouraged to seek a lifetime employment contract, much as the young men of Japan have always done. From the appeasement-oriented "gray-flannel type" to the consumption-

[7] So significant was employment that, as a daily substitute for unavailable work, many thousands of the unemployed lined up at employment offices that could offer no jobs. See E. Wight Bakke, *The Unemployed Worker,* The Institute of Human Relations (New Haven, Conn.: Yale University Press, 1940), Ch. 5.

oriented blue-collar worker, the dominant concern in employment appears to be a concern with the job as a property right and as a guarantee of security.

More will be said about the actual meaning of contemporary work and about the meaning favored by employers. Before moving on, however, it is important to underline the lesson grounded in this brief historical review: men—both businessmen and workingmen—have consciously manipulated the meaning of work, and the responsibility for the result is theirs. The meaning of work does not spring from some historic dialectic, cultural determinism, industrial imperative, or political conspiracy, but from the conscious molding of willful men.

INDIVIDUAL VARIATIONS IN THE MEANINGS ATTRIBUTED TO WORK

Considerable diversity of expectations and experience exists among contemporary workers, notwithstanding their common business-encouraged concern with security. As Table 3 suggests, concerns with work differ with the sex, age, and social class of the individual. For example, while male and female adolescents experience work in very similar ways, they differ in their experience from men and women in the next age bracket (20–35 years). Similarly, lower-middle-class men in the age bracket from 35 to 55 years value work especially for workplace friendships; they also grow increasingly concerned about finding themselves on an apparently permanent level of advancement. Lower-middle-class women in the same age bracket also value new adult relationships but are not preoccupied with job plateaus. Having returned to a second career on completion of the family's child-rearing phase, many such women view their work as a positive advance.

This basic pattern, complex as it already is, would have to be qualified even further to reflect the way the meaning of work varies according to an individual's race and religion. Membership in the Negro race, for example, reduces the range of jobs open to an individual. Among middle-class Negroes, accordingly, the accent on security is great; civil service jobs are sought as much for the security they promise as for the freedom from racial discrimination that exists within the government. In the lower class, the classic association of sex roles with work roles becomes problematic; Negro women may secure steady employment while Negro men may be condemned to an almost daily hunt for work in the "irregular economy" of odd jobs. In the upper class, the status, power, and income associated with the professions is disproportionately great; Negro physicians, dentists, and lawyers constitute a much-envied elite inside the Negro community. Work, in short, has many particular caste, enclave, or ghetto meanings for Negro-Americans, meanings largely foreign to the experience of the larger community of Caucasians.

Religion impinges upon the meaning of work. For example, the range of occupational attainments is seriously conditioned by discrimination. Jews are excluded from the management of many banks and utilities; Catholics and the members of various Protestant sects are barred from many "blue-chip" concerns. Preoccupation with security varies thereby with religious affiliation. Secondly, published data suggest that Protestants are more vocationally ambitious than Catho-

Table 3. Stages in the Meaning of Work for White Urban Dwellers

	LOWER WORKING CLASS (Operators and kindred workers; service workers; laborers, except farm and mine: $3,000-$6,000 per annum)	UPPER WORKING CLASS (Craftsmen, foremen, and kindred; some service workers: $6,000-$9,000 per annum)	LOWER MIDDLE CLASS (Clerical and kindred sales workers: $3,000-$12,000 per annum)	UPPER MIDDLE CLASS (Professional, technical, and kindred workers, managers, officials: $8,000-$20,000 per annum)
MALE Adolescent	ECONOMIC SUPPORT — Aid to parents; freedom from parents		CHARACTER GUIDANCE; COLLEGE SUPPORT	
20-35	PEAK AND PLATEAU		CAREER TAKEOFF — Confirmation of public acceptance	Confirmation of promise
35-55	PLATEAU — Personal valuation; ego orientation	Skill valuation; achievement orientation	PEAK AND PLATEAU — Social valuation; affability orientation	Career valuation; life-scheme orientation
55 plus	SECURITY CAPTIVE — Keep the job at all costs		CAREER PHASEOUT — Preparation for retirement	
FEMALE Adolescent	ECONOMIC SUPPORT — Aid to parents; self-enhancement		CHARACTER GUIDANCE; COLLEGE SUPPORT	
20-35	ECONOMIC SUPPORT — Aid to parents; peer friendships		CAREER TRYOUTS — Premarriage accent on challenge	
35-55	"EMPTY NEST" RETURN TO WORK — Economic support; search for friendship		"EMPTY NEST" CAREER ACCELERATION — Accent on service; response to "Feminine Mystique"	
55 plus	AFFILIATION CAPTIVE — Need to be with "the girls"		CAREER PHASEOUT — Preparation for retirement	

lics.[8] Finally, in the lower and working classes, the association of sex roles with work roles again becomes uncertain for members of particular religions. Some Catholic women, for example, are torn between a quasi-religious traditionalism that encourages them to stay at home and the economic realities of large families that make second incomes valuable or even necessary.

In sum, the meaning of work for a particular individual is conditioned by much that he brings with him to his first job—his personal history, character, identification, psyche, and values. All these aspects of the individual are in turn influenced by the social order of which business is a part, and through them business has a secondary impact on the meaning of work. Only if we take into account general changes in the meaning of work related to the milieu or to environmental pressures, as well as the individual's personal variability, are we in a position to appraise the primary impact of business on the contemporary meaning of work.

THE IMPACT OF BUSINESS ON THE MEANING OF WORK

The contemporary sociologist Thomas M. Lodahl distinguishes among three components of the meaning of work: job involvement, man's incorporation of work into his life; job satisfaction, man's appraisal of the social and material rewards of work; and job motivation, man's response to challenge in his work. Composed as it seems to be of concern with work as a defining, supportive, and enlarging force, Lodahl's distinction avoids the single-factor stress and the resulting fuzzy notions for the Mayoist, the Marxist, or the mass society or mass calamity schools.[9]

"Job involvement" draws its major cultural support from two related influences. First, the Protestant ethic continues to encourage certain men to associate their work with God's design for the world, and to associate their material success with God's personal endorsement. Second, a loss of religious communion encourages certain other men to seek civil communion in the workplace. The philosopher Eric Hoffer reminds us how recent is the emergence of this involvement phenomenon. Strange and unprecedented, as much as anything else this attitude gives modern Western civilization its unique character and marks it off from all its predecessors. Hoffer observes:

> That free men should be willing to work day after day, even after their vital needs are satisfied, and that work should be seen as a mark of uprightness and manly worth, is not only unparalleled in history but remains more or less incomprehensible to many people outside the Occident.[10]

Job involvement has settled deep into the American grain. Its hold on the American public is evident in the job-seeking emphasis of the new "War on

[8] See Gerhard Lenski, *The Religious Factor: A Sociologist's Inquiry* (New York: Doubleday, 1963), p. 88.
[9] "Patterns of Job Attitudes," *Administrative Science Quarterly*, Vol. 9 (March, 1964), p. 484.
[10] *The Ordeal of Change* (New York: Harper & Row, 1964), p. 28.

Poverty" and in the nightmares of social commentators who think many Americans are unequal to leisure, one of the challenges of man-displacing technology. In short, job involvement directs our attention to the culturally valued necessity of work and to the connection between gainful employment and manly self-esteem.

"Job satisfaction" concerns the extent to which conditions surrounding work come up to the employee's expectations. The main determinant here is psychological and involves the presence or absence of expected deprivations or remunerations in work. Its various focal points include pay, hours, working conditions, the character of supervision, the kind of product made, and the reputation of the company. The concept of job satisfaction is valuable for understanding employee response to improvements made in the material conditions surrounding work. Better working conditions, the *sine qua non* of employee-encouraged job satisfaction, make employees less unhappy, but better conditions do not satisfy deepseated needs for increasing self-esteem and personal growth. Such needs can only be reached through alterations in the challenge-content of work itself.

"Job motivation" is the component of the meaning of work most directly concerned with self-esteem and growth. Motivation is measured by the extent to which the information employees get about themselves from their work comes up to their preferred self-image. The satisfied worker can say, "I have grown as a man in my work, and my increased job responsibility is evidence of this." The main determinants of motivation are the presence or absence of expected inhibitions of personal growth in work, novelty, and responsibility. The discontented worker is likely to complain, "All they've hired are my hands; they want me to check my brains at the gate." During the second world war concern with positive motivation in work was characteristic; the model of the worker was the servicerendering employee. A similar concern can be found today in the sporadic calls by engineers and others for work that is far more challenging. The concept of job motivation helps explain work marked by the extra effort willingly given, work elevated by the "little difference" that means big differences for the psyche and the personality alike. But what is the impact of business on each of these three facets of the meaning of work?

Job Involvement

With respect to job involvement, or man's incorporation of work into his life, the extent to which business permits engineering to dictate an ever finer subdivision of tasks creates a kind of social invisibility in modern work. It is difficult today to assign a status to many factory and office titles, such as "stud torquer" or "650 Program Writer." Employees are reluctant and unable, outside the workplace, to use such esoteric job titles as their "price tags and identification cards," albeit such use was once commonplace. On the other hand, there is evidence of considerable in-plant pride in new "jazzed-up" titles. Outside the workplace, many workers use process, company, or industry identifications ("I work in meat preparation," "I work for ARA-Slater," or "I work in the food service industry") in seeking status with outsiders. However, the identification element of job involvement is increasingly challenged by refinements in the division of labor and tasks.

To the extent to which business gives up arduous apprenticeships that effectively separate experienced men from beginners, allocates about one-third of all employee posts to women, opens high-status posts to women, and assigns men to tasks that lack any real function, business undermines a second key ingredient in job involvement: the vindication of manhood once possible in work of a certain masculine and virile character. On the other hand, however, evidence indicates considerable male ingenuity in resisting innovations thought to be image-threatening (as with eye goggles and other "effeminate" safety items). Men have also had considerable success in preserving leadership positions in departments into which women workers have been integrated.

Finally, concern with workmates as a source of friendship and of support remains an important ingredient in job involvement. To the extent that business demands that men travel great distances to a central location and to the extent that it fosters only work-role allegiances among workforce members, the workplace may decline as a preferred locus of human activity. Data already confirm that little socializing is done after work hours by members of the same work group. Even at work, men prefer non-work-related daydreaming to extensive camaraderie. Many sum up their detachment toward their fellow-workers in the slogan, "I just work here."

The data, however, also reveal that the workplace, while often not the preferred locus of social relationships ("Who would prefer a dirty, fumy machine room to a pleasantly noisy tavern?"), nevertheless remains a vital locus for initiation and maintenance of social contacts among certain workmates. Significant in this regard are the well-financed attempts by personnel departments to nurture close and supportive ties among employees, attempts that include company newspapers, family picnics, recreation leagues, and retirement banquets.

In sum, business today may have a slight positive impact on contemporary job involvement. To be sure, business must accept responsibility for the increasing invisibility of job titles, for the erosion of the traditional masculine quality of certain work roles, and for the loss of human warmth in centralized worksites. However, business probably more than compensates for these effects through its various counter-efforts, including the conscious manipulation of inflated job titles, support of male-leadership posts, and maintenance of morale-boosting personnel programs. Evidence of the considerable strength of contemporary job involvement is available in the fact that American boys look forward to work, American men fear unemployment, American women rejoin the labor force soon after child-rearing, and aged Americans resist separation from work as long as humanly possible.

Job Satisfaction

The impact of business on job satisfaction is fairly easy to measure. Business has long been preoccupied with wages, supervision, job security, and other items it believes related to job satisfaction. Its impact on these factors has been both considerable and generally positive. There are some exceptions to these general effects, however. By maintaining discrimination in the wages paid to women and to

Negroes of both sexes, business has helped undermine the wage-related job satisfaction of many workers. Negro families, for example, had a median income in 1966 of $4,463, while that of white families was $7,722. More generally, by collaborating with unions in the compression of wage differentials (thereby demoralizing skilled workers) and endorsing the clockwork regularity of annual wage increases (thereby making routine what once was challenging) business has helped futher undermine wage-related job satisfaction.

The data suggest that adequate wages are now largely taken for granted by the members of giant industrial unions. The force of competition among companies for manpower, along with competition between business and labor for employee allegiance, are believed by many employees adequate safeguards of the workplace wage scale. What is taken for granted is moderately impressive: looking beyond the depressed wages of Negro workers and women workers, and, looking beyond the high-status/low-wage situation of 35 million employees in the service and public sectors of the economy, there is no denying that the standard set by the path-breaking, unionized bloc of 18,500,000 employees in manufacturing is very high. Since 1939, actual weekly wages of factory workers (exclusive of fringe benefits) have more than quadrupled, rising from $23 to $107. In the same period manufacturing wages have gone up nearly three times as fast as living costs, enabling most workers to keep fairly well ahead of inflation. At the very least, as Scott Paradise points out, "Even when men can say nothing else good about the work they have to do, they take some pride in the fact that they pay their own way and are supporting their own families."[11]

Supervision is another important component in job satisfaction. To the extent to which business tolerates the resurgence of a rigidly firm variety of supervision, it sacrifices some degree of job satisfaction. On the other hand, there are indications that, contrary to the oversimplification of some alienation theorists, business is not under grass-roots pressure to maintain a pro-employee style of supervision. Rather, workers differ widely in what they regard as "considerate" supervision. Staff specialists and skilled manual workers, for example, expect supervisors to evaluate them on job performance rather than on personal feelings, a strategic preference nearly completely reversed by unskilled manual workers. Overall, employees seem to prefer leaders who protect them against others in the organization and who "play fair" in resolving disputes among group members—both expectations with little or no relation to employee-centered leadership.

Job security also helps condition job satisfaction. To the extent that business has failed to quiet the anxieties of workers about automation and technological displacement, it has sacrificed much of the worker's sense of security in work. Data suggest that "the basic anxiety of factory workers is the job itself."[12] The anxiety

[11] "The Meaning of Work," *Detroit Industrial Mission Life and Work*, Vol. 2 (August, 1965), p. 1. See also David Bertelson, *The Lazy South* (New York: Oxford University Press, 1967).

[12] Robert Blauner, *Alienation and Freedom: The Factory Worker and His Industry* (Chicago: University of Chicago Press, 1964), p. viii. "With technological and population trends ever threatening to increase the already high levels of unemployment, the most serious and immediate social problem of our industrial economy is clearly not the nature of work, but the very existence of sufficient jobs."

remains despite the fact that unemployment may even now be fading as a national specter. During 1966, for example, unemployment fell to a 13-year low. (Only 4.5 per cent, or 3.5 of 78.5 million labor force members were unemployed.) In its stead loomed a reverse problem, a growing shortage of skilled workers. The expansion of the labor force that began in 1961 concentrated in the very places where some commentators had forecast that automation would cause trouble.[13]

Business, then, has a definite impact on job satisfaction. Some of its impact is negative; business must accept responsibility for discrimination in wages, for the formalization of compensation, for a resurgence of rigidly firm leadership, and for uncertainty about job tenure. In general, however, the impact of business on job satisfaction is positive. Business has consciously attempted to maintain high wage levels and to show a sensitivity to employee interests by being fair in such job security matters as non-discriminatory layoffs. Evidence of the generally high level of job satisfaction in the American labor force is available in a host of employee-attitude polls and in the high seniority levels of most American workers. Business has contributed much to this development and, thereby, to the current security-oriented meaning of work.

Job Motivation

Evaluating the impact of business on job motivation is more difficult. Business has long overlooked and, in certain cases, refused to look at the significance of personal challenge and psychological growth in work. Preoccupied with heightening job satisfaction, business has neglected creating aids to motivation. In short, the impact of business on job motivation appears minimal and perhaps even negative.

There are exceptional companies, of course. Through decentralization, job enlargement, job retraining, job rotation, and the creation of "utility man" posts to keep alive challenge in work, some companies have contributed much to motivation. These efforts, however, have been few in number and have therefore had limited impact. The general situation is that business, operating with a narrow image of Security-preoccupied Man, has underplayed possibilities for reversing the trend toward the triviality of work.

Responsibility is an important component in job motivation. To some extent business has sought to balance the negative impact on motivation of its exclusive control of the means of production by giving workers a voice in the formulation of work rules, safety rules, factory norms, and, via the suggestion system, even the operation of the work process itself. On the other hand, however, the data minimize the significance of much of this; workers relay to researchers a pervasive sense of divorce from control, of divorce from real power. They feel a sense of

---

[13] On improvements in the unemployment picture, see Daniel Bell, "The Bogey of Automation," *New York Review of Books* (August 26, 1965), pp. 23–25; "Help Wanted—Almost Everywhere," *Business Week* (October 16, 1965), pp. 28, 29; Robert M. Solow, "Technology and Unemployment," *The Public Interest* (Fall, 1965), pp. 17–26; Robert L. Heilbroner, "Men and Machines in Perspective," *The Public Interest* (Fall, 1965), pp. 27–36; Edwin L. Dale, Jr., "The Big Gun on Poverty," *New Republic* (August 7, 1965), pp. 13–15. Cf. Ben Seligman, *Most Notorious Victory: Man in an Age of Automation* (New York: The Free Press, 1967).

detachment that divides the world into "them" and "us," and that minimizes their sense of responsibility for the character of their livelihood and rationalizes almost any state of affairs.

Opportunity for advancement is another important component in job motivation. To the extent that business hires and promotes on the basis of merit and objective criteria rather than caste and personal or arbitrary criteria, it contributes to job motivation. However, the opportunity for advancement in any enterprise has objective limits, and many blue-collar workers have revised the American dream of individual success. Some dream of class mobility via union-secured general wage increases. Some are preoccupied with the mobility prospects of their children. Others prefer a personal retreat in marginal small-business ownership as a security-oriented prop for uncertain self-esteem. All of these responses are steps taken in realistic recognition of the disparity between the myth and the reality of advancement opportunity (blue-collar workers seldom rise above the level of foreman). Similarly, white-collar workers confront expanding educational requirements for significant promotions and the grim fact that opportunities grow smaller as one advances inside a pyramidal organization. Career lines grow vague, men become frozen in dead-end posts, and individuals come too late to realize how long ago their careers had reached a plateau.

Freedom helps condition job motivation. Business can increase employee freedom by protecting workers from inflexible supervisors and by giving them some latitude to be themselves at work. Union grievance machinery combines here with the efforts of various progressive personnel departments to provide some protection for individuality, even as self-conscious reactions against the *IBM Songbook* and the "gray flannel suit" have opened up some room for individual expression and non-conformity. The overall picture is less favorable, however; the workplace culture continues to be generally repressive. The doctrine of *en loco parentis* still seems to guide subordinate-supervisory relations. Unmalleable workers never get hired, or at least they never advance. Pervasive emphasis at work is placed on group or team efforts. Unrelenting pressure exists to merchandise one's personality. And a subtle dilution of job content in upper-echelon posts permits general sociability to replace real skill as a criterion of merit.

Business, then, has a generally negative impact on job motivation. To be sure, some firms have experimented with ways to preserve challenge and have encouraged adult and individualistic behavior in work. More typically, however, business disregards many challenge-aiding techniques, employs educational "caste" restrictions on advancement, and supports an other-directed social ethic. Revealing pleas for challenge are regularly sounded by the employees of large law firms or "law factories," overly specialized engineers, overly taxed school teachers, social workers ensnarled in red tape, assembly-line factory workers, and many others. While moderately involved in their work, and generally satisfied with it, most American workers appear to have little job motivation.[14] Business has

---

[14] Berger thinks the predominant kind of work is "*neither* fulfillment *nor* oppression, a sort of gray, neutral region in which one neither rejoices nor suffers, but with which one puts up with more or less grace for the sake of other things that are supposed

Table 4. "Work Meaning" Configurations by Occupational Group.

PER CENT OF 1960 LABOR FORCE	OCCUPATIONAL GROUPS (CENSUS TITLES)	INVOLVEMENT	SATISFACTION	MOTIVATION
18	Blue-collar semi-skilled	Moderate– low	Considerable	Low
15	White-collar clerical	Moderate– low	Moderate– low	Low
13	Blue-collar craftsman, foremen	Considerable– moderate	Considerable	Considerable– moderate
12	Service workers	Considerable	Moderate	Moderate
11	White-collar professional, technical	Considerable	Considerable– moderate	Considerable
10	White-collar managers, proprietors	Considerable	Considerable	Considerable– moderate
8	Farm workers (hired hands)	Considerable	Moderate– low	Low
7	White-collar sales personnel	Moderate– low	Moderate	Moderate– low
6	Blue-collar laborers	Low	Moderate– low	Low

contributed much to this development—and thereby to the current demeaning character of work.

TOWARD A NEW PERSPECTIVE ON WORK

Table 4 represents the author's rough and venturesome estimate of the extent of the job involvement, satisfaction, and motivation experienced by various categories of workers. To what degree is business responsible for these results? The evidence is uneven and contradictory, but it points to a slight degree of business responsibility for the current state of job involvement and a considerable degree of responsibility for both high job satisfaction and low job motivation.

to be more important." Peter L. Berger, "Some General Observations on the Problem of Work," in *The Human Shape of Work,* Berger, ed. (New York: Macmillan, 1964), p. 219.

No precise assessment of the impact of business on the meaning of work will be possible until the influence of other variables is better understood. Not enough is known about the effect on the meaning of work of early socialization trends, basic human personality needs, political and cultural variables, family problems, or related social phenomena. Many of our basic assumptions also must be examined anew. For example, how middle-class-bound are the concepts of "job motivation" and "personal growth"? And why should men not dislike certain kinds of work?

Above all, not enough is understood of the ultimate commitment of our industrial society or of the ultimate values against which employee attitudes and behavior can be judged pathological or reasonably adaptive.[15] On intuitive, emotional, or ideological grounds one can excuse business (with the Mayoists), exonerate business (with the students of bureaucracy), or condemn business (with the alienation theorists) for what one judges has become of work. A really convincing and refined judgment is impossible, however, until investigation reveals more information about the major variables involved and about the significance of individual differences in job involvement, job satisfaction, and job motivation.

Current Managerial Shortsightedness

While a precise estimate of the impact of business on the meaning of work is impossible, certain general observations can be made. It is possible to conclude that business is making mistakes in its current management of the meaning of work—mistakes as judged by the professed values of business itself. It is vital to distinguish here between the relatively unavoidable costs of industrial advance (the division of labor, the centralization of authority) and the costs of unnecessary distortions of industrial advance (meaningless work, relentless routines, stultifying conformity, premature human obsolescence). No doubt industrial advance is impossible without some loss of personal power and significance by individual workers, but industrial advance does *not* demand that the majority of employees be regarded only as units of production best manipulated by dollars and Muzak-lullabies.[16]

Business fails to follow adequately the dictates of its own production-maximizing values. Through its low regard of job involvement, its one-sided stress on job satisfaction, and its grossly inadequate concern with job motivation, business sacrifices productivity gains and adds greatly to its overhead. In the wide spectrum of business attitudes, some businessmen believe that an appeal to maximum self-interest actually exhausts the subject of human motives—when the experience of business during the second world war with Service-rendering Man clearly suggests otherwise—and that modern man is merely a cross between the economic

---

[15] An outstanding start in this connection has been made by Dr. Abraham Maslow, current president of the American Psychological Association. See especially the 36 necessary preconditions for Eupsychian Management Policy (e.g., Assume in all your people the impulse to achieve, Assume that people are improvable, etc.) in Abraham Maslow, *Eupsychian Management* (Homewood, Ill.: Dorsey, 1965), pp. 17–33, *passim.*
[16] See Melvin Tumin, "Business as a Social System," *Behavioral Sciences* (April, 1964), p. 130.

and social strawmen of yesteryear. Other businessmen seem to think that man's interest in order and man's need for security make unnecessary all novelty and challenge in his work. Evidence that neither of these assumptions is correct is provided by the indications that productivity levels today remain considerably below those possible with a more highly motivated labor force, by the costly mobility of restless lower-echelon employees, and by the flight from corporations to universities of challenge-seeking scientists and engineers.

Business has rather clearly erred in refusing to underwrite a meaningful, large-scale test of the effectiveness of motivation-enhancing techniques—even at the risk of test results recommending the radical overhaul of business itself. Rigidity here violates the high value business otherwise places on experimentation, and it ultimately threatens the dynamism at the very heart of our industrial order. Sociologist Melvin Tumin asks whether business might not

> serve its own avowed interests much more effectively if it restructured its operations and recast its themes in order to attempt to evoke the kind of identification with an enterprise, concern for its outcome, and sense of significant membership in it that have proven, in other institutions like the family and church, to be able to evoke extraordinary amounts of conscientious giving of one's best, without thought or concern for differentiated rewards?[17]

We may never know—so long as business continues to ignore or to pre-judge the matter in a most unbusinesslike way.

The Future

Trends in economic development and in organizational growth encourage new hope that we may yet achieve a dramatic breakthrough in our current impasse regarding that one of work's three components most in need of reform, job motivation.

Our economy is the world's first modern "service economy." More than half our employed labor force is now found outside traditional production areas, and, most significantly, increases in our labor force occur overwhelmingly in industries that provide services (education, sales, finance, etc.). As national income levels rise, the demand for goods rises less rapidly than does the demand for services. As man-displacing productivity grows in goods production, more workers turn to the services for employment. These trends serve, in combination, to point a clear path toward service-oriented economic growth.

Such growth has four positive implications for job motivation. First, service companies are characteristically small concerns. In the future, the large corporation is likely to be overshadowed by the hospitals, universities, research institutes, government agencies, and professional organizations that are the hallmarks of a service economy. To the extent to which smallness reduces formalism, stratification, and centralization, it may be expected to encourage democratic participation and personal growth. Second, small firms are characteristically competitive. To the extent to which competition encourages innovation and adaptiveness, it may be expected to provide personal challenge and opportunity. Third, service companies

17 *Ibid.*

make greater use of workers with higher education than do production firms. Since education creates a need for further personal development, it may be expected to stir unceasing employee pressure for creative options. Finally, service companies provide work of a particularly personal bent. Employees are closely related to their work and often render highly personalized service of a kind that offers ample scope for the development and exercise of personal skills.

The issue is not clearcut. Service companies employ many women workers, older workers, and part-time workers. Historically, these groups have made little concerted effort to secure gains with respect to work rules and other job motivation matters. Service companies are also poorly unionized. This results in an imbalance of employee-employer power and fails to insure surveillance and gadfly protection. It is also alleged that small firms do not allocate sufficient resources to product research. If this is true and continues to be true as the number of small firms grows, it could reduce educational requirements for employment, lead to a lessening in product competition, permit artificial rigidities in company structure, and in other ways seriously set back the promotion of job motivation. On the whole, however, the positive implications of the service trend appear more impressive and are more likely to be borne out.

Further evidence that the trend toward more services is a hopeful one is provided by students of organizational growth. Today's exponential growth in occupational specialties—especially the trend toward professionalism—is encouraging a slow but discernible movement toward an adaptive ideal of business organization. The adaptive type of organization is believed especially receptive to job motivation concerns. Professor (of management) Jerald Hage suggests that organizations exist on a continuum between two ideal types:[18]

ORGANIC MODEL (Emphasis on adaptiveness)	MECHANISTIC MODEL (Emphasis on production)
High complexity	Low complexity
Low centralization	High centralization
Low formalization	High formalization
Low stratification	High stratification
High adaptiveness	Low adaptiveness
Low production	High production
Low efficiency	High efficiency
High job satisfaction	Low job satisfaction
Communication through information and advice	Communication through instruction and orders
Loyalty to the tasks of the organization	Loyalty to the organization
Emphasis on expertise	Emphasis on local knowledge

[18] "An Axiomatic Theory of Organizations," *Administrative Science Quarterly*, Vol. 10 (December, 1965), p. 305. Reprinted by permission of the author and the *Administrative Science Quarterly*. See also Warren Bennis, "Beyond Bureaucracy," *Trans-Action* (July/August, 1965), pp. 31–35, and *Changing Organizations* (New York: McGraw-Hill, 1967).

Today's knowledge and information "explosion" accelerates the rate of change in new business programs and techniques. Business organizations accordingly tend to move toward increased complexity, with its accent on individual expertise, and toward increased adaptiveness, with its stress on organizational expertise. Especially where the output is service to clients, rather than manufacturing products, tomorrow's business organization will have less opportunity for the standardization of tasks and more need to show adaptiveness. The result for job motivation may be better than we can now easily imagine.

Speculation about the future is a matter of probabilities, of course, not certainties. But the economy is moving into services. Men are being automated out of deadening assembly-line posts. Escalation in educational and skill demands is bringing a new and a restless salaried class into being. Product innovation appears related to a certain amount of dynamic corporate change and development. Clean, continuous-flow, high-motivation production units are developing. And delayed workforce entrance, longer vacations, and earlier retirement are all scaling work back to more human and manageable dimensions. There is cause for confidence that this shift toward a service economy will strengthen the job motivation component of work provided only that men, particularly our critical business innovators and decision-makers, recognize the opportunity and improve on it.

CONCLUSION

Too often, original thinking concerning the impact of business on the meaning of work is replaced by a simple adherence to one or another of the ten ideological schemes reviewed in Table 1. Depending on our politics, our insight, and our learning, we are inclined to choose whatever scheme will best support us as we condemn, condone, or possibly even congratulate business for its part in shaping the current meaning of work. Such judgments, however, wither under exacting scrutiny. They merit replacement by insights based on more investigation into the situation actually prevailing in the marketplace.

New experimental programs should be based on the pragmatist's model of man as a rational, "satisficing" problem-solver rather than on some of the more stereotyped worker profiles. Human relations at work are not determined by an interplay between victims and villains, as some of the popular ideologies tend to imply. More attention should be paid to the consequences of the unevenness of business encouragement to greater job involvement, job satisfaction, and job motivation on the part of workers. Specifically, the profits and related gains to business that might result from motivationally oriented reforms at work should be fully investigated. As Maslow points out, hard-headedness, tough-mindedness, profits, and all the rest of it absolutely require considered attention to the ability of people to grow in work. Only when workers can grow are they likely to produce at their optimum level.

Much remains to be learned about the nature of work itself and its interelationship with the general culture. Investigators and practical businessmen alike should adopt a realistic skepticism toward "simple and sovereign" ideologies, alert themselves to the real gaps in our knowledge, and show a greater readiness to use our genuine, hard-earned insights. We may yet create both desired and actual work meanings we can transfer to our children without embarrassment, resignation, or regret—this in a world in which the impact of business on the meaning of work will honor business, workers, and the world itself.

SELECTED READINGS

LEONARD SAYLES, ED., *Individualism and Big Business* (New York: McGraw-Hill, 1963). A volume of essays concerned with the effects of large, complex organizations on the opportunities of individuals for creative and meaningful work; several essays by the editor take issue with the position that organizations are repressive.

CHRIS ARGYRIS, *Integrating the Individual and the Organization* (New York: John Wiley, 1964). A well-known critic of large organizations presents his views of the opportunities provided managers by the behavioral sciences to reorganize the firm in line with the psychological needs of individuals for "self-actualization."

DANIEL BELL, *The End of Ideology* (New York: The Free Press, 1960). A collection of well-known essays on various aspects of the social changes America experienced in the 1950's. Especially important in the present context is the frequently cited essay, "Work and Its Discontents: The Cult of Efficiency in America" (pp. 222–64).

ERICH FROMM, *Man for Himself* (New York: Holt, Rinehart and Winston, 1947). Combining the sociological insights that have come out of the Marxist tradition with the more intellectually radical thoughts of Freud in his later years, the author, a well-known psychoanalyst and social observer, pursues the effects of industrial living on personality.

ROBERT BLAUNER, *Alienation and Freedom: The Factory Worker and His Industry* (Chicago: University of Chicago Press, 1964). An interesting essay and four industry case studies combine data collected by the Roper Survey Corporation with data collected by the author. A few methodological weaknesses in the substantive chapters do not invalidate this intriguing volume.

VICTOR VROOM, *Work and Motivation* (New York: John Wiley, 1964). This is an inventory of a very large body of empirical findings on occupational choice, work satisfaction, and work performance.

part 5

BUSINESSMEN AND AMERICAN CULTURE

"America passed from barbarism to decadence in little more than three hundred years," a European observer once remarked, "a feat that was greatly facilitated by the fact that it skipped civilization entirely." For many foreign commentators the brash American democracy will always be something less than a "culture," and they will cite as proof our Ku Klux Klans, gaudy neon lights, Hollywood morals, junkyards, highway billboards, Los Angeles politics, Jacksonian inauguration parties, Teapot Dome scandals, race riots, urban slums, and countless other manifestations of peculiar taste, superficial interests, and perverted values. They will also contrast the "trapped" housewife with her multiple neurosis, the tax-conscious art collector, and the profit-minded impresario of TV westerns in America today with the courtly ladies or flowerlike peasant girls, the grand seigneurs, and the William Shakespeares of the European past. The smog over our urban centers, to make a poor joke, would seem to make an airtight case for the prosecution.

This arraignment of American culture as a whole requires no answer in the present context. But since "business values" are often singled out as the proximate cause of America's alleged shortcomings as a refined civilization, the essays in this final section have undertaken an examination of the impact of business on education, the creative arts, and the performing arts. Each concludes that business does influence artistic and intellectual endeavors in the United States—sometimes for good, sometimes for ill—and that it is in the best interests of our large corporations to support these endeavors. There is, apparently, no fundamental antipathy between the serious artist or intellectual and the serious businessman. According to Alfred North Whitehead, "a great society is a society in which its men of business think greatly of their functions." If our businessmen do think greatly of their work, they will not be content to live in a society where artistic and intellectual enterprises are allowed to languish.

chapter 12

BUSINESS AND EDUCATION

Marcia Freedman, a researcher with the Columbia University Conservation of Human Resources Project, is the holder of advanced degrees in both business and education. This background, together with her years of experience with research focused on manpower problems and as a consultant to business corporations and the government, gives her a unique vantage point from which to gauge the impact of business on education in America.

In a widely praised and provocative assessment of education in America, two leading scholars recently described the school as

> a transitional institution in which the process of education gradually separates the young from family and locality and prepares them to join the great corporate systems and to establish their own independent nuclear families. . . . From [its position between the nuclear family and the corporate structures of the public world] it derives its function of separating and directing the individual in his pre-adult life away from his family and toward integration in the superstructures.[1]

In her essay Dr. Freedman compares the past and present relationships of the "transitional institution" or school on the one hand and the "corporate systems" and "superstructures" on the other and concludes that the social distance between them is narrowing. American parents have long viewed education and economic success as intimately related. That modern business shares this attitude is shown by its efforts to hire highly educated personnel and to make use of the research conducted at educational institutions and by the startling growth of a new knowledge industry capable of shaping regional development in the United States.

Dr. Freedman documents three specific trends in the economic

[1] Solon T. Kimball and James E. McClellan, Jr., *Education and the New America* (New York: Random House, 1966), pp. 39–40.

*relationship between business and education: business aid to educa-
tion is increasing; business has come to view education, from an
explicitly technical perspective, as an industry subject to moderniza-
tion, and many firms have undertaken to supply the materials,
machines, and methods needed; and business and education have
entered into a new kind of collaboration and competition in connection with government welfare programs. All three trends show
that the influence of business on education is increasing. Dr. Freedman offers no theoretical structure to explain the nature of this
influence, but clearly it will be neither wholly good nor wholly bad.
Whether individually or through their governments, Americans
must carefully identify and encourage the positive aspects of the
concern of business with education and limit its negative aspects.*

*In reading the essay the reader may wish to keep in mind the
following questions.*

*1. What kind of evidence would the business community need
to determine the specific advantages of the use of educational
requirements as a screening device in selection procedures?*

*2. Dr. Freedman draws a distinction between businessmen as
citizens involving themselves in educational decision-making and
corporations "acting formally as corporations" involving themselves
in "setting public policy." What kind of restraints might we reasonably anticipate would reduce the risks Dr. Freedman sees in the
second kind of involvement? Which of these restraints would be
least likely to discourage corporations from their benevolent
involvements?*

*3. The trends Dr. Freedman reports seem to be largely irreversi-
ble. Is there a connection between these trends and the growth of
student unrest on some of our major college campuses? How can
we assure education the transitional role, of which Professors
Kimball and McClellan write, if it no longer occupies an interstitial
position between the family and "the superstructures"?*

MARCIA FREEDMAN \ BUSINESS AND EDUCATION

This essay attempts to trace the convergence of ideas, styles, and interests in
business and education. American education has been influenced by many institutions and movements; what is attempted here is not an accounting of all the forces
that have shaped the educational system but some empirical statements as to the
role of business.

INTRODUCTION

Lawrence A. Cremin has summarized the pragmatic justifications of American education: "Education is good economics, sensible politics, and sound defense; it trains character, helps people get ahead; and incidentally keeps them off the labor market for protracted periods of time."[1] To such pragmatic concerns, Cremin counters the vision of fostering human growth, "defined as the deliberate effort to achieve excellence in every domain of life," with the implied demand that "all our institutions . . . exert a continuing educative influence on individuals."[2]

All Classes Favor Education

The dualism expressed in these two views has permeated American attitudes toward education; in fact, preparation for the "good life" has always been understood as incorporating the promise of upward mobility, an article of faith buttressed by the realities of the much-publicized data on the money value of an education. Blue-collar workers, like their middle-class counterparts, have relatively high aspirations for their children, and feel that their sons in particular should have as much education as possible, even when they are unsure as to how this education can be financed.[3]

The very poor would seem to agree; a Detroit study reported that mothers characterized as "high-recipient" welfare clients "set high educational aspirations for their children and expected high levels of academic performance . . . especially where the father was absent. In pursuit of this goal the mothers seem to display none of the fatalism frequently attributed to them." Contrary to expectations, Negro mothers had higher aspirations than whites.[4]

Education and the Job Market

The consensus among people located in different social strata reflects the major role played by education in allocating occupational status. "Stay in school and get a better job" has been a slogan directed at young people; one result has been a tendency to characterize dropouts or "so-called 'early school leavers' [as] unprepared for employment."[5]

That educational achievement has become the prime ingredient in the contest

[1] *The Genius of American Education* (New York: Random House, 1966), p. 31.
[2] *Ibid.*, pp. 34–35.
[3] See Gladys L. Palmer, *The Reluctant Job Changer* (Philadelphia: University of Pennsylvania Press, 1962), p. 156.
[4] Oliver C. Moles, Jr., "Child Training Practices Among Low-Income Families," *Welfare in Review,* Vol. 3 (December, 1965), p. 8.
[5] National Association of Manufacturers, *This We Believe About Education* (New York, 1961).

for upward mobility is the result of two major historical trends—an increasing supply of educated people and a rise in demand resulting from technological change. The increase in supply, measured by the median years of schooling of the population, reflects the wealth of a nation that can afford both the necessary investment in educational facilities and the foregone production of the young. The increase in demand for educated workers reflects the economy's ever greater reliance on technology, with the long-run effect of raising the technical requirements for some jobs, while diminishing the number of unskilled occupations. Even in agriculture and materials handling, where mechanization has not raised skill requirements in every job, certain jobs have completely disappeared, with machines able to outproduce hand labor.

The preferences of employers have also had an important effect in emphasizing educational achievement. It is well recognized by economists that a loose labor market encourages employers to raise educational as well as training and experience requirements.[6] Given a range of educational levels in the population and a labor market short of full employment, an employer can decide to hire those people at the head of the queue regardless of the appropriateness of the match and regardless of possible implications for job satisfaction and performance.[7]

Managerial options also play a part in the changing occupational mix of the economy. For over a decade the number of white-collar workers has exceeded blue-collar workers; those directly engaged in production are now a minority. While this trend has been primarily the result of changes in production modes, it has been enhanced in some cases by a deliberate increase of white-collar staffs. Both technology and preferences have resulted in an increasingly bureaucratic work force and a concomitant increase in the polite aspects of social intercourse in the workplace. Middle-class styles of relationship, the American equivalent of "U" speech in Britain, are in some instances as important a requisite for the job as the relevant skill content.[8]

The Institutional Relationships of Business and Education

Much of the emphasis on education that permeates the American scene can be viewed historically as a predictable effect of industrialization and is to that extent independent of specific modes of business organization. Nevertheless, the intent of

[6] Lloyd G. Reynolds, *The Structure of Labor Markets* (New York: Harper & Row, 1951), pp. 73–74; National Commission on Technology, Automation, and Economic Progress, *Technology and the American Economy* (Washington: Government Printing Office, 1966), p. 23.

[7] Ivar Berg, "Educational Requirements, Employment, and the Urban Labor Market," in Eli Ginzberg, ed., *Manpower Strategy for the Metropolis* (New York: Columbia University Press). In press, 1968.

[8] Thus, Professor Bereday of Teachers College, Columbia University, devotes his Saturday afternoons to a class for 10 high-school girls, teaching them speech and deportment in order to improve their job and educational opportunities. "A Real-Life Higgins Descends on Harlem," *New York Times,* May 8, 1966.

this essay is to explore some of the institutional relationships of business and education. While it is possible to discern trends, no theoretical structure clearly emerges to explain the relationships. The material as presented is, therefore, largely descriptive. It falls into four major parts: (1) historical changes in educational emphasis on vocationalism and the shift of business attention from the secondary school to the university; (2) concomitant changes in the university and in the role of education in regional development; (3) direct business aid to education; and (4) expansion of education as a market and the resulting implications for heightened business influence on the educational process.

HISTORICAL VOCATIONAL EMPHASIS IN AMERICAN EDUCATION

Vocationalism became an issue in American education early in the history of the nation. With the transition to an industrial society, a number of interests converged to sponsor a general expansion of the scope and responsibility of the public schools and, specifically, the establishment of vocational curricula under public auspices. Over the years, however, the needs for such programs have been subtly transformed, and the attitudes and activities of businessmen toward them have changed accordingly.

Early Forms of Vocationalism

At a time when America was predominantly an agricultural nation, vocationalism found its expression in the farmers' institute idea, in the work of the committee on education of the National Grange, and most explicitly in the colleges founded under the Morrill Act of 1862.[9] Although devoted from the beginning to both the agricultural and the mechanical arts, the establishment of these colleges grew out of farm pressures. Originally, they served a much younger population than we are accustomed to think of as college-age. "Considering the age of the students, the course content, and the level of instruction, the early land-grant colleges performed a function similar to that of a good comprehensive high school today."[10]

With the growth of the high school, the land-grant colleges raised the level of their work to the highly skilled professional areas. In the meantime, industrialization brought with it a demand for skilled workers that could no longer be met by immigration alone. In the movement for federal support for vocational education, culminating in passage of the Smith-Hughes Act of 1917, business influence was decisive.

Impressed by the presentation at the Philadelphia Centennial Exposition of 1876 of instruction shops from the Moscow Imperial Technical School, several Ameri-

[9] Lawrence A. Cremin, *The Transformation of the School: Progressivism in American Education, 1876–1957* (New York: Random House, 1961), p. 42.
[10] Grant Venn, *Man, Education and Work* (Washington: American Council on Education, 1961), p. 46.

can educators took up the cause of manual training in the public schools. Originally, school shops were established as an aid to the academic instruction of students not preparing for college rather than as a means of skill acquisition, but "the businessmen who advocated and supported manual education" wanted "practical trade training to free them from growing regulation of apprenticeships."[11] Thus, the organizer of the New York Trades School held out "the promise that his graduates would work at lower wage scales and remain relatively free of union control. A $500,000 grant by J. P. Morgan to the New York Trades School in 1892 symbolized a rather general concurrence on the part of the business community."[12]

The history of the Smith-Hughes Act is an intriguing chapter in American legislative practice, an example of skillful lobbying, urban-rural tradeoffs, and the bringing together of strange political bedfellows.[13] By 1916, the U.S. Chamber of Commerce had added its support for the bill as a result of an overwhelmingly favorable response to a poll of local chambers.[14] While the support of labor was obtained only after the AFL perceived the inevitability of schools offering vocational training and decided to influence rather than oppose the movement, business enthusiasm was high from the beginning. The attitudes of business are well illustrated by those of the National Association of Manufacturers, which took up the cause of vocational education immediately after the founding of the organization.

Evolution of the Policies of the NAM

Given the general position of the NAM on all aspects of federal participation in local affairs, its early support not only for vocational education but ultimately for granting federal aid to encourage it is astonishing.[15] The Association's second annual convention, in 1897, discussed English and German technical schools connected with plants and recommended that industry help in organizing and promoting "practical arts, industrial, manual training or other technical schools, and that employees be urged to attend these schools. The need for commercial education in the public schools of the nation was also emphasized at this convention."

In the years 1900 through 1903, NAM conventions adopted resolutions advocating "the establishment of free public commercial and technical schools" or commercial and technical departments in high schools. A Committee on Industrial Education was appointed in 1904, and in the following year it presented an extensive study on industrial education in foreign countries. According to Fern:

---

11 Cremin, *The Transformation of the School, op. cit.*, p. 33.
12 *Ibid.*, p. 36.
13 For an excellent account, see *ibid.*, Chapter 2, which also contains references to the important source materials.
14 *Ibid.*, p. 56.
15 The material that follows is from George H. Fern's *A Brief Statement of the History and Activities of the National Association of Manufacturers in Education, 1857–1959*, Mimeographed Report (New York, 1959).

This report so forcibly indicated the need for trade schools in the United States that the entire membership was urged by resolution to foster industrial education, and the officers and members of the Association were constituted as a permanent committee pledged to urge upon public men, educators, manufacturers, and the people the necessity of a comprehensive system of trade schools throughout the country.[16]

By 1908, the committee had prepared a sample bill for consideration by state legislatures. The Association's support for trade schools, continuation schools, and compulsory education up to age 18 was reiterated at its annual conventions, and in 1913 for the first time the Association "expressed approval of Federal aid for vocational education through moderate appropriations for extension work in agriculture, continuation schools for industry, and for home economics."

In the years following passage of the Smith-Hughes Act, the NAM turned its attention to a variety of issues that had implications for education. It lobbied against federal legislation to regulate child labor while working to establish local standards for the improvement of child labor conditions. In 1931 the Association began to emphasize the importance of economic education, and it continues to do so. In 1961, the NAM made an official pronouncement on federal aid to education. After asserting that state and local resources are sufficient to support education, the statement concluded, "Specifically, federal grants for educational purposes should be terminated and federal promotional activity with respect to elementary, secondary and higher education should be halted."[17]

Presumably, among other grants to be terminated would be those emanating from the Smith-Hughes Act and its amendments and extensions since 1917. It is perfectly clear that manpower demands at the turn of the century carried more weight with the NAM than fear of government control, whereas today the reverse is true. If the need for school-based vocational training were again to become as great as the need for specific public services, one can assume that NAM ideology would be tempered on the subject of federal aid to education as it now is in respect to federal contributions for building highways.

In fact, however, business in general has long since lost its enthusiasm for vocational training in the schools. In contrast to the campaign for the Smith-Hughes Act, not one business spokesman testified at the hearings on the 1963 Vocational Education Act.

Current Business Attitudes Toward Vocationalism

The demands of business for vocationally trained students have not disappeared, but they are now being satisfied at a later stage in the educational enterprise. Modern pluralistic restatements of the Platonic ideal of the educative community consider the schools only one among many educational institutions, which typically

[16] *Ibid.*

[17] National Association of Manufacturers, *Industry Believes, 1965: Policies on Current Problems as Adopted by the Board* (New York, 1965), p. 15.

include the family, the church, and the mass media. Business also is said to contribute by investing in training, thus furnishing the worker with those increments of skill necessary to perform a specific job for the firm.[18]

The willingness of business to make this investment has been interpreted as a reassertion of its educational role.[19] In fact, however, the structure of production, rather than any conscious assumption of role, has been responsible for the rejection by business of the school as the site for blue-collar training. For the most part, the internal labor market of a large firm provides it with sufficient unskilled manpower. When gaps have occurred, they have been in the ranks of skilled craftsmen who are periodically in short supply. Although training activity in blue-collar occupations increases in boom periods, the issue has been at the margins of corporate concern.

Business and Higher Education

If blue-collar workers have not bulked large in company training plans, managerial personnel, who come to their jobs with high educational achievements, have received inordinate attention.[20] Large business investments in recruiting and training these workers reflect the new attitudes of business toward higher education and the highly educated. A theoretical underpinning for this emphasis is provided by recent work in the economics of education, which seeks to demonstrate the return to individuals from investment in human capital as well as the relationship of such investment to national economic growth.[21]

Business firms demonstrate their convictions about the productivity of the highly educated not only within the organization but in their outside activities. A recent survey of the National Industrial Conference Board describes the change in emphasis as follows:

---

[18] A survey by the Stanford Research Institute reported estimates as high as $30 billion for company expenditures on training; these estimates were made in the absence of reliable data, and may be exaggerated. Cf. *Training in Industry* (Palo Alto, Calif.: Stanford Research Institute, 1962).

[19] Cremin, *The Transformation of the School, op. cit.*, p. 57.

[20] See U.S. Department of Labor, Bureau of Apprenticeship and Training, *Training of Workers in American Industry* (Washington: Government Printing Office, 1964); and Neil W. Chamberlain, "The Role of the Union in Corporate Manpower Planning." Prepared for Conference of Labor Management Institute, October 14–15, 1965.

[21] Edward F. Denison, *The Sources of Economic Growth in the United States and the Alternatives Before Us* (New York: Committee for Economic Development, 1962); Theodore W. Schultz, *The Economic Value of an Education* (New York: Columbia University Press, 1963); and Gary S. Becker, *Human Capital*, National Bureau of Economic Research (New York: Columbia University Press, 1964). It is no historical accident that "this florescence of a new specialty in economics" has occurred simultaneously with widespread curriculum reform in the public schools and a sharp increase in the competition for college entrance; cf. Mary Jean Bowman, "The Human Investment Revolution in Economic Thought," *Sociology of Education,* Vol. 39 (Spring, 1966), p. 112.

Traditionally, companies have justified their aid-to-education programs on two grounds. First, as good corporate citizens, they have had an obligation to support education along with other community good works. Second, if business and private citizens did not give assistance to education, the educators would turn to the federal government for help—and federal control of education would follow.

Both of these arguments are still advanced to justify aid-to-education programs. But nowadays it is more common for companies to explain their support of education in terms of the practical benefits they get from education. They point out, for example, that the colleges and universities are steadily enlarging the frontiers of knowledge through research, the application of which provides commercial benefits to industry. They also point to the obvious fact that those institutions are furnishing industry with an ever-growing supply of trained manpower to fill executive and technical positions.[22]

Business has begun to back its belief in higher education with substantial monetary support. Stockholders have occasionally challenged corporate investments of this kind, but the new business policy has several times been given judicial sanction. In the famous Smith case of 1953 in New Jersey, the judge confirmed, among other things, the direct pecuniary advantage to the corporation of the reservoir of scientific and executive talent in the universities.[23]

What might be called the movement among businessmen to support education through corporate contributions began in 1943 in Indiana, specifically as a means of "saving" the independent college and obviating the possibility of federal aid.[24] The Smith decision gave the movement real impetus. The Council for Financial Aid to Education estimates that direct corporate support of education, mainly higher education, reached the level of $178 million in 1960, $200 million in 1962, and $250 million in 1964.[25]

THE EFFECTS OF VOCATIONALISM ON THE UNIVERSITY

The financial support of higher education by business is in part a recognition of dramatic changes in the role of the university. In theory at least, the higher learning of the nineteenth century was not supposed to inculcate specific skills. Thorstein Veblen gave expression to this ideal when he wrote in 1918:

[22] National Industrial Conference Board, *Industry Aid to Education*, Studies in Public Affairs, No. 1 (New York, 1965), p. 3.

[23] *Ibid.*, p. 4. For a discussion of the case (A. P. Smith Manufacturing Co. v. Barlow, *et al.*, 26 N.J. Super. 106 [1953]), see Richard Eells, *Corporation Giving in a Free Society* (New York: Harper & Row, 1956), Ch. 2.

[24] For details, see Donald E. Thompson, "Corporate Giving—A Partial Answer to the Financial Needs of Higher Education," *American Association of University Professors Bulletin* (Winter, 1961), pp. 321–24.

[25] Council for Financial Aid to Education, *1964 Corporation Support of Higher Education* (New York, 1965), p. 3.

> "Practical" branches of knowledge (Law, Politics, Accountancy, etc.) . . . have a place within the university precincts only by force of a *non-sequitur*. . . . The American business community is well enough as it is, without the higher learning, and it is fully sensible that the higher learning is not a business proposition.[26]

Veblen was conscious that a great falling away from this ideal had already taken place, however, and he called for reform. Modern commentators often frankly praise the very vocational courses and orientation that Veblen opposed. John Walsh, for example, has emphasized that the educational establishment is a vital cog in the economic machine:

> The importance of gearing education to social change and creating the right kinds and amounts of "human capital"—which concerns many economists these days—has been one of the main factors that has influenced higher education to forsake its own version of splendid isolation in recent years and begin to think and act more as if it were a part of the nation's total education system.[27]

Lewis A. Coser has discussed this philosophy and its backers:

> [An] influential group of educators and academic decision-makers has now publicized the opinion that the university ought in fact to be nothing but a training ground for marketable skills and for the absorption of professional norms, besides being a locale for specialized research. Bernard Berelson . . . puts the matter with commendable frankness: "The graduate school should aim at training the skilled specialist—not . . . at producing the 'educated man,' the 'cultured man,' the 'wise man' (nor, for that matter, the 'mere technician,' either."[28]

Perhaps a little discouraged by such thinkers, Columbia University's Jacques Barzun once went so far as to suggest that "the liberal arts tradition is dead or dying" and the trend is so clear that "to object would be like trying to sweep back the ocean."[29] The production of an educated elite in the traditional British style is not without its present-day defenders, however. Daniel Bell, for example, has warned against premature specialization and recommended a curriculum designed to educate men who know values as well as problem-solving methods.[30] But Coser believes that this elite has much the same utility as the skilled specialist, to provide leadership for "a more sophisticated establishment in desperate need of men with a wider vision to meet the research, planning and coordinating requirements of modern America. . . ."[31]

The unattached intellectuals of an earlier day, Coser argues, have been absorbed into the institutions of official culture, especially the university, and there is no

[26] *The Higher Learning in America* (New York: Hill & Wang, 1957), pp. 54–55.
[27] "ACE Study: Higher Education's Aloofness from Occupational Education Seems to Be Thawing," *Science,* 144 (June 12, 1964), p. 1321.
[28] *Men of Ideas* (New York: The Free Press, 1965), p. 284.
[29] Jacques Barzun, "College to University—and After," Address at Convocation of Hofstra University, December 11, 1963.
[30] *The Reforming of General Education* (New York: Columbia University Press, 1966).
[31] *Op. cit.*, p. 266.

lack of opportunity for them to circulate among practical men of affairs or indeed to become such practitioners themselves:

> Not only is the university expected to provide new skilled manpower; its professors are also expected to lend their own skills. There is now an intimate interplay between the university and the public, as well as private, bureaucracies, a continuous reciprocal flow and interchange between the universities and Washington, between private industry and the academy.[32]

The university that strives to meet the demands of these several constituencies has been designated by Clark Kerr as the "multiversity." Kerr celebrates and extols this new institution by invoking investment in human capital as the most important factor in economic growth. The university's role as the servant of that growth is thus not only legitimate but inevitable. The multiversity, he says, "is an imperative rather than a reasoned choice of elegant alternatives."[33]

THE ROLE OF EDUCATION IN REGIONAL ECONOMIC DEVELOPMENT

The growth of a new "knowledge industry" in the United States that is attempting to supply the voracious new demands of business and government is exemplified by the Route 128 syndrome. Route 128 is a highway crescent on the outskirts of Boston on which are located a large number of scientific and technical firms, "spun off" by the great universities of the area.[34] As a symbol of the relationship among business, government, and the university, it received official recognition in the Gilpatric report for the Department of Defense, which explained the concentration of defense contracts in California and Massachusetts by the research and development potential available in their strong university centers.[35] The demand for the geographical dispersion of such centers is explained by Kerr as "in part, the new realization of the role of a university as a factor influencing the location of industry."[36]

Research Centers and New Industries

The growing number of state commissions for economic development has obviously received the message. One of North Carolina's chief attractions to industry is the Research Triangle, a non-profit foundation that coordinates the research potential of Duke University, the University of North Carolina, and

[32] *Ibid.*, p. 357.

[33] Clark Kerr, *The Uses of the University* (Cambridge, Mass.: Harvard University Press, 1963), p. 6.

[34] For a detailed description, see Christopher Rand, "Profile: Center of a New World," Parts I, II, and III. *New Yorker,* Vol. 40 (April 11, 18, and 25, 1964), pp. 43–90, 57–107, 55–129.

[35] Roswell Gilpatric, *The Changing Patterns of Defense Procurement,* Office of the Secretary of Defense, June 19, 1962.

[36] Kerr, *op. cit.,* p. 70.

North Carolina State College. Founded in 1955, it owns a 4,300 acre campus in the center of the Triangle area for the location of industrial and governmental research facilities. The *Industrial Development Manufacturers Record*, in its reference study on the Triangle assures clients that "the emphasis is on practicality." The basic concept, according to an official of the research park, is "that once a scientific complex is established, industrialization of a high order will follow throughout the state."[37]

Kansas' development literature features a brochure on the University of Kansas Center for Research in Engineering Science, established in 1961. The president of Kansas State, although not adverse to practicality, has stressed the basic research orientation of the Center as an "effective counter-measure to the reputation of anti-intellectualism" in the midwest, which has caused that region to lag behind the east and west coasts in the development of an electronics industry.[38]

The Georgia Institute of Technology has taken a somewhat different tack. Its Industrial Development Division has opened five area offices to give technical assistance to industry and to development groups in outlying parts of the state. The most recent branch was supported by contributions from industry, emphasizing the close ties between business and the university and between both of these and the activities of development agencies.

Local Schools and Plant Sites

Further evidence of the influence of business is the increased importance attached to the quality of local school systems as a factor in industrial site selection. All state development commissions attempt to put their best foot forward in this respect, particularly where the state has a foundation aid program to insure minimum standards. The community audit forms of companies offering site-selection advice typically call for great detail on the local public schools. George Melloan describes Robert L. Yaseen, vice president of Fantus Factory Locating Service, a consulting firm, as having been "amazed" by the sharp rise in importance of schools in plant-site selection, and quotes him as follows:

> You would think there would be more interest in operating economics than in the local schools and that obligations to the stockholders would take precedence over the needs of company executives, but prevailing school conditions have become one of the primary factors in site selection.[39]

Among other examples of business interest in local schools, Melloan cites the practice of General Electric, which not only makes thorough surveys of all aspects

[37] *North Carolina's Research Triangle* (Atlanta: Conway Publications, 1963), pp. 38 and 51.
[38] James A. McCain, *University Research: A Regional Resource*, Center for Research in Engineering Science, University of Kansas (Lawrence, n.d.), p. 3.
[39] "School Scrutiny: Good Educational Systems a Key Factor in Locating Plants," *Wall Street Journal*, September 23, 1965. See also the discussion of this point by David Rogers and Melvin Zimet, p. 39.

of local schools in its site-selection studies but has been known to participate in campaigns to obtain passage of local legislation for new school financing. The International Paper Company Foundation, he reports, budgeted $385,000 in 1965 for aid to 26 school systems that educate the children of the parent company's employees around the nation.[40]

The change in attitude among businessmen toward public expenditures for elementary and secondary education is striking. Some business interests still oppose tax increases for school purposes, but the large corporations seem to be moving steadily in the opposite direction. Such influential corporate support generally implies better local education, but the effects of the trend are probably greater in small towns, where pupils are less strictly separated by social class in different neighborhood schools. In large cities, companies seldom exert much influence, although individual executives may serve on local (usually suburban) boards of education.

DIRECT BUSINESS AID TO EDUCATION

In addition to making financial contributions to higher education, companies give other forms of direct aid as a result of general civic-mindedness and concern for promoting both the company's image and its products. A National Industrial Conference Board survey of 300 companies[41] mentions the following forms of aid given:

> Financial aid to educational institutions
> Student scholarships and loans
> Contributions of equipment and material
> Teaching aids
> Contributing manpower to education
> Sponsorship of educational radio and television programs
> Teacher study awards
> Work-study programs
> Special courses and meetings for students and teachers

In another sample of 167 business concerns, about 25 per cent reported giving aid in the following categories: secondary education, teacher education and development, and equipment assistance.[42] Albert L. Ayars estimated the total annual expenditure by business and industry in support of elementary and secondary education to be about $160 million.[43] This is a very rough estimate, based on figures furnished by a smaller sample of companies. As for the kinds of aid given, Ayar's sample yielded the data shown in Table 1.

[40] *Ibid.*
[41] *Op. cit.*
[42] Council for Financial Aid to Education, *Aid-to-Education Programs of Some Leading Business Concerns* (New York, 1964).
[43] "How Business and Industry Are Helping the Schools," *Saturday Review* (October 17, 1964), p. 70.

Table 1. Per Cent of 248 Firms Furnishing Given Types of Aid.

TYPE OF AID	PER CENT		
	ELEMENTARY	SECONDARY	COLLEGE
Student field trips	24	66	55
Speakers	18	62	59
Student club programs	4	60	8
Student work experience programs	7	26	39
Help in training and guidance	4	42	38
Student award programs	3	29	18
Curriculum advisors	4	22	19
Meeting facilities and equipment	4	17	14
Teachers and professors on loan	1	5	16
Substitute or night school teachers	1	14	22
Student travel programs	—	3	5
Other programs	2	6	6
Help in Upgrading Teachers			
Plant visits	24	54	34
Workshops, seminars	7	54	34
Research & work experience	1	10	24
Special classes	1	3	3
Travel programs	1	2	1
Other programs	2	5	3

Source: Albert L. Ayars, "How Business and Industry Are Helping the Schools," *Saturday Review* (October 17, 1964), p. 70.

The Rationale for Non-Financial Contributions

With some exceptions, non-financial business aid to schools is more extensive at the secondary than at the primary school level. Although professional education organizations have set standards for acceptable materials and services,[44] it is difficult to appraise the real gain to the schools of these activities.

Some insight into the pros and cons of various forms of aid from the point of view of industry is provided by the NICB study. Generally speaking, companies have to decide if the returns in good public relations—and, in some cases, in sales—warrant the time and effort invested in activities that tend to proliferate without limit. This judgment is necessarily subjective, since ready measures are not available either as to costs or to benefits.

The Minnesota Mining and Manufacturing Company furnished the NICB with an example of a firm that undertook a large-scale effort both "to promote more

[44] The Business-Industry Section of the National Science Teachers Association, the American Association of School Administrators, and the Association for Supervision and Curriculum Development have all been active in this field.

effective teaching" and "to stimulate demand" for a product line. In 1963, the company invited schools to participate in a contest by submitting proposals for the use of the company's equipment for making and projecting transparencies. Five hundred schools all over the country were to receive awards, a $3,000 "package" of equipment. The company's publicity supervisor coordinated the entire program, which involved local 3M dealers and an outside public relations agency. The overhead attached to this project is not stated, but the equipment and materials given away as prizes alone came to $1.5 million.[45] The NICB report concluded:

> Management foresees two benefits to the company from this program. The comments and ideas it obtains from the winning schools should prove valuable in planning the design of new models for this product line. And the program and attendant publicity should stimulate demand for other products by educational institutions throughout the country.[46]

While not all business aid to schools is on such a scale or so closely tied to the company's product line, the 3M example is significant as an extension of more modest forms of company participation into a special marketing technique.

The Role of Trade Associations

In the production and dissemination of teaching aids, trade associations and other cooperative industry groups are more active than individual firms. Two of the largest national business organizations, the Chamber of Commerce and the National Association of Manufacturers, also have extensive educational programs.

A particular concern of the NAM has been the "economic illiteracy" of the population. According to one of the Association's leaflets,

> If people understand the operation of our economic system, they are less likely to believe that government has the miraculous power to increase wages, decrease consumer prices, reduce taxes, and raise public welfare expenditures, all at the same time. They may even be less likely to vote for the candidate who promises all these things![47]

In pursuit of this ideal, the Association has helped to promote various programs of economic education, many of them directed at high school teachers and financed by business and industry. One program, developed by DuPont and adopted by the Association, consists of a three-session course that has been used by 600 business firms and trade associations and more than 1,000 colleges and high schools. During 1961 and 1962, the NAM distributed almost three million copies of an 11-booklet series entitled *Industry and the American Economy*. The NAM also provided the funds for several film series, among them a National Educational Television series called "The American Business System."

[45] National Industrial Conference Board, *op. cit.*, pp. 41–42.
[46] *Ibid.*, p. 42.
[47] Education Division, National Association of Manufacturers, *The Choice: Economic Ignorance or Understanding,* Mimeographed Report (New York, n.d.), p. 2.

A recent educational project of the NAM has been the publication of a series of pamphlets, *Job Previews*, which describe the duties, requirements, wages, and methods of entry for particular jobs. The pamphlets are intended for the use of high school guidance counselors, and information for this series is gathered from business firms and other associations. The Association has also sponsored a program called MIND (Methods of Intellectual Development), which has included experimentation in programed learning techniques in basic education and typing for the poorly educated.

The U.S. Chamber of Commerce is also active in the publication of educational information—for example, brochures promoting friendly relations between businesses and schools and information on how industry has used school-based training programs. Much of the Chamber's material is provided in the form of continuing loose-leaf supplements to its *Education Projects for Business Organizations*, a sourcebook of ways for "explaining your business, increasing economic literacy, raising educational levels, guiding youth, meeting manpower needs, meeting education needs." The topics covered in the sourcebook include research, instruction, campaigns (for better schools and pay, redistricting, and scholarships), recognition (awards for teachers), and legislation.

EDUCATION AS AN INDUSTRY AND AS A MARKET

The relationship between business and the world of education is not limited to the production of useful knowledge and trained workers on the one hand and contributions of money, goods, and services on the other. As might be expected in our commercial society, we frequently think of the school itself as a business—both as a manager of a kind of production and as a customer. This point of view is not new, but now it seems more relevant than ever before. Education is now called a "growth industry," a phrase that implies fundamental changes in the relationship between business and education.

The School Administrator as Production Manager

One of the first observers to describe an educator as a production manager was Thorstein Veblen:

> [University administrators] must be able to show by itemized accounts that the volume of output is such as to warrant the investment. So the equipment and personnel must be organized into a facile and orderly working force, held under directive control of the captain of erudition at every point, and so articulated and standardized that its rate of speed and the volume of its current output can be exhibited to full statistical effect as it runs. [The] various universities are competitors for the traffic in merchantable instruction. . . .[48]

[48] *Op. cit.*, pp. 64–65.

Veblen's analysis has been extended to primary and secondary schools by Raymond E. Callahan, who has attributed the development of the school administrator's role to the imposition of "Taylorism" on the operation of the public schools. In the face of traditional reluctance to provide adequate financial support for education, school administration became in effect a search for cost-cutting without regard to the educational value of the "product."[49] Particularly in the period from 1910 to 1930, the strength of business and industrial groups was in direct contrast to the vulnerability of administrators; great pressure was brought to bear to operate schools economically, to adopt business values, and to follow the edicts of the time-and-motion-study experts. Superintendents accepted the role of business executive and plant manager, a role reinforced by teacher-training institutions in which acceptable dissertations were produced on such subjects as "Public School Plumbing Equipment."

In Callahan's view, the search for economies has continued with relative disregard for quality,[50] and school administrators, preoccupied with questions of finance, feel more comfortable in discussing buildings and budgets than the curriculum and the learning process.[51]

Educational Productivity and Remedial Mechanization

Callahan's thesis about the penuriousness of school administrators is one face of a coin. The other face is the thesis exemplified in the title of an article by Daniel Seligman, "The Low Productivity of the Education Industry." Seligman recognizes in passing the difficulties in determining quality of output, but his main concern is for rising educational costs and an alleged decrease of return on the educational dollar.[52]

The appearance of Seligman's article coincided with the orbiting by Russia of the first earth satellite and the immediate subsequent outcry in America for a reform in our educational system. Predictably, the critique that followed the Soviet triumph reflected the large technological bias in the American approach to almost any problem—a bias that shows itself in the greater readiness of our public authorities to make capital appropriations than to provide adequate operating

---

[49] *Education and the Cult of Efficiency* (Chicago: University of Chicago Press, 1962).
[50] As the educational market assumes more importance, business complaints about their counterparts on school boards are certain to multiply. Thus, an executive who "supervises an expanding educational market program, says the field is 'the toughest market there is to sell in!' He adds: 'A man in business is willing to take some chances but when he gets on a school board he becomes very conservative. He's afraid of being accused of buying frills!'" George Melloan, "Selling to Schools: Big Education Outlays, New Teaching Methods Create a Vast Market," *Wall Street Journal,* May 3, 1965.
[51] Callahan, *op. cit.,* pp. 251–53.
[52] *Fortune,* Vol. 58 (October, 1958), pp. 135–36 ff. In fact, the measurement of real output, as well as input, has created thorny problems for economists studying employment and productivity in the service industries. See, for example, Victor Fuchs, "The Growing Importance of the Service Industries," *Journal of Business of the University of Chicago,* Vol. 38 (October, 1965), pp. 344–73.

budgets, in our continuing search for labor-saving devices, and, above all, in our general belief that most problems have purely technical solutions. While most of the critics of education agreed on the need for massive infusions of cash, they also were careful to consider ways and means for overcoming the technological backwardness they discerned in the educational system.

According to Seligman, the Ford Foundation had long been convinced that whatever the merits of traditional emphasis on the primary role of the teacher, it would be impossible to improve education merely by training more and better teachers. Consequently the Foundation stood ready to finance experiments to enhance "productivity." Among the early experiments undertaken were the use of classroom television, new audio-visual aids, teacher aides, a four-quarter system to utilize academic plants full-time, and consultation on scientific management from private firms.[53]

Expansion of the Educational Market

In the ensuing decade, this type of experimentation in education proliferated. With the advent of teaching machines, language laboratories, and enormously complex and expensive computerized classrooms, the education market that had been dominated by small suppliers became an object of interest to some of the nation's largest corporations. In 1961, *School Management*, a magazine for school administrators, listed about 600 school suppliers; by 1965 it listed 1,700 with additions of about 50 per month.[54] The growing size of the market could be judged from the expansion of national expenditures for education. In 1950, they totalled about $9.3 billion, or 3.5 per cent of the gross national product. Between 1954 and 1964, these outlays rose 142 per cent to $33.7 billion, or 5.4 per cent of GNP, and a rise to $50 billion or 6.1 per cent of GNP has been projected by 1973. "Of particular interest to suppliers," Melloan notes, is that "a rising share of educational spending is going into equipment and materials, as opposed to teacher salaries and other costs . . . ." The fast growth in new teaching tools apparently amazed the suppliers themselves. Seymour Ziff, an executive of Dage-Bell, called the potential "frighteningly enormous."[55] Its enormousness was underscored by the funds available—for example, the $100 million authorized for school libraries, textbooks, and related materials in the Elementary and Secondary School Education Act of 1965 and the $65 million allocated to college libraries under the Higher Education Act of 1965.

Product Development and Organizational Change

The race for the educational market, and particularly to produce items involving new teaching technologies, has had the sanction of important leaders in the education field. Richard Bright, appointed director of research for the U.S. Office of

[53] Seligman, *op. cit.*
[54] Melloan, "Selling to Schools," *op. cit.*
[55] Quoted in Melloan, *ibid.*

Education in 1966, came to his new job from the post of director of instructional technology at Westinghouse. An electrical engineer, he predicted at the time of his appointment that in the American school of the near future, the textbook would disappear and be replaced by the computer as a source of information.[56] Francis Keppel, former dean of the Graduate School of Education at Harvard and subsequently U.S. Commissioner of Education and Assistant Secretary of Health, Education, and Welfare, gave a prominent place to the new technology in his book, *The Necessary Revolution in American Education*. Commenting on the need to increase research and development in education far beyond recent levels (under 1 per cent of total expenditures for the U.S.), Keppel welcomed the help of the private sector of the economy, which he thought should not only provide materials for learning, but which also

> has a role to play beyond merely filling orders. As in other aspects of society's life, it too could invest funds in research and development. [An important contribution of industry could be] its know-how in the organization and management of research and development enterprises and in distributing their results. In an area where education has little experience, the private sector is knowledgeable and well-staffed.[57]

If the private sector was "knowledgeable and well-staffed," its resources were apparently poorly distributed for profiting fully from the new opportunities in education, and a corrective series of acquisitions and mergers followed. Even a partial listing of these arrangements suggests what an enthusiastic attitude corporate managers took toward the scope and possibilities of the new market. A fine example of optimism occurred when the Xerox Corporation purchased Basic Systems, Incorporated, even though the latter had consistently lost money; the president of Xerox defended the move on the grounds that it was "a cluster of very, very unusual people, and what we really acquired was a group of brains."[58] During 1965 and 1966, the financial pages reported that Xerox had gone on to acquire University Microfilms of Ann Arbor and American Educational Publications from the Wesleyan University Press. IBM purchased Science Research Associates, a Chicago educational publisher, and entered into a licensing agreement with the financial reporting firm of Dun & Bradstreet. Raytheon acquired both D. C. Heath, a major textbook publisher in Boston, and Dage-Bell, the largest manufacturer of language laboratory equipment. Alfred A. Knopf, having acquired Pantheon, was purchased by Random House, and the combine in turn was merged with RCA. ITT acquired Howard W. Sams & Company, a publisher of text and vocational materials, which itself controlled Bobbs-Merrill and several training facilities. Sylvania Electric Products entered into a special agreement with Readers Digest, which in turn absorbed dictionary publisher Funk & Wagnalls. Two of the biggest giants of all, General Electric and Time, Incorporated, put up the capital

---

[56] "Textbooks and Technology: How Computers Will Change the Teacher's Role," *National Observer*, May 9, 1966.
[57] (New York: Harper & Row, 1966), p. 120.
[58] Gene Smith, "Xerox Corp. Sets Education Role," *New York Times*, May 14, 1965.

for the General Learning Corporation, with an estimated equity of $37.5 million. The importance of the venture was underlined when Francis Keppel left government service to become the first chairman of General Learning.

Several of these changes, like the purchase of Basic Systems and Science Research Associates, represent a first step into the dynamic educational field by industrial giants eager to maintain a rate of growth begun elsewhere. The mergers between electronic firms and publishing houses apparently are in anticipation of two more specific developments. One of these involves the greatly expanded use of programed education, "the combining of editorial materials and electronic technology in a systems approach to educational problems."[59] In the succinct language of David Sarnoff, chairman of RCA, "They [the publishers] have the software and we have the hardware."[60] The other development, a possibility for the longer run, is the creation of information utilities. The IBM-Dun & Bradstreet agreement, apparently promising instant dissemination of financial information tailored to the needs of individual customers, is likely to set a pattern for subsequent information utilities in other fields of knowledge. In the view of one observer, "These utilities will in fact be supplying information that was formerly presented in printed format by publishers."[61] John Diebold, the head of an international management consulting company, has pointed out that since the field will be very expensive to enter, it is likely to become monopolistic and have high rates both of capital consumption and of profit return.[62]

The development of vast information storage and retrieval systems is, of course, aimed at a far larger market than schools and universities alone. Professor Fritz Machlup has suggested that education has been joined by research and development, publishing, information machines, professional services, communications, and even entertainment, to become the "knowledge industry."[63] In this setting, education appears simply as a retailer of old knowledge, and we are returned once more to the Platonic notion of the educative community.

THE INTERACTION OF BUSINESS AND EDUCATION IN SOCIAL REFORM PROJECTS

In 1966, Merrill Lynch, Pierce, Fenner & Smith offered its clients a booklet called "The New American Horizon," which listed stocks of companies likely to benefit most from the Johnson Administration's "Great Society" plans. While stressing such items as the potential consequences for drug companies of Medicare and birth control plans, the report singled out for attention no fewer than eight publishing companies.

[59] William D. Smith, "Electronics and Books: Merger Path; Technology Stirs Search for Profits," *New York Times,* February 6, 1966.
[60] Harry Gilroy, "Electronics and Books: Merger Path; Trend Viewed Cautiously by Publishers," *New York Times,* February 6, 1966.
[61] Smith, *op. cit.*
[62] *Ibid.*
[63] *The Production and Distribution of Knowledge in the United States* (Princeton, N.J.: Princeton University Press, 1962).

The researchers now turning their talents to educational technology have also attempted to deal with other social problems. One of their basic tools is systems analysis, which involves, according to the president of Honeywell's Electronic Data Processing Division, "the skills of problem definition, of breaking down a massive and nearly incomprehensible set of factors into component parts that can be attacked prudently and efficiently."[64] This kind of engineering approach to problem-solving particularly appeals to American predilections. In 1965, the state of California contracted with several aerospace firms for feasibility studies designed to suggest

> whether dramatic new approaches might speed the solution of social and other problems in urban areas, where 70 per cent of Americans now live. Besides juvenile delinquency, fields in which California has contracted for preliminary studies include transportation of people and freight (North American Aviation, Inc.), information flow in government (Lockheed Aircraft Corp.) and waste management (Aerojet-General's life sciences division).[65]

An executive of Space-General Corp. (an Aerojet-General subsidiary), which had contracted for the study of delinquency, described the firm's capability this way:

> Our talent lies in the systems approach—being able to organize a vast complex problem by its components. . . . Whether we understand the relationships or not and without necessarily understanding any of the whys of those relationships, we can then expose that problem to all the technological devices and methods we use, for instance, in devising a grand plan to land a man on the moon.[66]

The change in the relationship between business and the community at large implied by these undertakings was summarized by Richard Cornuelle of the NAM: "The welfare state is more vulnerable to competition than to argument."[67]

The Competition Between Business and Educational Institutions in the Job Corps

Several companies have come into direct competition with educational institutions in connection with the training activities of the Job Corps. The operation of several large installations of the Job Corps was contracted to private companies that saw in these undertakings the same opportunities the aerospace companies saw in the California studies described above—a chance to get a foothold in the education business as a hedge against possible future declines in government defense spending and to acquire experience even at the cost of accepting limited profits now in return for the prospect of winning larger contracts in the future.

Among the companies holding Job Corps contracts in 1966 for the operation

[64] Walter Finke, as quoted in "Tackling the Big Ones," an editorial in the *Christian Science Monitor,* May 6, 1966.
[65] Mitchell Gordon, "Down to Earth; Aerospace Firms Seek to Turn Their Talents to Curing Urban Ills," *Wall Street Journal,* June 9, 1965.
[66] *Idem.*
[67] Quoted in Melloan, "Great Society Corp.; Businesses Undertake Broad Social Programs, Reap Gains Themselves," *Wall Street Journal,* April 7, 1966.

of residential vocational training centers were Federal Electric (a subsidiary of International Telephone and Telegraph), Litton Industries, Philco (Ford Motor Company), Economics Systems Corporation (AVCO), Science Research Associates (IBM), U.S. Industries, Burroughs Corporation, Packard-Bell Electronics, and General Precision Equipment. Some of these firms received contracts formerly held by non-profit institutions, on the grounds that private companies had done a better job.[68] This conclusion has been the subject of some controversy,[69] but the eagerness with which business has embraced competition with existing educational institutions is not at issue. Federal Electric, which operated the center at Camp Kilmer, New Jersey, once saw itself as the heir of the entire national effort: "We are going to run the best camp," said its president, "and get the best job-placement results and then submit a proposal in 18 months to take over the whole program."[70]

CONCLUSION

While the new role of business in education is by no means a unique instance of business involvement in decision-making in the public sector, it obviously raises several sensitive issues, most of which have been inadequately researched. We know that individual businessmen participate in the setting of educational policy, but studies in this field have not been designed either to measure their influence or to distinguish it from the political influence of other identifiable groups.[71] When businessmen serve on boards of education, they have the same opportunity as other citizens to act on their beliefs. Ultimately, the educational process is subject to the influence of every interest group, and in the case of the public schools—theoretically at least—to the electorate. Whatever businessmen do or do not do in this sphere deserves the same critical view as the behavior of any other group or, alternatively, of the workings of the system as a whole.[72]

[68] Sargent Shriver, the director of the Office of Economic Opportunity, made this judgment on the basis of the absence of "incidents" in business-run camps. The *New York Times*, in reporting on this statement, went on to say: "Job Corps officials feel that conclusions about who is best qualified to run a Job Corps center are subject to several considerations: the brevity of the experience, luck, especially when incidents occur away from the camp, and the possibility that the corporations have more sophisticated controls on adverse publicity." Joseph A. Loftus, "Business Lauded for Job Corps Role," *New York Times*, September 6, 1965.

[69] For a discussion of the issues, see National Committee on the Employment of Youth, "The Job Corps: A Dialogue," *American Child*, Vol. 48 (Winter, 1966). For a somewhat fuller discussion of the role of business in the Job Corps, see Ivar Berg and Marcia Freedman, "The Job Corps: A Business Bonanza," *Christianity and Crisis* (May 31, 1965), pp. 115–19.

[70] "Shriver and the War on Poverty," *Newsweek*, September 13, 1965.

[71] See S. V. Martorana, *College Boards of Trustees* (Washington, D.C.: Center for Applied Research in Education, 1963).

[72] For a cautionary tale of the effects of uncertainty among business influentials on the fate of a university, see D. S. Greenberg, "Pittsburgh: The Rocky Road to Academic Excellence," *Science*, 151 (February 4, 11, and 18, 1966), pp. 549–52, 658–62, and 799–801.

It is a different case when corporations, acting formally as corporations, openly involve themselves in setting public policy, with the consequent blurring of distinctions between the public and the private sector. Alfred C. Neal, president of the Committee for Economic Development, has asserted that

> the differences between organizations operating as businesses and those operating as governments are becoming more indistinct all the time. Governments conduct themselves in more businesslike ways, to the advantage of everyone. Businesses conduct themselves in more government-like ways, also to the advantage of everyone.[73]

Where this leaves our vaunted pluralism and the freedoms pluralism is supposed to protect is worthy of investigation. Henry S. Kariel has pointed out the dangers of allowing the search for consensus to suppress conflict and give to the private sector those opportunities for power that the Constitution was designed to frustrate in the public sector.[74] How much power of this kind business has accumulated already is uncertain, but it is extensive enough to have spawned a considerable literature about corporate responsibility, business statesmanship, and the legitimacy of responding to claims and exerting influence outside the classic competitive role.[75]

The giant corporations that recently entered the educational field clearly did so in order to reap new profits. They are bound to have a profound influence on educational policy unless their activities are subjected to extensive restraints. What will be the nature of the influence flowing from the profit motive? The market power of these firms will probably result in greater production and use of sophisticated equipment. At first firms may tend to check each other, but under the pressure of competition technical innovations may proliferate at a rate that will prevent their ever being evaluated. There is, after all, no regulatory body like the Food and Drug Administration that can order withdrawal of a worthless machine. If the process of merging continues apace, and if the knowledge industry is consolidated into a network of information utilities, there will be no possible check except government intervention.

A special danger inherent in the new involvement of corporate giants in education is that technalism may be pursued for its own sake, to the detriment of other programs that also compete for a share of the educational dollar. Lawrence Cremin has warned against the "heady idea" of some reformers who look to the eventual production of "teacher-proof" materials,

> so tightly and artistically constructed as to be impervious to misuse by ill-trained instructors. . . . But education is too significant and dynamic an enterprise to be left to mere technicians; and we might as well begin now the prodigious task

---

[73] Melloan, "Great Society Corp.," *op. cit.*
[74] *The Decline of Pluralism* (Stanford, Calif.: Stanford University Press, 1961).
[75] See, for example, Henry G. Manne, "Corporate Responsibility, Business Motivation, and Reality," *Annals of the American Academy of Political and Social Science*, Vol. 343 (September, 1962), pp. 55–64. See also the essays here by Clarence Walton, p. 83, David Rogers and Melvin Zimet, p. 39, and Ivar Berg, p. 147.

of preparing men and women who understand not only the substance of what they are teaching but also the theories behind the particular strategies they employ to convey that substance. A society committed to the continuing intellectual, aesthetic, and moral growth of all its members can ill-afford less on the part of those who undertake to teach.[76]

The danger, however, is not only in undermining teacher preparation but also in permitting the search for attractive new techniques to obscure long-standing problems in the organization and administration of public education. Efficiency alone does not produce quality or result in social change. Many issues, ranging from geographical inequities to the "role strains" of school principals, are not amenable to purely technical approaches. They are too complex for their solution to be entrusted to any single group in American life. Like other groups, business may contribute, but its methods, innovations, and influence merit continuous evaluation.

SELECTED READINGS

MARY JEAN BOWMAN, "The Human Investment Revolution in Economic Thought," *Sociology of Education*, Vol. 39 (Spring, 1966), pp. 111–37. This article summarizes, under sensible headings and to some extent in the familiar shorthand of economists, the contribution of the economics profession to an understanding of educated people as "human capital."

FRITZ MACHLUP, *The Production and Distribution of Knowledge in the United States* (Princeton, N.J.: Princeton University Press, 1962). An imaginative effort to map the "knowledge industry" in the United States, this volume is a mine of information about the many overlaps between the educational establishment and business enterprises.

EDWARD F. DENISON, *The Sources of Economic Growth in the United States and the Alternatives Before Us*, Supplementary Paper No. 13 (New York: Committee for Economic Development, 1962). This influential study, also recommended in connection with the essay by Gordon C. Bjork, examines the substantial contribution of education to total national income and to the growth in per capita income in the U.S. in the period 1929–57. Since on-the-job training as well as formal schooling is considered, the author's estimates must be evaluated with some caution. The findings reported suggest that corporations influence growth in a variety of indirect ways by their impact on the supply of and demand for "education."

SOLON T. KIMBALL AND JAMES E. MCCLELLAN, JR., *Education and the New America* (New York: Random House, 1962). Vintage Books (Random House) softcover edition, 1966. This is a first-rate and lucidly written statement of the function of American education as seen by a distinguished anthropologist and a philosopher. The authors regard the school as a "transitional institution," and from

---

[76] *The Genius of American Education, op. cit.*, pp. 56–57.

this perspective they thoroughly analyze the relationship between schools and American society, including the "corporate structures of the public world."

LAWRENCE A. CREMIN, *The Transformation of the School: Progressivism in American Education, 1876–1957* (New York: Vintage Books, 1961). Includes important historical material on vocationalism in the development of the public school system.

THORSTEIN VEBLEN, *The Higher Learning in America* (New York: Hill & Wang, 1957). This classic critique by the iconoclastic institutional economist first raised some of the questions pursued in this essay.

FRANCIS KEPPEL, *The Necessary Revolution in American Education* (New York: Harper & Row, 1966). Among the revolutions Mr. Keppel envisages in American education is one directed toward the large-scale reorganization of the public schools based primarily on a greatly expanded American capacity for research and development. He emphasizes the significance of private industry in helping to accomplish the technical aspects of this "necessary revolution."

chapter 13

BUSINESS AND
THE CREATIVE ARTS

ROBERT N. WILSON *is a distinguished social scientist who has made significant contributions to the sociology of the arts. In this essay he examines the impact of the American business system on artistic culture in the United States. Professor Wilson's balanced appraisal stands in contrast to a great deal of alarmist writing that has concerned itself with the same theme. Countless commentators have pointed to the soft-core autobiographies of actresses, ugly urban buildings, and the hideous design of many of the beached whales that crowd our highways as evidence of the violence done to aesthetic standards in a business society. Hardly a month goes by without some "little magazine" appearing with an article condemning the "wasteland" produced by television crews in the hire of corporations bent upon providing a visual chewing gum for tired American eyes. Drama critics bemoan the decline of the theater and point out that in a commercial society, in which aesthetic judgments must be made with a sober eye toward profit, we are likely to find more splashy musicals than serious drama and more situation comedies than inspired explorations of the human situation. Indeed, if the noisiest popular critics are to be believed, the Supreme Court's definition of pornographic material, in the celebrated Ginzberg case, as material that looks only to titillation and lacks any redeeming intellectual and aesthetic value, would seem to cover most of what is offered to culture-seeking Americans.*

Professor Wilson takes a longer and broader view of the matter. While he does not minimize the more unpleasant truths concerning the state of taste or the conditions facing artists in a business society, he recognizes the benefits that accrue to the arts and to artists from the interplay of freedom and affluence in a democratic business society. In a three-step sociological analysis, he examines the differences in the imperatives to which artists and businessmen respond, the differences in the role of artist and businessman in the structure of the social system, and the impact of business decisions upon the content of the arts and upon the atmosphere in which artists must work. In conducting this appraisal, he gives a great deal of weight to the bureaucratic character of modern business and modern society and so succeeds in identifying many more interesting tensions in the business-art nexus than have been delineated in analyses that focus on the motives *of business leaders and artists rather than the* structural contexts *in which work and art are embedded. Many questions will occur to the reader in response to this analysis.*

1. Professor Wilson indicates that the contemporary artist has more in common with the business entrepreneur of old than does the modern business leader. Why, then, do serious artists so often fail as vendors of their own work in contemporary America?

2. It could be argued that businessmen, both privately and as purchasers of art for their organizations, are too tolerant of avant garde *art and that this inhibits the maturation and reduces the self-discipline of young artists who find too-early and too-rewarding markets for their work. Might this observation help explain why more American artists do not rise from the output of popular art to the production of high culture?*

3. Professor Wilson points out that popular culture accepts business values, while high culture severely questions them. Acceptance is usually thought of as a quality of the mature and rebellion as a quality of the immature; why, then, do the later works of so many great artists represent higher culture than their early works? Which does more to undermine a value, a rebellion against it or the indifference sometimes implied by the creation of a wholly new value?

4. According to Professor Wilson, the creator of high culture is at odds with society. Make a case for the position that businessmen, too, are at odds with society, specifying the precise ways in which they differ in their confrontation with the status quo.

5. Compare and contrast the consequences to American society of the postures of the businessman and the creator of high culture as you have delineated them in response to the previous question.

ROBERT N. WILSON \\ HIGH CULTURE AND
POPULAR CULTURE
IN A BUSINESS SOCIETY

Artists and intellectuals became acutely vulnerable to pressures from the commercial nexus in eighteenth-century England. Greatly heightened levels of literacy in the population, joined with cheaper techniques of printing and distribution, exposed the purveyors of high culture to a market situation.[1] England in the Industrial Revolution can perhaps be taken as a precursor of what we should today term a "business society." Manufacturing, trade, and finance began to create an economic climate that affected all who worked in the arts—or in anything else. Of equal or larger significance, these activities were linked to political and religious themes to foster a climate of values sustaining the acquisitive thrust of a business society.

The shift from an economic base of aristocratic and other patronage to an increasingly open popular marketplace for art could be construed both as a favorable omen and as threatening exposure from the artist's point of view. It began to give him independence from the vagaries of whimsical patrons, making him more nearly his own man. Too, the expanded market offered a potential mass audience that could afford him a comfortable—in rare cases a handsome—income from the sale of his creations. At the same time, the writer or artist became willy-nilly an entrepreneur, confronted by the iron dictates of popular taste; often an amateur, not to say naïve, businessman, he was in many instances a ready victim of the manipulative printer or merchant. This was one meaning of London's Grub Street, the residence of poor writers so often mentioned in English literature: raw exploitation of the writer or would-be writer, whose literary skill often exceeded his talent for dealing with the exigencies of a developing business system.

THE DISCREPANCY BETWEEN BUSINESS AND AESTHETIC VALUES

Very early in the development of business societies in western Europe, artists and devotees of high culture began to enunciate a state of warfare between what they perceived to be the values of businessmen and the values of an aesthetic elite. Artists and intellectuals, being professionally articulate, were able to frame the terms of warfare and preempt the field of expression; businessmen and government officials, if they reacted at all, waged the battle by obdurate inattention

---

[1] A particularly astute and well-documented account of this transformation appears in Leo Lowenthal, *Literature, Popular Culture and Society* (Englewood Cliffs, N.J.: Prentice-Hall, 1961).

rather than by aggressive persecution of the artist. Although the artist objected then, and objects now, to many tangible features of a business system—the accumulation of material goods, the focus on money as a measure of man and his works, the rigorous efficiency of factory discipline, the single-minded stress on a narrow route to achievement—it is probably true that his fundamental argument was and is with the abstract structure of values that underlies the business society as he has experienced it. Thus Stendhal wrote, "Far be it from me to conclude that industrialists are not honorable. All I mean is that they are not heroic."

And César Graña, describing Baudelaire, poignantly expressed what the artist asserts against the business system: "a retention of the uncontrollable in human affairs and the philosophical anxiety and aesthetic intrigue of the world." Surely a taste for philosophical anxiety and aesthetic intrigue is quite far from the concerns of most members of a business society (or perhaps any society). Baudelaire at one pole and, say, Dickens' Gradgrind or Defoe's Crusoe at the other seemingly have little to say to one another. What, then, is the nature of the discrepancy in values between an aesthetic dandy and a successful manufacturer?

A clue to one aspect of the discrepancy is contained in Stendhal's complaint that industrialists are "not heroic." By this he means that they are calculating, not that they are cowardly. Business activity rewards the individual who can operate in a rational, foresighted, utilitarian manner, who pursues discrete goals and husbands his resources in a mode of disciplined efficiency. The businessman dreams realizable dreams. To the Romantic artist, especially, this apparently unexceptionable pattern of behavior is gross, demeaning, grubbily undignified. He calls for a non-utilitarian orientation, a gratuitous release of human resources, the quest for the unattainable. His favored discipline consists in the exigencies of the tragic muse, not in the factory time clock or the margin of profit. He inclines to prefer the lifelong aesthetic gamble, the staking of the self against immense odds of existence and creation, to the calculated risk of bringing off a commercial venture.

Another facet of the separation between artist and industrial man concerns their conceptualizations of experience. This difference in ways of seeing and talking is at least partly rooted in the existence of two fundamental patterns of communication, which Suzanne Langer has described as the "discursive" and "presentational" models. In discursive language—that of prose—words and images point to discrete aspects of experience; they tell someone about something in the fashion of logical pointing. In presentational language—that of poetry and the arts—the symbolic vehicles are directed to re-creating in the recipient an impression of a total slice of life, rather than to making statements or propositions. Discursive language compartmentalizes life, deals with it in parcels that can be wrapped and labeled; presentational language expresses and stimulates the rich whole of seamless experiencing at many levels of apprehension. High culture most nearly approaches the use of presentational language, while business and industry must clearly be conducted in discursive terms.

At bottom, the differences in value are almost certainly matters of that indefinable property called "style." When Sinclair Lewis jeers, in the opening sentences of *Main Street,* at the Ford cars and other small-town artifacts for which "Erasmus wrote in Oxford cloisters," he expresses a disappointment with plain American business style and a hunger for the grandeur of some alternative.

If the practitioners and audiences of high culture feel a disaffection, indeed a sharp enmity, for business society, what may be said of those dedicated to popular culture? Here, it seems, the polarization is a good deal less extreme. Popular culture is by definition closer to the dominant values and common tastes of the society in which it occurs; it is popular, in part, precisely because it is comfortable. The books, films, and drama of popular culture take advantage of business society in that they are supported by its affluence and its scheme of values. In turn, they tend to exalt those ideas, emotions, and customs that ensure a viable motivational base for the industrial-commercial enterprise. Popular culture is to a profound extent the creature of a business society, especially in its close connection to the ends and means of advertising. Indeed, we may find that one of the most important distinctions between high and popular culture is that popular culture accepts business values and exhorts its audience to do likewise, while high culture severely questions those values and easy assumptions.

WHAT IS A BUSINESS SOCIETY?

A major hazard to sensible discussion about the roles of artists and art in society has been the lack of precision in defining just what kind of art and what kind of society are in question. The serious poet or painter or composer, for instance, is probably always at odds with the society around him in some sense. His activity is rare and singular; he works alone; he assesses those perceptions and evaluations that most people around him take for granted (and perhaps *must* take for granted) in the conduct of their daily affairs. Similarly, the popular artist is presumably always in tune with whatever version of social order surrounds him. He reaffirms its key tenets, does not interrogate its foibles too extensively, caresses the surface of life as it is usually lived. He may probe the cracks in the façade of social consensus, but he is not likely to batter at its foundations.

Having generalized so boldly, one must try to specify what artists behave how in what sorts of societies. In the present context the burden is to characterize "business society," "high culture," and "popular culture" before much progress can be made in analyzing their relationships. By a business society I mean to denote the societies of western Europe, the United States, and Canada, those social structures marked by representative government, democratic polity, a more-or-less free economy in which entrepreneurial striving is prominent, and a developed industrial-commercial pattern. The business society is in this sense to be distinguished from industrial countries that do not have a strong entrepreneurial tradition or a relatively free marketplace (the U.S.S.R. being the type case) and from the so-called developing or underdeveloped societies. The primary referent of a business society is the contemporary United States.

Although a description of the United States in these terms could be a very elaborate essay, I shall confine my remarks to three major themes that are particularly relevant to the position of the artist and the processes of the arts. These are the primacy of the business calling, the organization of business enterprise, and the motivations and styles that accompany this calling and this form of organized effort.

We hear often today of Americans' disenchantment with business occupations and with the cluster of values centering on achievement of profit. Only a minority of college seniors frankly aspires to a business career. Public opinion polls show large percentages of the population to be skeptical about business ethics and the truth of advertisement and to question the contribution of business to the common good. Nevertheless, both the total distribution of vocations and the values demonstrated in everyday life leave slight doubt that Calvin Coolidge's words are as accurate now as when he spoke them in the twenties: the business of America *is* business. Our heralded affluence is as much the product of business values as of natural abundance, and that affluence in turn reinforces the rightness of energetic striving for gain. No matter that most men work for salary rather than profit, in offices rather than stock exchanges, what is important is the way they work and the promises for which they work. The way they work is dutifully, in the veritable spirit of the Protestant ethic; the promises for which they work are a combination of material plenty and that self-validation Max Weber traced from its religious origins.

With the exception of two professions—medicine and law—business occupations are perhaps the only ones in our society that usually require no explanation by their adherents: no apology, rationalization, or explication is called for. In a country without an aristocratic tradition exalting leisure and amateurism, the businessman could become—as he has—the natural aristocrat. Linked to this ready acceptance of business callings as inherently right and appropriate to the masculine role, we find the most obvious measure of their primacy in the money economy. Business roles are rewarded in the marketplace on a scale that far exceeds the compensation of any other occupational category; it is a commonplace, for instance, that men at the very highest levels of government triple or quadruple their salaries if they move into the business sector.

If business occupations indeed constitute the primary model for occupational life, so the patterns of organized effort in business pursuits are models for understanding the organization of work throughout the society. Work relationships in a business organization are fundamentally bureaucratic in type, distinguished by specialization, interlocking functions, discrete formulation of goals and definition of means, hierarchy of authority, and rational accountability of effort. Accompanying and enforcing these themes is a conception of technical expertness —exemplified by the engineer, the accountant, the machinist—resting on trained capacity for specified work performances. The calculability of effort directed toward scheduled achievements is a pervasive characteristic of business enterprise; it is one very important mode of what Max Weber foresaw as the rationalization of life, the disenchantment of the world. Above all, contemporary business implies membership in a bureaucratic structure and adherence to bureaucratic norms. It enjoins a coordinated network of relations to fellow members, the kind of intensive involvement and allegiance entailed in the vulgar designation "organization man."

Business callings and business institutions are underpinned by a distinctive American motivational complex that stresses the need for achievement, for the approval of one's peers, for the validation of self in tangible outcomes of striving. Although these motives are obviously not unique to the business society, they seem here to be peculiarly intense; what is crucial is not the desire for achievement itself but the zealous nature of the pursuit, the concentration on external criteria of individual worth, the calculated employment of human resources. Complementing these motivational springs of business effort is a style of life marked by activism, dutifulness, and the careful pacing of behavior toward a deferred reward. Considerations of functional efficacy are assumed to dominate the enterprise, so that we ordinarily ask, not "What kind of person is he?" but, "What can he *do?*"

WHAT ARE HIGH CULTURE AND POPULAR CULTURE?

It is patently impossible to attain perfect agreement about the boundaries of the two versions of cultural life with which we are concerned. We must at once note that our use of the term culture is narrower and more in keeping with common usage than with the anthropologist's concept. That is, we are confined to the intellectual-artistic sector of man's social heritage and patterned contemporary behavior and neglect the total range of styled choices that makes up the "culture" of a human group. Culture in our sense is connoted by those vehicles that are conserved, created, and transmitted to entertain and instruct through the imaginative representation of life. It embraces the arts, broadly construed to include novels, dramas, poems, paintings, sculpture, the dance, and music. It occurs in the traditional media—the book or performance—and the newer mass channels of television, movies, radio, magazines, and newspapers.

At their extremes, high and popular culture are relatively easy to distinguish. High or fine culture seriously aspires to comparison with the winnowed excellence of the past, with the few preserved exemplary works in the artistic and critical heritage. Popular culture, variously termed "mass" or "mediocre," aspires only to contemporary acceptance by large audiences, is designed almost wholly for amusement, and is governed by no canons more rigorous than the producer's guess at what will stimulate an easy enjoyment. High culture is demanding and asks of its audience an imaginative participation, a deep and alert responsiveness along a spectrum of sensibility. Popular culture is undemanding, requires of its audience minimal attentiveness, and is satisfied with superficial responsiveness often limited to "liking" or "disliking." But given these polar cases, we confront a fairly wide middle area of ambiguity. There would presumably be little dispute with the classification of, say, Picasso or T. S. Eliot as practitioners of high culture or the author of a television situation comedy as a promoter of popular culture. There is, however, that penumbra often designated as "middlebrow" or *kitsch* that seemingly aspires simultaneously to fastidious critical acceptance and mass response. Works and artists that do not fall clearly at either extreme inspire passionate debate among observers who feel that a division is crucial and must be rigidly maintained.

Devotees of high culture are given to despair about the state of the arts. They are inclined to argue that a mass business society inevitably imposes a sort of aesthetic Gresham's Law, in which bad art drives out good. The good, at any rate, is taken to be the enemy of the best; a combination of business values and the proficiency of the mass media lends to this enemy an overwhelming advantage. Thus the great variety and bulk of popular culture are assumed to drown out the lonely but elegant voice of high culture.

There are other apostles of high culture, however, of whom Edward Shils[2] is an example, who maintain that a pluralistic society can fittingly sustain varied levels of culture. They contend that popular culture is not by definition "bad" in total and that a business society is not inherently inimical to the creation and appreciation of works of high culture. One might conclude that a pessimistic view is poised in fatiguing and apparently limitless debate against an optimistic one. As César Graña once observed in analyzing the pessimist, "the open industrial society can produce neither a social structure nor a set of cultural images to which a certain kind of intellectual can pay homage." Shils, and writers such as David White or Gilbert Seldes, adopt an optimistic stance. They do not exalt popular culture, nor do they proclaim the business society as a champion of high culture. Rather, they note that this society *allows* for high culture and that it is up to sensitive creators and critics to show an energetic persistence in their callings.

We have, then, a series of questions, often too sharply posed. Can high culture coexist with a business society? Can high culture coexist with popular culture? Are both high and popular culture so pervaded by the values and styles of a mass industrial social system that art has forever lost its noble autonomy? Such angular alternatives, and their issue in a vivid rhetoric of all-or-nothing, must probably give way to more intricate problems and tentative solutions under sober examination. We shall try to inquire into the complex of relationships among American business society, its arts, artists, and audiences.

DIRECT ARTICULATION OF BUSINESS WITH HIGH AND POPULAR CULTURE

The most obvious, if not really the simplest, relationship between business and the arts is strictly economic. In a money economy where business generates the money, both high and popular culture are dependent on business for essential support. Business is the patron of the fine arts and the acknowledged master of the popular arts. Surpluses from business activity, the basis of our affluence, pay the bills for the enterprises of high culture; these monies foster university and foundation—and now government—provisions for subsidies of artists and their

[2] See "The High Culture of the Age," in Robert N. Wilson, ed., *The Arts in Society* (Englewood Cliffs, N.J.: Prentice-Hall, 1964).

works. Business fortunes and, increasingly, business salaries, go to buy paintings, to subscribe to symphonies, and to commission architecture and sculpture.

Popular culture is in great measure not so much the creature of business surplus as it is an integral part of expenditure in business institutions. Advertising is of course the primary route for this expenditure, and the products of popular culture are intimately attached to business because their media (television, radio, magazines) exist on business support. The historian David M. Potter describes advertising as the "characteristic institution" of an abundant society (the United States) and remarks on how little we know about this institution:

> But advertising as an institution has suffered almost total neglect. One might read fairly widely in the literature which treats of public opinion, popular culture, and the mass media in the United States without ever learning that advertising now compares with such long-standing institutions as the school and the church in the magnitude of its social influence. It dominates the media, it has vast power in the shaping of popular standards, and it is really one of the very limited group of institutions which exercise social control. Yet analysts of society have largely ignored it.[3]

And with reference to the context in which the popular artist functions:

> It is as impossible to understand a modern popular writer without understanding advertising as it would be to understand a medieval troubadour without understanding the cult of chivalry, or a nineteenth-century revivalist without understanding evangelical religion.[4]

Potter goes on to rehearse the basic argument advanced by many observers in recent years concerning the connection of media content to the desiderata of advertising. Popular culture, in this view, is constrained always by the businessman's understandable desire to reach the widest possible audience for his wares; the larger the audience, the more likely it is that a lowest common denominator of taste and subject matter will prevail. Thus popular art cannot shock, cannot be profound, cannot demand too much of its audience, and cannot treat matters that interest only a minority of readers, viewers, or listeners. In the words of an English critic quoted by Potter, American periodical writing "fixes the attention but does not engage the mind." And, contends Potter, this is exactly what the advertiser who supports the popular arts wants: to hold the audience without so stimulating or involving it that attention is seriously diverted from the accompanying commercial message.

Against this gloomy appraisal of the possibilities for popular culture there stand at least some significant examples of business support for works of popular excellence. Our business society has occasionally made fine drama available on television, has widely distributed many good books (the "paperback revolution" in publishing), and has generated the techniques of reproduction and distribution that make prints of good paintings accessible to the meanest wall space. Two

---

[3] *People of Plenty* (Chicago: University of Chicago Press, 1954), p. 167.
[4] *Ibid.*, p. 168.

questions may be raised about the mass dissemination of excellence, involving respectively the identities of the creator and the audience. The first reservation notes the propensity of purveyors, in a commercial climate, to bet on sure things; certifiable works of high culture from the past are preferred to the ambitious efforts of contemporaries. Thus we may receive Shaw or Sophocles on television infrequently but Samuel Beckett almost never. Publishers are willing to risk bringing out a large cheap edition of Wordsworth (aided by the fact that his works are in the public domain), but the works of modern poets like Ezra Pound or William Carlos Williams are much higher priced. The second question really asks whether the nature of the aesthetic transaction, the interplay between the artist and audience, is transformed by number, distance, or the perceptual set of respondents. Is Shakespeare-in-the-Park still Shakespeare? Is Homer less than or different from Homer if his verse is on sale in thousands of drugstores? Those who yearn for an elite audience whose sophistication matches the quality of the work of art are perhaps at one with Kingsley Amis in his contention about expanding university enrollments: more is worse. Yet we cannot be very sure—was the tiny audience of the past in uniformly deep communion with the artist's highest intentions? Is the mass audience of the present so inattentive or obtuse as to destroy the aesthetic relationship? How can the value of many people enjoying a poem at a certain, perhaps superficial, level of receptivity be weighed against the value of a precious few responding with a full engagement of their perceptual resources?

Direct articulation of business society with high and popular culture clearly entails more than the content of the arts and the character of the audience. Conspicuously, it involves the economic position of those who create. Business values and organizational genius insure that the successful practitioner of popular culture will be handsomely rewarded. Never in history has the really popular writer, for instance, found his craft more lucrative. Dickens, or even Scott Fitzgerald, looks like a marginal literary sharecropper when compared with Harold Robbins or Irving Wallace or any regularly employed screenwriter. In Hollywood, on Broadway, and in publishing the economics of a mass business society offer an enormous jackpot to lucky winners. The support given artists tends, however, to be unevenly distributed and wildly oscillating in amount; a few are highly compensated, many are rewarded sporadically and modestly, many do not survive.

Creators of high culture stand in a peculiarly ambiguous position. Their art is not economically feasible in a business society; with very few exceptions the painter, poet, or composer does not earn his way in the marketplace. It may well be argued that the fine arts have never been able to pay their own way and that the phenomenon specific to our society is not the fact of subsidy but merely a change in its sources. For church, state, or municipality, substitute universities, foundations, or business institutions themselves. An affluent business society probably offers more, and more varied, kinds of support for the serious artist than does any other social arrangement. Yet this economic flooring is not always granted to the artist as artist; it tends to come in the form of the "second job," the paying employment of the artist as teacher, editor, professional, or businessman—or even producer of popular culture. If the second job is avowedly non-creative and substantially different from the task of art, its demands obviously divert the artist from investing anything like full time and energy in his artistic vocation. (However, some artists—notably the insuranceman-poet Wallace Stevens and the physician-poet William Carlos Williams—have asserted that the running of careers in tandem is psychologically satisfying.) In general, second jobs that are close to the artistic endeavor but not identical with it, such as teaching and editing, appear most congenial to the continued generation of products of high culture.

The serious artist as intermittent producer of popular culture presents a very interesting case. A poet and university don who writes mystery novels (C. Day Lewis), a social historian who did the same (Bernard De Voto), the many novelists who work on film scripts—each of these may handle his money-making chore with aplomb, indeed with relish. On the other hand, some critics maintain that the rewarding opportunities afforded by popular culture are likely to seduce the artist, consuming his spirit with trivia. Ezra Pound, for instance, argued many years ago that the poet must be subsidized or else his art will suffer from the blandishments of the popular media:

> Villon is the stock example of those who advocate the starvation of artists, but the crux is here, to wit, that Villon had nothing whatsoever to gain by producing a bastard art. No harpies besought him for smooth optimism, for patriotic sentiment, and for poems "to suit the taste" of our readers. If he had nothing to lose by one sort of writing he had equally little to gain by any other.[5]

There is little evidence, however, that artists must inevitably be corrupted if they make excursions into the popular. We do not know that Fitzgerald or Faulkner was inferior as a novelist to what he might have been had he never served time in Hollywood; Richard Eberhart is not demonstrably a less able poet for the fact that his verse has appeared in a ladies' magazine of astronomical circulation. Perhaps the puristic critic underrates the artist's versatility as craftsman, his ability to work alternately at more than one level and for more than one audience.

INDIRECT IMPLICATIONS OF BUSINESS FOR HIGH AND POPULAR CULTURE

It is tempting to suggest that the business society entirely determines the course of culture. Commercial-industrial-technological values are pervasive; the artist grows up in this climate, and is accordingly surrounded (some might say bombarded) at every turn by the sights and sounds, the assumptions and proclamations of business. Yet to regard this as the whole story would be to commit ourselves to a species of vulgar Marxist determinism. For the creator does just that: creates. The artist envisions possibilities and wrenches perceptions in ways that neither he nor his family nor his class can predict. The root meaning of creativity is that the artist will make, will invent something fresh. Who can say that the business

[5] *Patria Mia* (Chicago: Ralph Fletcher Seymour, 1950).

society that influenced the authors of *Babbitt* and *Death of a Salesman* has not been equally influenced by those works, driven to examine its premises and its manners? The industrial climate that produced an Andrew Wyeth, a Martha Graham, a Richard Lippold, or an Alexander Calder, even a Gertrude Stein, has been in turn affected by those innovators.

Furthermore, the artist emphatically does not respond merely to his contemporary circumstances. The autonomy of art is grounded in its having a tradition, a series of products and evaluations that transcends particular times and places. In the republic of art are many mansions, and it is to these, as well as to the everyday environment, that any given artist owes his stimulus and his allegiance. One must then admit that although a modern poet is undeniably influenced by business, he is shaped as much or more by, say, classic Chinese poetry or the rhythms of Gerard Manley Hopkins. The living presence of a tradition, of the forms and themes that are the vessels for the artist's insight, points to a further aspect of independence in the universe of high culture; this is culture's capability of changing from within. As several social theorists, notably Sorokin and A. L. Kroeber, have maintained, the sophisticated patterns of high culture are distinguished by a potential for immanent change. What Kroeber termed "pattern fulfillment," the unfolding of art and science according to an internal logic of structural development, should make us wary of attributing the paths of artistic culture solely to the flux of its institutional environment.

There are, however, at least two ways in which a business society holds crucial indirect implications for high and popular culture. The first is the impact of business on the content of the arts themselves; the second is the influence of a business atmosphere on the people involved, on artistic career lines, aesthetic sensibility, and the audience's responsive capacity.

We have earlier remarked the stock argument that advertising pushes the popular media toward the bland and the superficial. There seems little doubt that this is in general true. Advertisers are cautious about disturbing their public, and an art that does not disturb can scarcely be a vital experience. One may ask, however, in how far the drive toward a comfortable and stereotyped popular culture is specific to business as such; it may always accompany a mass society, that is, a society marked by widespread literacy, interdependence, centralization, and shared awareness. Thus, although the United States is surely more nearly the prototype of a business society than is Britain, critics of recent shifts in popular culture in the two countries make quite similar analyses. For example, in America the critic S. I. Hayakawa has compared the leading themes of our blues and of "popular" music; he notes how much more closely the former hew to the facts of life, how much greater is their bite and pungency. But after indicting the lyrics of Tin Pan Alley as sugary unrealism, he notes a trend:

> The existence of the blues demonstrates that it is at least possible for songs to be both reasonably healthy in psychological content and widely sung and enjoyed. But the blues cannot, of course, take over the entire domain of popular song because, as widely known as some of them have been, their chief appeal, for cultural reasons, has been to Negro audiences—and even these audiences

have been diminishing with the progressive advancement of Negroes and their assimilation of values and tastes in common with the white, middle-class majority.[6]

Paralleling this nostalgia for the integrity of a minority version of popular culture, Richard Hoggart writes of commercial dominance in British society as destructive of an older working-class culture:

> Inhibited now from ensuring the "degradation" of the masses economically, the logical processes of competitive commerce, favoured from without by the whole climate of the time and from within assisted by the lack of direction, the doubts and uncertainty before their freedom of working-people themselves (and maintained as much by ex-working-class writers as by others) are ensuring that working-people are culturally robbed. Since these processes can never rest, the holding down, the constant pressure not to look outwards and upwards, becomes a positive thing, becomes a new and stronger form of subjection; this subjection promises to be stronger than the old because the chains of cultural subordination are both easier to wear and harder to strike away than those of economic subordination.[7]

If the "chains of cultural subordination" are worn by the mass audience for popular culture, it must also be remembered that the business dollars forging the chains sometimes supply countervailing forces. Business has on occasion supported the dissemination of such contrary content, to use only the example of television, as *Death of a Salesman*, "This Was The Week That Was" (a satirical review of current affairs), and certain excellent presentations of "Playhouse 90."

Overt business themes tend to be almost entirely absent from high culture; serious artists have rarely dealt with business in any direct fashion. In the popular media, representations of businessmen and business life seem to be polarized. Business is portrayed either as a dramatic jungle, corrupt and corrupting (*Executive Suite*) or as a non-problematic source of life-style (father's occupation in any situation comedy). Perhaps business is mainly a steady hum in the background, an unquestioned framework for the minutiae of domestic concerns. Certainly it does not engage the attention as a milieu for dramatic action, in the way statecraft and kingly plot did for Shakespeare or Sophocles, war for the Greek poets, knightly romance for the medieval singer.

BUSINESS VALUES AND ARTISTIC CAREERS

Artistic careers in high culture are almost diametrically opposed to the career lines favored by a business model. It might be said that the artist's fabled "deviance" in American society begins exactly in his not being a businessman. Why should his career be suspect and marginal? Perhaps in the first instance its difference

---

[6] "Popular Songs vs. the Facts of Life," in Bernard Rosenberg and David Manning White, eds., *Mass Culture* (New York: The Free Press, 1957), p. 401.
[7] *The Uses of Literacy* (Boston: Beacon Press, 1961), pp. 200–01.

inheres in its not being in the usual sense a career at all: training is haphazard, certification is virtually non-existent, reward is capricious, the location and stated hours for work are not given but personally chosen, the criteria for evaluation of artistic competence are amorphous and notoriously unstable in the short run. The practitioner of high culture (and to a considerable extent the producer of popular culture as well) is far closer in spirit to the nineteenth-century business entrepreneur than he is to the bureaucratic business or professional man of today. An artist typically works in solitude and is therefore not heavily enmeshed in coordinated relations to others. His role is diffuse and wide-ranging, not narrowly contrived to fulfill a very specific function; everything human and natural *is* somehow a part of his frame of action. The life of the emotions is an integral part of his work, not an intrusion to be tightly disciplined during the performance of a task. A writer or painter must renew himself daily in the battle to be creative, and this absorption may entail a conception of time different from that of most members of an industrial society. He is concerned with the immediacy of creative effort and the eternity of aesthetic judgment, not with the balance sheet of next week or the promotion of next month.

And indeed the study of artistic careers in the contemporary United States provides evidence that entry into the artistic role is difficult and that persistence in the role requires a hardy spirit. The neophyte is harassed both by the intrinsic difficulty of attaining competence and by the pressures interested parties exert to push him toward a business style. Mature artists probably suffer most from economic instability, an instability that is a direct consequence of non-membership in the organizational nets within which most of their fellows work. But they are not immune from the knowledge that most people in their society regard their work as remote, possibly frivolous, and—in the case of men—in an important sense unmasculine. The roots of the suspicion that male artists are not wholly male are several: the traditional allocation of aesthetic interests to women in America; the seemingly high, and highly visible, numbers of homosexuals in certain arts (for instance, the dance); and the presence of a sensuous "feminine" component in art that is inhibited by the strictly male discipline of the business occupations.[8]

If business careers and artistic careers are so baldly discrepant, it is likewise no secret that the prevailing values of a business society offend the aesthetic sensibility. Science, technology, commerce, mass prosperity, the riotous profusion of things and services—all these seem to be inseparable from a style of rational and optimistic calculation. A well-ordered life, a planned life, an existence free from accident and marked by a cautious control over ends and means—the explicit goal of a middle-class business credo—appears as a living death to the majority voice in modern letters. Graña states the case succinctly:

> The prudence and prudery of the middle classes may look with horror upon lust, waste, irresponsibility, superstition, and violence, and middle-class "reform" may seek to eradicate them from society as a whole. But for the literary imagina-

[8] Wilson, ed., *op. cit.*, chapters 1–4.

tion these traits are often the companions of amusement, charm, grace, courage, and the daily predicament of human triumph and failure and, within failure, survival, a spectacle always reassuring to those bored with the hygienic and relentless optimism of the present age.[9]

The Protestant ethical spirit, the rationalization of life, and the organization of work according to bureaucratic modes all militate against any ready acceptance of business society by those who create works of high culture. Artists are at once more playful and more serious than the business style can countenance. They are more playful, not in the sense of unbridled hedonism or trivial pleasure-seeking, but in their experimental and flexible posture toward the problems of life's meanings. They are more serious not in a tense sobriety, but rather more in a capacity to savor the bloody angles of existence and to accept the tragic mode as a real part of human affairs.

BUSINESS VALUES AND THE AUDIENCE

Opinions about the influence of a business society on the audience for the arts differ sharply. Some observers feel that the open industrial system, with its affluence and communicative élan, provides a varied opportunity for the wide consumption of both high and popular arts. Others are equally convinced that the milieu of business values is antithetical to true sensibility and alert responsiveness. To a considerable extent these differing views revolve around the old question of whether "bad" culture drives out "good," whether the flood of popular products dulls the senses and steals the time of the cultural consumer.

A species of cultural double-play is postulated by many critics: business supports popular culture, which in turn diverts the potential audience from attending to high art. Indeed, there is rather convincing research evidence that audiences of all sorts do spend a great deal of time responding to the mass media of popular culture, notably television. What is especially interesting about this research is the general homogeneity of habits among people of widely differing educational and occupational levels. Steiner, for example, discovered that those of high educational attainment—those, presumably, who would be most likely to renounce the seductions of popular culture for the rarer delights of high culture—actually exhibited viewing patterns quite similar to their fellows in American society at large. He concluded that "the program mix of different educational groups is strikingly constant . . . ."[10] Wilensky states:

> There is little doubt from my data as well as others' that educated strata—even products of graduate and professional schools—are becoming full participants in mass culture; they spend a reduced fraction of time in exposure to quality print

[9] César Graña, *Bohemian Versus Bourgeois* (New York: Basic Books, 1964), p. 207.
[10] Gary A. Steiner, *The People Look at Television* (New York: Alfred A. Knopf, 1963), p. 168.

and film. This trend extends to the professors, writers, artists, scientists—the keepers of high culture themselves—and the chief culprit, again, is TV.[11]

And again:

> . . . uniformity of behavior and taste is the main story. Nowhere else has a "class" audience been so swiftly transformed into a "mass" audience.[12]

Shils argues that the intellectuals have nobody to blame but themselves for this state of affairs. That is, devotees of high culture allow that culture to erode by their inattention and sloth; no one is "forcing" the arts to disappear from the mass business society. Contrarily, Clement Greenberg believes that the nature of an industrial system is such that consumers are compelled to "relax" away from the job and are unable to muster the energy that response to fine art demands. A business society, he contends, not only offers a diet of popular culture but trains and strains its members away from the kind of alertness required to apprehend products of high culture:

> To the exact end of greater productivity, capitalism, Protestantism, and industrialism have brought about a separation of work from all that is not work which is infinitely sharper and more exclusive than ever in the past. And as work has become more concentratedly and actively work—that is, more strictly controlled by its purposes, more efficient—it has pushed leisure out of the foreground of life and turned it into the negative instead of positive complement of itself. Work may be less arduous physically than it used to be, but its present standards of efficiency require one to key oneself to a higher pitch of nervous and mental effort, if only for the sake of the self-control and self-denial required by any kind of sustained activity directed solely toward an end outside itself. Leisure, in compensation, has become much more emphatically the occasion for flight from all purposefulness, for rest, respite, and recuperation. It is certainly no longer the sphere *par excellence* of realization, but a passive state, primarily, in which one's least passive need is for distraction and vicarious experience that will give those immediate satisfactions denied one during working hours by the constraint of efficiency. This in itself is a valid need, but when one's nerves insist that it be met with a minimum of mental exertion on one's own part only a base kind of culture can satisfy it, a kind of culture that has lost all efficacy as recreation (in the literal sense) and become entirely a matter of rudimentary entertainment and diversion—of the sort, exactly, that we see in lowbrow and much of middlebrow culture.[13]

What can one suggest to answer, or alleviate, Greenberg's persuasive indictment? In a business society, after all, business and culture are indissolubly wedded. Must business, despite its overt financial support for high and popular culture, inevitably debilitate the audience?

[11] Harold L. Wilensky, "Mass Society and Mass Culture: Interdependence or Independence," *American Sociological Review*, Vol. 29 (April, 1964), p. 190.
[12] *Ibid.*, p. 191.
[13] "Work and Leisure Under Industrialism," *Commentary*, Vol. 16, (July, 1953), pp. 57–58.

The United States as a business society has often been described as "pluralistic": it is marked by great variety of values, life-styles, occupations, material goods, and cultural forms. Although empirical findings indicate astonishing uniformity in television viewing, perhaps the total range of cultural response is more complex and diverse. Books, magazines, films, and other media afford immense opportunity for the satisfaction of more specialized tastes. As Wilbert E. Moore has averred:

> The very mass production that yields uniformity in some goods also yields the possibility of substantial variability in the combinations that particular consuming units may choose to put together.[14]

If cultural products are plural, one might ask whether the patterns of allegiance to the business style in occupational striving and discipline are not also plural. Is Greenberg's picture too sweeping, and can some considerable sectors of the audience retain or recapture the zest for high culture? There are at least some indications that a very rich business society may provide both the economic surplus for supporting artists and the leisure surplus for supporting audience receptivity. As the true revolution in production and information control that is commonly termed automation takes hold, it is conceivable that most members of the population will not only work fewer hours but will begin to cultivate a different attitude toward work and leisure. Enhanced leisure opportunities *may* lead people to reexamine life's meanings in a way that increases their potential interest in high culture. One cannot even dismiss the notion that our educational system may direct certain energies toward education for an informed and perceptive enjoyment of leisure.

Surely many of the relationships we have described between a business society and its various arts would apply to other types of society as well. Notably, much that pertains to the position of the mass media, the disciplines of industrial work, and the bureaucratic organization of effort would fit almost equally well the case of a non-business but large-scale industrial system, such as the Soviet system has now become and the system China is striving to create. Yet the presence of advertising, of a democratic polity and pluralism, of "venture capital" for the arts, and of certain types of artistic freedom probably will continue for some time to distinguish the business society of the modern West from other mass industrial complexes.

CONCLUSION

We may conclude that the United States enhances the vitality of high and popular culture by providing economic abundance, widespread leisure, pluralistic values in which the arts can find a place, and an open forum for expressive variety. As a

[14] *Social Change* (Englewood Cliffs, N.J.: Prentice-Hall, 1963), p. 109.

business society, America hampers the arts by its dedication to occupational efficiency and organization, its exaltation of the style of business callings, its insistence on profit as a measure of efficacy, and its assignment of recreation to the sphere of the trivial. On balance, it seems undeniable that the opportunities for the artist are as rich as they have ever been. The possibility of creating an audience of talented perceivers also appears great, given the foundation of very much expanded education and leisure. And we must never forget the stubborn element of autonomy in aesthetic pattern and artistic creativity: art and artist are not utterly formed by a business, or any other, society. A fitting note of optimism is struck by the distinguished biologist, Theodosius Dobzhansky:

> The variety of human genotypes, and hence of inclinations and abilities, is increased, not decreased, by hybridization. I suppose the same is true on the cultural level also. A large and complex society should be better able to provide for specialized talent and to tolerate unconformity than a small homogeneous group. I, for one, do not lament the passing of social organizations that used the many as a manured soil in which to grow a few graceful flowers of refined culture.[15]

SELECTED READINGS

CÉSAR GRAÑA, *Bohemian Versus Bourgeois* (New York: Basic Books, 1964). A truly elegant exercise in intellectual history. Describes with wit and depth the rise of a bohemian, anti-business ideology among French writers of the nineteenth century. Invaluable as a source of understanding the tradition of artists' quarrels with commercial values and styles.

LEO LOWENTHAL, *Literature, Popular Culture and Society* (Englewood Cliffs, N. J.: Prentice-Hall, 1961). An excellent, historically detailed account of the relations between high culture and popular culture. Especially revealing in its analysis of philosophical and aesthetic debates about the merits of various cultural forms and in its examination of the changing social roles of artists as industrialization proceeded.

ERIC LARRABEE, AND ROLF MEYERSOHN, EDS., *Mass Leisure* (New York: The Free Press, 1958). A collection of provocative fact and opinion about the uses of leisure in industrial society.

BERNARD ROSENBERG, AND DAVID MANNING WHITE, EDS., *Mass Culture* (New York: The Free Press, 1957). A reader containing widely varied articles about popular culture—its creators, audiences, content, and significance in contemporary life. Notable for its range of argument and for the fact that one editor is a friend, the other a foe, of popular culture.

[15] *Mankind Evolving* (New Haven, Conn.: Yale University Press, 1962), p. 325.

DAVID M. POTTER, *People of Plenty* (Chicago: University of Chicago Press, 1954). Perhaps the most original and compelling recent examination of things distinctively American. Sets forth an entertaining and quite convincing thesis about "economic abundance and the American character." Potter is acute in his description of advertising and its relation to popular culture.

ROBERT N. WILSON, ED., *The Arts in Society* (Englewood Cliffs, N.J.: Prentice-Hall, 1964). A series of articles examining the roles of artists and the products of high culture from a social-psychological perspective.

chapter 14

BUSINESS AND
THE PERFORMING ARTS

RICHARD EELLS *is a seasoned commentator on the place of the corporation in a pluralistic society, the significance of its activities as a patron of health and art, and its meaning as a dominant social institution. In his essay he reports briefly upon the quantitative dimensions of corporate philanthropy and the factors relevant to an estimate of the interest of the modern corporation in the maintenance of "a national cultural seedbed that is tillable."*

Professor Eells's argument favors extended corporate support of the arts. His data tells us, however, that while there has been an increase in such support, corporations presently give somewhat less than one-fourth the full amount they are encouraged to donate by tax regulations. Since tax arrangements make the public a partner in the corporations' beneficence, the discrepancy is all the more surprising. The economics of the performing arts are so precarious, according to a comprehensive 1966 study,[1] that this gap is a crucial one indeed. It has been reliably estimated, in another report, "that only slightly over half of all corporations in the United States give anything to the arts," and that "of the total contributions made by all corporations, only a tiny fraction—at most 3 to 4 per cent . . . goes to the arts." It was also noted that "larger companies seem to direct less of their contribution budget for civic and cultural activities than do smaller."[2] These figures provide a perspective for ap-

[1] William J. Baumol and William G. Bowen, *Performing Arts: The Economic Dilemma* (New York: The Twentieth Century Fund, 1966), pp. 1–11.

[2] *The Performing Arts, Rockefeller Panel Report on the Future of Theatre, Dance, Music in America: Problems and Prospects* (New York: McGraw-Hill, 1965), pp. 82–83. This volume makes it clear that even were the performing arts to solve such marginal problems as "featherbedding" and corrupt business practices in respect to ticket sales and book juggling, the issues would remain because there are so few opportunities to increase the "productivity" of the arts through technological changes.

praising optimistic views of the corporation as a major factor to be considered by the arts in their quest for support. The essay suggests several additional questions.

1. Corporations require, writes the author, a highly literate and demanding consumer public and a national cultural seedbed that is tillable. This requirement, he says, is the logical culmination of an economic system that prizes individual initiative and a liberal democracy that is premised on the notion of responsible citizenship. What assumptions need one make to establish the logical culmination he infers from the institutional arrangements to which he alludes?

2. What suggestion would you make in order to maximize such values as an enlightened public, unfettered competition, and support for the arts when two TV channels, in a major urban center, wish to present prize-winning and widely acclaimed dramas during "prime viewing hours" (when advertising sells best)? If the stations show these dramas by agreement on different dates, they risk violation of antitrust laws. By what logic would you defend your suggestion?

3. According to the study by Baumol and Bowen, cited above, the audience for the performing arts in America is an upper-income one, drawn in substantial part from the higher levels of corporate America. What courses, other than increased donations, might "socially responsible" business leaders consider in order to broaden the base for the consumption of culture?

4. What specific issues (with respect to the arts as well as to corporations) would be generated by these other undertakings, and how do they compare with the issues the author discusses in connection with the pros and cons of corporate donations to the performing arts? How might such specific issues be resolved?

RICHARD EELLS

BUSINESS FOR ART'S SAKE: THE CASE FOR CORPORATE SUPPORT OF THE ARTS

Business as a gainful occupation is often thought to exclude that "love of mankind" implied in philanthropy. The law governing corporate gifts long raised barriers against a corporate donative power except as it was exercised for the non-philanthropic purpose of deriving direct benefits for the donor company. Today, however, one commentator on changes in that law declares that "the business corporation may love mankind."[1] The old barriers have fallen in most states. Corporate boards generally enjoy wide discretionary authority to decide what benefits, indirect as well as direct, a gift may yield a company and even whether to make disinterested grants that benefit mankind. The attention of directors and executive managers now shifts from the legality of corporate giving to different issues: the hard questions of "how much" and "to whom." What managers need, but do not yet have, is an articulate policy in every donor company that will set up guidelines to help them decide how much to dedicate to specific activities, particularly to certain new areas such as the arts.

LEGAL RECOGNITION OF THE CORPORATE DONATIVE POWER

Fifty years ago, about the only business-giving was the personal philanthropy of the proprietors and company presidents of closed corporations. The prevailing legal position was that "a business corporation has nothing to give away." Since the husbanding of resources for making profits was considered the primary goal of the corporation, this precluded any diversion of corporate funds into the hands of outsiders. Unavoidable and expedient "business expenses" for the support of certain charities (community funds, for example) were allowed, but pure and unalloyed gifts were not.

Events in the last half-century have contrived to alter this traditional view. A pluralistic and democratic society committed to the principle that human affairs should be governed, so far as possible, by voluntary associations will also expect much from associations in the private sector. This applies specifically to business corporations as supporters of private non-business associations. If these associations and their activities are to be held in private and not public hands, business is confronted with the necessity of ensuring sources of private support and even of augmenting such support on a vast scale. Here the business corporation must play a large part, not because corporate wealth is an obvious target for fund-raisers, but because the corporation acknowledges the imperative to be in the forefront of certain fund-raising efforts that strengthen the free institutions in the corporate environment. The vigor of free institutions is now widely recognized as necessary for corporate survival and growth.

Legal sanction for this view has slowly emerged. Most of the states now have modified or abandoned the old common-law rule of direct benefit. Modernized "permissive" legislation authorizes (but does not direct) corporations to make greatly broadened categories of gifts. The permissive character of the legislation underlines two significant facts about donative power: (1) while corporations, as creatures of the state, have only the powers conferred upon them by their creator, yet (2) the powers thus conferred are in the nature of quasi-governmental powers

---

[1] B. S. Prunty, Jr., "Love and the Business Corporation," *Virginia Law Review* (April, 1960), p. 467.

exercisable in the private sector according to the discretionary judgment of the governing organs of corporations, and the donative power is no exception to the rule.

The liberal legislative approach to corporate donative power has begun to appear in federal as well as in state legislation. Congress amended the National Banking Act to grant the donative power to national banks. The Internal Revenue Code has, since 1935, authorized the deduction of charitable contributions for corporate income-tax purposes up to 5 per cent of taxable income.

The constitutionality of these statutes or their underlying principle has been affirmed by state and federal courts in a series of cases where dissident stock-holders have tried to prevent directors from exercising the donative power. In a Utah case testing the action of the Union Pacific Railroad[2] in creating a charitable foundation and making a donation to it, the court, even though it refused to apply Utah's new permissive legislation, had no difficulty upholding the gift under a liberalized interpretation of common-law principles. The leading New Jersey case, A. P. Smith Company v. Barlow,[3] upheld a corporate contribution to Princeton University, not only under New Jersey's permissive legislation but also under the state's common-law principles.[4]

THE SCOPE OF CORPORATE GIVING

The combination of favorable legislation and a changing view of the application of common law has led to a new climate for corporate giving and, particularly after the passage of the Revenue Act of 1935, an appreciable expansion of its amount. While total corporate contributions, as reported by the U.S. Treasury,[5] were rather small in the first years after 1935—only $30 million in 1936, for example, or 0.39 per cent of corporate net profits that year—by 1945 they had reached $266 million, or 1.24 per cent. This figure, however, was not exceeded until 1951, when the amount hit $343 million. A peak was reached in 1953 with $495 million; it declined, then rose again, reaching $595 million in 1962, or about 1.2 per cent.

While corporate giving has been a factor of vital and growing importance during the past four decades, it still comes to less than 7.5 per cent of total philanthropic donations in the United States. The American Association of Fund-

[2] Union Pacific Railroad Co. v. Trustees, Inc. *et al.*, 8 Utah (2nd) 101, 329 Pac. (2) 398 (1958).
[3] A. P. Smith Manufacturing Co. v. Barlow *et al.*, 26 N.J. Super. 106 (1953); affirmed, 98 Atl. (2nd) 581; appeal to the U.S. Supreme Court dismissed for want of a substantial federal question, 346 U.S. 861 (1953).
[4] For a detailed analysis of the A. P. Smith case see Richard Eells, *Corporation Giving in a Free Society* (New York: Harper & Row, 1956), Ch. 2.
[5] U.S. Treasury Department, Internal Revenue Service, *Statistics of Income, Corporation Income Tax Returns.*

Raising Counsel estimated[6] total philanthropic giving in 1965 at $11.3 billion and attributed it to the following sources:

SOURCE	AMOUNT IN MILLIONS	PER CENT
Individuals	$ 8,662	76.6
Foundations	1,125	10.0
Business corporations	780	6.9
Charitable bequests	733	6.5
Total	$11,300	100.0

This table does not fully reflect total corporate giving. The figures do not take into account the fact that some foundation gifts originate with business corporations. Nor do any of the standard tables show the full scope of corporate support in non-cash aid, which is substantial.

The recipients of most American philanthropy are not the usual recipients of corporate aid. The Association's estimates for the distribution of total American philanthropy in 1965 are shown below:

RECIPIENTS	PER CENT
Religion	49
Education	17
Welfare	13
Health	11
Foundations	4
Civic, cultural, etc.	4
Other	2
Total	100

What are the comparable percentages for the distribution of corporate giving? The best source for this information is the National Industrial Conference Board,[7] which has conducted studies of corporate giving since 1955. The Board's figures are merely estimates based on sample surveys that do not cover the entire field

[6] *Giving U.S.A.*, (New York: American Association of Fund-Raising Counsel, 1967), p. 11. The percentages have been calculated by the author.
[7] John H. Watson, III (Manager of Company Donations Department, Division of Business Practices, The National Industrial Conference Board), "Report on Company Contributions for 1965," *The Conference Board Record* (October, 1966), pp. 45–54. See also his *Industry Aid to Education: Studies in Public Affairs, No. 1,* A Research Report of the Conference Board, 1965.

of corporate enterprise; however, they are the best we have, and we may draw at least tentative conclusions from them.

The NICB's survey for 1965 covered 448 companies, which gave 0.68 per cent of their pretax income to various types of donees during the year. Most of the companies were manufacturing firms with a heavy concentration of electrical and non-electrical machinery makers, metal fabricators, and chemical and allied companies. The non-manufacturing companies were mainly from banking, finance, and real estate. Though some concerns were of modest size, the majority controlled assets of $100 million or more. The survey showed the following breakdown of the 1965 company contributions dollar:

RECIPIENT	PER CENT
Health and welfare	41.5
Education	38.4
Culture (cultural centers, performing arts, symphonies, little theaters, libraries, museums, and the like)	2.8
Civic causes (municipal and community improvement, good government, and the like)	5.8
Other (religious causes, groups devoted solely to economic education)	9.2
Non-identifiable (because the donee is unknown)	2.3
Total	100.0

CORPORATE SUPPORT FOR THE SEVERAL ARTS

Corporate giving for civic and cultural purposes has increased somewhat in recent years; the figures for these types of donation are probably somewhat understated. Nevertheless, the sums remain far below what they should be, and they confirm the conclusion of another important recent study that corporate giving is decidedly precedent-bound. This special study, undertaken for the Rockefeller Brothers Fund,[8] looked into corporate support of the performing arts and revealed that there was a general hesitancy on the part of corporations to spend much money for this purpose—even though many corporate executives wanted to do so— simply because it had not been done before.

Despite the widespread dependence on precedent in corporate giving, notable departures have occurred that may indicate a changing approach. Business now seems especially able to justify support for the "performing arts." In New York City, for example, corporations have given millions of dollars to the Lincoln

[8] *The Performing Arts: Rockefeller Panel Report on the Future of Theatre, Dance, Music in America: Problems and Prospects,* (New York: McGraw-Hill, 1965), Ch. 5, "Corporate Support for the Performing Arts," based in part on an analysis made by Richard Eells of responses from 100 corporations to a questionnaire on corporate support of the arts.

Center for the Performing Arts. The John F. Kennedy Center for the Performing Arts in Washington, D.C., is said to have received some of its projected dollar needs from corporate gifts.

Both institutions were created specifically to encompass all the performing arts. Support for the musical arts in particular has also been in evidence. Companies have contributed to building funds for the construction of concert halls; they are supporting radio and television broadcasts of symphony orchestras; grants are being made to various orchestras to cover operating needs and to send them on tour. Corporations have even joined together to make one large gift to a famous symphony orchestra that had fallen on hard times. And one of the largest corporations in the United States has recently established a grant to graduate students doing research in the field of music. Opera and ballet have also inspired corporate involvement. A major petroleum company has been sponsoring radio broadcasts of New York's Metropolitan Opera for 24 consecutive years, while a well-known shipping firm recently underwrote the cost of a new production of Aïda. As far back as the 1940's a major manufacturer of perfumes paid for the production of a new ballet. At the time, this was considered a precious move on the firm's part, but today it would not be so regarded.

Painting and design play vital economic roles in advertising and industrial design. Recently, one of the country's leading automobile manufacturers publicly announced a sizable grant to one of the country's leading art schools. The only explanation company executives gave was this: "It's long overdue." In so few words, the company acknowledged the contribution that art and design, artists and designers, had made to the company's livelihood over the years.

Architecture is an important art form that deserves better corporate support.[9] Well-designed metropolitan office buildings and glamorous community plants often involve economies that their corporate sponsors did not foresee when they decided on other grounds to pay for a good architect. An Italian paper company recently retained one of the world's great architects to design an expandable plant that would accommodate the firm's future needs; when the work was finished, company executives were not surprised to learn that they had helped to create a masterpiece of architecture, but they hardly expected to be hailed as the owners of the prototype industrial plant of tomorrow. The place of architecture in urban design, too, is of growing importance to business corporations, as Charles Abrams, Constantine A. Doxiadis, and others have shown.[10]

Television provides a medium not only for presenting literature in dramatized form but also for new forms of art born in the age of electronics. Television is more than an industry and an advertising medium. As a way to new art forms it offers opportunities for imaginative companies, and several have responded by sponsoring, or otherwise supporting, dramatic, musical, and visual art programs of the highest artistic merit. With the advent of public television there will be new opportunities to cultivate the "vast wasteland" by corporate donors who are not

[9] See Robert Sheehan, "Portrait of the Artist as a Businessman," Fortune (March, 1967), pp. 144 ff.
[10] See, for example, the publications of the Library of Urban Affairs, New York City.

advertisers but outright supporters of this medium of enlivening the arts for millions of people.

INNOVATION, CREATIVITY, AND FORESIGHT

How is this emerging collaboration of business and the arts to be explained? In one sense, of course, it is inevitable: as a major social institution, the modern corporation cannot avoid some involvement with so pervasive a concern of society as the arts. On a more pragmatic level, the arts are a factor in the corporate environment that business must adjust to, and, if possible, take advantage of. This is frequently the point of view of the corporate executive who is confronted with requests for gifts to symphonies, museums, and the like; he can rationalize the gifts negatively, as an unavoidable business expense under the heading of good will, or more positively, as an expenditure that will make the community more attractive for employees.

The significance of the relationship between business and the arts is not simply that it is unavoidable or promises obvious short-term advantages to one party or the other. Rather, the involvement can greatly benefit both principals in the long run. Joseph Schumpeter stressed the point that the dynamism of business depends primarily upon innovation; the fashioning of new products, the opening of new markets, the advancing of new industrial designs are all part of the innovative process for the businessman. The creative artist proceeds along similar lines, though in different ways, since he too innovates with new forms, new materials, new structures, and new blendings.

But the artist is not simply an innovator; probably more than anything else, his best works are likely to reflect the present state of the norms, tensions, and tendencies in our culture. The sensitive artist can provide terse indicators of present and future directions of the human condition. Art's symbolism is not always clear to the businessman; it will become clearer with the convergency of the two institutions of art and the corporation. The forward thrust of a free and open society depends in large measure upon both the vigorous and untrammeled artistic life of the community and the maturation of the corporation as a social institution. The cherishing of artistic creativeness by the corporate world will contribute toward a deeper and more comprehensive view of human life and will strengthen the concept of a plural society in which individual ideas and freedoms are themselves cherished. It is a tyrannical society that tries to dictate to the innovator and the artist; it is a free society that protects their individuality and stimulates their creativity.

THE CORPORATE IMAGE AND CORPORATE CITIZENSHIP

Corporations are not soulless creations that care nothing about the human condition, though often in the past they were described that way. At law, the business corporation was once dubbed a bloodless apparition, a fictitious legal "person" without a conscience. Critics attacked it as the mere instrument of selfish men who were bent only on amassing personal wealth and power. It was accused of having no sense of social responsibility. It was viewed with suspicion—if not downright hostility—as though corporate boards, like women condemned for sorcery by the Inquisition, had an inherent wickedness of heart. The corporation was presumably the citadel of tycoons who like Oscar Wilde's cynic "knew the price of everything, but the value of nothing." Its managers were said to equate all value with the dollar sign. Indifferent to anything that could not be explained in a profit-and-loss column, hostile to anything that threatened its single-minded thrust for gain, the corporation of this stereotype was far removed from the world of the artist.

This stereotype carried more than a grain of truth for some companies. Over the past two decades, however, a new corporate image has largely displaced the older one and justifiably so. The corporation has become more humane, at no small dollar cost. So far from having no heart at all, the modern corporation is actually feared by some for its heart and its new social conscience—for now it may seek to control as it contributes. On the other hand, the new image evokes thoughts of the great technological contributions that have been made to society by large companies. It focuses attention on their role in giving us a better life. It reminds us of how they strengthen the sinews of national and Western defense. And, most significantly for the present inquiry, it even hints at corporate benevolence and patronage: the good that is being done through corporate involvement with charitable, educational, and cultural activities without attempts to control.

Yet this involvement is not philanthropic in the sense of being purely altruistic love of mankind. Nor could it be, consistent with the basic purposes of a business corporation devoted to profitable productive processes. Corporate giving, correctly taken as an aspect of corporate policy, is not philanthropy in this sense at all; it is a prudent use of corporate assets, prudent in the sense that both payers and payees will benefit eventually. Sound corporate giving, whether for the arts or otherwise, is based on corporate donative policy drawn in instrumental terms. It is policy, that is to say, that makes donations auxiliary to the business activities of a company. Aid to education, for example, increases the supply of new knowledge and of educated and trained people, indispensable resources to the business sector.

Financial aid to the arts has a similar rationale. Because of the indirectness and the indefinite timing of returns to a particular donor company that can be measured in profit-and-loss statements, however, a new kind of corporate ecology is needed to link cause and effect, to state the necessary and sufficient conditions of justifiable grants-in-aid, and to provide indices for measuring results. For decades large-scale advertisers have been aware that measuring the effects of a given advertising expenditure is impossible; but rather than terminate an expense so vital to their survival simply to facilitate neat accounting, they continued to advertise and kept their critics at bay with a smokescreen of vague philosophizing about the corporate image and the sea level of product information. Corporations may have to adopt a similar policy for education and the arts; until far better analytical tools than we now have become available, payments to the arts should go forward simply as an aspect of "good corporate citizenship." At length, both from the sociology of the arts and the ecology of business enterprise, we shall have a stronger rationale for corporate support of the arts.

Corporate donative policy is not and cannot be reduced to a narrowly profit-centered and egoistic basis with no time dimension beyond the annual balance sheet. Nor can the criteria for selecting the recipient of corporate giving remain where they are today in all too many companies: keeping up with the Joneses, submitting to the biggest internal and external pressures to favor this or that charitable organization, choosing from the Internal Revenue Service's list of eligibles those donees that promise the best "tax bargains" for the donor company, or simply going along with last year's list as the easiest way out.

Against such sterile bases for corporate policy in relation to the cultural milieu, there is developing in the corporate community a new philosophy of corporate involvement in the ethical and aesthetic aspirations of American society. This development coincides with a profound revolution in the underlying structure of traditional capitalism. Among the most significant aspects of this revolution is the widespread diffusion of shareholding.[11] Some 3,000 incorporated companies are now listed on the recognized exchanges of the United States (some 26,000 of the one million corporations have securities that are quoted and have some degree of trading), and there are about 18 million shareholders. At one time, the savings of our people and institutions went primarily into insurance, savings banks, bond purchases, and mortgages; now they go increasingly into corporate equities. The individual and institutional shareholders of a corporation now constitute a significant "public" with which management must strive to maintain good relations. The great securities markets, the professional investment community, the regulatory

[11] Robert L. Heilbroner says in *The Limits of American Capitalism* (New York: Harper & Row, 1966), p. 85: "The concentration of stock—the single most important medium for the investment of large wealth—has shown no tendency to decline since 1922 (despite the great increase in small stockholders), and seems in fact to have increased: the top 2 per cent of families, who held just under two-thirds of all corporate stock in the 1920's, actually held more than three-quarters of all stock in 1953."

On the other hand, the long-range trend can be differently viewed, as is seen in the perceptive article by Paul P. Harbrecht, S.J., on "The Modern Corporation Revisited," *Columbia Law Review* (December, 1964), pp. 1410 and 1421–22: "As late as 1952, when the corporate system was well established, [stockholders] numbered only one out of sixteen Americans. The proportion of share purchasers must have been even smaller during the early growth of the corporations that formed the backbone of American business. What we know of the personal income levels of wealth distribution indicates that relatively few individuals had sufficient savings to enable them to invest in shares, which were risky propositions at best. Now one out of six adult Americans owns shares, although the dollar value of individual participation has been reduced. But the general trend is plainly toward greater participation in the benefits of enterprise." He contends further that an evolutionary movement in our economy toward "a systemic whole" operates "less for the benefit of the private few and more for the good of all society" by reason of three major developments: "(1) placing control of wealth in collective societies (corporations), (2) making claims on their income negotiable in financial markets, and (3) establishing the financial institutions to collect and use those claims as a basis for new claims that they offer to the public." These key financial institutions include pension funds, mutual funds, and life insurance companies.

commissions, the professional business schools, and the growing sector of the public press reporting on corporate enterprise all indicate a growing interest on the part of a vast public in the conduct of corporations.

The interaction between corporations and society affects the country's growth, its tone and temperament, and its vitality. The impact of a corporation varies partly with its size. The giants, the larger institutions, and the companies in the public service area provide stability. The enterprisers, the venture corporations, and the wildcatters provide aggressiveness and some of the old-time risk-taking zeal of the laissez faire period. In this broad spectrum of corporate capitalism one discerns a remarkable variety of indirect corporate influences on the immediate plant communities, on regions, on the scientific, educational, and cultural life of the nation. The venture corporations and the wildcatters are necessarily more "egoistic," while companies higher in the scale of size and institutionalization become "socially responsible" to a high degree.

Any move to expand the corporations' broad social role is likely to draw the fire of many economists, accountants, and lawyers, whose score or more of concepts of the firm[12] seldom leave any room for non-economic managerial motivations. Yet more and more top business leaders in the larger corporations do have a strong sense of so-called public or social responsibility, comparable to that of statesmen in the highest ranks of government, and they are being urged on by modern conditions to redefine the meaning of modern business. The consequences for the arts of this redefinition may be far-reaching.

The idea of "corporate citizenship" is coming to mean, for many executives, the identification of company goals with the noblest goals of the community that sustains the enterprise. Corporate enterprise—which now embraces many kinds of work and calls upon the country's best skills, talent, intellect, and artistic genius—is more aware than ever before of its dependence upon the entire sweep of human resources. The next step is corporate involvement and commitment with the institutional structures through which these human resources are sought out, nourished, trained, educated, professionalized, and utilized for the flowering of a greater civilization. Corporations require not only manpower; they require a highly literate and demanding consumer public and a national cultural seedbed that is tillable. This is the logical culmination of an economic system that prizes individual initiative and of a liberal democracy that is premised on the notion of responsible citizenship.

THE SOCIAL FUNCTIONS OF ART

Theories about the social functions of art have undergone some important changes in recent years. Since ancient times philosophers have been seriously concerned with theories of beauty, but in the United States aesthetics has little status as a

[12] Fritz Machlup, "Theories of the Firm: Marginalist, Behavioral, Managerial," *American Economic Review*, Vol. 57 (March, 1967), pp. 1–33, especially at pp. 26 ff., examines "the 21 concepts of the firm."

branch of philosophy and a focus of interest for thoughtful citizens. There is still a strong strain of suspicion here that art is only a luxury product of civilization, a cultural frill, a piece of social veneer. This attitude can be traced back to Puritanism, perhaps, but also to the authentic need of our new country to devote most of its attention to controlling the physical environment. While the need to take care of necessities first is genuine, however, it is no justification for turning concern about them into a religion; our reluctance to accept the artist as a pillar of our society now that it has become so wealthy and advanced in other respects is some evidence that this has been done.

The arts are a useful, and perhaps indispensable, path to knowledge of the worlds outside and within us, and as such they have always been cultivated in great cultures. Art, in Susanne K. Langer's phrase, is "cognition of feeling" through symbolic expression that extends our knowledge beyond the scope of actual experience; it seems to embody truths that cannot otherwise be made known—and this kind of knowledge is not simply limited to "non-scientific" categories. As Maritain has said, we are grateful to poets "not only as lovers of beauty, but also as men concerned with the mystery of their own destiny." Perhaps Bergson was justified in his view of art as "only a more direct vision of reality."

A people standing at the opening of a vast new era of knowledge about man and the universe in which he lives cannot afford to be narrowly doctrinaire about the available paths to truth. T. B. L. Webster, referring to another great transitional period when the ancient Greeks abandoned a primitive for a modern view of the world—a transition that took some 300 years—has pointed to their need at the time for new types of words, new forms of sentences, and new kinds of arguments to communicate their radically new views of things. It was a most difficult operation and not always successful, for the resistant old ways of thought kept recurring. Philosophers constructed arguments to prove their guesses; for help they turned to the hypotheses and evidence of the natural sciences and mathematics. Advance would not have been possible, Webster concluded, "without the close day-to-day cooperation between mathematicians, scientists, artists, and poets."[13]

Art also serves as an indicator of social trends, and as such, alone, cannot safely be overlooked in managerial scanning of the corporate environment, especially in essaying long-range planning and in the corporate ecology of new environments such as the so-called underdeveloped countries. Arnold J. Toynbee has said that, if we are attempting to ascertain the limits of any particular civilization in space or time, the aesthetic test is the surest as well as the subtlest. Sorokin's thesis[14] concerning the decay of our "sensate" and "ideational" cultures and the signs of an emergent "integral" sociocultural order—with the fine arts as an important index—is a comparable view. The ethical contributions of art to our society are

[13] "Communication of Thought in Ancient Greece," in A. J. Ayer *et al., Studies in Communication* (London: Martin Secker & Warburg, 1955), pp. 125–46.
[14] Pitirim A. Sorokin, *The Basic Trends of Our Times* (New Haven, Conn.: College & University Press, 1964), Ch. 1.

perhaps more obvious than its contribution as a social barometer. The American painter, Ben Shahn, has cited François Mauriac's pessimistic view that both the United States and the Soviet Union are technocracies that are "dragging humanity in the same direction of dehumanization," despite their mutual assumptions of antagonism. Man, according to Mauriac, is "treated as a means and no longer as an end—that is the indispensable conditioning of the two cultures that face each other today." Shahn holds that art is a bulwark against dehumanization; good art is directly a "product of the spirit," and the artist, in "the very business of keeping his integrity, begins to supply some of the moral stamina our country needs." The artist does more; he can contribute to the enrichment and awakening of "a country that has allowed too much of its magnificent endowment of freedom to slip away" because of its preoccupation with the acquisition of material wealth alone and neglect of its endowment of spiritual and cultural values.[15]

The relevance of such observations to corporate enterprise is not always recognized. While it is gradually being accepted that the modern corporation is a social institution of multivalue goals, it comes hard for some critics to concede that aesthetic values can be numbered among them. Corporate virtue as a goal in its own right is often accepted but seldom that quality which, for the ancient Greeks, indicated at once the morally good and the aesthetically beautiful. Perhaps the time has come to revive this connection in corporate policy. We are already near this in the corporate rationale for the support of general education, particularly scientific education. But while science and technology have helped us to come to terms with our physical environment and have bestowed on corporate enterprise untold wealth of knowledge, science cannot provide that vision by which we are elevated in mind and deed—a contribution of the humanities and not least of the arts. Alfred North Whitehead repeatedly warned of the grooving of our professional minds, trained too exclusively by intellectual analysis, into ways of thought that become sterile in the total comprehension of human life with all its myriad colorations and meanings; only the aesthetic experience could provide the necessary corrective.[16] For young and old alike there has to be—in a free society—*ready access* to the aesthetic experience and the chance to inculcate the habits of aesthetic apprehension, the education of the eye, the ear, and the tactile senses to those nuances of color, sound, and feeling that a civilized man must have both to survive and to evolve the high culture he aspires to.

These propositions lead directly to the problem of corporate goals in a society of high culture. President James M. Hester of New York University wonders whether in this respect we are not living off the idealistic capital of another era, and asks what we are to do to replenish these capital needs. It is an urgent issue for all policy-makers in both public and private sectors.

[15] "The Role of the Artist Today," *Washington Post,* December 1, 1963.
[16] *Adventures of Ideas* (New York: Macmillan, 1933), Chs. 17 and 18; *Science and the Modern World* (New York: Macmillan, 1925), pp. 256 ff; and *The Dialogues of Alfred North Whitehead As Recorded by Lucien Price* (New York: Mentor Books, 1956), *passim.*

BUSINESS, THE GOVERNMENT, AND ARTISTIC FREEDOM

Many Western writers and artists doubt that Western society is much superior to Soviet society as a milieu for freedom of artistic expression. Ben Shahn fears that he fights a losing battle because "some bright entrepreneur" is always looking for ways to "turn into big money every activity in which the artist engages, simply by cheapening it a little, by taking out the challenge, the meaning, the controversiality."[17] This complaint and others like it are hardly to be brushed aside as leftist propaganda. The arts suffer suppression in authoritarian regimes that they do not suffer here, yet dangers to the artist are also inherent in the free-enterprise system. Will business be able to provide leadership in guarding against these dangers or must the government intervene? Naturally, one cannot reasonably expect the artist to be insulated from the workings of the marketplace, and there would be a great clamor from the artistic community if artists were to be deprived of the rewards of entrepreneurial activity in the arts. On the other hand, the evidence is strong that the production of great art requires high-minded support of a kind not automatically afforded by the market mechanism. But who is to provide this support? The proper mix of public and private support of the arts remains a great unresolved issue in the United States.

The issue is too often posed as an alarming alternative: corporate support and freedom versus government subsidy of the arts and bondage for artists. Questions of social policy are rarely as simple as that; in this case, it seems that both business and the government must work together. Corporate support of the arts should be increased to preserve the essentially pluralistic character of American society, in this case the pluralism of its artistic sectors. But at the same time it will probably prove impossible to avoid a measure of public subsidy for the arts, and perhaps a much larger subsidy than is now regarded as acceptable in federal, state, and local governmental circles. Could corporate support by itself "bridge the gap between private art and commodity art" and "divorce art from money-making"? These questions were asked by Kenneth Tynan[18] in a discussion of the movement in America to create new centers of art. On the basis of British experience, Tynan doubted that Lincoln Center and our other centers would long survive if they relied solely on private subsidies. How long would the subsidies last, he asked, and would the foundations really come through? Uncertain private subsidies would, in his opinion, threaten the principles of continuity in the presentation of the heritage of dramatic literature. And private subsidies would be less democratic than public subsidies granted by an elective parliament.

In the United States it is almost certain that we shall settle for a mix of public and private subsidization of the arts as a supplement to the considerable stimulus provided by the marketing of artistic products. We want many centers of decision-

---

[17] Shahn, *op. cit.*

[18] "To Divorce Art from Money-making," *New York Times Magazine* (December 1, 1963), pp. 35 ff., and "Culture in a Democracy," *Musical America* (December, 1963), pp. 155–56.

making in the arts as well as in business, in education, and in other aspects of our national life. In this way, there is an encouragement of that freedom in the arts that we have so jealously guarded in other departments of life.

PLURALISM AND THE ART CENTER OR COUNCIL

The concept of New York's Lincoln Center is in some ways one of the great inspirations of the twentieth century. But, many critics have said, New York needs a number of theaters where the vast literature of the drama can be studied coherently and played with stylistic unity and probity. There should perhaps be a number of permanent companies pursuing special areas and forging their own styles. This is a task that cannot be assigned to the commercial theater. And the same argument, with little change, applies to the other performing arts, especially music and dance, and to other communities. Corporate support of the local repertory theaters all over the country can be a stroke in behalf of artistic freedom: the local companies need consult no central authority on repertorial or other artistic issues. In supporting this type of activity the companies are affirming the necessary connection of freedom for artists and freedom for others. A multiplicity of autonomous art centers, even within the same community if it is a vast metropolis, could thus be a deliberate policy objective in corporate support.

The emphasis must always be on pluralism. Care must be taken lest corporate giving be used to promote or preserve a monistic structure. At present, many corporate donors prefer to give to art centers or arts councils rather than to individual art groups or persons; in this way they believe they can escape having to decide which artists to help. But in avoiding this Scylla, what about the Charybdis on the other side of the channel—the danger that united funds threaten the very pluralism of artistic effort that has been so much praised? United funds are not so likely to encourage the unorthodox, which in the arts is sometimes the most creative.

If the need for pluralism in a democracy is genuine, the corporation should be prepared to support diversity and to counter orthodoxy by supporting individual artists and artistic enterprises. This is a hard practice to follow, for the donor must set up defensible donative policy criteria in artistic fields where fierce battles rage over questions of taste. Imagine a corporation concerned about its public image daring to support a revolutionary writer like James Joyce or a contemporary composer as controversial as Johannes Brahms was in his day. Brahms unveiled his First Symphony in 1876; as late as 1893, Philip Hale, author of scholarly program notes for the Boston Symphony, declared that the symphony was "the apotheosis of ignorance." Critics here and in Europe suggested signs in concert halls reading, "Exit in case of Brahms."

Will the corporate supporter of the arts today steer clear of the controversial writers, composers, choreographers, and performers, electing instead to aid a new Arts Establishment? If such is the choice, there is not only disregard for the new, the venturesome, and the creative but, more significantly, a counterproductive move toward uniformity and the well-grooved establishment. The very large Ford Foundation grants to ballet groups in 1963 ran into that charge, whatever may be said for the merits of the recipient dance companies.

Assuming a positive program of corporate support of the arts—positive, that is, from the standpoint of pluralistic doctrine—a vigorous growth of musical, dramatic, and ballet activity might result, if business companies set out deliberately to encourage the unorthodox, the new, and the untried. To accomplish this, business budgets would have to be geared to norms not now widely accepted in the world of corporate donors, norms that would defend the search for new talent as a kind of artistic risk comparable with business risk-taking. The corporation that takes a reasoned and intelligent lead in this kind of budgeting will make a new and favorable name for itself, and it will be acting in the best tradition of liberty. Liberty is sometimes defined as the mere absence of restraint, but it can also be regarded as a strong, positive force. As Joyce Cary has put it, "Liberty is creation in the act. It is therefore eternal and indestructible . . . it is always at work."[19]

John Steinbeck observed[20] that our species, the only creative species, has but one creative instrument: "the individual mind and the spirit of a man." The miracle of creation has always been, he insisted, in the lonely mind of a man and not in a group. There have been no "great collaborations," whether in music, in art, in poetry, in mathematics, or in philosophy. After the miracle of creation has taken place, a group might build and extend it, but "the group never invents anything." One might cavil at these sweeping propositions, but hardly with Steinbeck's fight "to preserve the one thing that separates us from the uncreative beasts," that is to say, "the free, exploring mind of the individual human." His fight for "the freedom of mind to take any direction it wishes, undirected," applies with especial force to the arts.

The mind free to wander, as Whitehead put it, was a condition precedent to man's great modern leap "from plough to Polaris." The conceptualizing processes of great seminal minds—in Einstein or Fermi, for example—appear to be closely akin to the creative processes of the artistic imagination. The work of supporting artistic freedom is difficult, but the higher interest of the modern corporation is to undertake it.

SELECTED READINGS

F. EMERSON ANDREWS, *Philanthropic Giving* (1950) and *Corporation Giving* (1952), both published by the Russell Sage Foundation, New York. Standard works on the historical development and current trends in American philanthropy.

RICHARD EELLS, *Corporation Giving in a Free Society* (New York: Harper & Row, 1956). An analysis of the appropriateness, the possibilities, and the limita-

[19] *Power in Men,* first published in 1939, republished in 1964 with an introduction by Hazard Adams (Seattle: University of Washington Press, 1964).
[20] *East of Eden* (New York: Bantam Books, 1962), pp. 113–14.

tions of corporate giving, with emphasis on a theory of corporate giving that strengthens a free society as a condition of corporate survival and growth.

RICHARD EELLS, "Corporate Giving: Theory and Policy," *California Management Review*, Vol. 1 (Fall, 1958), pp. 37–46. A statement of prudent investment principles as one method of formulating the donative policies of corporations.

RICHARD EELLS, *The Meaning of Modern Business: An Introduction to the Philosophy of Large Corporate Enterprise* (New York: Columbia University Press, 1960), Ch. 4: "The Dilemma of Corporate Responsibility."

RICHARD EELLS, "Executive Suite and Artist's Garret," *Columbia Journal of World Business*, Vol. 1 (Inaugural Issue, Fall, 1965), pp. 37–44. Calls for a meaningful dialogue between the world of art and business to discover their common purposes.

WILLIAM J. BAUMOL AND WILLIAM G. BOWEN, *Performing Arts: The Economic Dilemma* (New York: The Twentieth Century Fund, 1966). An explanation of the financial problems of live professional performing arts—theater, opera, music, and dance—in the United States.

CLARENCE C. WALTON, *Corporate Social Responsibilities* (Belmont, Calif.: Wadsworth, 1967), "The Corporation and the Arts," pp. 114–17, and "The Artistic Model," pp. 139–42.

CLARENCE WALTON AND RICHARD EELLS, EDS., *The Business System: Readings in Ideas and Concepts* (New York: Macmillan, 1967), Vol. 3, Part VI: "Business and the Realm of Values." A selection of readings concerning value theory— including problems of aesthetics and ethics—as a major component of a developing general theory of management.

RICHARD EELLS, *The Corporation and the Arts* (New York: Macmillan, 1967). Looking beyond the one-sided concept of corporate support of the arts, this study examines the mutual dependence of business and the arts as innovators and creators in a free, democratic society.

INDEX